Lecture Notes in Computer S
Edited by G. Goos, J. Hartmanis and J. v

Springer
Berlin
Heidelberg
New York
Barcelona
Hong Kong
London
Milan
Paris
Singapore
Tokyo

X. Sean Wang   Ge Yu   Hongjun Lu (Eds.)

Advances in Web-Age Information Management

Second International Conference, WAIM 2001
Xi'an, China, July 9-11, 2001
Proceedings

Series Editors

Gerhard Goos, Karlsruhe University, Germany
Juris Hartmanis, Cornell University, NY, USA
Jan van Leeuwen, Utrecht University, The Netherlands

Volume Editors

X. Sean Wang
George Mason University, Department of Information and Software Engineering
Fairfax, VA 22030-4444, USA
E-mail: xywang@gmu.edu

Ge Yu
Northeastern University, Department of Computer Science and Engineering
Shenyang, 110004, China
E-mail: yuge@mail.neu.edu.cn

Hongjun Lu
Hong Kong University of Science and Technology
Department of Computer Science
Clear Water Bay, Kowloon, Hong Kong, China
E-mail: luhj@cs.ust.hk

Cataloging-in-Publication Data applied for

Die Deutsche Bibliothek - CIP-Einheitsaufnahme

Advances in web age information management : second international conference ; proceedings / WAIM 2001, Xi'an, China, Jul y 9 - 11, 2001. X. Sean Wang ... (ed.). - Berlin ; Heidelberg ; New York ; Barcelona ; Hong Kong ; London ; Milan ; Paris ; Singapore ; Tokyo : Springer, 2001
(Lecture notes in computer science ; Vol. 2118)
ISBN 3-540-42298-6

CR Subject Classification (1998): H.2, H.3, H.4, I.2, H.5, J.1, C.2

ISSN 0302-9743
ISBN 3-540-42298-6 Springer-Verlag Berlin Heidelberg New York

Springer-Verlag Berlin Heidelberg New York
a member of BertelsmannSpringer Science+Business Media GmbH

http://www.springer.de

Printed in Germany

Typesetting: Camera-ready by author, data conversion by PTP-Berlin, Stefan Sossna
Printed on acid-free paper SPIN: 10839875 06/3142 5 4 3 2 1 0

Preface

We welcome you to the Second International Conference on E-commerce and Web Technology (ECWEB 2001) held in conjunction with DEXA 2001 in Munich, Germany. This conference, now in its second year, is a forum to bring together researchers from academia and commercial developers from industry to discuss the state of the art in E-commerce and web technology and explore new ideas.

We thank you all for coming to Munich to participate and debate the new emerging advances in this area. The research presentation and discussion during the conference will help to exchange new ideas among the researchers, developers, and practitioners.

The conference program consists of an invited talk by Hannes Werthner, University of Trento, Italy, as well as the technical sessions. The regular sessions cover topics from XML Transformations and Web Development to User Behavior and Case Studies. The workshop has attracted more than 80 papers and each paper has been reviewed by at least 3 program committee members for its merit. The program committee have selected 31 papers for presentation.

We would like to express our thanks to the people who helped put together the technical program: the program committee members and external reviewers for their timely and rigorous reviews of the papers, the DEXA organizing committee for their help in administrative work and support, and special thanks to Gabriela Wagner for always responding promptly.

Finally, we would like to thank all the authors who submitted papers, those presenting papers, and the attendees who make this workshop an intellectually stimulating event.

We hope you will enjoy this conference and make it a success.

September 2001

Sanjay Kumar Madria
Günther Pernul

Organization

General Chair:

Deyuan Gao	Northwestern Polytechnic University, China

Conference Chairs:

Hongjun Lu	Hong Kong University of Science & Technology, China
Akifumi Makinouchi	Kyushu University, Japan

Program Chairs:

X. Sean Wang	George Mason University, USA
Ge Yu	Northeastern University, China

Tutorial&Panel Chair:

Min Wang	IBM T. J. Watson Research Center, USA

Publicity Chair:

Qiang Zhu	The University of Michigan, USA

Organization Chairs:

Zhanhui Li	Northwestern Polytechnic University, China
Kaiming Shi	Northwestern Polytechnic University, China

WAIM Steering Committee:

Jianzhong Li	Harbing Institute of Technology, China
Hongjun Lu (**Chair**)	Hong Kong University of Science & Technology, China
Baile Shi	Fudan University, China
Jianwen Su	University of California, Santa Barabara, USA
Shan Wang	Renmin University, China
X. Sean Wang	George Mason University, USA
Ge Yu	Northeastern University, China
Aoying Zhou	Fudan University, China

The Second International Conference on Web-Age Information Management was organized by

Northwestern Polytechnic University, China

in cooperation with

China Computer Federation, Database Society

and sponsored by

Fujitsu Limited, Japan,
TechnoProject Limited, Japan, and
National Science Foundation, China

Program Committee

Vijay Atluri	Rutgers University, USA
Daniel Barbará	George Mason University, USA
Claudio Bettini	University of Milan, Italy
Sang K. Cha	Seoul National University, Korea
Arbee L.P. Chen	National Tshing Hua University, Taiwan
Wan-Sup Cho	Chungbuk National University, Korea
Carlo Combi	University of Udine, Italy
Alex Delis	Polytechnic University, USA
Guozhu Dong	University of South Australia, Australia
Susan Gauch	University of Kansas, USA
Stephane Grumbach	INRIA, France
Jiawei Han	Simon Fraser University, Canada
Xingui He	Beijing Institute of System Eng., China
Larry Kerschberg	George Mason University, USA
Hiroyuki Kitagawa	University of Tsukuba, Japan
Yasushi Kiyoki	Keio University, Japan
Jiajin Le	Donghua University, China
Hans-J. Lenz	Free University, Berlin, Germany
Jianzhong Li	Harbin Institute of Technology, China
Tianzhu Li	Hebei University, China
Zhanhuai Li	Northwestern Polytechnic University, China
Huan Liu	Arizona State University, USA
Ling Liu	Georgia Tech, USA
Weiyi Meng	SUNY at Binghamton, USA
Xiaofeng Meng	Renmin University, China
William Perrizo	North Dakota State University, USA
Niki Pissinou	University of Louisiana at Lafayette, USA
Peter Revesz	University of Nebraska-Lincoln, USA
Baile Shi	Fudan University, China
Kyuseok Shim	KAIST, Korea
Dan Suciu	University of Washington, USA
Chanjie Tang	Sihuan University, China
Shiwei Tang	Peking University, China
Fu Tong	Shanghai University, China
Vassilis Tsotras	University of California, Riverside, USA
Shunsuke Uemura	NAIST, Japan
Victor Vianu	University of California, San Diego, USA
Guoren Wang	Northeastern University, China
Haiyang Wang	Shandong University, China
Jason Wang	New Jersey Institute of Technology, USA
Min Wang	IBM T. J. Watson Research Center, USA
Nengbin Wang	Southeast University, China
Shan Wang	Renmin University, China

(Program committee continued)

Kyu-Young Whang	KAIST, Korea
Jef Wijsen	University of Mons-Hainaut, Belgium
Jiepan Xu	Nanjing University, China
Dongqing Yang	Peking University, China
Masatoshi Yoshikawa	NAIST, Japan
Jeffrey X. Yu	Chinese University of Hong Kong, China
Aidong Zhang	SUNY Buffalo, USA
Aoying Zhou	Fudan University, China
Lizhu Zhou	Tsinghua University, China
Longxiang Zhou	Institute of Mathematics, China
Qiang Zhu	University of Michigan, USA

External Referees

Maggie Y.C. Chang
George Chang
Pei-Yi Chen
Jie Chen
Zhihong Deng
Qin Ding
Kai Essig
Youlin Fang
Jun Gao
Zhiguo Gong
Katherine G. Herbert
Wei Huang
Yoshiharu Ishikawa
William Jockheck
Maleq Khan
Yong-Sik Kwon
Keunjoo Kwon
Shengen Li
Wang Lian
Xiuli Ma
Atsuyuki Morishima
Pratik Mukhopadhyay
Chen Ning
Jian Pei
Weining Qian
Huiyuan Shan
Xiaochun Tang
Chun Tang
Anthony Tung
Tengjiao Wang
Dalin Wang
Xiong Wang
Wei Wang
Lianghuai Yang
Michael M. Yin
Liang Zhang
Sen Zhang
Shihui Zheng

Program Committee (continued)

[illegible]

External Referees

[illegible]

Table of Contents

Multimedia Databases & High Dimensional Indexing (Session 1A)

Information Retrieval & Text Indexing (Session 1B)

Data Mining (Session 2A)

Semistructured Data Management (Session 2B)

Data Warehousing & Federated Databases (Session 3A)

Web Information Management & E-commerce (Session 3B)

Temporal, Spatial & High Dimensional Information Management (Session 4A)

Data Mining & Constraint Management (Session 4B)

Data Integration & Filtering (Session 5A)

Workflow & Adaptive Systems (Session 5B)

Session 1A
Multimedia Databases & High Dimensional Indexing

Regular Research Paper (30 minutes)
Spatial-match Iconic Image Retrieval with Ranking in Multimedia Databases

Regular Research Paper (30 minutes)
Similarity-based Operators in Image Database Systems

Short Research Paper (15 minutes)
An Efficient High-Dimensional Index Structure Using Cell Signatures for Similarity Search

Research Experience Paper (15 minutes)
Using Object-relational Database Systems and XML in the Context of a Wireless-oriented Multimedia Information System

Spatial-Match Iconic Image Retrieval with Ranking in Multimedia Databases

Jae-Woo Chang and Yeon-Jung Kim

Department of Computer Engineering, Chonbuk National University Chonju, Chonbuk 560-756, South Korea
{jwchang, yjkim}@dblab.chonbuk.ac.kr

Abstract. In multimedia database applications, it is necessary to retrieve multimedia documents to satisfy a user's query based on image content. For this, we represent an image as a set of icon objects, and then do indexing by regarding the icon object as a representative of a given document. When users request content-based image retrieval, we convert a query image into a set of icon objects and retrieve relevant images in the multimedia database. In this paper, we propose new spatial-match iconic image representation schemes supporting ranking, called SRC scheme using MBC(Minimum Bounding Circle) and SRR scheme using MBR(Minimum Bounding Rectangle). Because our SRC and SRR schemes combine directional operators with positional operators, they can represent spatial relationships between icon objects precisely and can provide ranking for the retrieved images.

1 Introduction

The applications of multimedia databases include digital library, architectural design, cartography, video on demand (VOD), digital newspaper, and electronic commerce. Records (i.e., Documents) used in the multimedia database applications are typically complex in their structure and contain various multimedia data, such as text, image, audio, video, and animation. When the traditional database systems deal with multimedia documents, they can support only query by text content (e.g., captions and keywords) because they mainly focus on formatted data and texts. However, the approach using text content has a couple of problems [1]. First, original keywords do not allow for unanticipated searching. Secondly, the caption is not adequate to describe the layout, sketch, and shape of images. For the multimedia database applications, we can consider a query like this: *Retrieve images which contain trees on the north side of a house and cars on the left side of the house.* To support the query, it is essential to support content-based image retrieval on multimedia documents.

Given a pixel-level original image, it is analyzed prior to storage so that icon objects can be extracted from its content. The icon objects are used to search the multimedia database and to determine whether an image satisfies a query's selection criteria. The purpose of our paper is to provide both effective representation and efficient retrieval of images when an original image is automatically or manually transformed into its iconic image including only icon objects. For this, we propose new spatial-match iconic image representation schemes supporting ranking in

X.S. Wang, G. Yu, and H. Lu (Eds.): WAIM 2001, LNCS 2118, pp. 3-13, 2001.

multimedia databases. Because our schemes combine directional operators with topological operators, they can represent spatial relationships between icon objects precisely. Because our schemes support ranking for the retrieved images, we can provide the image results retrieved in the order of relevance to a user query. In order to accelerate image searching and support image ranking, we also design an efficient access method based on an inverted file technique.

The remainder of this paper is organized as follows. In Section 2, we introduce a review of related work. In Section 3, we propose new spatial-match iconic image representations with ranking and we design an efficient access method to accelerate image searching in Section 4. In Section 5, we analyze the performance of our schemes. Finally, we draw our conclusions and suggest future work in Section 6.

2 Related Work

There have been some studies on spatial-match iconic image representation schemes [2], [3], [4], [5], [6], [7]. They can be classified into mainly two approaches. The first approach is based on directional information, for instance, 9DLT(Direction Lower Triangular) scheme [4]. The other approach is based on topological information, for instance, 2D C-string [3] and SMR(Spatial Match Representation) schemes [5]. In this section, we introduce the 9DLT and the SMR, which give much impression to our work.

Chang and Jiang [4] proposed the 9DLT scheme to describe spatial relationships between objects, i.e., icon objects. In the scheme, direction codes are denoted by nine integers, i.e., 1, 2, 3, 4, 5, 6, 7, 8, and 0, according to the direction of a target object from the reference object. For instance, the direction code 1 indicates that the target object is located at the north side from R(reference object), and the direction code 2 indicates the north-west side from R. The direction code 0 indicates that the target object and R are located at the same position in an iconic image. Using the directional codes, the 9DLT scheme easily describes spatial relationships between objects, being represented by (*object A, object B,* D_{AB}). Here, D_{AB} means the *9DLT directional code*, being one of integers from 0 to 8, which indicates spatial relationships between objects in terms of direction.

The SMR scheme proposed by Chang et al. [5] makes use of fifteen topological operators to describe spatial relationships between icon objects. The topological operators are made by applying the operators used for the specification of temporal relationships between time intervals to spatial environments [8]. A topological operator P_X (P_Y) denotes relationships between the projections p and q, respectively, of object A and B over the X-axis (Y-axis). The SMR scheme represents spatial string for both exact match and approximate match as follows. Here, $PA_X(PA_Y)$ is a topological operator for approximate-match.

- Exact match string : ST_E^{AB} = {(Object A, Object B, P_X, P_Y)}
- Approximate match string : ST_A^{AB} = {(Object A, Object B, PA_X, PA_Y)}

3 New Spatial-Match Iconic Image Representations with Ranking

For image indexing and retrieval, the 9DLT and the SMR have a critical problem that they can not support ranking on the retrieved image results since they adopt a signature file as their access method. Thus, we propose new spatial-match iconic image representation schemes which represent spatial relationships between icon objects by using both directional and positional operators. Our representation schemes can also support ranking for the retrieved results to a user query by adopting an inverted file as their access method. We call our representation schemes SRC(**S**patial-match **R**epresentation with Minimum Bounding **C**ircle) and SRR(**S**patial-match **R**epresentation with Minimum Bounding **R**ectangle), respectively.

3.1 Spatial-Match Representation of the SRC Scheme

To identify a salient object in an image, we use Minimum Bounding Circle(MBC)[9], being a circle which surrounds the object. Using MBC, we can represent the spatial relationships between two objects based on the projections of the objects on the X-axis and the Y-axis. In Figure 1, rc_X and rc_Y are the projected center point of the reference object on the X-axis and the Y-axis, respectively. Similarly, tc_X and tc_Y are the projected center point of the target object. rad_R and rad_T are the radius of the reference and the target objects, respectively. dis is the distance between the center point of the reference object and that of the target one, i.e., $dis = \sqrt{dis_X^2 + dis_Y^2}$. In addition, Ang is measured as an angle made between the centers of two objects when the reference object is considered as the center of the XY-coordinates.

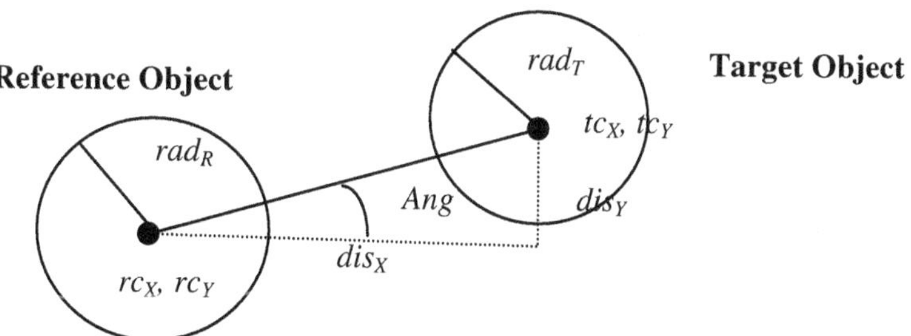

Fig. 1. Spatial relation between two objects in the SRC scheme

For spatial-match representation in the SRC scheme, we define seven positional operators such as *FA*(*Far-away*), *DJ*(*Disjoint*), *ME*(*Meet*), *OL*(*Overlap*), *CL*(*Is-included-by*), *IN*(*Include*), *SA*(*Same*). They are made from the positional operators of the SMR scheme in order to represent spatial relationship between two objects in the XY-coordinates. The spatial relation R^{AB} between two objects is determined as follows. Here DM means a distance multiplier for deciding *far-away*.

- $R^{AB} = FA$ iff $dis \geq (rad_R + rad_T) * DM$
- $R^{AB} = DJ$ iff $(rad_R + rad_T) < dis \leq (rad_R + rad_T) * DM$

- $R^{AB} = ME$ iff $dis = (rad_R + rad_T)$
- $R^{AB} = OL$ iff $(dis < rad_R + rad_T)$ $(((rad_R \leq rad_T)$ $(rad_R + dis > rad_T))$ $((rad_R > rad_T)$ $(rad_T + dis > rad_R)))$
- $R^{AB} = IN$ iff $(rad_R > rad_T)$ $(rad_T + dis \leq rad_R)$
- $R^{AB} = CL$ iff $(rad_T > rad_R)$ $(rad_R + dis \leq rad_T)$
- $R^{AB} = SA$ iff $(rad_T = rad_R)$ $(dis = 0)$

3.2 Spatial-Match Representation of the SRR Scheme

In order to identify a salient object in an image, a technique is needed to put the object in Minimum Bounding Rectangle (MBR)[10]. In other words, MBR is the rectangle that surrounds the object in terms of both the lower left corner (the minimum point on the X-axis and the Y-axis) and the upper right corner (the maximum point on the X-axis and the Y-axis). Using MBR, we can represent the spatial relationships between two objects based on the projections of the objects on the X-axis and the Y-axis. In Figure 2, rs_i and re_i are the projected minimum and maximum values of the reference object on the i-axis (i= X or Y), respectively. ts_i and te_i are the minimum value and the maximum value of the target object on the i-axis, respectively. As a result, rs_X is the projected minimum value of the reference object on the X-axis and re_X is the projected maximum value of the reference object on the X-axis. The same meaning is applied to rs_Y, re_Y, ts_X, te_X, ts_Y, te_Y.

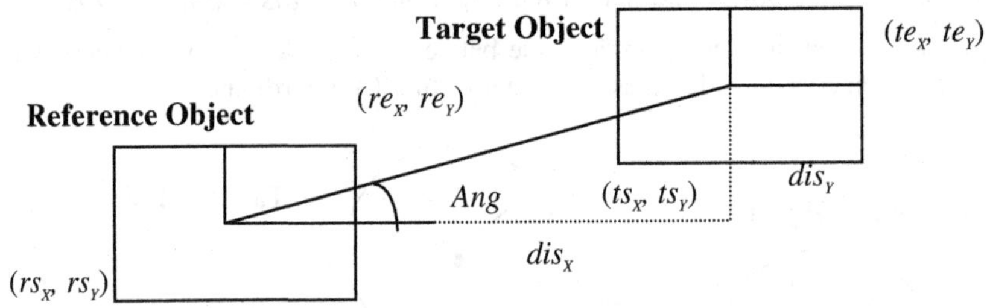

Fig. 2. . Spatial relation between two objects in the SRR scheme

Also, dis_X means the distance between the centers of two objects on the X-axis and dis_Y on the Y-axis. In addition, *Ang* is an angle measured between the centers of two objects when the center of reference object is considered as the center of the XY-coordinates. Based on the SMR positional operators [5], we use seven positional operators such as *FA*(*Far-away*), *DJ*(*disjoint*), *ME*(*Meet*), *OL*(*Overlap*), *CL*(*Is Included by*), *IN*(*Include*), *SA*(*Same*). The spatial relation R_i^{AB} between two objects for the i-axis is determined as follows:

- $R_i^{AB} = FA$ iff $dis_i \geq (re_i - rs_i + te_i - ts_i)/2*DM$
- $R_i^{AB} = DJ$ iff $(re_i - rs_i + te_i - ts_i)/2 < dis_i < (re_i - rs_i + te_i - ts_i)/2*DM$
- $R_i^{AB} = ME$ iff $dis_i = (re_i - rs_i + te_i - ts_i)/2$
- $R_i^{AB} = OL$ iff $(rs_i \leq ts_i$ $re_i < te_i)$ $(rs_i < ts_i$ $re_i \leq te_i)$ $(rs_i \geq ts_i$ $re_i > te_i)$ $(rs_i > ts_i$ $re_i \geq te_i)$
- $R_i^{AB} = CL$ iff $(rs_i \geq ts_i$ $re_i < te_i)$ $(rs_i > ts_i$ $re_i \leq te_i)$

- $R_i^{AB} = IN$ iff $(rs_i \leq ts_i \quad re_i > te_i) \quad (rs_i < ts_i \quad re_i \geq te_i)$
- $R_i^{AB} = SA$ iff $(dis_i = 0) \quad (\; re_i - rs_i = te_i - ts_i)$

The two-dimensional spatial relation R^{AB} between two objects is defined as follows. Here, R_X^{AB} and R_Y^{AB} indicate the spatial relationships between two objects A and B on the X-axis and the Y-axis, respectively.

- $R^{AB} = FA$ iff $R_X^{AB} = FA \quad R_Y^{AB} = FA$
- $R^{AB} = DJ$ iff $(R_X^{AB} \neq FA \quad R_Y^{AB} = DJ) \quad (R_Y^{AB} \neq FA \quad R_X^{AB} = DJ)$
- $R^{AB} = ME$ iff $(R_X^{AB} \neq FA \quad R_X^{AB} \neq DJ \quad R_Y^{AB} = ME) \quad (R_Y^{AB} \neq FA \quad R_Y^{AB} \neq DJ$ $R_X^{AB} = ME)$
- $R^{AB} = OL$ iff $(R_X^{AB} \neq FA \quad R_X^{AB} \neq DJ \quad R_X^{AB} \neq ME \quad R_Y^{AB} = OL)$
- $(R_Y^{AB} \neq FA \quad R_X^{AB} \neq DJ \quad R_Y^{AB} \neq ME \quad R_X^{AB} = OL)$
- $(R_Y^{AB} \neq CL \quad R_X^{AB} = IN) \quad (R_Y^{AB} \neq IN \quad R_X^{AB} = CL)$
- $R^{AB} = CL$ iff $(R_X^{AB} = CL \quad R_Y^{AB} = SA) \quad (R_X^{AB} = SA \quad R_Y^{AB} = CL) \quad (R_X^{AB} = CL$ $R_Y^{AB} = CL)$
- $R^{AB} = IN$ iff $(R_X^{AB} = IN \quad R_Y^{AB} = SA) \quad (R_X^{AB} = SA \quad R_Y^{AB} = IN) \quad (R_X^{AB} = IN$ $R_Y^{AB} = IN)$
- $R^{AB} = SA$ iff $R_X^{AB} = SA \quad R_Y^{AB} = SA$

We finally define a spatial string of two objects A and B as follows. Here, Ang is ranged from 0° to 360°.

- SS = (Reference Object A, Target Object B, R^{AB}, Ang)

3.3 Similar Topological Operators

When we analyze the seven topological operators, some topological operators, i.e., *IN* and *SA,* may have their similarity on spatial relationship, but they are determined to be different positional operators. For this, we classify the seven topological operators into two groups, i.e., *'disjoint'* and *'include'*. The *'disjoint'* group includes *far-away(FA), disjoint(DJ), meet(ME),* and *overlap(OL)* operators. The *'include'* group includes *include(IN), is-included-by(CL)* and *same(SA)* operators. We can compute their similarity between two operators as follows.

1. In the *'disjoint'* group, we determine their similarity between the four topological operators. The topological operators can be ordered according to their similarity, i.e., *FA – DJ – ME – OL.* For instance, *FA* has the highest similarity with *DJ* while it has the lowest similarity with OL.
2. In the *'include'* group, we also determine their similarity between the three positional operators, in the order of *CL – SA – IN*. For instance, *CL* has the highest similarity with *SA* while having the lowest similarity with IN.
3. Finally, we determine that there is no similarity between one of the topological operators in the *'disjoint'* group and one in the *'include'* group, except *OL*. In case of *OL*, we determine that *OL* has its similarity to *CL and IN* of the *'include'* group.

Figure 3 depicts a graph to describe their similarity between seven topological operators based on the above procedure. Using Figure 4, we can compute the similarity distance (sim_dis) between positional operators as the number of edges between nodes, as shown in Table 1.

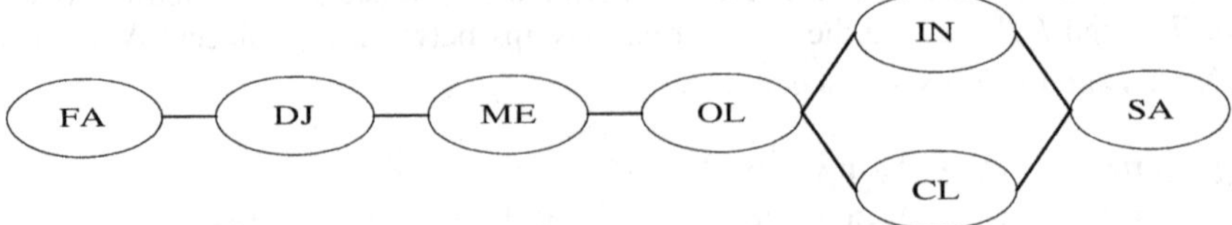

Fig. 3. Similarity graph of positional operators

Table 1. Similarity distance between positional operators

	FA	DJ	ME	OL	CL	SA	IN
FA	0	1	2	3	4	5	4
DJ	1	0	1	2	3	4	3
ME	2	1	0	1	2	3	2
OL	3	2	1	0	1	2	1
CL	4	3	2	1	0	1	2
SA	5	4	3	2	1	0	1
IN	4	3	4	3	2	1	0

3.4 Indexing Scheme with Ranking

To support ranking for providing the retrieved results in the order of their similarity to a user query, we devise a new weighting scheme which can rank the results based on the angle made between two objects and their positional operator. Let X be a spatial string in an iconic image and Y be a spatial string in an iconic query image. When two spatial strings X and Y are denoted by X=(A, B, R^{AB}, Ang) and Y=(QA, QB, QR^{AB}, $QAng$), respectively, the following formula (1) calculates a weighting value between X and Y ($0 < W^{XY} \leq 1$) if both conditions are satisfied. Otherwise, $W^{XY} = 0$.

- the two objects from each string are the same, i.e., $A = QA$ and $B = QB$, and
- the angle difference, i.e., |Ang-Qang|, is less than a threshold (θ).

$$W^{XY} = 1 - \frac{|Ang - QAng|}{\theta} * \delta \quad (1)$$

where,

$$\delta = \frac{1}{1 + \text{sim\_dis}(R^{AB}, QR^{AB})} \quad \text{if sim\_dis}(R^{AB}, QR^{AB}) \quad \text{thres\_dis}$$

$$\delta = 0 \quad \text{otherwise}$$

Here *sim_dis*(R^{AB} , QR^{AB}) means the similarity distance between R^{AB} and QR^{AB} and *thres_dis* means a threshold distance for deciding whether or not we consider the similarity distance between R^{AB} and QR^{AB}. That is, if *sim_dis*(R^{AB} , QR^{AB}) is greater than *thres_dis*, its position weight, δ, equals to 0. Because an iconic image commonly has multiple objects, the number of spatial strings for an image is calculated as $m(m-1)/2$, where m is the number of objects in an iconic image. Therefore, we can compute a weight W_{PQ} between an iconic image (P) in the database and an iconic query image(Q) as the following formula (2). Here, n is the number of spatial strings in Q and W_i^{XY} is the weighting value between the i-th spatial string of Q and its matching spatial string of P.

$$W_{PQ} = \frac{\sum_{i=1}^{n} W_i^{XY}}{n} \tag{2}$$

4 Inversion-Based Access Method

Since the 9DLT and the SMR schemes make use of a signature file [11] as their access methods, they have good performance in terms of storage utilization. However, due to the characteristics of the signature file, they have two disadvantages. First, they can not support ranking for the retrieved result. Secondly, since they do post scanning, it takes long time in a retrieval operation, especially when the number of spatial strings are large. Thus, our schemes use an inverted file [12] as its access method in order to support ranking and fast retrieval. Figure 4 shows the structure of an inversion-based retrieval method used for our schemes.

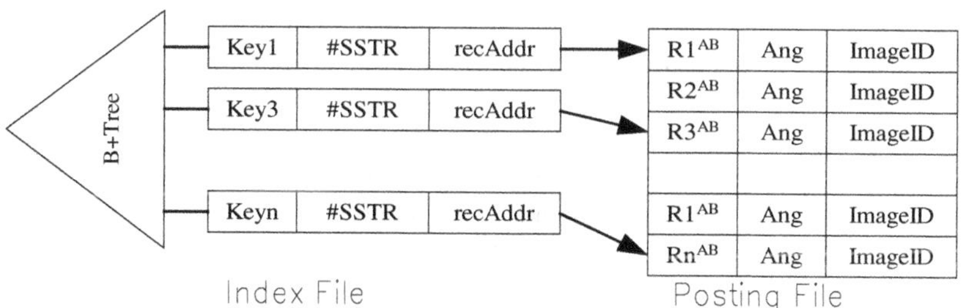

Fig. 4. The inverted file structure used for our schemes

To construct a key, we combine two object identifiers from a spatial string. For instance, suppose a spatial string (*A, B, OL, 234°*). We concatenate A and B to form a string 'AB', which is used as the key of the string. In Figure 4, *recAddr* means the address of posting file record corresponding to a given key in the posting file and *#SSTR* means the number of the spatial strings with the key. In addition, R^{AB} indicates the topological operator of a spatial string, *Ang* indicates the angle of a spatial string, and *ImageID* indicates the identifier of an iconic image related with a spatial string.

For inserting a spatial string being (*A*, *B*, R^{AB}, *Ang*) in a iconic image referred by *ImageID*, our scheme makes a key out of two object identifiers in the spatial string and search the key in our inversion-based retrieval method. If the key, i.e., 'AB', already exists in the index file, we read the posting file record pointed by the key and increase *#SSTR* by 1. Then, we insert R^{AB}, *Ang* , and *ImageID* into the posting file record. If the key does not exist in the index file, we make a new posting file record and set *#SSTR* to 1. Then, we insert R^{AB}, *Ang* , and *ImageID* into the posting file record. Finally, we insert the new key into the index file. For retrieval, we first make a set of spatial strings, being (*QA, QB*, QR^{AB}, *QAng*), from an iconic query image. Then, we construct a key from each spatial string and search the index file with the keys. If all of the keys do not exist in the index file, there is no iconic image satisfying the query in the database. Meanwhile, if one of the keys, i.e., '*QAQB*' is found in the index file, we read the posting file record with the key from the posting file. Then, we obtain a pair of W^{XY} *and ImageID* by comparing (QR^{AB}, *QAng*) with all of the spatial strings in the posting file record. Next, we compute W_{PQ} by averaging W^{XY} for each *ImageID* after finding a set of W^{XY} *and ImageID* pairs for all the spatial strings of the query image. Thirdly, we obtain the retrieved results by excluding iconic images having smaller W_{PQ} than a given value. We finally rank the results in the order of W_{PQ} and provide them to users.

5 Performance Analysis

For our experiment, we assume that an iconic image consists of icon objects each of which has its object identifier and its position. The position is described by two points in the XY-coordinates, such as the low left corner and the upper right corner. In addition, the threshold of angle difference , i.e., θ, is determined to be 45° because many people use eight directions, such as north, northeast, as so on. *thres_dis* is also determined to be one because adjacent topological operators in their similarity graph are definitely considered to be similar. Finally, we make use of the following data.

- For the database used for our experiment, we collect 150 images from interior design books.
- The iconic image transformed from each image has 3 to 20 icon objects.
- The icon objects used in the database are 53 different types.
- For the user query, we generate 45 iconic query images.
- Each iconic query image has 2 to 3 icon objects.

For the performance evaluation, we compare our SRC and SRR schemes with the 9DLT and the SMR in terms of retrieval effectiveness as well as system efficiency. In order to evaluate the retrieval effectiveness, we make use of recall and precision measures [13]. The test panel is composed of ten graduate school students from our department of computer engineering. Here, the 9DLT(E) and the 9DLT(A) stand for the exact match and the approximate match of the 9DLT scheme, respectively. Similarly, the SMR(E) and the SMR(A) stand for the exact match and the approximate match of the SMR scheme. For the precision and the recall, we adopt the 11-point measure [13]. Since the 9DLT and the SMR can not support ranking, we measure the performances in two ways for fair comparison, as shown in Table 2. One is for the ranking where the retrieved result is provided in the order of its relevance to a query. The other is for the non-ranking where the retrieved result is provided without ordering. In the case of the ranking, since the 9DLT and the SMR do not support the ranking, we rank the retrieved images in the order of the sequence retrieved. Table 2 shows the precision and recall of the 9DLT, the SMR, our SRC, and our SRR. In the case of the non-ranking, our SRR scheme is nearly the same as the 9DLT, but it is superior to the SMR in terms of the recall while it is inferior to the SMR in terms of the precision. In addition, our SRC scheme is lower than the 9DLT and the SMR in terms of the recall. In the case of the ranking, our SRR and SRC schemes are superior to the 9DLT and the SMR in terms of both the precision and the recall. Our SRC scheme has a good result in terms of the precision, while our SRR scheme has a good result in terms of the recall. That is, our SRC scheme holds about 7% higher recall and 16-19% higher precision, while our SRR scheme holds about 25% higher recall and 9-12% higher precision. Figure 5 shows the recall-precision graph of the 9DLT(A), the SMR(A), the SRC(40) and the SRR(40) with the 11-point measure. As shown in the graph, our SRC and SRR schemes show overall better performance than the 9DLT and the SMR.

Table 2. Comparison of retrieval effectiveness

Retrieval Effectiveness	Non-Ranking Recall	Non-Ranking Precision	Ranking Recall	Ranking Precision
9DLT (E)	71.3675	31.3010	26.9559	34.5807
9DLT (A)	71.3675	31.3010	26.9559	34.5807
SMR (E)	46.9810	56.3167	25.0000	30.8750
SMR (A)	62.4083	50.2611	26.6131	31.7019
SRC (40)	46.2806	30.1548	31.9964	59.0410
SRC (50)	36.9437	38.5424	39.7960	50.0905
SRC (60)	36.6734	41.1227	32.4071	40.3550
SRC (70)	43.6774	49.8143	28.1036	42.4512
SRR (40)	69.0556	36.3170	51.7525	43.4000
SRR (50)	57.6953	46.3286	58.2265	38.0101
SRR (60)	54.1238	47.3750	59.5278	35.4008
SRR (70)	49.4632	50.7071	58.7405	35.3712

In order to evaluate system efficiency, we compare our SRC and SRR schemes with the 9DLT and the SMR in terms of storage overhead (SO), insertion time, and retrieval time. SO is computed as *(index size / iconic image size)*100*. Table 3 shows the insertion, the retrieval time and SO. As shown in Table 3, the insertion operation of our SRC is about three times slower than that of 9DLT(E) and about twice slower than SMR(E). And our SRR is about five times slower than that of 9DLT(E) and about three times slower than SMR(E). This is because our SRC and SRR schemes require append operations to the posting file more frequently than the 9DLT(E) and the SMR(E). Meanwhile, the insertion operation of our SRC is three times faster than that of 9DLT(A) and about seven times faster than that of SMR(A). Similarly, our SRR is twice faster than the 9DLT(A) and about five times faster than SMR(A). This is because the 9DLT(A) and the SMR(A) take long time for making their signature files due to a large number of spatial strings.

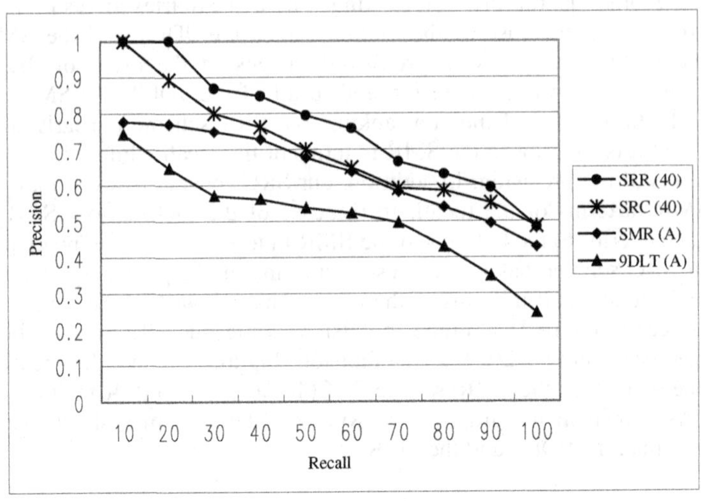

Fig. 5. Recall-precision graph

Table 3. Performance comparison in terms of system efficiency (sec.)

Efficiency	9DLT(E)	9DLT(A)	SMR(E)	SMR(A)	SRC	SRR
Insert Time	6.46	67.11	13.18	168.97	24.40	34.50
Retrieval Time	5.62	41.94	8.52	90.99	0.69	1.37
SO	19	63	24	90	471	651

The retrieval operation of our SRC is about eight times faster than the 9DLT(E), about sixty times faster than SMR(E), about twelve times faster than 9DLT(A), and about one hundred thirty times faster than SMR(A). And our SRR is about five times faster than the 9DLT(E), about seven times faster than SMR(E), about thirty times faster than 9DLT(A), and about seventy times faster than SMR(A). This is because our SRC and SRR schemes need not do post scanning because of using the inverted file. However, since our SRC and SRR schemes use the inverted file, they require about five to thirty times lager storage overhead than the 9DLT and the SMR. In addition, because the representation of our SRC scheme is simple than that of our SRR scheme, our SRC scheme is faster and takes little disk space than our SRR scheme.

6 Conclusions

In this paper, we proposed new spatial-match iconic image representations, called SRC and SRR, which combine the directional operators with the positional operators so that they might provide precise relationships between icon objects in an iconic image. Since our SRC and SRR schemes also support ranking for the retrieved result, they can rank the result in the order of their relevance to a user query. From our experiment, we showed that our SRC and SRR schemes should be superior to the 9DLT and the SMR in terms of retrieval effectiveness. In addition, our SRC and SRR schemes showed about six to one hundred thirty times faster retrieval efficiency than the 9DLT and the SMR, while they spent about eight to ten times more storage overhead. When we compare our SRC with our SRR, our SRR scheme is better in terms of retrieval effectiveness, while our SRC scheme is better in terms of system efficiency. Therefore, our SRC and SRR schemes are shown to be suitable for developing multimedia information systems which require ranking as well as fast retrieval. For future work, it is necessary to prove the superiority of our spatial-match iconic image representations by applying them to real multimedia database applications with a large amount of data.

References

1. V.N. Gudivada and V.V. Raghavan, "Design, and Evaluation of Algorithms for Image Retrieval by Spatial Similarity," ACM Transactions on Information Systems, Vol. 13, No. 2, pp.115-144, 1995.
2. S. K. Chang, Q.Y. Shi, and C.W. Yan, "Iconic Indexing by 2D strings", IEEE Transaction on Pattern Recognition and Machine Intelligence, 9(3): pp. 413-428, 1987.
3. S.Y. Lee and F.J. Hsu, "Spatial Reasoning and Similarity Retrieval of Images using 2D C-string Knowledge Representation," Pattern Recognition, Vol. 25, No. 3, pp. 305-318, 1992.
4. C.C. Chang and J.H. Jiang, "A Fast Spatial Match Retrieval Using a Superimposed Coding Techniques," International Symposium on ADTI(Nara, Japan), pp.71-78, 1994.
5. J.W. Chang, Y.J. Kim and K.J. Chang," A Spatial Match Representation Scheme for Indexing and Querying in Iconic Image Databases," ACM International Conference on Information and Knowledge Management, pp. 169-176, Nov. 1997.
6. M. Nabil, A.H. Ngu, and J. Shepherd, "Picture Similarity Retrieval Using the 2D Projection Interval Representation," IEEE Transaction on Knowledge and Data Engineering, Vol. 8, No. 4, 1996.
7. T. Tagashira and T. Amagasa and M. Aritsugi and Y. Kanamori, "Interval-Based Representation of Spatio-Temporal Concepts," 9th International Conference on Advanced Information Systems Engineering (CaiSE*97) Springer LNCS 1250, pp. 231-244, 1997.
8. J. Halpern and Y. Shoham, "A Prepositional Model Logic of Time Intervals", Journal of Association Computing Machinery, Vol. 33, pp.935-962, Oct. 1991.
9. M. Safar and C. Shahabi, "2D Topological and Directional Relations in the World of Minimum Bounding Circles," International Database Engineering and Applications Symposium, pp. 239-247, 1999.
10. D. Papadias, Y. Theodoridis, T. Sellis and M.J. Egnhofer, "Topological Relations in the World of Minimum Bounding Rectangles: a Study with R-trees," ACM SIGMOD on Management of Data, pp. 92-103, 1995.
11. C. Faloutsos and S. Christodoulakis, "Signature Files : An Access Methods for Documents and its Analytical Performance Evaluation, " ACM Transaction on Database Systems, 2(4) pp. 267-288, 1984.
12. G. Salton, and M. McGill, "An Introduction to Modern Information Retrieval," McGraw-Hill, 1983.
13. R.R. Korfhage, "Information Storage and Retrieval," Wiley Computer Publishing, pp.199-202, 1997.

Similarity-Based Operators in Image Database Systems

Solomon Atnafu[1], Lionel Brunie[1], and Harald Kosch[2]

[1] Information Systems Engineering Laboratory, INSA de Lyon
Bat.Blaise Pascal, 20 Avenue Albert Einstein, 69621 Villeurbanne, France
{Solomon.Atnafu, Lionel.Brunie}@lisi.insa-lyon.fr
[2] Institute of Information Technology, University Klagenfurt
Universitätsstr. 65-67, 9020 Klagenfurt, Austria
harald.kosch@itec.uni-klu.ac.at

Abstract. The integration of similarity-based data retrieval techniques into database management systems, in order to efficiently support multimedia data, is currently an active research issue. In this paper, we first demonstrate the necessity of introducing novel similarity-based operations in image databases, with example queries. Then, we introduce our image data repository model that is designed to support similarity-based operations under the object-relational database paradigm. We then define novel similarity-based algebraic operators that are frequently required and study their properties in image database management systems. Finally, we investigate the possibilities of extending the proposed image table model to support salient-based operations on image database systems.

1 Introduction

The importance of using the low level contents of image data for its identification, storage and operation purpose has been one of the active issues of research in the last decade. As a result, a number of research prototypes, applications, and commercial systems that support low-level content manipulation has been developed [12,2,13,8,14]. Thus, the use of low-level contents for similarity-based search has become a promising approach for image and video data management. Thus, in this paper, we focus on the management of content-based[1] image databases. A number of works are done to integrate image and other media data with content-based data retrieval methods using different techniques [8,3,6,7]. What most of the currently available content-based image retrieval systems do in common is that, for a given single query image, they search for the most similar images from a set of or database of images. This in principle can be associated to a content-based selection operation in a multimedia database systems. However, other more complex operations such as "content-based join operation"[2] (i.e. a

[1] *In this paper, the terms "content-based" and "similarity-based" are used interchangeably.*

[2] *See Section 4 for more details on this operation.*

X.S. Wang, G. Yu, and H. Lu (Eds.): WAIM 2001, LNCS 2118, pp. 14–25, 2001.

Similarity-based matching of two or more image tables) are not considered in the works done in this area. We believe that there is the need to consider such operations and to develop a formal framework for the similarity-based operations on image databases identical to that of the traditional database operators. Hence, the purpose of this paper is to identify and introduce the most needed similarity-based operations, to study their properties, to formalize the use of these operations, and to see the way of using these similarity-based operations in conjunction with the relational operators under an Object-Rrelational (OR) paradigm. The capability of an OR DBMS to support multimedia data is widely discussed in [11].

To demonstrate the practical significance of our work, consider that an image table consist of the attribute components: image, the feature vector representation [3] of the image, and a component that contains alphanumeric information about the image. Let EMP is an image table of employee of a company and contains the attribute components: photo of the employee, feature vector representation of the corresponding photo, the name of the employee, his/her occupation, etc. Let SI be an image table that contains images of individuals who appeared and entered by the front gate of the company where a surveillance camera is mounted, the corresponding feature vector representations of their images, the date and time at which each of the images was scanned or taken.

Suppose now that there is an investigation scenario of an event that is associated to the images in SI. SI alone can not give a complete information about a person whose photo is captured. It is therefore necessary, to perform some operations on the tables in order to get a complete information of a person whose image is in SI. Sinse, operations based on similarity measures do not perform accurate matching, a common practice is to search for a range of the most similar images. An investigator may pose the following query.

Query: *For pictures of individuals in SI that were scanned yesterday from 4 to 6PM, find their most similar images from EMP, with their corresponding name and address.*

Processing this query requires a relational selection on the SI table and then a "similarity-based join" on SI and EMP. This demonstrates the need for a combined use of relational and similarity-based operations on image tables. To facilitate similarity-based system of operations we also need a convienent image data repository model.

Thus, to introduce such system of operations in image database systems, we first present in Section 2 the related work in the domain. Section 3 introduces our model for an image data repository. In Section 4, the most commonly required similarity-based operators are introduced and their properties are studied. Section 5 demonstrates how our image table model can be extended to support operations on salient objects of an image. Finally, conclusions are given.

---

[3] *That is, a vector representation of an image in terms of its features such as color, texture, shape, etc.*

2 Related Work

A number of content-based image retrieval research prototype systems such as Photobook, Netra, Surfimage, VisualSeek, CAFIIR, STAR etc. [8,15,5,3] are currently in practice. Commercial database systems have also started to integrate content-based image retrieval modules in their systems. QBIC is a content-based image query system available commercially either in standalone form, or as part of other IBM products such as the DB2 Digital Library. It offers retrieval by any combination of color, texture or shape - as well as by text keyword [15]. However, it doesn't support operations such as the "similarity-based join". The VIR Image Engine from Virage is a well-known commercial system. It is available as a series of independent modules, that system developers can integrate in to their own programs. The engine provides the fundamental capability for analyzing and comparing images. But, it has no concept of persistent storage, user interfaces, query processing nor optimization [3]. It is a pure set of algorithms that is designed to be embedded in software and hardware systems where its capabilities are needed. This makes it easy to extend it by building new types of query interface, or additional customized modules to process specialized collections of images. As a result, the VIR Image Engine is available as an add-on to the existing database management systems such as Oracle8i Enterprise Edition [7]. The Excalibur Image DataBlade Module from Excalibur Technologies is a product that offers a variety of image indexing and matching techniques based on the company's own proprietary pattern recognition technology. This datablade module is incorporated in the Informix database system to support a content-based image storage and retrieval [6].

A common feature of the add-on modules integrated in these DBMSs is that, given a query image, they search its most similar images from a database of images using their respective content-based image retrieval engines. That is, the attempts so far didn't exceed from these one-to-many content-based image retrieval operations. A positive result of these works is that, one can use SQL based statements to store, and retrieve images using content-based feature representations. However, as said before, these systems are strongly limited in terms of supporting complex similarity-based operations and mixed queries involving both relational and similarity-based operations.

3 A Model for an Image Data Repository

The introduction of images in to a database management system has required different techniques to store, describe, and manipulate image data. W.I. Grosky et al have given a model that describes the information that can be captured by an image data to facilitate its storage and content-based retrieval [4]. According to this model, the information that an image data can posses may be seen as physical view (image matrix and image header) and logival view (global and content-based view). Thus, an image repository or an image table should manage to capture all these information regarding an image.

In this paper we introduce our novel image data repository model (which we also refer it as "*image table*"), that is defined under an OR paradigm.

Definition 3.1. (Image Table)

An object-relational image table is defined as a table of five components $M(id, O, F, A, P)$. Where:

- id is a unique identifier of an instance of M,
- O is a reference to the image object itself which can be stored as a $BLOB$ internally in the table or which can be referenced as an external $BFILE$,
- F is a feature vector representation of the object O.
- A is an attribute component that is used to describe the object using keyword like annotations and may be declared as a set of object types,
- P is a data structure that is used to capture pointer links to instances of other tables associated by a binary operation.

Note that, in an image table M, the item of primary importance for a content-based retrieval is the image itself. The image is described by its feature vector and all the remaining attributes are associated to the image. The three components O, F, and A can be used to capture sufficient information on an image data. P can be considered as a column whose content is a data structure that can store links to instances of other tables during binary operations such as similarity-based join. P has a value *null* in the base tables, but a non-null value in the resulting table of a similarity-based binary operation. More formally, when it contains a value, P can be expressed as a set of tuples of the form $(table,\ set\_of\_ids)$, where the component *table* denotes the associated table by a binary operation and set_of_ids is the set of its referenced id elements. After a similarity-based binary operation like a similarity-based join of M_1 and M_2(see Section 4 for the Definitions), the P component of the resulting image table, M', holds a link to a table M_2. Then, for each instance of M', P will contain elements of the form $(M_2, \{id_2^1, ..., id_2^h\})$, where h is the number of instances of M_2 associated by the operation.

With the help of this image table model, we can manage the requirements to integrate a content-based image data in an OR data management system more convienently. Furthermore, this model can be extended to support the storage of segmented objects of an image to enable us perform salient-based operations on image tables.

4 The Similarity-Based Operators

To define the novel similarity-based operators on image tables we use the method of content-based range query [9]. A content-based range query on a set of images S returns those image objects that are within distance[4] of ε from the query

[4] *Here, distance is defined as the distance between the feature vectors representing the images in a feature space*

image q. Thus, we define our similarity-based operators as given below. At the end of this section, we will show how the range query is advantageous over the k-Nearest Neighbour method [10] for similarity-based opearations in image database systems.

4.1 The Similarity-Based Selection Operator

The similarity-based selection operator is a unary operator on an image table performed on the component F based on the following definition.

Definition 4.1. (Similarity-Based Selection)

Given an image query object o with its feature vector representation, an image table M, and a positive real number ε; a similarity-based selection operation denoted by $\sigma_o^\varepsilon(M)$, is given by: $\sigma_o^\varepsilon(M) = \{(id, o', f, a, p) \in M | o' \in NN^\varepsilon(M, o)\}$, where $NN^\varepsilon(M, o)$ denotes the range query with respect to ε for query image object o and an image table M.

The similarity-based selection operation first uses the range query search method to select the image objects that are most similar to o from the objects in M (which is also expressed by the notation $NN^\varepsilon(M, o)$). Then, it identifies the instances of M whose image objects are selected to be similar to o.

4.2 The Similarity-Based Join Operator

A similarity-based join is a binary operator on image tables performed on the feature vector components as defined formally below.

Definition 4.2. (Similarity-Based Join Operation)

Let $M_1(id_1, O_1, F_1, A_1, P_1)$ and $M_2(id_2, O_2, F_2, A_2, P_2)$ be two image tables and let ε be a positive real number. The similarity-based join operation on M_1 and M_2, denoted by $M_1 \otimes^\varepsilon M_2$, is given by:
$M_1 \otimes^\varepsilon M_2 = \{(id_1, o_1, f_1, a_1, p_1') | (id_1, o_1, f_1, a_1, p_1) \in M_1 \; and \; p_1' = p_1 \cup (M_2, s\_id^\varepsilon(M_2, o_1)) \; and \; p_1' \neq null\}$, where $s\_id^\varepsilon(M_2, o_1) = \prod_{M_2.id}(\sigma_{o_1}^\varepsilon(M_2))$ (i.e. the *ids* contained by the projection on the *id* component of the associated instances of M_2).

Each instance of an image table and a resulting table of a multimedia join [5] is identified by its unique identifier, *id*. Note that if the content of p_1 is *null* (not pointing to M_2), then its instance will not be contained in the resulting table. This definition of a similarity-based join reflects the practical needs of content-based image retrieval. Figure 1. illustrates, the resulting tables of two similarity-based joins. The similarity-based operators defined above depend on "relative" measures. Due to this, the similarity-based operators possess different

[5] *In this paper and in [1], the terms "similarity-based join" and "multimedia join" are given interchangably.*

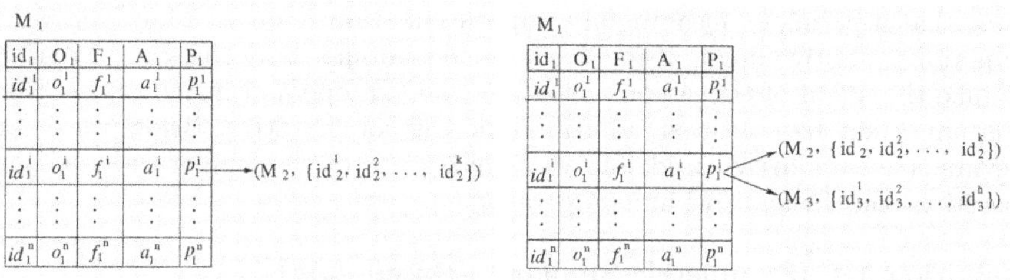

Fig. 1. The Similarity-based joins $M_1 \otimes^{\varepsilon} M_2$ and $(M_1 \otimes^{\varepsilon} M_2) \otimes^{\varepsilon} M_3$ respectively

.

algebraic properties than that of the relational ones. For example, contrary to the relational join operator, we observed that the similarity-based join operator $\otimes^{\varepsilon}$ is not commutative. This shows that in similarity-based join operation, the order of the image tables is meaningful. If an image table appears at the left of a similarity-based join, then its objects are taken as reference for the similarity operation. In the example Query of Section 1, the image table SI should appear at the left if we are interested to know about the individuals who entered the gate. Furthermore, the similarity-based join operator $\otimes^{\varepsilon}$ is clearly not associative. However, an operator without these properties of commutativity and associativity is difficult to be exploited for query optimization. We thus need to see possibilities of extending this operator so that it satisfies these useful properties.

4.3 A Symmetric Similarity-Based Join Operator

In view of the current practices of content-based query systems (where for a given image query object, we search for its most similar objects from a database of image objects), the similarity-based join defined above is what may be needed for many applications. However, its non-commutativeness and non-associativeness makes it lose the good properties that the relational join operator has. To make the similarity-based join operator suitable for similarity-based query optimization, we extend the similarity-based join operator to a *Symmetric Multimedia Join* operator in such a way that it satisfies the useful properties for query optimization. To facilitate this, let us first define the following basic operator, the *Additive Union.*

Definition 4.3. (Additive Union)

Let M_1 and M_2 be two image tables, the Additive Union of M_1 and M_2 denoted by $M_1 \uplus M_2$ is an image table that merges all the records of M_2 to M_1 or vice versa. The additive union contains all the instances that are either in M_1 or in M_2, without excluding none of the instances of M_1 or M_2.

To perform a similarity-based binary operation on two image tables, we assume that their feature vector component F are extracted identically in such a way that it permits a meaningful computation of range query. Moreover, when we perform additive union, if the A components do not have the same structure we take the union of the A components of the two operand image tables. Here it is important to note that additive union is commutative. Below we define a symmetric similarity-based join that makes use of the similarity-based join operation and the additive union operator.

Definition 4.4. (Symmetric Similarity-Based Join)

Let M_1 and M_2 be two image tables, the symmetric similarity-based join of M_1 and M_2 denoted by $M_1 \oplus^{\varepsilon} M_2$ is formally defined as:
$M_1 \oplus^{\varepsilon} M_2 = (M_1 \otimes^{\varepsilon} M_2) \uplus (M_2 \otimes^{\varepsilon} M_1)$.

Hence, a symmetric similarity-based join $\oplus^{\varepsilon}$ possesses the property of commutativity. i.e. $M_1 \oplus^{\varepsilon} M_2 = M_2 \oplus^{\varepsilon} M_1$. This follows directly from the commutativity of the additive union.

We can now generalize the symmetric symilarity-based join on more than two image tables and define a *Multi Symmetric Similarity-Based Join.* This definition reflects the characteristics of similarity-based operations and maintains useful properties for similarity-based query optimization.

Definition 4.5.(The Multi Symmetric Similarity-Based Join)

Let M_1, M_2, ... M_n be n image tables. The Multi Symmetric Similarity-Based Join, denoted by $M_1 \oplus M_2 \oplus ... \oplus M_n$ is defined as:

$$M_1 \oplus M_2 \oplus ... \oplus M_n = \biguplus_{i<j;\ 1 \leq i,\ j \leq n} M_i \oplus M_j$$

The way the multi symmetric similarity-based join operates is not identical to that of the multiway join known in relational database systems. Here, it doesn't consider intermediate resulting tables as operands. This property could rather be useful when considering the properties of content-based image retrieval. It is important to note here the order of the operands is not relevant on the result of a multi symmetric similarity-based join. Though order is not relevant for the result, the order of each pair of operands can effectively be utilized for query optimization purpose as in the case of relational join operation.

4.4 Relationships between the Symmetric and Non-symmetric Similarity-Based Joins

The *Extract* Operator: The Similarity-Based Join, stated in Definition 4.2 (which is non-symmetric), can be expressed in terms of the symmetric similarity-based join by by the use of an operator called *Extract* [1]. Hence, the following holds true.

$M_1 \otimes^{\varepsilon} M_2 = Extract_{M_1}(M_1 \oplus^{\varepsilon} M_2)$ and
$M_2 \otimes^{\varepsilon} M_1 = Extract_{M_2}(M_1 \oplus^{\varepsilon} M_2)$,

The *Mine* Operator: We stated above that the symmetric similarity-based join can be interpreted as the additive union of the two one sided joins (non-symmetric similarity-based joins). After having the resulting table for one of the one-sided joins, we present here the method to get the other without applying similarity-based operations. If for example we have the resulting table of $M_1 \otimes^\varepsilon M_2$ with its new P_1 component, we can make use of the contents of P_1 to get the instances of $M_2 \otimes^\varepsilon M_1$ by direct statistics collection. This follows from the idea that, given the same value of ε, if an object o_2 of M_2 is within a distance of ε to the object o_1 of M_1, then the converse is also true, by the symmetric property of distance. This is a property that we can get from the use of range query [9] (i.e. we can not have this advantage if we use for example the k-NN search method). Hence, we can compute the symmetric similarity-based join, $M_1 \oplus^\varepsilon M_2$, by performing only one of the one-sided joins and then using an operator called the *Mine* operator for the other. The major advantage of this approach is that, the *Mine* operator could be much less expensive than similarity-based join.

Let us first define and demonstrate the use of the *Mine* operator on a simple multimedia join, $M_1 \otimes^\varepsilon M_2$. Then, we will show how it can be generalized for any complex multimedia join expression.

Definition 4.6.(The Mine operator)

Consider the multimedia join $M_1 \otimes^\varepsilon M_2$. The *Mine* operator on $M_1 \otimes^\varepsilon M_2$, denoted as $Mine(M_1 \otimes^\varepsilon M_2)$ uses the component P of the resulting table of $M_1 \otimes^\varepsilon M_2$ and builds the table $M_2 \otimes^\varepsilon M_1$. Conversely, $Mine(M_2 \otimes^\varepsilon M_1)$ uses the component P of the resulting table of $M_2 \otimes^\varepsilon M_1$ and builds the table $M_1 \otimes^\varepsilon M_2$.

To demonstrate the use of *Mine* let us first distinguish the difference between non-referring and non-referenced instances of an operand image table of a multimedia join. For the multimedia join $M_1 \otimes^\varepsilon M_2$: %vspace-0.15cm

- if the object of an instance of M_1 has no similarity matching in M_2 by the multimedia join, we say that it is a non referring instance. Conversely,
- if an instance of M_2 is not associated by the similarity matching of the multimedia join, we say that this instance is a non-referenced instance of M_2.

Considering the multimedia join $M_1 \otimes^\varepsilon M_2$, suppose M_1 has a set of referring instances M_1' and non-referring instances $M"_1$. Note that, M_1' and $M"_1$ are disjoint and that $M_1 = M_1' \uplus M"_1$. Suppose also that M_2 has a set of referenced instances M_2' and a set of non-referenced instances $M"_2$. Note also that, M_2' and $M"_2$ are disjoint and that $M_2 = M_2' \uplus M"_2$. Then, the symmetric multimedia join expression: $M_1 \oplus^\varepsilon M_2 = (M_1' \uplus M"_1) \oplus (M_2' \uplus M"_2)$ will finally be reduced to: $M_1 \oplus^\varepsilon M_2 = (M_1' \otimes^\varepsilon M_2') \uplus (M_2' \otimes^\varepsilon M_1')$.

Thus, if $M_1' \otimes^\varepsilon M_2'$ is computed using the similarity-based join operation of Def. 4.2, the other (i.e. $M_2' \otimes^\varepsilon M_1'$) can be generated using the *Mine* operator or vice-versa. The Algorithm on Figure 2 demonstrates how the *Mine* operator computes $M_2' \otimes^\varepsilon M_1'$, from the resulting table of $M_1' \otimes^\varepsilon M_2'$. Note that, if an instance of M_1 is not referring in the join $M_1 \otimes^\varepsilon M_2$, then it can not be re-referenced by $M_2 \otimes^\varepsilon M_1$. Furthermore, dropping the non-referring and non-referenced instances from the resulting image table will not affect the commutative property of the symmetric similarity-based join.

Create table T = T(id, O, F, A, P)
Foreach instance *inst* of M' **Do**
    Foreach element id_2 of $inst.P_1'$ **Do**
        If id_2 is not in T
        Append $get\_instance(M_2, id_2)$ in T
        End If
        Update P of $T.id_2$ with $M'.id_1$
    End Do
End Do
Return(T).   /* $T = M_2 \otimes^\varepsilon M_1$ */

Fig. 2. Algorithm for the *Mine* operator

There is a great deal of work that can be done by a query optimizer to select the appropriate strategy. It is up to the query optimizer to choose which similarity-based join to do first and then use the *Mine* operator for the other. Hence, we can clearly see that the symmetric similarity-based join can be more effectively processed with query optimization techniques.

The *Mine* operator given above for a simple similarity-based join (i.e. a similarity-based join between two image tables) can be generalized to apply on complex similarity-based join expressions. The general principle is that, for each one-sided similarity-based join, we can compute the other sided join with the use of the *Mine* operator.

For a short description, let us consider the symmetric similarity-based join of three image tables M_1, M_2, and M_3, $((M_1 \oplus^\varepsilon M_2) \oplus^\varepsilon M_3)$. To compute $M_1 \oplus^\varepsilon M_2 \oplus^\varepsilon M_3$, the system needs to process six similarity-based joins (non-symmetric) based on Definition 4.2. However, we can only compute three of the similarity-based joins and the rest three can be generated using the *Mine* operator. In like manner, to compute a multi symmetric similarity-based join with n operand tables, we need to compute $n(n-1)$ non-symmetric similarity-based joins, out of which $n(n-1)/2$ of them can be generated using the *Mine* operator. Then, the results can be merged to form the multi symmetric similarity-based join based on Definition 4.5.

4.5 Other Operators on Image Tables

In relational database systems, the Intersection, Union, and Difference operators are among those operators that are commonly used. These operators can be adopted to be used on image tables of the schematic form $M(id, O, F, A, P)$ we considered in this paper. Below, we describe, the way how we can perform these operations on image tables.

- The **Intersection** of two image tables M_1 and M_2, denoted by $M_1 \cap M_2$, is the set of instances that are in both M_1 and M_2. M_1 and M_2 are required to have the same attributes. Comparison on the A component is based on the relational rules. We say that two F values are the same, if their feature vector representation match when placed in the feature space with a certain freedom of error, as far as this error doesn't have effect on the identicalness of the other components of the instances of the two tables. This error could be an error that emanate as an error during transforming the image to its feature vector representation. The F components of M_1 and M_2 must be created with the same feature measures and the A components need to have the same attribute elements.
- The **Union** of two image tables denoted as $M_1 \cup M_2$, is the set of instances that are in M_1 or M_2 or both. Comparison on the F and A components is done as discussed in the case of the intersection operation above.
- The **Difference** of two image tables M_1 and M_2, denoted as $M_1 - M_2$, is the set of instances in M_1 but not in M_2.

A cartesian product of two image tables may be defined as follows.

Definition 4.7. (Cartesian Product)

The Cartesian Product of two image tables M_1 and M_2 denoted by $M_1 \times M_2$ is defined ad:

$$M_1 \times M_2 = \{(id_1, o_1, f_1, a_1, p_1') | (id_1, o_1, f_1, a_1, p_1) \in M_1 \ and\ p_1' = (M_2, set\ of\ all\ ids\ of M_2)\}.$$

The use of the operators discussed in this section, will permite us to create a system of similarity-based algebraic operations on image databases, identical to the relational algebraic systems in RDBMS.

5 Supporting Salient Object Based Operations

An image is a complex item that may contain different objects of interest. The particular meaningful objects of interest in an image are referred in the literature as *Salient objects* [7]. In some other works it is referred as *Semcons* [18,19]. In these paper we use the term *salient objects*. In a content-based retrieval, we may be interested only on a particular object in an image. Hence, Multimedia Database systems should enable us to operate on these particular objects in an image. In current practices, content-based image retrieval systems have shown the effectiveness of using salient objects for image similarity-based comparisons. Effective similarity-based search engines such as facial image retrieval engines, medical images retrieval engines, etc. use the concept of segmentation. Segmentation is an important phenomena that deals with the process of identifying the objects of interest (or salient objects) within an image. The integration of segmented objects in similarity-based image retrieval operations is an important issue and will inevitably be supported by most of the future content-based multimedia data retrieval systems. Techniques of segmentation are discussed in [10,2].

Our model for an object-relational image table, $M(id, O, F, A, P)$, is designed in such a way that it can as well support the storage of segmented image data objects. Thus, operations on salient objects could be made possible. Supposing that the contents of the salient objects are extracted, O can be represented as $O = \{O^1, O^2, O^3, ...\}$, where each component O^i stores the data of each sub object. The component F stores the feature vector representation of each salient object in which case F stands for a set of sub feature vectors expressed as $F = \{F^1, F^2, F^3, ...\}$, where F^i is the feature vector representation of O^i. The component A can also be defined as $A = \{A^1, A^2, A^3, ...\}$ so that each A^i is used to store the semantic attribute data of a corresponding O^i. The component P of the model can as well be extended to store some spatial and hierarchical relationships among the segmented objects. In a system that supports segmentation, similarity-based operations is performed with reference to each of the component items (salient objects), in which case spatial relationships among the component objects are considered. The similarity-based algebraic operators we discussed in this paper, though now given for operations on a whole image, can be used to support operations on salient objects. Detailed works on this issue is a future work.

6 Conclusion and Future Work

The many successful research results in the domain of computer vision and patren recognition have made content-based image retrieval a promising approach. The integration of these facilities into DBMSs in order to efficiently support multimedia data management is what should follow next. We argue that one of the key issues to tackle this problem is the definition of a well formalized multimedia content-based operations useable for modeling, optimizing and processing *multimedia queries*. In this view, we presented a new schematic model for an *image table* based on an OR paradigm. In this model, a new pointer component called P has been introduced to capture links between image tables during binary operations. The introduction of P plays an important role for an effective image data management. We then have defined several novel similarity-based operators. The content-based operators we introduced, have rich semantics, are well formalized, and possess very useful properties. We further studied the properties of the novel operators and the possibilities of using them in combination with relational operators.

Future work includes, the design of a content-based query optimizer, the extension of the similarity-based operators to support operations on salient objects of images, and the implementation of these in to an OR data management system.

References

1. S. Atnafu, L. Brunie, and H. Kosch. Similarity-Based Algebra for Multimedia Database Systems. In *12th Australian Database Conference (ADC-2001)*, pages 115–122, Gold Coast, Australia, 2001. IEEE Computer Society.
2. S. Berchtold, C. Boehm, B. Braunmueller, D. A. Keim, and H. P. Kriegel. Fast Parallel Similarity Search in Multimedia Databases. *SIGMOD Conference*, pages 1–12, 1997. AZ, USA.
3. John P. Eakins and Margaret E. Graham. Content-Based Image Retrieval: A report to the JISC Technology Applications Programme. January 1999.
4. William I. Grosky and Peter L. Stanchev. An Image Data Model. pages 14–25. Lecture Notes in Computer Science 1929, Springer, 2000.
5. J.K.Wu, A.D. Narasimhalu, B.M. Mehtre, C.P. Lam, and Y.J. Gao. Core: A Content-Based Retrieval Engine for Multimedia Information Systems. *Multimedia Systems*, 3:25–41, 1995.
6. Informix Press. Excalibur Image Datablade Module User's Guide, March 1999. Ver. 1.2, P. No. 000-5356.
7. Oracle Press. Oracle8i Visual Information Retrieval Users Guide & Reference, 1999. Release 8.1.5, A67293-01.
8. Y. Rui, T.S. Huang, and S.F. Chang. Image Retrieval: Past, Present, and Future. *Journal of Visual Communication and Image Representation*, 10:1–23, 1999.
9. T. Seidl and H.P. Kriegel. Efficient user-adaptable similarity search in large multimedia databases. *VLDB'97, Athens, Greece*, pages 506–515, 1997.
10. T. Seidl and H.P. Kriegel. Optimal Multi-Step k-Nearest Neighbor Search. *SIGMOD*, pages 154–165, 1998. WA, USA.
11. M. Stonebraker and P. Brown. *Object-Relational DBMSs*. Mogan Kaufmann Pub. Inc, San. Francisco, 1999. ISBN 1-55860-452-9.
12. V. S. Subrahmanian. *Principles of Multimedia Database Systems*. Morgan Kaufmann Publishers Inc., San Fransisco, California, 1998. ISBN 1-55860-466-9.
13. V.Oria, M.T. zsu, L. Liu, X. Li, J.Z. Li, Y. Niu, and P.J. Iglinski. Modeling Images for Content-Based Queries: The DISMA Approach. pages 339–346, 1997. 2nd Int. Conf. on VIS, San Diago.
14. Jian-Kang Wu. Content-Based Indexing of Multimedia Databases. *IEEE Transaction of Knowledge and Data Engineering*, 9(6):978–989, 1997.
15. A. Yoshitaka and T. Ichikawa. A Survey on Content-Based Retrieval for Multimedia Databases. *IEEE Transactions on Knowledge and Data Engineering*, 11(1):81–93, 1999.

An Efficient High-Dimensional Index Structure Using Cell Signatures for Similarity Search

Jae-Woo Chang[1] and Kwang-Taek Song[2]

[1] Dept. of Computer Engineering, Chonbuk National University
Chonju, Chonbuk 560-756, South Korea
jwchang@dblab.chonbuk.ac.kr

[2] WOORIN R&D Laboratory
902, Hanjin Resort Officetel, 535-5, BongMyung-Dong,
Yusung-Gu, Taejeon, South Korea
ktsong@woorin.re.kr

Abstract. In this paper, we propose an efficient high-dimensional index structure using cell signatures for similarity search in multimedia database applications. Our index structure partitions a high-dimensional feature space into a group of cells and represents a feature vector as its corresponding cell signature. By using cell signatures rather than real feature vectors, it is possible to reduce the height of our high-dimensional index structure, leading to efficient retrieval performance. In addition, we present a similarity search metric for efficiently pruning search spaces based on cell signatures. Finally, we compare the performance of our index structure with that of its competitor like the X-tree. It is shown from experimental results that our index structure is better on retrieval performance than the X-tree.

1 Introduction

In multimedia database applications, it is necessary to support content-based retrieval on multimedia objects including image, video, or audio. For this, a request for images similar to a query image can be answered by similarity search in the high-dimensional vector space [1]. The similarity search is briefly defined as finding *k* objects 'most similar' to a given query object. As such, the similarity search corresponds to a search for the *k* nearest neighbors in the space. For content-based multimedia information retrieval, it is essential to support a query for retrieving the k-nearest neighbor objects. Especially, the retrieval on the k-nearest neighbor objects in a large amount of multimedia database requires significantly a great number of disk I/Os. To overcome this overhead, there have been studied on many tree-based index structures, like SS-tree[2], SR-tree[3], TV-tree[4], and X-tree[5]. Although the tree-based index structures generally work well for low-dimensional spaces, their performance is known to degrade as the number of dimension increases, which is called 'dimensional curse' phenomenon[6].

X.S. Wang, G. Yu, and H. Lu (Eds.): WAIM 2001, LNCS 2118, pp. 26-33, 2001.

To overcome the difficulties of high dimensionality, we propose an efficient high-dimensional index structure using cell signatures, which supports efficient retrieval on the k-nearest neighbor objects in multimedia database applications. Our index structure partitions a high-dimensional feature space into a group of cells and represents a feature vector as its cell signature for a cell including it. That is, we makes use of the approximation of feature vectors, called cell signature, so that we may reduce the number of page I/O accesses for searching objects in our index structure. In addition, we propose a new similarity search metric using cell signatures so as to improve the performance of our index structure.

The organization of this paper is as follows. In Section 2, we will review some conventional high-dimensional index structures. In Section 3, we propose a new high-dimensional index structure using cell signatures for efficient similarity search. In Section 4, we analyze the performance of our high-dimensional index structure. In Section 5, we draw our conclusions.

2 Tree-Based Index Structure

It is necessary to use tree-based index structures which provide an efficient access to multimedia data with high-dimensional feature vectors. Some previous work on indexing high-dimensional data has been done. First, D. A. White and R. Jain [2] presented an R-tree-like index structure, called the SS-tree. The central concept of the SS-tree is the use of spheres instead of bounding boxes in the directory. Although the SS-tree clearly outperforms the R*-tree, spheres tend to overlap in high-dimensional spaces. Thus, an improvement of the SS-tree was proposed in [3], where the concepts of the R-tree and SS-tree are integrated into a new index structure, the SR-tree. The directory of the SR-tree consists of spheres and hyper-rectangles such that the area corresponding to a directory entry is the intersection between the spheres and the hyper-rectangles. Therefore, the SR-tree outperforms both the R*-tree and the SS-tree.

Secondly, the TV-tree [4] is another R-tree-like high-dimensional index structure which uses the concept of telescope vectors. The telescope vectors divide attributes into three classes: ones being common to all data items in a sub tree, ones being ignored, ones being used for branching in the directory. The motivation for ignoring attributes is that a sufficiently high selectivity can often be achieved by considering only a subset of the attributes. Therefore, the remaining attributes have no chance to substantially contribute to query processing. Obviously, redundant storage of common attributes does not contribute to query processing, either. The major drawback of the TV tree is that the selectivity information about the behavior of single attributes is required.

Finally, the X-tree proposed by S. Berchtold etc. [5] improved retrieval efficiency by avoiding the overlap of data area in high-dimensional data space. The X-tree makes use of both an overlap free algorithm and a new concept of super node to avoid the overlap of directory nodes. As the dimensionality is increased, the overlap area is large. Therefore, the X-tree uses a hierarchical directory structure for low-dimensional data and a linear directory structure for high-dimensional data, which enables us to save storage space and provide fast retrieval. Its nodes are composed of directory nodes containing a minimum bounding rectangle (MBR) information and data nodes including the feature vectors of objects. The X-tree is known as an index structure supporting efficient k-NN search in high-dimensional data space. However, the fan-out of X-tree nodes is decreased as the dimensionality is increased [7].

3 High-Dimensional Index Structure Using Cell Signatures

3.1 Main Concept

In the conventional tree-based index structures, a leaf node contains **<VECTOR, oid>** where **oid** is an object-identifier used as a pointer to a data object and VECTOR is an n-dimensional feature vector of an object. A non-leaf node contains **<MBR, son_ptr>** where son_ptr is a pointer to its child node and MBR is an n-dimensional minimum bounding rectangle (MBR) which bounds all the entries in the descendent node. As dimensionality is increased, the size of an MBR in a non-leaf node is larger, leading to the smaller fan-out of the non-leaf node. To contain more entries in a non-leaf node, it is possible to store the signature of an MBR, instead of the original MBR, where the signature is an abstraction of an MBR. For this, we divide the space of a high-dimensional feature space into a group of cells and assign each cell to its own signature. In our index structure, we make use of equivalent intervals for space partitioning because the cells are hyper-cubes. Therefore, the number of bits for each dimension is used to determine how many partitions each dimension space is divided into. When using *b*-bit cell signatures, there are 2^b partitions for each dimension. To map an MBR into its signature, we introduce the concept of cell-based MBR(CMBR) in a high-dimensional space.

Definition 1. *Given an MBR R= $((l_0, u_0), (l_1, u_1), \ldots, (l_{n-1}, u_{n-1}))$ in D[0, 1] of n-dimension, a CMBR CR in a cell-based n-dimensional space is defined as follows where b is the number of bits for each dimension.*

$$CR = ((cl_0, cu_0), (cl_1, cu_1), \ldots, (cl_{n-1}, cu_{n-1}))$$
$$cl_i = \lfloor l_i \times 2^b \rfloor \times (1/2^b),\ cu_i = \lceil u_i \times 2^b \rceil \times (1/2^b)\ (0 \leq i < n)$$

For example, the CMBR CR11 of an MBR R11(0.33, 0.41, 0.54, 0.85) in a two-dimensional space is (0.25, 0.5, 0.5, 1). For a given CMBR, we generate the signature of the CMBR.

Definition 2. *For a given CMBR CR = $((cl_0, cu_0), (cl_1, cu_1), \ldots, (cl_{n-1}, cu_{n-1}))$ in a cell-based n-dimensional space, the signature of a CMBR CR is generated in the following where SIG is a function for generating b-bit number in each dimension..*

$$S(CR) = Sl_0Su_0Sl_1Su_1....Sl_iSu_i,\quad (0\quad i<n)$$

$$Sl_i = SIG(cl_i \times 2^b),\quad Su_i = SIG(cu_i \times 2^b).$$

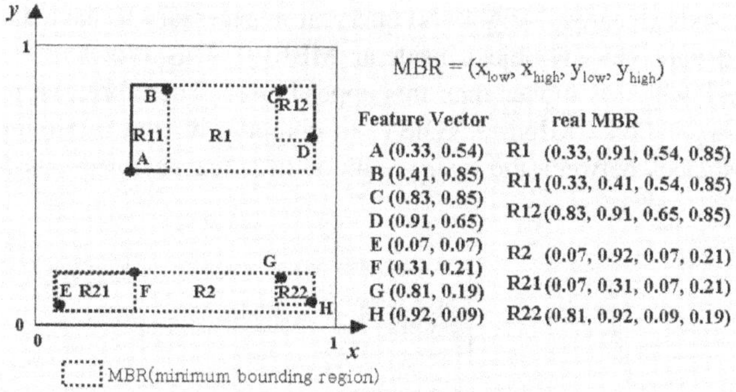

Fig. 1. Two-dimensional feature space

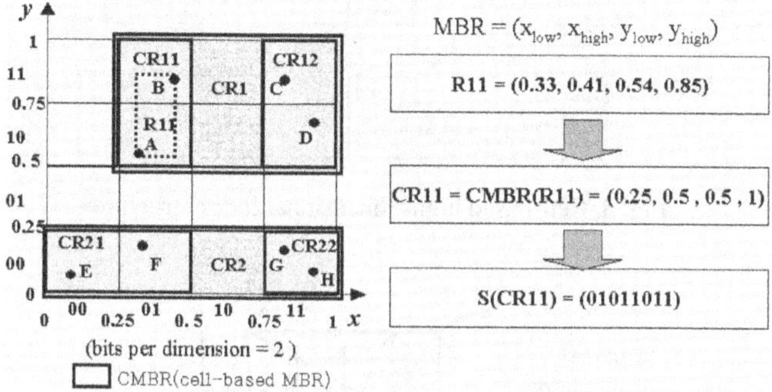

Fig. 2. Approximation of MBR in a cell-based two –dimensional space

Fig. 1 shows eight feature vectors and six MBRs surrounding them in two-dimensional feature space. And Fig. 2 shows the approximation of MBR in a cell-based two-dimensional space. Because two bits are used for each dimension, there are four partitions and sixteen cells for a two-dimensional space. Since the points of the partitions in the example are 0.25, 0.50, 0.75, and 1.0, points in the range of 0 to 0.25, 0.25 to 0.50, 0.50 to 0.75, and 0.75 to 1 can be mapped to cell signatures '00', '01', '10', and '11', respectively. In Fig. 2, MBR R11(0.33, 0.41, 0.54, 0.85) contains two object feature vectors, i.e., A<0.33, 0.54> and B<0.41, 0.85>. The CMBR CR11 containing the objects A and B is represent as (0.25, 0.5, 0.5, 1) by definition 1. The signature of CMBR CR11, i.e., S(CR11), is '01011011' by the definition 2. In the same way, we can generate the cell signatures for the other MBRs. Fig. 3 depicts our high-dimensional index structure when we insert the eight feature vectors in Fig. 1.

3.2 New Distance Metric for Similarity Search

For nearest neighbor search using the R*-tree, Roussopoulos[8] proposes an algorithm which reduces the number of visiting nodes by computing the minimum distance (MINDIST) and the minmax distance (MINMAXDIST) between a given query point and a MBR. In order to avoid visiting unnecessary MBRs in our index structure for answering a k-NN (Nearest Neighbors) query, it is necessary to have an upper bound of the k-NN distance to any object inside an MBR[9]. This allows us to prune MBRs with MINDIST which is higher than this upper bound. Therefore, we propose a new distance metric, called CMINMAXDIST, to compute all the minimum and all the maximum distances between the query point and feature vector points for each of n-axis.

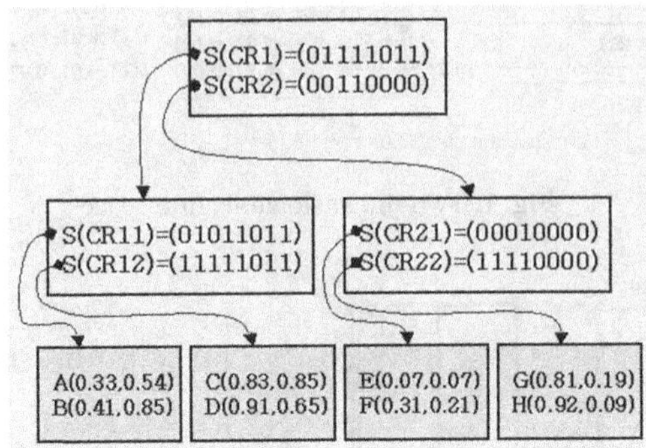

Fig. 3. Cell-based high-dimensional index structure

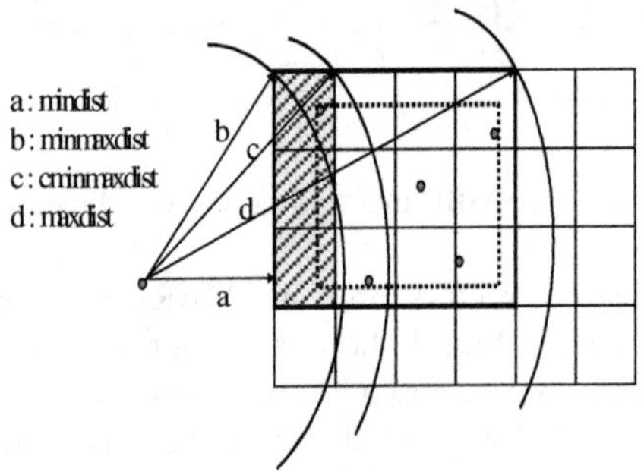

Fig. 4. Distance between the query point and the MBR

Fig. 4 illustrates MINDIST, MINMAXDIST and CMINMAXDIST in a two-dimensional space. For cell-based n-dimensional space, the conventional upper bound of the k-NN distance, MINMAXDIST, cannot guarantee the true k-th object for k-NN query. But the CMINMAXDIST can guarantees that there is a cell within the MBR at a distance less than or equal to CMINMAXDIST.

Definition 3. *The distance of a point P in E(n) from a CMBR CR in the same space, denoted CMINMAXDIST(P, CR), is :*

$$CMINMAXDIST(P, CR) = \min_{1 \le k \le n}(|p_k - crm_k|^2 + \sum_{\substack{i \ne k \\ 1 \le i \le n}} |p_i - crM_i|^2)$$

where

$$crm_k = \begin{cases} s_k + cd & \text{if } p_k \le \dfrac{s_k + t_k}{2} \text{ and } p_k < s_k \\ s_k & \text{if } p_k \le \dfrac{s_k + t_k}{2} \text{ and } p_k \ge s_k \\ t_k - cd & \text{if } p_k > \dfrac{s_k + t_k}{2} \text{ and } p_k > t_k \\ t_k & \text{if } p_k > \dfrac{s_k + t_k}{2} \text{ and } p_k \le t_k \end{cases}$$

$$crM_i = \begin{cases} s_i & \text{if } p_i \le \dfrac{s_i + t_i}{2} \\ t_i & \text{Otherwise.} \end{cases}$$

4 Performance Analysis

For our performance analysis, we implement our high-dimensional index structure and the X-tree under Solaris 2.6/SUN Enterprise 150. Our experiment is performed with two types of data sets: synthetic data and real data. The synthetic data set following the normal distribution is created by MATLAB. The real data set is made from color histograms of about 100,000 color images. We generate 15-and 20-dimensional feature vectors from the real color images. The syntactic data sets are created for 10, 12, 14, 16, 18, and 20-dimensions. Each data set consists of 100,000 feature vectors in the range of [0, 1] for each dimension. For each data set, we search for 100-NN queries.

The insertion time is measured as a total time for inserting feature vectors. Fig. 5 show the insertion time for syntactic and real data sets. For the syntactic data set, it takes about 33 seconds for 10-dimensional data and 69 seconds for 20-dimensional ones in the X-tree. In our index structure (named CS-tree), it takes about 35 seconds and 70 seconds because it needs time for calculating a signature of entries in the non-leaf node. The insertion times for the real data set are similar to those for the syntactic data set.

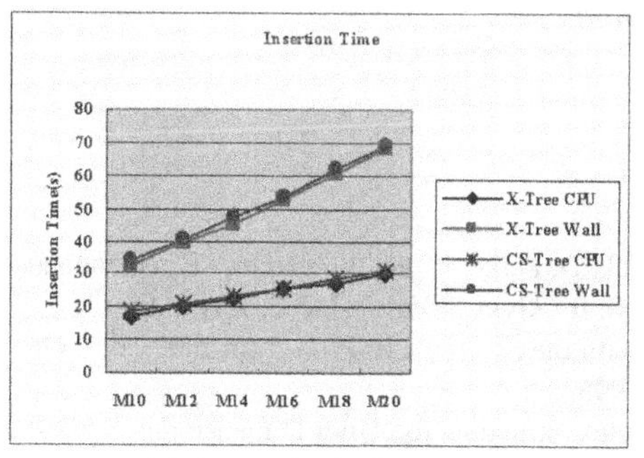

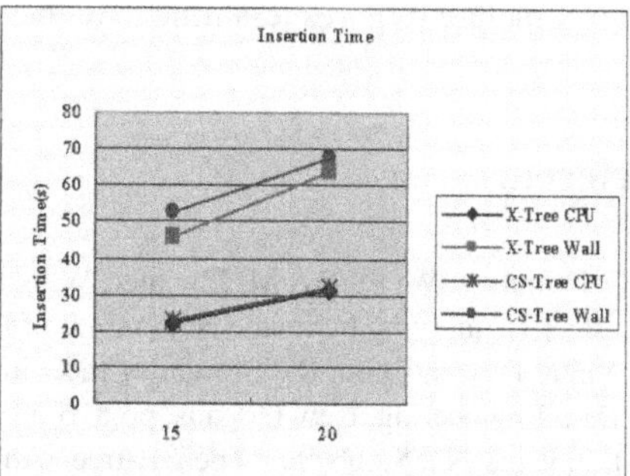

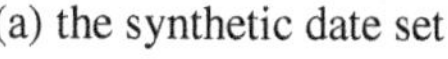

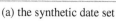

(a) the synthetic date set (b) the real data sets

Fig. 5. Insertion times

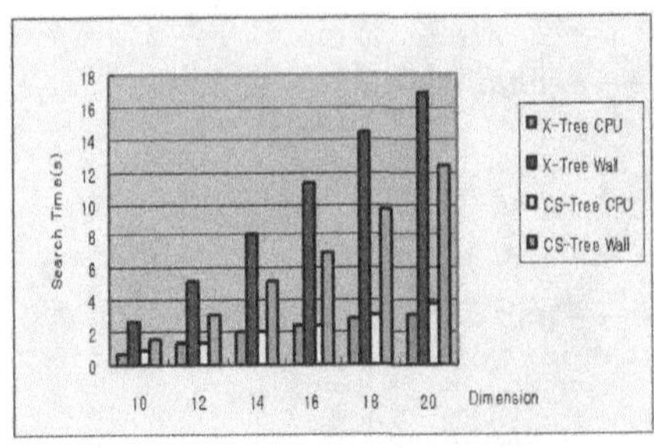

(a) the synthetic date set

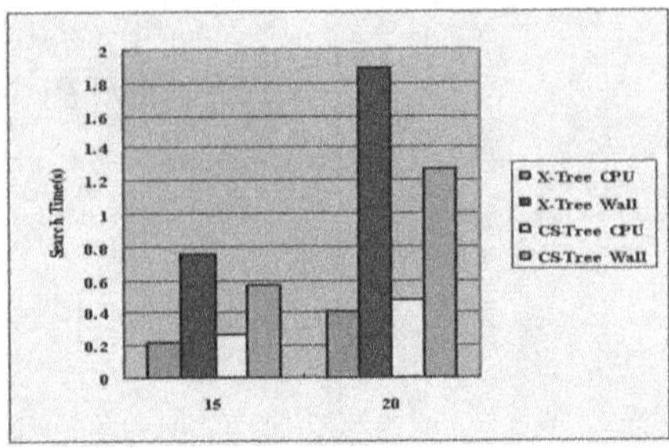

(b) the real data sets

Fig. 6. Search Time for k-NN search (k=10)

The k-NN search time is measured as a total time for searching for the k nearest neighbors to a given query vector. Fig. 6 (a) and (b) show search time (or response time) for k-NN search (k=100) in the synthetic and real data sets, respectively. Our high-dimensional index structure shows the best performance over the X-tree for all dimensions. That is, it takes about 0.6 second for the 15-dimensional real data set and about 1.2 second for the 20-dimensional real data set. When the number of dimensions is 20, our index structure achieves about 30% better performance on k-NN search than the X-tree.

5 Conclusion

We proposed a new high-dimensional index structure which overcome the difficulties of high dimensionality. In our index structure, the signatures of MBRs in a non-leaf node are used in order to increase the fan-out of the non-leaf node. Also, we newly defined upper and lower bounds by using new distance so that we might achieve good performance for the k-NN search. For performance evaluation, we implemented our index structure and compare its performance with those of the X-tree. The insertion times of our index structure is similar to those of X-tree. For the k-NN search, our index structure requires less time than the X-tree.

References

1. C. Faloutsos, W. Equitz, M. Flickner, W. Niblack, D. Petkovic, and R. Barber, "Effecient and effective querying by image content", J. of Intell. Inf. Sys., 3(3/4):231-262, July 1994.
2. White. D.A and Jain. R, "Similarity Indexing with the SS-tree", In Proc. 12th Intl. Conf. On Data Engineering, New Orleans, pp.516-523, 1996.
3. Katayama N., Satoh S., "The SR-tree: An Index Structure for High-Dimensional Nearest Neighbor Queries", Proc. ACM SIGMOD Int. Conf. on Management of Data, pp. 369-380, 1997.

4. K.I. Lin, H. Jagadish, C. Faloutsos, 'The TV-tree: An Index Structure for High Dimensional Data,' VLDB Journal, Vol. 3, pp. 517-542, 1994.
5. Berchtold S., Keim D., Kriegel H.-P., 'The X-tree: An Index Structure for High-Dimensional Data', 22nd Conf. on Very Large Databases, 1996, Bombay, India.
6. V. Pestov, "On the geometry of similarity search: Dimensionality curse and concentration of measure", Technical Report RP-99-01, School of Mathematical and Computing Sciences, Victoria University of Wellington, New Zealand, January 1999.
7. Arya, S. et al., 'An Optimal Algorithm for Approximate Nearest Neighbor Searching', In Proc. ACM-SIAM Symposium on Discrete Algorithms, pp. 573-582, 1994.
8. Roussopoulos N., Kelley S., Vincent F., 'Nearest Neighbor Queries', Proc. ACM SIGMOD Int. Conf. on Management of Data, 1995, pp. 71-79.
9. S. Berchtold, C. Bohm, D. Keim, and H. -P. Kriegel, 'A Cost Model for Nearest Neighbor Search in High-Dimensional Data Space', In Proceesings of ACM PODS Symposium on Principles of Database System, 1997.

Using Object-Relational Database Systems and XML in the Context of an Wireless-Oriented Multimedia Information System

Christoph Dittberner, Thomas Courvoisier, and Guntram Flach

Computer Graphics Center Rostock,
Joachim-Jungius-Str. 11, D-18059 Rostock, Germany
{dittbern, tc, gf}@rostock.zgdv.de

Abstract. In this paper, we present an architecture for access, exchange and presentation of information in a mobile computing environment. We focus our attention on new strategies for the adaptation and integration of database techniques regarding the management of multimedia data types at the particular conditions of mobile infrastructures. We believe that object-relational database systems e.g. Informix and Oracle8i are ideal repositories on the stationary server side for next generation multimedia applications, especially in inter-networked LAN or WAN environments.

Moreover, our approach illustrates the use and benefits of XML technology as a generic gateway to any mobile device. The basic idea of this paper is the integration of object-relational database technology and XML techniques in a Mobility Information Center (MIC) as a framework for mobile environments. The major aim is to optimize the data exchange and presentation by using media specific queries, data preprocessing and reduction methods within the database system. The server side data transformation and the presentation on mobile end system is controlled by RDF-based meta information and XML/XSLT technology. All these methods are influenced by contexts like local resources, environment parameters, and user preferences.

1 Introduction

The presented architecture is one main part of the project "Mobile Visualization" (MoVi)[1] [4, 5]. This project is focused on investigations which shall enable the graphic presentation of scientific data and of other, even multimedia data in a mobile environment. In the project MOVI, a new approach is developed which enables applications on mobile computers for exchange and visualization of multimedia objects with applications on stationary database servers via the Object Bus.

However, there are the well known problems of mobile computing which should be considered when designing an architecture for this purpose e.g. resource limited

[1] This research is supported by the DFG (German Research Association) under contract: UR 61/1-3

X.S. Wang, G. Yu, and H. Lu (Eds.): WAIM 2001, LNCS 2118, pp. 34-45, 2001.

mobile terminals, low bandwidth of the communication channels, location and time dependencies of data, variations in quality of transfer, and possible disconnections.

In the following, we focus our attention on the work packages *multimedia data management and access, data exchange* as well as *visualization and presentation.* These work packages address the investigation and development of strategies for the efficient exchange of multimedia objects over wireless and wired networks. All strategies consider the dynamically changing resources of mobile end systems and network resources.

Therefore, we need a suitable universal architecture which includes the several methods for the retrieval, transformation, exchange and presentation of data adapted to the specific environment (e.g. Web-based, conventional Client/Server- or mobile computing environment)

In the context of mobile environments (as a specialized environment case of our universal framework architecture), the question is how we can integrate known compression/conversion algorithms into the database system or how we can map the already developed request processing and information retrieval methods to server-side built-in operations. The aim is to use the new possibilities of object-relational database systems as stationary data servers by integration of combined features from document management, information retrieval and mobile computing.

In spite of the comfortable possibilities for management and retrieval of multimedia data in object-relational database systems [11], there is a need for application and device dependent presentation and visualization of the complex data structures on any client device. An universal interface to the database system is required in order to use the object-relational multimedia functionality and to realize the derivation of the application and device dependent visualization. In this context XML, the eXtensible Markup Language [13] as the universal format for publishing and exchanging data offers new solutions.

However, to realize this potential, it is necessary to be able to extract structured data from XML documents and store it in a database, as well as to generate XML documents from data extracted from a database. Therefore we developed the database independent *DaS* utility (*Da*tabase to XML *S*ervlet, [6]), which offer this functionality.

The remainder of this article is organized as follows: The next section contains a brief survey of a new communication architecture for selection, access and exchange of information in a mobile computing environment. We present a framework on the base of a Object Bus which enables applications to access globally distributed heterogeneous multimedia information in the Infoverse and to exchange it effectively with respect to mobile resources and other parameters of mobile computing. In Section III, we present our XML-based approach for the database access and the derivation of the device and environment specific transformation and presentation of multimedia object structures. We motivate the need for the integration of object-relational database technology into our framework architecture.

Furthermore, we describe and analyze the possibilities and restrictions of the developed RDF-based metadata repository for the distributed content search and the intelligent control of data preprocessing and transformation. Section IV provides an overview of our experimental framework application based on an Oracle8i database server for text document retrieval (*Inter*MediaText extension) and generic user interfaces on different clients (Web-Browsers, PDAs, WAP phones). Finally, we summarize the major results of this investigation and give and outlook on future activities.

2 Object Bus Architecture

The Object Bus Architecture of the Mobility Information Center (MIC, see figure 2) has to serve as a flexible platform for the efficient exchange of user data and applications between stationary data servers and mobile end systems. Our main concept is an object oriented approach with the *Object Bus* (OBus) as one central feature. This Object Bus serves as a transparent layer for mobile communication and is responsible for the delivery of messages.

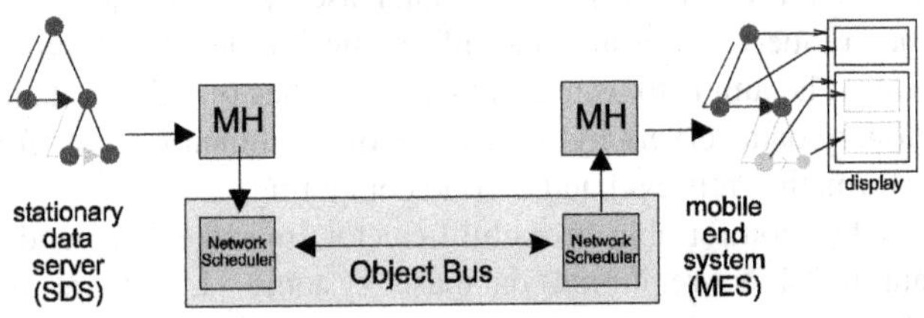

Fig. 1. Traversal and exchange of objects

This object bus was extended in order to face and minimize the problems caused by limited bandwidth, end system resource limitations, and frequent disconnections. Basic components of this extended object bus are *Network Schedulers* and context-sensitive *Request/Reply caches*. They use techniques like priority- and QoS-controlled communication, transparent data compression and context-controlled caching to provide basic solutions for these problems. The second main feature is the introduction of *Message Handlers* (MH) [5] that act in place of the communicating processes when exchanging structured objects (see figure 1). They notify each other about transfer procedures and transfer the objects.

The Message Handler serves to exchange requests and appropriate reply objects between processes and to enable the access to single units of information. That means, that they provide additional functionality to the application to enable a transparent access to remote objects. Due to their *object specific* design and their knowledge about type and structure of the data to be transferred they are able to use type and structure dependent methods for minimizing network traffic and response times like data reduction (e.g. compression, conversion) and detail-on-demand.

All these modules are implemented as CORBA clients and servers that communicate via the OBus. The complete database is stored at the stationary multimedia support server at the office or can be accessed via this server.

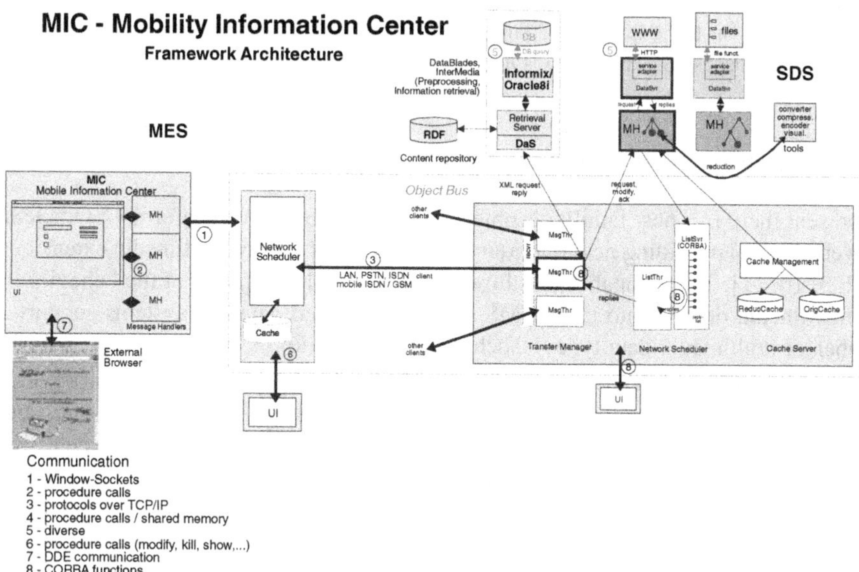

Fig. 2. Overview: Components of the System Architecture on MES and SDS

More details about the components of the Object Bus Architecture and the experimental validation results of our methods and communication protocols you will find in [5]. Based on this architecture, we present in the next section the integration of an object-relational database system as an extension of the Stationary Data Server (SDS) within the MoVi framework architecture (see figure 2). Furthermore we describe our XML-based approach for the database access and the derivation of the device and environment specific transformation and presentation of multimedia object structures.

3 Content Transformation and Visualization

The concept of our XML-based approach of content transformation and visualization aims as first at the determination of relevant data from the different information sources (databases, media servers, local files etc.) in order to convert them into the uniform data structure XML (eXtensible Markup Language [13]). Within this step of content integration relations can be provided among data from different sources. Additionally, data transformations and consistency checks are provided. In the following step the device and context specific multimedia object structure is automatically generated or can be requested on demand by the client (content mediation). A significant advantage of this approach is that in the first step of content integration the data are transformed on a very abstract level as a XML data structure. In the last step, the content mediation results in the required transformation of an media specific output format by means of XSLT stylesheets [12].

An essential part of this is the data preprocessing and server side content transformation on the data itself. Thereby, especially the new possibilities of object-relational databases (e.g. Informix, Oracle8i) are used and adapted in a suitable way.

3.1 Object-Relational Database Systems

At present there is a new family of object-relational DBMS (e.g. Informix , Oracle8i, Universal DB2) providing new important extensions, especially multimedia extensions [1, 2, 3, 10, 11]. These capabilities allow the direct implementation of the behavior of the multimedia objects into the DBMS. Object-relational database systems support a number of multimedia data types - such as images, audio, or video - in their built-in system provide class hierarchies. For instance the Informix Dynamic Server provides extensibility in four key areas: datatypes, user defined functions, index structures and the query optimizer. Other areas Informix has addressed are additional languages for writing extensions and server procedures, "smarter" BLOBs for enhanced large object support, support for access to external data and the ability to create "packages" of extensibility as DataBlade modules. All of these features are very important to enable the object-relational DBMS to handle a broader set of application requirements.

In the scope of the MoVi project the aim is to integrate known compression or conversion algorithms into the database system or to map the developed request processing and information retrieval methods to server-side built-in operations. So we reach the effect *to relieve the communication components of the MIC object bus architecture (e.g. Message Handlers) from this functionality* and to transfer this to the database backend side (SDS).

To support the information required by the MoVi architecture, the DBMS must also address the general problems in distributed systems, such as distributed and parallel query processing, distributed mobile transaction management, data location transparency and data replication. In addition, network issues such as limited bandwidth and network delays become important considerations, since they could adverse effects on the supported QoS (data compression and conversion).

The technical realization of the above functionality is done as *part of the Stationary Data Server (SDS)* in the system architecture of MoVi (see figure 2).
We believe, that the use of an *object-relational database system (e.g. Informix or Oracle8i) for multimedia data management, data preprocessing, QoS and information retrieval will be an excellent, integrated approach* in the MOVI framework.

On the other hand, there is the need for an application and device independent interface to the database system. Based on the XML technology, we present in the next section our approach of the XML/XSL integration of the Stationary Data Server (SDS) within the MOVI framework architecture.

3.2 DAS - *Da*tabase to XML *S*ervlet

XML, the eXtensible Markup Language [13], has quickly emerged as the universal format for publishing and exchanging data in the World Wide Web. Although XML was originally conceived as a replacement for HTML, it has emerged as a generic data exchange format. Its hierarchical structure and user-defined tags can be adapted to a wide variety of structured and semi-structured data, and many operations on XML documents – parsing, editing, validation, transformation can be performed independent of the actual tags in the document.

A key advantage of using XML as a data source is that its presentation is separate from its structure and content. The XML data defines the structure and content, and then a stylesheet is applied to it to define the presentation. XML data can be presented in a variety of ways (both in appearance and organization) simply by applying different XSL[2] stylesheets [12] to it. For example, a different interface can be presented to different users based on user profile, browser type, or other criteria by defining a different stylesheet for each different presentation style, or stylesheets can be used to transform XML data into a format tailored to the specific application that receives and processes the data.

However, to realize this potential it is necessary to be able to extract structured data from XML documents and store it in a database, as well as to generate XML documents from data extracted from database. To convert XML documents to relational tupels (in both directions), we need methods translating semi-structured

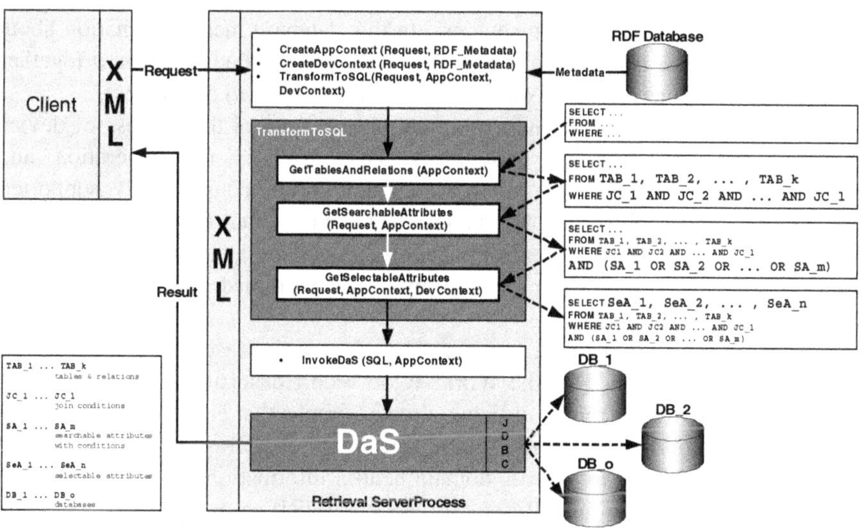

Fig. 3. Overview: Request Processing and SQL Query Generation

[2] XSL provides for stylesheets that allow you to transform XML into HTML or other text-based formats, rearrange or filter data.

queries over XML documents to SQL queries over tables and converts the results to XML.

Therefore, we developed the *DaS* utility [6] (*Da*tabase to XML *S*ervlet), that solves these problems. The utility is based on widely accepted standards – JDBC[3] for database access and DOM[4] for XML document access. The DaS utility was realized in two versions, as a servlet or as an integrated server module (see figure 2 and 3).

In the scope of the MIC framework, by using the DaS utility we have now the possibility to exchange XML structures over the object bus. On the mobile end system (MES) device dependent XSLT [12] stylesheets convert the XML document into the target presentation. This makes it possible to present context in the format best suited to target device (e.g. HTML, WML, Plain Text), influenced by contexts like local resources and user preferences.

In the following, the metadata use and management is briefly presented, restricted to the characteristics relevant to this paper. Then, the main features of the XML-based request processing and the prototype related to the MOVI solution are described.

3.3 RDF-Based Content Repository

As a first step the content repository was realized with tools for administration and analyzing of the given information sources. In this database meta information about data types, mime types and the maximum size of attribute values are stored together with device descriptions (e.g. kind and size of display, supported data types).

However, based on this information we are able to control the process of device dependent transformation on two levels. One level is the generation and transformation of the SQL query so that the query result consists only supported attribute fields (see also Section 3.4). The second level is to control the transformation on the attribute values itself. That means data preprocessing methods such as media specific conversion, compression of data by using multimedia extensions of the object-relational database system.

The content repository is based on the RDF (Resource Description Framework) specification [14], developed by the World-Wide Web Consortium (W3C). RDF is based on a concrete formal model utilizing directed graphs that elude to the semantics of resource description. To provide a serialized syntax of RDF graphs XML is used for encoding. RDF is able to express domain neutral information about any resource that can by named by a Uniform Resource Identifier (URI) as its address to be made available in machine understandable form.

The basic concept is that a Resource is described by a collection of properties called a RDF description. Each of these Properties has a property type and value.

---

3 JDBC is a java API for SQL-based access to relational databases.

4 DOM (Document Object Model) specifies an object model for XML documents, with objects for elements, PCDATA and entity references.

3.4 Request-Processing

In the following we present the process of request processing and the SQL query generation in more detail (see figure 3). Clients run at several end devices. On one hand there is the client running as an application e.g. on a palm handheld or a PC computer. On the other hand the client can run as a single thread/servlet on a WAP-enabled web server to support mobile WAP-phones or general internet browsers (XSLT controlled HTML/WML generation).

First of all the client generates an XML document used to structure the client-request (see figure 4). Therefore it has to determine the device context for instance display resolution, color depth, available memory, graphical capabilities (e.g. support of multimedia objects such as images, audio, video). Therefore, we have stored the needed information of each supported end device in the RDF-based content repository. The only task the client has to do is to determine on which end device it runs.

In the second step the user has the possibility to formulate his query depending on the application context. In the case of „VW-TextRetrieval" application (see also section 4) he can start the content based text retrieval of technical text documents.

After completion the client sends the request (see figure 5) to the Retrieval Server at the stationary data server side (see figure 3 and 4). On both side we have an XML - interface. The server parses the incoming XML-request and validates it to a specific command-DTD [6].

After that, it starts several tasks to process the request and generate the result XML structure.

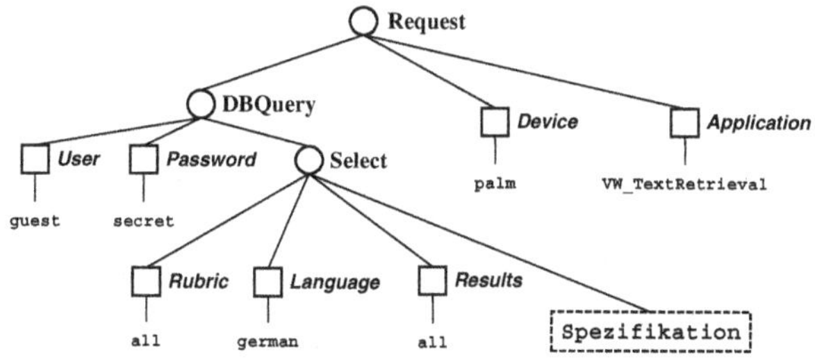

Fig. 4. Example - Client-Request

The first task is to create the application context (`AppContext`) depending on the incoming request. Therefore, we have to fetch all application relevant information needed to reproduce the database content from the RDF content repository database. These information is collected in a XML structure.

This structure represents metadata about the concerned database (e.g name of database, JDBC driver). On the other hand here we store the information about the relations (tables or joins) needed to generate the SQL query. Each table description consists of column descriptions whereby only information related to relevant columns is stored. In the column branch we also collect information about type, mimetype, minimum and maximum size of the attribute.

These values are used for instance to decide if the attribute values should be transmitted via a low network bandwidth. The `searchable` attribute of the column descriptions indicates whether a column contains relevant data for the retrieval process (e.g. the user query can match it) or not (e.g. column information only needed for joining tables). The `SearchMethod` attribute describes the dedicated functionality used by the SQL query (e.g. user defined or system specific functions) and in which way the results should be sorted. The `Selection` branch presents all attributes which could be transmitted to a client.

After that, in a similar process the XML-structure for the device context (`DevContext`) is created using information fetched from the RDF repository database. The device context consists of device descriptions as described above in this section.

After these three structures (`Request, AppContext, DevContext`) have been built, an empty „Select From Where"-query (SFW) is transformed into a filled one (see figure 3).

Now when all these tasks are completed the DaS utility is invoked to generate the result XML structure using the filled „SFW"-query and the application context as input parameters.

4 Prototype

In the scope of the iViP[5] project (integrated virtual product creation) we evaluated the developed architecture and new concepts within an industrial application scenario. The iViP project [7] aims on a modern software architecture, an open integration platform, additional system services and applications for supporting the whole product creation process. iViP does not only provide a framework, but also various innovative tools as complexity management for varaible design, support for the early design phase and specific simulation modules.
As a first step we realized with a project partner from the automotive industry (Volkswagen AG) an experimental system to demonstrate the presented data transformation, retrieval, request processing and visualization functionality as part of the stationary data server (SDS) within the MIC framework architecture. This prototype was developed on the base of the Oracle8i server in combination with the Oracle *Inter*MediaText extension.

The application context was the design and realization of a database archive for management and content based text retrieval for structured technical product standard descriptions (PDF documents). By means of the MIC framework architecture, the user is now able to use the generic user interfaces on different clients for instance web

---

5 The iViP project is partly funded by the German Federal Ministry for Education, Science, Research and Technology (BMBF) under grant 02PL10xxx and supervised by the project sponsor for production and manufacturing technologies (PFT).

browsers, PDAs or WAP phones for the access and content based text retrieval over these technical standards.

As an example, on the web-based user interface the user can choose an search term in order to start the content based text retrieval and get the following result list (see figure 5) of technical documents, which are ranked by a normalized rank factor. Furthermore, the user has the possibility to access the original PDF documents.

In the case of client requests from PDAs or WAP phones only a reduced document structure with included document abstracts is presented (see figure 6, 7).

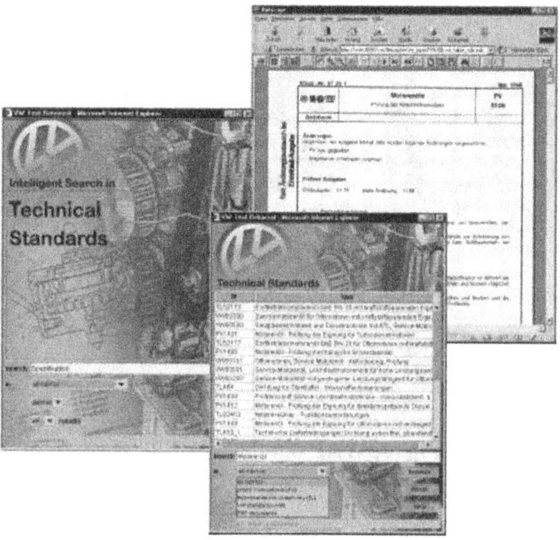

Fig. 5. Text Retrieval: Web User Interface

In addition to the transformation and selection strategies a reduction of delays and of used bandwidth can also be achieved by compression and conversion of media documents before transferring them. As another aspect, we will integrate Level-of-detail methods (e.g. Detail-on-demand,

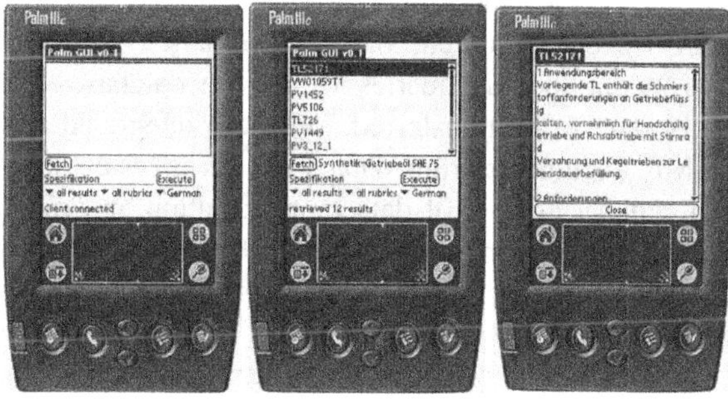

Fig. 6. PalmIIIc User Interface

Progressive Refinement) directly into the database system. These preprocessing methods can be carried out as user defined functions by developed DataBlade modules. These will be an excellent combination with the already developed data transformation and XML/XSLT-based presentation technique and framework components (Network Scheduler, Message Handler) with support for the methods above.

Fig. 7. WAP phone User Interface

5 Conclusion

In this paper, we have described some parts of our framework approach based on object-relational databases and XML techniques. The major aim is to get a basic system for mobile multimedia information exchange, retrieval and presentation, allowing applications to access globally distributed multimedia information and to exchange it effectively with respect to mobile resources and other parameters of the global environment.

Moreover, we considered especially the new possibilities of object-relational database technology by using content based information retrieval and reduction methods as well as media specific queries within the database system in order to reduce the amount of data to be transferred. With the integrated *DaS* utility we are able to generate XML documents from databases. As a result, based on the XML philosophy, we can achieve any set of data transformation and reduction as well as XSL controlled visualization to any mobile device like PDAs and WAP phone. The flexible server side data transformation and request processing is controlled by a RDF-based meta information schema.

In future work, studies will be performed in order to develop a suitable transaction management [8, 9] in the context of a mobile environment The major aim is to develop a new approach of a context based and transaction-driven multimedia data management with support for content based and media dependent request processing.

References

1. Aberer, K., Thimm, H., Neuhold, E.J. Multimedia Database Systems, In: *Handbook of Multimedia Computing*, Borko Furth (Editor), CRC Press, 1998
2. Aberer K., Klass W. Multimedia and its Impact on Database System Architectures. In *Apers, P.M.G, Blanken, H.M., Houtsma, M.A.W (Eds.). Multimedia Databases in Perspective.* Springer , 1997
3. Apers, P.M.G, Blanken, H.M., Houtsma, M.A.W (Eds.). Multimedia Databases in Perspective. *Springer* , 1997
4. Bönigk, J., Lukas,U.v., Interactive Exchange of structured multimedia Data with mobile hosts. In *Global Communication Interactive*, published by Hanson Cooke Ltd, 1997
5. Bönigk, J., Flach, G., System Architecture and Strategies for the Exchange of structured multimedia Data in the Context of mobile Visualization. In Proc. *5th Intl. Workshop on Mobile Multimedia Communication (MoMuc)*, October 1998
6. Courvoisier T., Flach, G. Integration of relational data structures into XML applications - *Da*tabase to XML *S*ervlet, DaS, *Proc. of GI. Workshop "Internet Databases"*, Berlin, 2000
7. Lukas, v. U. Enabling Cross-Enterprise Collaboration with iViP, In Proc. 8th European Concurrent Engineering Conference: Concurrent Engineering - the Path to Electronic Business, April 2001
8. Narasayya, V.R.: Distributed transactions in a Mobile Computing System, *First IEEE Workshop on Mobile Computing Systems and Applications*, 1994
9. Pitoura, E.; Bhargava, B.: Revising Transaction Concepts for Mobile Computing, , *First IEEE Workshop on Mobile Computing Systems and Applications*, 1994
10. Stonebraker, M., Object-Relational DBMSs – The Next Great Wave, Morgan Kaufmann, 1996
11. Westermann, U., Klas, W., Architecture of a DataBlade Module for the Integrated Management of Multimedia Assets, *First Int. Workshop on Multimedia Intelligent Storage and Retrieval and Retrieval Mangement (MISRM),* October 1999
12. World Wide Web Consortium, XSL Transformations (XSLT) Version 1.0, *W3C Recommendation*, 16 November 1999, http://www.w3.org/TR/1999/REC-xslt-19991116
13. World Wide Web Consortium, Extensible Markup Language (XML), Recommendation, 1998,
14. http://www.w3.org/TR/REC-mls/
15. World Wide Web Consortium, Resource Description Framework (RDF) Model and Syntax, *Recommendation*, 1999,
16. http://www.w3.org/TR/PR-rdf-syntax/

Session 1B
Information Retrieval & Text Indexing

Regular Research Paper (30 minutes)
Utilizing the Correlation between Query Keywords for Information Retrieval

Regular Research Paper (30 minutes)
Adjacency Matrix Based Full-text Indexing Models

Short Research Paper (15 minutes)
Goal-Oriented Information Retrieval Using Feedback from Users

Short Research Paper (15 minutes)
Classify Web Documents By Key Phrase Understanding

Utilizing the Correlation between Query Keywords for Information Retrieval

Tetsuya Yoshida, Daiki Shinkai, and Shogo Nishida

Dept. of Systems and Human Science, Grad. School of Eng. Science, Osaka Univ., 1-3 Machikaneyama-cho, Toyonaka, Osaka 560-8531, Japan
yoshida@sys.es.osaka-u.ac.jp

Abstract. This paper proposes a method to utilize the correlation between query keywords in information retrieval toward extrapolating their semantic information. In accordance with the rapid development of internet and WWW (World Wide Web), it has been getting more and more hard to pinpoint the appropriate document from the huge information resource. Various search engines have been developed to retrieve the appropriate information based on the keywords, however, it is hard for the user to specify the keywords enough to pinpoint the appropriate documents. Since there often exist some semantic correlation between the keywords, this paper proposes to finding out the another keyword by utilizing their semantic correlation in order to narrow the scope of seach. Experiments were carried out to investigate the effectiveness of the proposed method and the result hinted the effectiveness of our approach as a pre-processing to narrow the scope of search for search engines.

1 Introduction

Due to the rapid development of internet and WWW (World Wide Web) it has been getting more and more hard to pinpoint the appropriate URL(Uniform Resource Locator) or document from the huge information resource [3,6]. Most search engines provide the candidates for the appropriate URL based on the keywords which are specified by the user. However, it is often the case that may processes (e.g., And/Or search with multiple keywords, specification of search range, time stamp of documents) are required, and this can burden the user with cognitive overload.

Generally the retrieved documents are ordered and shown to the user according to the degree of importance, which is often calculated based on the frequency of the specified keywords in documents. However, since thousands of documents can be retrieved for one query, it is hard for the user to find out the truly appropriate document if the specification or description of query keywords is insufficient or incomplete.

This paper proposes a method to utilize the correlation between query keywords in information retrieval toward utilizing their semantic information. The correlation between query keywords is structured into a tree by utilizing a thesaurus and the semantic information is infered based on the relationshop between the nodes in the tree structure and the thesaurus [9]. It is expected that

X.S. Wang, G. Yu, and H. Lu (Eds.): WAIM 2001, LNCS 2118, pp. 49–59, 2001.

extrapolating the semantic information between query keywords will lead to a methodology for information systems by playing the role of "reading between the lines" in information retrieval.

This paper is organized as follows. Sect. 2 explains our framework of information retrieval to utilize the correlation between query keywords. Sect. 3 describes the details of the method for utilizing the correlation between query keywords specified by the user. Experiments have been carried out to investigate the effectiveness of our approach and the result is reported in Sect. 4 with discussion. Sect. 5 briefly gives the conclusion of this paper.

2 Framework of Utilizing the Correlation between Query Keywords

The system architecture proposed in this paper is shown in Fig. 1. As shown in Fig. 1, the system consists of:

- query keyword input module
- search engine
- the module for calculating the correlation between query keywords

Each module is briefly explained below.

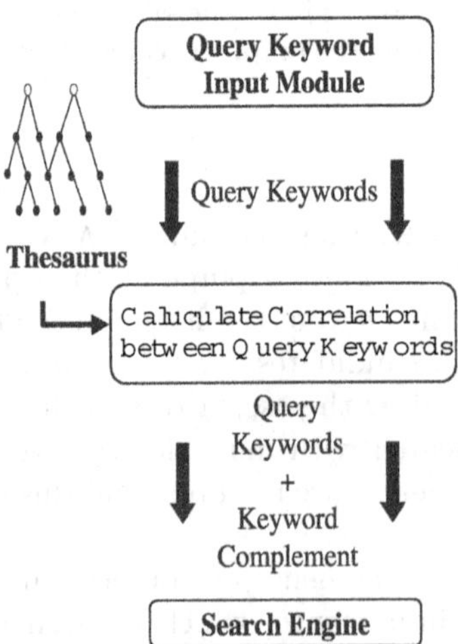

Fig. 1. System Architecture

2.1 Query Keyword Input Module

The system proposed in this paper requires the user to specify some nouns as the query keyword. This is because the thesaurus utilized in the system represents only the classification and relation between nouns. Normalizing adjective, verb, etc. into noun is left for further work. In addition, the system is designed so that the desired information can be appropriatelly retrieved within 5 cycles of interaction between the user and system. This is to reduce the burden of user on information retrieval, which is the aim of the proposed system.

2.2 Search Engine

In the system a search engine on WWW accepts the noun, which is calucated based on the method explained in Sect. 3 (the details of this module is explained in Sect. 3), as an extra query keyword in addition to the ones specified by the user. Currently the construction of search engine is not dealt with and existing search engines (e.g., goo (http://www.goo.ne.jp), InfoNavigator (http://infonavi.infoweb.ne.jp)) have been utilized. This is to focus on the effect of the module which utilizes the correlation between query keywords on the existing search engine for efficient information retrieval.

2.3 Thesaurus

A thesaurus, which defines or represents the relation between words, is utilized to construct the information retrieval system based on the correlation between query keywords. Since the relation of semantic meaning between words can be easily represented as numericals or distance in a thesaurus, it is suitable for computational or symbol processes to utilize as another keyword based on the hidden or implicit correlation between the them. For instance, a thesaurus is often utilized to calculate the degree of similarity between words in Natural Language Processing (NLP) [2,7]. Since the relation between words defined in a thesaurus can be considered as a graph as in a semantic network [5], it is possible to treat the neighboring words with high similarity and distant words with low similarity.

It would be possible to utilize the user profile, which describes the detailed information on the user, to carry out information retrieval specialied for each user [8]. However, describing the detailed information on each user requires a lot of work and it would be difficult to carry out information retrieval by adapting to the change in interests of user based on the fixed user profile. Thus, in our approach a thesaurus, which describes the common semantic information for users, is utilized to facilitate information retrieval in order to reduce the burden of user. The system proposed in this paper utilizes the "Modern Japanese Noun Thesaurus" which is constructed by Prof. Hagino in Tokyo Metropolican University [4].

3 Calculating the Correlation between Query Keywords

In general most information retrieval systems require additional keywords to narrow the scope of search to retrieve the desirable or appropriate information for the user. However, selecting the keywords for narrowing the scope of search can be hard for users and sometimes it can put too much burden on users. The aim of the proposed method in this paper is to extrapolate the hidden or implicit correlation between the query keywords and to utilize it as the additional keyword so that the scope of search can be effectively narrowed to facilitate information retrieval.

3.1 Profile Tree Algorithm

In our approach the system constructs the tree structure which includes all the query keywords specified by the user as its nodes. The tree is called a "profile tree" in our approach. To construct the profile tree, for each query keyword (noun) the system first construct the tree structure which includes the keyword as its root (this is called "keyword tree"). Since multiple keyword trees are constructed when multiple query keywords are specified, the system then tries to find out the node (noun) which is commonly included in the trees. Then, the tree structure which includes the common noun as its root is constructed as the profile tree. For instance, suppose Olympic and baseball are specified as the query keyword. Then, the algorithm for constructing the profile tree works as follows: (see Fig. 2,3)

Step. 1. Construct the keyword tree for each query keyword (Olympic and baseball) with the word as its root.
Step. 2. Compare nodes in both trees and search the common node in them (in Fig. 2, "ball game" is found out as the common node.)
Step. 3. By treating the common node as its root, construct the profile tree which includes the query keywords as its nodes.

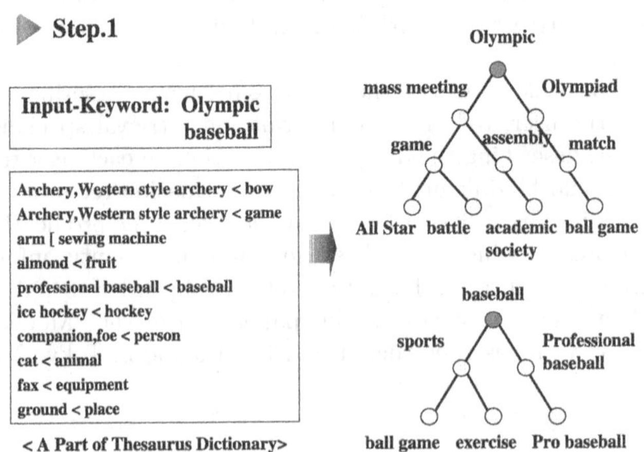

Fig. 2. Keyword trees for Olympic and baseball.

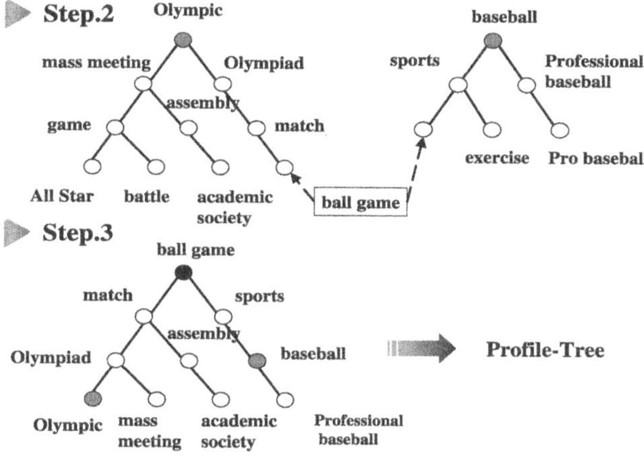

Fig. 3. An example of profile tree.

3.2 Similarity Measure

To select the noun as the another query keyword from the profile tree, the degree of similarity with respect to the specified query keywords is measured for each noun in the profile tree. Hereafter the noun for the another query keyword is called "*keyword complement*" in this paper, since it is utilized to "complement" the insufficient information conveyed by the specified query keywords from the user. Currently the system employs the similarity measurement equation which is often utilized in the research on NLP to measure the degree of similarity for synonym [7]. As for the profile tree in our approach, it is possible to treat the depth of the common upper node for two words as the similarity of these words. Suppose the depth of two words are d_i,d_j and the depth of the common upper node for these words is d_c. Then, the degree of similarity is defined as [7]:

$$similarity = \frac{d_c \times 2}{d_i + d_j} \tag{1}$$

As for the profile tree in Fig. 3, since $d_c = 1$, $d_i = 4$, and $d_j = 3$, the degree of similarity for Olympics and baseball is calculated as:

$$similarity = \frac{1 \times 2}{4 + 3} = 0.286$$

In general the depth of the root node is treated as 0 for the calculation of similarity in most thesauruses. This is because when the common upper node for two words is the root node, it is reasonable to interpret that there is no relation between these two words since the root node with no semantic meaning is often introduced arbitrary in order to make the network (graph) of words as a tree structure. In the thesaurus utilized in our system, since the symbol "?" is used as the root, it can treated that there be no relation between them when the common upper node for two words is detected as "?". However, since the profile tree is constructed by treeting the common noun in keyword trees as its root, it is possible to consider all the nouns (nodes) in the profile tree have some correlation or relevance in semantics. Thus, the depth of root node is treated as 1, not 0, in the calculation of the degree of similarity in (1) in our approach. For instance, Fig. 4 shows the degree of similarity for each node with respect to the profile tree in Fig. 3. The degree of similarity is calculated by treating the depth of "ball game", which is the root in the profile tree, as 1.

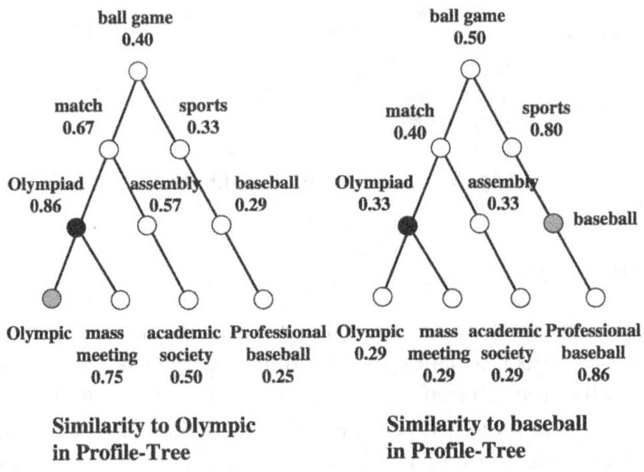

Fig. 4. An example of similarity calculation.

4 Experiment

Experiments have been carried out to investigate the effectiveness of the proposed method in Sect. 3 as a pre-processing to narrow the scope of search for search engines. Following the evaluation measurement in the research on Information Retrieval [1], precision is utilized to measure to what extent the generated keyword complement plays the role of narrowing the scope in search for information retrieval. On the other hand, recall is utilized to measure to what extent information retrieval is carried out to retrieved the necessary or desired information.

Precision is the ratio of the number of correct documents with respect to that of the overall retrieved ones, and measures the capability of not retrieving the incorrect documents. On the other hand, recall is the ratio of the number of actuallly retrieved documents with respect to that of the correct ones, and measures the capability of retrieving the correct documents without exception. Suppose the number of correct documents is A and that of actually retrieved documents is B. Then, precision and recall are calculated as: (see Fig. 5)

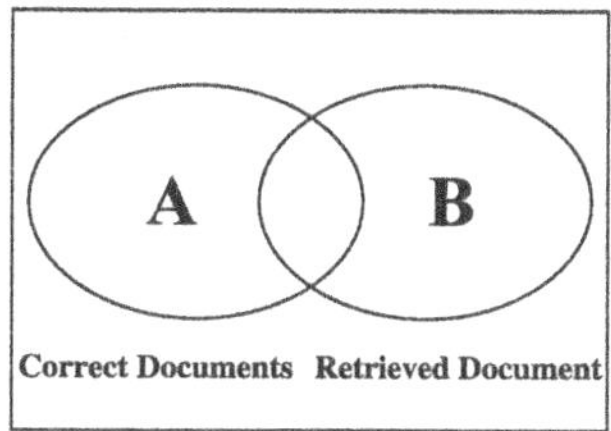

Fig. 5. The relation between the Precision and Recall.

$$Precision = \frac{A \cap B}{B} \qquad Recall = \frac{A \cap B}{A} \tag{2}$$

As for the document search in information retrieval, the recall gets lower when the user specifies inappropriate query keywords. On the other hand, if the user specifies the keyword which can be matched in may URLs, the recall gets higher but the precision gets lower. The effectiveness of the proposed system is measured in terms of the increase in both precision and recall by utilizing the keyword complement as the additional query keyword with respect to the original keywords. This is to measure to what extent the keyword complement is effective to remove unnecessary documents and also to retrieve the desirable documents without exception.

4.1 Relation between Similarity and Keyword Complement

The degree of similarity is calculated for all the nodes in the profile tree. However, since the degree of similarity is calculated with respect to the thesaurus, it is not necessarily the case that "the word with high degree of similarity = the word with the effecive complement role in information retrieval". Thus, experiments have been carried out to investigate to what extent the degree of similarity defined in (1) contributes to narrowing the scope of search in information retrieval.

In the experiment the word "sports" and "gamble" were used as the query keywords. The profile tree was constructed with respect to these words and the degree of similarity was calculated for all the nodes in the tree. The number of nodes in the tree was 217, all of which could be considered as the candidates for the keyword complement. The tuple of the words "sports, gamble, X", X is the candidate for the keyword complement, were used as the query keywords for a search engine, and precision and recall were calculated. This is to investigate the relation between the degree of similarity in the profile tree and the effectiveness of narrowing search in information retrieval. In the experiment whether the retrieved document is appropriate was judged subjectively by the user and thus the result depends on the user. Here, the correct documents (URLs) were determined by the user subjectively in order to measure precision and recall. As for all the nodes in the profile tree, Fig. 6 shows the relation betwen the degree of similarity, precision, and recall. Fig. 7 shows the relation betwen precision and recall with respect to each candidate for keyword complement[1]. No document was retrieved with 103 word out of 217 candidates for keyword complement, therefore, these were removed from the experimental data.

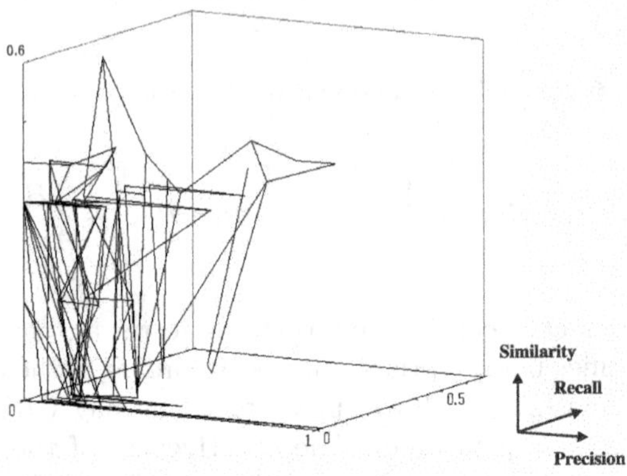

Fig. 6. The relation between the Similarity, Precision, and Recall.

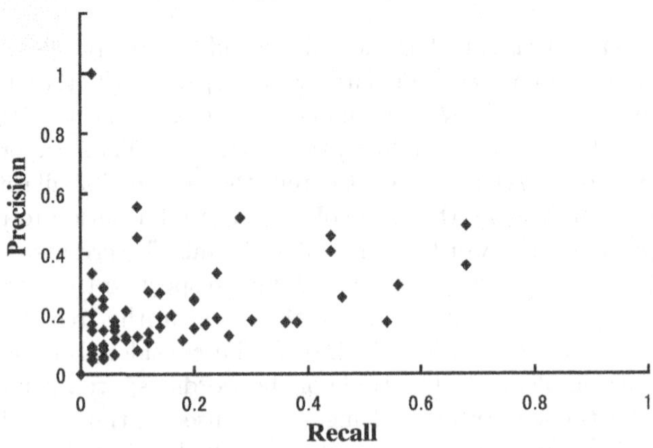

Fig. 7. Precision and Recall with the Keyword Complement.

[1] In the experiment goo was utilized as the search engine

4.2 Effectiveness of Information Retrieval via Keyword Complement

Experiments have been carried out to investigate the effectiveness of the keyword complement determined in the experiment in Sect. 4.1. In the experiment goo and InfoNavigator were used as the search engine. These search engines are effective when the user is familiar with the appropriate query keyword and when all the URLs which include the query keyword should be retrieved. However, it is difficult to carry out information retrieval with this kind of search engine when the user is not so familiar with the appropriate query keyword or when the exact desciption of query keyword is extremely complicated. Experiments were carried out to evaluate whether the generated keyword complement in our approach could contribute to augmenting such kind of search engines.

In the experiment the user specified "sports" and 'gamble" as the keywords. Then, the noun "race" was utilized as the keyword complement since it was high in both precision and recall from the result in Fig. 7. Fig. 8 shows the change of precision and recall by utilizing other word as another query keyword to the case in which the keyword complement is used. In the figure, the number "1 ~ 4" means the change of precision and recall with the additional keyword of:

1. the noun with the highest similarity
2. the lower word in the thesaurus
3. the noun selected by the user
4. the keyword complement

Also, Table 1 shows the change in the number of retrieved documents and that of corrent documents.

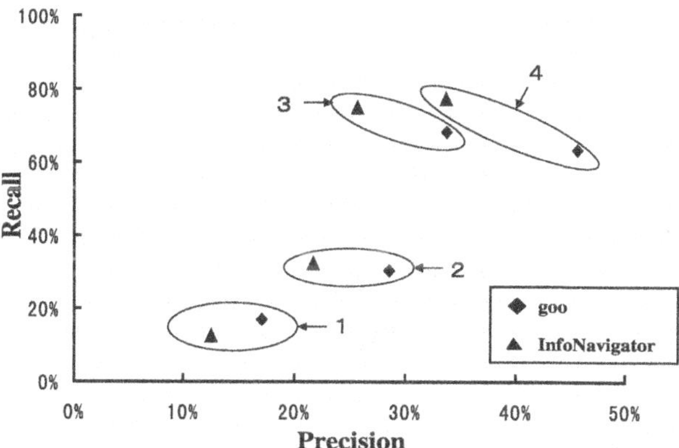

Fig. 8. Change of precision and recall with the keyword complement as the additional keyword.

Table 1. Change of the number of retrieved and correct documents. In the table, R represents the number of retrieved documents and R represents the number of corrent documents.

search engine	keyword	R	C	R ∩ C
goo	similarity	41	41	7
	thesaurus	45	41	18
	user	83	41	28
	keyword complement	57	41	26
Info-Navigator	similarity	40	40	5
	thesaurus	68	40	21
	user	117	40	30
	keyword complement	92	40	31

4.3 Discussion

Although the degree of similarity in a thesaurus is utilized to measure the correlation between the specified query keywords and the candidate for the keyword complement, Fig. 6 shows that the relationship "high degree of similarity = effective keyword complement" is not necessarily satisfied with. However, it is expected that utilizing the degree of similarity in some way will lead to finding out the effective keyword complement, since the similarity in a thesaurus still reflects the semantic meaning or correlation between words.

The aim of experiment in Sect. 4.2 was to investigate the effectiveness of keyword complement in terms of:

- increase in the degree of precision $\Rightarrow$ narrow the scope of search in information retrieval
- sustain the degree of recall $\Rightarrow$ retrieve correct documents without exception

The comparision with other words as the additional query keyword in Fig. 8 showed that utilizing the keyword complement proposed in this paper would contribute to both high degree of precision and recall[2]. However, the result remains at indicating or hinting that there exists some noun with high degree of precision and recall, and currently the system cannot automatically select such a word as the keyword complement from the profile tree.

5 Conclusion

This paper has proposed a method to utilize the correlation between query keywords in information retrieval toward utilizing their semantic information.

[2] Although in some case the keyword selected by the user also showed high degree of recall.

Semantic correlation between the specified query keywords is calculated based on a thesaurus in order to come up with "another" query keyword. The degree of similarity to calculate the semantic correlation is defined based on the degree of similarity for synonym in the research of NLP (Natural Language Processing). Experiments were carried out to investigate the effectiveness of the proposed method and the result hinted the effectiveness of our approach as a pre-processing to narrow the scope of search for search engines. to narrow the scope of search in information retrieval and to reduce the cognitive burden of the user in information retrieval. However, currently it is not possible to uniquely select the word as the best keyword complement based on the degree of similarity in a thesaurus. We plan to improve the algorithm for selecting the keyword complement so that the similarity can be utilized appropriately to uniquely select the effective word as the another keyword in information retrieval.

Acknowledgments. This research is partially supported by Kayamori Foundation of Informational Science Advancement.

References

1. Readings in Information Retrieval, 1997.
2. Recent Advances in Natural Language Processing, 1997.
3. D. Cabeza, M. Hermenegildo, and S. Varma. The PiLLoW/CIAO Library for INTERNET and WWW Programming using Computational Logic Systems. http://www.clip.dia.fi.upm.es/miscdocs/pillow /article/pillow.html, 1996.
4. T. Hagino. A Classification System of Meaning based on a Modern Japanese Noun Thesaurus, 1996. in Japanese.
5. Philip J. Hayes. On semantic nets, frames and associations. In *Proceedings of the Fifth International Joint Conference on Artificial Intelligence (IJCAI-77)*, pages 99–107, Cambridge, Massachusetts, August 1977.
6. S. W. Loke and A. Davidson. Logic web:enhancing the web with logic programming. *The Journal of Logic Programming*, 36:195–240, 1998.
7. M. Nagao. *Natural Language Processing*. Iwanami Publisher, 1996. in Japanese.
8. U. Shardanand and P. Maes. Social Information Filtering: Algorithm for Automating 'Word of Mouth'. In *Proceedings of CHI'95*, 1995.
9. D. Shinkai, T. Yoshida, and S. Nishida. Complement Keywords for Query toward Efficient Information Retrieval. In *1999 IEEE International Conference on Systems, Man, and Cybernetics (SMC'99)*, pages I 916–921, 1999.

Adjacency Matrix Based Full-Text Indexing Models[1]

Shuigeng Zhou[1], Jihong Guan[2], Yunfa Hu[3], Jiangtao Hu[3], and Aoying Zhou[3]

[1]State Key Lab of Software Engineering, Wuhan University, Wuhan 430072
zhousg@whu.edu.cn
[2]School of Computer Science, Wuhan University, Wuhan 430072
jhguan@wtusm.edu.cn
[3]Computer Science Department, Fudan University, Shanghai 200433
{yfhu, jthu, ayzhou}@fudan.edu.cn

Abstract. This paper proposes two new character-based full-text indexing models, *i.e.*, adjacency matrix based inverted file and adjacency matrix based PAT array. Formally, the former is a kind of reorganization of the traditional inverted file, and the latter is a kind of decomposition of the traditional PAT array. Both organize text-indexing information in the form of adjacency matrix. Query algorithms for the new models are developed and performance comparisons between the new models and the traditional models are carried out. The new models can improve query-processing efficiency considerably at the cost of much less amount of extra storage overhead compared to the size of original text database, so are suitable for applications of large-scale text databases, especially Chinese text databases.

1 Introduction

The rapid development and wide application of World Wide Web (WWW) leads to explosively increasing of online text information. More and more people surf the Web for information they need. Such a situation poses new challenge to researchers and scientists in the information retrieval field. That is, how to effectively and efficiently organize and manage massive text information on Web and how to accurately and completely search from Web what the users request [1,2]. Currently, the popular solution is Web search engine, which is essentially a text database where text-indexing model constitutes its core technique [3]. As the amount of text information exponentially increases and the number of user queries rapidly grows, query-processing efficiency becomes major bottleneck of Web search engines. Take AltaVista[4], one of the largest Web search engine systems under running, for example. In 1998, the overall AltaVista system was running on 20 multi-processor machines, all of them having more than 130Gb of RAM and over 500Gb of disk space. Only query processing consumes more than 70% of these resources [1].

To a great extent, the efficiency of information retrieval systems depends on the underlying text indexing models. That is the reason why efficient text indexing

[1] This work was supported by China Postdoctoral Science Foundation and National 863 Hi-Tech Foundation (No. 863-306-ZT04-02-2).

X.S. Wang, G. Yu, and H. Lu (Eds.): WAIM 2001, LNCS 2118, pp. 60-71, 2001.

techniques have been the hot topic in information retrieval area. Up to date, several text-indexing models have been developed, in which widely accepted are inverted files [1,2,5], signature files [1,2,6], PAT tree [1,2,7] and PAT array [1,2,8]. Owing to their advantage of fast response and easy implementation, inverted file and its variations have been used in most text database systems [9] and search engines [3].

This paper intends to develop new character-based full-text indexing models of higher efficiency. By seeing a text database as a directed graph and combining the concept of adjacency matrix of directed graph with the structures of traditional inverted file and PAT array, we propose two new full-text indexing models, which are called adjacency matrix based inverted file and adjacency matrix based PAT array respectively. The new models can improve considerably query-processing efficiency of IR systems at the cost of much less amount of extra space overhead compared to the size of original text database, thus are suitable for applications of large-scale text databases and can be used as an effective way to update the IR systems under running.

Note that in this paper a query is an arbitrary character string and the result is a set of documents containing the query string. In Section 2 we give some basic concepts and definitions. We introduce two new character-based full-text indexing models and their query-processing algorithms in Section 3 and Section 4 respectively. We compare the new models with traditional inverted file and PAT array in Section 5 and present some experimental results in Section 6. We conclude the paper in Section 7.

2 Preliminaries

Let Σ be an *alphabet*: a finite, ordered set of characters. For an arbitrary character l in Σ, there is an associated natural integer i, which indicates the position of l in Σ, and l is also denoted by l^i. In the case of Chinese text databases, Σ corresponds to the Standard Chinese Characters Base, such as GB2312-80, which includes Chinese characters, letters, digits, punctuation marks and other symbols that may appear in Chinese text documents. The region-position code[1] of each character assigned in GB2312-80 may be used as the character's position identifier in Σ (The alternative is the Unicode system). For English text collections, Σ is a set of letters, digits, punctuation marks and other symbols that may occur in English text, and the ASCII code of each character in Σ is taken naturally as its position identifier in Σ.

A *text string* or simply *string* over Σ is a finite sequence of characters from Σ. Specifically, a string has no characters at all is called the *empty string* and is denoted by ε. To avoid confusion, we generally use u, v, w, x, y, z, and the Greek letters to denote strings. The *length* of a string is its length as a sequence. We denote the length of a string w by $|w|$. Alternatively a string w can be considered as a function w:{1,…,$|w|$} Σ ; the value of $w(j)$, where 1 j $|w|$, is the symbol in the jth position of

---

[1] In GB2312-80, the characters are organized into groups. A group is called a region containing no more than 256 unique characters, each of which is distinguished by its position in the region. Thus each character in GB2312-80 is identified by a region code (1 byte) and a position code (1 byte), which are combined into its region-position code (2 bytes) as a whole.

w. To distinguish identical symbols at different positions in a string, we refer to them as different occurrences of the symbol. That is, the symbol $l\ \Sigma$ occurs in the jth position of the string w if $w(j)=l$.

Two strings over the same alphabet can be combined to form a third by the operation of *concatenation*. The concatenation of strings x and y, written xy, is the string x followed by the string y; formally, $w=xy$ if and only if $|w|=|x|+|y|$, $w(j)=x(j)$ for $j=1,\ldots,|x|$, and $w(|x|+j)=y(j)$ for $j=1,\ldots,|y|$. A string v is a *substring* of a string w if and only if there are strings x and y such that $w=xvy$. Both x and y could be ε, so every string is a substring of itself. If $w=xv$ for some x, then v is a *suffix* of w; if $w=vy$ for some y, then v is a *prefix* of w. If x is a substring of string w, then we denote $P(w, x)$ the set of positions of x occurring in w, or the occurrences of x in w.

For a string w, let us pad artificially at its right end with an infinite number of null (or any special characters that is not included in Σ). Then, a *semi-infinite string* (abbreviated to *sistring*) of string w is the sequence of characters starting at a certain position within w and continuing to the right.

Example 1. For string w_1:Once upon a time, in a far away land…
The following are some of the possible sistrings:

Sis_1: Once upon a time, in a far away land…
Sis_2: nce upon a time, in a far away land…
Sis_8: on a time, in a far away land…
Sis_{11}: a time, in a far away land…
Sis_{22}: a far away land…

Obviously, two sistrings starting at different positions are always different. For the simplification of description, meanwhile to guarantee that no one sistring be a prefix of another, it is enough to end the string w with a unique end-of-string symbol that does not appear in Σ. Thus, sistrings can be unambiguously identified by their starting position. That is to say, $P(w, x)$ is a singleton if x is a sistring of string w. The result of a lexicographic comparison between two sistrings is based on the text of the sistrings, instead of their positions. Therefore, in example 1 above, we have $Sis_{22} < Sis_{11} < Sis_2 < Sis_8 < Sis_1$.

Definition 1. A *text database TB* is a collection of text documents, each of which is a string over Σ. Neglecting the boundary between any two adjacent documents, a text database can be seen as a long string, whose length is the sum of the lengths of all documents in the text database. We denote $|TB|$ the length of text database TB. From the sistring point of view, text database TB corresponds to a sequence of sistrings.

In what follows, we treat a text database as a string when discussing inverted file, and see it in the sistring point of view while dealing with PAT array.

Definition 2. Suppose V is the set of all unique characters appearing in text database TB, $V=\{t_i\ |i=1\sim|V|\}\ \Sigma$. For each character t_i in V, it occurs at different positions in the string of text database TB. Let p_i be the set of positions that t_i occurs in TB□denote $p_i=\{p_{i1}, p_{i2},\ldots, p_{i|pi|}\}$ where $|\ p_i|$ is the occurrence number of t_i in TB, p_{ij} is the jth position where t_i occurs in TB (counting from the starting point of TB string). The *full-text indexing inverted file* can be written formally as follows.

$$\{<t_i, p_i>|\ (i=1\sim|V|)\}. \qquad (1)$$

Practically, indexed terms and the corresponding occurrences are stored separately. That is, to divide (1) into two parts:

$$\{<t_i, pt_i> \mid (i=1\sim|V|)\}, \quad (2)$$

$$\{p_i \mid (i=1\sim|V|)\}. \quad (3)$$

Above, pt_i is a pointer pointing to p_i. In (2), all indexed terms are sorted lexicographically and stored with corresponding pointers sequentially in the indexed file, while occurrences in (3) are stored sequentially in the posting file.

Definition 3. Suppose V is the set of all unique characters appearing in text database TB, $V=\{t_i \mid i=1\sim|V|\}$ Σ . Let TB be denoted by a string $w=c_1c_2\ldots c_n\$(n=|TB|)$ where c_i is the ith character in w and c_i V, \$ is the assumed unique end-of-string symbol that does not appear in $\sum$. String w corresponds to a sequence of sistrings:

$$Sis=<sis_1, sis_2,\ldots, sis_n> \quad (4)$$

where $sis_i = c_ic_{i+1}\ldots c_n\$$ indicates the ith sistring of w. Sorting the sistrings in (4) lexicographically, we get a new sequence of sistrings:

$$PSis=<psis_1, psis_2,\ldots, psis_n>. \quad (5)$$

Obviously, for each sistring $psis_i$ in $PSis$, there is a sistring sis_j in Sis that is equal to $psis_i$ while i and j are not necessarily the same. (5) is the *full-text indexing PAT array* of text database TB. In practice, the positions of sistrings, instead of the sistrings themselves, are used in (5).

Definition 4. For a text database TB, there exists a directed graph $TBG=<V_g, E_g>$ where V_g is the set of vertices, each of which corresponds to a unique character appearing in TB, *i.e.*, $V_g=V$; E_g is the set of directed edges, each of which corresponds to a pair of adjacent characters appearing in TB and its direction points from the first character to the second one. We call TBG the *directed graph of text database TB.*

Definition 5. As described in the graph theory, a weighted directed graph is a directed graph that each edge has an associated value. In the context of this paper, the value associated with each directed edge is the position of the character corresponding to the directed edge's source vertex. Considering that some adjacent-character pairs occur at different positions in the text database, that is, in the directed graph of text database there exists the case of multiple directed edges having similar starting and end vertices. We compact all directed edges with similar starting and end vertices to one directed edge and unite all values associated with these edges to a set of values. We call the result graph *compact weighted directed graph of text database*. In what follows, without specific declaration, while referring to weighted directed graph, we mean compact weighted directed graph. Formally, text database TB corresponds to a weighted directed graph $WTBG=<V_w, E_w, L_w>$ where $V_w=V$ is the set of vertices, E_w is the set of directed edges, and L_w is the set of values associated with all directed edges in E_w. Denote $L_w(l^i, l^j)$ the set of values associated with directed edge l^il^j, then $L_w(l^i, l^j) = P(TB, \text{“}l^il^j\text{”})$, and $L_w=\{L_w(l^i, l^j) \mid \forall l^il^j: l^il^j \quad E_w\}$.

Example 2. Given a Chinese text string w_2:"我们的国家，我们的人民；你们的国家，你们的人民，他们的国家，他们的人民。". There are totally eleven unique characters appearing in w_2, in which nine are Chinese characters, the rest two are punctuation marks. Theses unique characters constitute the vertices set V_w ={"我", "你", "他", "们", "的", "人", "民", "国", "家", "，", "。"}. Fourteen unique adjacent-character pairs constitute the directed edges set E_w ={"我们", "们的", "的国", "国家", "家，", "，我", "的人", "人民", "民，", "，你", "你们", "，他", "他们", "民。"}. Values associated with these directed edges are as follows: L_w ("我", "们")={1, 7}; L_w ("你", "们")={13, 19}, L_w ("他", "们")={25, 31}, L_w ("；", "我")={6}, L_w ("，", "你")={12, 18}, L_w ("，", "他")={24, 30}, L_w ("们", "的")={2, 8, 14, 20, 26, 32}, L_w ("的", "国")={3, 15, 27}, L_w ("的", "人")={9, 21, 33}, L_w ("家", "，")={5, 17, 29}, L_w ("民", "，")={11, 23}, L_w ("民", "。")={35}, L_w ("国", "家")={4, 16, 28}, L_w ("人", "民")={10, 22, 34}. Fig. 1 illustrates the weighted directed graph of string w_2.

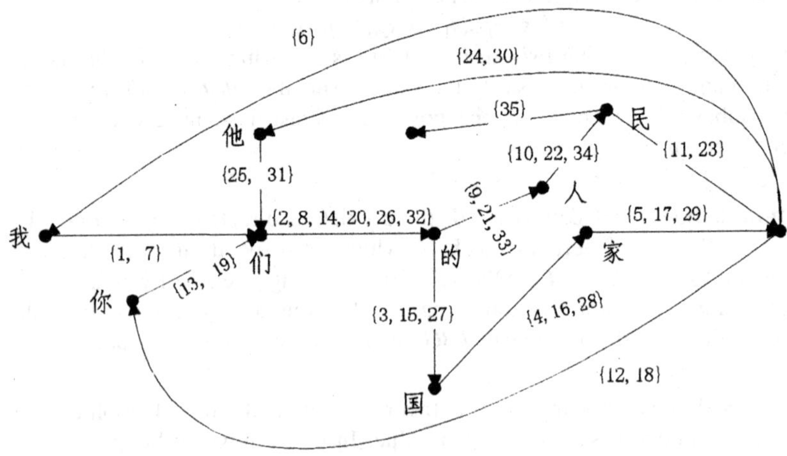

Fig. 1. Weighted directed graph of string w_2

3 Adjacency Matrix Based Inverted File and PAT Array

Definition 6. For a text database, there is a corresponding weighted directed graph that associates with an adjacency matrix. Thus, a text database has an adjacency matrix where each matrix element corresponds to a set of values associated with the corresponding directed edge. Formally, let V Σ be the set of all unique characters appearing in text database *TB*, and denote *D* the adjacency matrix of *TB*, we have

$$D=[d_{ij}], \qquad (6\text{-}1)$$

$$d_{ij}= d(l^i,l^j)=L_w(l^i, l^j) = P(TB, \text{“}l^il^j\text{”}). \qquad (6\text{-}2)$$

We call matrix *D* *adjacency matrix based full text indexing model* of text database *TB*.

Example 3. Given string w_2 in example 2, according to definition 6 and the weighted directed graph illustrated in Fig. 1, it is easy to build the adjacency matrix indexing model of w_2. Let V_w={“我”, “你”, “他”, “们”, “的”, “人”, “民”, “国”, “家”, “，”, “。”}. The text indexing model D is a 11×11 matrix:

$$D = \begin{vmatrix} \Phi & \Phi & \Phi & d_{14} & \Phi & \Phi & \Phi & \Phi & \Phi & \Phi & \Phi \\ \Phi & \Phi & \Phi & d_{24} & \Phi & \Phi & \Phi & \Phi & \Phi & \Phi & \Phi \\ \Phi & \Phi & \Phi & d_{34} & \Phi & \Phi & \Phi & \Phi & \Phi & \Phi & \Phi \\ \Phi & \Phi & \Phi & \Phi & d_{45} & \Phi & \Phi & \Phi & \Phi & \Phi & \Phi \\ \Phi & \Phi & \Phi & \Phi & \Phi & d_{56} & \Phi & d_{58} & \Phi & \Phi & \Phi \\ \Phi & \Phi & \Phi & \Phi & \Phi & \Phi & d_{67} & \Phi & \Phi & \Phi & \Phi \\ \Phi & \Phi & \Phi & \Phi & \Phi & \Phi & \Phi & \Phi & \Phi & d_{7\,10} & d_{7\,11} \\ \Phi & \Phi & \Phi & \Phi & \Phi & \Phi & \Phi & \Phi & d_{89} & \Phi & \Phi \\ \Phi & \Phi & \Phi & \Phi & \Phi & \Phi & \Phi & \Phi & \Phi & d_{9\,10} & \Phi \\ d_{10\,1} & d_{10\,2} & d_{10\,3} & \Phi & \Phi & \Phi & \Phi & \Phi & \Phi & \Phi & \Phi \\ \Phi & \Phi & \Phi & \Phi & \Phi & \Phi & \Phi & \Phi & \Phi & \Phi & \Phi \end{vmatrix}$$

in which d_{14}= L_w (“我”, “们”)={1, 7}, d_{24}= L_w (“你”, “们”)={13, 19}, d_{34}= L_w (“他”, “们”)={25, 31}, d_{45}= L_w (“们” , “的”)={2, 8, 14, 20, 26, 32}, d_{56}= L_w (“的” , “人”)={9, 21, 33}, d_{58}= L_w (“的” , “国”)={3, 15, 27}, d_{67}= L_w (“人” , “民”)={10, 22, 34}, $d_{7\,10}$= L_w (“民” , “， ”)={11, 23}, $d_{7\,11}$= L_w (“民” , “。 ”)={35}, d_{89}= L_w (“国” , “家”)={4, 16, 28}, $d_{9\,10}$= L_w (“家” , “， ”)={5, 17, 29}, $d_{10\,1}$= L_w (“； ”, “我”)={6}, $d_{10\,2}$= L_w (“； ” , “你”)={12, 18}, $d_{10\,3}$= L_w (“， ” , “他”)={24, 30}. The rest matrix elements are empty set Φ.

Practically, there are two different approaches to implement the adjacency matrix based full-text indexing model:

1) Seeing matrix element d_{ij} in D as a set of positions of adjacent-character pair l^il^j occurring in TB, and sorting all elements of d_{ij} in positional order, then d_{ij} is equivalent to the inverted list of indexed term l^il^j.
2) Treating matrix element d_{ij} as a set of positions of the sistrings whose prefix is the adjacent-character pair l^il^j, and sorting all elements of d_{ij} in lexical order of the corresponding sistrings, then d_{ij} is similar to the PAT array of sistrings with a prefix of l^il^j.

To distinguish this two different implementation approaches, we use $D^1$and D^2 to denote the implemented adjacency matrices of approach 1) and approach 2) respectively, and call D^1 the *adjacency matrix based full-text indexing inverted file*, D^2 the *adjacency matrix based full-text indexing PAT array*.

Formally, D^1 is a kind of reorganization of the traditional inverted file, *i.e.*, transforming the character-based inverted file to a kind of adjacent-character pair based inverted file and organizing all inverted lists in the form of adjacency matrix. Conversely, the traditional inverted file is a kind of compression of D^1, that is, to compact the adjacent-character pair based inverted file to the character-based inverted file. Analogously, D^2 is a kind of decomposition of the traditional PAT array, *i.e.*, splitting a long PAT array into a collection of short PAT arrays such that each short PAT array corresponds a set of sistrings having a similar prefix in the form of adjacent-character pair; on the contrary, the traditional PAT array is a kind of aggregation of D^2. Following are four algorithms for transformations between D^1 and the traditional inverted file, D^2 and the traditional PAT array. It is easy to prove the correctness of these algorithms in terms of definition 2, 3 and 6. Owing to the limitation of space, we give no detail here.

Algorithm 1. Build D^1 from traditional inverted file.
Input: indexing lists of any two indexing terms in text database:

$\{l^i{:}p_{i1},\cdots,p_{in}\}$,
$\{l^j{:}p_{j1},\cdots,p_{jm}\}$.

Output: $D^1=[d_{ij}]$.

Processing:

$$d_{ij} = L_w(l^i,l^j)$$
$$= \{k \mid \forall k\ (\exists p_{ik_1} \exists p_{jk_2} : p_{ik_1} = k \ and \ p_{jk_2} = k+1 \ while \ 1 \quad k_1 \quad n \ and \ 1 \quad k_2 \quad m)\}.$$

Algorithm 2. Build traditional inverted file from D^1.
Input: $D^1=[d_{ij}]$.
Output: $\{l^i{:}\ p_i\}$.
Processing:

$$p_i = \bigcup_{j=1}^{|V|} d_{ij}.$$

Here, " " indicates the set union operator.

Algorithm 3. Build D^2 from traditional PAT array.
Input: PAT array $PSis=\{psis_1, psis_2,\ldots, psis_n\}$.
Output: $D^2=[d_{ij}]$, $d_{ij} = L_w(l^i,l^j)$.
Processing:

1) Find the first sistring $psis_k$ matching with "l^il^j*" in *PSis* by binary search.
2) Starting from $psis_k$, search continuously in *PSis* the other sistrings matching with "l^il^j*" in the right and left directions till no such sistring can be found.
3) Assume $psis_{k1}$ and $psis_{k2}$ are the two sistrings that match with "l^il^j*" and locate at the most right and the most left positions in *PSis* respectively, then

$$d_{ij} = L_w(l^i,l^j)$$
$$= \{psis_{k1}, psis_{k1+1},\ldots, psis_k,\ldots, psis_{k2-1}, psis_{k2}\}(1 \quad k1 \quad k \quad k2 \quad n).$$

Algorithm 4. Build traditional PAT array from D^2.
Input: $D^2=[d_{ij}]$.
Output: PAT array $PSis=\{psis_1, psis_2,\ldots, psis_n\}$.
Processing:

$$PAT = \bigcup_{i=1}^{|V|}\bigcup_{j=1}^{|V|} d_{ij}.$$

Similarly, " " is the set union operator.

4 Query Processing Algorithms

4.1 Query Processing Algorithm Based on D^1

Query processing based on D^1 is essentially a kind of set operation. Following is a theorem about D^1 based query processing.

Theorem 1. Let "$l_1l_2 \ldots l_n$" be a query string, $q(l_1l_2 \ldots l_n)$ the query result, then

1) When n=2k, $q(l_1l_2...l_n) = d_{12}^{0} \quad d_{34}^{2} \ldots \quad d_{2k-3\,2k-2}^{2k-4} \quad d_{2k-1\,2k}^{2k-2}$;

2) When n=2k+1, $q(l_1l_2...l_n) = d_{12}^{0} \quad d_{34}^{2} \ldots \quad d_{2k-3\,2k-2}^{2k-4} \quad d_{2k-1\,2k}^{2k-2} \quad d_{2k\,2k+1}^{2k-1}$.

Here, $d_{ij}^{m} =< d(l_i, l_j) - m > = \{(x\text{-}m) \mid \forall x : x \quad d(l_i, l_j)\}$.

Proof: According to definition 6, it is easy to prove theorem 1. We omit the details here.

In order to improve query-processing efficiency, we must reduce the number of disk accesses or set intersections. Three techniques are available as follows.

- Reducing the number of set intersections. That is equivalent to reducing the number of matrix elements involved in set intersection. We can adopt the optimizing technique proposed in [10] to cut down matrix elements involved in query processing, which utilizes a directed graph method to optimize the search path at the cost of a little more space overhead.
- Reducing the number of elements in the sets involved in intersection operation. Taking use of the properties of query string, it is possible to cut down the number of elements in the sets involved in intersection operation. Here consider a special case: substring occurring repeatedly in the query string. Suppose "l_il_{i+1}"(1 i n-1) occurs twice in the query string $l_1l_2 \ldots l_n$ at an interval of k, then the valid elements for intersection operation in $d(l_i, l_{i+1})$ is $d(l_i, l_{i+1}) \cap < d(l_i, l_{i+1}) + k >$. Actually, there exist many of such cases, which we are not intended to enumerate completely here.
- Improving the efficiency of set intersection. If the text database is very large, the sizes of sets involved in query processing will be large too. Note that intersecting large sets is also time consuming. Given two sets A and B that include m and n elements respectively (Let m n), a more efficient way to carry out intersection between A and B is 1) sorting the elements of set A and set B in advance; 2) comparing the elements in the larger set with the elements in the smaller one. In such a way, m and n are the lower-bound and upper-bound of element comparisons needed for $A \cap B$ respectively.

4.2 Query Processing Algorithm Based on D^2

Algorithm 5. Query processing based on D^2

Input: Full-text indexing model D^2 and query string "$l_1l_2 \ldots l_n$".

Output: $q(l_1l_2 \ldots l_n)$.

Processing:

1) Based on D^2 and "$l_1 l_2$", obtain PAT array $d(l_1, l_2)=\{psis_1, psis_2, \ldots, psis_m\}$.
2) Search the first sistring $psis_k$ matching with "$l_1 l_2 \ldots l_n$*" in $d(l_1, l_2)$ by binary search.
3) Starting from $psis_k$, search continuously in $d(l_1, l_2)$ the other sistrings matching with "$l_1 l_2 \ldots l_n$*" in the right and left directions till no such sistring can be found.
4) Assume $psis_{k1}$ and $psis_{k2}$ are sistrings that match with "$l_1 l_2 \ldots l_n$*" and locate at the most right and the most left positions in $d(l_1, l_2)$ respectively, then

$$q(l_1 l_2 .. l_n) = \{psis_{k1}, psis_{k1+1}, \ldots, psis_k, \ldots, psis_{k2-1}, psis_{k2}\} (1 \quad k1 \quad k \quad k2 \quad m).$$

5 Comparisons with Traditional Indexing Models

Suppose the size of text database TB is N ($N=|TB|$), the number of unique characters in the text database is m ($m=|V|$), and the length of query is l_q. Furthermore, for the simplicity of analysis, we assume all characters occurring in the text database at equal probability. Thus the average size of elements in adjacency matrix D^2 is $E \quad N/(m*m)$.

5.1 Traditional Inverted File *vs.* D^1

1) Time cost for indexing building: $O(N)$.
2) Space overhead
   a) D^1:$O(N+m*m)$.
   b) Inverted file: $O(N+m)$.
3) Search time cost
   a) D^1: At most $(l_q+1)/2$ disk accesses and $(l_q-1)/2$ set intersections.
   b) Inverted file: l_q disk accesses and (l_q-1) set intersections. Furthermore, considering that the average size of matrix elements in D^1 is about 1/m of the size of inverted file, which will result in higher query-processing efficiency.

Note that 1) disk access is the major factor that influences the value of query efficiency; 2) for large- scale text database, we have $N>>m$ because m is limited and N can grow as the text database expands. That is to say, the extra space overhead of D^1 is much less than the size of original text database. In the case of English text collections, m is not greater than 256. While in Chinese text environment, m is generally between 6000 and 8000. Thus, adjacency matrix based inverted file model can achieve more 50% benefit of query efficiency at the cost of much less extra space overhead compared with the size of original text database.

5.2 Traditional PAT Array *vs.* D^2

1) Time cost for indexing building: $O(N \log(N))$.
2) Space overhead
   a) D^2: $O(N+m*m)$.
   b) PAT array: $O(N)$.

3) Search time cost
   a) D^2: At most $4\log_2(E)$ disk accesses and $2\log_2(E)$-1 comparisons.
   b) PAT array: At most $4\log_2(N)$ disk accesses and $2\log_2(N)$-1 comparisons.

Let us consider the worst case. For large-scale text databases, we still have $N >> m$, which means that the extra storage overhead of D^2 is negligible compared with the size of original text database. At the same time, D^2 benefits $8\log_2(m)$ disk accesses and $4\log_2(m)$ comparisons less than traditional PAT array. Specifically, suppose the size of text database N=640Mb□ at most 117 disk accesses are requested for traditional PAT array. In the case of English text collections, let m=256, then 64 disk accesses are cut down by D^2, *i.e.*, the improvement ratio of query efficiency is 54%. For the Chinese text environment, let m=6763(Taking GB2312-80 for example)□then 101 disk accesses are cut down by D^2, that is, a query efficiency improvement ratio of 86%. Certainly, we admit that the results are only approximate estimation, which may deviate somewhat from the realistic values. However, because each matrix element in D^2 is only part of the entire PAT array of the text database, D^2 will still outperform the traditional PAT array.

Finally, we have a comparison between D^1 and D^2. Note that there is no much difference in space overhead between D^1 and D^2. However, it is noteworthy to analyze the difference in their search time cost. Still, we consider disk access the major bottleneck of query efficiency. Obviously, query efficiency of D^1 is related to the length of query string, while query efficiency of D^2 depends on the size of matrix element involved in query processing. When disk accesses of the two models are equal, we have

$$(l_q+1)/2 \quad 4\log_2(E). \tag{9}$$

That is,

$$(l_q+1)/2 \quad 4\log_2(N/(m*m)). \tag{10}$$

From (10), we obtain

$$l_q \quad 8\log_2(N/(m*m))-1. \tag{11}$$

Equation (11) sets an approximate criterion about when to handle query using D^1 and D^2. We carry out further estimation in the following two specific cases:

1) In the case of English text database, let N=640M and m=256, we have l_q 105. That is to say, when the length of query is shorter than 105 characters, it is more efficient to handle queries using D^1 than using D^2. On the contrary, if the length of query is longer than 105 characters, D^2 is favorable.
2) Under the Chinese text environment, let N=640M and m=6763, we can obtain l_q 30, *i.e.*, when the length of query is shorter than 30 characters, it is more efficient to handle query using D^1 than using D^2. Otherwise, it is favorable to use D^2 to handle query.

For a certain text database, if the query is short, it is more efficient to process query by using D^1 than using D^2. Otherwise, it is favorable to use D^2. In realty, it is likely to accommodate the two query modes simultaneously in the same text database. In implementation, we can establish the indexing matrix according to D^2, then choose query mode (D^1 or D^2) in terms of query length.

6 Experimental Results

Experiments are carried out over a real world Chinese text database to validate the feasibility and efficiency of the new models. The test database includes 6556 Chinese text documents, and its size is 107Mb. We completed the experiments on a PC with a PIII 500MHz CPU and 512Mb RAM. The goal of experiments is to measure the improvement ratio of query processing efficiency of the new indexing models. We define the query processing efficiency improvement ratio as follows.

$$r = \frac{t_{old} - t_{new}}{t_{old}} 100\%. \tag{12}$$

Here, t_{old} represents the time consumed for handling one or more user queries with the traditional indexing models, *i.e.*, inverted file and PAT array, while t_{new} indicates the time used for handling the similar queries with the new indexing models, *i.e.*, adjacency matrix based inverted file and adjacency matrix based PAT array. To make our experimental results more reasonable and reliable, we chose manually 1000 different queries for testing. The query processing efficiency is evaluated on the average time cost in handling the 1000 different queries. Each query is a Chinese text string with from 2 to 25 Chinese characters, and its queried result is not empty. Table 1 lists the query number distribution over query length of the 1000 different queries. Obviously, the number of shorter queries is larger, while the number of longer is smaller, which conforms to the realistic situation of user query delivery.

The experimental results are presented in Table 2, which show that the new models can improve considerably the query processing efficiencies of the traditional inverted file and PAT array.

Table 1. Query number distribution over query length of the 1000 processed queries

l_q (characters)	2	5	7	10	12	15	17	20	22	25
N	150	150	150	100	100	100	100	50	50	50

Table 2. Experimental results of query processing efficiency improvement ratio

	D^1	D^2
Query processing efficiency improvement ratio (r)	52%	80%

Note that Chinese is quite different from English and other western languages:

- Chinese has a relatively large character set. GB2312-80 collects 6763 Chinese characters. While in English, the alphabetic table has only 26 unique characters.
- A Chinese word can be a single character, or two or more characters. According to the *Frequency Dictionary of Modern Chinese*, among the top 9,000 most frequent words, 26.7% are unigrams. In English, only "a" and "I" are single-character words.
- The written Chinese text has no delimiters to mark word boundaries. Extracting words (or keywords) from Chinese text is a complex task in natural language understanding area. On the contrary, English words are explicitly separated by blanks, which makes word extraction in English text be quite easy and simple.

Theses differences above make character-based indexing models be more suitable for Chinese text retrieval. Consider that both D^1 and D^2 are character-based full-text indexing model, and as far as query-processing efficiency is concerned, they all favor text databases with a relatively large character set. Thus, the new models are more suitable for applications of Chinese text databases.

7 Conclusion Remarks

In this paper, we investigate two new character-based full-text indexing models that can improve the query efficiency of IR systems considerably at the cost of much less amount of extra storage overhead compared to the size of original text database. Algorithms of query processing for the new models are developed. The performances of the new models are analyzed and compared with that of traditional indexing models. Experiments over real world Chinese text collection are carried out to demonstrate the effectiveness and efficiency of the new models. We also argue that the proposed new models are suitable for applications of large-scale text databases, especially Chinese text databases. Further research will focus on: 1) Exploring efficient building and updating algorithms for the new indexing models over large-scale text databases; 2) Investigating query optimization for the new indexing models; 3) Applying the new models to real-world IR systems.

Acknowledgments. We would like to thank the anonymous referees for helpful suggestions and insightful comments.

References

1. R. Baesa-Yates and B. Ribeiro-Neto. Modern Information Retrieval. Addison Wesley, Reading, Mass. 1999.
2. W. B. Frakes and R Baesa-Yates. Information Retrieval: Data Structures & Algorithms. Prentice Hall PTR, Upper Saddle River, New Jersey. 1992.
3. D. Sullivan. Search Engine Watch. http://www.searchenginewatch.com.
4. AltaVista, http://www.altavista.com.
5. A.Tomasic, H. Garcia-Molina and K. Shoens. Incremental updates of inverted lists for text document retrieval. In: *Proceedings of SIGMOD'94*, 1994. 289-300.
6. C. Faltousos and S. Christodoulakis. Signature files: an access method for documents and its analytical performance evaluation. *ACM Trans. On Office Information Systems*, 1984, 2(4): 267-88.
7. D. R. Morrison. PATRICIA- practical algorithm to retrieve information coded in alphanumeric. Journal of the ACM, 1968, 15(4): 514-534.
8. G. Navarro. An optimal index for PAT arrays. In: N. Ziviani, R. Baeza-Yates and G. Guimaraes, editors. Proceedings of the Third South American Workshop on String Processing. Carleton University Press International Informatics Series, V.4, Recife, Braizl, 1996. 214-227.
9. C. Tenopir and J. S. Ro. Full Text Database. Greenwood Press, 1990.
10. S. Zhou. Key techniques of Chinese text databases. PhD thesis, Department of Computer Science, Fudan University, China, 2000.

Goal-Oriented Information Retrieval Using Feedback from Users

Hiroyuki Toda, Toshifumi Enomoto, and Tetsuji Satoh

NTT Cyber Space Laboratories
1-1 Hikari-no-oka, Yokosuka-shi, Kanagawa-ken, 239-0847, Japan
{hiroyuki, eno, satoh}@isl.ntt.co.jp

Abstract. To allow people in closed groups such as clubs to more efficiently retrieve documents from the WWW, this paper proposes a retrieval system that incrementally optimizes a number of fixed search goals. Optimization involves observing how people in the group rate the documents returned in comparable searches. The search goal selected by the user allows the system to effectively (and automatically) prune the search results retrieved by free keyword searches. Tests show that the system provides better performance than existing search heuristics.

1 Introduction

With the growth of the WWW, the amount of information that can be accessed has exploded. As a result, users are demanding retrieval systems that can efficiently locate the desired information. Unfortunately, the basic function of ordinary retrieval systems is to return all documents that include the user specified keyword(s). Users are forced to manually prune the result list in order to get the documents desired.

The retrieval technique proposed herein uses the feature that users belonging to the same group will share the same search goals and will rate documents in much the same way. According to this consideration, we collect information on the search action of a group and use it to optimize the results of subsequent searches conducted by group members. A user belonging to a group can search more efficiently because the search history of prior users in the same group is utilized. We construct a prototype system based on this proposition and find that it yields much higher precision in terms of search results.

2 Current Problem and Related Work

An ordinary retrieval system receives keyword(s) as a query and locates the documents that include the keyword(s). Next, it sorts the document list by some statistical measure such as frequency of keyword appearance. This method is based on the concept that is "documents that are similar to the query are the desired documents".

X.S. Wang, G. Yu, and H. Lu (Eds.): WAIM 2001, LNCS 2118, pp. 72-79, 2001.

Unfortunately, most users tend to input no more than 3 keywords[1]. The retrieval system finds it difficult to achieve really efficient searches with so few keywords. One result is that there are too many undesired documents in the search results. Many methods are being researched to address this problem.

- **"Reliability" based methods**

A reliability measure, calculated from the appearance frequency of hypertext linkage, can be used to exclude useless documents. In brief, a document that has high "reliability" is linked to by many other documents. This approach is used in many papers, for example HITS[2] and PageRank[3]. Web search engines that based on this technique[4] are famed for their high precision. It fails, however, if the range of the documents and/or link relations are insufficient[5].

- **Methods based on "Popularity"**

The measure of popularity is assessed by how often the document is selected; useless documents can be excluded by setting the level of popularity desired.

However, this method depends on the ease with which popularity can be defined. If popularity is simply taken as the total number of times a document is selected, irrespective of the query, documents with many high-frequency words would always have high scores. When we use popularity, we must consider what is the best measure of popularity and how to measure it. For example, Directhit[6] uses much time the user spent to perusing the page to provide a more accurate measure of popularity.

- **"Page Type" methods**

A new indicator is called page type[7]. In this system, the users input the desired page type and keywords, and the system finds all pages of the type indicated that include the keywords. This method is effective when the user's search goal is clear.

Unfortunately, it demands that all documents be classified in terms of their page type ahead of time. Moreover, this method assumes that all documents fall neatly into different categories such as "catalog" and "want ad". Accordingly, it is too restrictive.

- **The others**

The use of natural language queries solves the problems of too-few query words and searching based on keyword inclusion. Such system extract meaning from the natural language query, which is then used to achieve more effective searches[8]. Unfortunately, this method cannot be used widely because of the high cost of making the knowledge base and the difficulty of analyzing queries and documents.

Zhu et al. measured search efficiency to examine many metrics and their combination; the goal was information quality. Though their result indicate importance of information quality, such metrics are not well specialized.

3 Proposed Approach

- **Goal-Oriented Searches**

We considered the low precision of ordinary search results is due to their failure to clearly discern the user's search goal. That is, two users may have different search goals but use the same keywords. In this situation, it seems impossible for both users to receive highly precise results. How then can we identify the search goal of a user? Though natural language processing can discern the user's search goal, it's too expensive.

This paper describes a system that presents the user with a list of preset goals. While the true set of user goals is infinite, there is a small fixed set of commonly used goals. Typical examples include locating new products and identifying the most common problems.

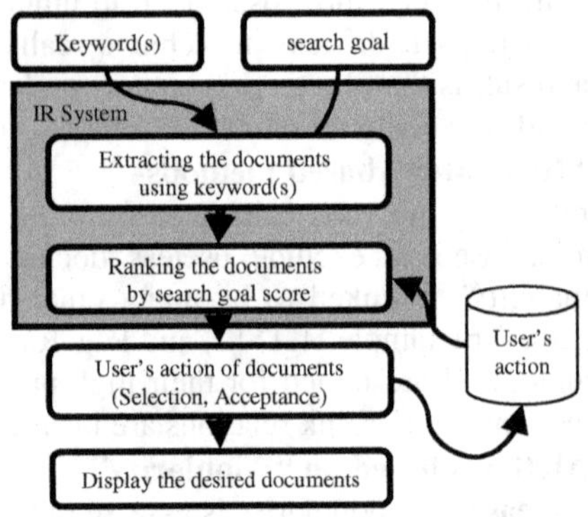

Fig. 1. Flow Chart of Proposed method

According to this consideration, the proposed retrieval system, "Search goal assistance" (SGA), utilizes preset search goals in addition to keywords. To make a search request, the user selects one search goal and inputs one or more keywords. SGA strips useless documents from the result list, so the user is presented with just the appropriate documents. A flow chart of SGA is given in Fig.1.

- **Document ranking using user feedback**

SGA is based on ranking indexed documents to achieve more effective searches.

Document i is given one "search goal score" (S_{ij}) for each of the j search goals. Search goal scores reflect the past responses of users who accessed the retrieval system. A user, who selects a search goal in making his search, is monitored, and information about which documents are selected from the result list and the user's assessment of the documents are collected and used to derive S_{ij}.

4 Details of Document Ranking

4.1 Calculating Basic Value

The search goal score S_{ij} is basically calculated from two measures: how often the document is selected by the users from among the search results (selection rate) and the how often the users rate the document as being appropriate (acceptance rate). Data on these measures is collected from the service logs of the retrieval system. SGA is assumed to hold n indexed documents and m search goals.

- **Selection rate**

The basic selection rate, c_{ij}, is the total number of times document i was selected from the result for search goal j. Because the result lists are ordered, documents on the first page are more likely to be selected than those on subsequent pages. To offset this effect, we weight document selection by using the term $F(r) = r^{2.08}$. r is the number of the page on which the document was displayed; the value 2.08 was determined from a review of the logs of a retrieval system used in our company. The weighted selection rate R_{ij} is given by

$$R_{ij} = \sum_{k=0}^{c_{ij}} (F(r))$$

- **Acceptance rate**

After a user selects a document, she is presented with an "Approval" button. If the user feels that the document suits her search goal, she clicks the button. The basic approval rate, e_{ij}, is the total number of times document i was found to be suitable for search goal j. The averaged acceptance rate E_{ij} is given by

$$E_{ij} = \frac{e_{ij}}{c_{ij}} \qquad \frac{\sum_{j=0}^{m} \sum_{i=0}^{n} \{c_{ij}\}}{N}$$

N is the number of combinations of search goals and documents existed in the log.

4.2 Calculating Search Goal Scores

The search goal scores are calculated using information held in the system logs. This following equation describes the straight time calculation of search goal score; all logs are given equal weighting. Search goal score S_{ij} is given by

$$S_{ij} = \sum_{t=1}^{l} \left(R_{ij}^{t} + \alpha\beta E_{ij}^{t}\right)$$

where l is total number of logs examined, t is the serial log number starting with the latest log, R^{t}_{ij} and E^{t}_{ij} are R_{ij} and E_{ij} as determined from the data in log t, α is the weight value needed to make the scale of the total acceptance rate equal to the scale of the basic selection rate; β is the used to properly weight the acceptance with respect to the evaluation by certain users.

A more practical score can be calculated by assigning higher weights to the youngest logs as they tend to be more up to date and relevant.

$$S_{ij} = \sum_{t=1}^{l} \left\{\left(R_{ij}^{t} + \alpha\beta E_{ij}^{t}\right) \; T(t)\right\} \quad \text{where } T(t) = \begin{cases} 1.0 - 0.1t\,(t \;\; 10) \\ 0\,(t \;\; 10) \end{cases}$$

5 System Overview and Implementation

We implemented a SGA prototype using the full text search system "TITAN"[9] as the starting point. The block diagram of the prototype, shown in Fig.2, indicates that there are two main blocks. Main parts are described below.

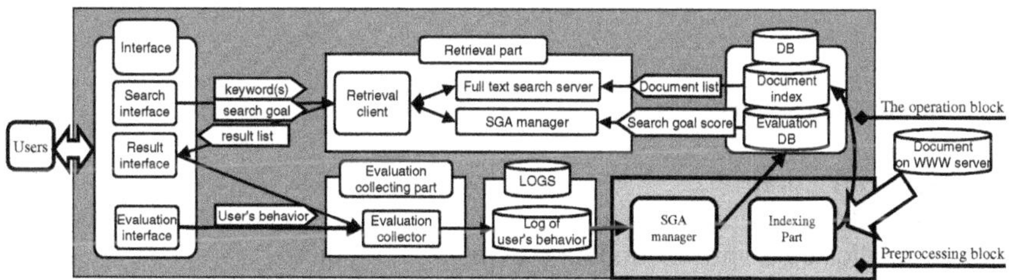

Fig. 2. Block diagram of the prototype

The operation block

This block consists of three parts and provides the search service and collects the user's responses.

– Interface

The user enters queries using this interface(see Fig.3). In addition to keywords, she selects one of the displayed search goals.

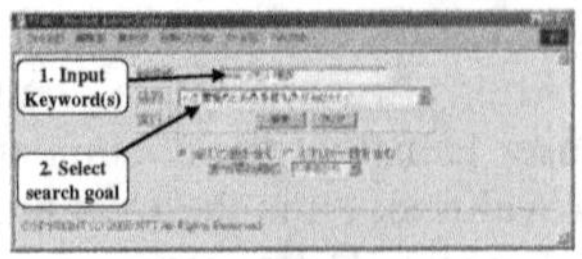

Fig. 3. Search Interface

If the user selects a document it is displayed in the lower browser pane (see Fig.4). If the user feels that the document well matches the search goal she clicks the "Approval" button.

– Retrieval part

This part receives the user's keyword(s) and search goal, completes the search, and displays the search result list to the user through the intermediary of the result interface. This part consists of full text search server and SGA manager. The former receives the keyword(s) and gets the list of document including the keyword(s). The latter receives the search goal and the list output by the full text search server. It gets the search goal score of each document in the list, for the search goal used from the Evaluation database. Next, it sorts by the search goal scores to make the result list.

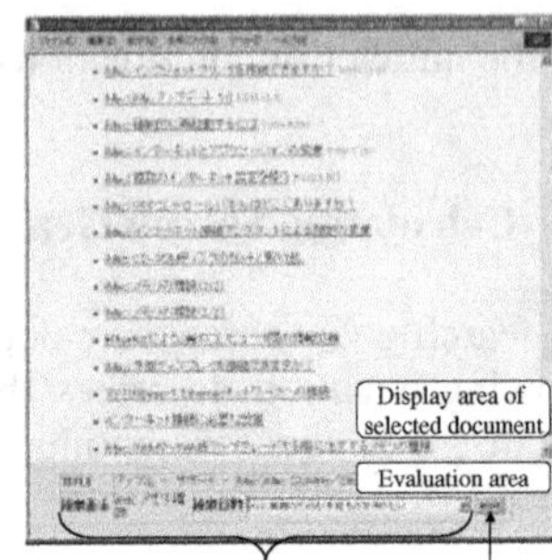

(http://www.apple.co.jp/support/otherimac/)

Fig. 4. Evaluation interface

– Action/collecting part

This part records the users actions in the result and evaluation interfaces and enters the data into the system logs as records. Each record holds the following data.

- Date - Document ID - Ranking of the document selected
- Keyword(s) - Search goal - User action ("Selection" or "Acceptance")

- **Preprocessing block**

This block consists of the indexing part and the SGA analyzer, which updates search goal scores of the documents; the scores are held in the evaluation database. Performance evaluation

6 Performance Evaluation

6.1 Evaluation Resource

- **Document collection**

We collected 2010 documents from two web sites[10][11] and a news group (fj.sys.mac) dedicated to information on Macintosh computers.

- **Search goal list**

9 search goals were manually acquired from the FAQ list[12] and the responses made by Macintosh users to a questionnaire. The search goal list is shown in Table 1. Our aim was to minimize the number of goals by using only the most-frequently used goals.

- **Evaluation data set (EDS)**

First we created EDS by presenting the 2010 documents to 5 subjects. Each subject was presented with the documents one by one and asked to select the search goals that the subject felt best matched the document as well as the most appropriate keyword(s). The keywords were to be taken from the document itself. In some instances the subject felt that none of the search goals were appropriate.

Fig.5 shows, as an example, a piece of EDS about document #33. It shows that for this document, 3 subjects selected search goal "b2" (its probability of search goal inclusion is thus 3/5) and the keyword "icWord".

Table 1. Search goal list

General information
a1 information of new product
a2 general topic such as product and event
a3 review and remark
Concrete information
b1 information of price
b2 information how to get
b3 information of time
Restrictive information
c1 detailed information
c2 information of method and material to actualize
c3 information of trouble shooting

```
<DOC ID = "33">
  <PURPOSE PID = "b2">
    <EVAL>3</EVAL>
    <WORD TIMES = "3">icWord</WORD>
  </PURPOSE>
(1){
  <PURPOSE PID = "c2">
    <EVAL>5</EVAL>
    <WORD TIMES = "5">mac</WORD>
    <WORD TIMES = "3">office</WORD>
    <WORD TIMES = "2">word</WORD>
  </PURPOSE>
}
</DOC>
```

Fig. 5. An example of evaluation data set (EDS)

6.2 Evaluation Method

At first, to train the SGA prototype, we created a virtual user.

1. The virtual user issued a series of 500 search requests. First, documents were randomly selected from EDS. Next, one of the search goals recorded for the document was randomly selected is as illustrated in Fig.5(1). Up to 3 of the keywords used with the selected search goal were selected according to the frequency with which they were used by the subjects in forming EDS.
2. The virtual user inputs a query and gets a result list.
3. The titles and summaries of all documents displayed in the result list were examined. If they (titles and summaries) contained all the keywords issued for that search the document was selected (page number was determined by assuming that 10 documents were displayed on each page).
4. The selected documents were checked against EDS. If their search goals were recorded in EDS, the virtual user "accepted" the document where the probability of acceptance equaled the probability of search goal inclusion.

The virtual user repeated processes 2 to 4 until 500 search requests were processed.

The above process was iterated 10 times and we got 10 logs.

After system learning was completed, we measured the recall-precision curve of the system using the following method.

1. We made a test list of 500 queries. This list was used in all subsequent evaluations.
2. We input each query to the system and got the result list.
3. For each document in the result list, we checked its search goals and keywords against those in EDS to determine if the document was correct or not.

Next, we measured the precision of the top 10 results. According to the logs of the retrieval system used by our company, most users use only the first page. Accordingly, we need to assess the system's performance as perceived by most people; it follows that this form of precision slightly differs from the standard R-precision measure. To sharpen the accuracy further, we consider only those search goals that were used by more 50% of the subjects as recorded in EDS.

6.3 Result

- **The effectiveness of using search goal**

We compare the proposed method to the simple feedback method. The simple feedback method(SFM) does not differentiate between the different search goals.

In the graph of the precision of the top 10 results, see Fig.6, we find that the precision of SFM doesn't rise even if the system is trained more extensively. Unlike the SFM, the precision of the proposed system increases as training progresses. These two graphs confirm the effectiveness of using search goal scores in boosting search efficiency.

- **The suitability of document evaluation**

To confirm the effectiveness of terms E_{ij} and R_{ij}, we created and tested the simple counting method(SCM). This method calculates the search goal scores as follows.

$$S_{ij} = \sum_{t=1}^{l} \left\{ \left(c_{ij}^{t} + \alpha\beta e_{ij}^{t} \right) T(t) \right\}$$

Recall-precision curves for the proposed method and SCM are plotted in Fig.7. The fact that SCM provides higher precision at low recall rates is explained as follows. With little or no training, SCM well captures the effect wherein the users pay most attention to just the first page; documents on subsequent pages are not well handled. The proposed method, on the other hand, provides better coverage and tends to rank all documents suitably.

Curves plotting the precision of the top 10 results as a function training times are given in Fig.6. The curves show that the proposed method yields better results as training proceeds.

The above results indicate, “the proposed method evaluates all documents more accurately” ”With adequate training, the proposed method yields higher performance than SCM”.

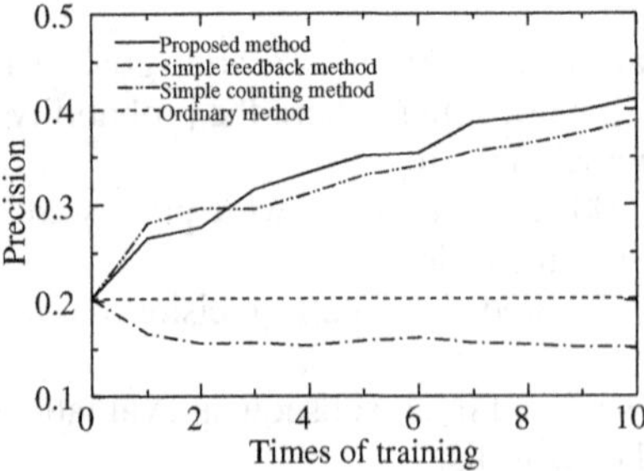

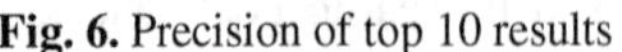

Fig. 6. Precision of top 10 results

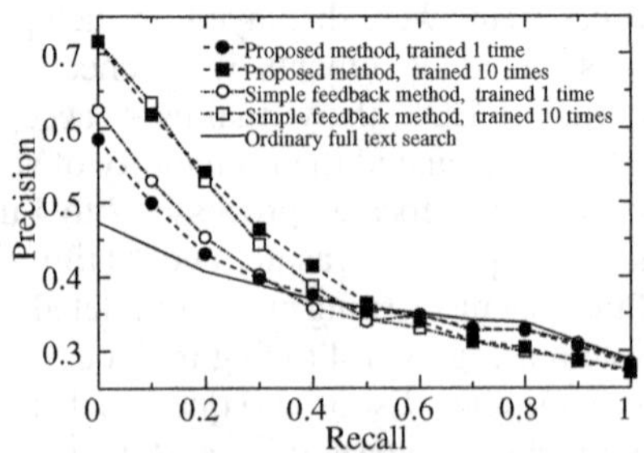

Fig. 7. Effectiveness of calculation method

- **Basic property using the proposal method**

If we compare the proposed method to the ordinary full text search method, we find that the former offers higher precision at low recall rates. At high recall rates, however, the ordinary method offers better precision at high recall rates.

The reason for this is that the current version of the proposed system appears to over emphasize the importance of selection compared to direct acceptance. Users often tend to select documents that are prominently displayed. This selection may force an unsuitable document to be placed ahead of a more suitable document that has yet to be selected. We found that such "neglected" documents tend to have vague or misleading titles and summaries.

7 Conclusion

This paper proposed a trainable document retrieval method suitable for closed groups, and implemented a prototype system. The method involves capturing user feedback and using the information to improve search performance. Each document is assigned a value, called the search goal score, for each predefined search goal. To initiate a search, the user inputs the keywords and the most appropriate search goal. Continued use of the system incrementally optimizes the search goal scores. Tests confirmed that the method described herein yields better search performance than conventional full text searching. It was also shown that the proposed responds well to training.

Future works include finding a way of assessing documents newly added.

References

[1] Witten, I. H., Moffat, A., Bell T. C.: "*Managing Gigabyes*", Morgan Kaufmann, 1999.

[2] Kleinberg, J. M. "Authoritative source in a hyperlinked environment", *the Journal of ACM*, 1999.

[3] Brin, S. and Page, L.: "The Anatomy of a Large-Scale Hypertextual Web Search Engine", *Proceedings of 7th WWW Conference*, 1998.

[4] "Google", http://www.google.com/

[5] Hawking, D., Voorheers, E.,: Craswell, N. and Bailey, P. "Overview of The TREC-8 Web Track", *Proceeding of TREC-8*, 1999.

[6] "Directhit", http://www.directhit.com/

[7] Matsuda, K. and Fukushima, T.: "Task-Oriented World Wide Web Retrieval by Document Type Classification", *Proceedings of the 1999 ACM International Conference on Inforamation and Knowledge Management*, 1999.

[8] Chun, Y., Ishima, M., Fujii, A., Ishikawa, T.: "A Utility-based Information Retrieval System for User Information Usage- UBIR", *The 3rd International Workshop on IRAL*, 1998.

[9] Hayashi, Y., Kikui, G. and Suzaki, S.: "TITAN:A Cross-linguistic Search Engine for WWW", *AAAI Spring Symposium Technical Report*, SS-97-05, 1997.

[10] "Apple Computer, Inc.", http://www.apple.co.jp/

[11] "MacWIRE Online", http://www.zdnet.co.jp/macwire/

[12] "FAQ and Answers list for Macintosh", http://www.csl.sony.co.jp/faq/mac-faq.sjis.html

Classify Web Document by Key Phrase Understanding[1]

Changjie Tang, Tong Li, Changyu Liu, and Yin Ge
chj-tang@263.net
Computer Department, Sichuan University, China, 610064

Abstract. In order to evaluate the security rank of document owner (sender or Web station), the documents discrimination is widely adopted to classify Web documents. The old strategy based on keywords matching often leads to low precision. This article proposes a new model called CKPU (Classifying by key Phrase Understanding) including the key sentence template, mining threshold vector, objective and, subjective discriminating. The experiment result shows that the algorithms are efficient for discriminating documents.

Keywords: File discrimination, Key sentence template, Phrase-understanding.

1 Introduction

To protect local host computer from unfriendly Web documents (black emails, malicious documents), evaluation the security rank of document sender (user or Web station) is widely studied [1,2,3]. However the existing strategy based on simple keywords matching often leads to low accuracy.

Let DOC be a supervised Web document. DOC can be viewed as combination of structured component and non-structural component. The structural part includes head, title, URL, author, and the other extractable parts by XML technique. The remains is non-structural part which can be viewed as a heap of sentences.

The process of structural part is relative simple and mature [11,12]. For non-structural part of DOC, the naive method does:(1) Predefine a set of key words and THRESHOLD. (2) Count the appearance of key words in DOC, denoted as COUNT. Calcify DOC as "negative" if COUNT > THRESHOLD, or "positive" otherwise. In fact it is based on simple word matching without programmatic analysis and language understanding. It is doomed to have the following deficiency: (a) Low precision. It may fail to detect unfriendly document and mistreating good documents as unfriendly one. (b) It is easy to be cheated by synonymy technique. (c) Low efficiency. As the information in key words is often not enough to make decision, it may need intervention of manpower. It leads low speed.

To solve these problems, we propose a new method named CKPU (Classifying by key Phrase Understanding). CKPU does three steps:(1) extracting the key sentences from teaching set, (2) Extracting the main grammatical elements,(3)Mining the discrimination rule for Web documents.

[1] Supported by the of National Science Foundation of China grant #60073046.

X.S. Wang, G. Yu, and H. Lu (Eds.): WAIM 2001, LNCS 2118, pp. 80-88, 2001.

2 The CKPU Model

We now describe the concepts of CKPU model (Classifying by key Phrase Understanding).

Definition 1 The *TeachDocs* is a set of Web documents selected by user satisfying following ENOUGH criteria: (1) *Typical enough* for the task by containing the typical negative and positive class of Web document for specific task.(2) *Clear enough* being already classified.(3) *Big enough.*

Note that, the knowledge about positive or negative criteria is hidden (or sampled) in the TeachDocs. It is the training set for data mining.

It is well-known that, most message-purpose article on Web are written in canonical news-style such that some sentences can express or summarize the main idea of a paragraph, to formalize it, we introduce:

Definition 2 The *Key sentence template* is a profile configured by user as following list, Where V_I is in {True, False} :

All-Sentence-In-Abstract = V_1
All-Sentence-In-First-Paragraph = V_2
All-Sentence-In-Last-Paragraph = V_3
First-Sentence-In-Each-Paragraph = V_4
Last-Sentence-In-Each-Paragraph = V_5
Sentence-Contain-word-XXXX = V_6
Sentence-Contain-word-YYYY = V_7 , ...,

If V_k=True, then the sentence specified by k-th rule will be selected as key sentences. This gives flexibility to user. The key sentence template is newly added to our prototype based on recent practice.

Definition 3 The *Key sentence set* KeySentenceSet of a document is the set of sentences selected by key sentence template. An element of KeySentenceSet is denoted as KeySentence.

The procedure to get key sentence from a Web document doc, denoted as *GetKeySetence* (doc, KeySentence), is straightforward according to key sentence template. Its details are omitted here.

The experience shows that, for document written in news-style, the 70% or more meaning of a sentence can expressed by SPO-Structure, (i.e. the expression of Subject, Predicate and Object). Thus we have;

Definition 4 Let S be in KeySentenceSet of a document. Its subject, predicate and object are denoted respectively as Sub, Pred and Obj. Let Null be the empty word. Then

1) The set KeyPhrase = {(Sub, Pred, Obj, CreditPhr)| At least two of Sub, Pred and Obj is not NULL} is called key phrase of S, where CreditPhr is a number indicating the contribution of the phrase to classification.
2) The set of key phrases of all document in TeachDocs, denoted as TeachPhraseSet, is called teach phrases; all the key phrases of one document of the TeachDocs is denoted as TeachPhrase.

An example to illustrate key sentences and phrase is shown in Figure 1.

Our CKPU method discriminates a document synthetically by the numbers of all negative phrases, positive phrases and average credit of all phrases. To formalize this we define the evaluation vector of a document:

Definition 5 (Evaluation vector of a document) Let doc be a Web document. Let Neg and Pos be the numbers of all negative and positive phrases respectively in doc. The positive and negative ratio are defined as Positive=Pos/n and Negative Negative= -Neg/n.. The average credit of all phrase of doc is defined as Credit= $_1{}^n$ $Credit_i$ /n, where $Credit_i$ is the credit of i-th phrases extracted from document doc. The evaluation vector of doc is defined as V = (Negative, Positive, DocCredit).

//Note that(1) since Neg >= 0, hence negative= -Neg/n. <= 0. (2) The //DocCredit in the evaluation vector of document doc is different from credit //of phrase that is denoted as CreditPhr.

Definition 6 (Gymnastics Mean) Let NumSet be a set of numbers, t and b are numbers, t>o, b>0 and 0<t+b<100. Then GymMean(NumSet), called gymnastics mean of NumSet with respect to (t, b), is defined as the mean of the elements in NumSet except the top t% and the bottom b% elements,

???/// Note that gymnastics mean value just likes the credit rule in the //sport games such as gymnastics and diving. The default value in our //prototype of t and b is 10.

Definition 7 (Threshold vector) Let TeachDocs be the teaching set, V_Set be the set of evaluation vectors of all document in TeachDocs.

1) The optimistic threshold vector of V_Set is defined as Opt_thres (V_Set) = (Neg_thres, Pos_thres, Credit_thres),where Neg_thres = Min { v_i.Negative | v_i in V_Set}, Positive = Min {v_i.Positive| v_i in V_Set}. Credit=Average({v_i.Credit| v_i in V_Set}).
2) The pessimistic threshold vector of V_Set is defined as Pes_thres (V_Set) = (Neg_thres, Pos_thres, Credit_thres), where Neg_thres = Max { v_i.Negative| v_i in V_Set}, Positive = Max {v_i.Positive| v_i in V_Set}. Credit =Average({v_i.Credit| v_i in V_Set}.
3) The Gymnastics threshold vector of V_Set is defined as Gym_thres(V_Set)= (Neg_thres, Pos_thres, Credit_thres), where Neg_thres = GymMean ({v_i.Negative | v_i in V_Set}), Positive= GymMean({v_i.Positive | v_i in V_Set}), Credit= GymMean ({v_i.Credit | v_i in V_Set}).

Based on the conceptual model above, the main idea of our semantic discriminating mechanism includes following two stages:

(1) Learning stage (Learn from TeachDocs, get evaluation vectors)

a) Extract TeachPhrase from TeachDocs by Parsing technique.
b) Evaluation each phrase p in TeachPhrase by setting p.CreditPhr to default (expert defined) values.
c) Calculate evaluation vector for each web document in TeachDocs.
d) Mining threshold vector from the set of evaluation vectors..

(2) Applying stage (discriminate specified Web document doc)

a) Extract key phrase from document doc by parsing technique.
b) For phrase p, get p.CreditPhr by matching p in TeachPhraseSet.
c) Calculate the evaluation vector V of doc.
d) Discriminate doc based comparing V with threshold vector.

3 Extracting Key Phrases

Extracting key phrases includes two main steps: (1) Extracting key sentence from document by user configured key sentence template. It is easy task in programming. (2)Calling grammar analyses module Gram.DLL to get key phrases. The module Gram.DLL is borrowed from the *XinYi Internet Chinese-English Translation System* (copyright 1996-2000) developed by our group [4]. The syntax knowledge are implemented as two knowledge bases. It uses verb as kernel of sentence and extracts phrases in the form of (subject, predicate) and (predicate, object). The main part of the verb rules are verb classification rules borrowed from Oxford Dictionary. The core of Gram.DLL is a non-determination algorithm. It uses back tracing mechanism to optimize the parsing process [4]. The default back-trace-depth is 5000. Its translating speed is more than 400 sentences per minutes on the platform with CPU 586-200. More detail and references can be found in [4].

4 Calculating Evaluation Vector and Threshold Vector

The evaluation vector V =(Negative, Positive, DocCredit) summarizes the feature of document and calculated by Algorithm 1. The main step is counting the number of Negative and Positive phrases.

Algorithm 1 (Calculating evaluation vector of a document)
Input Web document DOC, Stage; // Stage is in {Training, Applying}
Output evaluation vector V of DOC
Main Steps:

```
Get Key phrase KeyPhrase by module Gram.DLL. // see Section 3.
for each KeyPhrases p do {
if (Stage = = Training )
   if (doc is positive document) p.CreditPhr = positive_Default ;
      else p.CreditPhr = negative_Default // by expert experience; }
else  // (Stage = = Applying )
{  p.CreditPhr= TeachPhraseSet.p.CreditPhr;
   TotalCredit= TotalCredit+p.CreditPhr;
   TotalPharase = TotalPharase +1;
   if (p.CreditPhr>T_Phrase)  V.Positive= V.Positive +1;
   else V.Negative= V.Negative -1; // Thus V.Negative decrease
  .DocCredit=TotalCredit/TotalPhrase }  // end of else
} //end of for
 output V;
```

The cost of Algorithm 1 depends on the number of documents and size of KeySentence. Practice shows that it is efficiency. Once we have the set of the evaluation vectors of all DOC in TeachDocs, we can mine the threshold vector of TeachDocs as following Algorithm 2.

Algorithm 2 (Mining threshold vector)
Input VertorSet,i.e. the set of all evaluation vectors of TeachDocs,
Manner; //Manner in {Optimistic, Pessimistic, Gymnastics}
Output threshold vector T_Vector of TeachDocs
Steps:;
If (Manner= =Optimistic) T_Vector = Opt_thres(VertorSet); //Defintion 7
Else If (Manner= =Pessimistic) T_Vector= Pes_thres (VertorSet);
Else If (Manner= =Gymnastics) T_Vector= Gymnastics_thres (VertorSet);
Output T_vector;

5 Discriminating Web Documents

We now present two algorithms to discriminate Web documents. Algorithm 4 is named "objective" because it is based on the objective facts, that is, it only uses the ratio of negative phrases to positive phrases extracted from each document in TeachDocs.

Algorithm 3 (Objective Discriminating Algorithm)
Input The Web document doc to be discriminated and TeachDocs ,
Manner; //Manner; is in {Optimistic, Pessimistic, Gymnastics}
Ouput The discriminating conclusion of doc;
Main steps:
Extract key phrases from document doc, denoted as KeyPhrases;
For each phrase in KeyPhrases, get its Credit and its evaluation
vector V by Algorithm 1;
According to Manner, mine threshold vector of TeachDocs
by Algorithm 2 ,denoted as T_Vector;
If (T_Vector.Positive==0) then T_Vector.Positive=0.01;
If (V.Positive==0) then V.Positive=0.01; //avoiding zero as divisor
Judge_Ratio = (-V. Negative /V.Positive);
Threshod_Ratio = (-T_Vector.Negative /T_Vector.Positive)
If (Judge_Ratio >= Threshod_Ratio) the conclusion="No";
Else conclusion ="Yes"; //it is positive

The following Algorithm 5 is named "subjective" because it is based on the credit reflecting the subjective experience of expert.

Algorithm 5 (Subjective Discriminating Algorithm)
Input TeachDocs and the Web document doc to be judged;
Manner; //Manner; is in {Optimistic, Pessimistic, Gymnastics }
Output: The discriminating conclusion of doc;
Main steps:
Extarct TeachPhraseSet from TeachDocs ;
Acording to Manner, Mine threshold vector of TeachDocs
by Algorithm 2 , store as T_Vector;

Extract key phrases from document doc and stored in KeyPhrases;
Match each phrase of KeyPhrases and get its credit;
Get the evaluation vector V of d by Algorithm 1;
If (V.DocCredit<T_Vector.DocCredit)
the conclusion is “No”; //negative
Else conclusion is “Yes”; // Positive

6 Preliminary Experiment Results

The four training documents are about the stocks trend from http://finance.yahoo.com and http://biz.yahoo.com.

The key sentences extracted from the four teaching DOC’s are:

1.1.: The markets were up sharply after a government report showed job growth and wages rose less than expected in May.

1.2: Stocks began the day modestly higher in relatively quiet trading, with the major indexes posting relatively modest gains.

1.3: After a halting start, stocks continued to rally the day.

2.1: After rallying sharply to a seven month high over the past week, bonds pulled back this morning.

2.2: The Dow Jones Industrial Average dropped 43.43 points to 10982.42.

2.3 The Nasdaq Composite has lost 14.48 points to 3445 today, rallied to a double digit gain, but soon slipped back.

3.1 Just when it was starting to seem as though markets only go down, the Nasdaq reminded investors that it can go up, too.

3.2: Though the indexes wavered a bit during the day, tech stocks enjoyed a steady run-up.

3.3 The bond market, which began the day lower, got a boost from Cohen's comments as investors re-allocated funds

3.4: This suggests that recent rate increases have not slowed the economy.

4.1: The major market indexes were mostly off this morning following a quick move to the upside immediately.

4.2: The Nasdaq Composite soon gave up its gains.

4.3: The gross domestic product grew 2.4% for the first quarter according to a report issued last week.

4.4: Activision reported a loss of $2.07 per share on sales of $103.8 million.

The key TeachPhraseSet are expressed as a list of 6-tuple (Sentence number, Subject, Predict, object ,CreditPhr, Remark) as shown in Figure 1.Symbol "+" or "-" indicate the phrase is positive (stock is up) or negative. (stock is down).The evaluation vector computed by Algorithm-1 are shown in Table1.The Optimistic and pessimistic thresholds are in Table1.

(1.1) Markets, were, Up, +16, Doc 1 is Positive
(1.2) Stocks, began, higher, +10 , Doc 1 is Positive
(1.3) Stocks, continued, to rally, +16 Doc 1 is Positive
(2.1) Bonds, pulled, Back, -8, Doc 2 is negative
(2.2) Dow jones, dropped, , -10, Doc 2 is negative
(2.3) Nasdaq, lost, , -10, Doc 2 is negative
(3.1) Nasdaq, reminded, go up, +16, Doc3 is positive
(3.2) Stocks, enjoyed, run up, +16, Doc3 is positive
(3.3) Bond market, got, boost, +10, Doc3 is positive
(3.4) Rate increases, not slow, economy, +4, Doc3 is positive
(4.1) market indexes, were, off, -16, Doc 4 is negative
(4.2) nasdaq, Gave up, gains, -4, Doc 4 is negative
(4.3) gross domestic product , grew, 2.4%, +8, Doc 4 is negative
(4.4) Activision, reported, a loss, -16, Doc 4 is negative

Fig. 1. The key phrases of TeachDoc

Let DOC be the Web document to be discriminated. The key sentences extracted from DOC are as following:

(1) Investors seem optimistic that the markets can maintain yesterday's gains, but the temptation for profit taking may win out before the day is done.
(2) There was a sharp rally right after the opening as buyers emerged to nibble at some favorite issues that have been beaten down over the past few sessions.
(3) Shortly before 11:00 am, the Nasdaq index was up 71.67 points to 4573.
(4) Today's report suggests that the U.S. economy may show record growth during the first quarter of 2000.

Four key phrases extracted are as shown in Table 3. By matching phrase 2, 3, 4 in Table 2, we get the their credits. Note that phrase 1 cannot be matched successfully, thus it is assigned by experience and added into Table 2. The evaluation vector of document DOC is calculated by algorithm 1 as shown in Table4. According to the optimistic user, document DOC indicates that the trend of stocks market is going up. However, pessimistic user thinks that document DOC indicates it is going down.

It is interesting to try calculating threshold by gymnastics average. It gives a neutral (maybe more accuracy) result. In fact, it deduces the extent of the up-trend or downtrend of stocks market based on the evaluation vector of document, which is very helpful in some areas.

Table 1. Evaluation vector and threshold vector of the training Web documents

Evaluation vector	Doc Credit	Negative	Positive
Document1	14	-0/3	3/3
Document2	-9.33	-3/3	0/3
Document3	11.5	-0/4	4/4
Document4	-7	-3/4	1/4
Pes_threshold	2.29	0	1
Opt_threshold	2.29	-1	0

Table 2. Key phrases and their CreditPhr in TeachPhraseSet

Rec	Phrase	Credit Phr
#1	Market is up	16
#2	Run up	16
#3	Continue to rally	16
#4	Nasdaq lost	-10
#5	Nasdaq be up	16
#6	Dow Johns drop	-10
#7	Pull back	-8
#8	Be off	-16
#9	Begin higher	16
...	...	...

Table 3. Key phrase of the Web document to be discriminated

	<Sub, Pred, Obj>	Credit Phr
1	Investors seem optimistic	4
2	There was rally	16
3	Nasdaq was up	16
4	economy show growth	8

Table 4. Evaluation vector of the Web document doc to be discriminated

DocCredit	Negative	Positive
11	0/4	4/4

9 Conclusion and Future Work

We have proposed the CKPU method to discriminate Web file based on phrase understanding. Four algorithms, including extracting key phrase, mining threshold vector, objective and, subjective discriminating are introduced. The experiment result shows that the algorithms are efficient.

References

[1] "Email Remover, Anti-spams component", http://home.pacific.net.sg/~thantom / eremove.htm

[2] "Spam Hater",http://www.cix.co.uk/~net-services/ spam/ spam_ hater. htm

[3] Riloff, Ellen Lehnert, and Wendy ,"Information extraction as a basis for high-precision text classification", ACM Transactions on Information Systems Vol.12, No. 3 (July 1994), pp. 296-333

[4] YU Zhonghua, TANG Changjie and ZHANG, "The Grammar Analysis Strategy , for Machine Translation Systems", The Journal of Micro and Mini Computer System, Vol.21, No.3, 2000, pp.316 – 318.

[5] M. Jiang, S. Tseng, and C. Tsai, "Discovering Structure from Document Databases," In *Proceedings of PAKDD '99*, pp. 169-173, Apr. 1999.

[6] "Grammatical Trigrams description of statistic approaches for the modelization of the language". Htttp:// www. rxrc. xerox. com/ publis/ mltt /jadt/node2.html
[7] Hobbes Internet Timeline, http:// www.isoc.org/ guest/ zakon/ Internet / History/ hit.html
[8] H. Mannila and H. Toivonen, "Discovering Generalized Episodes Using Minimal Occurrence," In *Proceedings of the International Conference on Knowledge Discovery and Data Mining*, 1999.
[9] U. Fayyad and G. Piatetsky-Shapiro, *"Advanced in Knowledge Discover and Data Mining (Eds)"*, AAAI Press and The MIT Press, pp. 1-5, 1996.
[10] Tang Changjie, Yu Zhonghua, et. al. "Mine the Quasi-Periodicity From Web Data," *The Journal of Computer*, **23**(1), pp. 52-59.
[11] Peter Buneman. "Semi Structure", In Proceedings of the 16th ACM SIGACT-SIGMOD-SIGART symposium on Principle of database systems(PODS97), May 11-15,1997, Tucson. AZ USA, page 117-123.
[12] Brad Adelberg, "NoDoSE -- a tool for semi-automatically extracting structured and semi-structured data from test documents", In proceedings of ACM SIGMOD international conference on Management of Data, June 1-4,1998,Seattle,WA USA, Page 283-294.

Session 2A
Data Mining

Regular Research Paper (30 minutes)
Deriving High Confidence Rules from Spatial Data Using Peano Count Trees

Regular Research Paper (30 minutes)
A Distributed Hierarchical Clustering System for Web Mining

Research Experience Paper (15 minutes)
ARMiner: A Data Mining Tool Based on Association Rules

Short Research Paper (15 minutes)
An Integrated Classification Rule Management System for Data Mining

Deriving High Confidence Rules from Spatial Data Using Peano Count Trees*

William Perrizo, Qin Ding, Qiang Ding, and Amalendu Roy

Department of Computer Science, North Dakota State University,
Fargo, ND 58105-5164, USA
{William_Perrizo, Qin_Ding, Qiang_Ding,
Amalendu_Roy}@ndsu.nodak.edu

Abstract. The traditional task of association rule mining is to find all rules with high support and high confidence. In some applications, such as mining spatial datasets for natural resource location, the task is to find high confidence rules even though the support may be low. In still other applications, such as the identification of agricultural pest infestations, the task is to find high confidence rules preferably while the support is still very low. The basic Apriori algorithm cannot be used to solve these problems efficiently since it relies on first identifying all high support itemsets. In this paper, we propose a new model to derive high confidence rules for spatial data regardless of their support level. A new data structure, the Peano Count Tree (P-tree), is used in our model to represent all the information we need. P-trees represent spatial data bit-by-bit in a recursive quadrant-by-quadrant arrangement. Based on the P-tree, we build a special data cube, the Tuple Count Cube (T-cube), to derive high confidence rules. Our algorithm for deriving confident rules is fast and efficient. In addition, we discuss some strategies for avoiding over-fitting (removing redundant and misleading rules).

1 Introduction

Association rule mining [1,2,3,4,5], proposed by Agrawal, Imielinski and Swami in 1993, is one of the important methods of data mining. The original application of association rule mining was on market basket data. A typical example is "customers who purchase one item are very likely to purchase another item at the same time". There are two accuracy measures, support and confidence, for each rule. The problem of association rule mining is to find all the rules with support and confidence exceeding some user specified thresholds. The basic algorithms, such as Apriori [1] and DHP [4], use the downward closure property of support to find frequent itemsets, whose supports are above the threshold. After obtaining all frequent itemsets, which is very time consuming, high confidence rules are derived in a very straightforward way.

However, in some applications, such as spatial data mining, we are also interested in rules with high confidence that do not necessarily have high support. In still other applications, such as the identification of agricultural pest infestations, the task is to

* This work was partially supported by a U. S. – G. S. A. VAST grant. Patents are pending on the P-Tree Data Mining Technology.

X.S. Wang, G. Yu, and H. Lu (Eds.): WAIM 2001, LNCS 2118, pp. 91-102, 2001.

find high confidence rules preferably while the support is still very low. In these cases, the traditional algorithms are not suitable. One may think that we can simply set the minimal support to a very low value, so that high confidence rules with almost no support limit can be derived. However, this will lead to a huge number of frequent itemsets, and is, thus, impractical.

In this paper, we propose a new model, including new data structures and algorithms, to derive "confident" rules (high confidence only rules), especially for spatial data. We use a data structure, called the Peano Count Tree (P-tree), to store all the information we need. A P-tree is a quadrant based count tree. From the P-trees, we build a data cube, the Tuple Count Cube or T-cube which exposes confident rules. We also use the attribute precision concept hierarchies and a natural rule ranking to prune the complexity of our data mining algorithm.

The rest of the paper is organized as follows. In section 2, we provide some background on spatial data. In section 3, we describe the data structures we use for association rule mining, including P-trees and T-cubes. In section 4, we detail our algorithms for deriving confident rules. Performance analysis and implementation issues are given in section 5, followed by related work in section 6. Finally, the conclusion is given.

2 Formats of Spatial Data

There are huge amounts of spatial data on which we can perform data mining to obtain useful information [16]. Spatial data are collected in different ways and are organized in different formats. BSQ, BIL and BIP are three typical formats.

An image contains several bands. For example, TM6 (Thermatic Mapper) scene contains six bands, while TM7 scene contains seven bands, including Blue, Green, Red, NIR, MIR, TIR, MIR2, each of which contains reflectance values in the range, 0~255.

An image can be organized into a relational table in which each pixel is a tuple and each spectral band is an attribute. The primary key can be latitude and longitude pairs which uniquely identify the pixels.

BSQ (Band Sequential) is a similar format, in which each band is stored as a separate file. Raster order is used for each individual band. TM scenes are in BSQ format. BIL (Band Interleaved by Line) is another format in which all the bands are organized in one file and bands are interleaved by row (the first row of all bands are followed by the second row of all bands, and so on). In the BIP (Band Interleaved by Pixel) format, there is also just one file in which the first pixel-value of the first band is followed by the first pixel-value of the second band, ..., the first pixel-value of the last band, followed by the second pixel-value of the first band, and so on. See Fig. 1 for an example.

In this paper, we propose a new format, called bSQ (bit Sequential), to organize images. The reflectance values of each band range from 0 to 255, represented as 8 bits. We split each band into a separate file for each bit position. Fig. 1 also gives an example of bSQ format.

There are several reasons to use the bSQ format. First, different bits have different degrees of contribution to the value. In some applications, we do not need all the bits because the high order bits give us enough information. Second, the bSQ format facilitates the representation of a precision hierarchy. Third, and most importantly, bSQ format facilitates the creation of an efficient, rich data structure, the P-tree, and accomodates algorithm pruning based on a one-bit-at-a-time approach.

We give a very simple illustrative example (Fig. 1) with only 2 data bands for a scene having only 2 rows and 2 columns (both decimal and binary representation are shown).

BAND-1	
254	127
(11111110)	(01111111)
14	193
(00001110)	(11000001)

BAND-2	
37	240
(00100101)	(11110000)
200	19
(11001000)	(00010011)

BSQ format (2 files)
Band 1: 254 127 14 193
Band 2: 37 240 200 19

BIL format (1 file)

254	127	37	240
14	193	200	19

bSQ format (16 files)

B11	B12	B13	B14	B15	B16	B17	B18	B21	B22	B23	B24	B25	B26	B27	B28
1	1	1	1	1	1	1	0	0	0	1	0	0	1	0	1
0	1	1	1	1	1	1	1	1	1	1	1	0	0	0	0
0	0	0	0	1	1	1	0	1	1	0	0	1	0	0	0
1	1	0	0	0	0	0	1	0	0	0	1	0	0	1	1

BIP format (1 file)

254	37	27	240
14	200	193	19

Fig. 1. Two bands of a 2-row-2-column image and its BSQ, BIP, BIL and bSQ formats

3 Data Structures

We organize each bit file in the bSQ format into a tree structure, called a Peano Count Tree (P-tree). A P-tree is a quadrant based tree. The idea is to recursively divide the entire image into quadrants and record the count of 1-bits for each quadrant, thus forming a quadrant count tree. P-trees are somewhat similar in construction to other data structures in the literature (e.g., Quadtrees[10] and HHcodes [14]).

For example, given an 8-row-8-column image, the P-tree is as shown in Fig. 2 (PM-tree, a variation of P-tree, will be discussed later).

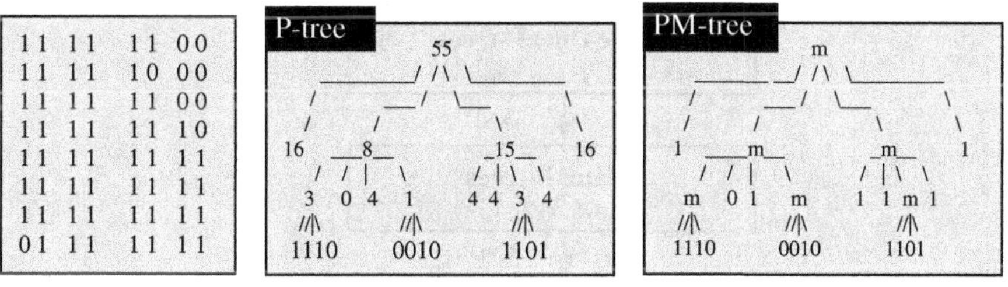

Fig. 2. 8*8 image and its P-trees (P-tree and PM-tree)

In this example, 55 is the number of 1's in the entire image. This root level is labeled as level 0. The numbers at the next level (level 1), 16, 8, 15 and 16, are the 1-

bit counts for the four major quadrants. Since the first and last quadrant are composed entirely of 1-bits (called a "pure-1 quadrant"), we do not need subtrees for these two quadrants, so these branches terminate. Similarly, quadrants composed entirely of 0-bits are called "pure-0 quadrants" which also terminate these tree branches. This pattern is continued recursively using the Peano or Z-ordering of the four subquadrants at each new level. Every branch terminates eventually (at the "leaf" level, each quadrant is a pure quadrant). If we were to expand all subtrees, including those for pure quadrants, then the leaf sequence is just the Peano-ordering (or, Z-ordering) of the original raster image. Thus, we use the name Peano Count Tree.

We note that, the fan-out of the P-tree need not be limited to 4. It can be any power of 4 (effectively skipping that number of levels in the tree). Also, the fanout at any one level need not coincide with the fanout at another level. The fanout pattern can be chosen to produce maximum compression for each bSQ file.

For each band (assuming 8-bit data values), we get 8 basic P-trees, one for each bit position. For band B1, we will label the basic P-trees, P_{11}, P_{12}, …, P_{18}. P_{ij} is a lossless representation of the jth bits of the values from the ith band. In addition, P_{ij} provides the 1-bit count for every quadrant of every dimension. Finally, we note that these P-trees can be generated quite quickly and can be viewed as a "data mining ready", lossless format for storing spatial data.

The 8 basic P-trees defined above can be combined using simple logical operations (AND, NOT, OR, COMPLEMENT) to produce P-trees for the original values in a band (at any level of precision, 1-bit precision, 2-bit precision, etc.). We let $P_{b,v}$ denote the Peano Count Tree for band, b, and value, v, where v can be expressed in 1-bit, 2-bit,.., or 8-bit precision. $P_{b,v}$ is called a value P-tree. Using the full 8-bit precision (all 8 bits) for values, value P-tree $P_{b,11010011}$ can be constructed by ANDing basic P-trees (for each 1-bit) and their complements (for each 0 bit):

$$P_{b,11010011} = P_{b1} \text{ AND } P_{b2} \text{ AND } P_{b3}' \text{ AND } P_{b4} \text{ AND } P_{b5}' \text{ AND } P_{b6}' \text{ AND } P_{b7} \text{ AND } P_{b8}$$

where ' indicates the bit-complement (which is simply the P-tree with each count replaced by its count complement in each quadrant).

From value P-trees, we can construct tuple P-trees, which is P-trees to record 1-bit counts for tuples. Tuple P-tree for tuple (v1,v2,…,vn), denoted $P_{(v1, v2, \ldots, vn)}$, is:

$$P_{(v1,v2,\ldots,vn)} = P_{1,v1} \text{ AND } P_{2,v2} \text{ AND } \ldots \text{ AND } P_{n,vn}$$

where n is the total number of bands.

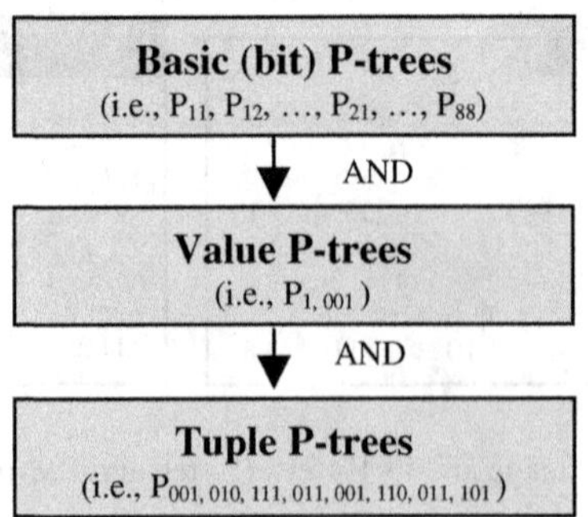

Fig. 3. Basic P-trees, Value P-trees (for 3-bit values) and Tuple P-trees

The AND operation is simply the pixel-wise AND of the bits. Before going further, we note that the process of converting the BSQ data for a TM satellite image (approximately 60 million pixels) to its basic P-trees can be done in just a few seconds using a high performance PC computer. This is a one-time process. We also note that we are storing the basic P-trees in the way which specifies the pure-1 quadrants only. Using this data structure, each AND can be completed in a few milliseconds and the result counts can be accumulated easily once the AND and COMPLEMENT program has completed.

In order to optimize the AND operation, we use a variation of the P-tree, called PM-tree (Pure Mask tree). In the PM-tree, we use a 3-value logic to represent pure-1, pure-0 and mixed quadrant. To simplify the exposition, we use 1 for pure 1, 0 for pure 0, and m for mixed quadrants. The PM-tree for the previous example is also given in Fig. 2.

The PM-tree specifies the location of the pure-1 quadrants of the operands, so that the pure-1 quadrants of the AND result can be easily identified by the coincidence of pure-1 quadrants in both operands, and pure-0 quadrants of the AND result occur wherever a pure-0 quadrant occurs on at least one of the operands.

For most spatial data mining, the root counts of the tuple P-trees (e.g., $P_{(v1,v2,\ldots,vn)} = P_{1,v1}$ AND $P_{2,v2}$ AND ... AND $P_{n,vn}$), are the numbers required, since root counts tell us exactly the number of occurrences of that particular pattern over the space in question. These root counts can be inserted into a data cube, called the Tuple Count cube (T-cube) of the spatial dataset. Each band corresponds to a dimension of the cube, the band values labeling that dimension. The T-cube cell at location, (v1,v2,...,vn), contains the root count of $P_{(v1,v2,\ldots,vn)}$. For example, assuming just 3 bands, the $(v1,v2,v3)^{th}$ cell of the T-cube contains the root count of $P_{(v1,v2,v3)} = P_{1,v1}$ AND $P_{2,v2}$ AND $P_{3,v3}$. The cube can be contracted or expanded by going up [down] in the precision hierarchy.

4 Confident Rule Mining Algorithm

We begin this section with a description of the AND algorithm. This algorithm is used to compose the value P-trees and to populate the T-cube. The approach is to store only the basic P-trees and then generate value P-tree root counts "on-the-fly" when needed. In this algorithm we will assume the P-tree is coded in its most compact form, a depth-first ordering of the paths to each pure-1 quadrant.

Let's look at one example (Fig. 4). Each path is represented by the sequence of quadrants in Peano order, beginning just below the root. Therefore, the depth-first pure1 path code for the first operand is: 0 100 101 102 12 132 20 21 220 221 223 23 3 (0 indicates the entire level 1 upper left quadrant is pure 1^s, 100 indicates the level 3 quadrant arrived at along the branch through node 1 (2nd node) of level 1, node 0 (1st node) of level 2 and node 0 of level 3, etc.). We will take the second operand, with depth-first pure1 path code: 0 20 21 22 231. Since a quadrant will be pure 1's in the result only if it is pure 1's in both operands (or all operands, in the case there are more than 2), the AND is done by: scan the operands; output matching pure1 paths. Therefore we get the result (Fig. 4).

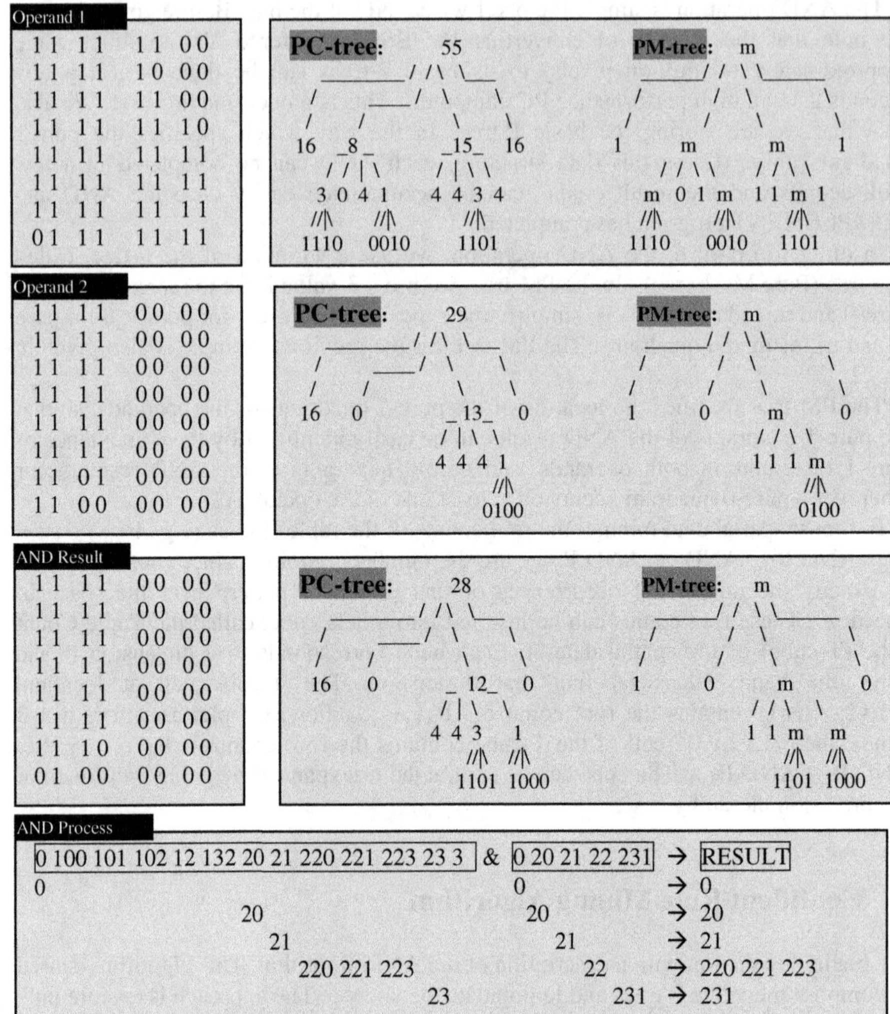

Fig. 4. Operand 1, Operand 2, AND Result and AND Process

In the following a T-cube based method for mining non-redundant, low-support, high-confidence rules is introduced. Such rules will be called confident rules. The main interest is in rules with low support, which are important for many application areas such as, natural resource searches, agriculture pest infestations identification, etc. However, a small positive support threshold is set, in order to eliminate rules that result from noise and outliers (similar to [7], [8] and [15]). A high threshold for confidence is set in order to find only the most confident rules.

To eliminate redundant rules resulting from over-fitting, an algorithm similar to the one introduced in [8] is used. In [8] rules are ranked based on confidence, support, rule-size and data-value ordering, respectively. Rules are compared with their generalizations for redundancy before they are included in the set of confident rules.

In this paper, we use a similar rank definition, except that we do not use support level and data-value ordering. Since support level is expected to be very low in many spatial applications, and since we set a minimum support only to eliminate rules resulting from noise, it is not used in rule ranking. Rules are declared redundant only if they are outranked by a generalization. We choose not to eliminate a rule which is outranked only by virtue the specific data values involved.

A rule, r, *ranks* higher than rule, r', if confidence[r] > confidence[r'], or if confidence[r] = confidence[r'] and the number of attributes in the antecedent of r is less than the number in the antecedent of r'.

A rule, r, *generalizes* a rule, r', if they have the same consequent and the antecedent of r is properly contained in the antecedent of r'. The algorithm is given in Fig. 5.

> Build the set of ***confident*** rules, **C** (initially empty) as follows.
> Start with 1-bit values, 2 bands;
> then 1-bit values and 3 bands; ...
> then 2-bit values and 2 bands;
> then 2-bit values and 3 bands; ...
> . . .
> At each stage defined above, do the following:
> Find all confident rules (support at least minimum_support and confidence at least minimum_confidence), by rolling-up the T-cube along each potential consequent set using summation. Comparing these sums with the support threshold to isolate rule support sets with the minimum support. Compare the normalized T-cube values (divide by the rolled-up sum) with the minimum confidence level to isolate the ***confident*** rules. Place any new confident rule in **C**, but only if the rank is higher than any of its generalizations already in **C**.

Fig. 5. Algorithm for mining confident rules

The following example contains 3 bands of 3-bit spatial data in bSQ format.

```
Band-1: B11         B12           B13
11 11 00 01    00 00 11 00    11 11 00 00
11 01 00 01    00 00 11 00    11 11 00 00
11 00 00 11    00 00 11 01    11 11 00 00
11 00 01 11    00 00 11 10    11 11 00 00
11 11 00 00    11 11 00 00    00 11 00 00
11 11 00 00    11 11 00 00    10 11 00 00
11 11 00 00    10 01 00 11    00 00 00 00
11 11 00 00    10 11 00 11    00 01 00 00

Band-2: B21         B22           B23
00 00 00 11    00 11 00 00    11 11 11 11
00 00 00 11    00 11 00 00    11 11 11 11
00 00 11 00    11 00 00 00    11 11 11 11
00 00 11 00    11 00 00 00    11 11 11 11
11 11 00 00    11 11 11 11    11 11 00 11
11 11 00 00    11 11 11 11    11 11 00 10
11 11 00 00    10 01 11 11    11 11 00 11
11 11 00 00    10 11 11 11    11 11 00 11

Band-3: B31         B32           B33
11 11 00 00    00 00 00 00    00 00 11 11
11 11 00 00    00 00 00 00    00 00 11 11
11 11 00 00    00 00 11 00    10 11 11 11
11 11 00 00    00 00 11 00    10 11 11 11
00 00 11 01    00 00 00 00    11 11 11 11
00 00 11 11    00 00 00 00    11 11 11 11
00 00 00 11    11 00 00 00    11 11 11 11
00 00 00 11    11 00 00 00    11 11 11 11
```

```
Band-1:

PM11                  PM12                PM13

mm10                  0mmm                10m0
1m10 0mm1             101m 11mm 0001      m10m
1101 0101 0001        0110 1010 0111      0010 0001

Band-2:

PM21                  PM22                PM23

0m10                  m011                111m
0110                  0110                0m01

Band-3:

PM31                  PM32                PM33

100m                  00m0                m111
1m01                  0010                00m1
0111                                      1010
```

Fig. 6. 8 8 image data and its PM-trees

Assume minimum confidence threshold of 80% and minimum support threshold of 10%. Start with 1-bit values and 2 bands, B1 and B2. The T-cube values (root counts from the P-trees) are given in Fig. 7, while the rolled-up sums and confidence thresholds are given in Fig. 8.

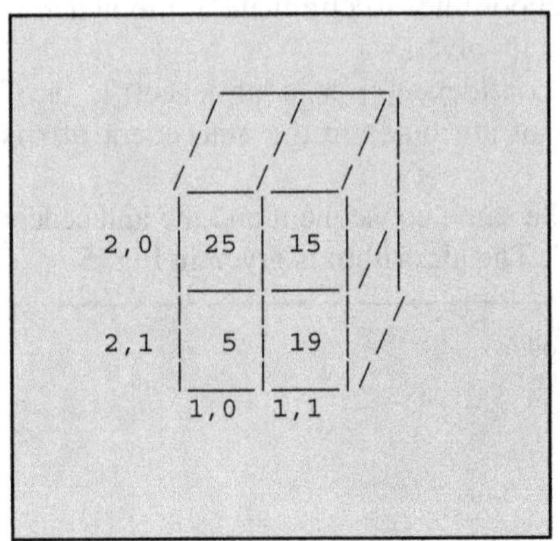

Fig. 7. T-cube for band 1 and band 2

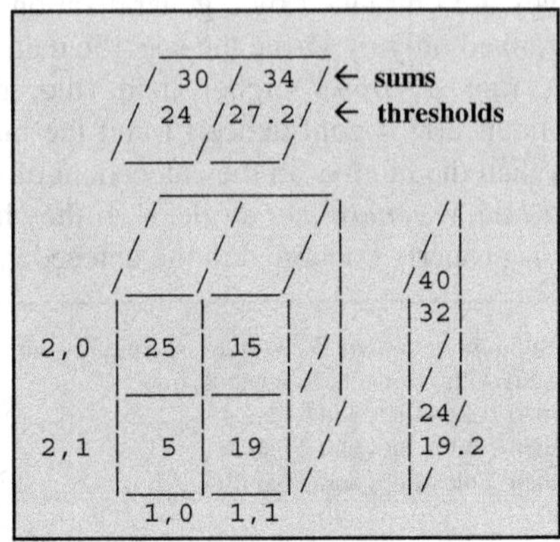

Fig. 8. Rolled-up sums and confidence thresholds

All sums are at least 10% support (6.4). There is one confident rule:

C:	B1={0} => B2={0}	c = 83.3%

Continue with 1-bit values and the 2 bands, B1 and B3, we can get the following T-cube with rolled-up sums and confidence thresholds (Fig. 9). There are no new confident rules. Similarly, the 1-bit T-cube for band B2 and B3 can be constructed (Fig. 10).

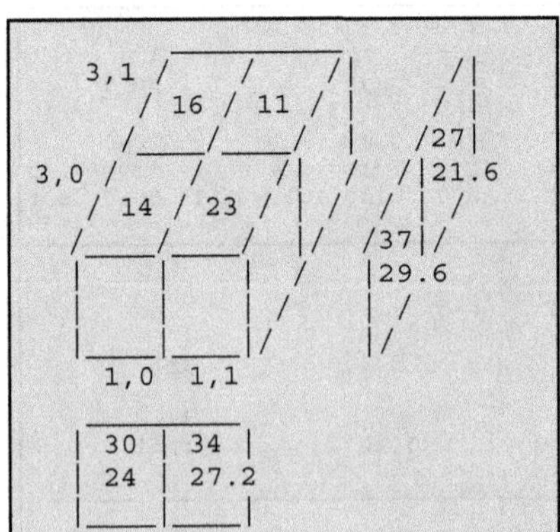

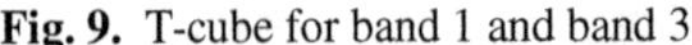

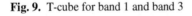

Fig. 9. T-cube for band 1 and band 3

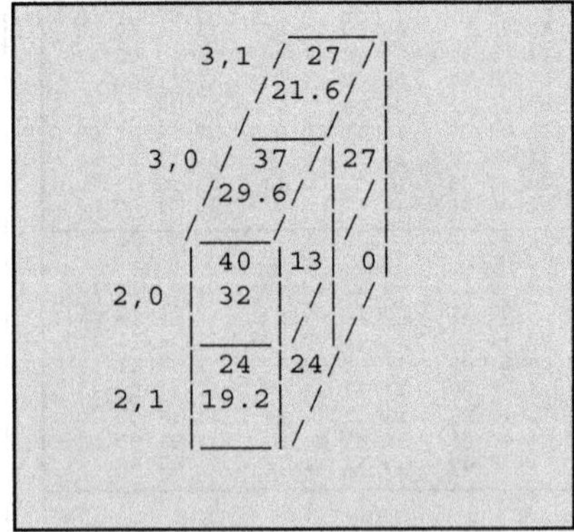

Fig. 10. T-cube for band 2 and band 3

All sums are at least 10% of 64 (6.4), thus, all rules will have enough support. There are two confident rule, B2={1} => B3={0} with confidence = 100% and B3={1} => B2={0} with confidence = 100%. Thus,

C:	B1={0} => B2={0}	c = 83.3%
	B2={1} => B3={0}	c = 100%
	B3={1} => B2={0}	c = 100%

Next consider 1-bit values and bands, B1, B2 and B3. The counts, sums and confidence thresholds are given in Fig. 11:

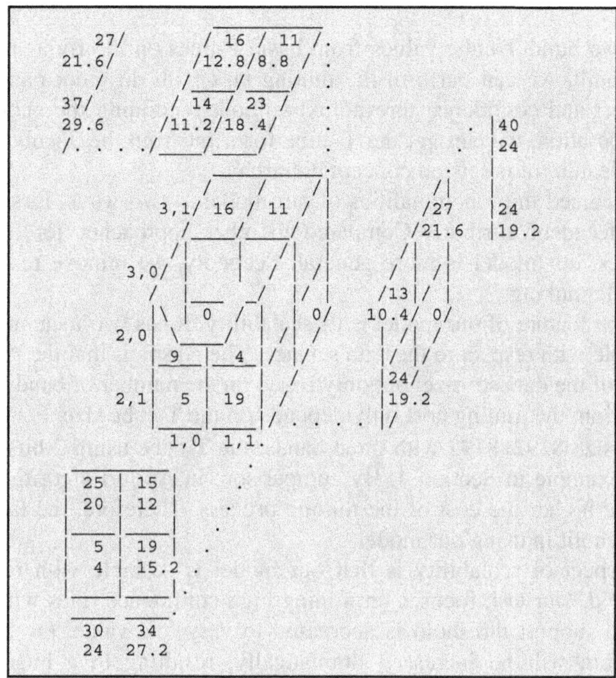

Fig. 11. The counts, sums and confidence thresholds for 1-bit values

Support sets, B1={0}^B2={1} and B2={1}^B3={1} lack support. The new confident rules are:

B1={1} ^ B2={1} => B3={0},	c = 100%
B1={1} ^ B3={0} => B2={1},	c = 82.6%
B1={1} ^ B3={1} =>B2={0},	c =100%
B1={0} ^ B3={1} => B2={0},	c =100%

B1={1}^B2={1} => B3={0} in not included because it is generalized by B2={1} => B3={0}, which is already in C and has higher rank. Also, B1={1}^B3={1} => B2={0} is not included because it is generalized by B3={1} => B2={0}, which is already in C and has higher rank. B1={0}^B3={1} => B2={0} is not included because it is generalized by B3={1} => B2={0}, which has higher rank also. Thus,

C:	B1={0} => B2={0}	c = 83.3%
	B2={1} => B3={0}	c = 100%
	B3={1} => B2={0}	c = 100%
	B1={1} ^ B3={0} => B2={1}	c = 82.6%

Next, we consider 2-bit data values and proceed in the same way. Depending upon the goal of the data mining task (e.g., mine for classes of rules, individual rules, …), the rules already in C can be used to obviate the need to consider 2-bit refinements of the rules in **C.** This simplifies the 2-bit stage markedly.

5 Implementation Issues and Performance Analysis

In our model, we build T-cube values from basic P-trees on the fly as needed. Once the T-cube is built, we can perform the mining task with different parameters (i.e., different support and confidence thresholds) without rebuilding the cube. Using the roll-up cube operation, we can get the T-cube for n bit from the T-cube for n+1 bit. This is a good feature of precision concept hierarchy.

We have enhanced the functionalities of our model in two ways. Firstly, we don't specify the antecedent attribute. Compared to other approaches for deriving high confidence rules, our model is more general. Secondly, we remove redundant rules based on the rule ranking.

One important feature of our model is its scalability. It has two meanings. First, our model is scalable with respect to the data set size. The reason is that the size of T-cube is independent of the data set size, but only based on the number of bands and number of bits. In addition, the mining cost only depends on the T-cube size. For example, for an image with size 8192 8192 with three bands, the T-cube using 2 bits is as simple as that of the example in Section 4. By comparison, in Apriori algorithm, the larger the data set, the higher the cost of the mining process. Therefore, the larger the data set, the more benefit in using our model.

The other aspect of scalability is that our model is scalable with respect to the support threshold. Our task focuses on mining high confidence rules with very small support. As the support threshold is decreased to very low value, the cost of using Aprioir algorithm will be increased dramatically, resulting in a huge number of frequent itemsets (combination explosion). However, in our model, the process is not based on the frequent itemsets generation, so it works well for low support threshold.

As we mentioned, there is an additional cost to build the T-cube. The key issue of this cost is the P-tree ANDing. We have implemented an efficient P-tree ANDing on a cluster of computers.

We use an array of 16 dual 266 MHz processor systems with a 400 MHz dual processor as the control node. We partition the 2048*2048 image among all the nodes. Each node contains data for 512 512 pixels. These data are store at different nodes as another variation of P-tree, called Peano Vector Tree (PV-Tree). Here is how PV-tree is constructed. First we build a Peano Count Tree using fan-out 64 for each level. Then the tree is saved as bit vectors. For each internal node (except the root), we use two 64 bit bit-vectors, one is for pure 1 and other is for pure 0. At the leaf level we only use one vector (for pure 1).

From a single TM scene, we will have 56 (7 8) Peano Vector Tree - all saved in a single node. Using 16 nodes we are covering a scene of size, 2048 2048.

When we need to perform ANDing operation on the entire scene, we calculate the local ANDing result of two Peano Vector Trees and send the result to the control node, giving us the final result.

We use Message Passing Interface (MPI) on the cluster to implement the logical operations on Peano Vector Trees. This program uses the Single Program Multiple Data (SPMD) paradigm. The following graph (Fig. 12) shows the result of ANDing time for a TM scene. The AND time varies from 6.72 ms to 52.12 ms for different lower bit numbers of the two P-trees.

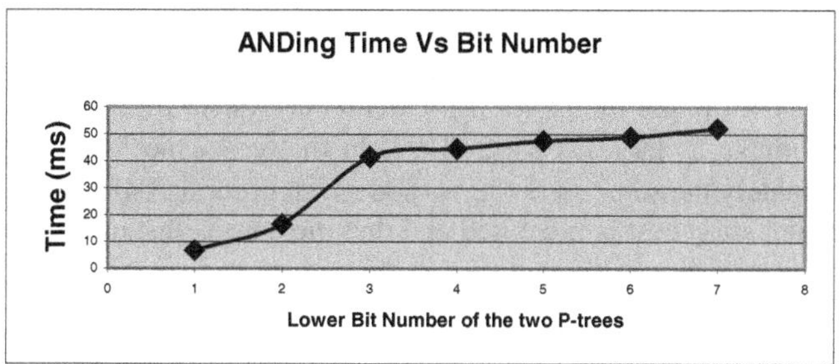

Fig. 12. P-tree ANDing time vs. Bit Number

With this high-speed ANDing, the T-cube can be built very quickly.

6 Related Work

The work in [6,7,8] deal with mining high confidence rules from non-spatial data and is therefore only marginally related. In [7] rules are found that have extremely high confidence, but for which there is no (or extremely weak) support. Some algorithms are proposed to solve this problem. There are two disadvantages of this work. One is that only pairs of columns (attributes) are considered. All pairs of columns, with similarity exceeding a pre-specified threshold are identified. The second disadvantage is that the similarity measure is bi-directional.

In [6], a brute-force technique is used for mining classification rules. They used association rule mining to solve the classification problem, i.e., a special rule set (classifiers) is derived. However, both the support and confidence are used in the algorithm even though only the high confidence rules are targeted. Several pruning techniques are proposed but there are trade-offs among those pruning techniques.

[8] and [15] are similar in that they both apply the association rule mining method to the classification task. They turn an arbitrary set of association rules into a classifier. A confidence based pruning method is proposed using the property called "existential upward closure". The method is used for building a decision tree from association rules. The antecedent attribute is specified.

Our model is more general than the models cited above and is particularly efficient and useful for spatial data mining.

The P-tree structure is related to Quadtrees [10,11,13] and its variants (such as point quadtree [13] and region quadtree [10]), and HHcodes [14]. The similarities among P-trees, quadtrees and HHCodes are that they are quadrant based, but the difference is that P-trees focus on counts. P-trees are not only beneficial for storing data, but also for association rule mining, since they also contain useful needed information for association rule mining.

7 Conclusion

In this paper, we propose a new model to derive high confidence rules on spatial data. Data cube techniques are used in our model. The basic data structure of our model, P-tree, has much more information than the original image file but is small in size. We build a Tuple Count cube from which the high confidence rules can be derived.

Currently we use the 16-node system to perform the ANDing operations for images with size 2048 2048. In the future we will extend our system to 256-nodes so that we can handle the image as large as 8192 8192. In that case, the P-tree ANDing time will be approximately the same as in the 16-node system for a 2048 2048 image since only the communication cost is increased and that increase is insignificant.

References

1. R. Agrawal, T. Imielinski, A. Swami. Mining Association Rules Between Sets of Items in Large Database. ACM SIGMOD 1993.
2. R. Agrawal, R. Srikant. Fast Algorithms for Mining Association Rules. VLDB 1994.
3. R. Srikant, R. Agrawal. Mining Quantitative Association Rules in Large Relational Tables. ACM SIGMOD 1996.
4. J. S. Park, M. Chen, P. S. Yu. An effective Hash-Based Algorithm for Mining Association Rules. ACM SIGMOD 1995.
5. J. Han, J. Pei, Y. Yin. Mining Frequent Patterns without Candidate Generation. ACM SIGMOD 2000.
6. R. J. Bayardo. Brute-Force Mining of High-Confidence Classification Rules. KDD 1997.
7. E. Cohen, et al. Finding Interesting Associations without Support Pruning. VLDB 2000.
8. K. Wang, S. Zhou, Y. He. Growing Decision Trees on Support-less Association Rules. KDD 2000.
9. V. Gaede, O. Gunther. Multidimensional Access Methods. Computing Surveys, 30(2), 1998.
10. H. Samet. The quadtree and related hierarchical data structure. ACM Computing Survey, 16, 2, 1984.
11. H. Samet. Applications of Spatial Data Structures. Addison-Wesley, 1990.
12. H. Samet. The Design and Analysis of Spatial Data Structures. Addison-Wesley, 1990.
13. R. A. Finkel, J. L. Bentley. Quad trees: A data structure for retrieval of composite keys. Acta Informatica, 4, 1, 1974.
14. HH-code. Available at http://www.statkart.no/nlhdb/iveher/hhtext.htm
15. B. Liu, W. Hsu, Y. Ma. Integrating classification and association rule mining. KDD 1998.
16. J. Dong, W. Perrizo, Q. Ding and J. Zhou. The Application of Association Rule Mining on Remotely Sensed Data. ACM Symposium on Applied Computing, 2000.

A Distributed Hierarchical Clustering System for Web Mining

Catherine W. Wen[1], Huan Liu[1], Wilson X. Wen[2], and Jeffery Zheng[3]

[1] Computer Science and Engineering, Arizona State University
cwen@asu.edu, hliu@asu.edu
[2] GoConnect, Australia
[3] CMST CSIRO, Australia

Abstract. This paper proposes a novel method of distributed hierarchical clustering for Web mining. The method is closely related to our early work of Self-Generated Neural Networks (SGNN), which is in turn based on both self-organizing neural network and concept formation. The complexity of the algorithm is at most O(MN*log*N). With the distributed implementation the method can be easily scaled up. The method is independent of the order the web documents presented. The method produces a natural conceptual hierarchy but not a binary tree. The method can include multimedia information into the same cluster hierarchy. A visualization mechanism has been developed for the clustering method and it shows the cluster hierarchy generated by the method has very high quality. The clustering process is fully automatic, and no human intervention is required. A clustering system has been built based on the proposed method, which can be used to automatically generate multimedia search engines, web directories, decision-making assistance systems, knowledge management systems, and personalized knowledge portals.

1 Introduction

Clustering technology plays an important role in Web mining [10] and has found many applications, such as Web search engines, Web directories, decision-making assistance, knowledge management, and personalized web knowledge portals [13], [17], [5]. The current clustering technology can be either hierarchical or non-hierarchical. Simple non-hierarchical clustering technology [1], [12], [2] is fast. Its time and space complexity is about O(MN), where M is the number of clusters generated and N is the number of instances to be clustered. This is quite reasonable when M<<N. However, they may produce sub-optimal results because they tend to generate large clusters in the early stage of clustering. Another disadvantage of the non-hierarchical clustering methods is that the results are normally dependent on the order the training instances are presented to the algorithms. Most hierarchical clustering methods [6], [2] are based on a structure called dendrogram, which is essentially a binary tree. The results

X.S. Wang, G. Yu, and H. Lu (Eds.): WAIM 2001, LNCS 2118, pp. 103-113, 2001.

generated by these methods are much better than the simple non-hierarchical methods. The results are normally independent of the order that the training instances are presented to the algorithm but need much larger computational amount (at least O(M*N*logN). Another problem of the algorithms based on dendrogram is that the conceptual structure human beings have for the real world is normally a more general hierarchy with multiple branches rather than a binary tree structure.

The Web presents its unique features and presents new challenges. It is massive and distributed with multimedia and semi-structured data. This paper proposes a novel method of distributed hierarchical clustering for Web mining. The method is closely related to our early work of Self-Generated Neural Networks (SGNN) [3], [15], [14] which is in turn based on both self-organizing neural network [9] and concept formation [4].

The algorithm takes a set of web pages collected by a web robot as input and generates a hierarchical network according to the conceptual similarity among the web pages. The method has been implemented in Java based on CORBA (Component Object Request Broker Architecture) [8] and can be used not only in automatic generation of a Web search engine and Web directories, but also in applications of decision-making assistance and personalized Web knowledge portals. The system generated can handle not only text information (HTML, Word, Excel, PDF, and Powerpoint) but also multimedia information (Images and sounds). Currently, a visualization mechanism has been developed to examine and browse through the cluster hierarchy. Other mining applications, such as decision-making assistance, knowledge management, and personalized knowledge portals, can benefit from the proposed method.

2 The Hierarchical Clustering Algorithm

The clustering process for each layer in the hierarchy is exactly the same as the classical non-hierarchical method:

Algorithm 1: *Single Layer Clustering* [2]
[Input:] A set of web documents D = {d_i}
[Output:] A cluster partition generated from {d_i} according to the similarity among the documents.
[Method:] *SimpleCluster(D)*

1. Assign the first document d_1 as the representative of the first cluster C_1.
2. For d_i, calculate the similarity S with the representative for each existing cluster.
3. If S_{max} is greater than a threshold value S_T, add the item to the corresponding cluster and recalculate the cluster representative; otherwise, use d_i to initiate a new cluster.
4. If an item d_i remains to be clustered, return to step 2.

Many similarity measures can be used here, such as [1], [2]

1. Dice similarity. For two documents D_i and D_j,

$$S_{D_i,D_j} = \frac{2\sum_{k=1}^{L}(w_{ik}w_{jk})}{\sum_{k=1}^{L} w_{ik}^2 + \sum_{k=1}^{L} w_{jk}^2}$$

where L is the length of the feature vectors and the summation is running through the whole vector (k = 1 to L).

2. Jaccard similarity.

$$S_{D_i,D_j} = \frac{\sum_{k=1}^{L}(w_{ik}w_{jk})}{\sum_{k=1}^{L} w_{ik}^2 + \sum_{k=1}^{L} w_{jk}^2 - w_{ik}w_{jk}}, \text{ or}$$

3. Cosine similarity.

$$S_{D_i,D_j} = \frac{\sum_{k=1}^{L}(w_{ik}w_{jk})}{\sqrt{\sum_{k=1}^{L} w_{ik}^2 \bullet \sum_{k=1}^{L} w_{jk}^2}}$$

We use cosine similarity for our system for its simplicity.We can use a centroid as the representative of a cluster:

$$C_i = \frac{\sum_{j=1}^{N} w_{ji}}{N},$$

where w_{ji} is the i-th component of the weight vector of the j-th item in the cluster and C_i is the i-th component of the centroid of the cluster.

It can be seen that Algorithm 1 is somewhat similar to Kohonen's LVQ with a fixed set of seed cluster representatives if we ignore the concept of the neighbourhood. Furthermore, it can be easily shown that the centroid formula is just a special case of the classical Hebb's rule [7] for synapse modification in neural networks:

$$w_{t+1} = w_t + \eta(e_t - w_t),$$

when the learning rate $\eta = \frac{1}{t+1}$, where w_t is the weight component at time t and e_t is the t-th training instance component.

To decide whether to generate a new cluster or simply put the current item into an existing cluster, there are many ways to select a threshold for Algorithm 1 and most of these methods are ad hoc. In [4], a heuristic method is used to avoid choosing a threshold. The item is compared for similarity with not only the cluster representatives but also the representative (or centroid) of the whole population. If the representative of the whole population is the one most similar to the current item, a new cluster will be initiated for the item, otherwise, the item is simply put in the cluster the most similar to it.

The following algorithm will further cluster each of the clusters generated in Algorithm 1 and eventually generate a cluster hierarchy.

Algorithm 2: Hierarchical Clustering

[Input:] A set of web documents $D = \{d_i\}$
[Output:] A cluster hierarchy generated from D according to the similarity among the documents.
[Method:] *ClusterHierarchy(D)*

1. Call *SimpleCluster(D)* to generate the first layer cluster partition $\{C^1_i\}$.
2. Set $j = 1$
3. Recursively, reduce the similarity threshold and call SimpleCluster(C^j_i) for all those clusters in $\{C^j_i\}$containing more than one item.

In [3], [14], an implementation of Algorithm 2 has been proposed as a network of self-generating neural networks in which each of the cluster consists of a Kohonen LVQ network, and the cluster in the hierarchy are connected with each other to form a network of neural networks. For simplicity, the calculation of the cluster representative was done by Hebb's rule of neural network updating. The decision rule for whether to generate new cluster or just put the current item into an existing cluster was the same as that in concept formation [4] because of its capability to form concept hierarchy.

It has been proven [16] that the results produced by the above algorithm is independent of the order in that the training instances are presented to the algorithm if the training instances are properly normalized and corresponding updating rule is used. Two kinds of normalization methods can be used here:

1. Length normalization

$$w'_{ij} = \frac{w_{ij}}{\sqrt{\sum_{k=1}^{L} w_{ik}^2}}$$

where, w'_{ij} is the j-th component of the i-th weight vector after normalization, and w_{ij} is the j-th component of the i-th weight vector before normalization.

2. Summation normalization.

$$w'_{ij} = \frac{w_{ij}}{\sum_{k=1}^{L} w_{ik}}$$

3 The Distributed Hierarchical Clustering Algorithm

The World Wide Web is a huge population of web pages. Thus, the scalability of a clustering system designed to deal with the WWW will be critical for its usefulness. One effective way to deal with scalability is by a parallel distributed system. It is easy to discovery the parallelism in the above algorithm. All the clusters in the hierarchy can be generated/searched in parallel after their parent clusters are generated/searched.

The implementation can be either any SMP computers or a set of computers connected through a fast Ethernet (say 100Mbps or GigaBps network). Fig. 1 shows how the clusters can be generated in parallel with the later – fast Ethernet implementation with CORBA or JAVA RMI.

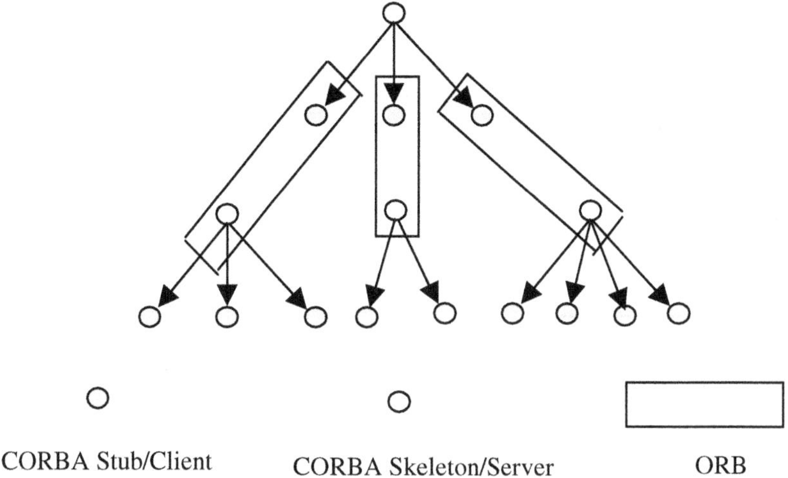

Fig. 1. A CORBA implementation of the algorithm

Each cluster in the hierarchy can be generated on a separated computer in the Ethernet. The parent layer, which acts as a CORBA client in this architecture, has a CORBA generated stub and the child cluster, acting as a CORBA server, has a CORBA generated Skeleton. The two sides communicate with each other through an ORB (Object Request Broker). The modified skeleton/server program basically implements Algorithm 1. After the parent layer is generated, it puts all its items, which were assigned to a particular child cluster, into an array in the stub/client program, the ORB will pass it as an IN parameter and call the remote object/method in the skeleton/server in the corresponding child cluster which implements Algorithm 1. Again, this process will continue recursively until all the web documents/items are exhausted and the whole cluster hierarchy is generated. The final resulting hierarchy itself will be distributed over the whole network

4 The System Implementation

The overall architecture of the implementation is shown in Fig. 2. From Fig. 2, it can be seen that the system contains the following components:

1. A Web robot, which collects the web pages to be processed.
2. A pre-processing unit, which extracts multimedia features from the web page files collected by the Web robot. These include:

a. Text files – keywords and key-phrases with weights which reflect the importance of the keywords and key-phrases to the web-pages.
b. Images files – all sorts of image features, such as colours, foreground, background, lines, edges, entropy, etc.
c. Sound files – all sorts of sound features represented with the LPC (Linear Predictive Coding) coefficients.

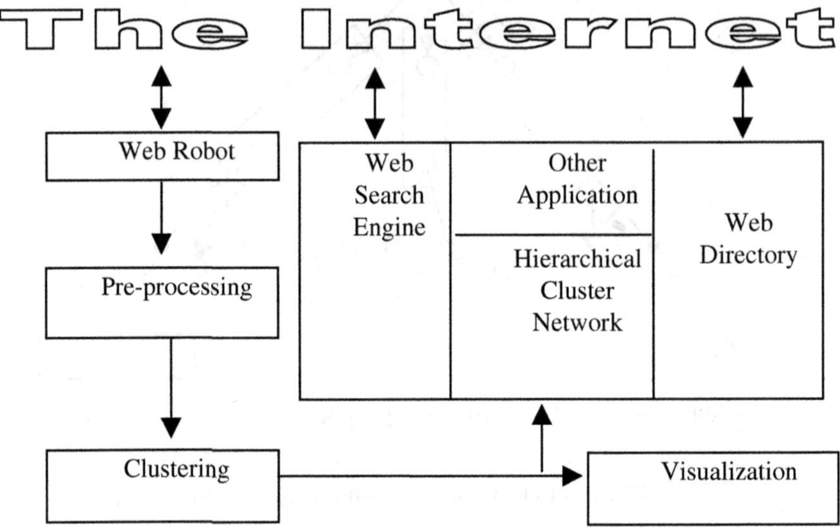

Fig. 2. The Overall System Architecture

1. A hierarchical clustering engine, which clusters the files according to their similarities into a cluster hierarchy. Considering the unique features of the Web, we need a clustering algorithm with the following characteristics:
   a. It is fast – For each layer only O(NM) similarities need to be calculated and compared, where M is the number of clusters in the layer, N is the number of files to be clustered, and normally we have M << N. The number of layers is O(log N).
   b. It is order independent – The resulting network is independent of the order in that the documents are presented if the feature vectors are properly normalized and corresponding updating rule is used.
   c. It is easy to discover parallelism – All the clusters in the hierarchy can be processed in parallel after their parent clusters are processed.
   d. It is fully self-generating – The hierarchy is generated by itself given a set of input web pages. No, structure design will be required.
   e. It is of concept-based clustering – The method is based on concept formation theory in artificial intelligence, and, thus, has strong concept formation capability.
   f. It is of content-based clustering for multimedia web pages/file – The search and browse can be content-based, that is using images or sounds as queries rather than using text describing them. The next

section will give detailed description of an multimedia clustering system based on the technology proposed here.

g. It is a unified multimedia cluster hierarchy – accommodating information of different media (text, image, sound, and video) in a single cluster hierarchy.

The clustering algorithm proposed in this paper is particularly designed to serve the needs.

1. A visualization mechanism is developed in the system which shows the structure of the cluster hierarchy and provides the capabilities to
   a. Examine the parameters of each node, including the feature-weight vector and some structure information.
   b. Browse the cluster hierarchy layer by layer, this is specifically usefully in the Web directory applications.

A snapshot of the visualization program is given in Fig. 3.

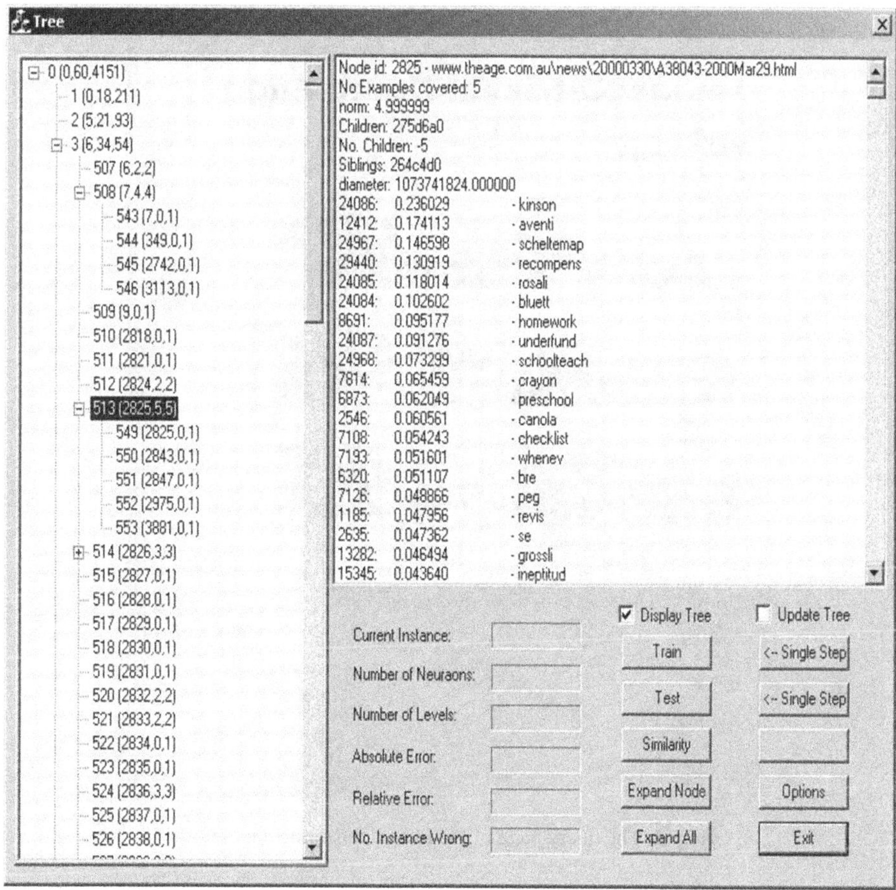

Fig. 3. Snapshot of the visualization subsystem

5 A Multimedia Information Clustering System

In this section a content-based multimedia information clustering system is described in detail to show the power of the technology proposed in this paper. The same program developed for the text information clustering system is used for both generating the cluster hierarchy and retrieval/browsing of the multimedia information. The only difference is that the multimedia (image/sound) features were extracted from the documents rather than text-only features (keywords/key-phrases). We use a new structural indexing technology to handle image features. Readers can check [19], [18] for details. The system described here is an image clustering system which extracts the image features (see the lower part of Fig. 4 for the details of the images features.

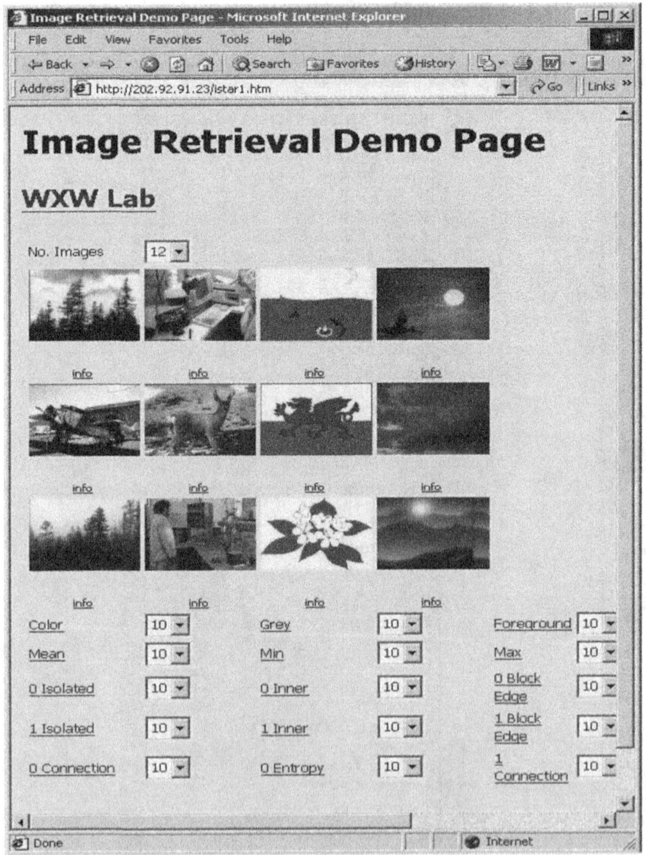

Fig. 4. The query page of the image clustering engine

The same principle can apply to a sound/music information clustering system. Again, the only difference is that the sound/music features represented by the LPC (Linear Predicated Coding) coefficients are extracted rather than text/image features.

The demo system has an image database containing about 500 images. As mentioned above, the system extracts the image features to form image feature vectors and then clusters them according to the similarity among the images. The resulting cluster hierarchy is then used as a content-based engine to provide the similarity based image retrieval capability. Clicking the image at the lower left corner of the image array to make a query with that particular image (with forest in the foreground but without clouds in the background). The content-based engine should find the most similar images to the query engine from the image database [11].

Fig. 5 shows that it achieved the exact goal that we expected it to achieve. As the first result, it returns the query image itself and the other two images returned are both satisfying the query criterion: "with forest in the foreground but without clouds in the background".

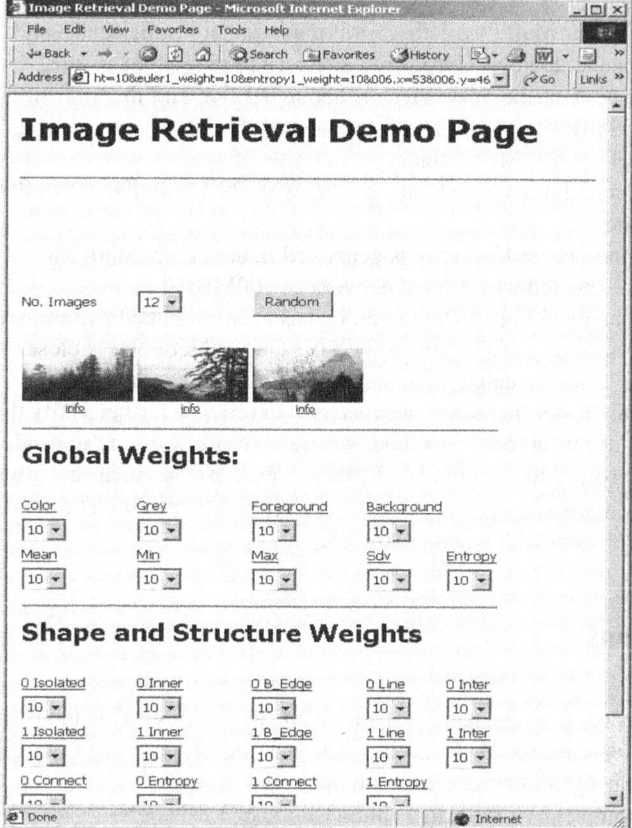

Fig. 5. Search result for the query in Fig. 4

An integrated multimedia information clustering system is in experiments, which handles combined queries like "I would like to buy a red Toyota Corolla like this."

Here, "this" will be represented with an image of a red car. A natural language front-end will extract the text features (keywords) from the query sentence and the image feature extraction mechanism (like the one we used in the demo system, here) will extract the image features. Then the cluster hierarchy will be searched to find what the user exactly wants.

6 Other Examples of Applications

A cluster hierarchy has been generated for some major Australian news Web sites. These include

1. The Australian (www.theaustralian.com.au) and Sydney Morning Herald (www.smh.com.au) in Sydney,
2. The Age (www.theage.com) and Herald-Sun (www.heraldsun.com.au)in Melbourne,
3. The Courier Mail (www.thecouriermail.com.au) in Brisbane, and
4. Some general News Corp. news site such as news.com.au. etc.

The total number of the Web pages is about 101,000 and the total size of the Web documents is 1.2GB. The resulting cluster hierarchy

1. takes about 400 MB in total ,
2. is generated in about 6 hours in a PC with P III 500MHz CPU, 256MB memory, and
3. the same cluster hierarchy is generated in about 3.5 hours with 3 similar PCs inter-connected with a local network of 100MBPS.

The quality of the resulting cluster hierarchy has been examined by both searching and browsing. The accuracy of the search with the cluster hierarchy is close to 100% and browsing through the visualized hierarchy shows the hierarchy contains a reasonably good conceptual cluster hierarchy as expected. In order to further verify the generality and robustness of our proposed method, we are currently working to produce a cluster hierarchy for some most popular Chinese Web sites, such as www.sina.com, www.263.com, www.chinaren.com, and www.dudu.net.cn, etc. The total number of web pages in this hierarchy is about 200,000.

7 Conclusions

Taking into account of the nature of the Web, we propose a method of distributed hierarchical clustering for Web mining. The method proposed has the following advantages comparing with other clustering methods:

1. The complexity of the algorithm is at most O(MN*log*N).
2. With the distributed implementation the method can be easily scaled up.
3. The method is independent of the order the web documents presented.
4. The method produces a natural conceptual hierarchy but not a binary tree.
5. The method can generate cluster hierarchy for multimedia information.

6. A visualisation mechanism has been developed for the clustering method and it shows the cluster hierarchy generated by the method has very high quality.
7. The clustering process is fully automatic, no human intervention is required.

A hierarchical clustering system has been built based on the proposed method which can be used to automatically generate multimedia search engines, web directories,

References

1. M. R. Anderberg, *Cluster Analysis for Applications*, New Yourk, Academic, 1973.
2. R. Baeza-Yates and B. Ribeiro-Neto, *Moden Information Retrieval*, Addison Wesley, ACM Press, 1999.
3. T. Caeli, L. Guan, and W. Wen, *Modularity in Neural Computing*, Invited paper, Proceedings of IEEE, Vol 87, No. 9, 1999
4. D. Fisher, *Knowledge Acquisition via Incremental Conceptual Clustering*, Machine Learning, vol 2, 1987
5. D. Gibson, J. Kleinberg, and P. Raghavan. *Inferring Web Communities from Link Topolgy*. In Conference on hypertext and Hypermedia. ACM, 1998.
6. D. Gordon, *A review of hierarchical classification*, J. Royal Statistical Society Series A, 150(2), 119-37, 1987
7. D.O. Hebb, The Organization of Behaviour, New York, Willy
8. Iona, *OrbixWeb Programmer's Guide*, Sept. 1998
9. T. Kohonen, *Self-Organization and Associative Memory*, Springer-Verlag, Berlin, 1984.
10. R. Kosala and H. Blockeel. *Web Mining Research: A Survey*. SIKDD Explorations, Newsletter of the ACM Special Interest Group on Knowledge Discovery and Data Mining. June 2 2000, Volume 2, Issue 1. pp 1-15.
11. Natsev, R. Rastogi, and K. Shim. *Walrus: A Similarity Retrieva Algorithm for Image Databases*. In Proc. 1999 ACM-SIGMOD Conf. On Management of Data (SIGMOD'99), pp 395-406.
12. S. Salton, *The Smart retrieval system*, Englewood cliffs, N.J., Prentice Hall. 1971.
13. J. Srivastava, R. Cooley, M. Deshpande, and P-N. Tan. *Web Usage Mining: Discovery and Applications of Usage Patterns from Web Data*. SIKDD Explorations, Newsletter of the ACM Special Interest Group on Knowledge Discovery and Data Mining. January 2000, Volume 1, Issue 2. pp 12-23.
14. W. Wen, *SGNNN: Self-Generating Network of Neural Networks*, invited paper, Australian Conference on Neural Networks, Brisbane, 1998.
15. W. Wen, A. Jennings, and H. Liu, *Self-Generating Neural Networks*, International Joint Conference on Neural Networks, Baltimore, 1992.
16. L. Wang, *On Competitive learning*, IEEE Transactions on Neural Networks, vol. 8, no. 5, pp. 1214-1217, Sept. 1997.
17. O.R. Zaiane, J. Han, and H. Zhu. *Mining Recurrent Items in Multimedia with Progressive Resolution Refinement*. In Proc. 2000 Int. Conf. Data Engineering (ICDE'00), pp 195-209.
18. Z.J. Zheng and C.H.C. Leung, *Graph Indexes of 2D- Thinned Images for Rapid Content-based Image Retrieval*, Journal of Visual Communication and Image Representation, Vol. 8, No. 2, pp. 121-134, 1997.
19. Z.J. Zheng and C.H.C. Leung, *Automatic Image Indexing for Rapid Content-based Retrieval*, in Proceedings of International Workshop on Multi-media Database Management Systems, IEEE Computer Society Press, 1996.

ARMiner: A Data Mining Tool Based on Association Rules*

Haofeng Zhou, Beijun Ruan, Jianqiu Zhu, Yangyong Zhu, and Baile Shi

Department of Computer Science, Fudan University,
Shanghai, 200433, P.R.China
haofzhou@fudan.edu.cn

Abstract. In this paper, ARMiner, a data mining tools based on association rules, is introduced. Beginning with the system architecture, the characteristic and the function are displayed in details, including data transfer, concept hierarchy generalization, mining rules with negative items and the re-development of the system. We also show an example of the tool's application in this paper. Finally, some expectations for future work are presented.

1 Introduction

The data mining technology has attracted lots of researchers and organizations for its brilliant prospects of application [1]. Due to prosperous research on it, a large number of applications have emerged and many prototypes have been produced. Some systems, for example, Intelligent Mine from IBM [2], DBMiner from Simon Fraser University [3] and Knight from Nanjing University [4], have been used successfully in many application domains like finance and commerce.

After developing AMINER [5], a data mining tools which adopts various kinds of data mining technology, we successfully constructed ARMiner, a data mining system based on association rules, as one component in AMINER. The goal of ARMiner is to develop data mining tools for intelligent POS system and support decision-making as an important tool in data warehouse.

2 Overview of the System

Around the world, there are two major kinds of architecture of data mining: one is process-oriented, for example, two multi-phase processing models proposed by Fayyad [6] and John [7] respectively. The other focuses on user and application, such as the user-oriented processing model invented by Brachman [8]. Actually, the other models can be classified into these two categories, such as three-tier architecture from IBM [9] and the Knight architecture from Nanjing University [4].

The architecture of ARMiner has the characteristics of both kinds. ARMiner consists of five components. The whole structure is shown in Figure 1.

* This paper was funded by the National 863 Projects of China No. 863-306-ZT02-05-1.

X.S. Wang, G. Yu, and H. Lu (Eds.): WAIM 2001, LNCS 2118, pp. 114–121, 2001.

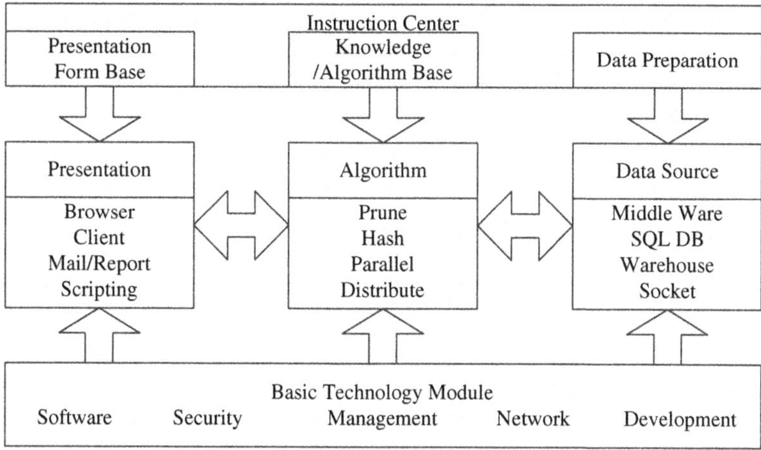

Fig. 1. The Architecture of ARMiner

Basic technology module: It refers the environment of software and hardware where the system is developed. As the physical foundation of implementation, it determines the efficiency of the final system.

Presentation module: It refers to the interface for users. It can be direct, like the interface of C/S architecture, or indirect, for example, the e-mail which users use to deliver data mining requests and accept the result.

Algorithm module: It is the core of the system. Guided by the instruction center, it selects suitable algorithms to mine the clean data processed from the data sources, applies some techniques like indexing, parallel computing and pruning ramifications to improve the efficiency and sends the mining result to presentation module.

Data source module: It prepares data for mining by transforming the raw data extracted in various ways from different sources, such as relational database, multidimensional database, data warehouse and even flat files. The raw data can be extracted through gateways such as ODBC, or by connecting databases in special ways, or by analyzing the data from data warehouse and other data sources. Large data set can be sampled to reduce the size of data. Then, the dirty data is removed by cleaning and the left is integrated for mining. In that way, every mining algorithm will face a unified interface.

Instruction center: As the headquarters of the system, it directs three modules, namely, presentation, algorithm and data source, to run properly. Presentation form base stores the definitions of forms in which the output is presented to the end users. Knowledge/algorithm base is used to control the management and execution of algorithms. Data preparation method base provides the methods for data source module during data transfer. There are two modes provided for executing instruction center: automatic mode and manual mode. The latter mode is reserved for manually controlling the mining process.

In the horizontal view, this architecture reflects the processing phases: data preparation, data mining and result presentation. In the vertical view, it focuses on application with the physical foundation and the reserved interface for manual control. Therefore, the characteristics of the precedent kinds of architecture are well combined into ARMiner.

3 The Role of ARMiner as a System

3.1 Functions of ARMiner as a Mining Tool

As a mining tool, ARMiner provides functions such as data preparation and association rules mining.

Data preparation includes data transfer and concept hierarchy generalization. The task of data preparation is to transform the raw transaction data according to the required structure and transfer the transformed data to the mining database of ARMiner.

The ultimate goal of data transfer is transferring the data from the sources to the mining database. In general, the data used by rule mining is transaction data, i.e., the data with the structure :$(TID, ItemID)$. Furthermore, to facilitate the work of displaying the rules, the description information of items, such as item name, should be transferred too. Therefore, the data to be transformed by ARMiner includes transaction set and item set.

During transformation, if there is no unique field as the primary key of the records in the original set, a new primary key is generated to substitute the old one. Then, the transaction data is transferred accordingly. This is called transformation-transfer and the counterpart is simple transfer. The proper transfer method is automatically chosen as the transfer rules are provided.

Data transfer provides ARMiner the proper data by importing the source data into the mining database.

The original transaction data often contains large amount of detailed data, where much useless knowledge may be discovered, and which can't reflect the abstract hierarchies in the real world. Therefore, it is important to generalize the original data after data transfer is finished. So, the concepts of domain knowledge are introduced here.

Many researchers have studied it and some algorithms are proposed [10][11][12]. However, these algorithms are usually bound to mining algorithms, that is, the concept hierarchies are take into account at the stage of generating large item sets. In that way, a problem occurs: as the knowledge of a domain isn't used, the algorithm of this kind will cause unnecessary cost. Hence, in ARMiner, we make concept hierarchy generation independent by separating it from the process of mining, and it can be regarded as a part of data preprocessing.

According to users' requirements, we process the raw data, convert them at more abstract levels. Then, from the new data set previously obtained, we remove the redundancy, and import these clean data into the mining database. The whole process is illustrated in the Figure 2.

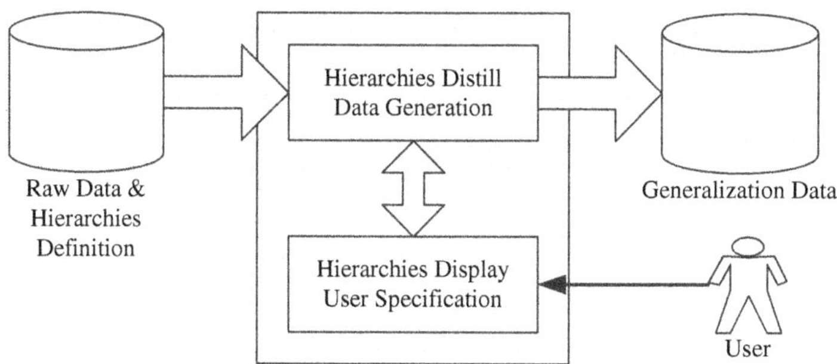

Fig. 2. Data Generalization Process

The display of concept hierarchies uses a tree to show the definitions of generalization levels. As an interactive process, generalization hierarchy selection allows users to choose the proper generalization levels. After the selection work is over, it delivers the generalization requirements to data generalization module. The module of concept hierarchy input and data generalization converts the hierarchies in tables into the ones with the program data structures, and transforms the raw data at the chosen levels, then stores these processed data into the mining database.

Association rule mining is the core technique of ARMiner. We not only introduce interestingness measure as a new kind of evaluation, but also provide an algorithm for association rules with negative items.

Interestingness measure is proposed to improve the previous evaluation system of association rule and there are various definitions[13][14][15]. Based on statistics, we define the interestingness measure of association rules of the form of $X \Rightarrow Y$ as $i = S(X)S(Y)/S(XY)$, where $S(X)$ is the support measure of X in the transaction set. If i, the interestingness measure of a rule, satisfies the condition of $0 < i < 1$, we will consider this rule valueless. ,However, as $i \geq i_m$ (i_m is the least interestingness measure and $i_m \geq 1$) ,it will be a valuable rule.

Based on the above definition, the evaluation of association rule contains three measure arguments: support, confidence and interestingness. Their statistical explanation is: given a rule $X \Rightarrow Y$, interestingness measure reflects the tightness of connection between X and Y, and confidence represents the connection direction in this condition, i.e., from X to Y or Y to X. Support measure shows whether this condition is common among the transactions.

Furthermore, by admitting negative items, we modify the definition of association rule and proposed the concept of negative itemset [16]. To obtain support measure of the negative item set, we devise a new algorithm, which computes support measure using the support measures of the positive literal set without rescanning the database.

Then, a mining algorithm is contrived for association rules with negative items. If the generated rules are not interesting to users, this algorithm is able to discover other rules (perhaps more interesting) by introducing negative item set automatically [16].

By these definitions and algorithms, we can discover the association rules whose semantics are more integrated, such as '$coffee \Rightarrow \overline{milk}$'.

3.2 Re-development Ability

During the development of the ARMiner, we encapsulate the system function into several API functions for re-development. These functions are classified into four categories: the mining algorithm functions, the rules generating functions, the data transformation functions and the concept hierarchy constructing functions.

The process of association rules mining can be divided into two phases: the large-set generation and the rules generation. The former is carried out by the mining algorithm functions whose interface is open, so we can use any algorithm which measure up the definition of the interface. In ARMiner , we currently provide the Apriori, AprioriTID [17] and DHP [18] algorithms, and we also can use other ones which have better performances. The second phase is implemented by the rules generating functions which include the original rules generation function mentioned by Agrawal and the new one mentioned above. By an option, the user can choose either of them.

During the transfer, with the transformation rules, data transformation functions will automatically choose either transformation transfer or simple transfer, and adjust the attributes of each field. The concept hierarchy constructing functions are used to analyze the original data and construct the hierarchies. To permit manual intervention in the process of mining, we made an independent operating interface for constructing hierarchies. Through this interface, users can freely select the wanted items in the displayed tree.

Implemented in the form of Dynamic Link Library(DLL), these functions can be seamlessly integrated with a few developing environments such as VC and VB. Therefore, the deployment of the system is greatly eased. We can use these API functions to enhance various kinds of existing information systems by providing decision support to them. Meanwhile, the interface definitions of API functions is the foundation of system extension. Following these definitions, more functions, such as mining algorithms with better performance and powerful guidance with more domain knowledge, will be added in.

4 The Application of ARMiner

The target database is a supermarket database where every item belongs to a definite category, for example, apple belongs to fruit, fruit belongs to food, and so on. First, using the domain knowledge implied in the concept hierarchy, we processed the transaction data of about one month. The hierarchy was constructed from the original data and the generalization items were selected, then the data was generalized. Now, we mined the database using interestingness measure and association rules with negative items. As the least support measure was 0.005 and the least confidence and interestingness were 0.06 and 1.15 respectively, we got the result as presented in Figure 3.

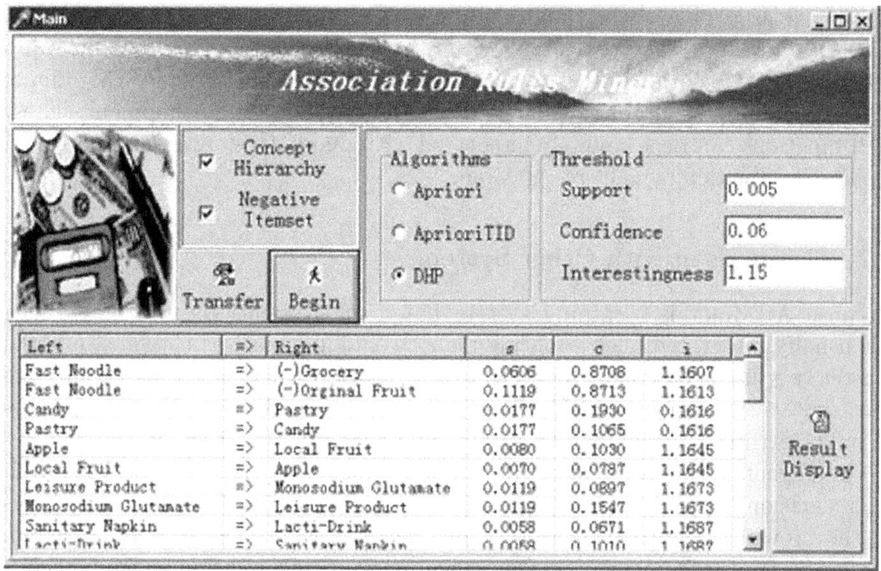

Fig. 3. The ARMiner Main Interface

As shown in this figure, the negative items are marked with '(-)'. If we had adopted only three threshold values to filter rules without consideration for negative items, some rules, such as "$fastnoodle \Rightarrow (-)groceries$", would not been discovered. This kind of rules appears just because the corresponding normal ones, such as $fastnoodle \Rightarrow (-)groceries$, bear interestingness less than 1. If only interestingness is used to filter rules, we would lose this kind of normal rules, needless to say, the ones with negative items. From the result, we detected some particular rules, such as '$sanitarynapkin \Rightarrow lacto - drink$', which is as weird as the classic sample of '$diaper \Rightarrow beer$'. Besides, the rule '$fastnoodle \Rightarrow \overline{fruit}$' means the former is for the busy life and the latter is for the leisure one.

Utilizing the API functions of ARMiner, we reconstructed an existing business information system. The users of this old system provided some specific requirements. For example, the hierarchy is not considered, but the negative items must be shown. In addition, the data transfer was avoided for the system was implemented directly upon the original system. Using the API functions, we successfully constructed a decision support module.

5 Relevant Topics

5.1 System Features

One of the advantages of ARMiner is that interestingness measure is introduced in system as a new evaluation to filter useless and uninteresting association rules. As a result, an improved algorithm is made to reserve the semantics implied in the association rules entirely. Moreover, ARMiner provides the mining algorithms and the preprocessing API functions for its re-development. These API functions can be seamlessly integrated with many developing environments, facilitating the deployment of ARMiner.

5.2 Comparison with Other Systems

Because ARMiner is a mining system based on association rules and others are usually integrated ones adopting many techniques such as classification and cluster, we just select their modules for association rules. Here, we choose two representative systems: IBM Intelligent Miner and Knight from Nanjing University. The former is a commercial system and the later is a research one.

Intelligent Miner is an integrated tool set based on DB2 and provides full-scale decision support. Its mining module for association rules strictly conforms to the previous definition of association rule and evaluation system. Although the problem of association rule generalization is considered and a batch of API functions are provided, this module has been screwed onto the foundation stone, DB2. By the Big Blue's great influence, its applications are populated extensively. However, ARMiner is independent of any database platform and can run on many platforms through ODBC. Rule generalization is also taken into account. Moreover, interestingness measure is introduced as a new evaluation argument. Meanwhile, ARMiner is able to discover the rules with negative items. Similarly, its API functions don't rely on any database.

Knight is a general-purpose mining tool, which uses ODBC and special database interfaces to implement its platform transparence. By guiding the knowledge discovery with syntax tree, it imports domain knowledge. Capable of four types of mining, it has been put into use in insurance area. In some similarity, ARMiner accesses databases through ODBC and introduces domain knowledge into system by concept hierarchies. The mining algorithms and data preprocessing function are encapsulated into Dynamic Link libraries. Therefore, the API functions are immediately provided for re-development as the system development is finished. ARMiner and its API functions have been used in several application areas.

6 Conclusion

The technology of data mining emerged to meet the requirements of actual practices. Its implementation will be helpful to the decision-make. Some of the efforts have been done in the ARMiner. It can use the domain knowledge through the concept hierarchy, and introduces the interestingness and algorithm that mines the rules with negative items, which make the semantics of the association rules more complete than ever; in addition, it also provide the API functions for the re-development, which leads to the more applications.

There are still some works we need to do in the future, e.g. we need to expand the algorithm implementation over the rules mining, and provide the complete function to the system.

References

1. Chen, M.-S., Han, J., Yu, P.S.: Data Mining: An Overview from a Database Perspective. IEEE Transactions on Knowledge and Data Engineering 6 (1996) 866-883
2. Agrawal, R., Mehta, M., Shafer, J.C., Srikant, R., Arning, A., Bollinger, T.: The Quest Data Mining System.In: Proc. of KDD (1996) 244-249
3. Han, J., Fu, Y., Wang, W., Chiang, J., Gong, W., Koperski, K., Li, D., Lu, Y., Rajan, A., Stefanovic, N., Xia, B., Zaiane, O.R.: DBMiner: A System for Mining Knowledge in Large Relational Databases. In: Proc. of KDD (1996) 250-255
4. Chen, D., Xu, J.: Knight:a General Purpose Data Mining System. J. Computer Research & Development 4 (1998) 338-343
5. Zhu, Y., Zhou, X., Shi, B.: Rule-based Data Minging Tool Kit:AMiner. Communication of High Technology 3 (2000) 19-22
6. Fayyad, U.M., Piatetsky-Shapiro, G., Smyth, P.: From Data Mining to Knowledge Discovery: An Overview. In: Advances in Knowledge Discovery and Data Mining. AAAI/MIT Press (1996) 1-34
7. John, G.H.: Enhancements to the data mining process[PhD Thesis], Dept. of Computer Science, School of Engineering, Stanford University (1997)
8. Brachman, R.J.: The Process of Knowledge Discovery in Database. In: Advances in Knowledge Discovery and Data Mining. AAAI/MIT Press (1996) 37-57
9. http://www.almaden.ibm.com/cs/quest/paper/whitepaper.html
10. Cheng, J., Shi, P.: Fast Mining Multiple-level Association Rules. Chinese J. Computers 11 (1998) 1037-1041
11. Han, J., Fu, Y.: Discovery of Multiple-Level Association Rules from Large Databases. In: Proc. of VLDB (1995) 420-431
12. Srikant, R., Agrawal, R.: Mining Generalized Association Rules. In: Proc. of VLDB (1995) 407-419
13. Zhou, X., Sha, C., Zhu, Y., Shi, B.: Interest Measure - Another Threshold in Association Rules. J. Computer Research & Development 5 (2000) 627-633
14. Brin, S., Motwani, R., Silverstein, C.: Beyond Market Baskets: Generalizing Association Rules to Correlations. In: Proc. of ACM SIGMOD (1997) 265-276
15. Savasere, A., Omiecinski, E., Navathe, S.B.: Mining for Strong Negative Associations in a Large Database of Customer Transactions. In: Proc. of Int. Conf. on Data Engineering (1998) 494-502
16. Zhou, H., Gao, P., Zhu, Y.: Mining Association Rules with Negative Items Using Interest Measure, In: Web-Age Information Management, Lecture Notes in Computer Science, Vol. 1846, Springer-Verlag Publisher (2000) 121-132
17. Agrawal, R., Srikant, R.: Fast Algorithms for Mining Association Rules in Large Databases. In: Proc. of VLDB (1994) 487-499
18. Park, J.S., Chen, M.-S., Yu, P.S.: An Effective Hash Based Algorithm for Mining Association Rules. In: Proc. of ACM SIGMOD (1995) 175-186

An Integrated Classification Rule Management System for Data Mining*

Daling Wang, Yubin Bao, Xiao Ji, Guoren Wang, and Baoyan Song

School of Information Science and Engineering, Northeastern University
Shenyang 110006, P.R.China
dlwang@mail.neu.edu.cn

Abstract. Classification rule mining plays significant roles in practical applications. While how to mine classification rules from a database efficiently is an important issue, how to manage and apply the mined rules effectively is the same important. This paper presents a classification rule mining management system, named SM-Classifier, which integrates the functionality of generation, querying, maintenance and application of classification rules. The architecture of SM-Classifier, the classification algorithm, the rule store structure, and the rule query operations are described.

1 Introduction

Nowadays, there are many different kinds of data mining methods to get various rules. Due to slow mining speed in large databases, it is not possible to mine the rules whenever demanding them. To solve this problem, it is necessary to build a rule management system, which can store the preprocessed data, the related data structure and the mined rules, and provide application interface.

Paper[1] proposed the concept of „pattern management", and analyzed the relationship between data management and pattern management. But it only gave a framework of pattern management, and didn't explains the details of the management. Literature[2] gave an algorithm of decision tree classification, described how to use the rules to classify new data, and discussed the involved problems like missing values. However, how to store and query rules, especially how to manage a large amount of rule sets from different data sources wasn't considered.

Mining classification rules is an important data mining technique with widely requirements in practical applications. Therefore, this paper presents the design of a classification rule mining management system with the goal to integrate the functionality of generating, querying, maintaining, and using classification rule.

The architecture of SM-Classifier is shown in Fig.1. SM-Classifier consists of the following major components:

---

* This work is partially supported by the Foundation for University Key Teacher, the Teaching and Research Award Program for Outstanding Young Teachers in Higher Education Institutions, and the Cross Century Excellent Young Teacher Foundation of the Ministry of Education of China.

X.S. Wang, G. Yu, and H. Lu (Eds.): WAIM 2001, LNCS 2118, pp. 122-129, 2001.

Preprocessing first transforms, cleanses, and integrates *Raw data* from different data sources, then samples and generates *Refined data.*

Rule storing stores the preprocessed data, the mined rules and the related data table. They are *Refined data, Training data*, *Rule set*, and *Mapping table.* If a decision attribute has too many values, we must aggregate these values into fewer values by mapping them from a large value space to a small value space. *Mapping table* is used to store the mapping relationship between old space and new one.

Classifying generates classification rules through mining from *Training dataset.*

Rule evaluating checks the accuracy of the mined rules.

Rule applying provides facility for user to look up mined rules by using *Query operations*, and to apply rules to classify new cases.

Rule Outputting supports to display rules and classified results in visual mode.

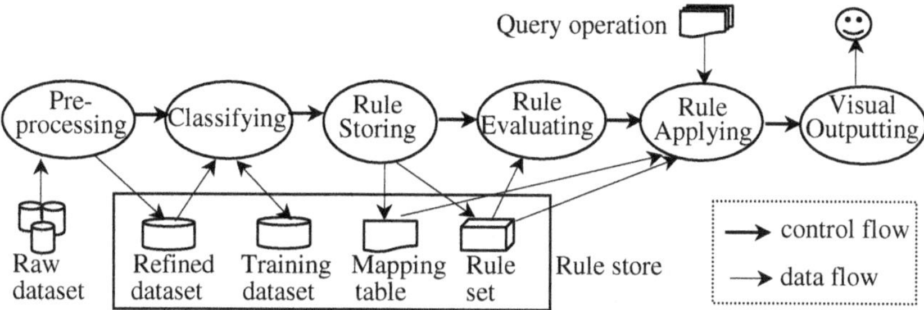

Fig. 1. Architecture of SM-Classifier System

2 Algorithm of Classification

There are many famous decision tree based classifying algorithms such as ID3[3], C4.5[2], and MedGen[4]. In these algorithms, the information gain is used as a criterion to select the attribute for a level of the decision tree so that the entropy can be minimized after a training dataset is divided into several subsets by the selected attribute. In this way, the average path length from every node to its leaf node is short and the average depth of the tree is small so that the tree has fast classification speed with high accuracy.

In SM-Classifier, we design an improved decision tree classification algorithm. The algorithm constructs the decision tree by using the C4.5 and MedGen methods but makes the following improvements by using the maximal correlation instead of the maximal information gain as in [2][3][4].

(1) When determining the classification order of the condition attributes, the condition attribute is selected, which has the maximal correlation between the condition attribute and the decision attribute.

(2) When determining the branching point of a numeral condition attribute, the value is selected, which has the maximal correlation between the condition attribute and the decision attribute.

For two values a_i $(i=1,2,...,m)$ of condition attribute A and b_j $(j=1,2,...,n)$ of decision attribute B, their frequency table is defined in Table 1. Where $f=N$ (N is the number of cases). We uses the equations (1) and (2) given in [5] to calculate the statistical variables χ^2 and Ψ_{coeff} .

Table 1. Frequency Table of Two Attributes

	b_1	b_2	...	b_n	SUM
a_1	f_{11}	f_{12}	...	f_{1n}	$A_1=\Sigma_j f_{1j}$
a_2	f_{21}	f_{22}	...	f_{2n}	$A_2=\Sigma_j f_{2j}$
⋮	⋮	⋮		⋮	⋮
a_m	f_{m1}	f_{m2}	...	f_{mn}	$A_m=\Sigma_j f_{mj}$
SUM	$B_1=\Sigma_i f_{i1}$	$B_2=\Sigma_i f_{i2}$	...	$B_n=\Sigma_i f_{in}$	$f=\Sigma_{i,j} f_{ij}$

χ^2 is used to calculate the correlation between A and B.

$$\chi^2 = \sum_{i,j}^{m,n} \frac{(f_{ij} - A_iB_j/f)^2}{A_iB_j/f} \tag{1}$$

Ψ_{coeff} is the correlation metric. The larger its absolute value is, the stronger correlation between A and B is. The correlation is weaker when the absolute value approaches 0. Thus we use Ψ_{coeff} to determine the order of attributes and the branching value when partitioning a numeral attribute in building the tree.

$$\psi_{coeff} = \begin{cases} \dfrac{f_{11}f_{22} - f_{12}f_{21}}{\sqrt{A_1A_2B_1B_2}}, & m = n = 2 \\ \sqrt{\chi^2/f} & , other \end{cases} \tag{2}$$

The reasons to use the correlation criterion rather than the information gain are as follows.

1. χ^2 can determine whether the correlation exists between a condition attribute and the decision attribute, and Ψ_{coeff} gives the correlation measure. They will not affect the classification accuracy when using the correlation to determine the order of condition attributes when building the decision tree.

2. In C4.5, the computation of gain involves *info*(T) and *info*$_x$(T). The former has time complexity $O(nlog_2n)$ and the latter has time complexity $O(n^2log_2n)$. In our algorithm, the computation of χ^2 and Ψ_{coeff} has time complexity $O(n^2)$. When $n>2$, $O(n^2log_2n)$ $O(n^2)$.

3. Information gain criterion has a strong bias in favor of tests with many outcomes[2]. For example, a primary key attribute in a data table contains unique value. *info*$_x$(T)=0 and the gain using this key attribute to partition the dataset is maximal. However, from the viewpoint of prediction, such a classification is useless. In our correlation metric, since f_{ij}=0 or 1 $(i=1,2,...,m, j=1,2,...,n)$, A_i=1 $(i=1,2,...,m)$, from experiments we know that the correlation between such a condition attribute and the decision attribute is less than the one of other attributes in most cases. Therefore, this attribute will not be selected and the bias can be avoided. Although C4.5 can use the information gain ratio to solve this problem, but the time complexity is increased.

In SM-Classifier system, the new classification algorithm is as follows:

Step 1: select a refined dataset D to create the decision tree.

Step 2: select the condition attributes $A_i(i=1,2,...,n)$ and a decision attribute B in D. A new training dataset D_1 is constructed with $A_i(i=1,2,...,n)$ and B by selecting part of the instances from D according to a given proportion.

Step 3: map multiple decision attribute values into a small number of values if the decision attributes has more than 3 values.

Step 4: remove the condition attributes having less correlation with the decision attribute from D_1 by computing χ^2. χ^2 between $A_i(i=1,2,...,n)$ and B is calculated for all condition attributes $A_i(i=1,2,\cdots,n)$ and decision attribute B. A new dataset D_2 is created with $A_i(i=1,2,...,m, m\ \ n)$ and B.

Step 5: compute Ψ_i $(i=1,2,...,m)$ of Ψ_{coeff} between every condition attribute A_i $(i=1,2,...,m)$ and the decision attribute B in D_2. Suppose $A_k=\{A_i|i=1,2,...,m,\ \Psi_k= MAX(\Psi_i)\}$, then D_2 is partitioned into $D_{21}, D_{22},...,D_{2p}$ according to every value of A_k. *Step 5* is executed recursively for every $D_{2j}(j=1,2,...,p)$ until one of the following conditions is satisfied.

(1) All instances in the sub-dataset belong to the same class.

(2) The percentage of the cases belonging to the same class is larger or equal to a given threshold τ.

(3) Each of the other condition attribute(s) in the sub-dataset has the same value, respectively.

Step 6: build the decision tree according to the result of *Step 5*. Every partition in *Step 5* generates a new node of the tree and every attribute value used in partitioning generates a branch of the new node. The Conditions in *Step 5* are used to generate leaf nodes: condition (1) corresponds to a single class, condition (2) corresponds to a single class but the cases less than τ are ignored, condition (3) corresponds to multiple classes. Each value in a leaf node has the form $<d, f>$, where d is the value of the decision attribute, and f is the frequency belonging to this class.

Since the tree has been pruned with threshold τ during building, the rules can be generated directly without needing pruning. Suppose that there are m branches in the tree, then every branch corresponds to a classification rule in the following form.

IF condition$_1$ *and* condition$_2$ *and* ... *and* condition$_m$ *THEN* decision

3 Store of Classification Rule

In order to introduce the rule store structure in SM-Classifier, we first give some definitions.

Definition 1: Let *RD* be a refined dataset preprocessed from any raw databases or datasets and *TD* be a training dataset from an *RD*.

Definition 2: Let *DT* be a decision tree generated from a training dataset.

Definition 3: Let *MT* be a decision attribute mapping table.

Definition 4: Let *RS* be a rule store including a set of *RD*s, a set of *TD*s, and a set of *DT*s, and a set of *MT*s.

At first, different raw datasets can be transformed into the unified format of SM-Classifier after preprocessing. We store the *RD*s in an *RDbase* in which each dataset corresponds to a single *RD*. Before classifying, a training dataset *TD* is extracted from the corresponding *RD*s and is stored in the *TDbase* in which each dataset corresponds to a single *TD*.

After classifying, the mined *DT* is stored in *DTbase* in which each set corresponds to a single *DT*. An *DT* contains all the nodes of the decision tree. Each node has a unique node ID. The non-leaf node has the structure:

nodeid, conditionattrname, $<condition_1, nodeid_1>$, ..., $<condition_m, nodeid_m>$

the leaf node has the structure: (n 3)

nodeid, decisionattrname, $<value_1, frequency_1>$,...., $<value_n, frequency_n>$

An *MT* can be generated when a decision attribute is processed. *MT* is stored in the *MTbase* in which each dataset corresponds to a single *MT*. An *MT* has two attributes: *Old* and *New*.

Each *RD* , *TD, MT* and *DT* has a unique identification (ID, usually a unique name), respectively. An *RStable* is defined to describe the relationship among *RD, TD, DT* and *MT*. *RStable* has the following structure.

RStable(RDid, TDid, MTid, DTid)

Every mining process generates one row in *RStable*, a training dataset in *TDbase*, a decision tree in *DTbase* and a mapping table in *MTbase*. Where *RDid, TDid, MTid, and DTid* are the IDs of the refined dataset, the training dataset, the mapping table, and the decision tree, respectively. If there is no mapping on the decision attribute, *MTid* is null. The structures of *RStable, RDbase, TDbase, MTbase,* and *DTbase* are shown in Fig.2

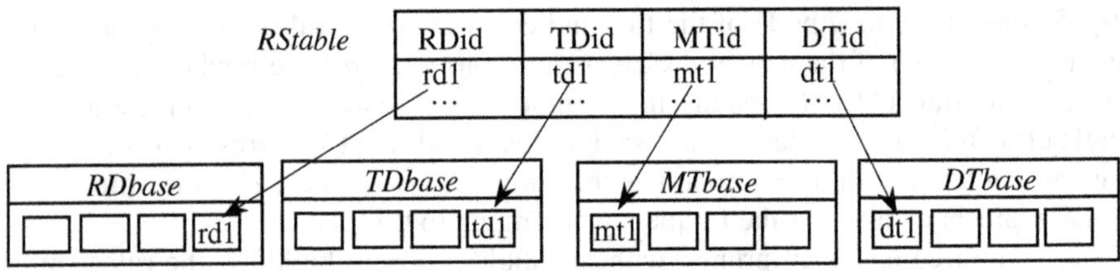

Fig. 2. Structure of *RStable, RDbase, TDbase, MTbase, DTbase*

4 Operation and Application of Classification Rule

To maintain the rules in the rule store, several modification operations are provided. The following are 5 major operations.

(1) *CreateData* (*tdID, rdID, attrlist, rate*)

This operation creates a new training dataset in *TDbase* by selecting the instances from a refined dataset in *RDbase*. *rdID* and *tdID* are the IDs of the refined dataset and the training dataset, respectively. *attrlist* is the attribute list that specifies the attributes to be selected, and *rate* is the percentage of the training dataset in the refined dataset. If *attrlist* is null, then all attributes will be selected.

(2) *CreateDecisionTree* (*dtID, tdID*)

This operation creates a decision tree in *DTbase* from a training dataset in *TDbase*, and save the nodes. *tdID* and *dtID* are the IDs of the *TD* and *DT*, respectively.

(3) *AppendRuleSet* (*rd, td, mt, dt*)

This operation appends a new row to *RStable*. Where *rd*, *td*, *mt*, and *dt* are the values of *RDid, TDid, MTid* , and *DTid* in *RStable*, respectively.

(4) *AppendMT(mtID, old, new)*

This operations appends a new row to *MT* in *MTbase*. Where *mtID* is the ID of the *MT*, *old* and *new* are the values of *OLD* and *NEW* in *MT*, respectively.

Therefore, a classifying process includes *CreateData* to select a training dataset, *AppendMT* when processing the decision attribute, *CreateDecisionTree* when generating the decision tree, and *AppendRuleSet* when generating the final result.

When a rule is outdated, we also provide some remove operations such as:

(5) *Remove(tdName)*;

This operation removes the row in *RStable* that matches *tdID*, and corresponding datasets in *TDbase*, *MTbase,* and *DTbase*, respectively. *tdID* is the ID of a training dataset to be removed.

To query the rules in the rule store, we define a query operation as follows.

(6) *Find (tdID, conditionattrs, decisionattrs)*

This operation can find one or more rules satisfying the requirements. *tdID* is the ID of a training dataset used to find the decision tree, *conditionattrs* is an ordered set that contains the pairs <condition attribute, condition> in the non-leaf nodes, *decisionattrs* is a set that contains the return values of the leaf node(s) that satisfy *conditionattrs*. If *conditionattrs* is null, the query will generate all the rules in the decision tree of *dtID*.

To apply classification rules to classify a new instance, the user first selects a training dataset name in *TDbase* and locates the corresponding decision tree in *DTbase*, then navigates the decision tree from the root to the leaf node with the values of the *conditionattr* from the new instance. The value of the leaf node is the classification result.

5 A Case Study

We have applied the system in a large iron-steel enterprise for product quality control. Now we take the parameter of steel-wire products for example to introduce the classifying process.

The user wants to analyze the influence of *EXIT_FUR, EXIT_RSM, TEMP_LAY* to *TS*. *EXIT_FUR, EXIT_RSM, TEMP_LAT* are condition attributes, *TS* is a decision attribute. The refined dataset is „wiredata“ and the training dataset is named „wiret1“. To get the training dataset, we first executes the following operation:

CreateData(„wiret1“,„wiredata“,“EXIT_FUR,EXIT_RSM,TEMP_LAY,TS“,50)

The resulting training dataset contains 587 instances , as shown in Table 2.

The preprocess of the decision attribute is needed because there are 81 values in *TS*. Suppose the ID of the new *MT* is „wirem1“, according to the domain knowledge, the user executes the operations as follow:

AppendMT („wirem1“, „350-495“, „Low“)
AppendMT („wirem1“, „500-995“, „Mid“)
AppendMT („wirem1“, „ 1000“, „High“)

Next, the following operation is executed to build the decision tree in *DTbase*. The ID of the decision tree is named „wiredt1“.

CreateDecisionTree („wiret1“, „wiredt1“)

In the correlation analysis, the correlation measure between *EXIT_FUR*, *EXIT_RSM, TEMP_LAY* and *TS* can be obtained through computing Ψ_{coeff}. They are: *EXIT_FUR (0.624)*, *EXIT_RSM (0.451)* and *TEMP_LAY (0.383)*, so they are valid. *EXIT_FUR* is selected first as the classifying node according to above result.

Table 2. Dataset of Case Study

TS	REDI_CTIO	ELON_GATI	EXIT_FUR
1170	36.0	9	1112
1200	37.0	11	1114
1190	34.0	9	1116
1180	38.0	10	1115
1180	37.0	9	1120
1190	33.0	10	1126
1190	33.0	9	1134
1190	41.0	8	1131
⋮	⋮	⋮	⋮

Moreover, the correlation between every value of *EXIT_FUR* and *TS* needs to be computed because of its numeral type, and the maximal result is selected to determine the next two branches of the node. The two branches are *EXIT_FUR 1089* and *EXIT_FUR>1089*. „wiretl“ is partitioned into two subsets. The two subsets are processed with above method recursively until getting the classification result, i.e. the decision tree as shown in Fig.3.

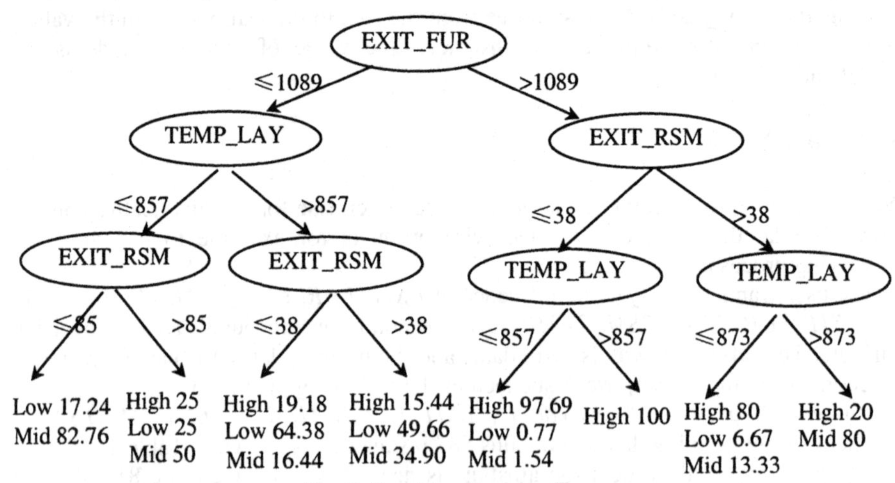

Fig. 3. Resulting Decision Tree

Some rules are generated from the decision tree such as:

1. *if EXIT_FUR>1089&EXIT_RSM>38&TEMP_LAY>873 thenTS=High20% TS=Mid80%*
2. *if EXIT_FUR>1089&EXIT_RSM>38&TEMP_LAY 873 then TS=High 80% TS=Low 6.67% TS=Mid 13.33%*
3. *if EXIT_FUR>1089 & EXIT_RSM 38 & TEMP_LAY>887 then TS=High 100%*

.....

Finally, the following operation is executed to store the description in *RSbase* :

AppendRS („wiredata“,„wiretl“, „wireml“, „wiredtl“)

Now the user can select „wiret1" as the training dataset and input the following values to classify the instance:

EXIT_FUR=1100; EXIT_RSM=35; TEMP_LAY=900;

After executing:

Find („wiret1",„EXIT_FUR=1100,EXIT_RSM=35,TEMP_LAY=900", "rule")

to get only one rule:

if EXIT_FUR>1089 & EXIT_RSM 38 & TEMP_LAY>887 then TS=High 100%

Final classification result is outputted as follow:

TS=High100% (1000)

6 Conclusion and Future Work

This paper presents a classification rule management system for data mining – SM-Classifier. We believe that rules management will become more and more important along with the development of data mining techniques.

This paper presents the architecture, construct a mining algorithm, designs the store structures, and defines some operations for rule management. They are also significant to manage other kinds of rules in data mining. Of course, because of differences in different types of rules, there are more work to build a general rule management system for all kinds of rules. Our future works include:

(1) A rules management system for general purpose will be built, which supports classification rules as well as association rules, clustering rules, sequential patterns and so on.

(2) The evaluation and optimization mechanism to rules should be added into the rules management system.

(3) A special rule query language will be developed to increase the usability of the rule management system.

We appreciate the valuable comments from anonymous reviewers and Prof.Yu Ge.

References

1. Parsaye, K.: From data management to pattern management. White paper, Information discovery, Inc., http:\\www.datamining.com (1998)
2. Quinlan, R.: C4.5 Programs for machine learning. Morgan Kaufmann Publishers. Inc. (1993)
3. Quinlan, R.: Induction of decision trees. Machine learning, 1(1), (1986) 81-106
4. Kamber, M.: Generalization and Decision Tree Induction: Efficient Classification in Data Mining. RIDE'97, Birmingham, England, April (1997)111-120
5. SAS Data Warehousing Overview Theory and Business Concepts. SAS Institute Inc. (1998)

Session 2B
Semistructured Data Management

Regular Research Paper (30 minutes)
Characterizing Web Document Changes

Regular Research Paper (30 minutes)
Identification of Syntactically Similar DTD Elements for Schema Matching

Research Experience Paper (15 minutes)
An XML Based Electronic Medical Record Integration System

Short Research Paper (15 minutes)
Enhancing XML Data Processing in Relational System with Indices

Characterizing Web Document Change

Lipyeow Lim[1], Min Wang[2], Sriram Padmanabhan[2], Jeffrey Scott Vitter[1], and Ramesh Agarwal[2]

[1] Dept. of Computer Science, Duke University, Durham, NC 27708-0129
{lipyeow, jsv}@cs.duke.edu
[2] IBM T. J. Watson Research Ctr., Hawthorne, NY 10532
{min, srp, ragarwal}@us.ibm.com

Abstract. The World Wide Web is growing and changing at an astonishing rate. For the information in the web to be useful, web information systems such as search engines have to keep up with the growth and change of the web. In this paper we study how web documents change. In particular, we study two important characteristics of web document change that are directly related to keeping web information systems up-to-date: the degree of the change and the clusteredness of the change. We analyze the evolution of web documents with respect to these two measures and discuss the implications for web information systems update.

1 Introduction

The World Wide Web is growing and changing rapidly [6]. The dynamic nature of web data poses a problem to information systems that either cache, summarize or index the web. These information systems typically have to sample or crawl the web periodically and update their local view of the web to reflect the changes in the web.

In dealing with this update problem, it is often helpful to know three characteristics of the change:

1. How *frequent* does a web document change?
2. How *much* has the content of a web document changed within a certain time interval?
3. How *clustered* are the changes in the web document?

Knowing the frequency of the change allows us to use variable crawling rates for documents with different change frequencies and thus conserve network bandwidth [4]. It also allows us to optimize for the common (most frequent) case, for example, by keeping data structures for frequently changing documents in memory [7].

Knowing how much the content of a web document has changed tells us how much the web has remained the same between two consecutive crawlings (samplings). Knowing the distribution of these changes tells us whether the changes are spread out in the changed document or whether these changes are

X.S. Wang, G. Yu, and H. Lu (Eds.): WAIM 2001, LNCS 2118, pp. 133–144, 2001.

well clustered and thus only affect small portions of each document. If changes are large and well spread out, rebuilding the local view of the web from scratch every time the web is crawled (sampled) may be more efficient than an incremental approach. On the other hand, if changes are small and clustered, an incremental approach may be more efficient.

The frequency of the web document change has been studied in previous work [5,3,2,1,4]. In [3], Cho et al. discuss how the frequency of change can be modeled by a Poisson process and how the frequency of change can be estimated from observed data. They also discuss the implications of these frequency estimates on crawling the web in [4]. Brewington et al. removed the memoryless assumption implicit in a Poisson process by modeling the web changes as a Renewal process [2,1]. They further defined a *freshness* metric to characterize how up-to-date a local information repository is compared to the web. Douglas et al. analyzed web changes using web access traces that yield distributions of web documents with respect to a variety of metrics [5]. However, because of the access-driven nature of their method, their results may not reflect the less popular documents on the web.

Despite the importance of the two other characteristics of the web change, no serious study has been done previously on these two issues. In this paper we address these two important questions: how much has a typical web document changed during two consecutive crawlings and how clustered are the changes.

We define two measures, a distance measure and a clusteredness measure, for analyzing and quantifying web document change. The distance measure characterizes the size of the change between two versions of a web document and the clusteredness measure characterizes how these changes are spread out within a web document.

The rest of the paper is organized as follows: In the next section, we have a general discussion on the types of changes between two samples of the web. In Section 3 we describe the data set that we used in our distribution analysis. In Section 4 and Section 5 we define the two measures for web document change and present our data analysis results with respect to these two measures. We discuss the implications of our data analysis on web information systems in Section 6 and conclude in Section 7

2 Types of Web Document Changes

In this section, we describe the types of changes that occur between two consecutive crawlings of the web. The set of web documents obtained from one crawling at a particular time is called a*sample* of the web and the time between two consecutive samples is called the *sampling interval.* We define a web document to be the sequence of words contained in a HTML file that has been stripped of scripting code and HTML syntax. Each HTML file or each document is associated with an URL and is assigned a unique document ID (*doc_id*). Each word occurrence within a document encodes the information $\langle word\_id, doc\_id, loc\_id\rangle$, which is also known as a *posting*, where *word_id* denotes the the unique ID identifying each word in the (English) vocabulary and *loc_id* denotes the position of that word occurrence in the document. Since each posting encodes all the information in a word occurrence on the web, the entire web can be encoded as a set of postings and a web information system can be viewed as a system maintaining the set of all postings (or a subset of it). For example, a web index is a web information system that stores this set of postings ($\langle word\_id, doc\_id, loc\_id \rangle$) sorted by *word_id*.

If we consider each sample as a set of documents, then between two consecutive samples S_n and S_{n+1}, any document can only belong to one of the following partitions (see Figure 1 top diagram),

$$\begin{cases} S_n \cap S_{n+1} & \text{common documents} \\ S_n - (S_n \cap S_{n+1}) & \text{deleted documents} \\ S_{n+1} - (S_n \cap S_{n+1}) & \text{inserted documents.} \end{cases} \tag{1}$$

In the Venn diagram at the top of Figure 1, a point represents a document, so

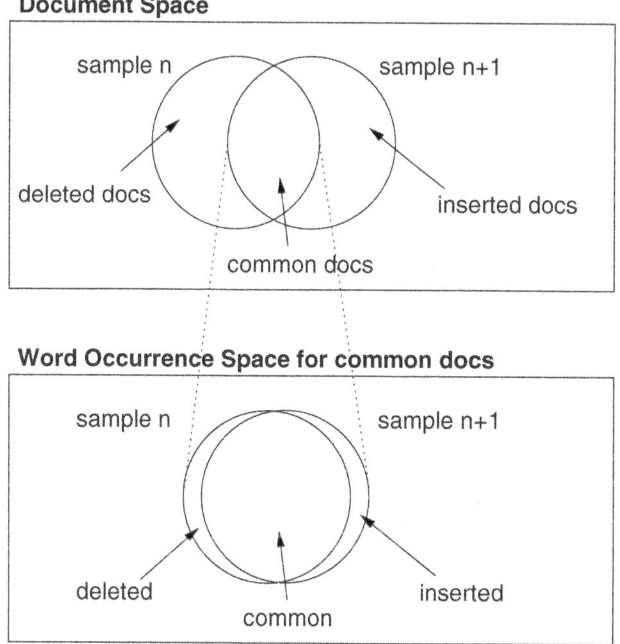

Fig. 1. Types of changes at the document collection level and the word occurrence collection level.

each circle represents a set of documents. Deleted documents are old documents that do not exist in the new sample anymore and they need to be removed from the system. Inserted documents are new documents that appears in the new sample only and they need to be inserted into the system. Common documents are the documents that are common between the two consecutive crawlings of the web. Some of these common documents might be unchanged and some of it might contain changes.

In this paper we are primarily concerned with the changes in the common documents. We have three reasons for this emphasis. The first is that techniques for inserting documents into information systems have already been well studied by the text retrieval community. Secondly, the common documents represents at least 50% of the documents currently maintained by the web information system at each update. Finally, of these common documents, most of the changes at each update are small as we will see in Section 4. If we consider the set of common documents as a collection of word occurrences (defined next), then between two consecutive samples, the overlap is significantly large.

We can further examine the set of common documents at the granularity of a word occurrence. A word occurrence corresponds loosely to a posting (a $\langle word\_id, doc\_id, loc\_id \rangle$ tuple) without the limitation of a numeric location ID; that is, it is shift invariant in some sense. In the Venn diagram at the bottom of Figure 1, each point represents a word occurrence. Each circle represents the set of word occurrences corresponding to the set of common documents of a particular sample. If we consider each circle as a sequence of word occurrences, the set of common word occurrences loosely corresponds to the longest common subsequence of the two sequences. Since most web information systems keep track of word occurrences, the number of common word occurrences gives an upper bound on the number of postings in the system that can remain unchanged upon an update.

3 Data Set Description

For our analysis we recursively crawled web documents starting from several seed URLs up to a maximum recursion depth of five levels. The list of seed URLs consists of www.cnn.com, www.ebay.com, www.yahoo.com, espn.go.com, and www.duke.edu. Our sampling interval is 12 hours (at 7 am and 7 pm EST). We collected data over a period of one month. For the data that we present here, we use 2 samples that are representative of the general update behavior.

Each document is preprocessed into a canonical form by stripping off any HTML tags and scripting code. Each character is transformed to its uppercase and extra white spaces are stripped.

Other characteristics of our data are summarized in Table 1. Note that although we perform our analysis over many samples of the web over many days, we only present the data analysis for a set of representative data since this is a clearer presentation than using 3D plots.

Table 1. Summary of the representative data set used for data analysis.

No. of docs at time n	6042
No. of docs at time $n+1$	6248
No. of deleted docs	2788
No. of inserted docs	2994
No. of common docs	3254
No. of common docs unchanged	1940

4 Degree of Change

We quantify the degree of the change between two versions of a document with a distance measure. We define our distance measure based on the idea of *edit distance*. Edit distance is usually defined as the minimum number of *edit operations* (insertions or deletions) required to transform one sequence to another. A document can be considered as a sequence of words or *word_id*'s and hence the ideas of edit distance map naturally to document distance as well. We define δ to be the minimal number of words deleted or inserted to transform one document to another. Our distance measure for two documents A and B can then be defined as

$$d(A, B) = \frac{\delta}{m+n}, \tag{2}$$

where m and n are the size (in words) of document A and document B respectively. Clearly, δ can be computed once the longest common subsequence of the two documents is known. If the two documents are the same, δ will be zero and the distance measure will be zero. If the two documents are completely different, δ will be equal to $m+n$ (since m old words need to be deleted and n new words need to be inserted) and the distance measure will be one.

We use this distance measure to obtain the distribution of the common documents that have changed with respect to the magnitude of change (Figure 2). The data points in our plots are computed by obtaining the distance of every old and new document pair and classifying them into bins where each bin corresponds to an interval of 0.5%. Each data point therefore corresponds to the number of documents in a particular bin. From the probability distribution plot with respect to our distance measure (Figure 2), we observe that most documents fall into the bins between distance 0 % and 20 %. From the corresponding cumulative distribution plot, we see that more than 90% of the documents have changes smaller than a distance of 20%. Moreover this behavior seems consistent across updates, i.e., over time, and it shows that the set of common word occurrences is very big and a large portion of the information maintained by the web information system can remain unchanged at an update.

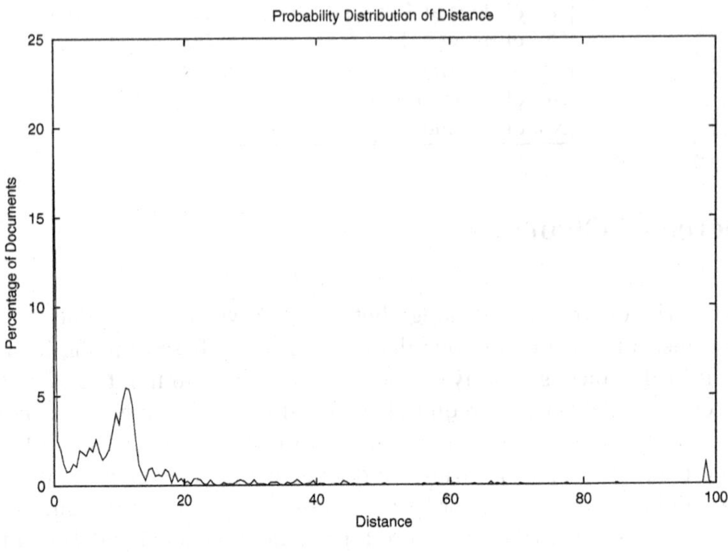

(a) Probability Distribution

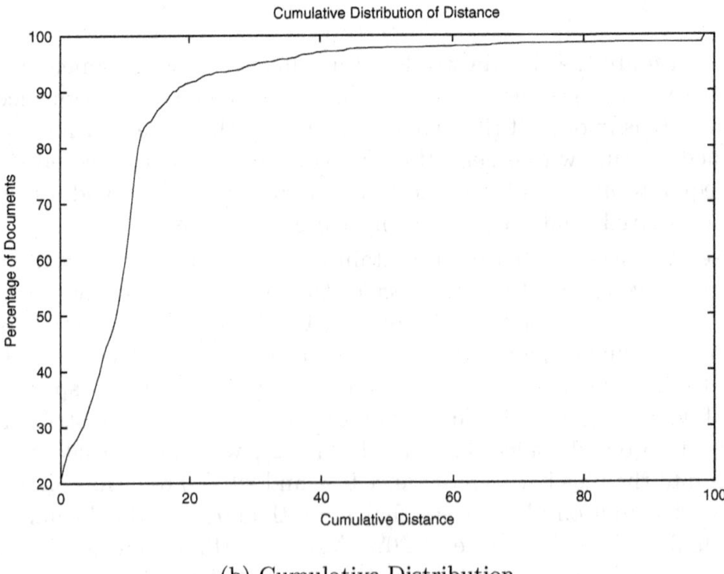

(b) Cumulative Distribution

Fig. 2. Distribution of documents with respect to our distance measure.

5 Clusteredness of Change

Besides the magnitude of change we are also interested in how clustered the changes are. For example, the insertion of a paragraph of 10 words to the beginning of a document is surely different from inserting the same 10 words at 10 different random and non-contiguous locations in the document. Why should this be of concern? Suppose the document is stored as an array of *word_ids*. The first type of change requires shifting all the words after the insertion point once by 10 cells. The latter type of change at random locations requires 10 separate shift operations. A similar argument can be constructed for linked-list or tree representation of the document; hence how localized a change is does affect the amount of computations required.

How do we measure clusteredness? One possibility is to use a clustering algorithm to find the position (the center) of each cluster and calculate the distance of each change from the nearest cluster (similar to the idea of statistical variance); however, this means that our clusteredness measure will be dependent on how good the clustering algorithm is and that is not desirable. Instead we resort to a simpler but effective method. We choose a block size and partition the document into blocks according to the size we have chosen. The fraction of the blocks affected by changes can therefore be used as a measure of how clustered the change is. The clusteredness of the changes required to transform document A to document B is

$$c(A, B, b) = 1 - \frac{\Delta}{\lceil m/b \rceil}, \tag{3}$$

where Δ is the number of blocks affected by the change, m is the size of the old document in words and b is the block size in words. If there are no changes, Δ will be zero and the clusteredness will measure one. If all the changes are clustered into one block and assuming that the block size b is sufficiently small, the clusteredness will be close to one. If the changes are distributed over all the blocks, Δ will be equal to $\lceil m/b \rceil$ and clusteredness will be zero.

The number of blocks affected by the change, Δ, can be determined in practice by first finding the (minimal) edit transcript between the old and the new document. An edit transcript is the sequence of edit operations required to transform the old document to the new document. In UNIX, the output of the `diff` command is a representation of the minimal edit transcript between two files. Using the edit transcript we can determine where the edit operations occur and count the number of blocks affected by the edit operations.

The block size b must be chosen such that it is much smaller than the document size m for this measure to be meaningful. Another possibility is to partition the document using HTML tags. One such tag is the paragraph tag `<p>`.

We study the distribution of the documents using this clusteredness measure. Since the clusteredness measure is only meaningful for documents that have changed, we perform our data analysis only on those documents. Two partitioning schemes are used: fixed size blocks (Figure 3) and `<p>`-tag blocks (Figure 4). From the probability distribution plot with respect to our clusteredness measure

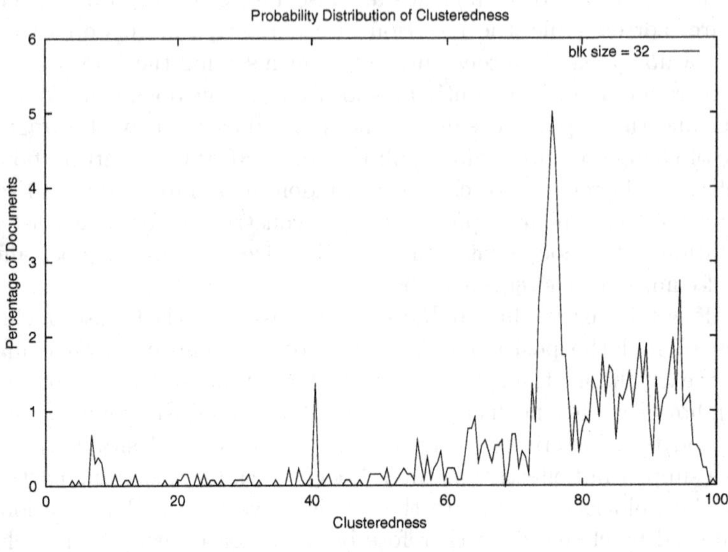

(a) Probability Distribution

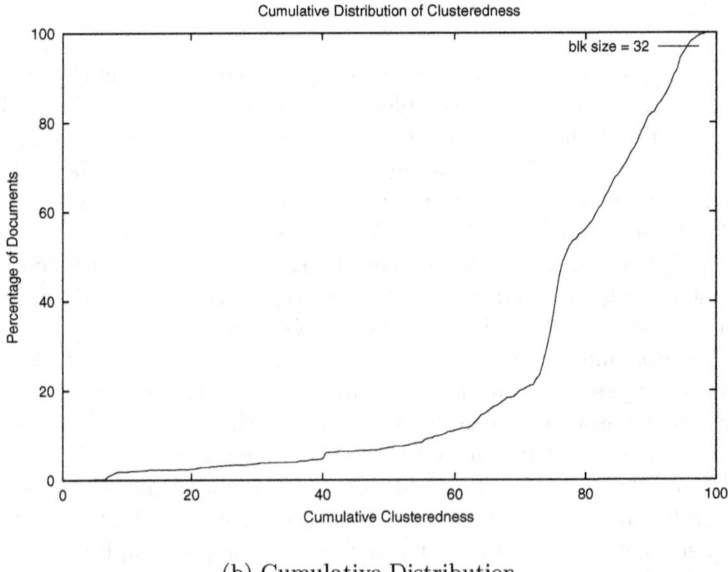

(b) Cumulative Distribution

Fig. 3. Distribution of documents with respect to clusteredness $c(A, B, 32)$.

$c(A, B, 32)$ (Figure 3), we observe that most document have changes that are more than 50% clustered, that is the changes affect less than half of the blocks. From the corresponding cumulative distribution plot, we see that only about 20% of the documents have changes that are less than 70% clustered. Using HTML paragraph tags, we observe in the probability distribution plot with respect to the clusteredness measure $c(A, B,$ <p>-tag) (Figure 4) that many document have changes that are more than 50 % clustered; however significant spikes occur consistently at the 0-0.5 % clusteredness bin. This is because some documents do not use the <p>-tag at all. For such documents there is only one block in total and any changes must occur in that block and hence $c(A, B,$ <p>-tag) is zero. This is consistent with the previous $c(A, B, 32)$-distribution plot (Figure 3) where no documents have changes distributed to every block. Other observable artifacts are the spikes at the 50% and 66% clusteredness marks. These are mostly due to the documents with only two to three paragraphs in total.

We observe that these plots show a very skewed distribution of documents across the clusteredness measure.

6 Implications for Web Information Systems

We show in Section 4 and Section 5 that the most changes in web documents are small and clustered. These skewed distributions expose an opportunity to improve the performance of web information systems by optimizing for the frequent case. In this section, we describe how we can exploit such distributions with a simple example. The example is chosen to illustrate the principles involved rather than for realism. For a non-trivial example, we refer the reader to our upcoming paper which will show how these techniques can be applied to updating web indexes.

Suppose we want to cache the entire web on a local file system. Our clusteredness results suggest that if each document is stored as several files each of size 32 words, then every update touches only a relatively small number of files. This means that we can leave a large portion of files untouched.

Using the same web caching example, suppose we would like to count the number of words that need to be touched during an update. A word occurrence is said to be *touched* if it is deleted or inserted or shifted in position. Further suppose that within a block/file that needs to be modified, only the words occurring after the starting position of the first change in the block need to be touched (since words occurring before the first change in the block remains unchanged). How does block/file size affect the number of words that need to be touched?

We measured the minimum number of words touched for different block sizes (using the same data set as the previous data analysis) and verified that as the block size gets smaller the number of edit operations decreases. It should be clear that if the block size is one word, this measure becomes the distance measure we defined in Section 4. Figure 5 shows the distribution plots of the documents with respect to the number of words touched normalized by the size of the old and the new document in number of words.

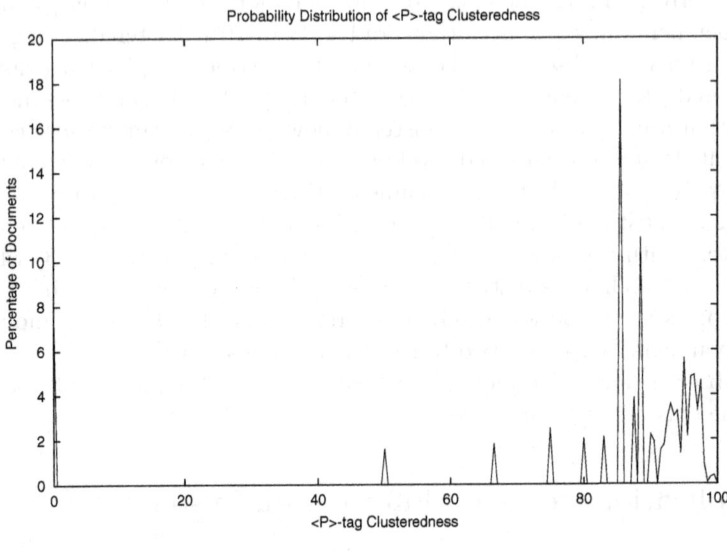

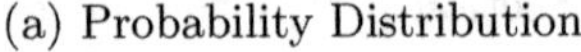
(a) Probability Distribution

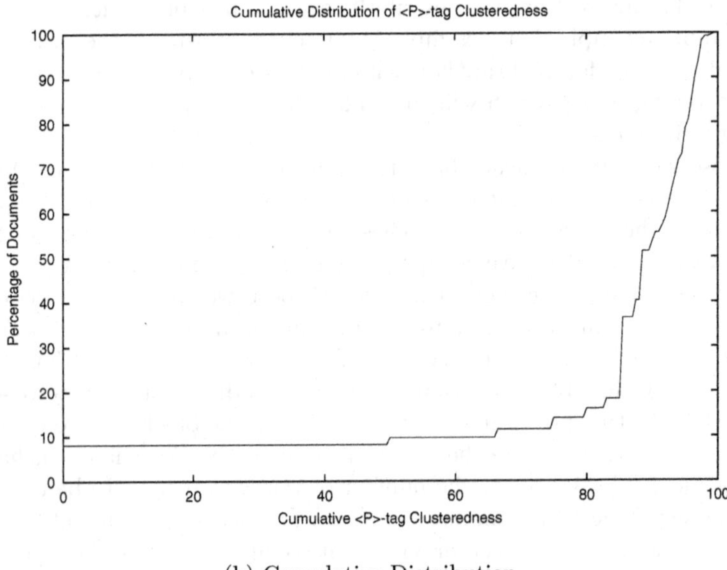

(b) Cumulative Distribution

Fig. 4. Distribution of documents with respect to clusteredness $c(A, B,$ <p>-tag).

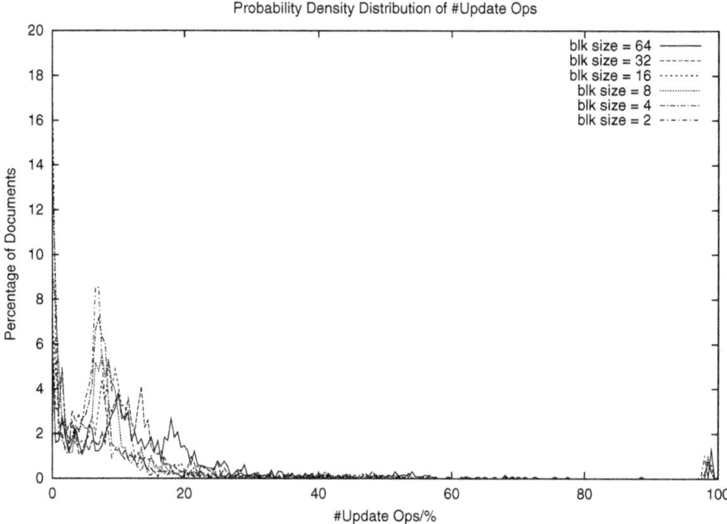

(a) Probability Distribution

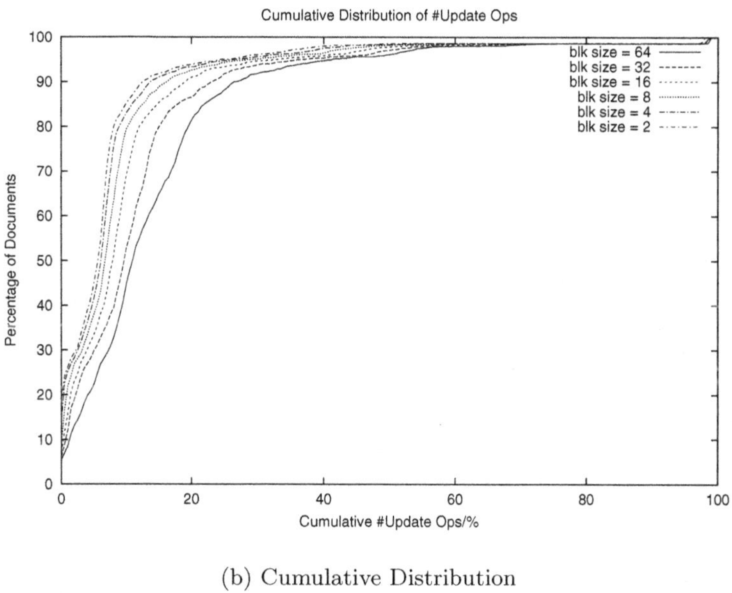

(b) Cumulative Distribution

Fig. 5. Distribution of documents with respect to the number of edit operations for different block sizes.

Note that in our caching example, there is a trade-off between the block/file size (hence number of files) and the size of the tables maintained by the file system. Extremely small block sizes should be avoided, because as block size gets smaller, the size of each of the tables maintained by the file system grows larger.

In practice, it is possible to determine the optimal block size by first finding the average cost of a file system table lookup relative to touching a word and then determining the block size that gives the optimal distribution for the two types of operation.

7 Conclusion

The dynamic nature of web data poses an challenging problem to web information systems on its efficient maintenance. In this paper we defined two measures, a distance measure and a clusteredness measure, to quantify some aspects of the dynamism of the web data so that we can have a basis on efficient maintenance of web information systems. Our analysis of the web document changes using these two measures have shown that we document changes are generally small and clustered, suggesting that update methods based on an incremental approach can be much more efficient compared with naive methods that need to rescan all the web data.

References

1. B. Brewington and G. Cybenko. How dynamic is the web? In *Proceedings of the Ninth International World Wide Web Conference*, May 2000.
2. B. Brewington and G. Cybenko. Keeping up with the changing web. *IEEE Computer*, 33(5):52–58, May 2000.
3. J. Cho and H. Garcia-Molina. Estimating frequency of change. *Submitted for publication*, 2000.
4. J. Cho and H. Garcia-Molina. The evolution of the web and implications for an incremental crawler. *26th International Conference on Very Large Data Bases*, September 2000.
5. F. Douglis, A. Feldmann, B. Krishnamurthy, and J. Mogul. Rate of change and other metrics: A live study of the world wide web. *Proceedings of the USENIX Symposium on Internet and Systems*, 1997.
6. S. Lawrence and C. L. Giles. Accessibility of information on the web. *Nature*, 400:107–109, 1999.
7. A. Tomasic, H. Garcia-Molina, and K. Shoens. Incremental updates of inverted lists for text document retrieval. *Proceedings of 1994 ACM International Conference of Management of Data (SIGMOD)*, pages 289–300, May 1994.

Identification of Syntactically Similar DTD Elements for Schema Matching

Hong Su[1], Sriram Padmanabhan[2], and Ming-Ling Lo[2]

[1] Computer Science Department, Worcester Polytechnic Institute, Worcester, MA, USA,
[2] IBM T.J.Watson Research Center, Hawthorne, NY, USA
suhong@cs.wpi.edu, {srp, mllo}@us.ibm.com

Abstract. XML Document Type Definition (DTD) enforces the structure of XML documents. XML applications such as data translation, schema integration, and wrapper generation require DTD schema matching as a core procedure. While schema matching usually relies on a human arbiter, we are aiming at an automated system that can give the arbiter a starting point for designing a matching that can best meet the requirements of the given application. We present an approach that identifies the syntactically similar DTD elements that can be potential matching components. We first describe *DTD element graph*, a data model for the DTD elements. We then define the distance between two *DTD element graphs*. We introduce the concept of *syntactically equivalent* and *syntactically similar* graphs. Then, we describe the algorithm to detect both schema equivalent and similar DTD elements. We have implemented the matching detection algorithm and several heuristics which improve performance. Our experimental results show reasonable precision of the algorithm in terms of recognition of correct matches.

1 Introduction

Database integration or global schema design [CMPQ+97][IFF+99] is a process that takes several schemas and integrates them into a view that provides a uniform interface for all the schemas. A crucial step for achieving a conceptually clean schema is to discover properties that hold among components in different schemas and then create semantic relationships between the schemas - a process known as *schema matching* [MIR93]. As XML emerges as an increasingly popular format for representation and exchange of data especially for e-commerce, it will lead to significant web data sharing and data integration. While the time required for constructing semantic matching may be justified for traditional data warehousing scenarios which are relatively static, it is unacceptable for e-commerce, where the information sources change frequently and hence applications must evolve much more quickly. Therefore, though the semantic matching will ultimately rely on a human arbiter, an automated system that can give an engineer a starting point for designing a "best" match, appears to be extremely valuable.

X.S. Wang, G. Yu, and H. Lu (Eds.): WAIM 2001, LNCS 2118, pp. 145–159, 2001.

For example, suppose there are two online shopping companies using XML describing the ordering information. While both have the concept of *patron* (*customer* or *client*) in their design model, they may end up with two syntactically different definitions describing *patron* as below:

Example 1.

```
<!Element customer (address, ssn, phone+)> <!Element client (location, ssn?, phone, phone?)>
<!Attribute customer id ID REQUIRED>       <!Attribute client id ID REQUIRED>
<!Element address (state, city, street)>   <!Element location (street, city, state)>
<!Element ssn #PCDATA>                     <!Element ssn #PCDATA>
<!Element phone #PCDATA>                   <!Element phone #PCDATA>
          DTD1                                       DTD2
```

Suppose later on, one company acquires the other, and therefore wants to build a database system to manage all the data. A naive approach is to simply union the schemas associated with each DTD. For example, to generate relation schema, if we adopt an approach which is a slight variance of the *Inline* approach proposed in [SHT+99], a relational schema generated for DTD1 looks like:

```
DTD1.customer (rowid, id, address.state, address.city, address.street, ssn)
DTD1.phone (customer_rowid, value)
```

Similarly, a relational schema generated for DTD2 looks like:

```
DTD2.client(rowid, id, location.street, location.city, location.state, ssn,
phone, phone)
```

Obviously a simple combination of the two disjoint schemas will result in: (1) conceptually unclean schemas which do not disclose any semantic relationship between the components in two DTDs; (2) bad scalability with the explosion of tables' number while more and more DTDs are integrated; and (3) unnecessary complexity of applications. For example, a statistical application for patrons' information has to collect data from distributed tables.

We need a mechanism to discover those semantically equivalent or similar components (we say these components *match*) to help generate an integrated conceptually clean schema. In this paper, we present a mechanism for detecting possible matches between components across DTDs. It consists of four phases:

1. DTDs are modeled as *DTD graphs* and a series of simplification transformations are performed to normalize the DTDs.
2. Initial matches are set up based on a series of matching criteria.
3. The initial matches are propagated by computing the matching likelihood of other component pairs based on their structural properties.
4. A "best" matching plan is selected from multiple matching plans based on the overall matching likelihood of the component pairs.

2 DTD Data Model

2.1 Simplification Transformation on DTD

In a DTD [W3C98], elements can in turn have sub-elements, attributes, or be empty. The structure of sub-elements is defined via a *content-model* of operators applied to its content particles. Content particles can be grouped as sequences (a,b) or as choices $(a|b)$. For every content particle, the content-model can specify its occurrence in its parent content particle using regular expression operators $(?, *, +)$. Attributes can be optional (*#IMPLIED*) or mandatory (*#REQUIRED*). Optionally, attributes can have a default or a constant value (*#FIXED*).

In a DTD, the declaration of sub-elements in an element's content model is ordered. The emphasis on order in XML comes from its origin as a document markup language. However applications that use XML for data exchange rather than a document are likely to ignore order. Hence in our discussion, order will not be our first concern.

The expressive power of regular expressions of DTD syntax can result in very complicated DTDs. We restrict our discussion to a simpler form of DTD. We perform similar transformations as those in [SHT+99] [DFS99] to simplify the DTDs into a *reduced DTD* in which every regular expression is a concatenation of expressions of the form p, or $p+$ where p is an element. The simplification transformations include:

1. Blurring non-null constraint: both p and p^+ has a not-null constraint, i.e., it is not allowed that p does not appear while this is allowed by $p?$ and p^*. We blur this difference by treating p and $p?$, p^+ and p^* the same.

Transformation example 1

$p? \rightarrow p$ $\qquad\qquad$ $p^* \rightarrow p^+$

2. Flattening: the transformation converts a group into a flat representation.

Transformation example 2

$(p|p') \rightarrow p, p'$ $\qquad$ $(p, p') \rightarrow p, p'$ $\qquad$ $(p, p')? \rightarrow p, p'$
$(p, p')^* \rightarrow p^+, p'^+$ $\qquad$ $(p, p')^+ \rightarrow p^+, p'^+$

3. Merging: for those sub-elements having the same name in a content model, merge all of them into a single one and record its occurrence. We can specify a constant SET_THR as a set threshold. Suppose n is the number of occurrence of a sub-element, if n is bounded and not larger than SET_THR, we denote them by p^n; if n is bounded but larger than SET_THR, we denote them by p^+; if n is not bounded, e.g., if there is a content model (p^+, p^*), we denote them by p^+. The set threshold can be adjusted according to the user's design habit.

For example, if it is known that the DTD designer tends to model a sequence of same sub-elements using a quantifier "*" or "+" only when the sub-element may appear more than three times, then we can set the SET_THR to 3.

Transformation example 3

$p, p', ..., p, ... \rightarrow p^2, p', ...$ (suppose $SET\_THR > 2$) $p, p', ..., p^+, ... \rightarrow p^+, p', ...$

This simplified DTD resulted from the transformation loses some information about:

1. Non-null constraint.

2. Grouping information. Grouping implies semantic association within the group's members. However, the flattening transformation may not be applied very frequently in that in a common DTD design, it is quite unusual for a DTD designer to generate content models with deeply nested structures [Sah00]. This is because the content model sometimes can be represented in a rather flat form while capturing the same semantic information conveyed in groups. For example, in Example 2, we can see a nested content model in DTD1 can be presented as a set of flat content models in DTD3 to avoid the loss of semantic information by flattening DTD1 to DTD2.

Example 2.

```
DTD1: <!ELEMENT paper ((title, paragraph*),(picture, caption?))>
DTD2: <!ELEMENT paper (title, paragraph*, picture, caption?)>
DTD3: <!ELEMENT paper (text, figure)>
      <!ELEMENT text (title, paragraph*)>
      <!ELEMENT figure (picture, caption)>
```

3. Relative orders of the elements. When we merge same sub-elements, it is possible that we loss the semantic information implied by the relative order between the to-be-merged sub-elements and their neighbors. For example, in Example 3, in DTD1, the surrounding sub-elements imply that the first *title* is the title of the paper while the second *title* is the title of the paper's references. However similar to Example 2, the DTD designer may tend to model it in a more clean way as shown in DTD3.

Example 3.

```
DTD1: <!ELEMENT paper (title, author, referenceid, title, author)>
DTD2: <!ELEMENT paper (title^2, author^2, referenceid)>
DTD3: <!ELEMENT paper (title, author, reference)>
      <!ELEMENT reference (referenceid, title, author)>
```

From the above discussion, we can see that if the designer of DTDs is skillful enough to provide some conceptual clean DTDs, the transformation we perform will cause less information loss.

2.2 Data Model of Reduced DTD

We build a DTD data model which is *an unordered directed cyclic graph.* Given a DTD, we represent it by a graph $G = (V, E, l, w)$ where V is a set of vertices, E is a set of edges, l is the labeling function and w is the weight function. In the graph, each vertex has a label $l(v)$ and each edge e is associated with a weight $w(e)$. Each vertex $v \in V$ falls into two categories:

1. Element vertex: each element vertex v represents an element. $l(v) =< N(v) >$ where $N(v)$ is v's name.

2. Attribute vertex: each attribute vertex v represents an attribute. $l(v) = < N(v), T(v), D(v), V(v) >$ where $N(v)$ is v's name, $T(v)$ is v's type, e.g., *CDATA, ID, IDREF, IDREFS, ENUMERATION* etc., $D(v)$ is v's default type, i.e., *#REQUIRED, #IMPLIED, #FIXED, #DEFAULT*, and $V(v)$ is v's default value (if any).

We denote the weight on edge e: $v_i \rightarrow v_j$ by $w(v_i, v_j)$ which indicates how many times v_j occurs in v_i's content model. Edge $e : v_i \rightarrow v_j$ falls into two categories:

1. sub-element inclusion edge: v_i and v_j are both element vertices. v_j is a sub-element of v_i. The weight of edge e is defined as following:

$$w(v_i, v_j) = \begin{cases} 1 & : \; quantifier\ for\ v_j\ in\ v_i\ is\ absence \\ SET\_THR & : \; quantifier\ for\ v_j\ in\ v_i\ is\ \text{"+"} \end{cases}$$

2. attribute attached edge: v_i is an element vertex while v_j is an attribute vertex. v_j is an attribute of v_i. Since when considering element, we do not differentiate between optional ("?") and exactly once (default), uniformly we do not differentiate between a required attribute (i.e., *#REQUIRED, #DEFAULT, #FIXED*) and the attribute which is optional (i.e., *#IMPLIED*). We then have $w(v_i, v_j) = 1$.

Given a DTD graph G and an element vertex e, we denote by $G(e)$ an *element graph* which represents the structure of element e. An element graph $G(e)$ is a subgraph of G that is composed of only vertices and edges that are reachable from e. We assume that in our scenario, all XML documents conforming to a same DTD have the same root element type. Hence rather than matching two DTD graphs G_1 and G_2, we match two element graphs $G_1(r_1)$ and $G_2(r_2)$ where r_1 and r_2 are the root element types of the XML documents conforming to DTD1 and DTD2 respectively. Figure 1 shows the element graphs of *customer* and *client* in Example 1.

2.3 Construction of a Directed Acyclic Graph (DAG)

It is possible that the root element graph is cyclic if there exists recursive element definitions in the DTD. To simplify the manipulation, we convert a cyclic graph to an acyclic graph. The process is composed of two steps:

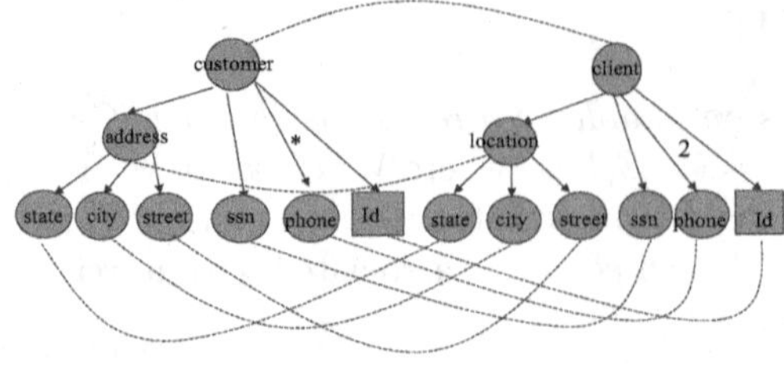

Fig. 1. Element Graphs

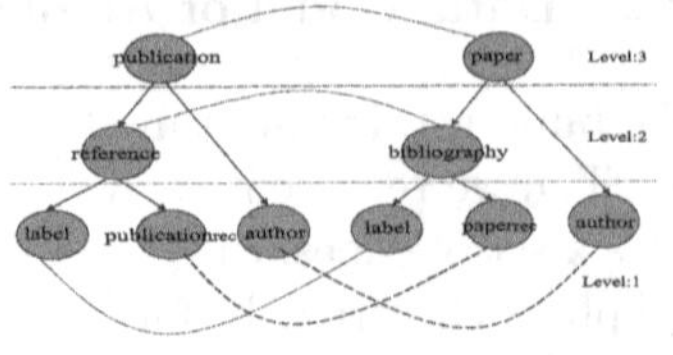

Fig. 2. Element Graphs of Recursive Element

Step A: Detection of recursive elements. Starting from the root, do a depth-first search over the graph. We say vertex u is the *ancestor* of vertex v if u is on a path in the graph from the root r to v. Mark u as a *recursive element vertex* if there exists an edge $v \to u$ and u is an ancestor of v.

Step B: Convert the cyclic graph to an acyclic graph. For each recursive element vertex u, create a new element vertex u_{rec}. We call the new vertex *leaf recursive vertex.* Direct all the edges entering u to u_{rec} instead.

3 Matching Criteria

3.1 Initial Leaf Vertices Matching

Once we have the DTD data model, the problem of finding the matching components in two DTDs is converted to find the matching vertices in two root element graphs. We call two matching vertices a *matching pair.* Intuitively, those vertices that have similar labels and hierarchical structure are promising matching pairs. Hence it is reasonable to match those leaf vertices who have the same labels and same structures (a single vertex). However, for those inner vertices, even if they have the same names, we do not take them as initial matches. This is because that the inner element vertices having the same name in two DTDs may actually have totally different content models.

We do not match the leaf recursive vertices that have the same labels because the leaf recursive vertex actually represents an inner element vertex. In section 4 we will discuss how to process recursive vertices separately. Now we give a formal description of the non-recursive leaf vertices matching.

Matching Criterion 1 *Non-recursive leaf vertices matching: two non-recursive leaf vertices $v \in G(r)$ and $v' \in G(r')$ match if they satisfy one of three following conditions:*
(1) Both v and v' are attribute vertices, $N(v) = N(v')$ and $T(v) = T(v')$.
(2) Both v and v' are element vertices and $N(v) = N(v')$.
(3) v is an element vertex while v' is an attribute vertex of type CDATA and $N(v) = N(v')$.

3.2 Element Graphs' Distance

To evaluate the matching quality of two element vertices, we introduce the notion of *element graphs' distance.* The notations we use in the definitions include: (1) $C(v)$ which indicates the set of children vertices of element v; and (2) $eleLabelMatch(v, v')$ which indicates whether the labels of two element vertices v and v' are equivalent (1 for equivalent, 0 for not equivalent). We then give a set of related definitions.

Definition 1. *Common Part of two matching vertices v and v', denoted as CommonPart(v, v').*
If two vertices v and v' match, a common part v'' denoted by $commonPart(v, v')$ is constructed as following:
(1) If v and v' are matching leaf vertices, construct an element vertex v'' that $N(v'') = N(v)$.
(2) If v and v' are matching inner vertices, construct an element vertex v'' that $N(v'') = N(v)$. For each matching pair (c, c') where $c \in C(v)$, $c' \in C(v')$, add an edge between v'' and $commonPart(c, c')$ with weight of commonWeight(v, v', c, c').

Definition 2. *Common direct children of vertices v and v', denoted as CommonDirect(v, v').*
If for an edge $u \rightarrow v$ with weight w, there exists an edge $u' \rightarrow v'$ with weight w' and v matches v', then we say element u and u' has a common direct child $commonPart(v, v')$ with a common weight of $min(w_1, w_2)$ (we use $min(i, j)$ to represent the smaller one between number i and j) which is denoted as commonWeight(u, u', v, v').

Definition 3. *Element v's graph size, denoted as graphSize(v).*

$$graphSize(v) = \begin{cases} 1 & : \quad C(v) = \Phi \\ \sum_{i=1}^{|C(v)|} w(v, c_i) * graphSize(c_i) + 1, \quad c_i \in C(v) & : \quad C(v) \neq \Phi \end{cases}$$

Definition 4. *Element graphs' distance:*
We use $commonDirect(v, v')$ to denote the set of common direct children of two element vertices v and v', we define the graph distance: $graphDis(v, v')$

$$= 1 - \frac{\sum_{i=1}^{|commonDirect(v,v')|} commonWeight(v,v',c_i,c_i') * graphSize(c_i'') + eleLabelMatch(v,v')}{max(graphSize(v), graphSize(v'))}$$

$$c_i'' \in CommonDirect(v, v')$$

Intuitively the distance between two element graphs represents how many vertices in the two element graphs overlap. This is similar to the graph distance metric based on the maximal common subgraph [BS98]

Example 4. In Figure 1, suppose $SET\_THR = 3$, $graphSize(customer) = graphSize\ (address) + graphSize(ssn) + graphSize(phone) * SET\_THR + graphSize(id) + 1 = 10$. Similarly, we have $graphSize(client) = 9$. The vertices connected by the dashed line at the bottom satisfy non-recursive leaf vertices matching criterion. Elements *address* and *location* match according to the inner matching criterion which will be introduced in section 4. Hence element *customer* and *client* have 4 direct common children. The first one is *address* with weight 1, the second is *ssn* with weight 1, the third is *ssn* with weight $min(SET\_THR, 2) = 2$, and the fourth is *id* with weight 1. Then $graphDis(customer, client) = 1 - (4*1+1*1+1*2+1*1)/max(10, 9) = 0.2$.

4 Detection of Hierarchically Equivalent Elements

In some scenarios, user may have strict requirement that only those components with the same hierarchical structures can be considered as a promising matching pair. Here we give the criterion for such kind of matching:

Matching Criterion 2 *Hierarchically equivalent matching:*
Two element graphs $G(v)$ and $G(v')$ are equal if there exists a bijection function f: $C(v) \rightarrow C(v')$ such that, for each pair of (u, u') where $u \in C(v)$, $u' \in C(v')$ and $u' = f(u)$, it satisfies:

(a) if u is not a leaf vertex, i.e., an inner element vertex, $G(u)$ and $G(u')$ are equal;

(b) if u is a non-recursive leaf vertex, u matches u';

(c) $w(v, u) = w(v', u')$.

We say two elements are hierarchically equivalent *if their element graphs are equal.*

In this section, we describe the algorithm for detecting hierarchically equivalent elements. We first introduce the notions of *vertex level* and *reduced topology structure* to help prune the search space.

4.1 Vertex Level and Reduced Topology Structure

Definition 5. *Level of a vertex v:*
(a) level(v)=1, if vertex v is a leaf vertex;
(b) level(v)=Max(level(c))+1, $c \in C(v)$, if vertex v is not a leaf vertex.

From the definition of hierarchically equivalent matching, we can see each vertex matches one vertex in another element graph and the matches are ancestor-order preserving. For easy comparison of the graph structure, we use a representation called *reduced topology structure* to capture part of the topology structure information. If the reduced topology structures of two elements are not equivalent, the two element definitely do not have same topology structure. Hence comparing the representations first can help prune search space.

The reduced topology structure representation for an element graph is composed of a sequence of representations for each vertex in the element graph. Each vertex in the graph is represented by a pair (l, o) where l and o indicate the level and out-degree of the vertex respectively. We sort the vertices by level first from higher to lower, and then sort the vertices that are on the same level by out-degree from higher to lower. We illustrate this Example 5.

Example 5.

```
<!Element publication (reference?, author)>
<!Element reference (label, publication)>
<!Element author (#PCDATA)>
<!Element label (#PCDATA)>
              DTD1
```

```
<!Element paper (bibliography?, author)>
<!Element bibliography (label, paper)>
<!Element author (#PCDATA)>
<!Element label(#PCDATA)>
              DTD2
```

In DTD1, we have a recursive element *publication*. In DTD2, we have a recursive element *paper*. The element graphs of *publication* and *paper* are shown in Figure 2. Vertex *publication* is represented as (3,2), *reference* is represented as (2,2) and *label*, $publication_{rec}$, *author* are all represented as (1,0). Then the reduced topology of element *publication* is {(3,2) (2,2) (1,0) (1,0), (1,0)}.

4.2 Detection Algorithm

If two elements' content models are hierarchically equivalent, the two element vertices must be on the same level. Hence the basic idea is, starting detection from the lowest level, comparing pairs of vertices on this level, and repeating the detection to next higher level one by one until reaching the highest level.

Definition 6. *Matching plan:*
A matching plan P is a set of matching pairs (v, v') satisfying, for any pair of (v_1, v'_1) and (v_2, v'_2) in P,
(1) $v_1 = v_2$ iff $v'_1 = v'_2$ (one-to-one)
(2) v_1 is an ancestor of v'_1 iff v_2 is an ancestor of v'_2 (ancestor order preserved).

Equality of Two Recursive Element Vertices. Some leaf vertices are recursive leaf vertices. In Section 3, we introduce the matching criterion for non-recursive leaf vertices by comparing their labels, and now we need to decide whether two recursive leaf vertices match. The process to find matching pairs of recursive elements is as below: **Step A: Grouping.** The recursive elements that have the same reduced topology structures are grouped together.
Step B: Choosing matching pair candidates. Within each group, choose any pair of elements (v, v') where $v \in$ DTD1, $v' \in$ DTD2, and both v and v' satisfy the condition that besides the recursive leaf vertex that reflects itself, there is no other recursive leaf vertices in its set of component leaf vertices. All these pairs are the matching pair candidates to be compared in Step C.

Step C: Extracting element graphs. For each matching pair candidate (v, v'), extract the element graphs $G(v)$ and $G(v')$ from the root element graphs. If the recursive elements happen to be the root elements, this step can be skipped.
Step D: Comparing. First, we suppose that v_{rec} matches v'_{rec}, then we apply the strategy of *propagating up matches* starting from the two matching recursive leaf vertices (we will describe the algorithm later). The algorithm will generate a matching plan. If (v, v') appears in the matching plan, we take the assumption as true, i.e., v_{rec} matches v'_{rec} and correspondingly v matches v'. Otherwise, we do not match v and v'.

Propagating up Matches. Once we have matched leaf vertices in two root element graphs $G(r_1)$ and $G(r_2)$, we propagate up the matches. For every matching pair (v, v') where $v \in G(r_1)$, $v' \in G(r_2)$, v and v' are merged, that is, all edges entering v' are moved to enter v, all edges leaving v' are removed and hence v' is not connected to $G(r_2)$. We repeat the matching process until there is no matching pairs that can be generated. To improve the performance of the propagating process, we consider two vertices for a comparison only if (1) there is at least one pair of children of these two vertices that matches and (2) their reduced topology structures are the same.

The algorithm *detection of equivalent non-recursive elements* is as following:

-*Input:*
  two root element graphs: $G(r_1)$, $G(r_2)$
  the level that detection begins from: detectLevel
-*Output:*
  a matching plan of this level $S = \{(a_i, b_i)|(0 \leq i \leq min(|G(r_1)|, min(|G(r_2)|))$

SetOfPairs equiDet(RootEleGraph $G(r_1)$, **RootEleGraph** $G(r_2)$, **int detectLevel)**

1. if *detectLevel* = highest level in $G(r_1)$ or $G(r_2)$
   return Φ;
2. Set *parentSet* $\leftarrow \Phi$;
   for each node n that satisfies:
     (a) n is on the level *detectLevel*
     (b) in-degree of n is larger than 1
   do {
     parentSet $\leftarrow$ the direct parents of n that are on the level *n+1*;
     for each pair (*a*,*b*) that satisfies:
       (a) $\{a,b\} \subseteq$ *parentSet*
       (b) a and b belong to different DTDs
       (c) the pair (*a*,*b*) has not been marked as compared
     do
       if $graphDis(a, b) = 0$ {
         add an edge (*a*,*b*) into the distance graph for the current level *disG(detectLevel)*
         mark this pair as compared.
       }
   }

```
3. int i=0;
   for each combination {(a0i,b0i), (a1i,b1i), ..., (ami, bmi), ...} in disG(detectLevel)
     do {
        i++;
        copy current DTD graph G(r1) and G(r2 to DTD graph G(r1i) and G(r2i);
        merge each pair (aj, bj) in the combination accordingly in G(r1i) and G(r2i);
        add all the pairs (a0i, b0i), (a1i, b1i), ..., (ami, bmi), ... to set mergePairsi;
        mergePairsi <- mergePairsi + equiDet(Gi, detectLevel + 1);
     }
4. choose the mergePairsk which has the maximal size.
   return mergePairsk.
```

Example 6. We differentiate the vertices having the same name in two DTDs by a lower index. For example, the vertex with label "author" in DTD1 is denoted by $author_1$. In Figure 2, element *publication* and *paper* have the same reduced topology structure of {(3,2) (2,2) (1,0) (1,0), (1,0)}. We then make an assumption that the recursive leaf vertices $publication_{rec}$ and $paper_{rec}$ match and apply the algorithm of propagating up matches based on the matching pairs on the first level, i.e., $\{(label_1, label_2), (publication_{rec}, paper_{rec}), (author_1, author_2)\}$. We use a dashed line to connect the leaf matching pairs. Starting from the first matching pair $(label_1, label_2)$, we choose (*reference, bibliography*) for a comparison since they are the parents of $label_1$ and $label_2$ respectively and they are on level 2. We then find they two match. There is no other vertices on level 2, then we propagate the matches to level 3, and finally find *publication* matches *paper*. This is in concordance with the assumption. The assumption is true, i.e., *publication* is equivalent to *paper*.

5 Detection of Hierarchically Similar Elements

For some applications, two components are allowed to match even if their hierarchical structvures are slightly different. Hence we introduce the notion of *hierarchically similar matching.*

Matching Criterion 3 *hierarchically similar matching:*
Given a distance threshold t *($t \leq 0.5$), we say two vertices v and v' are a* hierarchically similar *matching pair if $graphDistance(v, v') \leq t$.*

We can prove a distance threshold t that is less than 0.5 ensures that for a matching pair (v, v'), at least one sub-element of v matches a sub-element of v'. The detail can be found in [SPL01].

Two hierarchically similar elements can be on different levels. Hence for choosing the matching pair candidates, compared to hierarchically equivalent matching, we only keep the condition that they should have at least one pair of matching children but drop the other condition that they must have the same reduced topology structures.

We propagate up the matches in several rounds. In each round, we only consider the parents of those matching pairs which are newly generated in last round. We compare the parents to see whether they satisfy the matching criterion. However, for a matching pair (v, v'), a parent of v may match several parents of v'. Hence at each round, the matching plan is not unique. Different matching plans at this round may lead to different matching plans at next round. We call a matching plan at round k that has not terminated a *partial matching plan at round k*, the newly generated set of matching pairs at round k as the *local matching plan at round k* and the one that has terminated at round k as the *final matching plan at round k.* Hence if a matching process terminates at round k, the final matching plan at round k is the union of partial matching plan at round $k-1$ and local matching plan at round k.

One way to decide among these options is to exhaustively enumerate all possible final matching plans and pick the one that will generate least *total distance.* We define total distance as below:

$$TotalDistance = \sum_{FinalMatchingPlan} GraphDis(v, v') \qquad (v, v') \in FinalMatchingPlan$$

However this will result in a factorial large number of final matching plans. The enumerating algorithm is obviously expensive. Another option is using a greedy algorithm. We define a local distance as below:

$$LocalDistance = \sum_{LocalMatchingPlan} GraphDis(v, v') \qquad (v, v') \in LocalMatchingPlan$$

In each round, we always choose the local matching plan with the least local distance and filter out the other local matching plans. Such an algorithm may not be optimal but gains the time. Due to the space limitation, the algorithm for matching hierarchically similar elements can be found in [SPL01].

6 Implementation and Performance

In order to evaluate the solutions, we have run experiments to investigate the accuracy of our algorithm. We collect DTDs from a DTD repository [Org98]. The DTDs we are using as examples are a *JournalList.dtd* and a *DocBook.dtd* both of which describes publications' information. The reason why we choose these DTDs are: (1) both of the DTDs are practical DTDs; (2) what they most fit as example DTDs is that JournalList.dtd is a DTD loosely based on *DocBook.dtd* [Doc00]. The changes from *DocBook.dtd* is given in the readme document of *JournalList.dtd* which perfectly serves as a guideline for our manual matching; (3) the scale of this DTD is moderate. *JournalList.dtd* has 48 elements and some of the elements describing the formatting information share common attributes defined in an entity. *DocBook.dtd* has 69 elements.

The readme document of *JournalList.dtd* summarizes the changes from *DocBook.dtd*. The kinds of changes include: (1) the content models of some elements have been reduced; (2) some elements contain new sub-elements that are not present in *DocBook.dtd*; and (3) some elements have been made EMPTY.

Let us analyze these kinds of changes to see whether they can be handled by our algorithm. For adding new elements or deleting elements from the content model, it can be handled if the change falls into the range that the threshold allows. But as for the third kind of change that all the content particles in an element's content model are totally moved which results in an EMPTY content model, our algorithm cannot handle that. An element of type EMPTY will be modeled as a leaf vertex in the DTD graph. It will only be matched to other leaf vertices rather than inner vertices. However, since we allow those elements whose hierarchical structures have slight difference that falls below the threshold to match, missing of matches between such kind of components is somewhat offset.

Our algorithm for detecting hierarchically similar elements turns out to generate quite precise recognition of matching components in the two DTDs. We set the distance threshold to 0.2. For 44 matching pairs we can manually set up by referring to the *readme* document, it recognizes 39 pairs. As we have expected, some of the parents of the matching pairs which we have missed are still matched because they have some other matching sub-elements or attributes.

We investigate the performance of our algorithm further by changing the original *JournalList.dtd*. This time we introduce more kinds of changes. We rename the elements or attributes. Figure 3 shows the accuracy rate for detecting different kinds of changes. It shows that renaming the leave elements will have more negative impact on the accuracy for detecting matching components.

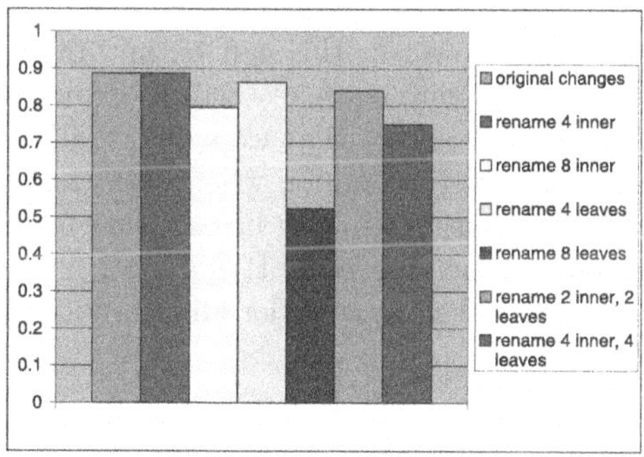

Fig. 3. Accuracy for detecting different kinds of changes

7 Related Work

Schema matching is mostly studied with relational schema. *ARTEMIS* [CA99] performs schema analysis according to the concept of affinity which is based on the similarities of names, structures as well as domain types. However, relational schema is rather flat while the schema of XML is hierarchical. *Transcm* [MZ98a] [MZ98b] is a rule-based approach that simplifies heterogeneous data translation. Rules are provided to the system to guide how to match a component in the source schema with a corresponding component in the target schema. It heavily relies on user interaction. For example, if a component of the source schema matches several components in the target schema, it cannot pick a most possible one but has to ask for user to determine one. [DDL00] is a learner-based approach that focuses on finding all one to one mappings between the leaf nodes (elements) of two schema trees. It does not match source-schema elements at higher level which requires developing learning methods that deal with structures.

Some work [CRGMW96,CGM97] has been done in change detection in hierarchically structured information. They are all dealing with a general tree model which does not incorporate the domain characteristics of schema of XML.

8 Conclusion and Future Work

XML based schema matching is likely to play an important role in e-commerce applications which rely on data integration and dynamic data sharing across distributed services (e.g., Emarkets). We have studied the problem of providing an automated tool for initial schema matching among DTDs. Our experimental evaluation using industry standard DTDs show that these algorithms are effective in identifying element and sub-tree matches. Renaming of elements reduces accuracy of the algorithms. However, this can be improved by using synonym dictionaries or domain-specific ontologies. We will be exploring these approaches as part of future work. Another issue that we would like to address is ambiguity. Ambiguity is likely to be very common when performing schema matching. For example, a one-to-one relationship can be modeled in several ways such as element and sub-element, or element and attribute, or element and an IDREF to another element. We would like to consider all alternatives as we perform the matching algorithm.

References

[BS98] H. Bunke and K. Shearer. A graph distance metric based on the maximal common subgraph. In *Pattern Recognition Letters 19 (1998)*, 1998.

[CA99] S. Castano and V. D. Antonellis. A schema analysis and reconciliation tool environment for heterogeneous databases. In *IDEAS*, 1999.

[CGM97] S. S. Chawathe and H. Garcia-Molina. Meaningful Change Detection in Structured Data. In *SIGMOD*, 1997.

[CMPQ+97] H. Carcia-Molina, Y. Papakonstantinou, D. Quass, A. Rajaraman, Y. Sagiv, J. Ullman, and J. Widom. The TSIMMIS project: Integration of heterogeneous information sources. *Journal of Intelligent Information Systems*, 1997.

[CRGMW96] S. S. Chawathe, A. Rajaraman, H. Garcia-Molina, and J. Widom. Change detection in hierarchically structured information. In *SIGMOD*, 1996.

[DDL00] A. Doan, P. Domingos, and A. Levy. Learning source descriptions for data integration. In *WebDB International Workshop on the Web and Databases*, 2000.

[DFS99] Alin Deutsch, Mary F. Fernandez, and Dan Suciu. Storing semistructured data with STORED. In *SIGMOD*, 1999.

[Doc00] DocBook.org. The docbook dtd. http://www.docbook.org/intro.html, August 2000.

[IFF+99] Z. G. Ives, D. Florescu, M. A. Friedman, A. Y. Levy, and D. S. Weld. An adaptive query execution system for data integration. In *SIGMOD*, 1999.

[MIR93] R. J. Miller, S. Y. E. Ioannidis, and R. Ramakrishnan. The use of information capacity in schema integration and translation. In *VLDB*, 1993.

[MZ98a] T. Milo and S. Zohar. Schema-based data translation. In *WebDB International Workshop on the Web and Databases*, pages 33–41, 1998.

[MZ98b] T. Milo and S. Zohar. Using schema matching to simplify heterogenous data translation. In *SIGMOD*, 1998.

[Org98] XML Org. XML.Org Registry Open for Business. www.xml.org/registry, 1998.

[Sah00] A. Sahuguet. Everything you ever wanted to know about DTDs, but were afraid to ask. In *WebDB*, 2000.

[SHT+99] J. Shanmugasundaram, G. He, K. Tufte, C. Zhang, D. DeWitt, and J. Naughton. Relational databases for querying XML Documents: Limitations and Opportunities. In *VLDB*, pages 302–314, Edinburgh, Scotland, UK, September 1999.

[SPL01] H. Su, S. Padmanabhan, and M. L. Lo. Identification of Syntactically Similar DTD Elements for Schema Matching. In *Technical Report*, January 2001.

[W3C98] W3C. *XML*^{TM} . http://www.w3.org/XML, 1998.

An XML Based Electronic Medical Record Integration System[1]

Hongyan Li[1], Shiwei Tang[1,2], Dongqing Yang[2], and Yi Yu[3]

[1]National Laboratory on Machine Perception, Center for Information Science, Peking University, Beijing, 100871, P. R. China
lihy@cis.pku.edu.cn
[2]Department of Computer Science & Technology, Peking University, Beijing, 100871, P. R. China
{tsw,dqyang}@pku.edu.cn
[3]PeridotHealth Systems Pte Ltd, Singapore 486118
yuyi@peridothealth.com

Abstract. In a domain specific information integration system CareHaven, a top-to-down integration strategy is adopted and XML is used as integration media. The main functional components of CareHaven and the disposal of user queries are fully explained in this paper. In the fulfilling of converting XML based query request to SQLs understood by data sources, we decompose the query request to sub requests that are easier to convert. Each sub request is converted with the aid of the mapping data. And the results of all sub requests is combined into one XML documents conformed to a certain DTD.

1 Introduction

In modern medical information domain, many information resources such as Electronic Medical Record(EMR) and service applications such as sophisticated image analysis tools are distributed in different systems. However, these systems and applications are independent and do not work together seamlessly. CareHaven [1], a medical information integration system based on web applications jointly developed by Center for Information Science of Peking Univ. and PeridotHealth Systems Pte. Ltd. of Singapore, aims to exploit the emerging community healthcare market with unique and comprehensive solutions to link different medical systems for users.

Standards ensure the feasibility of information integration. In medical field, there is an international standard Health-Level7(HL7 [2]) evolved at 1987 and uses for medical information interchange. On the other hand, XML supports an ideal basis for information integration. So, it's very natural to use XML to describe EMR, and the DTD of those XML documents could be established according to HL7. Thus, we use the top-to-down information integration in CareHaven: we have a global DTD that is understood and abided by every data resources.

---

[1] This work was supported by National Key Fundamental Research and Development Plan (973) of China under grant G1999032705.

X.S. Wang, G. Yu, and H. Lu (Eds.): WAIM 2001, LNCS 2118, pp. 160-167, 2001.

2 System Architecture

There are three main building blocks for the architecture of CareHaven [1]: Original Sub-System(OSS), Information Repository Center(IRC) and Information Coordinating Agent(ICA). OSS is the original data source of CareHaven. It may be Hospital Information System which wants to be integrated with other systems. IRC is the access and storage center for the integrated data, which includes XML documents and the global DTD. It's in charge of the management, query and maintenance of those data. Each OSS has its own ICA to communicate with IRC. Integrated information is issued through Web Server, which also provides such services as eCommerce. Users can view them by browsers at client site.

An IRC and all its linked ICAs and OSSs compose an autonomic meta-system which can be extended without any influence to the whole system. Meta-systems are independent from each other and use their IRC to communicate with each other.

Like many bottom-up information integration systems(TSIMMIS [3], Garlic [4], etc.), CareHaven follows the mediator approach for integrating heterogeneous sources. In bottom-up systems, the wrappers export XML views of the information at associated source. While the mediators are responsible for selecting, restructuring, and merging information from those views and for providing the integrated XML views, which contains such information as data organization and schema relationship among sources. Thus, the converting of mediator queries to source queries is much easier. But the global DTD(also a integrated views of the system) in CareHaven is generated from HL7 instead of data sources and represents no useful information of OSS. To have maximum compatibility to data sources and translate the XML based query requests in IRC to queries understood by data sources, a unique method is used. That is, to obtain mapping data from conceptual model of data sources, and decompose XML based query request to sub requests that are easier to convert with the aid of the mapping data. Later, the results of all sub requests is combined into one XML documents conformed to a certain DTD. So, our main components act differently as mediators and wrappers in bottom-up systems. A detail description is given to them in the following.

3 IRC

3.1 Data Organization in IRC

IRC uses an ORDBMS(Oracle8i) to manage information. It can manages and disposes the following data: ① Global DTD, which is generated by DTD Builder according to HL7 at the initialization of the whole system. ② Such relational data as user information. ③ Some integrated information existed as XML documents.

It's unnecessary and impossible to store all integrated information in IRC. For example, the entire information of a patient may be integrated into one EMR. For the summary information(the brief introduction of a patient and the concise description of his every episode in every hospital) in EMR, it is accessed frequently and occupies little memory and disk space and has little chance to change, so it is used as a kind of information index of EMR and stored in IRC in the form of XML documents. For the detail information(such as the detail description of a certain episode in a certain hospital) of EMR, it is converted to XML data only when there is such a real requirement. In this way, the frequency of communication between IRC and OSS is decreased and the query efficiency is improved.

3.2 The Support of Data Queries

To support the data queries is the key function of IRC. The following process is used in fulfilling of data queries.

[Process of queries in IRC]

(1) User issues the query request Q at client site.

(2) Q is sent to Web Server where the user's privilege to issue Q is verified. Then Q is passed to IRC.

(3) Query Transformation module in IRC decides if Q is a legal one firstly. If so, it decomposes Q to Q_1 that can be executed in its own meta-system and Q_2 that should be executed in other meta-system, and sends Q_2 to corresponding IRC.

(4) Query Execution module decomposes Q_1 to Q_{11} that relates to only summary information in IRC and Q_{12} that involves only detail information.

(5) DTD Builder module generates the query DTD required by Q_{12} on the basis of global DTD. Query DTD and Q_{12} are sent to corresponding ICA.

(6) The summary information existed as XML data in IRC is parsed by Parser module, and Q_{11} is executed by Query Execution module.

(7) Query Result Assembling module combines the result of Q_{11}, Q_{12}, and Q_2 to RX in XML document.

(8) RX is passed to XSL Processor module and converted to HTML data.

(9) Those HTML data are returned to Web Server. And the result to Q is displayed to user at client side.

4 ICA

In CareHaven, the integrated information is presented as XML documents in case it is extracted form OSS. It is the fundamental functions of ICA to convert XML based query requests to the queries understood by OSS and convert the result from OSS to XML document conformed to a certain DTD. Since RDBMS and ORDBMS are the main types of medical information management system, CareHaven achieves the conversion of XML requests to the SQL supported by those DBMSs firstly.

When an OSS is added into CareHaven, its administrator uses a human-machine interactive Interface for the generation of Mapping Data for query conversion. And Query Decomposer module in ICA can split the complex query request into such sub requests that can be converted to SQLs easily by Query Transformer module. OSS executes those SQLs and gives the results to Result Wrapper module where the results are transformed and combined to an XML document conformed to a certain DTD. The XML document is sent back to the request sender, surely a certain IRC.

We'll explain those processes in full details in the following.

4.1 Query Request Representation

The query request passed from IRC to ICA is composed of the following:① Query DTD which specifies the DTD related only to a query request. Surely it's a sub DTD of global DTD. The use of query DTD can avoid the traversing of all nodes in global DTD in query conversion. ② Query Request Targets. Multiple targets are allowed in one request. But every target must have an element in query DTD and a corresponding item in request result. ③ Query Request Condition. Every variable in the condition must have a corresponding element in query DTD.

So, the query request is represented according to the global DTD which is the critical basic of our translation framework and must observe the following constraint:

[Constraint1] The construction of global DTD used in the top-to-down information integration system should be of a tree type. Thus, all elements in DTD could be distinct from each other by their own names.

Every element in global DTD is traversed to see if it has a source in an OSS when this OSS is added into CareHaven. The relationship between DTD element and its source is reserved as a kind of mapping data. At the run time, mapping data is used for translation XML based query request to SQL in OSS. If the global DTD is of a tree type, every element has a distinct source or has no source at all in a certain OSS.

4.2 Mapping Data Generation

[Definition1] If an element E in global DTD has a source D in OSS M, we say D is the origin of E in M. Let D=O_M(E). Otherwise, we say E has no origin in M.

The query request conversion in CareHaven is capability-based. The query capabilities of the underlying OSS are fully used to extract the necessary information from it.

[Definition2] Suppose an element E in global DTD has an origin D in OSS M. According to *Constraint1* D is unique. If D can be presented as such a SQL statement: *SELECT A FROM* $T_1,\ldots,T_n(n\geq 1)$ *WHERE W*, we say E has a basic origin D in E. Let OS_M(E) indicate the set of expressions in SELECT clause, OF_M(E) indicate the set of tables(or views) in FROM clause, and OW_M(E) indicate the set of conditions in WHERE clause. OS_M(E), OF_M(E) and OW_M(E) is called to be the original query target, original query range and original query condition of E in M respectively.

All attributes in OS_M(E) and OW_M(E) are attached with the tables which they belong to. Suppose there is an attribute *a* in table *T*, then *a* is represented as *T.a* instead of *a* in OS_M(E) and OW_M(E). Although *T.a* is the equivalent of *a* in semantics, it'll bring more convenience in later query conversion.

A DTD element may have an origin in an OSS. But that origin may be not a basic one. For example, when an element represents composed information, it can hardly have a basic origin in any OSS. To find all DTD elements that have their basic origins is one of the basic functions of Interface.

The mapping between DTD elements and their basic origins in OSS is inadequate to generate the origin of query request. Surely the join relationship among tables(views) in OSS should be considered. Join operation should be taken on the tables arbitrarily. So the acquiring of the join relationship among those tables(views) that contribute to integration information also needs the help of OSS administrator.

Another important work for OSS administrator to do is to define the necessary conversion rules for codifying the domain semantics. For instance, the value of a DATE may be organized as '2000/12/20' in one OSS, while the same value may be represented as '12.20.2000' in another OSS. When translating the query request condition, which always contains some values, the conversion rules are absolutely necessary to perform semantic mapping.

The above two kinds of relationships and rules are collected through Interface module supplied by ICA and converted to Mapping Data. Further, there is a constraint on join relationship among tables(views) in OSS in order to automatically obtain the join condition when those tables(views) are involved.

[Constraint2] Among tables(views) that contribute to the integration information in OSS, there should be only one conditional join path(directly or indirectly) from one table(view) to another. When two tables(views) are involved in offering integration information, the join condition of their join relationship must be abided by unconditionally.

4.3 Query Conversion

In CareHaven, the query request is generated according to global DTD, it is always too complex to convert to SQL easily. We'd better to decompose it before conversion.

Following steps are followed in query translating.

[Step1] Query request R should be decomposed to a set of sub requests according to its condition. For each sub request, it has the same targets as R and is converted into Disjunctive Normal Form. That decomposition loses no semantics since the result of R equals to the union of results of all sub requests. And the constraint dependencies [5] among those sub requests are maintained in this decomposition.

[Definition3] The element E in global DTD is basic origin reachable in OSS M if it satisfies one of the following conditions: ① E has basic origin in M; ② All children of E in global DTD is basic origin reachable in M.

[Definition4] For such query request condition C that contains no operator OR, if every variable X in C has basic origin in M and $OS_M(X)$ has only one element, then C has its basic origin in M.

[Definition5] For such sub request R generated by *Step1*, it is called to have an origin in OSS M if it satisfies both of the following conditions; it is called to have no origin in M if it doesn't satisfy condition ② or all DTD elements corresponding to all targets in R are not basic origin reachable in M; it is called to have partly origin in M if it satisfies condition ② but only some DTD elements corresponding to some query request targets in R are basic origin reachable in M. The conditions are: ① All DTD elements corresponding to all query request targets in R are basic origin reachable in M; ② The query request condition of R has basic origin in M.

[Step2] For each sub request R generated by *Step1* and has partly origin in OSS M, let's take the query request target of R one by one. If the DTD element corresponding to a certain target T is not basic origin reachable in OSS M, then T is removed from R. And a corresponding NULL element will be inserted into the future XML result document of R.

[Step3] For each sub request R generated by *Step1* and *Stpe2* and has origin in OSS M, let's take the query request target of R one by one. If the DTD element corresponding to a certain target T has no basic origin in OSS M, then T is replaced from R with its children in DTD. This process is repeated until every target in R has a basic origin.

Query Decomposer module in ICA fulfills *Step1~3* by the use of query DTD and Mapping Data. The output of Query Decomposer is a set of sub requests. Each one has origin in the OSS and every target of each one has basic origin. Of course, the decomposition information must be sent to Result Wrapper module to assemble the correct result document of the original query request. Sometimes all sub requests generated by *Step1* have no origin in OSS. Result Wrapper would return a NULL result document in that case.

We'll concentrate on the disposal of sub request generated by Query Decomposer in the following. That's just the work of Query Generator module.

In a sub request Q, every target has the same condition as query request condition. It's very natural to convert every target to a SQL under that condition and then compose those SQLs to the SQL related to Q. Above all, we need to translate query request condition to its origin in OSS. But let us define two operators firstly.

[Definition6] $JT_M(TS_1, TS_2)$ and $JC_M(TS_1, TS_2)$ are two operators, where TS_1 and TS_2 are two table sets in OSS M. Search the conditional join path amony the tables(views) in TS_1 and those of TS_2. Whenever a new join path is found, the tables on that path are added to JT_M and the join conditions are added to JC_M. JT_M and JC_M must be Φ if either TS_1 or TS_2 is Φ or no such join path is found.

[Step4] Suppose the query request condition C of a sub request is composed of a set of sub conditions that shouldn't be subdivided. Every sub condition has basic origin in OSS M since C has a basic one. For a sub condition C_i, let X be a variable in C_i, replace X with $OS_M(X)$, judge whether the data type of $OS_M(X)$(may be obtained from the CATALOG of DBMS) is compatible to that of X in C_i. If so, rewrite C_i with the aid of conversion rules in mapping data when necessary(the Algorithm SCM in Reference [5] can be applied in that rewriting). Otherwise an error is raised since the data type of source data is incompatible to that of needed. After the replacement of all variables in C_i and no error raised, C_i evolves to a new condition C_i'. Let F be the union of all original query range of all variables in C_i. We get the original query range of C_i in M, that is F $JT_M(F, F)$, and its original condition C_i' $JC_M(F, F)$. Repeat the same process, all sub conditions of C may be translated to their origins in M.

In this step, when a sub conditions involves the values of attributes of different tables, the join conditions(if any) of those tables must be abided according to *Constraint2*. Let's take a condition, that is *E+F>3*, for example. Suppose *E* is provided by attribute *a* of table *A* while *F* is provided by attribute *b* of table *B* in an OSS. And from *A* to *B* has a join path *A* *C* *B*. Obviously, the values of *A.a* and *B.b* must be obtained under the join condition, that is $A.a_1=C.c_1$ *and* $C.c_2=B.b_2$. So the original query condition of *E+F>3* is $\{A.a+B.b>3, A.a_1=C.c_1$ *and* $C.c_2=B.b_2\}$. And the original query range of it is {*A*, *B*, *C*} instead of {*A*, *B*}.

[Step5] For two conditions C_i and C_j(each one may be a sub condition in *Step4* or a combined condition in *Step5*), let C_{ij} be a combined condition of C_i AND C_j, let

$J=OF_M(C_i)\ \ OF_M(C_j)$. Then $OW_M(C_{ij})=OW_M(C_i)\ \ OW_M(C_j)\ \ JC_M(OF_M(C_i)–J, OF_M(C_j)–J)$ and $OF_M(C_{ij})=OF_M(C_i)\ \ OF_M(C_i)\ \ JT_M(OF_M(C_i)–J, OF_M(C_j)–J)$.

In this step, if C_i and C_j have their effect on the same range of tables, then either C_i contains C_j or C_j contains C_i is met. So either $(OF_M(C_i)–J)$ or $(OF_M(C_j)–J)$ is Φ. That deduces both JC_M and JT_M are Φ. And the original query condition of C_i and C_j should be united directly to that of C_{ij}. Otherwise, the join conditions(if any) of tables in $(OF_M(C_i)–J)$ to tables in $(OF_M(C_j)–J)$ must be abided according to *Constraint2*. We needn't consider join conditions among tables in J because they are disposed already in previous steps.

Step4 and *Step5* are used to get the original query condition $OW_M(C)$ and the original query range $OF_M(C)$ of sub request condition C in the OSS M.

[Step6] For each query request target T_i of a certain sub request Q, it must have a corresponding element D in query DTD. Let C be the query request condition of Q and M be the OSS. Let $J=OF_M(D)\ \ OF_M(C)$. Then $OS_M(T_i)=OS_M(D)$ and $OF_M(T_i)=OF_M(D)\ \ OF_M(C)\ \ JT_M(OF_M(D)–J, OF_M(C)–J)$ and $OW_M(T_i)=OW_M(D)\ \ OW_M(C)\ \ JC_M(OF_M(D)–J, OF_M(C)–J)$.

This step is used to generate the origin of every query request target T_i under the condition of C. If the corresponding DTD element of T involves the same range of tables as C, then either $OF_M(C)$ contains $OF_M(D)$ or $OF_M(D)$ contains $OF_M(C)$ is met, and their original query conditions should be united to that of T. Otherwise, the join conditions(if any) of tables in $(OF_M(D)–J)$ to those of $(OF_M(C)–J)$ must be abided.

After we gain the origins of all query request targets under the query request condition of a sub quest, the following step is taken to combine them into the origin of the original sub request.

[Step7] For two query request targets T_i and T_j (each one may be a target of a certain sub request or a combined target in *Step7*), let T_{ij} be the combined target of T_i and T_j. Let M be the OSS and $J=OF_M(T_i)\ \ OF_M(T_j)$. Here J is not NULL since T_i and T_j have the same query request condition. Then $OS_M(T_{ij})=OS_M(T_i)\ \ OS_M(T_j)$ and $OF_M(T_{ij})=OF_M(T_i)\ \ OF_M(T_j)\ \ JT_M(OF_M(T_i)–J, OF_M(T_j)–J)$ and $OW_M(T_{ij})=OW_M(T_i)\ \ OW_M(T_j)\ \ JC_M(OF_M(T_i)–J, OF_M(T_j)–J)$.

[Step8] Repeat *Step7* till all targets are combined into only one(named T). Now we can get the SQL statement associated with the sub query request. The SELECT clause is composed of all elements in $OS_M(T)$, while FROM clause is composed of all elements in $OF_M(T)$. And WHERE clause is gained by union all elements in $OW_M(T)$ with AND operator.

5 OSS

There are two ways for OSS to provide information: passive way and active way. When OSS provides the result for a SQL converted by ICA, we say it work in passive way. But when the original data in the OSS is changed, OSS should send a message through Messaging module in ICA to IRC for notification in passive way. Lately, IRC will update the corresponding summary information in its database to maintain the consistency of summary information since it is a copy from OSS.

6 Conclusions and Further Work

In order to integrate scattered medical information sources across heterogeneous network environment, a multi-tier system is adopted in CareHaven, where a top-to-down integration strategy is used. CareHaven uses XML as integration media, provides an ICA for each existing OSS. ICA converts the XML based query request to SQL understood in attached OSS, detects any date changes in that OSS and sends it to IRC that manages global DTD as well as some integrated data and deals with the user queries. CareHaven ran successfully on the data supported by hospital information system of National University Hospital and Tan Tock Seng Hospital in Singapore. It may bring an idea to those domain specific information integration systems. There are many works to be done in the future, such as conversion query request to queries in other types of OSS besides RDBMS and ORDBMS, the design of query optimization on the basis of our system features, fulfilling the service integration besides data integration, facilitating flexible but high quality security mechanisms, etc.

References

1. Hongyan L., Shiwei T.: CareHaven: A Web Based Medical Information Multi-Tier System. In: Proc. of the 2000 China Hospital Information Network Conference, Beijing (2000) 55–60
2. HL7 SGML/XML SIG, HL7 Document. Patient Record Architecture, Draft. (1999)
3. Papakonstantinou Y., García-Molina H., Gupta A., Ullman J.: A Query Translation Scheme for Rapid Implementation of Wrappers. In: Tok Wang Ling (ed.): Proc. Of the 4th international Conf. on Deducive and Object-Oriented Databases, Springer-Verlag, Singapore (1995)
4. Roth M. T., Schwarz P. M.: Don't Scrap It, Wrap It! A Wrapper Architecture for Legacy Data Sources. In: Matthias J., Michael J. C., Klaus R. D., Frederick H. L., Pericles L., Manfred A. J. (Eds.): Proceedings of 23rd International Conference on VLDB, Morgan Kaufmann, Athens, (1997) 266-275
5. Chen-Chuan K. Chang, Hector Garcia-Molina.: Mind Your Vocabulary: Query Mapping Across Heterogeneous Information Sources. In: Alex D., Christos F., and Shahram G. (eds): Proc. of the 1999 ACM SIGMOD International Conference on Management of Data. Association for Computing Machinery, Pennsylvania, (1999) 335-346

Enhancing XML Data Processing in Relational System with Indices*

Yuqi Liang, Aoying Zhou, Shihui Zheng, Long Zhang, and Wenyun Ji

Computer Science Department, Fudan University
200433,Shanghai, China
{yqliang, ayzhou, shzheng0, lzhang, wyji}@fudan.edu.cn

Abstract. Using relational database to query XML documents is becoming a common and viable practice. To meet the request of retrieving XML data on Web, which are usually semi-structured or unstructured, the current database system need to be enhanced with the capabilities of dealing with path expressions and searching for information in text. In this paper, various index mechanisms, which can enhance the query engine of RDBMS with the capabilities of evaluating path expressions and supporting keywords search, are discussed. And some simple experiments are carried out to show the effectiveness of those indices.

1 Introduction

Recently, using database to manage XML documents is becoming a common practice. A number of solutions to store and query XML data in relational databases have been proposed [2,4,8]. However, most of XML documents on Web are semi-structured or unstructured. On one hand, XML data are usually modeled as directed graph and XML query navigates the nested structures of XML by path expressions. On the other hand, in the situations that XML data are nearly unstructured or their structures are unknown, keyword search seems to be a more suitable way to locate the information in which user is interesting. To meet the request of retrieving XML data on web, the current database system need to be enhanced with the capabilities of dealing with path expressions and searching for information in text. For those purpose, various index mechanisms, which can enhance the query engine of RDBMS with the capabilities of evaluating path expressions and supporting keywords search, are presented in this paper. They are extended join index, reference index, path index and full-text index. All those indices are implemented by way of relational tables. And some experiments are carried out to examine the effectiveness of those indices.

The rest of the paper is organized as follows. Section 2 gives some base techniques of storing XML document in RDBMS. Section 3 presents the index techniques. The experiment results are presented in Section 4. Finally, Section 5 briefly discusses related work and concludes the paper.

* This work was supported by National Natural Science Foundation of China and 973 Foundation of China.

X.S. Wang, G. Yu, and H. Lu (Eds.): WAIM 2001, LNCS 2118, pp. 168-175, 2001.

2 Preliminaries

In this section, we will give some base techniques of storing XML data with RDBMS.

2.1 Storing XML Documents in Relational System

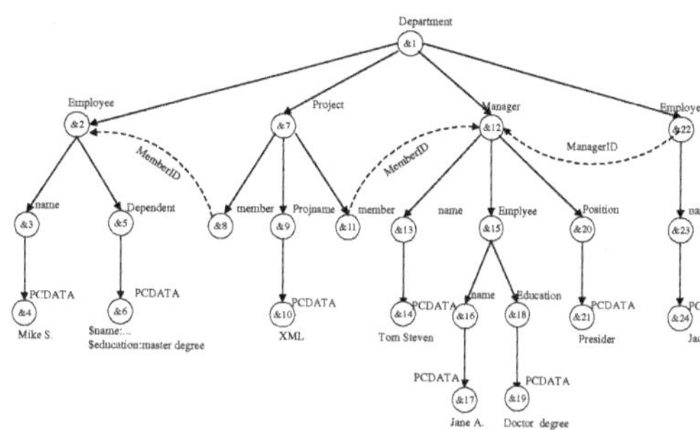

Fig. 2. A data graph

In discussion, we take a way similar to the SHARED mapping method in [8] to map XML documents into relational data. At first, the DTD of an XML document is simplified as a DTD graph. In the DTD graph, root nodes and nodes which are directed by more than one nodes or by a '*' node are mapped as relational schemas, other nodes are inlined into the relations corresponding to their nearest ancestor. An XML document can be represented by a directed graph, named as *data graph.* The data graph is evolved from the DOM tree after parsing that XML document. Every node has a unique object identifier. In addition, the reference between an IDREF and an ID attribute is specified by a dashed line, directed from the node having IDREF attribute to the element node that it refers to. According to the generated schemas, XML documents conforming to the DTD are mapped and stored as relation tables in some relational database system. For example, Figure 1 shows a DTD about the information of a department. Element *department, manager, employee, project, dependent* and *name* will be mapped as separate relational schemas. Element *education, projname* will be inlined into the relation *employee* and *project* respectively. Note every relational table has two additional columns: *ID* and *ParentID.* The column *ID* is maintained by the RDBMS as the primary key of the schema corresponding to the object identifier in *data graph* and the column *ParentID* is maintained as the foreign key referring to the key of the relation schema generated by its parent node in the DTD graph. For example, relation *project* has the schema as: Projcet(ID,Projname,ParentID). Figure 2 gives an example data graph satisfies the DTD in Figure 1.

```
<!ELEMENT department(manager*,employee*,project*)>
<!ELEMENT manager(employee*,name,position)>
<!ATTLIST manager ID ID #REQUIRED>
<!ELEMENT employee(name,education?,dependent*)>
<!ATTLIST employee ID ID #REQUIRED ManagerID IDREF
#IMPLIED>
<!ELEMENT project (member*,projname)>
<!ATTLIST member memberID IDREF #IMPLIED>
```

Fig. 1. An Example DTD

2.2 Path Expression Query and Query Conversion

The primary characteristic of XML query language is that it supports *General Path Expression* (GPE), which has the formation as $g_1.g_2.\ldots.g_n$. Here, g_i is a regular expression. The path expression composed of only elements is called *Single Path Expression* (SPE). Moreover, we use a subset of Lorel[1] as query language for presentation in this paper. An example of Lorel query is following:

```
Q1:  Select department.manager.employee
      Where department.manager.name ="Tom Steven"
```

Q1 selects the employees for manager *Tom Steven* in a department. Our query language has eliminated variables in Lorel by substituting each variable with the path expression, to which it is bound. Generally, in RDBMD, GPE expression is evaluated in two steps. First exploit DTD graph and the statistical information of XML data to eliminate regular operators in the GPE expression, and then convert it to a group of SPE expression. Next rewrite each query with only SPE expression into SQL statement, where each SPE expression is evaluated by a sequence of joins of the relation that the path involves.

3 Index Technique

In this section, we describe some index techniques implemented to enhance the query engine with the capabilities of evaluating path expressions and keyword search.

3.1 Extended Join Index (Ejindex)

Note that in the generated SQL statement, join between relations is to evaluate a path of a SPE expression. So we can pre-execute such intermediate join operation. In particular, we extend the join index [3], build index on two or more relations and keep the primary key *ID* of the rightmost relation and the column *ParentID* of the leftmost relation. The extended join index of R_1 *join* R_2... *join* R_k *on* R_i. $ID=R_{i+1}.ParentID$ ($1 \le i \le k$) is the relation *EJI(ID,ParentID)*:

```
EJI={ Select Rk.ID, R1.ParentID
       From   R1,…,Rk Where Ri.ID=Ri+1.ParentID 1≤i≤k }
```

With such extended join index, relation R_0 *join* (R_1 *join* R_2... *join* R_k) *join* R_{k+1} *on* R_i. $ID=R_{i+1}.ParentID$ ($1 \le i \le k$) is equal to the relation R_0 *join EJI join* R_{k+1} *on* $R_0.ID=EJI.ParentID$ *and* $EJI.ID=R_{k+1}.ParentID$, for the intermediate join operations have been pre-executed by the extended join index.

3.2 Reference Index (Rindex)

To evaluate a path expression traversing IDREF attribute, we have to replace the IDREF with all the possible elements it may refer to. Note ID attribute is an identifier of an element node and IDREF refers to that ID. So in the relational schema, the column mapped from ID and IDREF attribute can also be treated as primary key and foreign key. We can build a reference index on ID and IDREF, gather all the tuples that an IDREF attribute may refer to, and keep the IDs of the referring and the referred elements. Meanwhile such reference index may join with other relation, we also keep the *ParentID* of the tuple, in which the referring element is stored. For examples, let S be an element mapped as separate relational schema. The IDREF attribute of S is stored as a column named IDREF. R_i ($1 \le i \le k$) is the relation that S.IDREF may refer to. The reference index on S.IDREF is built as follows:

```
S_IDREF={UNION (Select Ri.ID as RefID,S.ID,S.ParentID
                    From Ri,S Where Ri.ID=S.IDREF)}
```

With the reference index *S_IDRef*, the GPE expression R_1.*S.IDRef*.R_2 can be evaluated by R_1 *join S_IDRef join R2 on* R_1. *ID=S_IDRef.ParentID and S_IDRef.RefID=*R_2.*ParentID.*

3.3 Path Index (Pindex)

For a given path expression, it's crucial to locate all the tuples bound to it. To achieve it quickly, we maintain a path dictionary in the system. Note if the reference between ID and IDRef leads to a loop in the data instance, we can compulsively decide that the loop in data instance be calculated just once. Hence the path set, which can reach a given node, will be fixed and finite, and the number of different path sets will be finite too. For a node *e*, the path set of *e* is all the path starting from root node and ending at node *e*. we denote it as *inpath(e.)*

$$\text{inpath(e)}=\{p \mid p=e_1.e_2 \ldots.e \text{ , e is a root node}\}$$

For any two nodes e and e', we say they are equivalent *iff inpath(e)=inpath(e')*. Based on node equivalence relationship, we can classify all nodes into different equivalent classes, and give each different *inpath* an identifier, denoted as *PathID*. The path set attached to a tuple in a relation is the *inpath* of the element node that generates that relation. The path index is implemented as follows:

1. Add an additional table: *PathDict(PathID,Path)* , keeping all the paths in a path set with identifier *PathID.*
2. Add a column *PathID* to every generated relational table.

Now tuples in the generated relational tables and the paths will be associated through *ID* and *PathID*. For any path, we can get a set of *PathIDs* from the relation *PathDict*, whose path set includes that path, then we can retrieve eligible tuples in the relational table corresponding to those *PathIDs*. On the other hand, for any tuple, we can get *PathID* in it, then look through *PathID* in the relation *PathDict*, we can get the path set attached to that tuple.

Using path index, a path expression can be evaluated efficiently. First, we can choose those path instances matching the path expression from relation *PathDict*. Then, according to the association between the path and the tuples, we can bind GPE expression with eligible tuples.

3.4 Implementing Keyword Search with Full Text Index

Keyword search is important to query XML data when user does not know the exact structure of XML data. As mentioned in [5], path expression query is not adequate fro query content in XML date. For example, in Figure 2, if user wants to retrieve all the employees who have *education* information, which may exist in the tag of element *education* (node &18), or in the content of element *dependent* (node&6). Rather than regular path expression query, a more nature query specification would be "find all of the employees contains word *education*". To solve this problem, we propose to add a predicate called **contains** to test whether a keyword exists in an XML element. The predicate **contains** has three parameters: 1) an *Element* expression for locating a special element. 2) a *Word* need to be tested its existence in that element, 3) *Location* of the keyword, for the keyword may exist in a tag name, the content of an element, an attribute name, or the value of the attribute. With predicate **contains**, the above retrieval example can be specified as following:

```
Q2:  Select     employee
      Where     contains("employee","education",any)
```

In Q2, we used **any** as the alias for the expression of 'tag|content|attribute| attribute_value', which means the word "education" may occur in any location.

For evaluating predicate **contains,** we build full text index in RDBMS. Different from traditional Information Retrieval systems, the full text index is kept in the granularity of elements. For every word appeared in an XML document, we generate a separate relation for it:

```
FI_Word(TableName,Element,Location,ID)
```

Here, *TableName* records the name of relational table in which the word appears. *Element* corresponds to the column name of that table, i.e. the tag name in an XML document. *ID* is the primary key of the tuple. *Location* records the position of word. Next we will show how to process of predicate *contains(Element,Word,Location)*. First, we check whether the element contains the keyword according to the keyword and its *Location* (It can be fulfilled by checking whether the *ID* of a tuple appears in the column *ID* of the word index). If not, we expand the *Element* expression with all its possible sub-elements. Then we can evaluate predicate **contains** by checking whether the sub-elements contain keyword. For the sake of the efficiency, we can define a threshold for the depth of the sub-element to expand the *Element* expression.

For query Q2, note element *employee* inlines its sub-element *name, education* and attribute *ID.* It also has a sub-element *dependent,* which is to generate separate relation. Except these two relation, there are no other offspring elements of *employee* will generate separate relation. So we need just check whether there are "education" information contained in *employee* and *dependent* to evaluate the predicate **contains.** Thus Q2 will be translated into:

```
  Select    employee.ID From employee,FI_education
  Where     employee.ID = FI_education.ID
  And       FI_education.tablename='employee'
UNION
  Select    employee.ID From employee,dependent,FI_education
```

```
Where     employee.ID = dependent.ParentID
And       dependent.ID=FI_education.ID
And       FI_education.tablename='dependent'
```

Here, *FI_education* is a word index that keeps the information of keyword *education.* Note the word index does not keep the information of keyword's relative position to the other element. Provided only with such word index, we cannot tell directly that which element has an offspring containing the keyword. After we get the tuples containing the keyword in word index, for it is not the element we want to retrieve, we have to compute equijoin with the parent relation to test whether the tuple containing keyword belongs to the offspring of the element that we want to retrieve. While the parent relation of the tuple in the word index is not fixed, we cannot perform the equijoin with single SQL statement. To settle this problem, we propose to add an additional relation:

```
ancestor(ID,AncestorID,element)
```

The table *ancestor* records the *ID* of a tuple, which contains keyword information. The column *AncestorID* keeps the *ID* of the ancestral tuple of that tuple, *element* keeps the column of the ancestral tuple bringing the offspring tuple. i.e., for a record of *(TID, AID, E)* triple in relation *ancestor*, the element attached to the tuple *AID* can reach the element attached to the tuple *TID* through some path, which must traverse element *E*. Now for any tuple in the generated relation and a keyword, the tuple has an offspring element containing the keyword, if the *ID* of that tuple exists in the equijoin relation between the *word* index of that keyword and the relation *ancestor.* With relation *ancestor*, we can provide another bottom-up evaluation of predicate *contains(Element,Word,Location).* First look through the *word* index, get the possible tuple containing keyword information. Finally, refer to the relation *ancestor* to see whether the candidate tuple has offspring element containing keyword.

4 Experiments

The experiment is performed on a 500MHZ Pentium III machine running Windows 2000 professional version and SQL Server v7.0. The XML data tested in our experiment is all of the Shakespeare's plays in XML format, which are available from the Oasis Web site and are about 8M large. We also build a synthetic XML documents as follow: first a small tree-structured "template" XML document concern about DBLP publication was created with several ID and IDREF attribute, and then the template file is replicated to produce document with adequate size about 4M.

Table 1 gives the type and size of four indices, where index size is the total number of tuples in the index relations. Note the relation table *ancestor* 's size is 685,498, which is not included in table 1. Table 2 gives the six queries performed in the experiment. For query Q1 to Q3, according to the different query plan (see [9] for details), we perform the queries in two ways, including the naive query conversion (denoted as GS query plan) and the query conversion with indices (denoted as GSI query plan). For query Q4 to Q6, we also perform the queries in two ways. One performs a top-down retrieving without using relation *ancestor*, we denoted it as TD query plan. The other one, performs a bottom-up retrieving with the help of the relation *ancestor*, is denoted as BU query plan. Table 3 and table 4 lists for each query and for each query plan, the number of the SQL statements, the total number of joins, and the elapsed time for executing those queries.

According to the performance of Q1 to Q3, the using of indices reduces the number of joins, the number of the generated SQL statements. As a result it reduces the time for evaluating this queries substantially. While for query Q4 to Q6, the result shows that all queries can be carried out in several seconds, it means that our solution to support keyword search is feasible.

Table 1. The type and size of indices

	Index Number	Index Size
Path index	2	1,536
Extended join index	10	198,703
Reference index	1	4,091
Full text index	22,917	1,214,818

Table 2. The test queries and the result size

Query	Description	Result Size
Q1	Select play.#.title	1,047
Q2	Select play.act.scene.speech.line where play.title like "%Hamlet%"	2,279
Q3	Select dblp.inproceedings.(cite.idref)^2.title	3,600
Q4	Select play.#.speech Where contains(play.#.speech,"love",any)	2,126
Q5	Select play.act.scene.speech.line Where contains(play.title,"hamlet",any)	4,104
Q6	Select play.#.speech.line Where contains(play.#.speech,"subhead",tag) And contains(play.#.speech.line,"love",any)	8

Table 3. The performance of query Q1 to Q3

Query	Number of SQL Stmts		Number of Joins		Elapsed time (seconds)	
	GS	GSI	GS	GSI	GS	GSI
Q1	8	1	16	0	1.52	0.03
Q2	7	1	31	2	4.82	0.67
Q3	6	1	36	5	3.25	0.26

Table 4. The performance of query Q4 to Q6

Query	Number of SQL Stmts		Number of Joins		Elapsed time (seconds)	
	TD	BU	TD	BU	TD	BU
Q4	6	1	12	2	1.69	1.55
Q5	1	1	6	7	0.64	1.64
Q6	6	2	19	8	5.27	3.01

5 Related Work and Conclusion

Storing XML data with relation DBMS has been studied extensively [2,4,8]. We implemented a prototype of repository for XML data according to the SHARED method in [8] and built some indices for query conversion and keyword searching. All indices are implemented as relations. Join index, for computing joins between two relations, is studied in [3]. We extended it to multiple relations. Path index [6,7] is a powerful mechanism for evaluating path expression in semi-structured data. Our path dictionary integrates it into RDBMS and uses it to reduce joins. Moreover, we fulfilled the integration of regular XML query and keyword search, building full text index in RDBMS to support keyword search. However, as like [5], we create a table for each keyword, element pairs, which would result too much relational tables. We also maintain a global *ancestor* table, which makes the query conversion more easily implemented. According to the above discussion, some experiments were carried out, and the result of experiments shows that our approach is efficient. Even the queries with complex GPE expression or keyword search can be carried out efficiently with those indices.

References

1. S. Abiteboul, D. Quass, J. Mchugh, and et al. The Lore Query Language for Semistructured Data. *International Journal on Digital Libraries*, 1(1): 68-88, April 1997.
2. Deutsch, M. Fernandez, D. Suciu. Storing Semistructured Data with STORED. *Proceedings of the 28th SIGMOD International Conference on Management of Data*, May, 1999.
3. Patrick Valduriez, Join Indices, ACM Transactions on Database Systems, Vol.12, No.2, pages 218-246, June 1987.
4. D. Florescu, D. Kossmann. *A Performance Evaluation of Alternative Mapping Schemes for Storing XML Data in a Relational Database*. Technical Report 3684, INRIA, March 1999.
5. D. Florescu, D. Kossmann. I.Manolescu. *Integrating Keyword Search into XML Query Processing*. In proceedings of the ninth international WWW Conference, Amsterdam, Netherlands, May 2000.
6. R. Goldman and J. Widom. DataGuides: Enabling Query Formulation and Optimization in Semistructured Databases. *Proceedings of the Twenty-Third International Conference on Very Large Data Bases,* pages 436-445, Athens, Greece, August 1997.
7. T. Milo, D. Suciu: Index Structures for Path Expressions. In *ICDT'99, the 7th International Conference, Jerusale,Israel,* pages 277-295, 1999.
8. J. Shanmugasundaram, K. Tufte, C. Zhang, and et al. Relational Databases for Querying XML Documents: Limitations and Opportunities. *Proc. of the 25th International Conference on Very Large Databases*, Edinburgh, Scotland, September 1999.
9. Y. Liang, A. Zhou, S.Zheng, and et al. Enhancing XML Data Processing in Relational System with Indices. Technical Report, Fudan University, Feb. 2001.

Session 3A
Data Warehousing & Federated Databases

Regular Research Paper (30 minutes)
A Multidimensional Data Model Supporting Complicated Aggregations

Regular Research Paper (30 minutes)
Comparing String Similarity Measures for Reducing Inconsistency in Integrating Data From Different Sources

Short Research Paper (15 minutes)
Revisit on View Maintenance in Data Warehouses

Research Experience Paper (15 minutes)
Experiences with a Hybrid Implementation of a Globally Distributed Federated Database System

A Multidimensional Data Model Supporting Complicated Aggregations

Hongxing Tan [1,3], Wenwen Qi [2], and Longxiang Zhou [3]

[1] School of Computer Science, Henan University, Kaifeng, 475001, PRC
thx@mail.henu.edu.cn
[2] Department of Mathematics, Henan University, Kaifeng, 475001, PRC
qww@mail.henu.edu.cn
[3] Institute of Mathematics, Chinese Academy of Sciences, Beijing, 100080, PRC
lxzhou@math08.math.ac.cn

Abstract. A data cube is a collection of multidimensional data not only of one level, nor of all levels by one aggregation function, but of all levels by all aggregation functions admissible in an OLAP system. We propose a multidimensional data model that produces such kind of data cubes so that aggregation data of different levels can be kept consistent. The multidimensional data of different levels in a data cube are organized with so called aggregation nodes. We also define the operations on a data cube and illustrate the expressive power of the model by expressing analysis queries.

1 Introduction

Multidimensional data model plays an important role in OLAP applications. It describes the structure and operations of the multidimensional data, provides the basis of programming languages of OLAP systems and even determines the storage scheme of the data in some extent.

It has attracted many research interests to model multidimensional data. Gray et al. [2] defined operator CUBE to extend SQL and present a multidimensional view of relational data. Li and Wang [5] defined a multidimensional data model based on the so-called grouping algebra. Agrawal et al. [1] defined a multi-dimensional data model with the focus on operations on multidimensional data. Lehner [3] studied the problem of unbalanced dimensions and heterogeneous levels. Vassiliadis [7] defined a multidimensional data model in which each cube contains a basic cube so that operation *drill down* can be expressed explicitly. Pedersen and Jensen [6] considered the case that measures do not functionally depend on the dimensions in a multi-dimensional data set. Li and Gao [4] studied the problems of defining a data cube when levels of a dimension can not construct a lattice.

Except that the data cube defined in [2] contains aggregation data of all levels by an aggregation function, all kinds of data cubes just mentioned contain aggregation data only of one level by one aggregation function.

In an OLAP system, multidimensional data can be aggregated with more than one aggregation function to many levels. For example, daily sales can be summed into monthly sales, which then can be averaged into yearly average sales. The data of

X.S. Wang, G. Yu, and H. Lu (Eds.): WAIM 2001, LNCS 2118, pp. 179-190, 2001.

higher levels are dependent on those of lower ones so they should be kept consistent. It is difficult for existing multidimensional data models to describe such kind of aggregations and consistence.

This paper addresses such problems and proposes a novel multidimensional data model whose salient features are:

- ✓ The data cube in the new model contains data set of all levels by all aggregation functions admissible in an OLAP application;
- ✓ Navigation operations such as *roll up* and *drill down* are implemented with operations *select* or *join* for data of all levels logically exist in a cube;
- ✓ Aggregation restraints are defined in the model;
- ✓ Each operation deals with data of one certain level in the cube.

Example 1. To motivate the work described in this paper, let us use a running example of a company. When considering the sales of this company, three are the major dimensions: *time*, *customer* and *product*. The dimensions, along with their levels are depicted in Fig. 1.

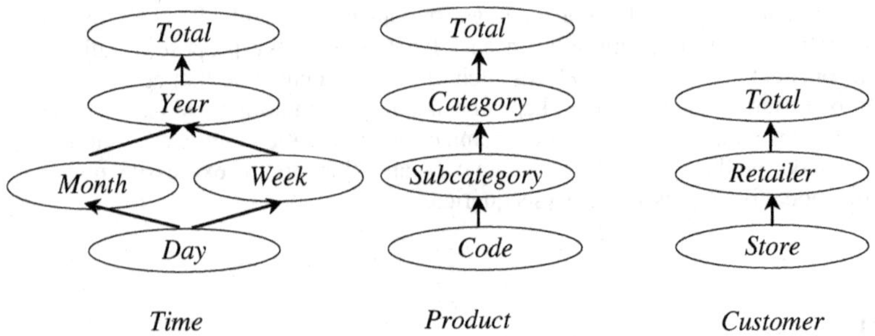

Fig. 1. Dimensions and Dimension Levels

This paper is organized as follows. We define the dimension structure in section 2 and measures in section 3. Multidimensional data are described in section 4. The operations of the model are given in section 5. In section 6, we employ several analysis queries to illustrate the expressive power of the new model. The conclusions of this paper are given in section 7.

2 Dimensions

A dimension consists of several levels, each of which in turn consists of a number of members. There is a partial order on those levels, according to which a containment relationship between members exists. For example, dimension *time* consists of levels of *year*, *month*, and so forth. 1999.1 and 1999.2 are members of level *month* and are contained in 1999, a member of level *year*.

For every dimension, we define its top level as *Total*, which has only one member *all*.

Definition 1 (Dimension Schema) A dimension *D* is a 4-tuple <*Members*, *Levels*, *level*, $\preceq$, *parent*> where

1. *Members* is the set of *D*'s members, and *all* *Members*;

2. *Levels* is the set of *D*'s levels, and *Total*   *Levels*;
3. *level* is a function on *Members*   *Levels*. Given *o*   *Members* and *l*   *Levels*, *level*(*o*) = *l* means member *o* belongs to level *l*, i.e., *o* is a member of *l*.

   All members of level *l* comprise the domain of *l* denoted by *DOM*(*l*), i.e., *DOM*(*l*) = {*o* | *o*   *Members*   *level*(*o*) = *l*}.

   Function *level* satisfies that

   (a) Any member in *Members* must belong to a certain level,

   (b) *DOM*(*Total*) = {*all*}.
4. $\preceq$ is a partial order on *Levels*, and <*Levels*, $\preceq$> constructs a lattice called the *dimension lattice* of *D*. *Total* is the maximum element of the dimension lattice.

   Given l_1, l_2 *Levels*, if $l_1 \preceq l_2$ and they are adjacent, we call l_2 the direct higher level of l_1 and l_1 the direct lower level of l_2, which is denoted by l_1 l_2.
5. *parent* is a function on *Members* where
   a) Given o_1, o_2 *Members*, if *parent*(o_1) = o_2 then *level*(o_1)   *level*(o_2),
   b) Given l_1, l_2 *Levels* and l_1 l_2, for each member o_1 on l_1 there exists a member o_2 of l_2 such that *parent*(o_1) = o_2.

Definition 2 (Multidimensional Level) Let the set of dimensions $\boldsymbol{D} = \{D_1, D_2, \ldots, D_d\}$, *d*   1. A multidimensional level on $\boldsymbol{D}$ is a *d*-tuple $<l_1, l_2, \ldots, l_d>$ where l_i D_i.*levels*, 1   *i*   *d*. The set of $\boldsymbol{D}$'s multidimensional levels is denoted by ***D***.*ML*.

Elements in ***D***.*ML* construct a lattice called the multidimensional lattice of ***D*** where $<l_1, l_2, \ldots, l_d> \preceq <l_1', l_2', \ldots, l_d'>$ $\forall i$(1   *i*   *d* $l_i \preceq l_i'$). We denote the minimum element of a multidimensional lattice by *bv*.

Given the dimension set ***D*** = {*Product*, *Customer*}, ***D***.*ML* is shown in Fig. 2.

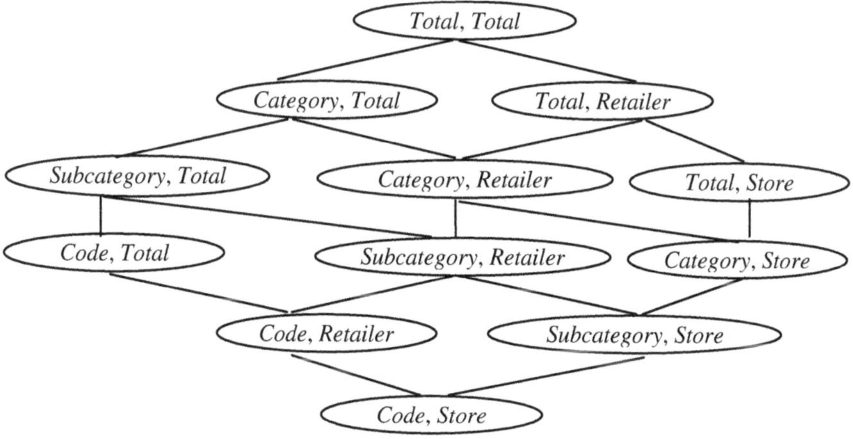

Fig. 2. The multidimensional lattice of {*Product*, *Customer*}

3 Aggregating Measures

This section discusses how to aggregate measure data. The measure data in an OLAP system may be of different levels that are determined by the levels of the dimensions on which the measures functionally depend. The measure data should be aggregated along with all those dimensions instead of only some one.

Definition 3 (Single Aggregation) Let the set of dimensions $\boldsymbol{D} = \{D_1, D_2, \ldots, D_d\}$ and the set of admissible aggregation functions $F = \{f_0, f_1, f_2, \ldots, f_n\}$ where f_0 is a trivial function. A single aggregation *agg* on $<\boldsymbol{D}, F>$ is a triple $<ml_s, f, ml_t>$ where ml_s, ml_t $\boldsymbol{D}.ML, f$ F and $ml_s \preceq ml_t$.

Function f_0 does nothing on input data, i.e., in a single aggregation $<ml_s, f, ml_t>$, $ml_s = ml_t$ only if $f = f_0$. We have f_0 in F only for convenience of expression, e.g., base data can also be treated as aggregation data for $<bv, f_0, bv>$ is a single aggregation. Aggregations within which $f = f_0$ are called trivial, and those within which f f_0 are called non-trivial. In the remainder of this paper, an aggregation is always referred to a non-trivial one unless mentioned specially.

Several single aggregations can be linked together to form a complicated aggregation process called an aggregation path.

Definition 4 (Aggregation Path) Let the set of dimensions $\boldsymbol{D} = \{D_1, D_2, \ldots, D_d\}$ and the set of admissible functions $F = \{f_0, f_1, f_2, \ldots, f_n\}$. An aggregation path *ap* on $<\boldsymbol{D}, F>$ is the concatenation of several single aggregations on $<\boldsymbol{D}, F>$: $ap = <agg_1, agg_2, \ldots, agg_k>$ where $agg_i.ml_s = agg_{i-1}.ml_t$, k 1, $1 < i$ k and $agg_1.ml_s = bv$.

Aggregation path $<agg_1, agg_2, \ldots, agg_k>$ can also be denoted by $< ml_1 \ ^{f_{t_1}} \ ml_2 \ ^{f_{t_2}} \ldots \ ^{f_{t_k}} \ ml_{k+1}>$ where $ml_i = agg_i.ml_s$, $ml_{i+1} = agg_i.ml_t$, $f_{ti} = agg_i.f$, 1 i k.

The stop level of an aggregation path carrying with process information is called an aggregation node. We denote the set of all the aggregation nodes of $<\boldsymbol{D}, F>$ by $V(\boldsymbol{D}, F)$.

An aggregation path and its aggregation node are equivalent except that a path emphasizes on the aggregation process and the node emphasizes on the level the process reaches. We always denotes a node with the path, i.e., if the aggregation node of aggregation path *ap* is *v*, then we say $v = ap$.

We denote the stop level of aggregation node v by $v.ml$, then $v.ml = ap.agg_{|ap|}.ml_t$. $v.ml.l_i$, which is the level of $v.ml$ on dimension D_i, can be denoted by $v.l_i$.

In the multidimensional lattice shown in Fig. 2, examples of aggregation paths are

$<<Code, Store>$ ^{sum} $<Code, Retailer>>$,

$<<Code, Store>$ ^{sum} $<Code, Retailer>$ ^{max} $<Subcategory, Retailer>>$ and

$<<Code, Store>$ ^{sum} $<Subcategory, Retailer>>$.

Definition 5 (Decomposable Aggregations) Let X be a set of values, aggregation function f is decomposable if and only if for any partition $\{X_1, X_2, \ldots, X_I\}$ of X, I 1, there exist aggregation functions g and h such that $f(X) = g(\{h(X_i) \mid 1$ i $I\})$. Here we say that f can be decomposed into g and h, denoted by $f = g \bullet h$.

Definition 6 (Combinable Aggregations) Aggregation functions g and h are combinable if and only if there exists an aggregation function f such that f can be decomposed into g and h.

It means agg_i is carried out on the result of agg_{i-1} that there exist two adjacent single aggregations agg_{i-1} and agg_i in an aggregation path. If $agg_{i-1}.f$ and $agg_i.f$ are combinable, we can combine agg_{i-1} and agg_i into one aggregation agg where $agg.ml_s = agg_{i-1}.ml_s$, $agg.ml_t = agg_i.ml_t$ and $agg.f = agg_i.f \bullet agg_{i-1}.f$.

By combing all the combinable adjacent aggregations in an aggregation path, we can get the *canonical path* of the aggregation path.

Definition 7 (Canonical Aggregation Path) Let the dimension set $\boldsymbol{D} = \{D_1, D_2, \ldots, D_d\}$ and the admissible aggregation function set $F = \{f_0, f_1, f_2, \ldots, f_n\}$. Given aggregation path *ap* on <***D***, *F*>, *ap*'s canonical path *cp* is an aggregation path where all the adjacent combinable aggregations in *ap* are combined.

For example, in the multidimensional lattice shown in Fig. 2, the canonical aggregation path of the aggregation path

<<Code, Store> ^{sum} *<Code, Retailer>* ^{sum} *<Subcategory, Retailer>>* is
<<Code, Store> ^{sum} *< Subcategory, Retailer>>*, and that of
<<Code, Store> ^{count} *<Code, Retailer>* ^{sum} *<Subcategory, Retailer>>* is
<<Code, Store> ^{count} *< Subcategory, Retailer>>*.

The result of any aggregation path is the same as that of its canonical one, so in the remainder of this paper, when an aggregation path is mentioned, we always refer to the canonical one.

Definition 8 (Subpath Set) Let the dimension set $\boldsymbol{D} = \{D_1, D_2, \ldots, D_d\}$ and the admissible aggregation function set $F = \{f_0, f_1, f_2, \ldots, f_n\}$. The subpath set *SP* of an aggregation path *ap* on <***D***, *F*> is the set defined as follows:

1. For any single aggregation agg_i in *ap*, <$ap.agg_1, \ldots, ap.agg_i$> *SP*;
2. For any aggregation path *p* in *SP* and a single aggregation agg_i in *p*, if $agg_i.f$ can be decomposed into *g* and *h* and there exists an multidimensional level *ml* in ***D***.*ML* such that $agg_i.ml_s \prec ml \prec agg_i.ml_t$, then aggregation path <$p.agg_1, \ldots, p.agg_{i-1}, p.agg$> *SP* where $agg.ml_s = agg_i.ml_s$, $agg.ml_t = ml$, $agg.f = h$;
3. No more aggregation path belongs to *SP*.

The subpath set of an aggregation path includes all the possible intermediate steps that the aggregation path may pass. For example, in the multidimensional lattice shown in Fig. 2, the subpath set of *<<Code, Store>* ^{count}*<Subcategory, Retailer>>* equals to

{*<Code, Store>*, *<<Code, Store>* ^{count}*<Code, Retailer>>*,
<<Code, Store> ^{count}*<Subcategory, Retailer>>*,
<<Code, Store> ^{count}*<Subcategory, Retailer>>*}.

Definition 9 (Reachability) Let the dimension set $\boldsymbol{D} = \{D_1, D_2, \ldots, D_d\}$ and the admissible function set $F = \{f_0, f_1, f_2, \ldots, f_n\}$. Given two aggregation nodes v_1 and v_2 in <***D***, *F*>, v_2 is reachable from v_1 if and only if there exist *k* aggregation nodes $v_1', v_2', \ldots, v_k'$, k 1 such that $v_1' = v_1$, $v_k' = v_2$ and for each 1 $i < k$, let $v_i' = \langle agg_1, agg_2, \ldots, agg_{k_i} \rangle$, there exists a single aggregation $agg_{k_{i+1}}$ such that $v_{i+1}' = \langle agg_1, agg_2, \ldots, agg_{k_i}, agg_{k_{i+1}} \rangle$. We denote that v_2 is reachable from v_1 by $v_1 \mapsto v_2$.

Definition 10 (Summarizability) Let the dimension set $\boldsymbol{D} = \{D_1, D_2, \ldots, D_d\}$ and admissible aggregation function set $F = \{f_0, f_1, f_2, \ldots, f_n\}$. Summarizability of measure *M*, *AGG*(*M*), is a subset of the aggregation nodes of <***D***, *F*> in which there do not exist two elements v_1 and v_2 such that $v_1 \mapsto v_2$. For any aggregation node *v*, if there exists in *AGG*(*M*) an element v' such that $v' \mapsto v$, then the measure data of *v* is invalid.

4 Multidimensional Data

Based on dimension and measure we have defined, this section discusses how to describe multidimensional data. First we define multidimensional data schema which is abbreviated to MD Schema.

Definition 11(MD Schema) An MD schema C is a 5-tuple $<\boldsymbol{D}, \boldsymbol{M}, F, AGG>$, where

1. $\boldsymbol{D} = \{D_1, D_2, \ldots, D_d\}$ is the set of dimensions;
2. $\boldsymbol{M} = \{M_1, M_2, \ldots, M_m\}$ is the set measures;
3. $F = \{f_0, f_1, f_2, \ldots, f_n\}$ is the set of admissible aggregation functions where f_0 is a trivial one;
4. AGG is the summarizability constraint description, which is a function on $\boldsymbol{M}$ $\rho^{V(\boldsymbol{D}, F)}$. For each M_i in $\boldsymbol{M}$, no two nodes in $AGG(M_i)$ are reachable from each other. For each element v in $V(\boldsymbol{D}, F)$, if there exists node v' in $AGG(M_i)$ such that $v' \mapsto v$, then the measure data of M_i in v is invalid.
5. $\boldsymbol{D} \quad \boldsymbol{M} = \quad$.

Given MD schema $C = <\boldsymbol{D}, \boldsymbol{M}, F, AGG>$, the terms defined on $<\boldsymbol{D}, F>$ are also valid on C, e.g., single aggregations, aggregation paths and aggregation nodes, etc. We denote the set of all aggregation nodes in C by $V(C)$. In the remainder of this paper, we always denote the number of dimensions and measures in a cube by d and m respectively.

Given MD schema C, the instances of C are composed of the aggregation data of every aggregation node.

Definition 12(Aggregation Data) Given MD schema $C = <\boldsymbol{D}, \boldsymbol{M}, F, AGG>$ and an aggregation node v in C, the domain of v $DOM(v) = \quad {}_{i=1}^{d}DOM(v.l_i) \quad {}_{i=1}^{m}DOM(M_i)$. An instance of v, $v.inst$, is a subset of $DOM(v)$ where every two elements $<o_1, o_2, \ldots, o_d, r_1, r_2, \ldots, r_m>$ and $<o_1', o_2', \ldots, o_d', r_1', r_2', \ldots, r_m'>$ of $v.inst$ satisfy that:

$<o_1, o_2, \ldots, o_d> = <o_1', o_2', \ldots, o_d'> \quad <r_1, r_2, \ldots, r_m> = <r_1', r_2', \ldots, r_m'>$.

For element $x = <o_1, o_2, \ldots, o_d, r_1, r_2, \ldots, r_m>$ in $v.inst$, $<o_1, o_2, \ldots, o_d>$ is called the coordinate of x denoted by $co(x)$; $<r_1, r_2, \ldots, r_m>$ is called the measure data of x denoted by $me(x)$.

Aggregation data of higher levels are calculated from those of lower ones. Given two aggregation nodes v_1 and v_2 in C such that $v_1 \mapsto v_2$ and an instance of v_1, to say $v_1.inst$, we can get an instance of v_2, to say $v_2.inst$, from $v_1.inst$. We denote such a process by $v_2.inst = Roll\text{-}Up(v_1, v_2, v_1.inst)$.

For any aggregation node v of an MD schema, v is always reachable from bv. Given an instance of bv, $bv.inst$, we can always get an instance of v, $v.inst$, from $bv.inst$: $v.inst = Roll\text{-}Up(bv, v, bv.inst)$.

If $v_1 \mapsto v_2$ and a subset of $v_2.inst$ is given as $v_2.inst_1$, then we can select from $v_1.inst$ the data used to calculate $v_2.inst_1$. We denote such a process as $Drill\text{-}Down(v_1, v_2, v_1.inst_1, v_2.inst)$:

$$Drill\text{-}Down(v_1, v_2, v_1.inst_1, v_2.inst) = \{x \mid x \quad v_1.inst \quad \exists y\,(y \quad v_2.inst_1 \quad co(y) = v_2(co(x)))\}.$$

Definition 13(Cube) Given MD schema $C = <\boldsymbol{D}, \boldsymbol{M}, F, AGG>$, an instance of C is called a cube on C, denoted by c, $c = \{v.inst \mid v \quad V(C) \quad v.inst = Roll\text{-}Up(bv, v, bv.inst)\}$.

We should point out it is only from the logical point of view that a cube consists of the data on every aggregation nodes. In fact, we seldom calculate the data of all nodes because not only is the amount of data too large, but also applications usually use only a small part of them. If the instance of an aggregation node has been calculated and becomes available, we say that the node has been materialized.

Given a cube c and one of its aggregation node v, we use $inst(c,v)$ to denote the data of v. Once c's base data, i.e., $inst(c, bv)$, is given, all the data of c are determined. Therefore, we need only $inst(c, bv)$ to describe the data of c.

In the remainder of this paper, we usually use c to denote a cube on MD schema C sometimes with subscript or superscript.

Definition 14(Multidimensional database) A multidimensional database *MDDB* is a set of cubes.

5 Operations on Multidimensional Data

This section presents the operations of the new model we define. Note that navigation operations such as *roll up* and *drill down* are not included because data of all aggregation nodes exist logically within a cube.

Operation 1: *Select*

select is used to select a subset of the data in a cube given an aggregation node and predicate on the node. The predicate may include restrictions on both dimensions and measures.

select σ

Input: cube c, aggregation node v in C, predicate p on $inst(c, v)$

Output: cube c'

$c' = \sigma^{v}_{p}c,\ C' = C$

$inst(c', bv) = Drill\text{-}Down(bv, v, inst(c, bv), \{x \mid x \quad inst(c, v) \quad p(x)\})$

For example, let query Q = "Get sales for product p_1 in each month of 1999.", Q can be expressed as $\sigma^{v}_{code = p_1 \quad year(day) = 1999}c$ where $v = (bv \quad ^{sum} <code, store, month>)$.

Manipulating data based on aggregation nodes is one of the salient features of this model. For example, in operations *select* and *join*, aggregation nodes should be provided. In the remainder of this paper, if the given node is bv, it can be omitted from the operation. For example, selecting data from bv in cube c by predicate p can be expressed as $\sigma_{p}c$.

Operation 2: *Intersect*

When intersecting two cubes. We should combine the measure data within the same coordinates of two cubes into one. Therefore, an extra operator is necessary to get a new value from the data in the same coordinates of the two aggregation nodes. We denote the operator by ϕ that takes the two measures as input and output either one of the inputs or the result of some calculation on them.

intersect
Input: cube c_1, c_2, $C_1 = C_2$, operator ϕ
Output: cube c
$c = intersect(c_1, c_2, \phi), C = C_1 = C_2$
$inst(c, bv) = \{x \mid x \quad DOM(C.bv)$
$\exists x_1, x_2(x_1 \quad inst(c_1, bv) \quad x_2 \quad inst(c_2, bv)$
$co(x) = co(x_1) = co(x_2) \quad me(x) = \phi(me(x_1), me(x_2)))\}$

Operation 3: ***Union***

By union two cubes we get the data in either of them when we are faced with the problem of how to deal with the measure data of the same coordinates of the two cubes. The solution is similar to that in operation *intersect*, i.e., we need an extra operator, to say φ. Given two cubes c_1 and c_2, we denote the result of operation *union* by c, then for each coordinate $<o_1, o_2, \ldots, o_d>$ in bv, the measure data $<r_1, r_2, \ldots, r_m>$ of each coordinate in c may be calculated in three cases:

1. If the measures in both c_1 and c_2 are null, then that of c is also null;
2. If there is data in only one of c_1 and c_2, to say $<r_1', r_2', \ldots, r_m'>$, then $<r_1, r_2, \ldots, r_m> = <r_1', r_2', \ldots, r_m'>$;
3. If there are data in both c_1 and c_2, to say $<r_1', r_2', \ldots, r_m'>$ and $<r_1'', r_2'', \ldots, r_m''>$ respectively, then $<r_1, r_2, \ldots, r_m> = \varphi(<r_1', r_2', \ldots, r_m'>, <r_1'', r_2'', \ldots, r_m''>)$.

Union
Input: cube c_1, c_2, $C_1 = C_2$, operator φ
Output: cube c
$c = Union(c_1, c_2, \varphi), C = C_1 = C_2$
$inst(c, bv) = \{x \mid x \quad DOM(C.bv)$
$(\exists x_1(x_1 \quad inst(c_1, bv) \quad co(x) = co(x_1)$
$\exists \; x_2(x_2 \quad inst(c_2, bv) \quad co(x) = co(x_2)) \quad me(x) = me(x_1))$
$\exists x_2(x_2 \quad inst(c_2, bv) \quad co(x) = co(x_2)$
$\exists \; x_1(x_1 \quad inst(c_1, bv) \quad co(x) = co(x_1)) \quad me(x) = me(x_2))\}$
$inst(Intersect(c_1, c_2, \varphi), bv)$

Operation 4: ***Minus***

This operation is used to get the data that are of c_1 but not of c_2.

Minus –
Input: cube c_1, c_2, $C_1 = C_2$
Output: cube c
$c = c_1 - c_2, C = C_1 = C_2$
$inst(c, bv) = \{x \mid x \quad inst(c_1, bv) \; \exists \; x_2(x_2 \quad inst(c_2, bv) \quad co(x) = co(x_2)\}$

Operation 5: Remove Dimension

This operation is used to remove a certain dimension from a cube occurring when in an aggregation node the dimension has only one member whose corresponding measure data is not empty. This restriction confirms the functional dependence of measures on dimensions. To perform this operation, we should first select such an aggregation node and the dimension to remove. *bv* of the result cube is the give node to remove dimension.

Remove dimension RD

Input: cube c, aggregation node v in c and $D_i \quad C.\mathbf{D}$

$\forall x_1, x_2(x_1, x_2 \quad inst(c, v) \quad x_1.o_i = x_2.o_i)$; ($x.o_i$ denotes the project on D_i of x)

Output: cube c'

$c' = RD_{D_i, v}(c)$

Let $C = \langle \mathbf{D}, \mathbf{M}, F, AGG\rangle$, $\mathbf{D} = \{D_1, D_2, ..., D_d\}$, then $C' = \langle \mathbf{D}', \mathbf{M}, F, AGG'\rangle$ where

$\mathbf{D}' = \{D_1', D_2', ..., D_{i-1}', D_{i+1}', ..., D_d'\}$,

$D_j'.Members = \{o \mid o \quad D_j.Members \quad v.l_i \preceq level(o)\}$,

$D_j'.Levels = \{l \mid l \quad D_j.Levels \quad v.l_i \preceq l\}$,

$D_j'.f = \{\langle o, l\rangle \mid \langle o, l\rangle \quad D_j.f \quad o \quad D_j'.Members \quad l \quad D_j'.Levels\}$,

$D_j'.parent = \{\langle o_1, o_2\rangle \mid \langle o_1, o_2\rangle \quad D_j.parent \quad o_1, o_1 \quad D_j'.Members\}$,

$1 \quad j \quad d$ and $j \quad i$;

$AGG' = \{\langle M_j, V_j'\rangle \mid M_j \quad \mathbf{M} \quad V_j' \quad \rho^{V(C)}$

$\exists\ v_1, v_2(v_1, v_2 \quad V_j' \quad v_1 \mapsto v_2)$

$\exists\langle M, V_j\rangle\ (\langle M, V_j\rangle \quad C.AGG \quad M = M_j$

$\forall v'(v' \quad V_j \quad \exists v(v \quad V_j \quad v \mapsto v'))\}$

Assume that a is the member on dimension D_i in $inst(c, v)$, then

$inst(c', C'.bv) = \{\langle o_1, o_2, ..., o_{i-1}, o_{i+1}, ..., o_d, r_1, r_2, ..., r_m\rangle \mid$

$\langle o_1, o_2, ..., o_{i-1}, a, o_{i+1}, ..., o_d, r_1, r_2, ..., r_m\rangle \quad inst(c, v)\}$.

Operation 6: Remove Measure

This operation is used to remove a measure that we do not care about any more.

Remove Measure RM

Input: cube c, measure M_i, $M_i \quad C.\mathbf{M}$

Output: cube c'

$c' = RM_M(c)$

Let $C = \langle \mathbf{D}, \mathbf{M}, F, AGG\rangle$, then $C' = \langle \mathbf{D}, \mathbf{M} - \{M_i\}, F, AGG'\rangle$ where

$AGG' = \{\langle M_j, V_j\rangle \mid \langle M_j, V_j\rangle \quad AGG \quad j \quad i\}$.

$inst(c', bv) = \{\langle o_1, o_2, ..., o_d, r_1, r_2, ..., r_{i-1}, r_{i+1}, ..., r_m\rangle \mid \exists r_i(\ r_i \quad DOM(M_i)$

$\langle o_1, o_2, ..., o_d, r_1, r_2, ..., r_{i-1}, r_i, r_{i+1}, ..., r_m\rangle) \quad inst(c, bv)\}$

Operation 7: ***Join***

Join is used to join two cubes c_1 and c_2. A coordinate in c_1 will be related to more than one coordinate in c_2, and a new measure will be generated from the measures in the two given cubes.

The difference between relation join and cube join includes two aspects. First, cube join may generate new measure but not new dimensions. Secondly, cube join is not commutable because not only is the relationship between the coordinates of the cubes c_1 and c_2 one to many, but also the function used to generate new measure is not always commutable.

Join $\bowtie$

Input: cube c_1 and one of its aggregation nodes v_1, cube c_2 and one of its aggregation nodes v_2, predicate p, new measure M and the create function f

Output: cube c

$c = c_1.v_1 \bowtie_{p}^{M=f(M_1,M_2)} c_2.v_2$, where $\boldsymbol{M}_1$ and $\boldsymbol{M}_2$ are the measure sets of C_1 and C_2 respectively.

Let $C_1 = <\boldsymbol{D}_1, \boldsymbol{M}_1, F_1, AGG_1>$, $\boldsymbol{D}_1 = \{D_1, D_2, ..., D_d\}$, then $C = <\boldsymbol{D}, \boldsymbol{M}, F_1, AGG_1>$, where $\boldsymbol{D} = \{D_1', D_2', ..., D_d'\}$,

$D_i'.Members = \{o \mid o \quad D_i.Members \quad v_1.l_i \preceq level(o)\}$,

$D_i'.Levels = \{l \mid l \quad D_i.Levels \quad v_1.l_i \preceq l\}$,

$D_i'.level = \{<o, l> \mid <o, l> \quad D_i.level \quad o \quad D_i'.Members \quad l \quad D_i'.Levels\}$,

$D_i'.parent = \{<o_1, o_2> \mid <o_1, o_2> \quad D_i.parent \quad o_1, o_2 \quad D_i'.Members\}, 1 \quad i \quad d$;

$\boldsymbol{M} = \boldsymbol{M}_1 \quad \{M\}$.

$inst(c, C.bv) = \{x_1 \quad <r> \mid x_1 \quad inst(c_1, v_1) \quad r \quad DOM(M)$

$\exists! x_2(x_2 \quad inst(c_2, v_2) \quad p(x_1, x_2) \quad r = f(me(x_1), me(x_2)))\}$

where $x_1 \quad <r>$ means the conjunction of x_1 with $<r>$, i.e., if $x_1 = < o_1, o_2, ..., o_d, r_1, r_2, ..., r_m >$, then $x_1 \quad <r> = < o_1, o_2, ..., o_d, r_1, r_2, ..., r_m, r>$.

$\exists! x_2$ means there exists only one x_2.

For example, we can calculate the percentage of each month's sales of those of the year given the month and year sales as follows.

Assume that the basic sales data are stored in cube c_1, let

$v_1 = <bv \quad ^{sum}<Total, Month, Total>>$, $v_2 = <bv \quad ^{sum}<Total, Year, Total>>$,

$c_2 = c_1$,

then the result is $c_1.v_1 \bowtie_{year(c_1.Date)=year(c_2.Date)}^{percent=c_1.Sale\,/\,c_2.Sale} c_2.v_2$.

So far we have introduced all the operations of the new model we defined. The operations mentioned in literatures mainly include *slice/dice*, *roll up*, *drill down* and CUBE, etc. Now we discuss how to express them within the new model.

slice/dice. *slice* means to select all the measure data corresponding to a member of a certain dimension; and *dice* means to select the measure data corresponding to a subset of the members of each dimension. Both of them can be expressed easily with operation *select*.

roll up and *drill down* mean to get measure data of higher and lower level from data of certain levels respectively. The results of these two operations are in the different aggregation nodes of the same cube as the given data.

Operator CUBE [2] is used to calculate the cube defined on a single aggregation function. Because the cube we defined contains data of all the aggregation nodes, the result of CUBE is a special case of the cube.

roll up, *drill down* and CUBE operator cause no changes on the data of a cube, so they are not included in the operation set of the new model.

6 Query Examples

In this section, we will illustrate the expressive power of the new model by expressing analysis queries taken from [1]. We assume that the sales data described in example1 are stored in cube *c*.

Q1. For store *s* and for each product, give the fractional increase in the sales in each month of 1999 relative to the same month in 1998.

1. For store *s*, select sales of 1999 and 1998 respectively:

   $c_1 := \sigma_{Store = s \quad Year(Day) = 1999}(c),\ c_2 := \sigma_{Store = s \quad Year(Day) = 1998}(c)$

2. Join c_1 and c_2, the join condition is that the months are the same but years are not equal. The new measure equals to $(c_1.Sale - c_2.Sale) / c_1.Sale$:

   Let $v = \langle bv \quad ^{sum} \langle Store, Month, Category \rangle\rangle$,

   $c_3 := c_1.v \bowtie^{Increment=(c_1.Sale - c_2.Sale)/(c_1.Sale)}_{m(c_1.Month)=m(c_2.Month) \quad year(c_1.Month) \quad year(c_2.Month)} c_2.v$ where

   m(*Month*) means the month value of *Month* where *Month* carries the information of year while *m*(*Month*) not, e.g., *m*(1999.1) = 1.

   c_3 is the required result.

Q2. For each product category, select total sales of this month for the product that had the highest sales in that category of last month.

1. Calculate the sales in 1999.10 from basic data:

   $c_1 := \sigma_{Month(Day) = 1999.10}(c)$

2. Associate the sales with products:

   $v_1 := \langle bv \quad ^{sum} \langle Total, Month, Code \rangle\rangle$

   $v_1' := \langle bv \quad ^{sum} \langle Total, Month, Code \rangle \quad ^{max} \langle Total, Month, Category \rangle\rangle$

   $c_1' := c_1$

   $c_1 := c_1.v_1 \bowtie_{c_1.Month=c_1'Month \quad Catagory(c_1.Code)=c_1'Catagory \quad c_1.Sale=c_1'Sale} c_1'.v_1'$

   c_1 is the required result.

Q3. Select stores of which the total sale of every product category increased in each of 1997-1999.

1. Select sale data in 1997 – 1999 from the basic data respectively:

   $c_1 := \sigma_{Year(Day) = 1997}(c),\ c_2 := \sigma_{Year(Day) = 1998}(c),\ c_3 := \sigma_{Year(Date) = 1999}(c)$

2. Select the store of which the total sale of every product category increased in 1997:

   $v := \langle bv \quad ^{sum} \langle Store, Category, Year \rangle\rangle$

   $c_2 := c_2.v \bowtie_{c_2.Year = c_3.Year - 1 \quad c_2.Store = c_3.Store \quad c_2.Category = c_3.Category \quad c_2.Sale < c_3.Salre} c_3.v$

3. Select the store of which the total sale of every product category increased in 1998:

   $c_1 := c_1.v \bowtie_{c_1.Year = c_2.Year - 1 \quad c_1.Store = c_2.Store \quad c_1.Category = c_2.Category \quad c_1.Sale < c_2.Salre} c_2$

   c_1 is the required result.

7 Conclusions

We propose a novel multidimensional data model one of whose salient features is that it describes aggregation data in all levels based on aggregation nodes.

It has attracted many research interests to model multidimensional data, e.g., [1, 3, 4, 5, 6, 7] and a survey can be found in [8]. Most of those models define a cube as the data set of one certain aggregation node, so the data of different cubes (aggregation nodes in our model) are independent on each other. In our model data of all aggregation nodes exist logically and are kept consistent. Access to data of any level can be carried out with only operation *select* and navigation operations such as *roll up* and *drill down* are not necessary any more.

The problem of determining data of which aggregation nodes should exist physically, i.e., which aggregation nodes should be materialized is not trivial. In fact, given a cube *c*, data of every aggregation node of *c* and those cubes derived from *c* can be treated as materialized views of *inst*(*c*, *bv*). So the above problem is that of selection of materialized views, which is beyond the scope of this paper.

References

[1] R. Agrawal, A. Gupta, S. Sarawagi, Modeling Multidimensional Databases, ICDE '97: 232-243

[2] J. Gray, A. Bosworth, A. Layman, H. Pirahesh, Data Cube: A Relational Aggregation Operator Generalizing Group-By, Cross-Tab, and Sub-Totals, Microsoft Technical Report MSR-TR-95-22, 1995, available at http://www.research.microsoft.com/~gray/

[3] W. Lehner, Modeling Large Scale OLAP Scenarios, EDBT '98: 23-27

[4] J. Li, H. Gao, A Multidimensional Data Model for Data Warehousing, Journal of Software, China, 2000, 11(7): 908-917

[5] C. Li, X. Wang, A Data Model for Supporting Online Analytical Processing, CIKM '96: 81-88

[6] T. B. Pedersen, C. S. Jensen, Multidimensional Data Modeling for Complex Data, ICDE '99: 336-345

[7] P. Vassiliadis, Modeling Multidimensional Databases, Cubes and Cube Operations, SSDBM '98

[8] P. Vassiliadis, T. Sellis, A Survey of Models for OLAP Databases, SIGMOD Record, 28(4), Dec. 1999: 64-69

Comparing String Similarity Measures for Reducing Inconsistency in Integrating Data from Different Sources

Sergio Luján-Mora and Manuel Palomar

Departamento de Lenguajes y Sistemas Informáticos, Universidad de Alicante,
Campus de San Vicente del Raspeig
Ap. Correos 99 - E-03080 Alicante, Spain
{slujan, mpalomar}@dlsi.ua.es

Abstract. The Web has dramatically increased the need for efficient and flexible mechanisms to provide integrated views over multiple heterogeneous information sources. When multiple sources need to be integrated, each source may represent data differently. A common problem is the possible inconsistency of the data: the very same term may have different values, due to misspelling, a permuted word order, spelling variants and so on. In this paper, we present an improvement from our previous work for reducing inconsistency found in existing databases. The objective of our method is integration and standardization of different values that refer to the same term. All the values that refer to a same term are clustered by measuring their degree of similarity. The clustered values can be assigned to a common value that could be substituted for the original values. The paper describes and compares five different similarity measures for clustering and evaluates their performance on real-world data. The method we present may work well in practice but it is time-consuming.

1 Introduction

Information fusion is the process of integration and interpretation of data from different sources in order to derive information of a new quality. Integrating databases into a common repository has become a research topic for many years. Information fusion is a very complex problem, and is relevant in several fields, such as Data Re-engineering, Data Warehouse, Web Information Systems, E-commerce, Scientific Databases, etc.

One of the main problems in integrating databases into a common repository is the possible inconsistency of the values stored in them, i.e., the very same term may have different values. This problem is known as the *field matching problem*, and it is part of the Data Cleaning task. This is an important issue, because erroneous datasets propagate error in each successive generation of data.

The problem of the inconsistency found in the values stored in databases may have two principal causes:

X.S. Wang, G. Yu, and H. Lu (Eds.): WAIM 2001, LNCS 2118, pp. 191–202, 2001.

1. Single-source: Databases may contain duplicate values concerning the same real-world entity (inconsistency) because of data entry errors (misspelling, typing errors), because of unstandardized abbreviations, or because different people can use different values to name the same term (spelling variants, permuted word order, transliteration differences). For instance, a database that stores the names of the departments of a university may have several different forms (e.g., the use of upper-case letters or abbreviations): *"Department of Software and Computing Systems"*, *"Dep. of Software and Computing Systems"*, *"D. of software and computing systems"*, etc.
2. Multi-source: On the other hand, this is a common problem in environments where multiple databases must be combined: equivalent data in the multiple sources must be identified (knowledge discovery, data mining, data warehouse, data re-engineering, etc.).

In Figure 1, we present an example to show the aim of our proposal. Let us suppose that we have different databases (particularly, different relational tables) and the sources have different criteria for representing values in affiliation names. For example, with reference to the affiliation of researchers who work at the University of Alicante, we may easily find that there are different values for this university: *"Universidad de Alicante"* or *"Universidad Alicante"* (in Spanish) and *"Alicante University"* (in English).

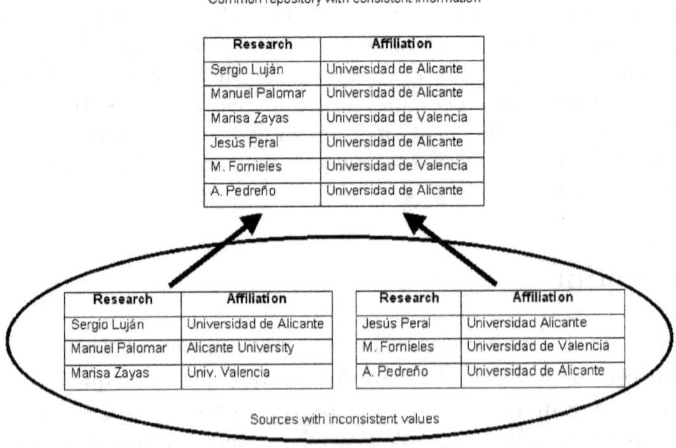

Fig. 1. Solving inconsistency into a common repository

The remainder of the paper is structured as follows: Section 2 outlines the possible causes that give rise to the different variants that appear for the same term and introduces our method for reducing inconsistency found in existing databases; Section 3 explains the core of our study and details the technical aspects; Section 4 provides an evaluation of the method; and finally, our conclusions are presented in Section 5.

2 Analysis of the Problem

This section exposes the origin of the problem and present and intuitive proposal of our method to reduce inconsistency.

2.1 Causes

After analysing several databases with information both in Spanish and in English, we have noticed that the different values that appear for a given term are due to a combination of the following causes:

1. The omission or inclusion of the written accent: *"Asociación Astronómica"* or *"Asociacion Astronomica"*.
2. The use of upper-case and lower-case letters: *"Department of Software and Computing Systems"* or *"Department of software and computing systems"*.
3. The use of abbreviations and acronyms: *"Department of Software, University of Alicante"* or *"Dep. of Software, Univ. Alicante"*.
4. Word order: *"Miguel de Cervantes Saavedra"* or *"Cervantes Saavedra, Miguel de"*.
5. Different transliterations[1]: *"Kolmogorov"* or *"Kolmogorof"*, *"Chebyshev"* or *"Tchebysheff"*.
6. Punctuation marks (e.g., hyphens, commas, semicolons, brackets, exclamation marks, etc.): *"Laboratorio Multimedia (mmlab)"* or *"Laboratorio Multimedia - mmlab"*.
7. Errors: Misspelling (apart from the written accent), typing or printing errors (absence of a character, interchange of adjacent characters, etc.), phonetic errors: *"Gabinete de imagen"* or *"Gavinete de imagen"*, *"Bill Clinton"* or *"Bill Klinton"*.
8. Numbers: *"Area 51"* or *"Area fifty-one"*.
9. Extra words: *"Royal Yacht Club"* or *"Yacht Club"*.
10. Different denominations and synonyms: *"Seismological Register Unit"* or *"Seismic Register Unit"*.
11. Use of different languages: *"Tribunal de Cuentas"* (Spanish), *"Court of Auditors"* (English) or *"La Cour des Comptes"* (French).

There has been great interest in studying the quality of the information stored in databases for a long time [9,10], and diverse methods have been developed for the reduction of the inconsistency found in databases [1,2,4,8,7].

[1] Transliteration is the general process of converting characters from one particular script to another one, such as converting from Greek, Russian Cyrilic alphabet or Japanese Katakana (Kana) to Latin. It is very important to note that this transliteration is not translation. It is simply converting the letters from one script to another, not translating the underlying words.

2.2 Intuitive Proposal of a Method to Reduce the Inconsistency Found in Databases

The method we propose in this paper improves our previous work [7]. We have added new distances, developed different evaluation measures and employed a different clustering algorithm. These improvements result in a better performance of the method.

Our algorithm resolves all the problems detailed in Section 2.1, except the four last causes, which depend on how different the two strings that represent the same term are. The method that we propose can be divided into six steps [7] (the improvements presented in this paper affect the fourth step, *Clustering*): Preparation, Reading, Sorting, Clustering, Checking, and Updating.

3 Technical Description of the Method

In this section, technical aspects of our method are described. We start by introducing a previous processing for obtaining better results in Section 3.1. Section 3.2 describes how the similarity between two strings is considered. Section 3.3 presents the algorithm itself and finally, Section 3.4 explains the last step of the method, i.e., checking that the obtained clusters are correct.

3.1 Previous Processing

The strings undergo a previous processing to obtain better results from the clustering. The objective of this processing is to avoid the three first causes of the appearance of different forms for the same term (see Section 2.1): i.e., accents, lower-case/upper-case and abbreviations. The accents are eliminated, the string is converted to lower-case and the abbreviations are expanded.

3.2 String Similarity

The similarity between any two strings must be evaluated. There are several similarity measures; in our research, we employ five measures: Levenshtein distance (LD), invariant distance from word position (IDWP), a modified version of the previous distance (MIDWP), Jaccard's coefficient (JC), and the minimum of the four previous measures (CSM).

The *edit distance* or *Levenshtein distance* (LD) [5] has been traditionally used in approximate-string searching and spelling-error detection and correction. The LD of strings x and y is defined as the minimal number of simple editing operations that are required to transform x into y. The simple editing operations considered are: insert a character, delete of a character, and substitute a character with another. In our method, we have taken a unitary cost function for all the operations and for all of the characters.

If two strings contain the same words (variant forms of the same term) but with a permuted word order, the LD will not permit their clustering. To solve this problem, we introduce another distance that we call the *invariant distance from word position* (IDWP) [6]. It is based on the *approximate word matching* referred to in [2]. To calculate the IDWP of two strings, they are broken up into words (we consider a word to be any succession of digits and letters of the Spanish alphabet). The idea is to pair off the words so that the *sum* of the LD is minimised. If the strings contain different numbers of words, the cost of each unpaired word is the length of the word.

We also use a *modified IDWP* (MIDWP). We add a new matching condition: if two strings fulfil Equation 1, we assume they match perfectly[2] (in that case, we consider their LD is zero):

$$LD(x, y) \leq 1 + \frac{|x| + |y|}{20} \ . \tag{1}$$

The last measure we have employed is the *Jaccard's coefficient* (JC) [11], the ratio of the matching words in x and y to all the words in x and y:

$$JC(X, Y) = \frac{|X \cap Y|}{|X \cup Y|} \ , \tag{2}$$

where X and Y are the set of words of the strings x and y respectively.

In order to compare the above-mentioned measures, we need the JC subtracted from one (1 - JC). Besides, the LD, IDWP, and MIDWP are divided by the length of the longest string. Thus, all the measures obtain a similarity value from 0 (x and y are the same string) to 1 (x and y are totally different).

Finally, we also combine the four previous similarity measures (*combined similarity measure*, CSM): we choose the minimum of the four similarity measures for every pair of strings.

3.3 Algorithm

The goal of clustering is to find similarity between strings and cluster them together based on a threshold of similarity between the strings. In related work [2, 7], the clustering algorithm employed is basically the *leader algorithm* [3]. This algorithm is chosen as opposed to more elaborate algorithms (e.g., *k-means algorithm*, *Fisher algorithm*) because the more elaborate algorithms are slower and the number of clusters is unknown. The *leader algorithm* is very fast, requiring only one pass through the data, but it has several negative properties: the partition is not invariant under reordering of the cases and the first clusters are always larger than the later ones. This is intrinsic to the algorithm: the comparison between a new string and the existing clusters is made only until a cluster that meets the condition is found, without considering the possibility that a better value of the criteria is met later, for another cluster.

The clustering algorithm we propose in Table 1 resolves the first-clusters-larger problem: it uses a *centroid*[3] method and the comparison for every string is made with all the existing clusters for the time being.

[2] If there is less than one mismatch every 10 characters, we assume that the strings match perfectly (near perfect).

[3] In this research, the *centroid* (also called *center of mass* or *center of gravity* in physics) is representative of all the strings in its cluster.

Table 1. Clustering algorithm

```
Input:
S: Sorted strings in descending order by frequency (s_1,...,s_m)
α: Threshold

Output:
C: Set of clusters (c_1,...,c_n)

Variables:
b, d, i, j, k

    Begin with string s_i (i = 1)
    Let the number of clusters be k = 1
    Classify s_i into the first cluster c_k
    Increase i by 1
    Do While i ≤ m { // For all the strings
        Begin working with the cluster c_j (j = 1)
        Calculate the distance between the string s_i and the
        centroid of cluster c_j: d = D(s_i, c_j)
        Let the best cluster be c_b (b = 1)
        Increase j by 1
        Do While j ≤ k { // For all the existing clusters
            If D(s_i, c_j) < d then {
                Let the lower distance be d = D(s_i, c_j) and
                the best cluster be b = j
            }
            Increase j by 1 // Next cluster
        }
        If d < α then { // Closer and close enough cluster
            Assign string s_i to cluster c_b
            Recalculate the centroid of cluster c_b
        }
        Else { // New cluster
            Increase k by 1
            Create a new cluster c_k and classify s_i into the new
            cluster
        }
        Increase i by 1 // Next string
    }
```

The algorithm chooses the strings, from greatest to smallest frequency of appearance, since it assumes that the most frequent strings have a greater probability of being correct, and thus, they are taken as being representative of the rest. As seen in Table 1, it depends on one parameter α (threshold). The algorithm makes one pass through the strings, assigning each string to the cluster whose *centroid* is closer and close enough (distance between the string and the *centroid* lower than α) and making a new cluster for cases that are not close enough to any existing *centroid*. The distance D is calculated using one of the similarity measures explained in Section 3.2.

The *centroid* of a cluster must be recalculated every time a new string is assigned to the cluster. The *centroid* is chosen to minimise the sum-of-squares criterion:

$$\sum_{i=1}^{n}(D(s_i, C))^2 \ , \tag{3}$$

where n is the number of strings assigned to the cluster and C is the *centroid*.

3.4 Revision and Updating

The final step of the method consists of visual checking the obtained clusters and detecting possible errors to correct them. In the original database, the strings of a cluster are replaced by its *centroid* (it represents its cluster). Therefore, almost all variants of a term are put together under a single form.

4 Experimental Results and Evaluation

We have used four files for evaluating our method[4]. They contain data from four different databases with inconsistency problems: files A, B, and D contain information in Spanish, while file C in English. The method has been implemented in *C* and *C++*, running in *Linux*.

4.1 File Descriptions

Table 2 gives a description of these four files. The *optimal number of clusters* (ONC) indicates the number of handcrafted clusters. The three last columns contain the number of single strings with (W) and without (WO) the expansion of abbreviations, and the rate of reduction (on expanding the abbreviations, the number of single strings is reduced, since duplicates are removed). We have done all the tests with and without the expansion of abbreviations.

The amount of duplication of a file is measured by the *duplication factor* (DF) [1], which indicates how many duplicates (textual or not textual) of each record appear in the file, on the average. Table 3 shows the DF and the standard deviation (SD) of the four files. It also shows the reduction (Red.) of the DF when the abbreviations are expanded.

[4] These test files are available at
`http://www.dlsi.ua.es/~slujan/files/clusterfiles.tgz`.

Table 2. File descriptions

File	Size (Bytes)	ONC	Strings in file	Strings WO	Strings W	Reduction (%)
A	10,399	92	234	234	145	38.0
B	1,717,706	92	37,599	1.212	1.117	7.8
C	108,608	57	2,206	119	118	0.8
D	24,364	226	596	584	505	13.5

Table 3. Duplication factor (DF) and file consistency index (FCI)

File	Duplication factor					File consistency index				
	WO	SD	W	SD	Red. %	WO	SD	W	SD	Red. %
A	2.54	1.00	1.58	0.84	37.8	0.31	0.29	0.12	0.26	61.2
B	13.17	5.39	12.14	5.23	7.8	1.72	1.26	1.11	1.14	35.4
C	2.09	2.88	2.07	2.80	0.9	0.33	1.18	0.31	1.13	6.0
D	2.58	1.16	2.23	1.08	13.6	0.53	0.44	0.27	0.27	49.0

The DF shows how many duplicates of each record exist, but it does not indicates if the duplicates look like each other or not. We have developed a coefficient (consistency index) that permits the evaluation of the complexity of a cluster: the greater the value of the coefficient is, the more different the strings that form the cluster are. A null value indicates that the cluster contains only one string. The *consistency index* (CI) of a cluster of n strings is defined as:

$$CI = \frac{\sum_{i=1}^{n}\sum_{j=1}^{n} LD(x_i, x_j)}{\sum_{i=1}^{n} |x_i|} . \tag{4}$$

The *file consistency index* (FCI) of a file that contains m clusters is defined as the average of the consistency indexes of all the existing clusters in the file:

$$FCI = \frac{\sum_{i=1}^{m} CI_i}{m} . \tag{5}$$

The FCI for hand-generated clusters of the files A, B, C, and D is shown in Table 3. As the FCI is an average, the table also shows the standard deviation (SD). It is obvious that the clusters of file B are more complex than those of files A, C, and D. In all cases, however, the FCI is reduced when expanding the abbreviations, since the discrepancies between the strings of a given cluster tend to diminish. With respect to file C, the reduction of FCI when the abbreviations are expanded is minimum, because the reduction of strings is not appreciable: only 0.8% versus 38.0% (file A), 7.8% (file B), and 13.5% (file D) (Table 2).

4.2 Evaluation Measures

We have evaluated the quality of the produced clusters when our method is applied by using four measures that are obtained by comparing the clusters produced by our method with the optimal clusters (ONC):

1. NC: number of clusters. Clusters that have been generated.
2. NCC: number of completely correct clusters. Clusters that coincide with the optimal ones: they contain the same strings. From this measure, we obtain *Precision*: NCC divided by ONC.
3. NIC: number of incorrect clusters. Clusters that contain an erroneous string[5]. From this measure, we obtain the *Error*: NIC divided by ONC.
4. NES: number of erroneous strings. Strings incorrectly clustered.

4.3 Evaluation and Discussion

As we have already mentioned, the clustering algorithm depends on one parameter (α). We have done all the tests on setting its value from 0.0 to 0.599, in 0.001 steps.

Table 4. Precision and Error: previous / current work

File		Previous work Precision (%)	Previous work Error (%)	Current work Precision (%)	Current work Error (%)	Similarity measure	α
A	WO	70.7	7.6	81.5	8.6	CSM	[0.236, 0.249]
	W	84.8	0	89.1	0	MIDWP	[0.153, 0.166]
B	WO	67.4	8.7	71.7	9.7	CSM	[0.270, 0.288]
	W	72.8	6.5	77.1	2.1	CSM	[0.174, 0.176]
C	WO	85.9	1.7	89.4	1.7	JC	[0.471, 0.499]
	W	84.2	1.7	87.7	1.7	JC	[0.471, 0.499]
D	WO	43.8	16.8	53.0	15.9	IDWP	[0.435, 0.437]
	W	67.7	6.2	76.1	2.6	MIDWP	0.187

We compare the performance of the five similarity measures. The result of the experiments using the four files and the similarity measures are summarized in Table 4 (column **Current work**). The table shows the highest precision and the corresponding error obtained in each file when the LD, IDWP, MIDWP, JC, and CSM are used. The corresponding threshold (α) also appears. Note that the similarity measure that produces the best results varies from a file to another. Moreover, the expansion of abbreviations improves the precision and diminishes the error in all cases (except file C). Besides, the best precision, with a lower error, is obtained at a lower threshold when the abbreviations are expanded.

[5] A subset of a correct cluster is not considered as incorrect.

In Table 4, we also compare the precision and error obtained in our previous work [7] and in the current work. The test files A, B, C, and D used in the previous work are the same of this paper. As you can see, the new method achieves better results: the precision increases and the error keeps very similar values or even diminish. In some cases, the precision rises 10 units.

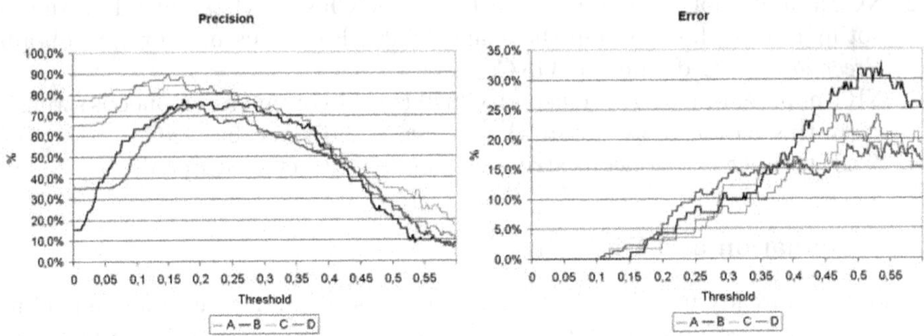

Fig. 2. Precision and error obtained with CSM and expansion of abbreviations

The left graph in Figure 2 shows the dependency of precision from the threshold (α) for all four files when the combined similarity measure (CSM) with expansion of abbreviations is applied (the graph obtained without expansion of abbreviations is very similar to this one). The four curves have a similar shape, with a peak between 0.1 and 0.25.

Figure 2 also shows the effect of varying the threshold (α) in the error. The right graph compares the error for all four files when the combined similarity measure (CSM) with expansion of abbreviations is applied. The error is insignificant when the threshold is under 0.15. For a threshold under 0.35, the error is below 15%.

Finally, Figure 3 displays precision (left) and error (right) achieved with the modified invariant distance from word position (MIDWP) and expansion of abbreviations. The shape of these two graphs is very similar to Figure 2. This time, there is a peak between 0.15 and 0.3. When the results obtained with the other similarity measures (LD, IDWP and JC) are plotted, the graphs also present a similar shape.

The threshold that obtains the best precision is certainly difficult to determine, because it varies from a data set to another one. But the Figures 2 and 3 insinuate a value between 0.1 and 0.3.

5 Conclusions and Future Work

Referential integrity provided by relational database management systems prevents users or applications from entering inconsistent data. Databases with an inadequate design may suffer data redundancy and inconsistency. On the other

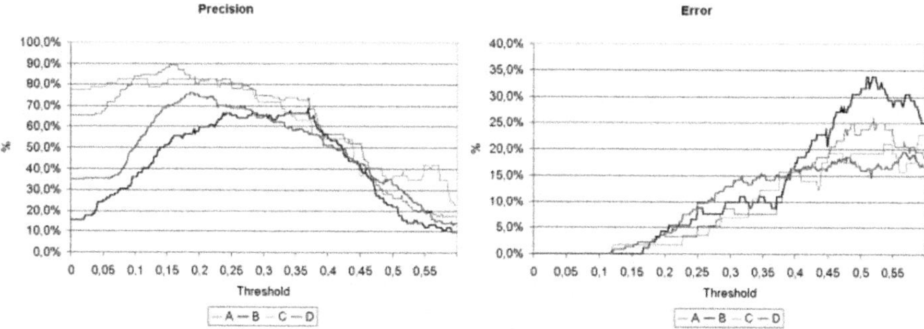

Fig. 3. Precision and error obtained with MIDWP and expansion of abbreviations

hand, there is an increasing need to integrate data and provide a uniform view of data. This paper has discussed techniques for improving data quality by using clustering to find different values that refer to the same term and replacing all values in a cluster with a unique form. So, we have presented an automatic method for reducing the inconsistency found in existing databases. Our method clusters strings based on their proximity to the existing clusters: the distance between a cluster and a string is determined as the difference between the *centroid* of the cluster and the string. The method we have proposed achieves successful results with a considerably low error rate, although it does not eliminate the utility of reviewing the clusters obtained.

The final number of clusters and the effectiveness of the method strongly depends on the threshold value fixed by the user. The threshold lets the user adjust the behavior of the method: a very small threshold (conservative) will produce a large number of small clusters and a decrease in the number of matching values that should be clustered, meanwhile a very large (aggressive) one will produce a small number of large clusters and an increase in the number of falsely matched values. Based on the data obtained in our research, we propose the use of a threshold between 0.1 and 0.3.

Our first contribution is an algorithm that is domain-independent and language-independent. Previous related work deals with special cases of the field matching problem (customer addresses, census records, bibliographic databases, etc.). The second contribution is the use of two methods for evaluating the similarity between two strings: the invariant distance from word position, derived from the Levenshtein distance, and the combined similarity measure. Last but not least, we present the consistency index that permits the evaluation of the complexity of a cluster: the greater the value of the coefficient is, the more different the strings that form the cluster are.

Currently, we are working on improving the algorithm in order to cluster the multilingual values. We are applying dictionaries and other techniques relating to natural language processing (e.g., removing stop words, lexical analysis).

We are also planning to investigate other heterogeneity problems: record matching (merge/purge problem) and schema level conflicts (attribute naming conflicts, format heterogeneity, and so on).

References

[1] D. Bitton and D. J. DeWitt. Duplicate record elimination in large data files. *ACM Transactions on Database Systems*, 8(2):255–265, June 1983.

[2] J. C. French, A. L. Powell, and E. Schulman. Applications of Approximate Word Matching in Information Retrieval. In F. Golshani and K. Makki, editors, *Proceedings of the Sixth International Conference on Information and Knowledge Management (CIKM 1997)*, pages 9–15, Las Vegas (USA), November 10-14 1997. ACM Press.

[3] J. A. Hartigan. *Clustering Algorithms.* A Wiley Publication in Applied Statistics. John Wiley & Sons, New York (USA), 1975.

[4] M. A. Hern ndez and S. J. Stolfo. Real-world data is dirty: Data cleansing and the merge/purge problem. *Journal of Data Mining and Knowledge Discovery*, 2(1):9–37, 1998.

[5] V. I. Levenshtein. Binary codes capable of correcting deletions, insertions, and reversals. *Cybernetics and Control Theory*, 10:707–710, 1966.

[6] S. Luján-Mora. An Algorithm for Computing the Invariant Distance from Word Position. Internet: http://www.dlsi.ua.es/~slujan/files/idwp.ps, June 2000.

[7] S. Luján-Mora and M. Palomar. Clustering of Similar Values, in Spanish, for the Improvement of Search Systems. In M. C. Monard and J. S. Sichman, editors, *International Joint Conference IBERAMIA-SBIA 2000 Open Discussion Track Proceedings*, pages 217–226, Atibaia, São Paulo (Brazil), November 19-22 2000. ICMC/USP.

[8] A. E. Monge and C. P. Elkan. An efficient domain-independent algorithm for detecting approximately duplicate database records. In *SIGMOD Workshop on Research Issues on Data Mining and Knowledge Discovery (DMKD'97)*, pages 23–29, Tucson (USA), May 11 1997.

[9] A. Motro and I. Rakov. Estimating the Quality of Databases. In T. Andreasen, H. Christiansen, and H. Larsen, editors, *Proceedings of FQAS 98: Third International Conference on Flexible Query Answering Systems*, volume 1495 of *Lecture Notes in Artificial Intelligence*, pages 298–307, Roskilde (Denmark), May 1998. Springer-Verlag.

[10] E. T. O'Neill and D. Vizine-Goetz. The Impact of Spelling Errors on Databases and Indexes. In C. Nixon and L. Padgett, editors, *10th National Online Meeting Proceedings*, pages 313–320, New York (USA), May 9-11 1989. Learned Information Inc.

[11] C. J. V. Rijsbergen. *Information Retrieval.* Butterworths, London (UK), 2 edition, 1979.

Revisit on View Maintenance in Data Warehouses

Weifa Liang[1] and Jeffrey X. Yu[2]

[1] Department of Computer Science,The Australian National University
Canberra, ACT 0200, Australia
[2] Department Systems Engineering and Engineering Management
Chinese University of Hong Kong, Hong Kong

Abstract. The complete consistence maintenance of SPJ-type materialized views in a distributed source environment has been studied extensively in the past several years due to its fundamental importance to data warehouses. Much effort has been taken based on an assumption that each source site contains only one relation and no multiple appearances of a relation is allowed in the definition of views. In this paper a generalized version of the view maintenance problem that not only a relation may appear many times in the definition of the view but also a site may contain multiple relations is considered. Due to unpredictability of the communication delay and bandwidth between the data warehouse and the sources, the materialized view maintenance is very expensive and time consuming. Therefore, one natural question for this generalized case is whether there is an algorithm which not only keeps the view complete consistent with the remote source data but also minimizes the number of accesses to the remote sites. In this paper we first show that a known SWEEP algorithm is one of the best algorithms for the case where multiple relations are included in a site. We then propose a complete consistency algorithm which accesses remote sources less than $n-1$ times for the case where multiple appearances of a relation is allowed and n is the number of relations in the definition of the view.

1 Introduction

Data warehouses store materialized views in order to provide fast access to the integrated data from various local and/or remote sources [4]. They can be used as an integrated and uniform basis for decision support, data mining, data analysis, and ad-hoc querying across the source data. One of the fundamental problems in data warehousing is the view maintenance problem which aims at maintaining the content of a materialized view at a certain level of consistency with the source data when the updates commit at the remote sources.

Many incremental maintenance algorithms for materialized views have been introduced for centralized database systems [2,7,5]. There are also a number of similar studies in the distributed environments [3,8,12,14,15,9]. These previous works have formed a spectrum of solutions ranging from a fully virtual approach

X.S. Wang, G. Yu, and H. Lu (Eds.): WAIM 2001, LNCS 2118, pp. 203–211, 2001.

at one end where no data is materialized and all user queries are answered by interrogating the source data [8], to a full replication at the other end where the whole databases at the sources are copied to the warehouse so that the view refreshments (updates) can be handled in the warehouse locally [6,11]. In order to keep the content (data) of a view consistent with the source data, the approach most commonly used is to maintain the warehouse at night time when the warehouse is not available to users, while the user query can be processed in the day time when the maintenance transactions are not running. Following [14, 1], we here only consider maintaining materialized views through reducing the number of accesses to the remote site without using any auxiliary views. The complete consistence maintenance of a SPJ-type materialized view has been investigated in the past several years [14,1,10]. All these previous studies are based on the assumption that each source site contains only one relation and no multiple appearances of a relation are allowed in the definition of the view. In this paper we consider a generalized case which allows that (i) a relation may appear many times in the definition of the view; and (ii) a site may contain multiple relations. We first show that the SWEEP algorithm is one of the best such algorithms to make the view complete consistent. In other words, there is no maintenance algorithm which accesses the remote sites less than $n-1$ times but keeps the view complete consistent with the source data. We then propose a complete consistency algorithm which accesses the remote source less than $n-1$ times to evaluate the view update for the case with multiple identical relations in the definition of the view.

2 Preliminaries

A *data warehouse* is a repository of integrated data which collects and maintains a large amount of data from multiple distributed, autonomous and possibly heterogeneous sources. A typical data warehouse architecture is defined in [13]. On the source side, associated with each source there is a monitor/wrapper which collects the data of interest and sends the data to the warehouse. The monitor/wrapper is responsible for identifying changes and notifying the warehouse. On the data warehouse side, there is an integrator which receives the source data, performs necessary data integration and translation, adds any extra desired information such as the timestamps for historical analysis, and requests the warehouse to store the data. In effect, the warehouse caches a materialized view of the source data. The data is then readily available to user applications for querying and analysis. The communication between the source and data warehouse is assumed to be reliable FIFOs, i.e., messages are not lost on their way between the source and the warehouse and delivered in the order in which they originally are sent. No communication is imposed between any two sources. In fact, they may not be able to communicate with each other.

A warehouse state (source state) ws (ss) represents the content of the data warehouse (sources) at a given time point. The warehouse state changes whenever one of the views in it is updated. A source state ss_j is a vector that contains n components, and the ith component, $ss_j[i]$ is the state of source i which represents the content of source i at that given time point. Let $ws_0, ws_1, \ldots, ws_f$ be the sequence of the warehouse states after a series of source updates $ss_0, ss_1, \ldots, ss_q$, V be a materialized view, and $V(ws_j)$ be the content of V at warehouse state ws_j. Assume that V is derived from n sources, where each source has a unique identity i, $1 \leq i \leq n$. Further, assume that source updates are executed in serializable fashion across sources, and ss_q is the final state of the sources. $V(ss_j)$ is the result of computing the view V over the source state ss_j. That is, $V(ss_j)$ is evaluated over all R_i at the state $ss_j[i]$, $1 \leq i \leq n$. Given a materialized view V, V is *complete consistent* with the source data if, for every source state ss_i, there is a corresponding warehouse state ws_j such that $V(ss_i) = V(ws_j)$. Assume that initially $V(ws_0) = V(ss_0)$. That is, there is a complete order preserving mapping between the states of the view and the states of the sources.

In this paper we focus on the maintenance of SPJ materialized views such that they are completely consistent with the remote source data. Let V be a SPJ-type view derived from n relations $R_1, R_2, \ldots, R_n$, defined as follows.

$$V = \pi_X \sigma_P (R_1 \bowtie R_2 \bowtie \ldots \bowtie R_n), \tag{1}$$

where X is the set of projection attributes, P is the selection condition which is the conjunction of disjunctive clauses, and R_i is in a remote source j, $1 \leq j \leq K$ ($K \leq n$). Updates to the source data are either insertions or deletion of tuples. A modification is treated as a deletion followed by an insertion. Furthermore, the views in the warehouse are based on bag semantics.

3 Multiple Relations within a Single Site

In this section we consider the complete consistency maintenance of materialized views when a site contains multiple relations. As mentioned by its authors, the SWEEP algorithm [1] can be easily extended to deal with this case, which treats a site containing d relations ($d > 1$) as d different sites virtually. Thus, the evaluation of an update to the materialized view is implemented through visiting the site at least d times. To avoid multiple visits to a site, one natural question is to ask whether it is possible to evaluate the update by visiting each site just once instead of d times as suggested by the SWEEP algorithm? In the following we dedicate ourselves to answer this question. Unfortunately, we show that there is no algorithm that keeps the view complete consistent with the source data by visiting each site just once. Therefore, the SWEEP algorithm is one of the best algorithms to achieve the complete consistency.

It is well known that each SPJ type view can be represented by an undirected join-graph $G(N, E)$, where each node in N represents a relation, and there is an edge between two nodes if there is a join condition which only involves two relations. Note that each appearance of a relation in the definition of the view is treated as a different node in the graph. Let $G[S]$ be an induced subgraph by a subset of nodes S ($S \subseteq N$). An auxiliary view $V_S = \bowtie_{R_{i_j} \in S} R_{i_j}$ can be defined using S. If $G[S]$ is disconnected, then V_S is a *direct* product of the $|S|$ relations, which is usually avoided because this leads to very high join cost. Let S_i be the set of relations used by V in site i with $|S_i| > 1$, $1 \leq i \leq K$.

Theorem 1. *Given a SPJ view with multiple relations from a site, there is no algorithm that visits the site just once and keeps the view completely consistent with the remote source data.*

Proof. Assume that there is a source update δR_i at source i. To respond the update, there is a view update δV to be evaluated. Without loss of generality, assume that the site j contains $|S_j|$ relations and $G[S_j]$ is connected. Otherwise, it can be applied to each connected component of $G[S_j]$.

Let $\delta V_{i,j-1}$ be the partial result of δV after having visited sites containing $R_{i+1}, R_{i+2}, \ldots$, and R_{j-1}, where δR is either an insertion ΔR or a deletion ∇R. Now it is about to visit site j at the first time. In order to visit this site just once, all evaluation involved the relations at site j must be done through this visit. For simplicity, let $S_j = \{R_{j_1}, R_{j_2}, R_{j_3}\}$. Assume that R_{j_1} and R_{j_3} have updated δR_{j_1} and δR_{j_3} during the period from t_1 to t_2, where t_1 is the moment that the data warehouse starts evaluating the source update δR_i and t_2 is the moment that site j received the query of evaluating the partial result of δV and $\delta V_{i,j-1}$. Clearly $t_1 < t_2$. Since site j is visited just once, the evaluation involving R_{j_2} and R_{j_3} must be considered too during this visit. Let $\delta V'_{i,j}$ be the partial result received by the data warehouse at t_3 after finishing the evaluation at site j, which has been contaminated, where

$$\begin{aligned}\delta V'_{i,j} &= \delta V_{i,j-1} \bowtie V_{S_j} = \delta V_{i,j-1} \bowtie (R_{j_1} + \delta R_{j_1}) \bowtie R_{j_2} \bowtie (R_{j_3} + \delta R_{j_3}) \\ &= \delta V_{i,j-1} \bowtie (R_{j_1} \bowtie R_{j_2} \bowtie R_{j_3}) + \delta V_{i,j-1} \bowtie (R_{j_1} \bowtie R_{j_2} \bowtie \delta R_{j_3}) \\ &+ \delta V_{i,j-1} \bowtie (\delta R_{j_1} \bowtie R_{j_2} \bowtie \delta R_{j_3}) + \delta V_{i,j-1} \bowtie (\delta R_{j_1} \bowtie R_{j_2} \bowtie \delta R_{j_3}). \quad (2)\end{aligned}$$

Note that the contamination can be cleaned up using the logs of R_{j_1}, R_{j_2} and R_{j_3} in UMQ from t_1 to t_3. One important fact is the data warehouse does not have the knowledge of the subsequent updates δR_{j_1} and δR_{j_3} at the moment it issues the query $\delta V_{i,j-1} \bowtie R_{j_1} \bowtie R_{j_2} \bowtie R_{j_3}$ to site j. So, it is impossible at that time for it to send queries to the site in order to evaluate $R_{j_1} \bowtie R_{j_2} \bowtie \delta R_{j_3}$, $\delta R_{j_1} \bowtie R_{j_2} \bowtie \delta R_{j_3}$, and $\delta R_{j_1} \bowtie R_{j_2} \bowtie \delta R_{j_3}$, while $\delta V_{i,j} = \delta V'_{i,j} - \delta V_{i,j-1} \bowtie (R_{j_1} \bowtie R_{j_2} \bowtie \delta R_{j_3}) - \delta V_{i,j-1} \bowtie (\delta R_{j_1} \bowtie R_{j_2} \bowtie \delta R_{j_3}) - \delta V_{i,j-1} \bowtie (\delta R_{j_1} \bowtie R_{j_2} \bowtie \delta R_{j_3})$. Thus, there is no way to remove the contaminated data if the algorithm allows to visit each site just once. If $G[S_j]$ is disconnected, then for each connected component $G[S_{j_i}]$, an auxiliary view $V_{S_{j_i}}$ can be derived, and the above argument can be applied. Therefore, the theorem follows. ■

4 An SPJ View with Multiple Appearance of Relations

In this section we consider the complete consistency view maintenance for the case where multiple appearances of a relation are allowed in the definition of the view. We start with a simple algorithm for it. Basically, the simple algorithm is similar to the SWEEP algorithm except some minor modifications. Assume that the source update is δR_i, the update δV to V will be evaluated by visiting the other sources (except R_i) one by one. Let $\delta V_{j-1,i}$ be the partial result of δV after visiting distinct remote relations (sources) $R_{i-1}, R_{i-2}, \ldots$, and R_{j-1}. Now the simple algorithm is about to visit next source R_j. If R_j is a copy of R_i, then the partial result $\delta V_{j,i}$ of the update δV becomes $\delta V_{j,i} = \delta V_{j-1,i} \bowtie \delta R_i$, which can be evaluated at the data warehouse without querying the remote source containing R_i because δR_i which is located in the queue UMQ, is available locally. Otherwise, assume that a relation $R_{j'}$ has been visited before ($j < j' < i$) and R_j is a copy of $R_{j'}$ ($R_{j'} = R_j$), the evaluation of the partial result $\delta V_{j,i} = \delta V_{j-1,i} \bowtie R_j$ is done exactly as it is done in the SWEEP algorithm, i.e., the algorithm treats R_j as a different $R_{j'}$ and visits the site containing R_j again.

Having finished the evaluations of $\delta_{1,i}V$ and $\delta_{i,n}V$, $\delta V = \delta_{1,i}V \bowtie \delta_{i,n}V$ is evaluated locally and merged to V, and the updated view is complete consistent with the remote source data, which is stated in the following lemma. The proof of this lemma is similar to that for SWEEP, omitted.

Lemma 1. *For a given SPJ-type view with multiple appearances of a relation in its definition, the view maintained by the simple algorithm is complete consistent with the remote source data.*

4.1 An Improved Algorithm

Unlike the case where multiple relations are located in the same site for which we have shown that $O(n)$ accesses to remote sites is needed, we here show that the number of accesses to remote sources can be reduced by visiting each site only once. If V consists of K distinct relations, then the simple algorithm still requires $O(n)$ accesses to the remote sources. In the following an improved algorithm is presented, which aims to improve the number of accesses to the remote sources.

Following the assumption that there are only K distinct relations among the n relations in the definition of V, let a distinct relation R_{j_i} appear k_{j_i} times in the definition of V. Clearly $\sum_{i=1}^{K} k_{j_i} = n$. Let $Predicate(R_{j_i})$ be the set of join condition clauses in the definition of V, associated with R_{j_i}. It is obvious that $|Predicate(R_{j_i})| = k_{j_i} \leq K$. Let $All_{R_{j_i}}$ be the set of attributes in R_{j_i} and $C_{R_{j_i}} = \{A \mid A$ is an attribute of R_{j_i}, A is appeared in Q, and $Q \in Predicate(R_{j_i})\}$ be a subset of attributes of R_{j_i} which includes the attributes of R_{j_i} in the join condition clauses of V. Denote by $P_{R_{j_i}} = (All_{R_{j_i}} \cap X) \cup C_{R_{j_i}}$, the set of projection attributes of R_{j_i} which must be included in the schema definition of the incremental update expression δV of V.

Assume that k_i is the number of appearances of R_{i_1} in the definition of V. Let $R_{i_1} = R_{i_2} = \ldots = R_{i_{k_i}}$. The key idea behind the proposed algorithm is that one of the k_i copies of R_{i_1} will serve as the *representative* of its other $k_i - 1$ copies. To evaluate an update δV due to a source update, the remote site is visited by only accessing the representative of a relation. For the subsequent evaluation of δV, if the relation is met again, the algorithm does not need to access the remote site containing the relation again, and evaluates the update, based solely on the previously partial result in the data warehouse. As results, only K accesses to the remote sites are needed in order to update V.

The proposed algorithm is presented as follows. If a relation is appeared only once in the definition of V, its treatment during evaluation is exactly the same as that in the SWEEP algorithm. Otherwise, let a relation R_j with multiple copies have been scanned first during the evaluation of δV. Then, R_j will become the representative of the other copies of the relation. The role of a representative is as follows. When dealing with the joining of R_j and the previous partial result of δV, it is required that the schema of the partial result of δV is not only just including those attributes of R_j in X (i.e., the attributes in $X \cap All_{R_j}$ based on the current join condition) but also including the other attributes of R_j in P_{R_j}. With the update evaluation continues, assume that the next scanning source is R_k which is a copy of the representative R_j. This time the data warehouse is able to evaluate the partial result of the update to V, using only the current partial result in the warehouse and the join condition associated with R_k without querying the remote site containing R_k. Thus, the number of accesses to the remote sites will be determined by the number of representatives of relations in the definition of V, instead of $n-1$ in the simple algorithm. In the following we show that the view maintained by the improved algorithm is complete consistent with the source data.

Theorem 2. *Let V be the joins of n relations with some of the relations are identical. Assume that $V = R_1 \bowtie R_2 \bowtie \ldots \bowtie R_n$ and an update δR_i at a remote site R_i, then the evaluation an update δV to V to respond the source update proceeds. Let $\delta V_{k,i} = \delta R_i \bowtie \ldots \bowtie R_j \bowtie \ldots \bowtie R_k$ be the partial result of the update δV. During the evaluation of δV, assume R_k is being scanned and R_k is a copy of R_j that had been visited before, then $\pi_{A_{R_j}} \rho_{P_{R_j}} \delta V_{k,i} = \pi_{A_{R_j}} \rho_{P_{R_j}} (\delta V_{k-1,i} \bowtie R_k)$, i.e., $\delta V_{k,i} = \pi_{A_{R_j}} \rho_{P_{R_j}} \delta V_{k-1,i}$.*

Proof. For the simplicity, we assume that there is only a duplicate relation R_j in the definition of V. If there are more than 2 duplicates of R_j or multiple identical relations, it can be proven inductively. To respond a source update δR_i, the update δV to the view is as follows.

If R_i is the duplicate ($R_j = R_i$), δR_i will be used to replace all appearances of R_i in the definition of V, and there is no difference from the SWEEP algorithm, so, the theorem holds. Otherwise, the duplicate R_j is different from R_i. Following the SWEEP algorithm, to evaluate δV, it scans the other sources from both sides. One is from its current position to the left, and scans $R_{i-1}, R_{i-2}, \ldots, R_1$; another is from the current position R_i to the right, and scans $R_{i+1}, R_{i+2}, \ldots, R_n$. During the scanning, the two copies of R_j will appear in one of the following three positions. (i) Both copies are appeared at the left side. In this case, the first appearance of R_j will be its representative. Let R_k be the second appearance of R_j, then the evaluation of $\delta V_{j,i}$ is similar to its corresponding counterpart in the SWEEP algorithm except it includes more attributes of R_j by our definition, and the evaluation of $\delta V_{k,i}$ can be carried out in the data warehouse using $\delta V_{k-1,i}$ and the current condition associated with R_k. (ii) One copy of R_j is appeared at the left side and another is appeared at the right side. For this case, assume that the evaluation of δV starts from the left, then the representative of R_j is at the left side. The evaluation of δV then moves to the right, and the second appearance R_k of R_j will be at the right side. (iii) Both copies are appeared at the right side, which is similar to case (i), omitted.

We now focus on case (i). To evaluate $\delta V_{k,i}$, it can be done by sending a query $\delta V_{k-1,i} \bowtie R_j$ to the site containing R_j. Let $\delta V'_{k,i}$ be the partial result returned from the site after evaluating the query, which may contain the contaminated data. To obtain $\delta V_{k,i}$, the algorithm will offset the contaminated data by evaluating $\delta V_{k,i} = \delta V'_{k,i} - (\delta V_{k-1,i} \bowtie \cup_{j_i=j} \delta R^x_{j_i})$ at the data warehouse, where $\delta R^x_{j_i}$ is one of the updates to R_j occurred from the moment of δR_i occurred to the moment that $V'_{k,i}$ is received by the data warehouse. Let $\delta V''_{k,i} = \pi_{c_k(R_k)} \delta V_{k-1,i}$, where $c_k(R_k)$ is the current join condition associated with R_k. Then we have $\delta V_{k,i} = \delta V''_{k,i}$. To prove this claim, we first show that $t \in \delta V_{k,i}$ for any tuple $t \in \delta V''_{k,i}$. Let $t_{c_j}[R_j]$ be the set of attributes of R_j associated with the current join condition $c_j(R_j)$. From now on we abuse this concept further, $t_{c_j}[R_j]$ is also used to represent the values of these related attributes in tuple $t \in \delta V''_{k,i}$. Thus, for any tuple $t \in \delta V''_{k,i}$, both $t_{c_j}[R_j]$ and $t_{c_k}[R_k]$ are true. Then, we say that tuple t must be in $\delta V_{k,i}$, because $t_{c_j}[R_j]$ is true in $\delta V_{k-1,i}$ and $t_{c_k}[R_k]$ is true by the current join condition. Therefore, $\delta V''_{k,i} \subseteq \delta V_{k,i}$.

We then show that for any tuple $t' \in \delta V_{k,i}$, it must be in $\delta V''_{k,i}$ too. Since $t' \in \delta V_{k,i}$, $t'_{c_k}[R_k]$ must be true. While t' is obtained through the join of $\delta V_{k-1,i}$ and R_k, $t'_{c_j}[R_j]$ must be true due to that it is in $\delta V_{k-1,i}$. Thus, $t' \in \delta V''_{k,i}$. We therefore have $\delta V_{k,i} \subseteq \delta V''_{k,i}$. The theorem then follows. ■

We now can see that the maintenance time of V is improved dramatically because the number of remote accesses is $O(K)$, not $O(n)$. It must also be mentioned more space for the storage of the partial result is needed due to the fact that all attributes in $\cup_{R \in V} C_R$ must be included in the schema definition of the partial result, while they may not be included in the schema of δV in the `SWEEP` algorithm. Apart from that, in the `SWEEP` algorithm, the evaluation of $\delta V_{1,i}$ and $\delta V_{i,n}$ can be done concurrently. The proposed algorithm, however, cannot achieve this parallelism because there is only one representative for the multiple copies of a relation. In the following we extend our algorithm and make it have such kind of parallelism.

4.2 An Extension with Concurrency

To respond a source update δR_i, the proposed algorithm first evaluates $\delta V_{1,i} = R_1 \bowtie \ldots \bowtie R_{i-1} \bowtie \delta R_i$, then evaluates $\delta V_{i,n} = \delta R_i \bowtie R_{i+1} \bowtie \ldots \bowtie R_n$, and finally evaluates $\delta V = \delta V_{1,i} \bowtie \delta V_{i,n}$ and merges the result δV to V. Now, for the given δR_i, let V_L (V_R) be the set of distinct relations in the sequence of $R_1, R_2, \ldots, R_{i-1}$ ($R_{i+1}, R_{i+2}, \ldots, R_n$). We now extend the proposed algorithm to make it have the parallelism. That is, the algorithm proceeds the evaluation of $\delta V_{1,i}$ and $\delta V_{i,n}$ independently. Thus, there are two representatives for each $R \in V_L \cap V_R$. One is used for the evaluation of $\delta V_{1,i}$; another is used for the evaluation $\delta V_{i,n}$. It is not difficult to show that the updated view after merging $\delta V = \delta V_{1,i} \bowtie \delta V_{i,n}$ to V is completely consistent with the source data. We therefore have the following lemma.

Lemma 2. *Assume that there are K distinct relations in the definition of V consisting of n relations. To evaluate the update δV to V concurrently due to a source update δR_i, the number of accesses to the remote sources is as follows. If $V_L \cap V_R = \emptyset$, then the number of remote source accesses is no more than K; otherwise, the number of remote source accesses is at most $K + |V_L \cap V_R| \leq 2K$.*

Proof. If $V_L \cap V_R = \emptyset$, then, there is no relation with multiple appearances at the both sides (the left and the right sides) when evaluating the update to the view. Thus, all the other copies of a relation must be at the same side, and one of the copies will serve as the representative of the relation. Due to $V_L \cap V_R = \emptyset$, the evaluation at the left and the right sides can be carried out independently.

If $V_L \cap V_R \neq \emptyset$, then for each relation $R \in V_L \cap V_R$ with multiple copies in the left side, its first appearance will serve as the representative of its other copies in the left side. Similarly, its first appearance in the right side will serve as the representative of its other copies in the right side. Thus, there are two representatives for each $R \in V_L \cap V_R$, which are located in both sides respectively. While the number of accesses to the remote sources is determined by the number of representatives in the definition of V, thus, the number of accesses to the remote sources is $K + |V_L \cap V_R| \leq 2K$. ■

Acknowledgment. The work was partially supported by both a small grant (F00025) from Australian Research Council and the Research Grants of Council of the Hong Kong Special Administrative Region (Project No. CUHK4198/00E).

References

1. D. Agrawal et al. Efficient view maintenance at data warehouses. *Proc. of the ACM-SIGMOD Conf.*, 1997, 417–427.
2. J.A. Blakeley et al. Efficiently updating materialized views. *Proc. of the ACM-SIGMOD Conf.*, 1986, 61–71.
3. L. Colby et al. Algorithms for deferred view maintenance. *Proc. of the 1996 ACM-SIGMOD Conf.*, 1996, 469–480.
4. *IEEE Data Engineering Bulletin, Special Issue on Materialized Views and Data Warehousing.* 18(2), June, 1995.
5. T. Griffin and L. Libkin. Incremental maintenance of views with duplicates. *Proc. of the ACM-SIGMOD Conf.*, 1995, 328–339.
6. A. Gupta, H. Jagadish, and I. Mumick. Data integration using self-maintainable views. *Proc. 4th Int'l Conf. on Extending Database Technology*, 1996, 140–146.
7. A. Gupta, I. Mumick, and V. S. Subrahmanian. Maintaining views incrementally. *Proc. of the ACM-SIGMOD Conf.*, 1993, 157–166.
8. R. Hull and G. Zhou. A framework for supporting data integration using the materialized and virtual approaches. *Proc. of the ACM-SIGMOD Conf.*, 1996, 481–492.

9. W. Liang et al. Making multiple views self-maintainable in a data warehouse. *Data and Knowledge Engineering*, Vol.30, 1999, 121–134.
10. W. Liang et al. Maintaining materialized views for data warehouses with the multiple remote source environments. *Proc of WAIM'00.*, LNCS, Vol.1846, 2000, 299–310.
11. D. Quass et al. Making views self-maintainable for data warehousing. *Proc. of Int'l Conf. on Parallel and Distributed Information Systems*, 1996, 158–169.
12. A. Segev and J. Park. Updating distributed materialized views. *IEEE Trans. on Knowledge and Data Engineering*, 1(2), 1989, 173–184.
13. J. Wiener et al. A system prototype for warehouse view maintenance. *Proc. of Workshop on Materialized Views*, 1996, 26–33.
14. Y. Zhuge et al. View maintenance in a warehousing environment. *Proc. of the ACM-SIGMOD Conf.*, 1995, 316–327.
15. Y. Zhuge et al. Multiple view consistency for data warehousing. *IEEE ICDE'97*, Birmingham, UK, 1997, 289–300.

Experiences with a Hybrid Implementation of a Globally Distributed Federated Database System

Xuebiao Xu[1], Andrew C. Jones[1], Nick Pittas[1], W. Alex Gray[1], Nick J. Fiddian[1], Richard J. White[2], John Robinson[2], Frank A. Bisby[3], and Sue M. Brandt[3]

[1] Dept. of Computer Science, PO Box 916, Cardiff University, Cardiff, CF24 3XF, UK
{X.Xu | andrew | N.Pittas | alex | nick}@cs.cf.ac.uk
[2] Biodiversity & Ecology Research Division, School of Biological Sciences, University of Southampton, Southampton, SO16 7PX, UK
{R.J.White | J.S.Robinson}@soton.ac.uk}
[3] Biodiversity Informatics Laboratory, Centre for Plant Diversity & Systematics, The University of Reading, Reading, RG6 6AS,UK
{F.A.Bisby | S.M.Brandt}@reading.ac.uk

Abstract. The SPICE project is developing a globally distributed federated database of biological knowledge, forming a 'catalogue of life' by harnessing specialist expertise on classification of groups of organisms. The component databases are heterogeneous, and are joined to the federation in various ways. We explain how our federated approach partitions the task of maintaining a consistent classification into manageable sub-tasks. We use both CORBA and XML and, while CORBA is widely used for interoperable systems and XML is attractive for data exchange, some problems have arisen in practice. We discuss the problems encountered when incorporating CORBA ORBs from multiple vendors, compromising true platform independence. We also discuss the non-trivial effort required to achieve stability in CORBA-based systems, despite the benefits offered by CORBA in this respect. We present preliminary results, illustrating how performance is affected by various implementational choices.

1 Introduction

With the rapid growth of the Internet and the prevalence of web-based applications, there is an increasing need for fast query engines that can operate with widely distributed, cross-institutional data sources. In the SPICE (SPecies 2000 Interoperability Coordination Environment) project [8] we are exploring the development of such a system for the Species 2000 federated 'catalogue of life' [13]. This will eventually comprise about 200 species databases containing information regarding over 1,000,000 species in total. As we shall see, key requirements for SPICE include autonomy of the databases in the federation, resulting in heterogeneity both at the schema and platform level; the ability to accommodate change, both in the databases already present and in the addition of new ones, and the ability to function acceptably when parts of the federation are unavailable or under excessive load. Such unpredictability and change are inevitable in a large-scale, globally-distributed federated system [1]. Accordingly, it is inappropriate to use a traditional method to construct and execute a query plan.

X.S. Wang, G. Yu, and H. Lu (Eds.): WAIM 2001, LNCS 2118, pp. 212-222, 2001.

Instead, we wish each global query to be decomposed into sub-queries in an intelligent manner, so the system can adapt to fluctuations in computing resources, data characteristics, user preferences and data source availability.

In this paper we show that interoperation between ORBs from multiple vendors can prove difficult in practice, and that even when using a platform such as CORBA, robustness has to be designed explicitly into the system. We also provide some initial performance results from our system. In Section 2 we explore the general Computer Science context within which SPICE is placed. Section 3 explains the specific indexing problem that we are seeking to address, then presents the overall architecture adopted and describes SPICE in use. We also justify the use of a CORBA-based architecture, supplemented by the facility to query databases using CGI/XML. In Section 4 we discuss the problems presented by allowing interoperation between ORBs from various vendors, then in Section 5 we discuss other practical implementation issues including the use of appropriate threading models. Section 6 presents preliminary results regarding how the various approaches we are exploring affect system performance. In Section 7 we discuss further research planned in the SPICE project.

2 Research Background

If heterogeneous data from different data sources is to be combined, tools and infrastructure for *data integration* are required. Data integration using the mediated approach [15] with an object-oriented data model is a popular approach to heterogeneous data source integration [4, 5, 7, 10, 14]. In this approach, data sources can be encapsulated in *wrappers*, providing an interface to these sources using a common query language and/or a common data model. Wrappers are intended to reduce, or remove altogether, data source heterogeneity as seen by the mediator. Implementation of the wrappers may vary substantially from one wrapper to another. In some cases, including that of SPICE, the nature of the schema and the restricted range of queries for which support is required mean it is more appropriate to define an object-oriented common data model than to implement a full query language.

In the last decade or so, enabling technologies have emerged that are useful for building interoperable systems. Of particular relevance to us, the Object Management Group has defined CORBA (Common Object Request Broker Architecture), which provides a platform for communication between distributed, heterogeneous systems (e.g. [6, 11, 12]), and XML is becoming increasingly adopted as a way of exchanging structured and semi-structured information. ORB implementations that offer good performance, reliability and scalability are now available (e.g. Visibroker and Orbix). Also, many ORB vendors are integrating their products with high-performance, highly reliable middleware messaging systems. A comprehensive set of object services is defined for CORBA, providing such facilities as naming, transactions and persistence: such services are essential to real-world distributed object applications. All these make CORBA a practical infrastructure for projects such as SPICE.

At the same time, the World-Wide Web community is rapidly embracing XML as a new standard for data representation and exchange. XML as a standard for exchanging semi-structured information over the Internet is becoming increasingly supported by many software components such as compilers, import/export filters, query interfaces and sophisticated editors and browsers [3, 9]. Like HTML, XML is a subset of SGML. However, whereas HTML tags serve the primary purpose of describing how to display a data item, XML tags describe the data itself. XML is thus an attractive means of data exchange: we shall see in this paper that both CORBA and XML have an important role to play in the SPICE project.

3 The SPICE System

We shall now explain the scientific problem we are addressing, the approach we are taking to implement a suitable solution, and how the SPICE system is used.

3.1 The Problem

The SPICE project aims to develop a prototype infrastructure solving the Computer Science problems facing the Species 2000 project in its goal of creating a global catalogue of life. Using the catalogue, one should be able to search for a species online, and retrieve information including the accepted scientific name in the global classification provided by Species 2000, and synonyms from other classifications.

For biological and sociological reasons, the Species 2000 team believes that responsibility for maintenance of this catalogue must be divided up, each database holding information about some particular sector of the taxonomic hierarchy. For each database, information is drawn from a community having appropriate expertise. It is anticipated that the complete system will comprise about 200 such sectors. These individual sectors, it is argued, must be under the complete control of appropriate experts, and maintained remotely at suitable centres of excellence. Above this is placed a taxonomic hierarchy. Two aspects of the architecture of this catalogue of life were therefore specified by the Species 2000 team: it must be a federated database of some sort, and each component database must cover a particular region of the taxonomic hierarchy unique to that database. It follows that the SPICE project entails research into the practicalities of developing and maintaining a restricted kind of distributed ontology, in which terms are related by subsumption and synonymy.

The Species 2000 team had also defined (informally) the data that it was desirable to handle within the system—e.g. accepted scientific name and synonyms of an organism and taxonomic hierarchy details. The presence of taxonomic hierarchies (currently just one hierarchy) within the system means that we can regard the SPICE as a federated database system with a hierarchical access tree. But our main problem is how to obtain efficient access when the user's queries are *not* made against such structures. In an *un*sophisticated implementation each of the 200 or so data sources might be consulted on every occasion: we need to assess the performance of various approaches to solving this problem. We have been able to define a common data model, so a natural way of handling the schema and platform heterogeneity inherent in the federation is to wrap data sources to conform to this data model—a tightly coupled federation is appropriate. We adopt this approach in SPICE.

3.2 The SPICE Architecture

The prototype architecture of the SPICE system is given in Fig. 1. SPICE can be regarded as a 4-tiered system. On the upper side, an HTTP servlet is used to provide the interactions with clients coming from remote web browsers. The middleware part comprises two layers: the coordinator—called, in SPICE, the *common access system* (CAS)—and the database wrappers. The coordinator interacts with the HTTP server to get the parameters of user queries, determines which wrapped data source(s) must be consulted, queries the databases via their wrappers, assembles the results and sends them back to the HTTP server. The wrappers transform between the underlying component database data model and the Common Data Model (CDM) that has been defined for the coordinator. There are, in fact, two implementations of the CDM, intended to provide two distinct kinds of access, in which the wrappers behave either as CORBA objects or as servers that return XML documents in response to CGI requests. Two, rather than just one, kinds of wrapper-coordinator interfaces are provided because generation of wrappers is intended to be mostly under the control of the database providers, with differing skills. CORBA and CGI/XML were judged to be the most likely platforms that anticipated providers would be able to adopt readily.

The individual databases are called Global Species Databases (GSDs): in fact, in some cases they could be flat files or other structures that one might hesitate to call databases. Two of the GSDs are somewhat special, because they hold the taxonomic hierarchy and an *annual checklist* respectively, although they are accessed using the same CDM as the other GSDs. It will be noted that we have adopted XML as the language in which configuration information is stored, as well as being the language in which query results are represented.

It will be observed that by allowing heterogeneity of the kinds described—apart from anything else, some GSDs may perform much more efficiently than others—we have set a significant problem for ourselves. How can currency of data returned be balanced against database performance, so that the entire system continues to work satisfactorily as load increases? It was for this reason that we set out to explore how various parameters affected performance, e.g. whether the amount of data to be transferred had any bearing on whether the CGI/XML or the CORBA approach yielded better performance; whether standard techniques for getting through firewalls caused significant implementation or performance problems; whether interoperability between ORBs from different vendors could be maintained in practice, and whether the CDM adopted would work with all manner of legacy biodiversity databases.

3.3 SPICE in Operation

A deliberate design decision has been taken to ensure that the SPICE system can be accessed readily by users having no specialised hardware, and not wanting to install SPICE-specific software on their machines. We have therefore implemented an HTML interface, accessible over the World Wide Web, that makes minimal demands on browser capabilities. Initially the user enters a search term (e.g. *Taenio**) and the system responds with a series of pages containing all the species in the GSDs having a scientific name (either an *accepted name* or a *synonym*) matching the search term.

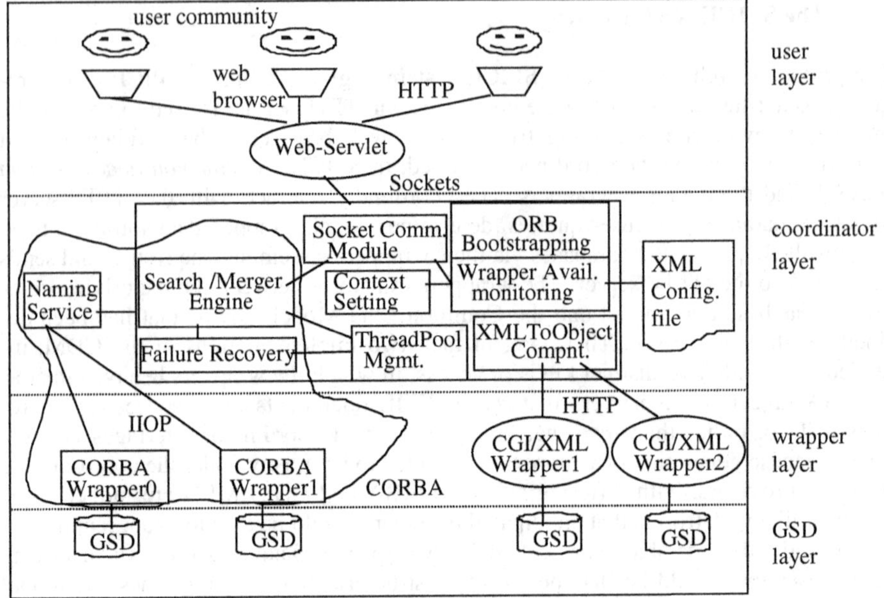

Fig. 1. Prototype architecture of the hybrid SPICE system

A small amount of information is displayed in these result pages for each species. One can also retrieve the full associated *standard data* required for every species in the catalogue of life. We plan to add user interface facilities to navigate through taxonomic hierarchies and access a static *annual checklist,* in addition to the dynamic, changing taxonomy represented by the GSDs. We shall also add 'onward links', via which more detailed species data can be retrieved from a number of sources. But the remainder of this paper concerns the primary question currently facing us: how can interconnectivity using software from multiple vendors be achieved effectively, and what are the parameters against which efficient access strategies must be developed?

4 Interoperation among ORBs

The CORBA standards aim to achieve interoperability across a wide variety of platforms and CORBA implementations, but we have encountered significant problems in practice. We want to support Visibroker and Orbix 2000 as they are major CORBA implementations; JacORB, in contrast, was selected as our third ORB since it is free and supports Java, which is the main language used in implementing SPICE.

4.1 Features Provided

A general problem with interoperating among ORBs is that each vendor only implements a *subset* of the CORBA standard. Although it is perhaps unsurprising that this is the case (in the case of other standards, such as SQL, the same phenomenon can be seen) the consequences in the case of CORBA are fairly severe. For example:

- CORBA services not provided by JacORB include *life cycle, externalisation, persistent objects* and *queries;*
- Visibroker's smart agent can only find objects running on Visibroker's ORBs;
- IDL types vary from one vendor to another, and
- some objects that can be marshalled in one ORB's environment cannot be marshalled in another environment, as different CORBA IIOP protocols are used. Special measures are needed to make such remote CORBA objects known.

To make interoperation among these ORBs feasible we have chosen a fairly low 'common denominator'. Using Interoperable Object References (IORs) has simplified matters, but we have nevertheless encountered various difficulties as explained above.

4.2 Implementational Heterogeneity

To some extent, the above kinds of problems can be identified by inspection of the product literature: an architecture relying only on features common to all relevant ORBs can be devised. A more frustrating problem, significantly impairing the portability of code written within systems such as SPICE, is the variation in the way that individual features are accessed—if they can be accessed at all! For example, we use a *naming service* to set up inter-object communication, but this service varies between ORBs. In some ORBs, the mechanism for booting this service is file-based; in others it is Web-based; in yet others it is internally embedded in the CORBA system. To solve this problem we have built our own naming agent within the CAS. Again, in the discussion that follows, it should be noted that some ORB implementations have built-in multithreading support that can be exploited merely by changing the link libraries, whereas others require explicit coding to use threads. Other problems are that (a) even for the same IDL file, the Java class mappings of Visibroker and Orbix are slightly different even though this has been standardised by the OMG, and (b) the treatment of null objects, in/out/inout parameters and firewall issues varies between vendors, versions and releases: some CORBA ORBs do not even allow null objects to pass between different machines because of the casting difficulties this introduces.

5 Practical Implementation Issues

The main implementation issues, other than those imposed by the way that the various ORBs work, relate to system stability and choice of an appropriate execution model.

5.1 System Stability

In SPICE, operation can continue if individual databases are unavailable, but it is nevertheless desirable to monitor their availability. We shall first explain how this is done, then consider the more general problem of recovery from (unexpected) failure.

Wrapper Availability Monitoring. In a distributed system like SPICE, where autonomy of the component databases is assumed, it is quite common for some of the remote databases to become unavailable via their wrappers for fixed periods of time. It is even possible that at any time some wrappers may unexpectedly fail to respond. The CORBA naming service may fail to bind or resolve too. If no monitoring service were provided within the coordinator for obtaining wrapper availability status, much time would be wasted in handling exceptions generated when failure occurs. We therefore include an embedded monitoring agent that can update each wrapper's availability status periodically so that it can be used in the generation of each query execution plan. In addition to this, an XML document is used to explicitly describe the participating GSD connection details, so that configuration can easily be updated. If a new GSD is to join (or leave) the system, we only need to add one element and assign (or change) the values for the corresponding attributes in the configuration file.

Failure Recovery. A wide range of unexpected failures could potentially occur in all parts of the SPICE system. Detection and recovery of such failures is important for system stability both at the CAS, the remote databases and in between. Here, we consider the most important failure modes that might arise in the servlet, the coordinator and the wrappers. The detection and recovery policies adopted are also described.

Servlet failure can occur if a user starts a SPICE session but does not disconnect properly, so the session does not close. SPICE will never know when to release resources for the session, e.g. the coordination service thread. At the very least the overall response time would deteriorate if no recovery policy were used. To avoid such problems, the Java session class used is extended with a private property recording the last access time, and a *time-out* policy is introduced. A *cleanup* thread running within the servlet periodically polls every available session object to see whether it should be discarded. If so, the appropriate resource recovery is performed.

A second problem is that the web-server and the coordinator are running separately over a substantial period of time. Situations can arise where, for example, the coordinator may stop unexpectedly without notifying the servlet, and then restart again. During this period some old sessions running on the servlet side will still be trying to communicate with the old coordinator resources. To cope with such failure, a *time-stamp* policy is used. Another private property recording the start time of the corresponding coordinator is added to the session class. Instances of the coordinator class also record their own start time. For each servlet access, the corresponding session must compare its coordinator start time with the start time of the current coordinator. If they differ the servlet will either automatically cause the coordinator to reallocate the corresponding resources or start a new session to replace the old one.

A third problem arises because the naming service is running separately from the coordinator and the CORBA wrapper: it does not provide such capabilities as notification, and we cannot alter this because it is not under our control. If the naming service is down, or has restarted unexpectedly, incorrect bindings can occur or, less fatally, the system performance may slow down because of unnecessary resolution of object references. To overcome this, a new class that periodically checks the availability of the object corresponding to the naming service, automatically updating it when the naming service is restarted, has been implemented.

5.2 Concurrency Control and Threading Policy

There are two obvious areas in which concurrency is desirable in SPICE: multiple users should be able to access the system concurrently, and each user session may be able to complete execution more quickly if separate threads are allocated for execution of each sub-query. The ability for the wrappers to accommodate multiple threads simultaneously is also desirable. In fact, some wrappers only allow a single database access thread—notably certain *divided* wrappers, because of a simplistic implementation of the CGI protocol—but we wish to exploit opportunities for concurrency when they arise. Among other things, we use distinct instances of a *transaction* class for each user, and within each transaction a new thread is created to service each request.

Threads provide an attractive mechanism for introducing concurrency. In SPICE, a thread can be allocated to each wrapper access if desired: the queries handled by SPICE are trivially decomposable into separate queries for each database. For example, if one is seeking all occurrences of species matching *Vi**, this query is forwarded to the wrapped databases, then the results are assembled by the coordinator as they are received. At present we are comparing three distinct strategies for the execution of a set of sub-queries during one SPICE user query. The three approaches are as follows:

1. Sequential execution without using threads;
2. Session-based thread without using thread pools, and
3. Multi-threads using thread pools.

In case (1), execution of the given query on a set of selected GSDs is done sequentially. There are no overlaps between the times when the sub-queries are being processed. In case (2), execution of the given query on a set of selected GSDs is done via concurrent execution of multiple threads. These threads exist only during the period that the current query is being processed. For an individual global query overlaps exist between sub-query execution threads. However, no overlaps exist between sub-query executions for different queries, as each wrapper supports only a single thread in this model. In case (3), a fixed set of threads for sub-queries is created and all resources are pre-allocated during the coordinator initialisation period. At least two queues are needed to store the *id*s of all the idle threads and all the busy threads for sub-query execution. When a query request comes in, it is assigned to a thread by using a scheduling policy that obtains an idle sub-query thread. If all threads are busy, the request is buffered in a queue until a sub-query thread become free. Execution is similar to case (2), but threads are *located* rather than *created* for an individual query.

The second and third of these policies would appear to offer obvious benefits over the single-thread approach, but how do the threaded approaches compare? This is one of the questions to which we provide a preliminary answer in the next section.

6 Early Performance Comparisons

The SPICE coordinator is implemented on Windows NT: wrappers are implemented on both Windows NT and Linux platforms. We will present an overview of some very preliminary experimental results obtained from running the system The results demonstrate how the techniques presented above affect the response time.

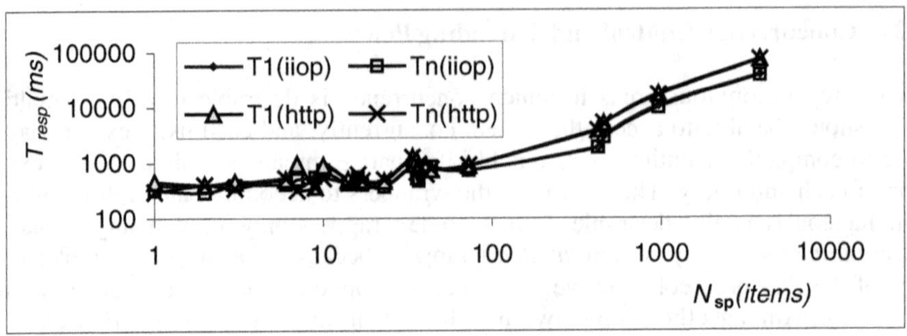

Fig. 2. Comparison of response time between CORBA and CGI/XML wrapper

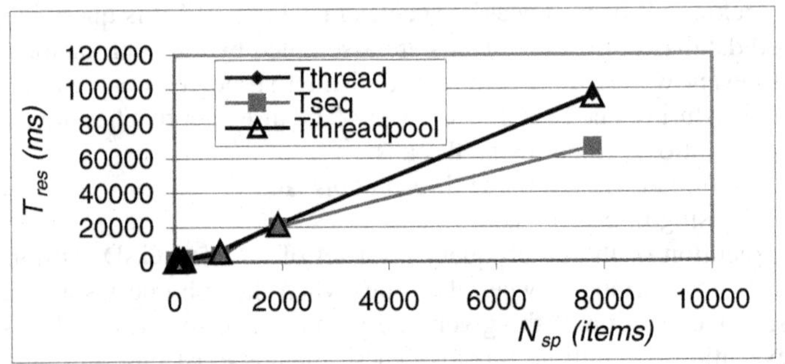

Fig. 3. Comparison of response time of sequential, threads and threads with pooling

In order to provide a basis for comparison, we have developed both a CGI/XML wrapper and a CORBA wrapper for the same GSD (the ILDIS International Legume Database & Information Service), and the comparison of the response time for the two wrappers is shown in Fig. 2. $T_1(_{iiop})$ and $T_n(_{iiop})$ are the response times for the first and *n*-th (*n*>=2) search using the CORBA wrapper respectively, while $T_1(_{http})$ and $T_n(_{http})$ are the first and *n*-th searching time for the CGI/XML wrapper. In the latter case, the time taken to parse and translate between XML and CORBA objects is included in the values given.

From our experience, for the same query the differences between these two approaches are slight when the size of the result set (which is approximately proportional to the number of species returned) is relatively small (*n*<=10). Indeed, sometimes the CGI/XML wrapper can respond faster than the CORBA wrapper. But as the number of species returned increases, the CORBA wrapper becomes much faster than the CGI/XML wrapper, especially when the numbers of species reaches about 100. For the CORBA wrapper, the response difference between the first time access and the *n*-th time (*n*>2) is much more significant than for the CGI/XML wrapper. It seems that for the first access, there is much more work to be done in the CORBA environment than subsequently, while in the Web environment, this is not the case.

In Fig. 3, we show another experimental result comparing the response time of the three different execution approaches mentioned in Section 5.2: sequential (T_{seq}), thread without pooling (T_{thread}) and thread with pooling ($T_{threadpool}$). Each of these trials was run with the coordinator connected to four different CORBA wrappers running remotely from the coordinator at another site in the UK. A certain amount of network latency was thus introduced. Generally we have found that:

$T_{threadpool} < T_{seq} < T_{thread}$ (n<=50), and

$T_{seq} < T_{threadpool} < T_{thread}$ (n>50)

where n is the numbers of species returned. The crossover point for these results evidently depends on a number of variables, but it seems that the thread with pooling approach appears to be much better than the thread without pooling approach. This implies that the construction of one thread object is much more time consuming than searching for and obtaining a pre-existing thread object from the thread pool and passing some parameters to it for execution.

As for the sequential approach, it is more efficient than the thread with pooling approach only when the number of species returned is relatively large (>1000). The reason is perhaps that, the benefits achieved by concurrent execution are liable to be lost if the overhead of swapping between threads increases as the resource requirements of each thread increases.

7 Conclusions and Future Work

In this paper, we have presented a web-based system (SPICE) that enables a user conveniently and efficiently to search multiple autonomous distributed species databases by using two different kinds of wrappers. A system that is resilient to change has been achieved, using XML-based descriptions of the participating databases, monitoring wrapper availability, etc. We have explored system performance, discovering that a CGI-based approach to wrapper connection appears to scale up less well than a CORBA-based approach, and that a major overhead associated with creating new threads appears to exist, at least in the Visibroker CORBA implementation. We have shown that interoperation between CORBA implementations from multiple vendors is difficult to achieve, and that using CORBA does not automatically ensure system stability. There is a need for CORBA vendors to take compatibility with other vendors' products more seriously.

As continuing work, we are exploring the use of caching techniques [2] to improve the system performance and we are building a test-bed to carry out more extensive testing of the effect on performance of varying a range of parameters and implementational decisions, e.g. to explore what happens when large numbers of queries are submitted simultaneously. The results of these tests will be used to inform the policy regarding when to use the caches and when to access the data directly. It should be noted that the large variability of wrapper performance is outside our control and therefore needs to be accommodated effectively within the SPICE system. In the future we may be able to regain a certain amount of control over aspects of wrapper implementation because we are implementing semi-automatic wrapper development tools for third parties to use. We are also working on the integration of a taxonomic hierarchy into the system, which will enable additional access methods based on navigation of the hierarchy. It is important to note that although system-level performance is important, it is also desirable to achieve scalability by innovation at the knowledge level. We are currently devising plans for how to achieve this.

Acknowledgements. The research reported here was funded by a grant from the Bioinformatics Initiative of the UK BBSRC and EPSRC. We are grateful to the Species 2000 team for co-operation and access to all project details; to D. Gee, J. Shimura and Y. Ichyanagi for access to earlier CAS prototypes, and to various Species 2000 member database organisations for access to their data and systems.

References

[1] R. Avnur and J.M. Hellerstein. Eddies: Continuously Adaptive Query Processing. In *Proc. SIGMOD '00*, pages 261-272, 2000. ACM Press.

[2] J. Basu, M. Poess and A.M. Keller. High Performance and Scalability Through Associative Client-Side Caching. In *Workshop on High Performance Transaction Systems (HPTS)*, Pacific Grove, California, 1997.

[3] T. Bray, J. Paoli, and C. Sperberg-McQueen. *Extensible Markup Language (XML) 1.0,* February 1998. W3C Recommendation available at: http://www.w3.org/TR/1998/REC-xml-19980210.

[4] O. Bukhres and A. Elmagarmid (eds.). *Object-Oriented Multidatabase Systems.* Prentice Hall, 1996.

[5] S. Cluet, C. Delobel, J. Simeon and K. Smaga. Your Mediator Needs Data Conversion! In *Proc. SIGMOD '98,* pages 177-188, 1998. ACM Press.

[6] D. Curtis. *Java, RMI and CORBA*, OMG White Paper, 1997. Available at: http://www.omg.org/news/whitepapers/wpjava.htm

[7] H. Garcia-Molina, Y. Papakonstantinou, D. Quass, A .Rajaraman, Y. Sagiv, J. Ullman, V. Vassalos and J. Widom. The TSIMMIS Approach to Mediation: Data Model and Languages. *Journal of Intelligent Information Systems (JIIS),* 8(2):117-132, 1997.

[8] A.C. Jones et al. SPICE: A Flexible Architecture for Integrating Autonomous Databases to Comprise a Distributed Catalogue of Life. In *Proc. DEXA 2000*, pages 981-992, 2000. Springer-Verlag.

[9] J.C. Mamou et al. XML repository and Active Views Demonstration. In *Proc. VLDB '99,* pages 742-745, 1999. Morgan Kaufmann.

[10] F. Naumann and U. Leser. Quality-driven Integration of Heterogeneous Information Systems. In *Proc. VLDB '99,* pages 447-459, 1999. Morgan Kaufmann.

[11] R. Orfali, D. Harkey and J. Edwards. *The Essential Distributed Objects Survival Guide,* John Wiley & Sons, 1996.

[12] J. Siegel. OMG Overview: CORBA and the OMA in Enterprise Computing. *Communications of the ACM,* 41(10):37-43, 1998.

[13] *Species 2000: Indexing the World's Known Species.* Available at: http://www.sp2000.org

[14] A. Tomasic, L. Raschid and P. Valduriez. Scaling Access to Heterogeneous Data Sources with DISCO. *IEEE TKDE,* 10(5):808-823, 1998.

[15] G. Wiederhold. Mediators in the Architecture of Future Information Systems. *IEEE Computer,* 25(3):38-49, 1992.

Session 3B

Web Information Management & E-commerce

Regular Research Paper (30 minutes)
Link Based Clustering of Web Search Results

Regular Research Paper (30 minutes)
Three-tier Clustering: an Online Citation Clustering System

Short Research Paper (15 minutes)
Introducing Navigation Graphs as a Technique for Improving WWW User Browsing

Short Research Paper (15 minutes)
The Evolution of the Contract Net Protocol

Link Based Clustering of Web Search Results

Yitong Wang and Masaru Kitsuregawa

Institute of Industrial Science, The University of Tokyo
{ytwang, kitsure}@tkl.iis.u-tokyo.ac.jp

Abstract. With information proliferation on the Web, how to obtain high-quality information from the Web has been one of hot research topics in many fields like Database, IR as well as AI. Web search engine is the most commonly used tool for information retrieval; however, its current status is far from satisfaction. In this paper, we propose a new approach to cluster search results returned from Web search engine using link analysis. Unlike document clustering algorithms in IR that based on common words/phrases shared between documents, our approach is base on common links shared by pages using co-citation and coupling analysis. We also extend standard clustering algorithm K-means to make it more natural to handle noises and apply it to web search results. By filtering some irrelevant pages, our approach clusters high quality pages into groups to facilitate users' accessing and browsing. Preliminary experiments and evaluations are conducted to investigate its effectiveness. The experiment results show that clustering on web search results via link analysis is promising.

Keywords: link analysis, co-citation, coupling, hub, authority

1. Introduction

Currently, how to obtain high-quality information from the Web efficiently and effectively according to user's query request has created big challenges for many disciplines like data engineering, IR as well as data mining because of features of the Web (huge volume, heterogeneous, dynamic, semi-structured etc.) Web Search engine is the most commonly used tool for information retrieval on the web; however, its current status is far from satisfaction for several possible reasons:

1. Information proliferate on the Web;
2. Different users have different requirements and expectations for search results;
3. Sometimes search request cannot be expressed clearly just in several keywords;
4. Synonym (different words have similar meaning) and homonym (same word has different meanings) make things more complicated;
5. Users may be just interested in „most qualified" information or small part of information returned while thousands of pages are returned from search engine;
6. Many returned pages are useless or irrelevant;
7. Many useful information/pages are not returned for some reasons

So many works [1][2][3] [15][18] try to explore link analysis to improve quality of web search results or mine useful knowledge on the web since links of one page could provide valuable information about „importance" or „relevance" of the page under

X.S. Wang, G. Yu, and H. Lu (Eds.): WAIM 2001, LNCS 2118, pp. 225-236, 2001.

consideration. [1] proposes that there are two kinds of pages in search results: „hub page“ and „authority page“ and they will reinforce each other. Its preliminary experiments indicated that HITS [1] could present some „high-quality“ pages on the query topic.

While HITS may provide a choice for 6th item and 7th item of what we discussed above, further studies are needed for other items. We think that clustering of *web search results* would help a lot. While all pages in search results are already on the same general topic, by presenting search results in more narrow and detailed groups users could have an overview of the whole topic or just select interested groups to browse. In the rest of this paper, when we talk about *web search results/search results*, we mean web pages returned from web search engine on a specific query topic. We use URLs or pages interchangeably when referring to search results.

Although traditional document clustering algorithms that based on term frequency could be applied to web pages, we would like to reconsider clustering of web search results by taking account of some features of web page:

1. *Hyperlink* between web pages is the main difference between text documents and web pages. It may provide valuable information to group related pages.
2. Most web pages in search results are usually *top pages* of web sites, which mean that they probably just include some links and pictures instead of concrete contents. (This makes term-based clustering algorithms poorly worked)
3. Web pages are written in multiple languages. (Term-based clustering algorithms are difficult to be applied to web pages written in languages other than English.)

We also emphasize some requirements for clustering of web search results, which has been stated in [7]:

1. Relevance: *Not all web pages* but high-quality pages in search results need to be clustered. Clustering should separate related web pages from irrelevant ones.
2. Overlap: One web page could *belong to more than one cluster* since it could have more than one topic.
3. Incrementality: In order for speed, clustering procedure should start to process one page as soon as it arrives instead of waiting all information available.

In this paper, we study contributions of link analysis to clustering of web search results. Our idea is very simple: *pages that share common links each other are very likely to be tightly related.* Here, common links for two web pages p and q mean common *out-links* (*point from p* and *q*) as well as common in-links (*point to p* and *q*). Especially, we only consider *non-nepotistic links* (hyperlinks between pages from different websites) since we think that hyperlinks within the same website are more to reveal the inner-structure (like site-map) of the whole website than implying a semantic connection. Our approach combines link analysis and extension of cluster algorithm *K-means* so that it can overcome disadvantages of standard K-means and meet requirements for clustering of web search results.

The paper is organized as follows: next section is an assessment of previous related works on clustering in web domain. In section3, a detailed description of the proposed approach is given. Subsequently in section4, we report experiment results on different query topics as well as evaluations. The paper is concluded with summary and future work directions.

2. Background

Clustering analysis has a long history and serves for many different research fields, like data mining, pattern recognition as well as IR. Vector Space Model, also called *TFIDF* method is the most commonly used one for document representation in IR, which based on terms frequency. Various measurements of similarity between different documents could be applied and one popular way is *Cosine* measurement. *K-means* and *agglomerative hierarchical clustering* are two commonly used methods for document clustering in IR. K-means is based on the idea that a center point (*Centroid*) can represent a cluster. K-means cluster *N* data points into *K* flat (one-level) groups. The advantage of K-means is its speed and its disadvantage is that the quality and structure of final clusters will depend on the choice of k value and k initial centroids. In contrast to K-means, hierarchical clustering creates a nested sequence of partitions, with a single, all-inclusive cluster at the top and singleton clusters of individual points at the bottom. According to [5], hierarchical clustering produces „better" clusters with high time complexity. Detailed description and comparison of document clustering could be found in [5][10][13].

2.1 Prior Related Work on Clustering Search Results

Related work can be classified into following categories: clustering hypertext documents in a certain information space and clustering web search results. As for clustering web search results, some works are basing on the whole document and some works are focusing on clustering snippet attached with each URL in search results in order to achieve speed. Snippet is considered as a good summary to capture the main idea of the page under consideration.

[9] propose a hierarchical network search engine that clusters hypertext documents to structure a given information space for supporting various services like browsing and querying. All hypertext documents in a certain information space (e.g one website) were clustered into a hierarchical form based on contents as well as link structure of each hypertext document. By considering about links within the same website, related documents in the same website could be grouped into one cluster. However, our target is not general situation but search results classification, which clusters search results into more narrow and detailed groups.

[11] explores clustering hypertext documents by *co-citation analysis* (its explanation is in section2.2). First, co-citation pairs are formed with their co-citation frequency. Co-citation pairs whose co-citation frequencies are above pre-specified *threshold* will be kept for further processing. Final clusters are generated by iteratively merging co-citation pairs that share one document. [11] also indicated that its approach could be applied to WWW. However, if AB is a co-citation pair that co-cite document set *f1* and BC is another co-citation pair that co-cite document set *f2*, then document C is added to cluster AB regardless of whether *f1* and *f2* are disjoined or not will sometimes lead to arbitrary decision.

Scatter/Gather [11] is a document browsing system based on clustering, using a hybrid approach involving both k-means and agglomerative hierarchical clustering.

It proposes in [7] an algorithm called suffix Tree Clustering (STC) to group together snippets attached with web pages in search results. The algorithm use techniques that construct a STC tree within linear time of number of snippets. Each node in this tree captures a phrase and associates it with snippets that contain it. After obtaining base clusters in this way, final clusters are generated by merging two base clusters if they share majority (50%) members. Since snippets usually bring noises and outliers, [8] proposes an algorithm called fuzzy relational clustering (RFCMdd) based on the idea of identifying k-medoids. [8] compassionates [7] with the ability to process noises and outliers brought by snippets. However, snippets are not always available in search results and they are also not always a good representation of the whole documents for their subjectivity.

2.2 Link Analysis

[1][2][3][15][18] study contribution of link analysis to improve the quality of search results as well as mine communities on the Web. [1] proposes that there are two kinds of pages in search results: hub and authority.

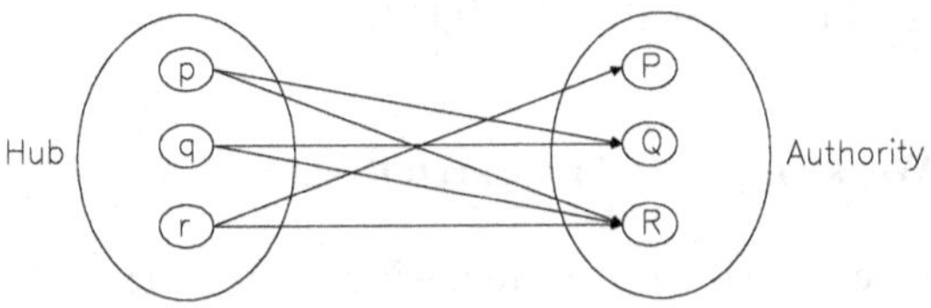

Fig. 1. Potential hub pages and authority pages in search results

Co-citation [21] and bibliographic *coupling* [20] are two more fundamental measures to be used to characterize the similarity between two documents. *Co-citation* measures the *number of citations* (*out-links*) *in common* between two documents and *coupling* measures the number of documents (*in-links*) that cites both of two documents under consideration.

In the above Fig.1, *p* and *q co-cite Q* and *R* and their co-citation frequency is 2; *P* and *R are coupled* by *r* and their coupling frequency is 1.

This could also be proved from the computation in HITS [1] about „hub" value and „authority" value of each page:

$$Hub(p) = \underset{p->p'}{\quad} Authority(p') = \underset{p->p'\,q->p'}{\quad} Hub(q) \text{ (p, q share common out-links)}$$

$$Authority(p) = \underset{p'->p}{\quad} Hub(p') = \underset{p'->p\ p'->q}{\quad} Authority(q) \text{ (p, q share common in-links)}$$

If one page has many out-links and also has high co-citation frequency with other pages, it may be „good hub" and clustered with other pages into one group with high possibility. So do authority pages. Both *co-citation and coupling* are considered in our approach when measuring the similarity between one page and the correspondent cluster.

3. Clustering Based on Link Analysis

Just as indicated above, the underlying idea of our approach is that pages that *co-cite* (share common out-links) or are *coupled* (share common in-links) are with high probability to be clustered into one group. For each URL P in search results R, we extract its all out-links as well as top n in-links by services of AltaVista. We could get all distinct N out-links and M in-links for all URLs in R.

3.1 Definition

- Representation of each page P in R

  Each page P in R is represented as 2 vectors: P_{Out} (N- dimension) and P_{In} (M-dimension). The *ith* item of vector P_{Out} is to indicate whether P has a out-link as the *ith* one in N out-links. If has, the *ith* item is 1, else 0. Identically, the *jth* item of P_{In} is to indicate whether P has an in-link as the *jth* one in M in-links. If has, the *jth* item is 1, else 0.

- Similarity measure

  We adopt traditional *Cosine* measure to capture common links (in-link and out-link) shared by pages P, Q that under consideration:

  Cosine $(P, Q)=(P \bullet Q)/(\|P\|\,\|Q\|) = ((P_{Out} \bullet Q_{Out})+(P_{In} \bullet Q_{In}))/(\|P\|\,\|Q\|)$, *where*

  $\|P\|^2 = (\sum_{1}^{N} P_{Out\,i}^{\,2} + \sum_{1}^{M} P_{In\,j}^{\,2})$ (Total number of out-links and in-links of page P),

  $\|Q\|^2 = (\sum_{1}^{N} Q_{Out\,i}^{\,2} + \sum_{1}^{M} Q_{In\,j}^{\,2})$ (Total number of out-links and in-links of page Q),

  $(P_{Out} \bullet Q_{Out})$ is dot product of vector P_{Out} and Q_{Out} to capture common out-links share by P and Q whereas $(P_{In} \bullet Q_{In})$ is to capture common in-links shared by P and Q. $\|P\|$ is length of vector P.

- Center Point of Cluster

  Centroid or center point C is used to represent the cluster S when calculating similarity of page P with cluster S. $|S|$ is number of pages in cluster S. Since centroid is usually just a logical point, its item values could be smaller than 1. So, we have:

  $C_{out} = \frac{1}{|S|} \sum_{P_i \in S} P_{i\,Out}$, $C_{In} = \frac{1}{|S|} \sum_{P_i \in S} P_{i\,In}$. *Similarity* (P, S)=*Cosine* (P, C)

  $= (P \bullet C)/(\|P\|\,\|C\|) = ((P_{Out} \bullet C_{Out})+(P_{In} \bullet C_{In}))/(\|P\|\,\|C\|)$

  $\|C\|^2 = (\sum_{i} C_{Out\,i}^{\,2} + \sum_{j} C_{In\,j}^{\,2})$, $\|P\|^2 = (\sum_{1}^{N} P_{Out\,i}^{\,2} + \sum_{1}^{M} P_{In\,j}^{\,2})$

- Near-Common Link of Cluster

  Near-common link of cluster means links shared by *majority members* of one cluster. If one link is shared by 50%members of the cluster, we call it „50% near-common link" of the cluster and the link shared by all members of the cluster is called *common link of cluster.*

3.2 Clustering Method

Here we introduce a new clustering method by extending standard K-means to meet requirements for clustering of web search results as well as to overcome disadvantages of K-means. In standard k-means, N data points are clustered into K groups. Value K and K initial centroids have to be pre-defined to start clustering procedure. Our clustering method is:

- Filter irrelevant pages

  Not all web pages in search results but high quality pages (in our case, only pages whose sum of in-links and out-links are at least 2 are processed) join clustering procedure. By filtering some irrelevant pages, we could improve the *precision* of final results.

- Define similarity threshold

  Similarity threshold is pre-defined to determine whether one page could be clustered into one cluster. Since similarity is meant to capture common links shared by different pages, similarity threshold could be easily defined and adjusted.

- Use *near-common link of cluster* to guarantee intra-cluster cohesiveness

  By adjusting to different values, we found 30% near-common link is appropriate and we require that every cluster should have at least one 30% near-common link to guarantee its quality and intra-cluster cohesiveness.

- Assign each page to clusters

  Each page *is assigned to existing clusters* if (a) similarity between the page and the correspondent cluster is above *similarity threshold* and (b) the page has a link in common with *near common links* of the correspondent cluster. If none of current existing clusters meet the demands, the page under consideration will become a new cluster itself. Centroid vector is used when calculating the similarity and it is *incrementally* recalculated when new members are introduced to the cluster. While one page could belong to more than one cluster, it is limited to *top 10* clusters based on similarity values. All pages that join clustering procedure are processed sequentially and the whole process is iteratively executed until it converges (centroids of all clusters are no longer changed). While the final result may be sensitive to the processing order, we would further examine it by changing processing order.

- Generate final clusters by merging *base clusters*

  When the whole iteration process converges, *base clusters* are formed. Final clusters are generated by recursively merging two base clusters if they share majority members. *Merging threshold* is used to control merging procedure.

The algorithm described above has same *time complexity* (*O(nm)*) with standard K-means, where *n* is the number of pages that join clustering procedure and *m* is the number of iterations needed for clustering process to converge (The convergence is guaranteed by K-means algorithm). Since $m \ll n$, the proposed approach is linear to the number of URLs/ pages that join clustering procedure.

In the proposed approach, not all URLs in search results will join clustering procedure and also not all URLs that join clustering procedure will be grouped with others. We think that this is more natural to handle noises and conforms to heterogeneous feature of the Web. There are three parameters in our approach that may affect quality of final results: *number of in-links*, *similarity threshold* and *merging threshold*, we have tried different values in experiments to investigate their effects.

4. Experiments and Evaluation

4.1 Experimental Environment

We carry out experiments on different query topics to check efficiency and effectiveness of the proposed approach. The whole process is divided into four steps:

- Data collection
  In order to test effectiveness, efficiency and scalability of the proposed approach, we carry out experiments with datasets on different query topics, different search engines with different numbers of search results. Since the approach is based on link analysis, different numbers of in-links are also examined. Table 1 gives summary of datasets. We download all pages in search results and extract all out-links for each page as well as its in-links by AltaVista.

- Data cleaning
  Since there are so many mirrors or duplicates on the Web, it will mislead clustering process if preserving these duplicates. We adopt a non-aggressive method to remove mirrors or duplicates in search results. Two pages p and q are said duplicate if (a) they each have at least 8 out-links and (b) they have at least 80% of their links in common. The page with higher common link percentage will be removed. As a result, its associated out-links and in-links are also deleted. Table2 shows how many pages in search results actually join clustering procedure after data cleaning and poor-quality pages (sum of in-links and out-link is less than 2) removal for different topics.

- Applying algorithm proposed in section3 to form base clusters

- Final clusters generation
  By applying the proposed algorithm, we obtain base clusters. Final clusters are generated by merging two base clusters if they share majority (e.g.75%) members. The cluster that has higher common member percentage is merged into the other one. To merge cluster A into B, we union members of both A and B under the cluster name B. Table2 shows final clusters obtained for datasets with specified similarity threshold for different query topics.

4.2 Experiment Results

Some statistics about experiments as well as final results are shown in below tables. According to Table2, only 60%-70% pages in search results are preserved for clustering. When requiring more in-links, more information is used for clustering, so pages that join clustering and pages that are clustered into groups also increase.

Table 1. Information of testing dataset

Dataset	Topic	Number of Pages in Search Result	Search Engine	Number of in-Links required
1	Jaguar (1)	750	Google	100
2	Jaguar (2)	750	Google	20
3	Data mining	200	AltaVista	100
4	Java	400	Yahoo	100

Table 2. Some statistics of experimenting after data cleaning

Topic/ Similarity Threshold	Number of Pages that join clustering	Avg. Out-Links / Avg. In-links	Iterations when converge	Merging threshold	Number of final clusters
Jaguar (1) /0.1	449	10.1 / 11.0	8	0.75	50
Jaguar (2) /0.1	438	10.3 / 6.4	7	0.75	55
Data mining /0.1	120	13.9 / 20.6	3	0.75	15
Java /0.1	295	7.8 / 53.1	5	0.75	21

Table 3. Distributions of clusters based on size with merging threshold 0.75

Topic/ Similarity Threshold	Total clus-ters	Size 2-3	Size 4-5	Size 6-10	Size 11-20	Size 21-40	Size 40-60	Size 60-80	Size above 80	Singlet-on clusters
Jaguar (1) /0.1	50	29	6	8	2	2	2	1	0	163
Jaguar (2) /0.1	55	31	8	7	4	3	2	0	0	160
Data mining /0.08	14	10	2	1	1	0	0	0	0	60
Java/ 0.08	23	15	2	2	2	1	0	0	1	105

Table3 gives final cluster size distribution for different topics. As results reveal, one page could belong to more than one cluster or belong to singleton cluster, which means that it cannot be grouped with others. Since it is possible for „query topic“ to have more than one meaning under different contexts, table3 indicates that the proposed approach could capture main semantic categories around query topic on the web as well as other small groups, which in most cases are pages from the same website.

Table 4. Results of final clusters with different similarity thresholds

Similarity Threshold	Topic	Number of final clusters	Singleton cluster	Maximum Cluster Size	Number of clusters with size >3
0.1	Data mining	15	66	13	5
0.08	Data mining	14	60	20	4
0.06	Data mining	12	53	20	8
0.1	Java	21	129	89	6
0.08	Java	23	105	107	8

Table 5. Examples of some main clusters for Topic „Jaguar“

No.	Main topic	URLs in the cluster with this topic
1	*Jaguar Car*	http://www.jagweb.com/ http://www.jaguarcars.com http://www.classicjaguar.com/...
2	*Jaguar Club*	http://www.jag-lovers.org/ http://seattlejagclub.org/ http://www.jagclub.com/...
3	*Magazine on Jaguar car/club*	http://www.kreiha.de/jaguar-magazin-online http://www.jagweb.com/jagworld/ http://www.jcna.com/....
4	*Jaguar Game*	http://atarihq.com/interactive/ http://www.millcomm.com/forhan/jaguar.html http://www.lpl.arizona.edu/~breid/videogames/jaguar.html...
5	*Mammal: Big Cat*	http://www.bluelion.org/jaguar.htm http://lynx.uio.no/catfolk/onca-01.htm http://www.gf.state.az.us/frames/fishwild/jaguar.htm#1...
6	*Touring: Jaguar Reef Lodge*	http://www.belizenet.com/jagreef.html http://www.divejaguarreef.com/ http://www.jaguarreef.com/jagreef/qtvr.html...
7	*Jaguar Racing Car*	http://www.jaguarracing.cz/ http://www.dmoz.org/Sports/Motorsports/Auto_Racing/Formula_One/Teams/Jaguar http://www.jaguar-racing.com/uk/html/...

Table4 compares final clusters with different similarity thresholds. By decreasing similarity threshold, we could see that more pages are clustered, maximum cluster size increases, which means more pages belong to main group. Moreover, some medium-size clusters emerge and distinctions between clusters are also not so clear. Table5 presents examples of some main clusters of dataset1. From table5, we could see that pages in the same cluster do share similar topic and contents under the general query topic.

4.3 Entropy-Based Evaluation

Validating clustering algorithm and evaluating its quality is complex because it is difficult to find an objective measure of quality of clusters. We decide to use *Entropy* to measure the quality of clusters. Entropy provides a measure of „goodness“ for un-nested clusters by comparing the groups produced by the clustering technique to known classes. In our initiative evaluation, we manually check each page that joins the clustering procedure and then give our judgment. Each page is given two estimates: relevance (to the query topic), main topic and then create *classes* manually. Although it is time-consuming and it could lead to bias in our evaluation, we plan to carry out user experiment to counteract potential bias. We adopt the computing of Entropy introduced in [10]: Let CS is a cluster solution and for each cluster j, its entropy is $E(j) = -\sum_{i} p_{ij} \log(p_{ij})$ · p_{ij} is used to compute the „probability“ that a member of cluster j belongs to the given class i. The average entropy for a set of clusters is calculated as the sum of entropies of each cluster weighted by its size: $E_{CS} = \sum_{j=1}^{m} \frac{n_j * E(j)}{n}$, where n_j is the size of cluster j, m is the number of clusters and n is the total number of data points. Our evaluations focus on topic „Jaguar“ with different merging thresholds.

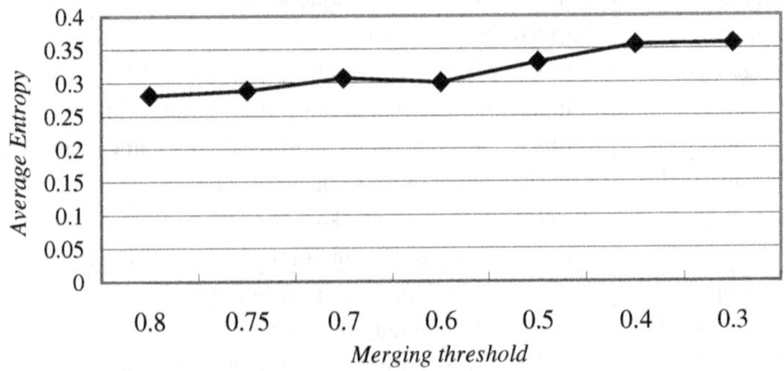

Fig. 2. Effects of merging threshold on Entropy for Topic „Jaguar“

Fig.2 shows overview of the effects of merging threshold on the quality of clusters. It indicates that higher merging threshold gives better results and the proposed approach is insensitive to the changes of merging threshold when merging thresholds are bigger than 0.6. In order to get in-depth understanding, we examine entropy distribution for every cluster with different merging thresholds and the results is shown in Fig.3. Cluster1, 2, …, 24 are in descendent order based on their sizes. For cluster22, since its entropy values are 0 for all merging thresholds, there is no correspondent bar. As merging threshold decreases from 0.8, we could see that some clusters will be merged into other clusters and thus correspondent bars will disappear. While cluster1 has the biggest cluster size for merging threshold 0.8, it is no longer the biggest one with the merging threshold less than 0.75. Instead, cluster3 is the biggest cluster when merging threshold is less than 0.75. This is also demonstrated by its high entropy values. Fig.3 suggests that small-size clusters are very stable and have high qualities since they have low entropy values. According to hand-check results, cluster12, 16 and 21are not semantically interpretable and this is in accordance with their high entropy values revealed in Fig.3. We consider introducing some heuristics to trim them out and adapt the approach to various situations. As for big-size clusters, they have relatively high entropy values and are tempt to change into higher values when merging threshold decreases. While we would like to continually check the result of merging threshold 0.9, 0.75 and 0.8 are our recommendations to generate reasonable clusters.

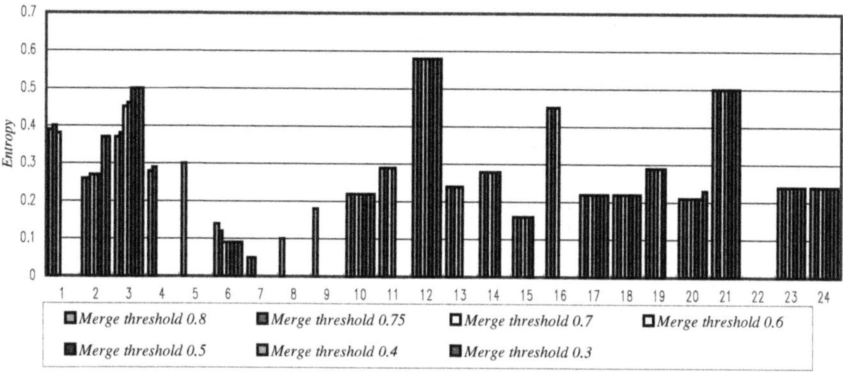

Fig. 3. Entropy of each cluster ordered by cluster size for Topic „Jaguar"

5. Conclusion

In this paper, we propose a new approach to cluster web search results based on link analysis. Our motivations are that currently users are more and more plagued by the inefficiency of web search engine and we would like to study how link analysis could contribute for clustering on search results. Since it is very important for scalability in web domain because of huge volume of information, time complexity of the proposed approach is linear to the number of pages join the clustering procedure. Our approach explores link analysis to filter irrelevant (with query topic) pages and cluster „high-quality" pages into groups to facilitate users' accessing and browsing, which only few works focus on this aspect. In order to get in-depth understanding about effectiveness of the proposed approach to cluster search results, we carry out experiments on different query topic: Jaguar, data mining, Java and evaluate experiment results using entropy metric. We also extend standard K-means algorithm to overcome its disadvantages like compulsory choice of K value and k initial centroids to make it more natural to handle noises. Experiment results indicate that the proposed approach could generate reasonable clusters when merging threshold 0.75 or 0.8 is given.

Since technique of using link analysis to cluster search results is still primitive, further experimenting as well as detailed analyses and interpretation of experiment results are our next step works. Comprehensive comparing with other related research is also needed.

References

1. Kleinberg 98 *Authoritative sources in a hyperlinked environment.* In proceedings of the 9th ACM-SIAM Symposium on Discrete Algorithms (SODA), January 1998.
2. Ravi Kumar *et. al.* 99 *Trawling the Web for emerging cyber-communities.* In Proceedings of 8th WWW conference, 1999, Toronto, Canada.
3. Brin and Page 98 *The anatomy of a large-scale hypertextual web search engine.* In Proceedings of WWW7, Brisbane, Australia, April 1998.
4. Oren Zamir and Oren Etzioni *99 Grouper: A Dynamic Clustering Interface to Web Search Results.* In Proceedings of 8th WWW Conference, Toronto Canada.
5. Richard C. Dubes and Anil K.Jain, *Algorithms for Clustering Data*, Prentice Hall, 1988
6. Oren Zamir and Oren Etzioni 97 *Fast and Intuitive clustering of Web documents,* KDD'97, pp287-290
7. Oren Zamir and Oren Etzioni 98 *Web document clustering: A feasibility demonstration.* In Proceedings of SIGIR' 98 Melbourne, Australia.
8. Zhihua Jiang *et. al. Retriever: Improving Web Search Engine Results Using Clustering.* http://citeseer.nj.nec.com/275012.html.
9. Ron Weiss *et. al.* 96 *Hypursuit: A Hierarchical Network Search Engine that Exploits Content-Link Hypertext Clustering.* ACM Conference on Hypertext, Washington USA,1996
10. Michael Steinbach *et. al. A Comparison of Document Clustering techniques.* KDD'2000. Technical report of University of Minnesota.
11. James Pitkow and Peter Pirolli 97 *Life, Death and lawfulness on the Electronic Frontier.* In proceedings of ACM SIGCHI Conference on Human Factors in computing, 1997
12. Cutting, D.R. *et. al.92 Scatter/gather: A Cluster-based approach to browsing large document collections.* In Proceedings of the 15th ACM SIGIR, pp 318-329; 1992
13. A.V. Leouski and W.B. Croft. 96 *An evaluation of techniques for clustering search results.* Technical Report IR-76 Department of Computer Science, University of Massachusetts, Amherst, 1996
14. Broder *et. al.* 97 *Syntactic clustering of the Web.* In proceedings of the Sixth International World Wide Web Conference, April 1997, pages 391-404.
15. Bharat and Henzinger 98 *Improved algorithms for topic distillation in hyperlinked environments.* In Proceedings of the 21st SIGIR conference, Melbourne, Australia, 1998.
16. Chakrabarti *et. al.* 98 *Automatic Resource Compilation by Analyzing Hyperlink Structure and Associated Text.* Proceedings of the 7th WorldWide Web conference, 1998.
17. Florescu, Levy and Mendelzon 98 *Database Techniques for the World-Wide Web: A Survey.* SIGMOD Record 27(3): 59-74 (1998).
18. Gibson, Kleinberg and Raghavan 98 *Inferring Web communities from link topology.* Proc. 9th ACM Conference on Hypertext and Hypermedia, 1998.
19. Agrawal and Srikant 94 *Fast Algorithms for mining Association rules,* In Proceedings of VLDB, Sept 1994, Santiago, Chile.
20. M.M. Kessler, *Bibliographic coupling between scientific papers*, American Documentation, 14(1963), pp 10-25
21. H. Small, *Co-citation in the scientific literature: A new measure of the relationship between two documents*, J. American Soc. Info. Sci., 24(1973), pp 265-269

Three-Tier Clustering: An Online Citation Clustering System*

Haifeng Jiang, Wenwu Lou, and Wei Wang

Dept. of Computer Science
Hong Kong University of Science and Technology, Hong Kong, China
{jianghf,wwlou,fervvac}@cs.ust.hk

Abstract. In this paper, we present a three tier clustering method where data objects are described by a number of feature dimensions. Using the approach, similarity along each feature dimension of objects are first computed. The inter-objects similarity are then computed from inter-feature-dimension similarity using a Bayesian multi-causal model. Objects are finally clustered based on the computed similarity. An online citation entry clustering system was built using the approach. It accepts user queries in the form of name of authors. Such queries are sent to citation/bibliography search engines. The returned entries are clustered based on feature dimensions such as authors, title, place of publication, etc. After clustering, entries from different authors with the similar name form different clusters, that are presented to the user. Preliminary experiment results indicated the effectiveness of the proposed clustering approach. The architecture of three-tire clustering framework, feature representation of a citation entry, a brief network model for inter-object similarity computation, and a special cluster evaluation technique are discussed in detail.

1 Introduction

The World Wide Web has become a global source of information. People can virtually get any information required from the Web. One type of information is bibliography and citations. A number of authoritative Web sites have been established to provide such information, such as CiteSeer [7], DBLP [6], etc. While the developers of those sites have spent a large amount of efforts in providing as accurate as possible results for user queries, the current situation seems not that satisfactory. For example, when we search for citations of a particular researcher, e.g., H. Lu, CiteSeer will return a list of papers together with citation information. However, by carefully analyzing the returned results, we will find that the entries returned are not exactly what we wanted. In addition to entries for the queried author, there are also entries for some researchers whose names are the same as (or similar to) the name in queries. This observation motivated

* This work is partially supported by a grant from the Research Grant Council of the Hong Kong Special Administrative Region, China (AOE97/98.EG05) and a grant from the National 973 project of China (No. G1998030414)

X.S. Wang, G. Yu, and H. Lu (Eds.): WAIM 2001, LNCS 2118, pp. 237–248, 2001.

us to work on the following problem: given a set of entries returned from those Web sites for citation and bibliography, automatically identify those entries for a particular real-world author. Our objective is to develop an online system that further processes the search results returned by those search engines and present to the user with more accurate search results. The problem is basically a document/text clustering problem. However, it differs from the traditional document clustering problem, which makes it not as trivial as it seems. First, most bibliography and citation entries contain less information than whole documents. If we are considering an online system and limit ourselves to use only the text in the entry without further access of detailed information related to the entry such as contents of the paper, only a few lines of text is available. Second, we do not have a priori knowledge about the entries that would be returned. That is, we are clustering a set of dynamically generated documents online. It is difficult to apply traditional information retrieval models directly.

To address the problem, we developed a novel clustering approach, three-tier clustering, as follows: each citation entry is a data object with a number of feature dimensions, such as author list, paper title, place of publication, etc. The first tier of the clustering approach is to find the similarity among objects along each feature dimension. The second tier is to combine the evidences of similarity from all feature dimensions into one similarity measure. The third tier of the approach applies a clustering algorithm to the objects to form clusters. Compared with clustering algorithms proposed in the literature, the novelty of this approach is that it allows us to integrate domain knowledge into a clustering algorithm:

1. It enables us to apply different functions to measure the similarity of objects along different feature dimensions. In our application, although both author names and paper titles consist of words, the measurement of similarity should be obviously different.
2. It enables us to distinguish the importance of different feature dimensions in determining the similarity of objects.

An citation entry clustering system has been implemented to investigate the effectiveness of the above approach. The current system concentrates on name queries, one of the most frequently used query types for online citation/bibliography database search. The system takes names of authors as a query, sends it to a citation/bibliography Web site(s). The results returned are clustered and presented to the user in the form of clusters. Each cluster contains entries from one real-world author, and the user can choose to view only those results for the author that s/he is querying for.

Figure 1 is part of the clustering result presented to the user who issues a query to CiteSeer for citation information of *H. Lu*. We can see that, a same name contained in different entries may correspond to different real-world authors. For this particular example, clusters 1, 2, and 3 are in fact belong to three different real-world authors.

In addition to the new clustering approach described above, the other unique features of online citation entry clustering system include:

Cluster results: Please select one or more clusters to browse

Size	Name	The author's working Area		
49	H LU	query, systems, optimization , database, dynamic , parallel , join	drill down	☐
30	H LU	branes, solitons, brane, string, supergravities, theory, bound	drill down	☐
19	H LU	memory, shared, networks, software, workstations, distributed	drill down	☐
5	H LU	methods, block, matrices, iterative, incomplete, applications	drill down	☐

Show selected papers | Clear all selections

Fig. 1. The major clustering result for name query "H LU"

1. After computing the similarity among citation entries, we use a Link-node Hierarchical Clustering algorithm (PLHC) for clustering. The algorithm is a compromise between single-link and complete-link hierarchical clustering algorithms. By PLHC, the negative effect of noisy objects can be reduced to an acceptable level.
2. The system is interactive. The result of clustering is presented in such a way that the user can "merge" clusters by selecting multiple clusters or "split" a cluster by drill down.
3. In general, clustering results are evaluated based on the tightness among data objects within a cluster and closeness between clusters. In our application, we modified two widely used evaluation metrics in information retrieval, precision and recall, to fit in our application.

The remainder of the paper is organized as follows. Section 2 briefly describes the system and Section 3 focuses on the three tier clustering approach. The results of some preliminary performance study are shown in Section 4. Section 5 concludes the paper.

2 The Reference Architecture of the Clustering System

Figure 2 depicts the reference architecture of the citation entry clustering system based on three-tier clustering. There are five main components in the system: *Query input interface*, *Wrappers*, *Search results integrator*, *Three-tier clustering module* and *Result presenter*. A user inputs a name query and chooses a source to which the query would be sent.

Wrappers are designed for source sites from which the citations are gathered. The Wrapper Multiplexer sends the query to the source sites. Wrappers involving the query will receive the results, that are converted into an internal representation. The results are are cleaned and integrated before clustering if multiple data sources are involved. The three-tier clustering module groups the citation entries into clusters. The details of three-tier clustering approach will be discussed in the following section. The result of clustering are then presented to the user through the Result Presenter.

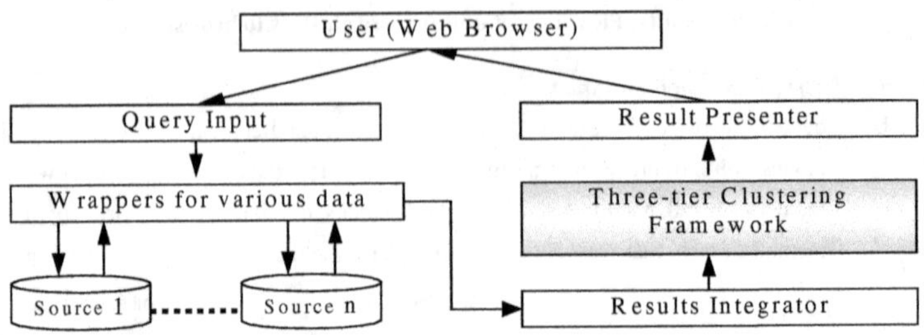

Fig. 2. Reference Architecture of the Clustering System

The system is implemented mainly by CGI programming. Wrappers are written in Perl 6.0 Scripting language, which has many easy-to-use modules for web applications. The result Integrator module and the three-tier clustering framework are implemented with C++ for performance consideration.

3 A Three-Tier Clustering Framework

Clustering groups objects (patterns, data items or feature vectors) into clusters such that the individual objects within a cluster are in some way characterized by an internal coherence and/or an external isolation. The clustering problem has been addressed in the context of many disciplines, including pattern recognition, artificial intelligence, information retrieval and data mining. As the World Wide Web attains a central position in the information economy of today, clustering techniques are also finding interesting applications in facilitating web browsing [3,4] and improving the performance of similarity in search engines [2,11].

Document clustering using only textual features such as words or phrases has been extensively studied [8,13,15]. Almost all clustering algorithms treat the attributes of data objects uniformly. For example, documents are described by a set of keywords. While this might be reasonable for certain applications, it may not reflect the semantics of attributes completely. As such, we extend the problem to more general case as follows. Let $O = \{o_1, o_2, \ldots, o_N\}$ be a set of objects to be clustered. Instead describing each object o_i by a number of *features*, we describe each object along a number of a *feature dimensions*, $\{F_1, F_2, \ldots, F_k\}$. In the case of citation entries, an entry is described by: *queried author name, author list, paper title, place of publication, and etc.* In other words, terms in each feature dimension, e.g., word *Stone* in the author list and the paper title, are treated differently.

With such representation, we proposed a three-tier clustering framework. The first tier of the framework is to find the similarity among objects along each feature dimension. The second tier is to combine the evidences of similarity from all feature dimensions into one similarity measure using a Bayesian network multi-causal model. The third tier applies a clustering algorithm to the objects to form clusters. In this section, we describe the details of these three tiers.

3.1 Feature Dimension and Inter-feature-Dimension Similarity

Most clustering algorithms represent objects to be clustered using multidimensional vectors, where each dimension is a single feature [5]. As mentioned above, we propose to represent objects with multiple feature dimensions. The rationale is as follows: First, features, even in the same domain, may have different semantics. For example, the same word in an citation entry could be part of the authors' name, a word in the title, etc. With different semantics, the similarity should be defined differently. Second, different features may play different role in the clustering process. Some are more important than the others. In fact, such a feature grouping approach has been adopted in some literatures implicitly, such as [11], in which the words, out-links and in-links in hypertext documents are treated as different dimensions that contribute differently to similarity calculation.

Since features in each feature dimension are homogeneous, we can devise very meaningful similarity functions to calculate the inter-feature-dimension similarity. Let's take name of authors as an example. Since an author name has many variations in abbreviative formats [12], a brute-force comparison algorithm does not work for names. For example, a full author name *Hongjun LU* may have several possible printed formats, such as *H. LU, H. J. LU* , etc. With separate feature dimension, we can define a *NameSimilarity* function, which calculates the similarity (0 - 1) of two names by considering all possible variations that a name can take. For the feature dimension of coauthor names, the inter-feature-dimension similarity is the normalization of the summation of all the pair-wise name similarities calculated by *NameSimilarity.*

3.2 Calculating Inter-object Similarity with a Bayesian Network

Similarity between objects can be computed from computed inter-feature-dimension similarity. We used a Bayesian network for this purpose.

A Bayesian Network N is a triplet (V, A, T), where: (1) V is a set of variables; (2) A is a set of arcs, which together with V constitutes a directed acyclic graph $G = (V, A)$; (3) $T = \{P(v|\pi_v) : v \in V\}$, where π_v stands for the set of parents of v. In words, T is the set of the conditional probabilities of all the variables given their respective parents.

For each pair of object i and object j, The inter-feature-dimension similarities have direct influences to the final inter-object similarity. Intuitively, we can have Bayesian network structure shown in Figure 3(a). Note that $s_i, s_2, \ldots, s_k$ are the inter-feature-dimension similarities and S is final inter-object similarity. More details about Bayesian Network can be found in [14].

Given the structure of the BN, we need to specify the conditional probability table or CPT for each node. We are interested in the conditional probability table $P(s|s_1, s_2, \ldots, s_k)$ in that the inter-object similarity can be obtained from that table. To simplify the constructing of CPT of BN nodes, we propose constructing the CPT of node s (or the inter-object similarity function) by exploiting local structure in the BN, i.e. the causal independence [16] and context-specific independence [17].

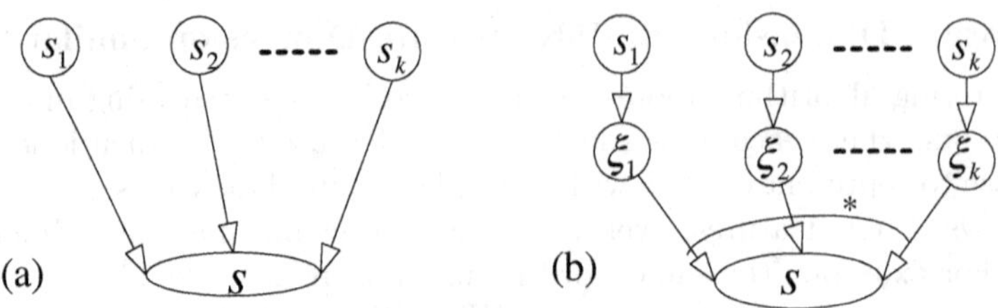

Fig. 3. (a) A Bayesian network to calculate the inter-object similarity. (b) Exploiting causal independence in conditional probability.

Causal Independence. Causal independence refers to the situation where the causes $c_1, c_2, \ldots, c_k$ influence e independently. Causal independence allows us to break a conditional probability into factors that involve fewer variables:

$$P(e = a|s_1, s_2, \ldots, s_k) = \sum_{a_1 * \ldots * a_k = a} P(\xi_1 = a_1|s_1) \ldots P(\xi_k = a_k|s_k)$$

where ξ_i is the contribution of s_i to s, $*$ is the base combination operator and s is called the independent cause variable, as shown in Figure 3(b).

Context-specific Independence. Context-specific independence (CSI) refers to conditional independence that is true only in specific context. Let X, Y, Z, and C be four disjoint sets of variables. X and Y are independent given Z in context $C = \gamma$ if $P(X|Z, Y, C = \gamma) = P(X|Z, C = \gamma)$, whenever $P(Y, Z, C = \gamma) > 0$. When exploiting context-specific independence, we are actually looking for some dominant feature dimensions that shield the effect of other feature dimensions to the final inter-object similarity. So far as we know, no literatures have ever formally stated such independence between sub-similarities for similarity calculation.

Now let us see how the above Bayesian multi-causal model can be used in our citation clustering problem. Given the inter-feature-dimension similarities, we apply the Noisy-OR causal independence model with some context-specific independence considerations. The inter-object similarity s can be expressed as $P(s = 1|s_1, s_2, s_3, s_4)$, that is, the probability of similarity being 1 given the four inter-feature-dimension similarities. With a Noisy-OR model, this probability can be calculated as:

$$P(s = 1|s_1, s_2, s_3, s_4) = 1 - P(s = 0|s_1) * P(s = 0|s_2) * P(s = 0|s_3) * P(s = 0|s_4)$$

where $P(s = 0|s_i)$ can be calculated from $P(s = 1|s_i)$. One observation about $P(s = 1|s_i)$ is that if $s'_i \geq s''_i$, then $p(s = 1|s'_i) \geq_P (s = 1|s''_i)$.

In our online citation clustering system, we use linear functions to define the conditional prob-abilities: $P(s = 1|s_i) = a_i * s_i$, that is, the contribution of one feature dimension similarity s_i equals to a_i . The reason for using linear functions is that the conditional probabilities defined by linear functions subject to the observation stated above. Since there are no training data to decide what the conditional probability function should be, a linear function is a natural choice. Our later experiments show that it works quite well. The values of a_i for different feature dimensions are assigned according to our observation and knowledge for the current version of the system.

Context-specific independence is also considered. For example, if $s_1 = 0$, then the final inter-object similarity must be 0 regardless of the values of s_2, s_3, s_4, meaning that if two queried author names are so different, then it is impossible that the two citation entries belong to same real-world author. But $s_1 = 1$ does not imply $s = 1$.

3.3 Proportional Link-Node Hierarchical Clustering

There are many clustering approaches. At the top level, there is a distinction between hierarchical and partition approaches. Hierarchical algorithms are more versatile than partition algorithms. On the other hand, the time and space complexities of the partition algorithms are typical lower than those of the hierarchical algorithms.

We adopted hierarchical clustering approach in our citation clustering system since it produces a nested series of partitions, making it possible for the user to participate in the clustering process to drill down or roll up the clustering results in a Web application. Another reason is that the time and space complexities of the hierarchical algorithms are not that critical since the number of entries returned for a author is usually not very large.

Among the hierarchical clustering algorithms, the single-link and complete-link hierarchical clustering algorithms are most popular. The problem for these two algorithms is that the single-link algorithm is too sensitive to noisy objects while the complete-link algorithm is too strict to have reasonably large clusters.

We present a Proportional Link-node Hierarchical Clustering algorithm, denoted as PLHC, which is a compromise between single-link and complete link hierarchical clustering algorithms. By PLHC, whether or not two sub-clusters would be merged together is decided by the proportional number of objects that contribute links between the two sub-clusters. By doing so, the negative effect of noisy objects is reduced to an acceptable level. The detailed algorithm is shown in Algorithm 1.

4 A Preliminary Performance Study

To study the effectiveness of our clustering approach, a series of experiments were conducted. Queries were issued to collect citation entries that are manually clustered based on our knowledge. The same queries were issued through the system and the results were compared with the manually clustered results.

4.1 Evaluation Metrics

The performance was evaluated to see how well the system can help the user get those citation entries that belong to the real world author intended done

Algorithm 1 The Proportional Link-node Hierarchical Clustering: PLHC

```
List pair_similarity_list;{sorted list, containing pair- wise similarities}
Place each citation entry in its own cluster;
while (pair_similarity_list not empty) do
   pair = RemoveHead(pair_similarity_list);
   cno1 = FindCluster(pair.o1);
   cno2 = FindCluster(pair.o2);
   if (cno1 == cno2) then
      continue;
   end if
   num_node1=CalcLinkNode(cno1, cno2); {link node in cno1}
   num_node2=CalcLinkNode(cno2, cno1); {link node in cno2}
   if (num_node1/SizeOfCluster(cno1) > THRESHOLD &&
   num_node2/SizeOfCluster(cno2) > THRESHOL) then
      MergeCluster(cno1, cno2);
   end if
end while
Output a nested hierarchical tree
```

manually by the user. We use the traditional metrics in information retrieval study, the precision and recall, to evaluate the system. Since we allow a user to pick a number of clusters as results, the two metrics are modified as follows:
Precision = (# of author's entries picked) / (# of total entries picked)
Recall = (# of author's entries picked) / (# of author's entries returned)

Author entries are defined as the citation entries that indeed belong to the author intended by the user.

4.2 Effectiveness of the System

In this section, we report the results of two sample queries. Two queried author's names are *H LU* and *G XU* respectively. The returned data is first cleaned for the purpose of evaluation. A paper entry is removed from the test set if one of the three citation fields (authors, title and publication) is missing. We also regard a paper entry illegal if none of its author contains the queried name. For example, a citation entry returned where *G* and *XU* are separated in two names was removed. For author *H LU*, CiteSeer returns around 140 citation entries. After cleaning, 91 entries are left. We manually cluster them with our knowledge into 5 clusters (5 real world authors). For query *G XU*, 86 cleaned entries are clustered into 3 clusters. Here we assume the manual clustering is correct. This is reasonable because we used all the information we could have to do the clustering, including visiting the author's web page. The details are shown in Table 1.

Recall that the user will be asked to choose one or more clusters to see their details. Let us denote this process as a Pick. And then we can calculate the precision and recall metrics according to the technique described above. In order to get Precision and Recall values for all the solution clusters (or all the real world queried authors) in a data set, we need to make Pick's with different

Table 1. Manual clustering results for clusters for the two sample queries

CNO	Size	Description
1	39	Database, data mining
2	25	Physics
3	13	Operating systems
4	9	S H LU
5	5	J H LU

(a) Query 1: H LU

CNO	Size	Description
1	47	Network communication
2	29	Computer graphics
3	12	Computer vision

(b) Query 2: G XU

intentions. Consider the data set for query *H LU*. There are five solution clusters and each cluster i belongs to real world author HLU_i. We will make 5 Pick's and Pick i is made with an intention of picking up HLU_i's paper entries. By doing this, we are able to calculate the precision and recall for each of the solution clusters in a data set.

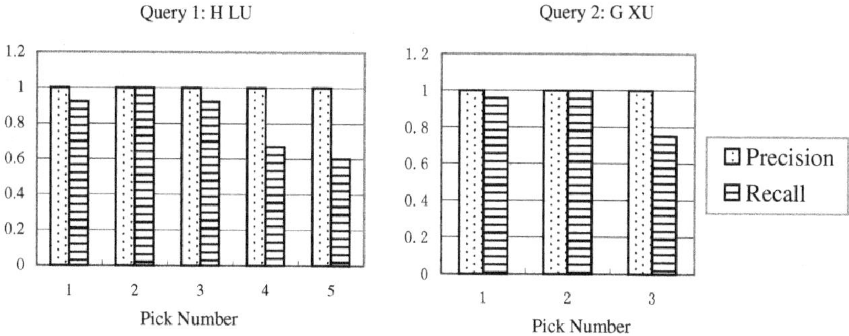

Fig. 4. Precisions and Recalls for different Picks

Figure 4 shows the precisions and recalls for different Pick's of both sample queries.

The results can be summarized as the following:

1. For any Pick of both sample queries, we can always achieve very high retrieval precision. It seems unlikely that paper entries belonging to two different real world authors will be put in the same cluster by our algorithm. High retrieval precision keeps the user away from irrelevant entries and provides better browsing experience.
2. For most Pick's, a recall above 85% can be obtained. But there are some Pick's, such as Pick 4 and 5 in Query 1 and Pick 3 in Query 2, whose recalls are relative low. A major reason is that solution clusters corresponding to

these Pick's are relatively small in size. The above three solution clusters are in size of 9, 5, and 12 respectively.

3. Citation entries contain very limited information, typically several author names and no more than 10 title words. So it is more likely that two paper entries sharing the same real world queried author will be put in two different clusters than two citation entries from two different real world authors will be clustered together. This results in the fact that precision is higher than recall for all Pick's of the two data sets.

4.3 Interpretation of Cut Values

The choice of a threshold value is always a controversial aspect for many algorithms that need one. For example, a data-mining algorithm that mines association rules would require support and confidence values rather than automatically decide the best values by the algorithm itself. In our online citation entry clustering system, we use a pre-defined cut value for the PLHC algorithm. The problem of adaptively finding the best cut value or near-best cut value is worth working on. In our approach, we investigate the interpretations of different cut values and then use the one that meets our clustering objective best. Generally speaking, the precision of the clustering result is proportional to the cut value used by the clustering algorithm, and the reverse for the relationship between recall and cut value. In other words, the smaller cut value we use, the lower precision the result clustering would be.

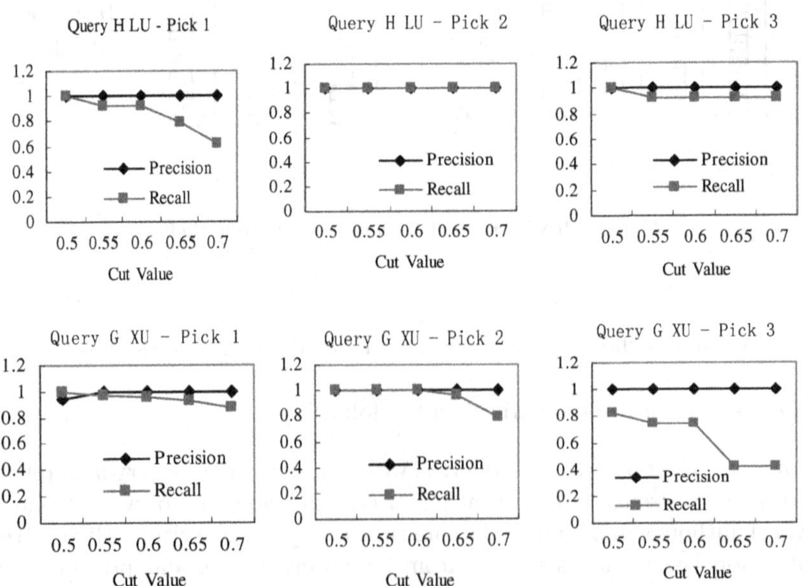

Fig. 5. Precisions and recalls for Pick's obtained by different cut values

Another interesting founding about the cut value from the experiment results is that the clustering results will not deteriorate much as long as the cut value varies in a semantically reasonable range (Note that the interpretation of cut values greatly depends on how the similarity function calculates the inter-object similarity.) This shows in some way that the belief network model applied to calculate the inter-object similarity works well. Figure 5 below shows the precisions and recalls of Pick's from different clustering results obtained by different cut values. The drawback of pre-defined cut value is also reduced much by the interactive Result Presenter, in which the user is allowed to roll up clusters (pick up more than one cluster) or drill down a particular cluster.

5 Conclusions

In this paper, we present an online citation entry clustering system based on a three-tier clustering framework. Using our system, a user first issues a name query, which is passed to online citation/bibliography search sites. Rather than showing the returned citation entries directly to the user, we first cluster all the citation entries according to the queried author names. Then, the result clusters are shown to the user with annotations. The user can choose a cluster of paper entries he/she is interested in. Our preliminary experiments show very encouraging results.

One possible future work is to refine algorithms for computing inter-feature-dimension and inter-object similarities. Consider the feature dimension of title words. Currently, we just count the common words between two titles to calculate the similarity of that dimension. This approach doesn't always work well because a same word may have different meanings in various contexts, while two different words could possibly implicate the same research area. So, a better solution is to identifying the real semantics of each word in a citation title and then calculating the inter-feature dimension similarity with such semantics.

In the application level, our next version would support queries to multiple data sources. In order to do so, more work in the data cleaning will be needed. One obvious issue is that citation entries returned by multiple data sources may have many duplicates, which have to be removed before clustering.

References

1. S. Brin, L. Page. *The Anatomy of a Large-Scale Hyper-textual Web Search Engine.* Proc. Of the 7th International World Wide Web conference,1998.
2. Rodrigo A. Botafogo, *Clustering Analysis for Hypertext Systems*, ACM- SIGIR'93 - 6/93/Pittsburgh, PA, USA.
3. Douglass R. Cutting, David R. Karger, Jan O. Pedersen, John W. Tukey, *Scatter/Gather: A Cluster-based Approach to Browsing Large Document Collections*, 15th Ann Int'l SIGIR'92, Denmark - 6/92.
4. Douglass R. Cutting, David R. Karger, Jan O. Pedersen, *Constant Interaction-Time Scatter/Gather Browsing of Very Large Document Collections*, 16th Ann Int's SIGIR'93/Pittsburgh PA USA - 6/93.

5. R. O. DUDA and P. E. HART, *Pattern Classification and Scene Analysis*, John Wiley and Sons, Inc., New York, NY, 1973.
6. Computer Science Bibliography, http://www.informatik.uni-trier.de/~ley/db/.
7. Lee Giles, Kurt Bollacker, Steve Lawrence. *CiteSeer: An Automatic Citation Indexing System.* Proceedings of the 3rd ACM Conference on Digital Libraries, pp. 89-98, 1998 [short listed for best paper award].
8. A.K. JAIN, M.N. Murty and P.J. FLYNN. *Data Clustering: A review. ACM Computing Surveys*, Vol. 31, No. 3, September 1999.
9. S. Lawrence and C.L. Giles. *Accessibility of information on the Web.* Nature, 400(8), July 1999, 107-109.
10. M. F. Porter. *An algorithm for suffix stripping.* Program, 14:130–137, 3 1980.
11. Dharmendra s. Modha, W.Scott Spangler. *Clustering Hypertext with applications to Web Searching*, Reseach Report RJ 10160(95035), Proceedings of ACM Hypertext Conference, May 30 - June 3, 2000.
12. *ACC: Sample Function to Format Names in Several Different Ways*, http://support.microsoft.com/support/kb/articles/Q149/9/53.asp
13. Rasmussen, E. *Clustering algorithms in Information Retrieval: Data Structures and Algorithms.* (1992), W. B. Frakes and R. Baeza Yates, Eds., Prentice Hall, Englewood Cliffs, New Jersey, pp. 419–442.
14. Stuart J. Russell. (1995), *Artificial intelligence : a modern approach*, Chapter 15, Prentice Hall.
15. Willet, P. *Recent trends in hierarchic document clustering: a critical review.* Inform. Proc. & Management (1988), 577–597.
16. N. L. Zhang and D. Poole (1996), *Exploiting causal independence in Bayesian network inference*, Journal of Artificial Intelligence Research, 5, 301-328.
17. N. L. Zhang and D. Poole (1999), *On the role of context-specific independence in Probabilistic Reasoning*, IJCAI-99, 1288-1293.
18. Research Index, the NECI Scientific Literature Digital Library. Available at http://citeseer.nj.nec.com/cs.
19. The Collection of Computer Science Bibliographies. Available at http://liinwww.ira.uka.de/bibliography/.

Introducing Navigation Graphs as a Technique for Improving WWW User Browsing

Christos Bouras[1,2], Agisilaos Konidaris[1,2], Eleni Konidari[3], and Afrodite Sevasti[1,2]

[1] Computer Technology Institute-CTI, Kolokotroni 3, 26221 Patras, Greece
{bouras, konidari, sevastia}@cti.gr
[2] Department of Computer Engineering and Informatics, University of Patras, 26500 Rion, Patras, Greece
[3] Child Development Centre, Department of Psychology, Heraclion, Greece
kondel@otenet.gr

Abstract. In this paper we show that users move from page to page, in the WWW, by following similar browsing patterns when they have similar browsing experience. Similar browsing patterns do not absolutely imply that the same URL's are visited. They only mean that users react in similar ways to similar web sites and follow almost foreseen routes. In order to prove this conclusion we introduce the Navigation Graph technique to trace users' web browsing patterns. We also categorize sites according to their structure by using a commercial tool. Having done these, we analyze the results of the navigation graphs and present them, pointing out the problems that users may encounter. Finally, in order to answer to these problems, we propose enhancements that can improve the performance of web browsers and web servers.

1 Introduction

The extensive use of the World Wide Web (WWW) in our days has established it as the dominant mean for accessing information. The WWW users comprise a heterogeneous group, the members of which have diverse social and professional backgrounds. The information provided and circulated through it, is the element that makes the WWW popular and imminently concerns all users.

It is interesting, however, to examine how the WWW users react to the information presented to them through WWW pages. Depending on the Web sites' structure, organization, presentation, design and appearance, users with different backgrounds and experiences seem to exhibit different reactions. These reactions concern the level of users' perception, their suppleness in navigation, their competence to access the specific information required and the degree of browsing optimization they can achieve. Another significant factor that is worth investigating in combination with the users' behavior, is the structural configuration of Web sites. This configuration is a factor that substantially affects the users' behavior and use of the WWW. It is also directly related to the efficiency and popularity of each Web site.

In this work, the above issues are thoroughly investigated. Initially, an analysis of the structural configurations of Web sites and how this configuration affects the users' behavior, is presented. Consecutively, the term of 'Navigation Graphs' is presented

X.S. Wang, G. Yu, and H. Lu (Eds.): WAIM 2001, LNCS 2118, pp. 249-256, 2001.

and thoroughly defined. WWW users' behavior is then examined with respect to the corresponding Navigation Graphs' formation. Based on the latter, the navigating behavior of groups of users with diverse characteristics is being traced, categorized and analyzed. Finally enhancements and improvements to the current organization of Web Sites and the WWW, with respect to the users' needs and gain are suggested.

2 Web Site Mapping

The WWW as we know it today consists of an impressive amount of Web Sites, each one of which comprises of a set of Web pages, containing a varying number of hyperlinks to other resources. From the early stages of the WWW's expansion, there have been attempts to visualize the internal organization of Web Sites and their interconnection in the WWW. These attempts were initiated by the ascertained problems of Web navigation and aspired to conclude to methods for moderating those problems. Here, a short reference will be made to those navigation problems that consist common knowledge among the users and developers of Web Sites.

According to [1], the two major navigation problems on a World Wide Web site are:

- **disorientation:** the tendency to lose sense of location and direction in a non-linear environment
- **cognitive overhead:** the additional effort and concentration necessary to maintain several tasks or trails at one time

In [2] more problems of Web navigation are mentioned. These are:

- **absence of physical context:** the reader sees only one page at a time
- **increased need for graphical context cues:** the reader's idea of what the web site contains must be presented and reinforced on each page
- **lack of control over the arrivals at one page:** the reader can arrive at any page by a variety of methods

Table 1. The results of a global WWW usability study

Percentage of WWW users	Result reported
17.8%	Difficulty in finding pages already visited
8.8 %	Difficulty in visualizing previous and future WWW locations
6.4 %	Difficulty in determining current location
87.7 %	Browsing the Web in an opportunistic manner

Many usability studies support the literature developed about Web navigation problems: according to [3], many users of the WWW cannot find pages already visited and cannot visualize where they are, or where they have been browsing. The results of a global WWW usability study [4] are shown in Table 1.

Another study ([5]) has shown that the 'Back' function of browsers is heavily used to return to a page, but that the history list is not. After all, the use of the history list doesn't resolve most navigation problems and does not contribute at all to the user's orientation within the pages of a Web site or within many visited Web sites.

In [6], it is clearly stated that people follow web links not only because of the page that might immediately be brought up but also because of some eventual set of pages they wish to see which may include, or may be found, inside the next linked page. This ascertainment shows that users often do not behave as the designer of a Web Site would want them to, and this causes poor utilization of the WWW.

In all the above cases, problems of Web navigation are being investigated and the Web users' behavior is analyzed. In most cases users have been asked questions and statistics have been produced according to their answers. In our case study, in the next paragraphs, users have only been asked one question. The question is:

– Do you consider yourself experienced or inexperienced?

The first step towards our analysis is site mapping and is described in the following section.

2.1 Web Site Mapping Results

In order for our experimental results to be produced, we used the log files of an HTTP proxy server over a period of one week. The population of the users that were connected to the WWW through our proxy server was dissimilar, with respect to the users' navigational experience, age and interests. The emerging log files contained approximately 1500 different Web Sites and 100 different users.

From these log files, all different Web Sites were extracted and their Site Maps were created using the I/O/D 4 Web Stalker [11]. The diagrams that occurred were then categorized according to their graphical representation and properties. From this indicative, extended sample of Web Sites, four categories of Web Sites were identified:

1. **Linear Web Sites.** This was one of the most rare cases of Web Site structure. In this category of Web Sites, all the site's pages contain a unique hyperlink to another page. Therefore, there is only one way to 'arrive' to a page and one way to 'depart' from it.
2. **Star-like Web Sites.** In this category of Web Sites, a central Web page (which is usually the home page of each Web Site) contains hyperlinks to all the other pages of the Site. The rest of the pages are only one 'hop' away from the home page and two 'hops' away from one another.
3. **Coherent Web Sites.** In this category of Web Sites, all pages contain hyperlinks to many of the other pages of the Site. The degree of coherency increases with the number of links existent among the pages of the Web Site.
4. **Non-structured Web Sites.** This category contains Web Sites that do not have a special pattern of Site Map. For these cases of Web Sites, the hyperlinks among pages do not follow any rules and have been incidentally created, according to the Web Site's developer needs. Such a Web Site can have a random Site Map layout, of any shape and structure.

Of course several existent Web Sites have a hybrid structure. In fact, the most popular configuration is that of the coherent Web Site with star-like components.

3 Navigation Graphs

Based on the categorization of Web Sites already presented, we can now proceed to the analysis of the users' navigational behavior. There are several already implemented tools that can be used to follow the trail of a Web user and record it. Most of these tools "translate" the user's actions into a directed graph that consists of nodes and arrows.

In [7] the authors have developed a prototype system called 'Footprints' which allows the tracing of users behavior while navigating in existent Web Sites. Internet Cartographer [8] is an application that works alongside the Web browser to classify and map all pages visited by the user. The map can also be used to find Web sites. SurfSerf [9] is another helper application that produces two-dimensional graphs of the Web browsing procedure. It demonstrates the structure of the sites visited and how they are linked together. Natto View [10] is a dynamic 3D visualization tool of the Web and finally, WebPath is another tool that visualizes the users' navigation, thoroughly described in [3].

3.1 Navigation Graphs' Definition

We have introduced a special methodology in order to visualize the vague concept of navigation in the WWW. This methodology consists of the use of what we call "Navigation Graphs" (NG).

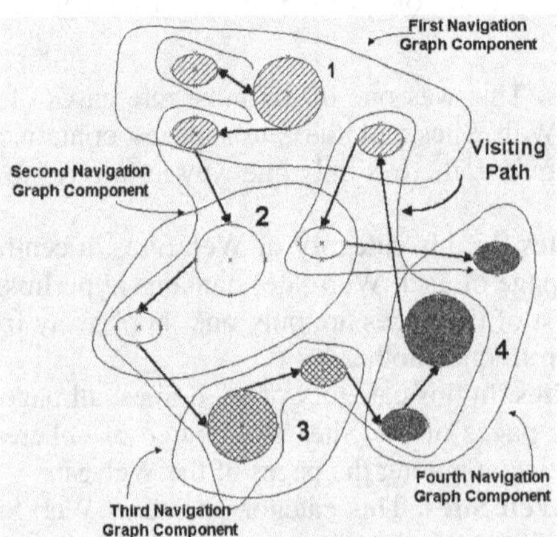

Fig. 1. A Navigation Graph

NGs are graphs that are able to picture the whole procedure of WWW navigation. For the formation of a NG, the URLs written in the navigation bar of the users' browser are taken into consideration in order of appearance.

In our NG notation, visits to pages within a site are represented as ovals, visits to new sites as circles and movements as directed lines (arrows). In Figure 1, all visited pages within a certain site are enclosed inside a perimeter line. Everything inside this line is a NG component that can be examined separately. Another element of Figure 1 is the curved line that connects the visited pages and is defined as the Visiting Path (VP). The arrows that connect NG components are defined as the backbone of the VP.

3.2 Connections between NG Components

For our analysis in this work, we have chosen to study a NG that consists of all four possible Web site structures, starting with a component with hybrid Web Site structure (coherent and star-like). This NG was chosen due to the evident popularity of this hybrid Web Site, together with the randomness of the rest of components of a NG. In the following section we will examine the VPs created by both inexperienced and experienced users in a NG that consists of the same components.

3.3 The VP of an Inexperienced User

The NG that we chose to examine is the one shown in Figure 2 (A). In the NG of Figure 2 (A) Site A is a Web Site that has the hybrid, coherent and star-like structure (a search engine in our case), Site B is a Web Site that is non-structured, Site C is a Web Site that has the linear structure and Site D is a Web site that has the coherent structure.

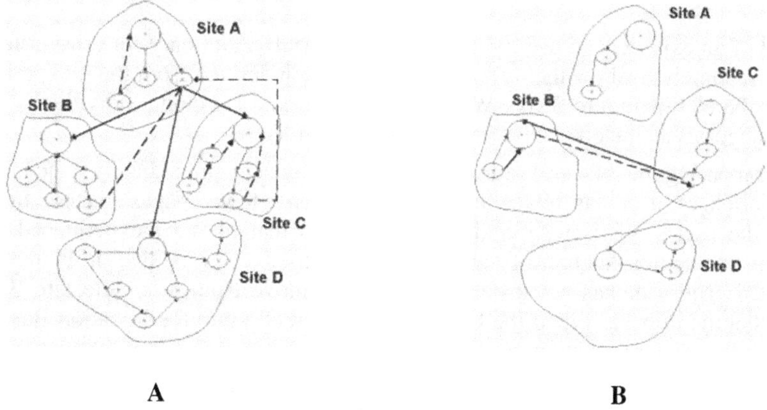

Fig. 2. The NG with the VP created by an inexperienced (A) and an experienced (B) user

The first observation made is that the VP consists of many loops. After observing similar loops in VPs of many inexperienced users, we have concluded that loops are a basic characteristic of Web behavior of inexperienced users. Of course loops are not always due to the user's lack of experience. It is clear that the structure of Site C (linear) is a structure that invokes loops independently of the user's experience. Consequently, many loops in non linear structured sites, and mostly loops in the backbone of the VP, are an indication of a Web user's lack of experience.

The topology of a NG's backbone is a very interesting result in our study. It is an indicator of user experience but also provides valuable hints on how a Web Site should be structured. In Figure 2 (A), one can see that the topology of the backbone of the NG is star-like and the user is using the BACK button in order to return to the central node. This indicates that the user is using a certain page (most likely a Web search engine result page) as a basis for his/her navigation. This behavior is very common amongst WWW users (experienced or not). There are certain Web pages, or sites, that are the basis of many users' VPs. These sites may change from session to session, or even during a session. In our opinion this is an issue that has to be examined very carefully. It is commonly accepted that a substantial number of users, use certain pages as "milestones" in their navigation. These pages must be treated with special care both from the server's side and the client's side. A suggestion for this problem is given in following sections.

The NG of Figure 2 (A), also gives us an indication of the user's knowledge on browser capabilities. The usage frequency of the "Back" button is a metric of user inexperience. Regarding Figure 2 (A), it is obvious that the user takes advantage of the functionality of the "Back" button a lot (dashed lines). It is obvious that the user's browser belongs to the fourth browser generation, because it provides more than one-step-back capabilities, and the user is aware of that.

The use of the "Back" button is not always positive, in determining user experience. Inexperienced users tend to use the "Back" button of a browser more than it should be used. This can lead to loops and insufficient use of Web resources.

3.4 The VP of an Experienced User

The VP of an experienced user will be examined briefly, and only for cross-reference purposes, namely to show the difference with the path derived from the inexperienced user. In the NG of Figure 2 (B), Web Sites A, B, C and D belong individually to the same categories as the ones represented in Figure 2 (A).

By comparing the NGs of Figures 2 (A) and (B), we can immediately conclude that the experienced user has fewer arrows, fewer loops, fewer pages visited. In other words, the user's VP is restricted with respect to that of the inexperienced users. Another interesting feature of the experienced user's NG is that it is not fully connected. The user has not used a hyperlink to move from Site A to site B. This means that the user has typed the URL of Site B directly into the Location Bar of his browser. This is another indication of the user's experience.

The only similarity that we can derive from the two NGs is the use of a page as a navigation "milestone". This is very important and leads us to believe that such pages are used by almost all users and, as already mentioned above, should be given special attention.

4 Results

In this section we will present the results that were the outcome of the Proxy files analysis process, the site categorization technique and the NG formation of most of the user navigation patterns found in the proxy files. The results provided by the NG patterns are the following:

- Inexperienced users often fall into browsing loops
- Inexperienced users use the "Back" button more often that experienced users
- Experienced users type URL's almost as often as they use bookmarks
- Both experienced and inexperienced users make the same browsing "mistakes" over and over
- Both experienced and inexperienced users follow the same or similar browsing patterns many times. This means that they often visit the same site and move to the same "next" site

The results of our research would not be the same if we did not know in advance if a user was considered experienced or inexperienced. Browsing patterns can heavily rely on every user's perception abilities. It is obvious that a user can not be easily categorized as experienced or inexperienced. We were able to do this by asking the user in advance if he considered himself experienced or inexperienced. After forming the experienced users NGs we realized that most of them followed similar patterns. The same happened with inexperienced users. Only these NGs were taken into consideration in the results that were mentioned above. This was done in an attempt to eliminate any possible false answers by users.

5 Proposed Enhancements of the Web Navigation Procedure

Our study of Web Navigation and Web Site structure with the use of NGs has led to some interesting ideas on how the whole WWW client-server model could be improved in order to facilitate the WWW users. The proposed enhancements apply to both clients and servers in the WWW. All the proposed enhancements aim at eliminating the users' browser problems that were the result of the Navigation Graph study. According to this general rule we propose enhancements that aim at making the user's browsing pattern as linear as possible since "loops" in navigation are not considered as a good practice. The proposed enhancements are the following:

- **Automated bookmark creation**. In the case of inexperienced users help could be provided in the form of automatic creation of bookmarks based on NGs. A browser that used NGs to record users' browsing patterns would be able to create bookmarks, for the user. These bookmarks could be based on "milestone" pages and help users in future web browsing sessions.
- **Help feature enhancement**. The use of NGs could lead to the provision of personalized help and tips. This would be possible since the browser would "know" by examining the user's NG about the problems that he/she may be encountering. This would result in the creation of personalized help and navigation tutorials.
- **NG archiving**. This could lead to the provision of "reminders" that would examine the current NG and when finding a relation with an older one, pass information concerning possible next links to the user enabling him to choose.
- **Client sided personalized statistics**. With the use of NGs browsers could provide personalized statistics, like how long a user has remained on a page or how often he/she has visited it.

- **Provision of site-category specific help**. By using NGs the browser could define a site's categories (as presented previously in this paper) and present useful information on how to navigate in the specific site.
- **Special treatment of "milestone" pages by the clients and servers.** Since "milestone" pages are generally considered to be very important to users, their "special treatment" by WWW clients and servers could be potentially beneficial. "Special treatment of "milestone pages may include: Client automatic bookmarking, Client caching, Server caching, Server response priority, Server script pre-execution.

6 Conclusions

The basic conclusion of our work is that the Web navigation and browsing procedures are highly individualized but also follow common patterns. A general remark though, is that most users would be happy if this procedure (visualized as the VP in this work) would become more linear. People do not like to go around in circles or come up with the same results. Diversity and variety is a popular demand in the case of the WWW.

NGs may be used to achieve two goals, the first being that of decoding the vast world of the WWW and the other being that of decoding the user navigational patterns within it. By defining and using NGs, we have come to certain conclusions that may help developers improve their Web Sites and allow users to utilize the full potential of the WWW.

References

1. Conklin, J.: Hypertext: An Introduction and Survey, IEEE Computer (1987) 20(9): 17-41
2. Kahn, P.: Mapping Web Sites: Planning Diagrams to Site Maps, A seminar of a series from Dynamic Diagrams, Inc found at http://www.dynamicdiagrams.net/seminars/mapping/maptoc.htm
3. Frécon, E. Smith, G.: WebPath - A three-dimensional Web History, IEEE Symposium on Information Visualization (InfoVis '98), Chapel Hill, NC, USA
4. GVU's WWW Surveying Team.: GVU's 8th WWW User Survey', October-November 1997, found at http://www.cc.gatech.edu/gvu/user_surveys/survey-1997-10/
5. Cartledge, L., Pitkow, J.: Characterising Browsing Strategies in the World-Wide-Web, Proc. of the 3rd international World Wide Web Conference, Germany, 1996.
6. Furnas, G.: Effective View Navigation, Proceedings of CHI'97, ACM Press, 1997
7. Wexelblat, A., Maes, P.: Footprints: Visualizing Histories for Web Browsing, MIT Media Lab, 1998
8. Inventix Software: Makers of Internet Cartographer, found at: http://www.inventix.com/
9. SurfSerf, found at: http://www.surfserf.com/
10. The Natto View, found at: http://www.mos.ics.keio.ac.jp/NattoView/
11. I/O/D Index, found at: http://www.backspace.org/iod/

The Evolution of the Contract Net Protocol

Lai Xu and Hans Weigand

INFOLAB,Tilburg University, P.O.Box 90153
Tilburg, The Netherlands
{lxu,Weigand}@kub.nl
http://infolab.kub.nl/people/{lxu,weigand}

Abstract. Contracts are a powerful co-ordination mechanism in distributed systems. The contract net protocol has been applied since about 1980. The CNP distributes tasks to different problem-solving nodes. TRACONET extended CNP with a bidding and awarding decision process based on marginal cost calculations. The CIA(Cooperative Information Agent) framework introduced the notion of obligations, which was broadened by CAS (Contractual Agent Societies) to support the fluid organisation of agent societies. Finally, the TPA framework (Trading Partner Agreement) introduced by IBM, although not agent-based, uses contracts as well, it uses executable contract in particular. We will analyse these four different contract model related researches (CNP, TRACONET, CAS and TPA) to compare their capabilities, background assumptions and limitations. We propose an integrated architecture and discuss the essential requirements still to be met.

1 Introduction

In 1980, the contract net protocol (CNP) [10] [11] for decentralised task allocation was one of the most important paradigms developed in distributed artificial intelligence (DAI). In 1993, the TRACONET (TRAnsportation COoperation NET) system [9] was presented; the formalisation is based on marginal cost calculations based on local agent criteria. The TRACONET system was seen as an extension of CNP in commitment strategy. A Cooperative Information Agent (CIA) model was described by Verharen in his Ph.D. thesis[12]. The CIA model is based on the Language/Action Perspective. These commitments are laid down in contracts. MIT Adaptive Systems and Evolutionary Software (ASES) introduces the concept of Contractual Agent Societies (CAS) as a metaphor for building open information systems that can automatically configure themselves through a set of dynamically negotiated social contracts. In January 2000, IBM submitted a specification for defining and implementing electronic contracts using TPA (trading-partner agreement). A TPA expresses the rules of interaction between the parties in the TPA while keeping each party process completely independent from the other parties. [8].

The paper is organised as follows: first describe the evolution of the contract net protocol along the steps of CNP (section 1.1), TRACONET (section 1.2),

X.S. Wang, G. Yu, and H. Lu (Eds.): WAIM 2001, LNCS 2118, pp. 257–264, 2001.

CIA (section 1.3) and CAS (section 1.4). Section 1.5 describes the TPA approach. Section 2 shows how the combination of CAS and TPA can provide a next step in the evolution. In section 3, we will discuss the evolution of CNP from a more general view. We finish with a conclusion and an indication of requirements that are still to be met(section 4).

1.1 Contract Net Protocol(CNP)

In the CNP, the network is assumed to consist of loosely coupled asynchronous agents, each agent can communicate with every other agent by sending messages. In the role of contractor, an agent can *decompose* a task into subtasks, send *requests for bids* on each specific subtask to all the other agents, *select* the most appropriate bid and *allocate* the task to that subcontractor.

The CNP is based on some assumptions. The announcement request message is not cancelled or changed; The contractor or subcontractor does not die; Counter proposing isn't allowed, and an agent can decide whether or not to bid to an announcement [3][7].

1.2 Transportation Co-operation Net (TRACONET)

In TRACONET, agent resources are overlapping, so each agent first solves its local problem, then an agent can potentially negotiate with other agents to buy or sell some services. An agent first calls its local optimiser to get the local "prices", based upon which the agents start the negotiations.

The negotiation process works likes described in the following example: in **the announcing stage**, an agent tries to buy some other agent's services at a price. The agent will use a special algorithm to choose a set of services from other agents and announces them in order to get bids from them. In **the bidding stage**, an agent reads the announcements sent by the other agents, and evaluate the cost using a special algorithm. If the maximum price mentioned in the announcement is higher than the local price, a bid is sent with the latter price. Otherwise, no bid is sent for this announcement. In **the awarding stage**, because there isn't a fixed timeout, the explicit loser messages have to be sent to every losing agent. After an award is sent to the winning agent, the agent will change its current state, the resources of every agent will be reloaded, and their tasks also will change.

In TRACONET, a party can send a **counterproposal message**. The other parties then can accept it, terminate the negotiation or counterproposal, etc. The level and stage of commitment is dynamically negotiated along with the negotiation of task.

In TRACONET, every agent still has a similar structure, and supports the overlapping function. The agents still work in a closed environment, every agent trusts each other without heterogeneous agents. The TRACONET has a peer 2 peer structure.

1.3 Cooperative Information Agent (CIA)

In the CIA, an agent has a number of tasks, it can be perform (in principle, an extensible set). Which tasks are executed, is determined by the contracts that the agent has set up with other agents. Typically, the agent relies on subcontractor agents, the relationship is also based on contracts. The agent contract is based on an agreement between at least two parties. The model, however, does also allow agents to send unauthorised requests to other agents; the receiving agent can ignore such a request, but it can also respond by proposing a contract (with mutual commitments). If the first agent accepts this proposal, there is a contract, and authorised interactions can start. The semantics of contracts can be described by means of illocutionary deontic logic, the logic of obligations, authorisations and speech acts. For more details, we refer to [13].

The aspect highlighted by the CIA model is that it is based on the notion of delegation. First, the agent himself can't be expected to be cooperative automatically. A contract should describe a mutual commitment, with reciprocal benefits. Second, the agent (principal) delegating some work to another agent has a need to control the activities of the other agent from a distance, while at the same time, the executing agent has a need to protect is relative autonomy. The contract should contain control procedures that find a balance between these two needs.

1.4 Contractual Agent Societies (CAS)

Crucial to the CAS [2] [4] model is the distinction between mutually trusted agents and mutually untrusted agents. A CAS is a set of mutually trusted agents; when an untrusted agent wants to join the society, it would first have to negotiate social contracts with the socialisation agent. During a socialisation process, the agent and socialisation agent engage in an explicit negotiation concerning the agent's capabilities and the society's norms. As a result of the negotiation between the agent and the society, a social contract is created, A social contract is a commitment of an agent to participate in a society and obey its norms.

Once admitted into the society, to locate another member of the society, member agents must send a request message to the matchmaker agent, describing the requested service. The matchmaker then broadcasts the request to all potentially eligible members. Interested members may then contact the sender directly by sending it a bid message. After they locate one another, they use exactly the same language they used to interact with the socialisation service agent to negotiate a new social contract that will define their partnership.

Once an acceptable bid has been received, the two parties can start communicating directly, or negotiate and form a private contract through the notary service. If a contract is unilaterally cancelled by one of the parties, the notary service informs the reputation agent. Also, if a contract is breached the notary informs both the reputation agent and the matchmaker. Member agents responsible for breaching more than N contracts lose their "good standing" with the

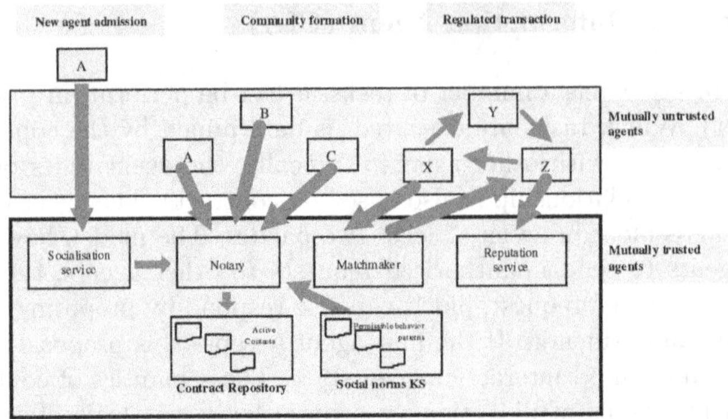

Fig. 1. Possible architecture of a Contractual Agent Society

society. As a consequence, they are banned from further use of the matchmaker. Figure 1 depicts one possible conceptual architecture of the society[2].

CAS focuses on developing an efficient, robust and open e-marketplace. There are no limiting assumptions in this system, on the other hand CAS has to face many challenges that include heterogeneity, limited trust, possibility of system failures, rapid adaptation and so on. CAS provides a certain level of support, so that heterogeneous agents can communicate with each other, and respond to changes amongst their members.

1.5 Trading-Partner Agreements(TPA)

In January 2000, IBM submitted a specification for defining and implementing electronic contracts using TPA (trading-partner agreement). The purpose of the TPA is to express the terms and conditions to which the parties to the TPA must agree in a form in which configuration information and the interaction rules that must be executable can be automatically generated from the TPA in each party's system. TPA doesn't complete the description of the application but only gives a description of the interactions between the parties. The application must be designed and programmed in the usual manner. Figure 2 shows the main elements provided by TPA.

A TPA is an XML document from which code is generated at each of the trading partner's computers. The semantics are defined by a textual design document and are embodied in rules and understood by the authoring tool that aids in the creation of a valid TPA. In order to utilise an electronic TPA, each party needs the authoring tool that prepares a TPA, the registration tool that extracts and stores TPA information to the registration database, and the code generation tool that uses TPA information and the registration database to generate into the executable file.

Overall Properties
Role
Identification
Communication Properties
Security Properties
Actions
Sequencing Rules
Error Handling

- Overall include TPA's name, starting and ending dates, and similar global parameters
- Role includes the means to define a TPA in terms of generic roles.
- Identification specifies the organisation names of the parties and various contact information.
- Communication include communication protocol, communication addresses
- Security include authentication and non-repudiation protocols, certificate parameters etc.
- Actions include an action menu which list the actions that the other party can request and various characteristics of those actions.
- Sequencing rules specify the order in which actions can be requested on each server.
- Error handling rules are various conditions related to error conditions.

Fig. 2. Key TPA elements

2 Combination of CAS and TPA

In the agent society, a business application can consist of:

- Interfaces: the service interfaces presented to agents; the application will also depend on the service interface definitions for any agent it uses from other applications in a subcontracting mode.
- Action methods: the implementations of each short running action that can occur in providing the service; each action involves responding to a specific event.
- Scheduling rules: the definition of the application's trigger events, i.e., combinations of response messages, time-outs and user requests, which will trigger execution of an action, and the rules to determine which action is to be scheduled when events occur.

An application available at an agent is defined as a named service with a collection of communicative action methods. A service invocation is composed of multiple actions. When a message arrives at the agent, it causes processing of an instance of that named application immediately, or it is put on the agenda. The *ServiceInvocation* implementation is a set of event driven scheduling rules. There is one *EventHandler* for each *ServiceInvocation*. The methods in the *EventHandler* correspond to different trigger events relevant to this *ServiceInvocation*. TPA generation and execution is shown in Figure 3.

The CAS is one open system in which agents can configure themselves using TPA. When agent A wants to join a CAS-based agent society, agent A first has to negotiate a social contract with the socialisation agent. In this process, a draft TPA will be proposed by the socialisation agent. The TPA objects are generated from the TPA at agent A and the socialisation agent. This request to join the society is communicated to the TPA object in the socialisation agent. The response message is received by agent A's TPA object, which evaluates the rules and draft items, if it supports the business rules, communication protocol, etc. it will configure itself. Otherwise, the agent can ask the socialisation agent a component with business rules and communication protocol that this society can support. Finally, agent A sends the "agree" message to the socialisation agent. A formal social contract will be formed and stored in the contract base.

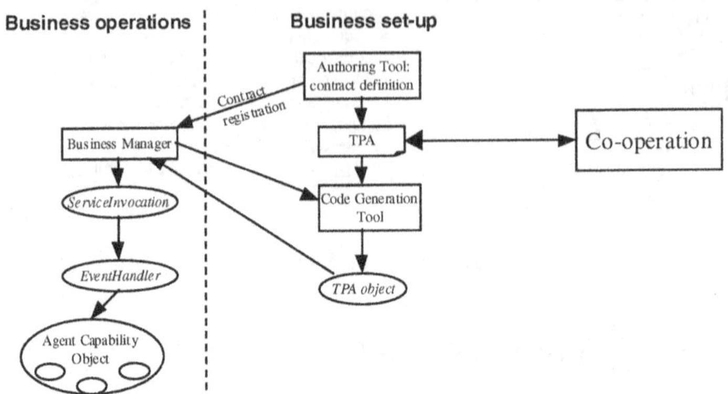

Fig. 3. The implementation of the socialisation process using TPA

The socialisation process was a simple two-partner negotiation process. When one member agent wants to negotiate and form private contracts with other member agents, maybe the member agents will create subcontracts to co-ordinate with other agents, or connect to their own business logic unit, etc. This is a very complicated multi-partner negotiation process. In our paper [14], we discuss how to implement the social contract and private contract at CAS. Further information will be discussed in a future paper.

3 Discussion

In contract net protocol, the early work of the classic CNP, makes many assumptions about agent behavior. Unlike the original CNP, the framework of TRACONET is extended to handle task interactions by clustering tasks into sets to be negotiated over as atomic bargaining items. In TRACONET the terminate negotiation command was added. The agent can cancel the deal on a task set. The counterproposing mechanism is allowed in TRACONET.

CAS defines a general set of principles for developing heterogeneous multi-agent systems. CAS includes mutually trusted and mutually untrusted agents, and adds the two-level concept; it is different from the old peer-to-peer infrastructure. CAS extends CNP and TRACONET, and CNP and TRACONET can be used in CAS as a subset of CAS's contracts.

TPA is a general contract in an inter-business environment, although it is not special for agent systems. If we view the agent as a part of software or as a component, TPA is easy to use in an agent-based system. TPA contains an

XML-based TPA language(tpaML). The action item and sequencing rules item are still open for extension, and the TPA offers a good framework for the contract specification.

As society and the problems that face it become more and more complex, agents have to become more and more intelligent. In 21st century, e-commerce is a distributed computing environment with dynamic relationships between a large number of autonomous service requesters, brokers and providers [1]. Agents are software systems, that are capable of interacting with other agents in a flexible and autonomous way [6]. We have noticed the trend of contracts, from a solution of concrete problems (CNP), local optimisation (TRACONET), simulate a civil society(CAS), to automatic execution in IT e-commerce environment(TPA), each model more complex than the last. We will point out some important changes:

Original design function: CNP provides a solution to how agents with different functions can co-operate in a closed environment; TRACONET's design gives agents with similar functions the ability to optimise for max-profit for each agent in a closed distributed network; CAS's goal is to make heterogeneous agents work in a safe and efficient way. Finally, TPA describes the peoblem how the contract can be automaticly executed in the system. From the solution of a distributed system, to QoS guarantees, the new agent systems can be applied to the open automated marketplace of contract net agents.

Architecture of agent system: The CNP and TRACONET provide a peer-to-peer architecture of agents; agents in this kind of system have similar structures, and monitor the negotiation process by themselves. CAS provides a two-level structure, it supports a communication platform for heterogeneous agents, and it emphasises social norms and central control, this kind of design efficiently prevents exceptions from occurring in the system.

Agent roles: In CNP and TRACONET, an agent can take on contractor and subcontractor roles. CAS is a two level concept, all mutually trusted agents have responsibility for the agent society; In the mutually untrusted level, there are member agents. Each role has been allocated to different agents. This way is more flexible and efficient in an open environment.

From distributed knowledge-sources to a centralised knowledge-base: In CNP, each agent has distinct knowledge-sources; in TRACONET, each agent has overlapping function resources. In CAS, the social norms and exception handling work as a centralised knowledge-resource.

4 Conclusion

Agent technologies and multi-agent systems are becoming more widely used for constructing e-commerce systems [5]; agent-mediated e-commerce systems have a great potential. Next generation contract net protocols have to be designed to support this kind of new environment. It will combine the properties of belief-based knowledge bases, reinforcement learning, self-adaptive systems, QoS guarantee, etc., to be very efficient to support e-marketplaces and dynamic-agents. New contract design should specify how an agent is to be loaded with new functions, change its behaviour dynamically and exchange program objects. Unlike the original contracts with fixed design, the new generation of contracts' desigen will be decided by the characteristics of the environment. What is also crucial for its adaptation is that these contracts are properly embedded in their environment. This means, among others, that the legal status of the contracts has been guaranteed. It also means that there is a secure identification system to guarantee the identity of agents and to relate them to real-world persons or companies.

References

1. Q. Chen, M. Hsu, U. Dayal, M. Griss: Multi -agent co-operation, dynamic workflow and XML for e-commerce automation. HP Laboratories Palo Alto, 1999.
2. C. Dellarocas and M. Klein: Civil Agent Societies: Tools for inventing open agent-mediated electronic marketplaces. Proceedings of the Workshop in Agent-Mediated Electronic Commerce (co-located with IJCAI'99), Stockholm, Sweden, July 1999.
3. C. Dellarocas and M. Klein. Designing robust, open electronic marketplaces of contract net agents. Proceedings of the 20th International Conference on Information Systems (ICIS), Charlotte, NC, December, 1999.
4. C. Dellarocas and M. Klein.: An Experimental Evaluation of Domain-Independent Fault Handling Services in Open Multi-Agent Systems. ICMAS-2000, The International Conference on Multi-Agent Systems, 2000.
5. M. Griss: My Agent Will Call Your Agent... But Will It Respond?: HP Laboratories Palo Alto, 1999.
6. Jennings, N.R., Sycara K. and Wooldridge M. : A roadmap of agent research and development: Autonomous agents and multi-agent system 1 (1) 1998.
7. M. Klein and C. Dellarocas.: Domain-Independent Exception Handling Services That Increase Robustness in Open Multi-Agent Systems.: ASES Working Report ASES-WP-2000-02.m Cambridge MA USA, Massachusetts Institute of Technology. 2000.
8. M. Sachs, A. Dan, T. Nguyen, etc,: Executable Trading-Partner Agreements in Electronic Commerce,: IBM Research Report, 2000.
9. Sandholm, T.: An Implementation of the Contract Net Protocol Based on Marginal Cost Calculations. Eleventh National Conference on Artificial Intelligence (AAAI-93), Washington DC, pp. 256-262, 1993.
10. Smith, R.G.: The Contract Net Protocol: High-level Communication and Control in a Distributed Problem Solver. IEEE Trans. On Computers C-29 (12): 1104-1113,1980
11. Smith, R.G., and Davis,: Frameworks for Co-operation in Distributed Problem Solving.: IEEE Trans. on System. Man and Cybernetics 11 (1): 61-70,1981
12. Verharen, E.,: A Language/Action Perspective on Cooperative Information Agents.: Ph.D. Thesis, Tilburg University,1997.
13. H. Weigand, E. Verharen, F. Dignum,: Integrated semantics for information and communcation systems.: In: R. Meersman (Ed), Proc. IFIP WG 2.5 Database application semantics, Chapman and Hall,1997.
14. H. Weigand, L. Xu,: Contract In E-commerce.: 9th IFIP 2.6 Working Conference on Database Semantics,2001.

Session 4A

Temporal, Spatial & High Dimensional Information Management

Regular Research Paper (30 minutes)
Semantic Compression of Temporal Data

Regular Research Paper (30 minutes)
Efficiently Computing Weighted Proximity Relationships in Spatial Databases

Regular Research Paper (30 minutes)
Compressing the Index – A Simple and Yet Efficient Approximation Approach to High-Dimensional Indexing

Semantic Compression of Temporal Data

Claudio Bettini

DSI - Università di Milano, Italy

Abstract. In a temporal database a specific semantics is usually intended by the database designer regarding how the values of certain attributes evolve over time and how these values change when considered in terms of different time granularities. In this paper we show how this semantics can be exploited to compress the original database. Differently from traditional compression techniques, queries can be evaluated directly against the compressed database.

1 Introduction

Many database applications store and manage time-related information, like bank transactions, product orders, employment histories, etc.. Temporal database management systems offer time management functions as opposed to traditional DBMS which leave most of time management to the specific applications. When data is associated with time in a temporal database [TW99], its semantics is usually specified in terms of the data being valid at the given time (called "valid time"), or as being added to (or deleted from) the DB at the given time (called "transaction time"). Usually information is only added to temporal databases, since the user may be interested to know what was the value of a certain attribute at an instant in the past or what was believed to be true in the database at a certain instant in the past. This leads to huge amount of data to be stored in a database. Despite the fact that computer memory costs have decreased dramatically over the past years, data storage still remains an important cost factor for large scale temporal database applications. If we consider applications in the field of mobile databases where portions of databases must be distributed to mobile devices such as PDAs or smartphones, data storage can become one of the critical factors.

Several data compression techniques have been investigated and applied in the field of databases. These techniques are based on finding and exploiting data redundancy that can be easily found in the data in terms of character distribution, character repetition, high usage patterns, and positional redundancy. A simple example may be representing sequences of zeros and blanks by a special character, followed by the length of the sequence. A more complex technique is Huffman coding, based on the conversion of fixed-sized pieces of data into variable-length codes, or LZW which converts variable-length strings into fixed-length codes. A good review of these techniques and their advantages/disadvantages in the context of databases can be found in [RVH93]. Experimental studies on compression in the IBM's DB2 database are reported in

X.S. Wang, G. Yu, and H. Lu (Eds.): WAIM 2001, LNCS 2118, pp. 267–278, 2001.

[IW94]. Other interesting compression techniques exploiting the particular structure of data have been recently proposed in [LS00] for XML documents.

When the semantics of data is considered, it is easy to find new forms of redundancy with respect to those identified by the techniques cited above. In particular, a rich semantics is usually associated to time-dependant data by the database designer regarding how the values of certain attributes evolve over time and how these values change when considered in terms of different time granularities. For example, when storing the average street price of products in terms of months, we may assume that explicit values persist until a new value is given, or that if a price value is missing it is possible to take the average of the previous and next known values for the same product; as another example, when storing the monthly rainfall amount in a certain region, we may assume that the rainfall amount in terms of years is just the sum of the ones given for the months of each year.

In [BWJ96] we introduced the notion of *semantic assumption* to formalize the semantics associated to temporal database schemas. We also showed how user queries involving data not explicitly present in the database can be transformed by the system using the formalization of the assumptions in order to be answered. Previous work on concepts similar to semantic assumptions include [CW83,SS87,SSR94]. In this paper, we adopt the same notion of semantic assumption together with the formal characterization of time granularities as deeply investigated in [BJW00], and we elaborate on the concept of *minimal representation* of temporal relations. Indeed, based on semantic assumptions, some of the explicit values stored in the database can be dropped leading to an equivalent relation, since these values will be automatically derived exploiting the assumptions. Intuitively, a minimal representation is obtained by dropping all possible values and/or changing the time-granularity associated with the relation. By substituting each temporal relation with its minimal representation according to semantic assumptions we obtain a compressed database equivalent to the original one. Our approach does not exclude the application of more traditional compression techniques over our compressed database.

Section 2 introduces the concepts of *temporal database with granularities* and *semantic assumption.* Section 3 defines our notion of semantically compressed database, and it describes how compression can be achieved. The problem of evaluating queries against a compressed database is addressed in Section 4, and Section 5 concludes the paper.

2 Temporal Databases and Semantic Assumptions

Intuitively, a temporal database is a collection of facts associated with one or more temporal contexts, modeling, for example, validity time, transaction time, or other time dimensions. Different facts may be associated with temporal contexts expressed in terms of different time granularities. For example, a bank transaction may require a timestamp in seconds, while the presence of an employee in a department may be expressed in days. A temporal database which allows facts to be expressed in terms of different granularities is intuitively called a temporal database with multiple granularities.

In this work we focus on relational databases and on validity time only. In this case, we model the database as a set of relations, each one with an implicit time attribute. The attribute value is used as a timestamp for the corresponding tuple and it is expressed in terms of a specific time granularity for each relation. An example is shown in Figure 1.

Item	StPrice	Time
I1	\$30	1st-q-2001
I2	\$100	1st-q-2001
I1	\$35	2nd-q-2001
I1	\$40	3rd-q-2001
I1	\$50	2nd-q-2002

Fig. 1. The PRICE temporal relation storing street prices in different quarters

In order to formalize this database model and investigate how database instances can be compressed, we first need to elaborate on the notion of time granularity.

2.1 Databases with Multiple Time Granularities

We first briefly present the mathematical characterization of time granularities as found in the granularity glossary [BD+97]. The *time domain* is a set of primitive temporal entities used to define and interpret time-related concepts. It is denoted by the pair $(T, \leq)$, where T is a nonempty set of *time instants*, and $\leq$ is an order relationship on them. and $\leq$ is a total order on T. For example, integers $(\mathbf{Z}, \leq)$ and real numbers $(\mathbf{R}, \leq)$ are examples of time domains.

Definition 1. *A* granularity *is a mapping G from the integers (the* index set*) to subsets of the time domain such that: (1) if $i < j$ and $G(i)$ and $G(j)$ are nonempty, then each element of $G(i)$ is less than all elements of $G(j)$, and (2) if $i < k < j$ and $G(i)$ and $G(j)$ are nonempty, then $G(k)$ is nonempty.*

The definition covers standard granularities like `day`, `month`, `week`, and `year`, bounded granularities like `year-since-2000`, granularities with noncontiguous granules like `business-day`, and gap-granularities (i.e., granularities with non-convex intervals as granules) like `business-month`.

As an example, `quarter-since-2000` can be defined as a mapping G, with $G(1)$ mapped to the subset of the time domain corresponding to the first quarter of year 2000, $G(2)$ to the second, and so on, with $G(i) = \emptyset$ for $i < 1$.

The index of a granule is used as an internal encoding to reference the granule. Independently from the integer encoding, there may be a "textual representation" of each granule, termed its *label*, that is used for input and output. This representation is generally a string that is more descriptive than the granule's index (e.g.,"August 1997", "1997/8/31").

If the values of the attribute `Time` in the PRICE relation is expressed in terms of the granularity `quarter-since-2000`, the indexes of its granules involved in the relation are 5, 6, 7 and 9, represented by the labels 1st-q-2001, 2nd-q-2001, 3rd-q-2001, 2nd-q-2002, respectively.

We now introduce the notion of temporal database with multiple granularities following [WJS95,BWJ96].

Definition 2. *A* temporal module schema *is a pair* (R, G) *where* R *is a relation schema and* G *a time granularity. A* temporal module *is a triple* (R, G, ϕ) *where* (R, G) *is a temporal module schema and* ϕ *is a mapping, called a* time windowing *function, from the integers to* $2^{\mathbf{Tup}(T)}$ *where* $\mathbf{Tup}(T)$ *is the set of all tuples on the time domain, such that* $\phi(i) = \emptyset$ *if* $G(i) = \emptyset$ *for each* i*, and* $\bigcup_i \phi(i)$ *is a finite set.*

Intuitively, the function ϕ gives the tuples (facts) that hold at a time granule $G(i)$ of granularity G. Referring to the PRICE relation, the corresponding temporal module schema is $(R,$ `quarter`$)$ where R=\{`Item, StPrice`\}, while the windowing function for the module is:
ϕ(1st-q-2001)=\{⟨ I1, \$30⟩, ⟨ I2, \$100⟩\}, ϕ(2nd-q-2001)=\{⟨ I1, \$35⟩\}, ϕ(3rd-q-2001)=\{⟨ I1, \$40⟩\}, ϕ(2nd-q-2002)=\{⟨ I1, \$50⟩\}, $\phi(i) = \emptyset$ for all other time values.

Note that temporal modules can represent infinite relations. For example we may set $\phi(i)$=\{⟨ I1, \$50⟩\} for all $i >$2nd-q-2002.

A *temporal database with multiple granularities* is simply a finite set of temporal modules, while a *database schema with multiple granularities* is a fixed set of temporal module schemas.

2.2 Semantic Assumptions

Semantic assumptions provide a formal specification of how unknown, yet implicit, values can be deduced from data explicitly present in the database. In particular, we are interested in information unknown for a particular instant (of the time same time granularity used in the database), and in information unknown for instants of different granularities. *Instant* semantic assumptions are used to derive the first type of information, while *granularity* semantic assumptions the latter.[1]

Hence, instant assumptions can be used to derive information at certain instants of time, based on the information explicitly given at different instants, considering a single time granularity. Such derivation can be done in a variety of ways. For example, (i) we may assume that the values of certain attributes persist in time unless they are explicitly changed; (ii) we may assume that a missing value is taken as the average of the last and next explicitly given values;

[1] In [BWJ96] the terms point-based and interval-based are used instead of instant and granularity respectively, but we believe the new terms are more intuitive.

or (iii) we may take the sum of the last three values. We adopt a general notion of instant assumptions such that, in principle, any interpolation function to derive information from explicit values can be used [BWJ96].

The *persistence* assumption has been widely used in practice. With $P_X(Y^{persis})$, we denote the assumption of the attributes XY being persistent with respect to the attributes X. This intuitively means that if we have explicit values for X and Y at a certain granule of time, these values will persist in time until we find an instant at which we have explicit values that are the same for the attributes X but different for Y. Note that the information derived by a persistence assumption always includes the original information (projected on XY).

If we generalize the persistence example, a temporal semantic assumption relies on the use of certain methods (called *interpolation methods*) to derive implicit values from explicit ones. An interpolation method is used to derive a value of an attribute by "interpolating" values of the same attribute at different granules of time. Examples of other interpolation methods are *average*, taking the average of the previous and next stored value, or *last-k-avg*, taking the average of the last k stored values. Consider the PRICE temporal relation. The company managing this data may decide the following policy: "If the price for an item in a quarter is missing it is assumed to be the average between the previous and next stored values for that item.". This is formally specified by the assumption $P_{\texttt{Item}}(\texttt{StPrice}^{avg})$ where avg is a logical formula template describing the interpolation. For example, there is no value in the PRICE table for the street price of product 'I1' for the fourth quarter of 2001. However, if the designer specified the above semantic assumption, a value of \$45 for item I1 is implied for the fourth quarter of 2001 as well as for the first quarter of 2002.

In general, if X, $Y_1, \ldots, Y_n$ are pair-wise disjoint attribute sets, and $meth_1$, …, $meth_n$ are interpolation methods, the expression $P_X(Y_1^{meth_1} \cdots Y_n^{meth_n})$ denotes the assumption using method $meth_i$ to derive implicit values of attributes Y_i with respect to attributes X, for each $i = 1, \ldots, n$.

We call *granularity* assumptions the semantic assumptions that can be used to derive information for a certain granule of one time granularity from information at granules of a different time granularity. Referring to our PRICE relation, the designer could have associated with this relation an assumption that says: "If a given item price is stored in the relation for a given quarter, the same price can be considered a good estimate for any month (or day, hour, etc.) of that quarter."

According to this assumption, the relation in Figure 2 is implied by that in Figure 1. In general, with $I_X(A^{\downarrow})$ we denote the assumption of the attribute A being *downward hereditary* with respect to the attributes in X. This intuitively means that if we have an explicit value for the attribute A with respect to certain values for X at a certain granule of granularity G, then for each granule of any other granularity that is covered by it, A has that same value with respect to the same values for X. The above assumption on the PRICE relation would be specified by $I_{\texttt{Item}}(\texttt{StPrice}^{\downarrow})$. Similarly, with $I_X(A^{\uparrow})$ we denote the assumption

Item	StPrice	Time
I1	$30	Jan-2001
I1	$30	Feb-2001
I1	$30	Mar-2001
I2	$100	Jan-2001
I2	$100	Feb-2001
I2	$100	Mar-2001
I1	$35	Apr-2001
I1	$35	May-2001
I1	$35	Jun-2001
I1	$40	Jul-2001
I1	$40	Aug-2001
I1	$40	Sep-2001
I1	$50	Apr-2002
I1	$50	May-2002
I1	$50	Jun-2002

Fig. 2. A temporal relation storing street prices in different months

of the attribute A being *upward hereditary* with respect to X. Intuitively, if we have the same value for the attribute A with respect to the same X at different granules, that value is also the value of A for the same X for each granule of any other granularity that is the union of some of these granules. In our example, the price of an item for a granule of time composed of several quarters (e.g. a year) is that of each quarter provided that the same value for that item is stored for all these quarters. With $I_X(A^{\updownarrow})$ we denote the assumption of the attribute A being *liquid* with respect to X; i.e., it is both downward and upward hereditary. In our example, this would be $I_{\mathtt{Item}}(\mathtt{StPrice}^{\updownarrow})$.

In general, a granularity assumption relies on the use of certain "conversion" methods. If X, Y_1, ..., Y_n are pair-wise disjoint attribute sets, and $conv_1$, ..., $conv_n$ are conversion methods, $I_X(Y_1^{conv_1} \cdots Y_n^{conv_n})$ is the interval assumption that allows to convert values of Y_i according to method $conv_i$ with respect to values of attributes X, for each $i = 1, \ldots, n$. Conversion methods include average, sum, last, etc.. In the case of average or sum, intuitively, the value for an attribute at a certain granule $H(i)$ of a target granularity H can be obtained by aggregating, according to the method, the values present in the database relation for granules included in $H(i)$. For example, an assumption may state that the yearly rainfall amount is given as the sum of the monthly rainfall, or that yearly street price of a product is given as the average of the quarterly street price.

Instant and granularity assumptions can be combined by applying instant assumptions first, and granularity assumptions later [BWJ96].

Minimal closure. A temporal module is called a *closure under a set of assumptions* Γ if it explicitly contains all the information implied by the assumptions. It is *minimal* if it does not contain any "extraneous" tuples.

In the PRICE example any closure under $P_{\texttt{Item}}(\texttt{StPrice}^{avg})$ must include ϕ(4th-q-2001)={⟨ I1, \$45⟩}, and ϕ(1st-q-2002)={⟨ I1, \$45⟩} in addition to those explicitly given. A minimal closure does not contain any other tuple. In this case the minimal closure is finite. Note, however, that minimal closures can be infinite; for example this happens when persistence assumptions are given.

In [BWJ96] we have shown that the minimal closure under instant assumptions is unique if each attribute in the temporal module is involved in one assumption. Notice that if this condition is not satisfied, the implied tuples would have at least one attribute for which any value is possible, since no assumption exists to determine which one should be given. For simplicity, in the rest of the paper we assume that this condition is always satisfied.

For granularity assumptions the minimal closure is intended with respect to a target granularity. For example, the relation in Figure 2 represents the minimal closure of the price relation under the $I_{\texttt{Item}}(\texttt{StPrice}^{\updownarrow})$ assumption with respect to the target granularity `month`. If we consider the minimal closure under both the given instant and granularity assumptions, the implied tuples for the missing months should also appear.

Another crucial notion is that of equivalence among temporal modules under a set of assumptions.

Definition 3. *Two temporal modules are said to be* equivalent *if they have the same minimal closures. When the modules have different granularities, they must have the same closures in terms of both granularities.*

3 Semantic Data Compression

Previous work has considered the value of semantic assumptions for answering user queries asking for data not explicitly present in the database. In this paper we focus on the value of semantic assumptions for compressing the database. For example, according to the semantic assumption $P_{\texttt{Item}}(\texttt{StPrice}^{avg})$, we observe that the tuple corresponding to the price value of item I1 in the second quarter of year 2001 can be dropped from the relation, since it is implied by the assumption.

A natural question is if, given a database and a set of assumptions, there exists a minimal representation of the database such that no tuple implied by the assumptions appear in any of the temporal modules.

3.1 Minimal Representation of a Temporal Module

A partial order on temporal modules can be easily defined as follows: Given $M = (R, G, \phi_M)$ and $M' = (R, G, \phi_{M'})$, $M \preceq M'$ if $\phi_M(i) \subseteq \phi_{M'}(i)$ for each i. We write $M \prec M'$ if $M \preceq M'$ and $M \neq M'$.

When only instant assumptions are considered, the minimal representation can be easily defined as follows:

Definition 4. *A temporal module M' is said to be* a minimal representation of M under a set of instant assumptions Γ *if M' is equivalent to M under Γ, and there is no temporal module M'' such that M'' is equivalent to M and $M'' \prec M'$.*

Referring to our example and considering the assumption $P_{\texttt{Item}}(\texttt{StPrice}^{avg})$ it is easily seen that the temporal module resulting from dropping the tuple $\langle I1, \$35\rangle$ from ϕ(2nd-q-2001) is a minimal representation of the PRICE relation.

In the presence of granularity assumptions, the notion of minimal representation is more involved, since, in principle, we have many (possibly an infinite number) of granularities to consider.

However, since the goal is having a windowing function with as few tuples as possible, it is clear that only granularities which have coarser granules than those appearing in the original temporal module are to be considered. For example, a module in terms of months is not a candidate for the minimal representation of PRICE since for each month in each quarter the value of the windowing function would be replicated, with the result of having many more tuples to be stored in the database. A temporal module in terms of years may be a reasonable candidate since each year is a grouping of quarters. Unfortunately, for the considered instance of the PRICE relation, the granularity assumption $I_{\texttt{Item}}(\texttt{StPrice}^{\updownarrow})$ does not lead to a set of tuples in terms of years. This would happen if, for each item, the same street price was stored in the quarters of 2001, and the same for 2002. In this case we would have a minimal representation of PRICE with one tuple for each item and each year.

When granularity assumptions are present, the above definition must take into account the target granularity.

Definition 5. *A temporal module M' is said to be* a minimal representation of M in a granularity G' under a set of assumptions Γ *if M' is equivalent to M under Γ, and there is no temporal module M'' in G' such that M'' is equivalent to M and $M'' \prec M'$.*

The minimal representation of temporal module M over all the granularities is identified as the temporal module equivalent to M having the most compact representation.

Definition 6. *Let $||\phi_M(i)||$ denote the number of tuples in $\phi_M(i)$. Then, given two modules $M = (R, G, \phi_M)$ and $M' = (R, G', \phi_{M'})$ with the same schema relation but different granularities, we can say that M has a more compact representation than M' if $\sum_i ||\phi_M(i)|| < \sum_j ||\phi_{M'}(j)||$, where i and j range over all indexes for which there is an explicit value of the windowing function in M and M', respectively.*

In practice, many granularities should not even be considered as candidates. For example, when `quarter` is the granularity of the original relation, finer granularities like `month`, `day`, or `hour` have no chance to lead to a more compact representation. Moreover, granularities must be chosen carefully in order to preserve the equivalence. Indeed, the choice of a coarser granularity in order to achieve more compression can easily lead to loss of information and introduce a sort of approximation.

The minimal representation is unique for particular assumptions (e.g., persistence), but not in general. Indeed, consider the following variant of the PRICE temporal module: ϕ(1st-q-2001) $= \{\langle I1, \$30\rangle\}$, ϕ(2nd-q-2001) $= \{\langle I1, \$35\rangle\}$,

ϕ(3rd-q-2001) = $\{\langle I1, \$40\rangle\}$, ϕ(4th-q-2001) = $\{\langle I1, \$45\rangle\}$, ϕ(1st-q-2002) = $\{\langle I1, \$50\rangle\}$, ϕ(2nd-q-2002) = $\{\langle I1, \$55\rangle\}$. Using the instant assumption we may drop the tuples for the second and fourth quarter of 2001, or alternatively we may drop those for the third quarter of 2001 and for the first quarter of 2002. In both cases we obtain a minimal representation.

3.2 Deriving a Compressed Temporal Module

Compressing temporal modules in our approach means deriving one of their minimal representations and using it for query-answering instead of the original representation. The minimal closure of a temporal module under a set of instant assumptions can be derived as follows: If m and n are the first and last instant for which the windowing function of the original module is nonempty, the minimal closure can be obtained by a query to the system asking for all tuples at all instants included between m and $n+1$. The value for $n+1$, in particular, can be considered the value of the windowing function of the minimal closure for all instants greater than n. As presented in [BWJ96] and briefly discussed in the next section, the database system transforms the query returning an answer that takes into account all the assumptions.

Assuming we have an algorithm to decide the equivalence of two temporal modules by deriving and comparing their closures, a trivial algorithm to derive the minimal representation of a temporal module $M = (R, G, \phi)$ under instant assumptions is the following:

> For each i such that $\phi(i) \neq \emptyset$, for each tuple t in $\phi(i)$, delete t from $\phi(i)$ if the resulting module is equivalent to the original one.[2]

Several optimizations are possible; for example, we should only consider tuples such that there exist other tuples with the same base attribute for at least one of the assumptions, and there are assumptions for which a group of "contiguous" tuples can be deleted by examining only the first and last tuple of the group.

Until now we have not considered granularity assumptions. In order to derive the minimal representation of a temporal module M in terms of a granularity G', we submit a query asking for all the data in M in terms of G'. Again, the system transforms the query according to all the instant assumptions and to the granularity assumptions useful to convert data into G'. The results in [BWJ96] guarantee that all the data in M that can be expressed in terms of G' are returned by the query.

We should now check if the new module is equivalent to the original one. Since they are in different granularities, the closure of the new module in terms of granularity G must be the same as the closure of the original module. If this is the case we can now use the instant assumptions in order to derive a minimal representation in terms of G'. The procedure is analogous to the one illustrated above for the original module. In principle this procedure should be applied to

---

[2] The algorithm assumes the original temporal module to be finite, and this is probably always the case if it comes from a relational database, but it can also be easily adapted to deal with the infinite case.

$$\begin{array}{l}\Psi^{\mathtt{M}}_{PV(W^{avg})}(w_1,\ldots,w_n,t) = \mathtt{M}(w_1,\ldots,w_n,t) \vee \\ \quad (\exists t_1,t_2,v_1,\ldots,v_n,u_1,\ldots,u_n)\ (t_1 < t\ \wedge\ \mathtt{M}(v_1,\ldots,v_n,t_1) \\ \qquad \wedge\ (\forall t'',z_1,\ldots,z_n) \\ \qquad\quad (t_1 < t'' \leq t \Rightarrow \neg(\mathtt{M}(z_1,\ldots,z_n,t'')\ \wedge\ (\forall i \in \mathrm{Ind}^{\mathtt{M}}_V)\ z_i = v_i)) \\ \qquad\quad \wedge\, t < t_2\ \wedge\ \mathtt{M}(u_1,\ldots,u_n,t_2) \\ \qquad \wedge\ (\forall t'',z_1,\ldots,z_n) \\ \qquad\quad (t \leq t'' < t_2 \Rightarrow \neg(\mathtt{M}(z_1,\ldots,z_n,t'')\ \wedge\ (\forall i \in \mathrm{Ind}^{\mathtt{M}}_V)\ z_i = u_i)) \\ \qquad \wedge\ (\forall i \in \mathrm{Ind}^{\mathtt{M}}_V)\ w_i = v_i = u_i \\ \qquad \wedge\ (\forall i \in \mathrm{Ind}^{\mathtt{M}}_W)\ w_i = \frac{v_i+u_i}{2})\end{array}$$

Fig. 3. The formula template for the *avg* method

each granularity defined in the system; however, as explained above, many of those granularities should not even be considered as candidates. The structure and the relationships between granularities provide useful heuristics to optimize the compression process.

Finally, the windowing functions of the computed minimal representations are easily compared for the most compact representation. This process leads to the selection of the temporal module that will be used in the compressed database.

4 Querying Compressed Data

Accordingly to what we have seen above, a compressed database is simply a set of temporal modules with associated assumptions with the property that each of them is the minimal representation of one of the original modules. Hence, we can use the same techniques proposed in [BWJ96] in order to answer any user query. The main idea consists of expressing interpolation and conversion methods in terms of a query language and automatically transform user queries by including these methods, so that any tuple implied by the assumptions and selected by the query is returned to the user. Since this procedure is proved to be correct in [BWJ96] when starting from the original database, and here we guarantee that the compressed database is equivalent to the original one, the procedure is correct in our case too.

In [BWJ96] we have used a many-sorted first order logic as a query language and later we have shown how to apply the same technique to SQL-like query languages. The specification of interpolation and conversion methods must be independent from the specific schema, hence the corresponding logic formulas have parameters in place of specific attribute names. As an example, the logical parametric expression for the *avg* method is illustrated in Figure 3. In the formula V and W are parameters as well as the number n of data attributes of the predicate $\mathtt{M}()$ (and corresponding variables). The symbol $\mathrm{Ind}^{\mathtt{M}}_V$, where V is a set of attributes, can be used to indicate the set of indices (positions) of attributes in

$$\Psi^{\mathtt{M},G'}_{I_V(W\updownarrow)}(x_1,\ldots,x_n,t) = (\forall b{:}\mathtt{bl})(\mathbf{IntSec}_{\mathtt{bl},G'}(b,t) \Rightarrow \\ \quad (\exists w_1,\ldots,w_n,s{:}G) \\ \qquad (\mathbf{IntSec}_{\mathtt{bl},G}(b,s) \wedge \mathtt{M}(w_1,\ldots,w_n,s) \\ \qquad \wedge (\forall j \in \mathrm{Ind}^{\mathtt{M}}_{VW})x_j = w_j))$$

Fig. 4. The formula template for the $\updownarrow$ method

V appearing in M when the "parameterized" scheme is instantiated.[3] Intuitively the formula takes all original tuples at instant t (first disjunct), then looks for tuples at preceding (t_1) and succeding (t_2) instants for which there is a tuple with the same attributes in V, making sure that there are no intermediate instant t'' with the same property. The value for each attribute in W not appearing in V is taken as the average of the values identified at t_1 and t_2. Consider, for example, the query "Give me the price of item $I1$ in the second quarter of 2001", which is formally expressed as:

$$\{y,t : \mathtt{quarter} \mid (\exists x)(\mathtt{PRICE}(x,y,t) \wedge x = I1 \wedge t = \text{2nd-q-2001})\}.$$

Note that if the PRICE temporal module has been compressed, the value asked by the query is not stored and an empty answer would be returned by a conventional database system. In our approach, the user query is transformed by the system so that in place of predicate PRICE() an appropriate instantiation of the formula template for the *avg* method is used. Then, the desired value is derived and returned to the user.

Consider now granularity assumptions: as an example of conversion method, Figure 4 reports the specification of liquidity ($\updownarrow$). The predicate $\mathbf{IntSec}_{\mathtt{bl},G}(b,s)$ in the formula is used to test the intersection between granules of different granularities. In this case, it returns true if $\mathtt{bl}(b)$ intersects $G(s)$ where bl is a basic granularity, intuitively finer than all other ones.

An example of query involving granularity assumptions is: "Give me, for each month in 2001, the street price of item I1", which is formally expressed as follows.

$$\{y,t : \mathtt{month} \mid (\exists x)(\mathtt{PRICE}(x,y,t) \wedge x = I1 \wedge \text{Jan-2001} \leq t \leq \text{Dec-2001})\}.$$

Since the query is evaluated against the compressed database, which is in terms of quarters, PRICE() is substituted by the system with PRICE-MONTHS(), given by the logical expression for the assumptions, with instantiated parameters. For example, by instantiating the logical expression for the $\updownarrow$ method we obtain:

$$\Psi^{\mathtt{PRICE,month}}_{I_{\mathtt{Item}}(\mathtt{StPrice}\updownarrow)}(x,y,t) = (\forall b{:}\mathtt{bl})(\mathbf{IntSec}_{\mathtt{bl,month}}(b,t) \Rightarrow \\ \quad (\exists w_1,w_2,s{:}\mathtt{quarter}) \\ \qquad (\mathbf{IntSec}_{\mathtt{bl,quarter}}(b,s) \wedge \mathtt{PRICE}(w_1,w_2,s) \\ \qquad \wedge x = w_1 \wedge y = w_2))$$

[3] For example, assume $\mathtt{M} = (\langle A,B,C,D,E\rangle, G)$ and $V = \{B,C,E\}$. Then $\mathrm{Ind}^{\mathtt{M}}_V = \{2,3,5\}$.

Then, the predicate PRICE is substituted with the formula including the application of the *avg* method. Of course the query will be optimized as usual during query processing; for example by applying the conversion only for the 12 months required. We refer the interested reader to [BWJ96] for details on how assumptions are combined and integrated into user queries.

5 Conclusion and Further Issues

We have presented a preliminary study on the application of the concepts of semantic assumption and time granularity for reducing the space needed to store temporal databases. The main applications we have in mind are in the field of mobile databases. For lack of space we have not addressed the issues related to maintaining the compressed database upon updates, which can be addressed with techniques similar to those used for maintaining materialized views. Future research includes investigation of the algorithms, experiments on real data, the application to "concrete" data models and query languages, and the formal study of the trade-off between compression and efficiency of query processing. Another interesting issue is the fact that in many cases there are semantic assumptions of which the designer is not aware of, and candidates may be proposed by data mining techniques.

References

[BD+97] C. Bettini, C.E. Dyreson, W.S. Evans, R.T. Snodgrass, X.S. Wang. A glossary of time granularity concepts. In *Temporal Databases: Research and Practice*, LNCS 1399, pp. 406–413, Springer, 1998.

[BWJ96] C. Bettini, X. Wang, and S. Jajodia. Temporal Semantic Assumptions and Their Use in Databases. *IEEE Transactions on Knowledge and Data Engineering*, 10(2):277–296, 1998.

[BJW00] C. Bettini, S. Jajodia, X.S. Wang. *Time Granularities in Databases, Data Mining, and Temporal Reasoning.* Springer, 2000.

[CW83] J. Clifford and D.S. Warren. "Formal semantics for time in databases." *ACM Transactions on Database Systems*, 8(2):214–254, June 1983.

[IW94] B.R. Iyer, D. Wilhite. Data Compression Support in Databases. *Proc. of the 20th VLDB Conference*, pp. 695–704, Santiago, Chile, 1994.

[LS00] H. Liefke, D. Suciu. XMill: an Efficient Compressor for XML Data. *Proc. of the SIGMOD Conference*, pp. 153–164, 2000.

[RVH93] M.A. Roth, S.J. Van Horn. Database Compression. *Sigmod Record*, 22(3):31-39, 1993.

[SS87] A. Segev and A. Shoshani. "Logical modeling of temporal data." In *Proc. of the SIGMOD Conference*, pp. 454–466, 1987.

[SSR94] E. Sciore, M. Siegel, and A.S. Rosenthal. Using semantic values to facilitate interoperability among heterogeneous information systems. *ACM Transactions on Database Systems*, 19(2):254–290, 1994.

[WJS95] X.S. Wang, S. Jajodia, V.S. Subrahmanian. Temporal modules: an approach toward federated temporal databases, *Information Sciences*, 82:103–128, 1995.

[TW99] V.J. Tsotras, X.S. Wang. Temporal Databases, in *Encyclopedia of Electrical and Electronics Engineering*, John Wiley & Sons, 1999.

Efficiently Computing Weighted Proximity Relationships in Spatial Databases

Xuemin Lin[1], Xiaomei Zhou[1], Chengfei Liu[2], and Xiaofang Zhou[3]

[1] School of Computer Science and Engineering, University of New South Wales Sydney, NSW 2052, Australia. lxue@cse.unsw.edu.au
[2] School of Computer and Information Science, University of South Australia Adelaide, SA 5095, Australia. Liu@cs.unisa.edu.au
[3] Department of Computer Science and Electrical Engineering University of Queensland, QLD 4072, Australia. zxf@csee.uq.edu.au

Abstract. Spatial data mining recently emerges from a number of real applications, such as real-estate marketing, urban planning, weather forecasting, medical image analysis, road traffic accident analysis, etc. It demands for efficient solutions for many new, expensive, and complicated problems. In this paper, we investigate the problem of evaluating the top k distinguished "features" for a "cluster" based on weighted proximity relationships between the cluster and features. We measure proximity in an average fashion to address possible nonuniform data distribution in a cluster. Combining a standard multi-step paradigm with new lower and upper proximity bounds, we presented an efficient algorithm to solve the problem. The algorithm is implemented in several different modes. Our experiment results not only give a comparison among them but also illustrate the efficiency of the algorithm.

Keywords: Spatial query processing and data mining.

1 Introduction

Spatial data mining is to discover and understand non-trivial, implicit, and previously unknown knowledge in large spatial databases. It has a wide range of applications, such as demographic analysis, weather pattern analysis, urban planning, transportation management, etc. While processing of typical spatial queries (such as joins, nearest neighbouring, KNN, and map overlays) has been received a great deal of attention for years [2,3,20], spatial data mining, viewed as advanced spatial queries, demands for efficient solutions for many newly proposed, expensive, complicated, and sometimes ad-hoc spatial queries.

Inspired by a success in advanced spatial query processing techniques [2,3,8, 20], relational data mining [1,18], machine learning [7], computational geometry [19], and statistics analysis [11,21], many research results and system prototypes in spatial data mining have been recently reported [2,4,5,10,12,14,16]. The existing research not only tends to provide system solutions but also covers quite a number of special purpose solutions to ad-hoc mining tasks. The results include efficiently computing spatial association rules [13], spatial data classification and

X.S. Wang, G. Yu, and H. Lu (Eds.): WAIM 2001, LNCS 2118, pp. 279–290, 2001.

generalization [10,14,16], spatial prediction and trend analysis [5], clustering and cluster analysis [4,12,17,23], mining in image and raster databases [6], etc.

Clustering has been shown one of the most useful tools to partition and categorize spatial data into *clusters* for the purpose of knowledge discovery. A number of efficient algorithms [4,17,22,23] have been proposed. While most existing clustering algorithms are effective to construct "clusters", they are ineffective to provide the reasons why the clusters are there spatially. Moreover, in many applications clusters are naturally existing; for example, a cluster could be a residential area. Therefore, it is equally important, if not more, to find out spatial properties of clusters based on their surrounding "features". The proximity is one of the most common measurements to represent the relationship between clusters and features. In [12], the problem of computing k closest features surrounding a set (cluster) of points in two dimensional space based on average/aggregate proximity relationships was investigated.

The problem of computing k closest features has a number of useful real applications. For instance, in a spatial database for the real-estate information, a set of points represents a residential area where each point represents a house/land parcel. A polygon corresponds to a vector representation of feature, such as a lake, golf course, school, motor way, etc. In this application, buyers or developers may want to know why some residential area is so expensive. Consequently they may want to know the k closest features. As pointed in [12], in such an application it is better to measure the proximity relationship in an average fashion to address a possible nonuniform data distribution. Furthermore, in such an application it may be more important to know that a residential area is only 5 kilometres away from the downtown area rather than 500 meters away from a swimming pool. This suggests that we should put weights when evaluate features, so that the obtained top k features are also based on their importance. In this paper, we investigate the problem of computing the *weighted k closest features* (WK); that is, each feature is associated with a weight. We will formally define the WK problem in the next section.

In WK, we assume that the "proximity value" between a cluster and feature has not been pre-computed, nor stored in the database. A naive way to solve WK is to first precisely compute the proximity value between each feature and a given cluster, and then to solve the WK problem. However, in practice there may be many features far from being part of solution to WK; and thus they should be ruled out by a fast filtering technique. The filtering technique developed in [12] for unweighted problem is not quite suitable to WK, because it specifically designed to solve unweighted problem. Motivated by these, our algorithm adopts a standard multi-step technique [2,12,13] in combining with novel and powerful pruning conditions to filter out uninvolved features. The algorithm has been implemented in several different modes for performance evaluation. Our experiments clearly demonstrate the efficiency of the algorithm.

The rest of the paper is organized as follows. In section 2, we present a precise definition of WK as well as a brief introduction of an adopted spatial database architecture. Section 3 presents our algorithm for solving WK. Section 4 reports our experimental results. In section 5, a discussion is presented regarding various modifications of our algorithm; this will be together with the conclusions. Note, due to the space limitation we do not provide the proofs of the theorems in this paper; the interested readers may refer to a long version [15] of the paper for these.

2 Preliminary

In this section we precisely define the WK problem. A *feature* F is a *simple* and *closed* polygon [19] in the 2-dimensional space. A set C of points in the two dimensional space is called *cluster* for notation simplicity. Following [12], we assume that in WK a cluster is always *outside* [19] a feature. Note that this assumption may support many real applications. For instance, in real-estate data, a cluster represents a set of land parcels, and a feature represents a man-made or natural place of interest, such as lake, shopping center, school, park, and entertainment center. Such data can be found in many electronic maps in a digital library.

To efficiently access large spatial data (usually tera-bytes), in this paper we adopt an extended-relational and a SAND (spatial-and-non-spatial database) architecture [3]; that is, a spatial database consisting of a set of spatial objects and a relational database describing non-spatial properties of these objects.

Below we formally define WK. In WK, the input consists of: 1) a cluster C_0; 2) a set $\Pi = \{\pi_j : 1 \leq j \leq m\}$ of groups of features (i.e., each π_j is a group of features); and 3) k to indicate the number of features to be found.

Given a feature F and a point p outside F, the length of the actual (working or driving) shortest path from p to F is too expensive to compute in the presence of tens of thousands of different roads. In WK, we use the shortest Euclidean distance from p to a point in the boundary of F, denoted by $d(p, F)$, to reflect the geographic proximity relationship between p and F. We believe that on average, the length of an actual shortest path can be reflected by $d(p, F)$. We call $d(p, F)$ the *distance* between p and F. Note that F may degenerate to a line or a point. Moreover, for the purpose of computing lower and upper proximity bounds in Section 3, the definition of $d(p, F)$ should be extended to cover the case when p is inside or on the boundary of F; that is, $d(p, F) = 0$ if p is inside of or on the boundary of F.

To address a possible arbitrary distribution of the points in C, we use the following *average proximity* value to quantitatively model the proximity relationship between F and C:

$$AP(C, F) = \frac{1}{|C|} \sum_{p \in C} d(p, F).$$

As mentioned earlier, in WK we will rank the importance of a feature by a positive value. More important a feature is, smaller its weight is. A weight can be assigned to a group of features by either a user or the system default. A set

$\{w_j : 1 \leq j \leq m\}$ of positive values is also part of the input of WK. WK can now be modelled to find the k features in $\sum_{j=1}^{m} \pi_j$ such that those k features lead to the k smallest values of the following function:

$$WAP(C_0, F) = W_F AP(C_0, F) \ \text{ where } F \in \sum_{j=1}^{m} \pi_j.$$

Here, W_F is the weight of F; that is, $W_F = w_j$ for $F \in \pi_j$. Note that in [12], the proximity between a cluster and a feature is measured in an aggregate fashion; that is, $\sum_{p \in C} d(p, F)$ is used there instead of using $\frac{1}{|C|} \sum_{p \in C} d(p, F)$. However, it should be clear that to compute the k closest features to a given cluster these two measurements are equivalent. This means that the top k feature problem in [12] is a special case of WK where all the weights are 1.

3 Algorithms for Solving WK

In this section, we present an efficient algorithm for solving WK. The algorithm is denoted by CWK, which stands for **C**omputing the **W**eighted K closest features.

An immediate way (brute-force) to solve WK is to 1) compute $WAP(C_0, F)$ for each pair of a given cluster C_0 and a feature F, and then to 2) compute the k closest features based on their WAP values. Note that $WAP(C_0, F)$ can be easily computed in $O(|C_0||F|)$ according to the definition of $WAP(C, F)$. Consequently, the brute-force approach runs in time $O(|C_0| \sum_{j=1}^{m} \sum_{F \in \pi_j} |F|)$. Practically, there may be many features involved in the computation; each feature may have many edges; and the given cluster may have many points. These make the brute-force approach probably computational prohibitive in practice. Our experiment results in Section 4.3 confirm this.

One possible way to resolve this problem is to adopt a multi-step paradigm [2,12,13]. First, we use a filtering step to filter out the features, and then do precise computation of WAP values for those candidate features only. A simple and very effective technique was proposed in [12] to solve WK with all weight equal to 1: *draw a circle encompassing the cluster and then keep the features with an intersection to the circle as the candidates.*

If we want to apply the above technique generally to WK with different weights, we may have to draw different circles for different groups of features due to different weights. Because for each group of features we have to keep at least k features, there may be too many candidates left and the filter may not be powerful enough,

In this paper, we propose a filtering technique based on the lower and upper bound for WAP values. Instead of computing the actual value of $WAP(C_0, F)$ in quadratic time $O(|C||F|)$, we may compute a lower bound and an upper bound for $WAP(C_0, F)$ in a linear time $O(|F|)$ with respect to the size of F. By these bounds, for the given cluster C_0, we can rule out the features, which are definitely not closest to C_0 in a weighted sense; Thus we do not have to precisely compute the weighted average proximity values between these eliminated features and C_0. This is the basic idea of our algorithm. In our algorithm CWK, we have not integrated our algorithm into a particular spatial index, such as R-trees, R^+-trees, etc, due to the following reasons.

- There may be no spatial index built.
- The WK problem may involve many features from different tables/electronic thematic maps; and thus, spatial index built for each thematic map may be different. This brings another difficulty when making use of spatial indices.
- A feature or a cluster, which is qualified in WK, may be only a part of a stored spatial object; for instance, a user may be interested only in certain part of a park. This makes a possible existing index based on the stored spatial objects not quite applicable.
- The paper [12] indicates the existing spatial indexing techniques do not necessarily support well the computation of *aggregate* distances; the argument should be also applied to average distance computation.

The algorithm CWK consists of the following 3 steps:

Step 1: Read the cluster C_0 into buffer.

Step 2: Read features batch by batch into buffer, compute lower and upper bounds of $WAP(C_0, F)$ for the given cluster C_0. Then determine whether or not F should be kept for the computation of $WAP(C_0, F)$.

Step 3: Apply the above brute-force method to the remaining features to solve problem WK.

In the next several subsections we detail the algorithm step by step. Clearly, a success of the algorithm CWK largely relies on how good the lower and upper bounds of WAP are. The goodness of lower and upper bounds means two things: 1) the bounds should be reasonably tight, and 2) the corresponding computation should be fast. We first present the lower and upper bounds.

Note that for presentation simplicity, the algorithms presented in the paper are restricted to the case when features and clusters qualified in WK are stored spatial objects in the database. However, they can be immediately extended to cover the case when a feature or a cluster is a part of a stored object.

3.1 Lower and Upper Bounds for Average Proximity

In this subsection, we recall first some useful notation. The *barycenter* (*centroid*) of a cluster C is denoted by $b(C)$. A *convex* [19] polygon encompassing a feature F is called a bounding convex polygon of F. The smallest bounding convex polygon of F is called the *convex hull* [19] of F and is denoted by P_F. An *isothetic* [19] rectangle is orthogonal to the coordinate axis. The minimum bounding rectangle of F refers to the minimum isothetic bounding rectangle of F and is denoted by R_F.

Given two minimum bounding rectangles R_C and R_F respectively for a cluster C and a feature F, an immediate idea is to use the shortest distance and the longest distance between R_C and R_F to respectively represent a lower bound and an upper bound of $AP(C, F)$. However, this immediate idea has two problems.

The first problem is that when two rectangles intersect with each other (note that in this case C and F do not necessarily have an intersection), the shortest and longest distances between R_C and R_F are not well defined. The second problem is that the bounds may not be very tight even if the two rectangles do not intersect. These also happen similarly for convex hulls. Below, we present new and tighter bounds.

Our lower bound computation is based on the following Lemma.

Lemma 1. $\sum_{i=1}^{K}\sqrt{x_i^2+y_i^2} \geq \sqrt{(\sum_{i=1}^{K} x_i)^2 + (\sum_{i=1}^{K} y_i)^2}$

Theorem 1. *Suppose that C is a cluster, F is a feature, and P is either the convex hull or the minimum bounding rectangle of F. Then, $AP(C,F) \geq d(b(C),P)$; in other words $d(b(C),P)$ is a lower bound of $AP(C,F)$.*

Clearly, the above lower bound is tighter than the shortest distance between two bounding rectangles.

Suppose that p is an arbitrary point. For a cluster, we use $\lambda(p,C)$ to denote the maximum distance between p to a point in C. Below is an upper bound of AP.

Theorem 2. *Suppose that p is an arbitrary point, C is a cluster, and F is a feature. Then $AP(C,F) \leq d(p,F) + \lambda(p,C)$.*

It is clear the right hand side in the inequality of Theorem 2 can be used as an upper bound of AP; and can be computed in time $O(|F|)$ once the computation of $\lambda(p,C)$ is done. We believe that this bound may be tighter than the longest distance between the minimum bounding rectangles. However, we cannot generally prove this because the tightness of the upper bound depends on the choice of p. In our algorithm, we will choose the *centroid* of a cluster C in the upper bound computation since it has to be used to obtain a lower bound. Note that generally $d(b(C),P_F)$ and $d(b(C),F)$ respectively in the lower and upper bounds cannot replace each other if F is not a convex polygon.

3.2 Read in the Relevant Cluster

In Step 1, we first read in the cluster C_0, which are specified by a user, into buffer. Then, we compute the centroid $b(C_0)$ and the maximal distance $\lambda(b(C_0),C_0)$. Clearly, this step takes linear time with respect to the size of C_0.

3.3 Read in and Filter out Features

This subsection presents Step 2. Consider that the total size of features to be processed may be too large to fit in buffer simultaneously. Features should be read into buffer batch by batch.

Note that in WK, our primary goal is to make a candidate set as close as possible to the actual solution; this means a small set of candidates will be expected to be left in the main memory after filtering step. Therefore, we may store the detail of the candidates in the main memory for a further processing. Particularly, the filtering step developed in CWK is to:

1. initialize the candidate set by assigning the first k features, and then,
2. examine the rest of the features one by one to determine whether or not they are candidates. In case that a new candidate is added, we should also check whether or not certain features included in the candidate set should be removed.

The following lemma can be immediately verified.

Lemma 2. *For a cluster C and a feature F with weight W_F,*

$$W_F d(b(C), P_F) \leq WAP(C,F) \leq W_F(d(p,F) + \lambda(p,C)).$$

Lemma 2 means that $W_F d(b(C), P_F)$ is the lower bound of $WAP(C,F)$ denoted by LB_F, while $W_F(d(p,F) + \lambda(p,C))$ is the upper bound of $WAP(C,F)$ denoted by UB_F.

Lemma 3. *Suppose π is a set of candidate features, Y is the k'th smallest UB_F for every $F \in \pi$. Then, F' is a feature in the solution of WK only if $WAP(C,F') \leq Y$. Thus, $LB_{F'} \leq Y$.*

Suppose that a new feature F is processed, Lemma 3 says that if LB_F for F is greater than Y, than F should not be considered as part of the solution of WK.

Consider the situation that a new F is added to π and the Y is updated (changed smaller). Then, a feature F' in π may no longer be a candidate if $LB_{F'} > Y$; and thus we have to remove F' from π. A naive way to do this is to scan the whole π to determine whether or not there is feature to be removed. To speed up this process, we can divided π into two parts A and B, where B is the set of candidates to be removed. We make A and B two ordered linked lists to store the candidates, let A has the fixed length of k, and use X to store the current largest lower bound of F in A. Each element F in A or B stores the identifier FID, LB_F and UB_F, and the spatial description of F. A and B are initially set to empty. The elements in A and B are sorted on the lexicographic order of (LB_F, UB_F) for each F.

Specifically, to process a F, CWK first computes the values of LB_F and UB_F for $WAP(C,F)$. Then, add the first k features to A according to a lexicographic order of (LB_F, UB_F). For the rest of the features, if $LB_F \leq Y$, it will be a candidate and kept in A or B. More specifically, F will be added to A in a proper position if $(LB_F, UB_F) < (LB_{F'}, UB_{F'})$, where F' is the last element of A; and then F' will be moved to B. When $(LB_F, UB_F) \geq (LB_{F'}, UB_{F'})$, F will be added to B. Once a new F is added to the A or B, X and Y should be updated. Each time after Y is reduced, we also need to check B to remove those features whose lower bounds are bigger than Y. Below is a precise description of Step 2.

```
Step 2 in CWK:
A ← ∅; B ← ∅;
Read in features;
for the first k features in π do
  { compute lower and upper bounds LB_F and UB_F for each feature F;
  keep them in A and compute X and Y; }
π = π - { the first k features in π };
for each F ∈ π do
  { compute LB_F and UB_F;
  if LB_F < Y then
    if LB_F > X or (LB_F = X and UB_F ≥ Y) then B ← F else
    { move last element of A into B;
    A ← F;
    Update X and Y;
    if Y reduced then remove features F ∈ B with UB_F > Y; }
  }
```

Once a batch of features are processed by the above procedure, we do not keep them in buffer except the candidate features in A and B.

3.4 Precise Computation

After filtering process in Step 2, the full information of remaining features for solving WK is kept in A and B. Then, we apply this information to perform a precise computation of WAP values using brute-force method.

3.5 Complexity of CWK

In Step 1, we read in the user specified cluster C_0 and do some relevant computation, this step takes linear time with respect to the size of C_0.

In Step 2, we do the filtering process to read in and filter out features, the main expenses here are to compute the lower and upper bounds of WAP for each F, and to possibly insert a F to A or B. These together run in $O(\sum_{i=1}^{n}|F_i| + n\log(|A|+|B|))$, here n is the number of total features.

Step 3 takes time $O(\sum_{F\in(A\cup B)}|C||F|)$ to compute WAP for the remaining features.

Note that the brute-force algorithm runs in time $O(\sum_{i=1}^{n}|C||F_i|)$. Clearly, in practice, the time complexity of the brute-force method is much higher than that of CWK, because $|A\cup B|$ is much smaller than n. This is confirmed by our experiment results in Section 4.

3.6 Variations of CWK

We implement the algorithm CWK in three different modes in order to evaluate the performance. The differences are the bounding shapes of a feature to be taken while doing the filtering process. The first mode is denoted by CWK-R, which uses only minimal bounding rectangles of features to compute the lower and upper bounds of $WAP(C, F)$. An alternative mode to CWK-R is to use the minimum bounding convex hulls instead of the minimal bounding rectangles, we denote this mode by CWK-P. The third mode, denoted by CWK-RP, adopts a multiple-filtering technique: 1) minimal bounding rectangles are firstly used to obtain the ordered linked list A and B, and then, 2) the minimum bounding convex hulls are computed for features stored in A and B to repeat Step 2 to get two new ordered linked list A' and B' before processing Step 3.

In next section, we will report our experiment results regarding the performance of the brute-force method, CWK-P, CWK-R, and CWK-RP.

4 Implementation and Experiment Results

The brute-force method and the three modes of CWK algorithm have been implemented by C++ on a Pentium I/200 with 128 MB of main memory, running Window-NT 4.0. In our experiments, we evaluated the algorithms for efficiency and scalability. Our performance evaluation is basically focused on Step 2 onwards, because the methods [3] of reading in clusters and features are not our contribution. Therefore, in our experiment we record only the CPU time but exclude I/O costs.

In the experiments below, we adopt a common set of parameters: 1) a feature has 30 edges on average, 2) a cluster has 200 points on average, and 3) the features are grouped into 20 groups.

In our first experiment, we generate a database with 50 clusters and 5000 features, and $k = 5$. We implement our algorithm for each cluster. The experiment results depicted in Figure 1 are the average time. Note the algorithm CWK-P, CWK-R, CWK-RP are respective abbreviated to "P", "R", "R-P" in the diagram.

From the first experiment, we can conclude that the brute-force method is practically very slow. Another appearance is that CWK-P is slower than CWK-R. Intuitively this is because that in CWK-P, the computation of a lower bound for each feature is more expensive than that in CWK-R. We also observed that CWK-RP appears the most efficient. This because that the second filtering phase in CWK can still filter out some features; and thus the number of features left for the precise computation is reduced. In short, we believe that CWK-P should be intuitively and significantly slower than CWK-R and CWK-RP when the number of features increases; this has been confirmed by the second experiment.

The second and third experiments have been undertaken through two dimensions. In the second experiment, we fix the k to be 15 while the number of features varies from 5000 to 50,000. Again, we run the 3 algorithms for each cluster and record the average time. The results are depicted in Figure 2.

In the third experiment, we fix the number of features to be $50,000$ while k varies from 5 to 75. Each algorithm has been run against each cluster and the average time is recorded. The experiment results are depicted in Figure 3.

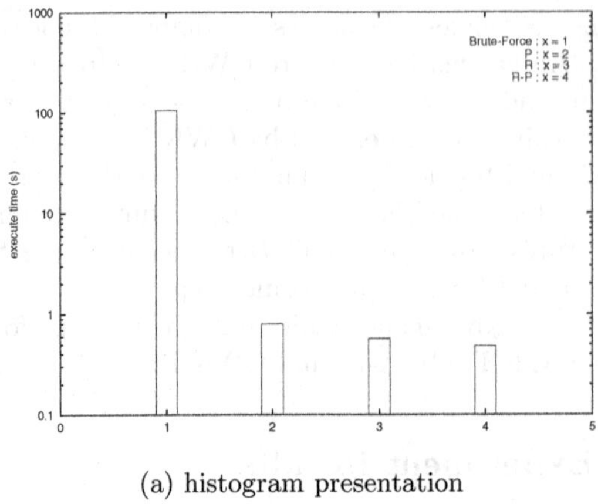

(a) histogram presentation

Algorithm	Average Run Time (s)
Brute-force	105.055
P	0.802
R	0.572
R-P	0.483

(b) table presentation

Fig. 1. Average execution time for four algorithms

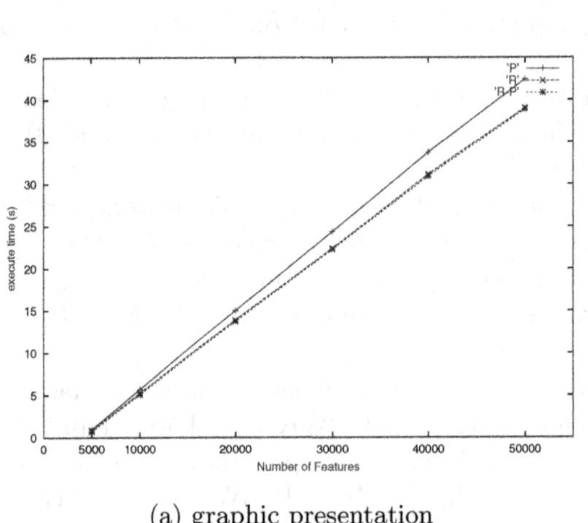

(a) graphic presentation

#FE	Algorithm	Average Run Time (s)
5000	P	0.975
	R	0.906
	R-P	0.760
10000	P	5.697
	R	5.244
	R-P	5.097
20000	P	14.988
	R	13.881
	R-P	13.720
30000	P	24.375
	R	22.400
	R-P	22.291
40000	P	33.747
	R	31.140
	R-P	30.922
50000	P	42.433
	R	39.302
	R-P	38.871

(b) table presentation

Fig. 2. Average execution time for three algorithms by different DB sizes

These three experiments suggest that CWK-RP and CWK-R is faster than CWK-P on average, and the performance of CWK-RP is faster than CWK-R. From the second and third experiment results, we see that the choices of different k values and different DB sizes will not change the above observation. The second experiment also shows the scalability of algorithm CWK.

The three conducted experiments suggest that our algorithm is efficient and scalable. Furthermore, we can see that although an application of convex hulls to

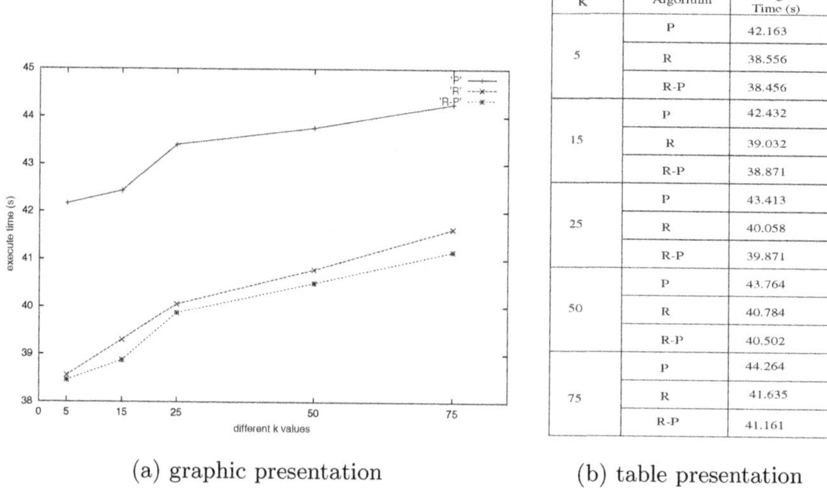

K	Algorithm	Average Run Time (s)
5	P	42.163
	R	38.556
	R-P	38.456
15	P	42.432
	R	39.032
	R-P	38.871
25	P	43.413
	R	40.058
	R-P	39.871
50	P	43.764
	R	40.784
	R-P	40.502
75	P	44.264
	R	41.635
	R-P	41.161

(a) graphic presentation (b) table presentation

Fig. 3. Average execution time for three algorithms by different K

the filtering procedures is more accurate than an application of minimal bounding rectangles, it is more expensive to use directly. Thus, the best use of convex hulls should follow an application of minimal bounding rectangles; that is, it is better to apply the CWK-RP mode.

5 Conclusion and Remarks

In this paper, we investigated the weighted top k features problem regarding average/aggregate proximity relationships. We presented an efficient algorithm based on several new pruning conditions, as well as various different modes of the algorithms. Our experiment results showed that the algorithm is quite efficient.

The problem WK, as well as the algorithm CWK, may be either generalized or constrained according to various applications. The interested readers may refer to our full paper [15] for details.

References

1. R. Agrawal and R. Srikant, Fast Algorithms for Mining Association Rules, *Proceedings of the 20th VLDB Conference*, 487-499, 1994.
2. M. Ankerst, B. Braunmuller, H.-P. Kriegel, T. Seidl, Improving Adaptable Similarity Query Processing by Using Approximations, *Proceedings of the 24th VLDB Conference*, 206-217, 1998.
3. W. G. Aref and H. Samet, Optimization Strategies for Spatial Query Processing, *Proceedings of the 17th VLDB Conference*, 81-90, 1991.

4. M. Ester, H.-P. Kriegel, J. Sander and X. Xu, A density-based algorithm for discovering clusters in large spatial databases, *Proceedings of the Second International Conference on Data Mining KDD-96*, 226-231, 1996.
5. M. Este, H.-P. Kriegel, J. Sander, Spatial Data Mining: A Database Approach, *SSD'97*, LNCS 1262, 47-65, 1997.
6. U. M. Fayyad, S. G. Djorgovski, and N. Weir, Automating the analysis and cataloging of sky surveys, *Advances in Knowledge Discovery and Data Mining*, AAAI/MIT Press, 1996.
7. U. Fayyad, G. Piatetsky-Shapiro, P. Smyth, and R. Uthurusamy, Eds. *Advances in Knowledge Discovery and Data Mining*, AAAI/MIT Press, Menlo Park, CA, 1996.
8. R. H. Guting, An Introduction to Spatial Database Systems, *VLDB Journal*, 3(4), 357-400, 1994.
9. J. Han, Y. Cai, and N. Cercone, Dynamic Generation and Refinement of Concept Hierarchies for Knowledge Discovery in Databases, *IEEE Trans. knowledge and Data Engineering*, 5, 29-40, 1993.
10. J. Han, K. Koperski, and N. Stefanovic, GeoMiner: A System Prototype for Spatial Data Mining, *Proceedings of 1997 ACM-SIGMOD International Conference on Management*, 553-556, 1997.
11. L. Kaufman and P. J. Rousseeuw, *Finding Groups in Data: an Introduction to Cluster Analysis*, John Wiley & Sons, 1990.
12. E. M. Knorr and R. T. Ng, Finding Aggregate Proximity Relationships and Commonalities in Spatial Data Mining, *IEEE Transactions on Knowledge and Data Engineering*, 8(6), 884-897, 1996.
13. K. Koperski and J. Han, Discovery of Spatial Association Rules in Geographic Information Databases, *Advances in Spatial Databases*, Proceeding of 4th Symposium (SSD'95), 47-66, 1995.
14. K. Koperski, J. Han, and J. Adhikary, Mining Knowledge in Geographic Data, to appear in *Communications of ACM*.
15. X. Lin, X. Zhou, C. Liu, and X. Zhou, Efficiently Computing Weighted Proximity Relationships in Spatial Databases, (http://www.cse.unsw.edu.au/~lxue), 2001.
16. H. Lu, J. Han, and B. C. Ooi, Knowledge Discovery in Large Spatial Databases, *Proceedings of Far East Workshop on Geographic Information Systems*, 275-289, 1993.
17. N. Ng and J. Han, Efficient and Effective Clustering Method for Spatial Data Mining, *Proceeding of 1994 VLDB*, 144-155, 1994.
18. J. S. Park, M.-S. Chen, and P. S. Yu, An Effective Hash-Based Algorithm for Mining Association Rules, *Proceedings of 1995 ACM SIGMOD*, 175-186, 1995.
19. F. Preparata and M. Shamos, *Computational Geometry: An Introduction*, Springer-Verlag, New York, 1985.
20. H. Samet, *The Design and Analysis of Spatial Data Structures*, Addison-Wesley, 1990.
21. G. Shaw and D. Wheeler, *Statistical Techniques in Geographical Analysis*, London, David Fulton, 1994.
22. X. Xu, M. Ester, H.-P. Kriegel, Jorg Sander, A Distribution-Based Clustering Algorithm for Mining in Large Spatial Databases, *ICDE'98*, 324-331, 1998.
23. T. Zhang, R. Ramakrishnan and M. Livny, BIRCH: an efficient data clustering method for very large databases, *Proceeding of 1996 ACM-SIGMOD International Conference of Management of Data*, 103-114, 1996.

Compressing the Index - A Simple and yet Efficient Approximation Approach to High-Dimensional Indexing

Shuguang Wang, Cui Yu, and Beng Chin Ooi

Department of Computer Science
National University of Singapore
3 Science Drive 2, Singapore 117543
{wangshug, yucui, ooibc}@comp.nus.edu.sg

Abstract. An efficient tunable high-dimensional indexing scheme called the iMinMax(θ) was proposed to map high-dimensional data points into single dimension value based on the minimum or maximum values among all dimensions [7]. Unfortunately, the number of leaf nodes needs to be scanned remains large. To reduce the number of leaf nodes, we propose to use the compression technique proposed in the Vector Approximation File (VA-file) [10] to represent vectors. We call the hybrid method, the iMinMax(θ)*. While the marriage is straight forward, the gain in performance is significant. In our extensive performance study, the results clearly indicate that iMinMax(θ)* outperforms the original iMinMax(θ) index scheme and the VA-file. iMinMax(θ)* is also attractive from a practical view point for its implementation cost is only slightly higher than that of the original iMinMax(θ). The approximation concept that is incorporated in iMinMax(θ)* can be integrated in other high-dimensional index structures without much difficulty.

1 Introduction

Indexing of high-dimensional data space has become increasing important in many new applications, such as multimedia databases, data mining, and geographical information systems. Efficient support to determine which portions of the data space are relevant to users' request becomes vitally important. The goal of this paper is to demonstrate the limitations of currently available index structures, and present a new index structure that considerably improves the performance in indexing high-dimensional data.

Numerous multi-dimensional indexing structures have been proposed. Many of these structures are conventional data-partitioning index structures. Search space is pruned in the search process in this type of index method. For example, the R-tree [4], R*-tree [1], and the latest iMinMax(θ) [7] are all typical data-partitioning index methods. Performance of existing multi-dimensional indexing methods degrades rapidly as the dimensionality increases, which is also known as "dimensional curse". In order to alleviate the problem of performance degradation, iMinMax(θ) adopts a different approach that reduces a high-dimensional

X.S. Wang, G. Yu, and H. Lu (Eds.): WAIM 2001, LNCS 2118, pp. 291–302, 2001.

data space to a single dimensional data space. Besides the data-partitioning index methods, there have been attempts to produce the space-partitioning methods. Examples include gridfiles [5], quad trees [3], K-D-B trees [8], skd-trees [6] and VA-file [10] [9] divide the data space into predefined partitions regardless the distributions of the data. The VA-file is not solely based on space partitioning, but rather on a hybrid of space-partitioning and signature methods. Each predefined partition of the data space is assigned a signature (bit stream) that is a small approximation to a data object. Queries are compared with every signature of the object first, and then a much smaller set of candidate objects will be visited to find the real answer set.

The iMinMax(θ) has been shown to perform very well by filtering out data points based on the attribute which has maximum or minimum value, but there are still some cases that it suffers rather high I/O cost. This is partly due to the problem of high-dimensional data space, where a very small query has very large width along each dimension, causing a large portion of data space to be checked. Due to the high percentage of data points being mapped into similar representative index values, iMinMax(θ) may still visit a big number of leaf nodes. On the other hand, the VA-file does well to minimize the search space and scan the signatures sequentially.

In this paper, we introduce the iMinMax(θ)* which is a marriage of iMinMax(θ) and VA-file — VA-file within iMinMax(θ). The iMinMax(θ)* uses the iMinMax(θ) as the base structure, and the VA-file approximation scheme in its leaf nodes. Hence, the iMinMax(θ)* inherits the strengths of both index schemes. Filtering of the subqueries, which can prune large portion of the search space, still holds in iMinMax(θ)*. The major difference or improvement in iMinMax(θ)* is that it stores the signature instead of data vectors in the B^+-tree, which is the underlying indexing structure used in iMinMax(θ). The advantage is two-fold: Firstly, the size of the index structure shrinks by a factor of eight; secondly, it supports the efficient sequential scan. The index can be readily integrated into existing DBMS, or even their kernel, cost effectively.

The rest of this paper is organized as follows. We introduce the principles of both iMinMax(θ) and the VA-file in Section 2. In Section 3, we present the proposed improved index structure and discuss in detail the search algorithms that the index structure supports in Section 4. The performance study is presented in Section 5, and finally we conclude in Section 6.

2 Basic Concept of iMinMax(θ) and VA-File

The iMinMax(θ)* is a hybrid of two index schemes: iMinMax(θ) and VA-file. Here, we shall provide the basic concept of each method.

2.1 iMinMax(θ) Approach

The iMinMax(θ) is dynamic and height-balanced, insertions and deletions can be intermixed with queries and no global reorganization is necessary. The variable

θ is a tuning knob to optimize the index for different data distributions. It can be tuned according to the property of the data set to improve the performance by distributing the data points across ranges. The iMinMax(θ) supports efficient range search by evaluating "optimal" subqueries and pruning those subqueries selecting answers in the Min/Max edge [7].

Intuitively, the iMinMax(θ) is a B$^+$-tree like structure that stores multidimensional data vectors and pointers to the data pages containing the actual data records. A non-leaf node is exactly like the classical B$^+$-tree node, except that the index values are real numbers transformed from multi-dimensional data vectors. A leaf node contains entries of the form (*key, v, ptr*) where *key* is the data point index key value, v is the multi-dimensional vector whose transformed value is the key, and *ptr* is the pointer to the data page containing information related to v.

Essentially, iMinMax(θ) transforms high-dimensional points to single-dimensional values as follows. Let x_{min} and x_{max} be respectively the smallest and largest values among all the d dimensions of the data point (x_1, x_2, ..., x_d) $0 \leq x_j \leq 1$, $1 \leq j \leq d$. Let the corresponding dimension for x_{min} and x_{max} be d_{min} and d_{max} respectively. The data point is mapped to y over a single dimensional space as follows:

$$y = \begin{cases} d_{min} * c + x_{min} & : \ if\ x_{min} + \theta < 1 - x_{max} \\ d_{max} * c + x_{max} & : \ otherwise \end{cases}$$

Note*:Multiplying d_{min} and d_{max} with "c" makes iMinMax(θ) suitable for more common cases.

The transformation actually partitions the data space into different partitions based on the dimension which has the largest value or smallest value, and provides an ordering within each partition [11].

The main problem in iMinMax(θ) is as following. For a range query, the search space or portion of the data space visited is still considerably large. And all data vectors are stored in the leaf nodes, and then a large amount of the range query I/O cost is wasted on traversing the false candidates in the leaf nodes. When the data set size or dimensionality increases, and data spread sparsely in the whole data space, the situation becomes even worse.

2.2 VA-File Approach

The VA-file (Vector Approximation file) is based on the idea of object approximation by mapping a coordinate to some value that reduces storage requirement. The basic idea is to divide the data space into 2^b hyper-rectangular cell where b is the tunable number of bits used for representation. For each dimension, i bits are used, and 2^i slices are generated in such a way that all slices are equally full. The data space consists of 2^b hyper-rectangular cell, each of which can be represented by a unique bit string of length b. A data point is then approximated by the bit string (signature) of the cell it falls into.

There are only two types of the data stored in the index structure, signature and its corresponding data vectors. They are stored separately in different files and can be selected according to their relative positions. In the signature file, a sequence of bit arrays is stored in sequence of the insertion. And in the data vector file, an array of data vectors is stored in the same sequence as that in the signature file.

The VA-file is a typical data-partitioning method, and the structure is simple and flat, which is different from other complex high-dimensional tree structures. It stores the high-dimensional vectors as complete objects without the transformation. Insertion and deletion can be easily implemented, however deletions may cause periodically global reorganizations because the structure is not dynamic. Efficient search is supported by the filtering technique on the signature file. Search queries are first compared with all approximations, and then the final answers are determined when the remaining smaller set of candidate objects are visited. The performance of the VA-file is affected by the number of bits (b) used. Higher b reduces the false drop rate, but increases the I/O cost of scanning the signature file.

The main problem of the VA-file is the following. The precision of the signature affects the size of the query hyper-cube. The generation of the signature of the range query is to map a float vector to a small number of bits, where it loses much accuracy. Signature is good enough to identify a vector in a high-dimensional data space, e.g., the signature of size 20 bits (4 bits per dimension) in 5-dimensional data space can address 100M different data points. However, when a range query in selectivity s is evaluated in the d-dimensional data space with signature in b bits per dimension, the selectivity to the VA-file actually can be as large as $((\lfloor s^{1/d} * 2^b \rfloor + 2)/2^b)^d$, which is more than 1.1^d times of the original selectivity assuming signature size is 4 bits per dimension.

3 Compressing the Indices

In Section 2, we have reexamined the design principles of the iMinMax and VA-file, and also possible optimization criteria. In what follows, we take those criteria into consideration in designing a new index scheme, iMinMax(θ)*. It draws the strengths of both iMinMax(θ) and VA-file, making it a much more efficient index.

iMinMax(θ) is a dynamic and height balanced structure. The discriminating values in the internal nodes are drawn from the domain of the reduced single dimensional space. Its insert and search algorithms are fairly similar to those of B^+-trees. For a new record, the mapping function is used to derive the iMinMax value, and the VA compression technique is used to derive the bit string vectors. The insert algorithm then traverses the tree to search for the right leaf to insert a new index key and record. The algorithm is outlined below.

We outline the InsertLeaf-, InsertOverflow-, InsertVector-, and Split- algorithms of iMinMax(θ)* below.

Algorithm InsertLeaf

```
IL1  Set L to be the leaf node found
     Set I to be the leaf internal node just 1 level upper than L
     Set v to the vector to be inserted
     Set apx to be the signature of v
IL2  If I is root and empty
       Create a new leaf node L' and add apx into L
       Make L and L' two siblings
       Create a new vector node V and add v into V node
       Make V as a child of L
       Return
     End if
IL3  If L is not full
       Add the apx into L
       Add the v into the corresponding V node
       Return
     Else if L is full and key of last entry is
     the same as the data vector
       /* for the case with too many duplicates */
       Return InsertOverflow
     Else
       Return Split
     End if
```

Algorithm InsertOverflow

```
IO1  Set O to be the overflow node reached
     Set v to the vector to be inserted
     Set apx to be the signature of v
IO2  If O is not full
       Add apx into O
       Add v into corresponding vector node
       Return
     Else
       If next overflow node exist
         Set NO to be next overflow node
         Return InsertOverflow
       Else
         Create a new overflow node NO
         Add the apx in NO
         Create a new vector node V
         Add the v in V and make V as a child of NO
         Return
       End if
     End if
```

Algorithm Split

```
S1  Set L to be the leaf node to be split
    Set n to be the number of data vectors
    with the same key value of the last entry in L
    Set k to be the key value of the data vector to be inserted
    Set k' to be the key value of the last entry in L
    Set v to the vector to be inserted
    Set apx to be the signature of v
S2  If n is greater than leaf node fan out and k > k'
      Create a new leaf node L'
      Add apx into L'
      Create a new vector node V
      Add v into V and make V as a child of L'
      Make L and L' two siblings
      Return
    Else if n is not less than half of the leaf node fan out
      Shift last n signatures in L to L'
      Add apx into L'
      Add v into corresponding vector node
      Make L and L' two siblings
      Return
    End if
    If n is greater than the leaf node fan out and k < k'
      Create a new leaf node L'
      Shift all signatures with key value not less than k to L'
      Add apx in L'
      Make L and L' two siblings
      Create a new vector node V
      Add v into V and make V as a child of L'
      Return
    End if
```

Besides the additional InsertVector algorithm, the insertion in iMinMax(θ)* is slightly more complex than that in iMinMax(θ). The complexity is resulted from replacing the high-dimensional data vectors with much smaller approximation bit streams. Storing the data vectors in a lower level also makes the insertion more complicated.

The size of the approximation of the data vector is a user-predefined number in bits. For generic applications, 4-6 bits are allocated to each dimension. Comparing with those multi-dimensional vectors which are several bytes per dimension, the approximation can be a factor of 8 times smaller. Consequently, leaf nodes in iMinMax(θ)* can hold 7 times more leaf entries than that in iMinMax(θ). In other words, iMinMax(θ)* possibly traverses about 7 times less number of leaf nodes than the original iMinMax(θ) to find all the candidates. This is how iMinMax(θ)* reduces I/O cost by condensing the tree index. The signature helps not only to minimize the search space but also speed up the scan when subqueries are evaluated. Given the signatures of a set of vectors and a query, efficient bit-wise operations can be used to minimize the CPU query cost. Using the signature also enables iMinMax(θ)* to be much more efficient for answering partial queries than iMinMax(θ)

The key in the iMinMax(θ) is used to improve the accuracy when it filters out the false drops. This is why iMinMax(θ) is still superior in terms of performance even though signature scheme suffers from bad accuracy in higher dimensional data space. Furthermore, due to the way iMinMax(θ) distributing the data points over d partitions, iMinMax(θ)* inherits such strong point and is hence less affected by data distributions.

4 iMinMax(θ)* Search Algorithms

In our implementation of iMinMax(θ)* we adopted the original iMinMax(θ) as the underlying index structure. However, in order to incorporate with the approximation space method, leaf node entries store only the keys and signatures in the form of (key, signature). And each leaf node will store those leaf node entries and pointers to the pages where the corresponding high-dimensional data vectors reside. Storing the signature instead of the high-dimensional data vectors in the leaf entries improves the efficiency as more entries are stored in each node, and hence fewer nodes are scanned. As mentioned in the previous section, we retrieve the data vectors by the relative position of its corresponding signature, so we do not have to store other information that may cause overhead.

The search method supported in iMinMax(θ)* is very similar to iMinMax(θ) search algorithm, except the additional complexity to generate the signature of the queries and deal with it in the high-dimensional space and select the correct data vector corresponding to the signature found.

Before every search, queries have to be mapped from the high-dimensional data vectors to the single-dimensional keys, and the θ used in the transformation has to be tuned to get the better performance [7]. Since leaf entries only store the signatures, the approximation need to be generated for each query before it is compared with the signatures in the leaf entries.

4.1 Point Search Algorithm

The function PointSearch outlines the point search algorithm. The function TransQuery is the same as that in iMinMax(θ) and the function Traverse is the same as that in typical B$^+$-tree.

For each point query, iMinMax(θ) traverses from the root node to the leaf, and then check for the right data points. If no such leaf node is found, which means there is no answer point to the query, NULL value is returned. If a matching tuple, normally the first match is found in some leaf node, the signature values of the query and the data vector will be compared to find a candidate. After the candidates stored in the same page are determined, they will be selected to compare the query values and determine the final answer set.

We note that it is possible to have some false drops after the first comparison between signatures; therefore the second comparison is necessary for most of the cases. All matching points including those stored in the adjacent pages will be retrieved also.

Point search algorithm.

```
FUNCTION PointSearch (p: Point Query; r: B+ Tree Root)
  VAR key: One-Dimensional Key; l: Leaf Node; s: Signature;
  VAR k: INT; v: Data Vector; a: Answer Set
  key:= TransQuery (theta); [7]
  s:= GenSignature(p);
  l:= Traverse(key, r);
  IF l== NULL THEN
    RETURN NULL
  ELSE
    FOR k:= 0 to n DO
      IF s == s' THEN
        v:= GetVector(k);
        IF v == p THEN
          a:= a + v;
        END IF
      END IF
    END FOR
    RETURN a;
  END IF
END PointSearch
```

4.2 Range Search Algorithm

Range search is slightly more complex than point search, for a range query consists of two parts, start point and end point. And certain subqueries can be pruned without evaluation [7]. The following shows the outline of the range search algorithm. Other than the additional complexity, the range query selects the data points within a range rather than the exact matches. Again answers reside in adjacent pages will be retrieved to find the complete answer set.

Range search algorithm

```
FUNCTION RangeSearch ((ps, pe): Range Query; r: B+ Tree Root)
  VAR key: One-Dimensional Key; l: Leaf Node; (ss, se): Signature;
  VAR k: INT; v: Data Vector; a: Answer Set;
  key:= TransQuery ((ps, pe)); [7]
  (ss, se):= GenSignature((ps, pe));
  IF NOT prune() THEN
    l:= Traverse(key, r);
    FOR k:= 0 to n DO
      IF ss {\pounds} s' {\pounds} se THEN
        v:= GetVector(k);
        IF ps <= v <= pe THEN
          a:= a + v;
        END IF
```

```
      END IF
    END FOR
    RETURN a;
  ELSE
    RETURN NULL
  END IF
END RangeSearch
```

5 Performance Evaluation

5.1 Experimental Setup

We ran the experiments on SUN workstation under Solaris using C implementation of iMinMax(θ), VA-file and our iMinMax(θ)*. In iMinMax(θ) and the iMinMax(θ)*, we used the B^+-tree as the single-dimensional index structure. For the experiments, we set the page size for data/node pages to be 4096 bytes. The retrieval of a page of data is counted as one I/O. No buffer or cache is assumed so each page fetched into the memory incurs an I/O. In [11], it has been shown that for iMinMax(θ) and the Pyramid tree, the buffer space has little impact on the performance, as there is hardly any referencing except for consecutively repeated queries. The queries generated for the experiments do not overlap and hence the access paths of the queries are different.

In this section we provide experimental result on the range queries. The VA-file assumes the uniformly (at least close to uniformly) distributed data set, and we shall show its performance in the experiments on uniform data. All data sets were obtained by using the procedure used in [7] which generates uniformly and normally distributed clusters in a d-dimensional data space. For every set of experiments, a total of 500 range queries are tested. The range queries are also generated by the procedure used in [7]. In [11], it has been shown that the CPU cost behaves in the similar trend, and due to space constraints, we shall concentrate on I/O costs here.

5.2 Effect of Dimensionality

In the first set of experiments, we vary the number of dimensions from 8 to 50 to see how increasing in data dimensionality affects the performance of iMinMax(θ)* The number of index objects is 10^5 in this set of experiments.

Figure 1 shows how these three structures perform to answer a range query in selectivity 0.1%. One noticeable observation is that the data-partition method, the VA-file, deteriorates most when the dimensionality increases to 50. For all dimensionalities the iMinMax(θ)* perform the best. In summary, the iMinMax(θ)* outperforms iMinMax(θ) by up to 25%. The result shows space-partitioning method may not be suitable for window queries, but it can help to filter the false drops if it is incorporated with other space-partitioning structures.

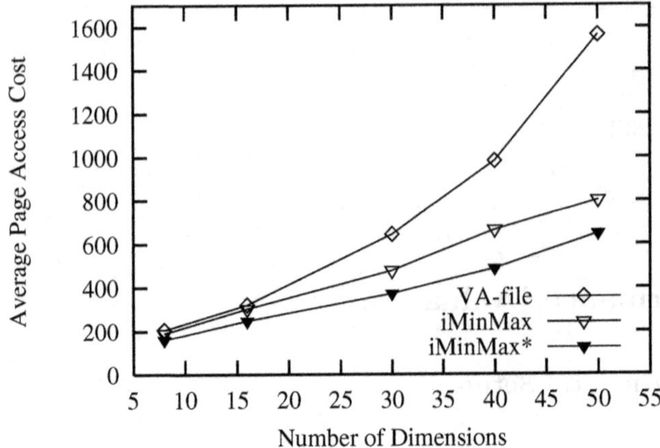

Fig. 1. Effect of dimensionality on uniformly distributed data

5.3 Effect of Data Sizes

Another major challenge in the design of iMinMax(θ)* was to ensure scalability of performance with respect to the size of the indexed data set. Here we only address the aspect of performing well on the range queries. We do not address the aspect of efficiently building the tree, for iMinMax(θ)* clearly takes a little more time and I/O to generate and store the signatures of the data vectors.

In this set of experiment, we fix the number of dimensions at 30, and the selectivity of the range queries at 0.1%. Figure 2 shows the results when the data set size varies from 100k to 500k points. We do not include the performance of the VA-file in this experiment. The reason is that for a 30-dimensional range query in selectivity 0.1%, the selectivity of the signature of this query can be $(((\lfloor 0.1\%^{1/30} * 16\rfloor + 2) / 16)^{30}$ (See the formula in Section 2.2) or 17 times larger assuming signature size is 4 bits per dimension. Its performance is therefore much worse than that of the other two structures. The results demonstrate that iMinMax(θ)* scales well in the data set size, and it suffers less from the I/O range search cost.

5.4 Effect of Data Distributions

In real databases, data points follow any distribution. A good index structure must perform well on all data sets in all distributions. In this experiment, we present the performance of iMinMax(θ) and iMinMax(θ)* on skewed normally distributed data. We fixed the dimension at 30, the data points clustered around 0.6, and the range queries were generated with same distribution. Each of the queries has query side 0.4. Figure 3 shows the result for the normally distributed data. It shows iMinMax(θ)* outperforms iMinMax(θ) again by a wide margin while the data set size increases.

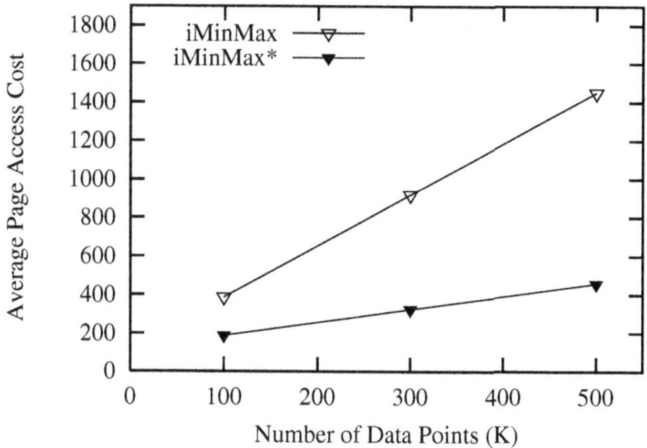

Fig. 2. Effect of varying data sizes

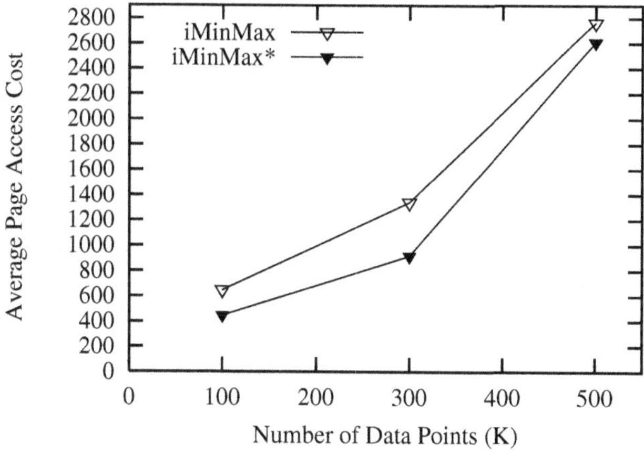

Fig. 3. Effects of varying data set size for normally distributed data

6 Conclusion

High-dimensional query is one of the most common queries in the multimedia information systems. It is therefore essential to have an efficient index scheme for supporting high-dimensional queries. Our results show that use of approximation significantly reduces the size of the leaf level index and enables a high-dimensional index to perform well for skewed data distributions, and scale up well for large data sets.

Our proposed index, iMinMax(θ)* integrates the strengths of both the VA-file and iMinMax(θ). In this paper, although only iMinMax(θ) index is considered, other hierarchical multi-dimensional indexes, such as the R-tree, could clearly be modified in a similar way. This is in fact similar in philosophy to the effort in providing larger node side in the R-tree [1].

Encouraged by the results obtained, our future work will concentrate on improving the performance of existing methods. For example, the precision of the approximation can be improved by increasing the number of approximation bits depending on the distribution of the data along each dimension. We will also look into extending iMinMax(θ) for approximate similarity and K-nearest neighbor search as in [11].

References

1. S. Berchtold, D.A. Keim, H.P. Kriegel:The X-tree: an index structure for high-dimensional data. Proc. Very Large Data Bases VLDB'96 (1996) 23–27.
2. N. Beckmann, H-P.Kriegel R. Schneider, B. Seeger: The R*-tree, An efficient and robust access method for points and rectangles. Proc. ACM SIGMOD Int. Conf. On Management of Data SIGMOD'90 (1990) 322–331.
3. R. Finkel and J. Bentley:Quad-trees: A data structure for retrieval on composite keys. ACTA Information (1974) 1–9.
4. A. Guttman:R-tree: A dynamic index structure for spatial searching. Proc. ACM SIGMOD Int. Conf. On Management of Data SIGMOD'84 (1984) 47–54.
5. J. Nievergelt, H. Hinterberger, and K. Sevcik:The grid file: An adaptable symmetric multikey file structure. ACM Transactions on Database Systems 1984 38–71.
6. B. C. Ooi: Efficient query processing in geographical information system. Lecture Notes in Computer Science #471, Springer-Verlag, 1990.
7. B.C. Ooi, K.L. Tan, C. Yu, and S. Bressan:Indexing the Edges - A simple and yet efficient approach to high-dimensional indexing. Proc. ACM SIGMOD-SIGACT-SIGART 19th Symposium on Principles of Database Systems PODS'2000 (2000) 166–174.
8. J. Robinson: The k-d-b tree: A search structure for large multidimensional dynamic indexes. Proc. ACM SIGMOD Int. Conf. On Management of Data (1981) 10–18.
9. R. Weber and S. Blott. An approximation based data structure for similarity search. Technical Report 24, ESPRIT project HERMES (no. 9141) (1997)
10. R. Weber, Hans-J. Schek, and S. Blott: A quantitative analysis and performance study for similarity-search methods in high-dimensional spaces. Proc. Int. Conf. Very Large Data Bases VLDB'98 (1998) 194–205.
11. C. Yu: High-dimensional indexing. PhD Thesis. National University of Singapore (2001)

Session 4B
Data Mining & Constraint Management

Regular Research Paper (30 minutes)
Finding Dense Clusters in Hyperspace: An Approach Based on Row Shuffling

Regular Research Paper (30 minutes)
Modelling Classification Performance for Large Data Sets – An Empirical Study

Regular Research Paper (30 minutes)
Mapping Referential Integrity Constraints from Relational Databases to XML

Finding Dense Clusters in Hyperspace: An Approach Based on Row Shuffling

Daniel Barbará and Xintao Wu

George Mason University, ISE Dept., MSN 4A4 Fairfax VA 22030, USA,
dbarbara,xwu@gmu.edu
This work has been supported by NSF grant IIS-9732113

Abstract. High dimensional data sets generally exhibit low density, since the number of possible cells exceeds the actual number of cells in the set. This characteristic has prompted researchers to automate the search for subspaces where the density is higher. In this paper we present an algorithm that takes advantage of categorical, unordered dimensions to increase the density of subspaces in the data set. It does this by shuffling rows in those dimensions, so the final ordering results in increased density of regions in hyperspace. We argue for the usage of this shuffling technique as a preprocessing step for other techniques that compress the hyperspace by means of statistical models, since denser regions usually result in better-fitting models. The experimental results support this argument. We also show how to integrate this algorithm with two grid clustering procedures in order to find these dense regions. The experimental results in both synthetic and real data sets show that row-shuffling can drastically increase the density of the subspaces, leading to better clusters.

1 Introduction

The area of clustering has received an enormous attention in the database community lately. The problem of clustering is to partition a dataset consisting of N points embedded in a d-dimensional space into k groups or clusters such that points in a single group have similar characteristics, while points in different groups are dissimilar. Many algorithms[13,5] assume that the number of clusters, k, is known a priori and aim to find the k clusters that optimize a certain predefined metric. When the dimensionality of the data set is high, clustering becomes difficult, since it is likely that the density of any region of the data space is low . Commonly (as in the IBM Intelligent Miner [8]), the high dimensionality problem is approached by asking the user to specify the subspace (subset of dimensions) for cluster analysis. Researchers have tried to automate the search for dense subspaces [1] by using a partitioning approach in which the data space is divided in cells (of equal size), measuring the number of points inside the cells and connecting adjacent high-density cells to form clusters. This last step is performed by finding a minimal cover of adjacent cells.

There are many situations in which the order of values in a domain is irrelevant. Consider, for instance, dimensions such as *color*, *product*, *companies*.

X.S. Wang, G. Yu, and H. Lu (Eds.): WAIM 2001, LNCS 2118, pp. 305–316, 2001.

In those examples there is no natural ranking for the values in the dimensions domain (e.g., it is irrelevant in which order we list "red," and "blue" in the *color* domain, or in which order we list "shirts," and "pants" in the product attribute). This fact can be exploited to find denser subspaces in the data set. Consider, for instance, the example of Figure 1 (a) which shows a data space with two categorical attributes, e.g., *product* (D_1) and *color* (D_2) . The shadowed cells may mean sales of a particular combination of product and color exceeding some threshold, while the white cells may mean the sales of the combination did not exceed that threshold. We want to find clusters that explain which combinations of color and products are big sellers. If the index of the categorical values was assigned randomly such as in figure 1(a), the shadowed cells appear approximately randomly distributed and making it difficult to merge those dense cells into big clusters. But if we map the index value along D_2, $\{0,1,2,3,4,5,6,7,8,9\} \Rightarrow \{5,9,6,0,8,7,2,3,4,1\}$, we get relatively evenly distributed dense cells in Figure 1 (b). An even better result, shown in 1 (c), is obtained if we continue the process on D_1,$\{0,1,2,3,4,5,6,7,8,9\} \Rightarrow \{7,3,8,1,4,9,6,0,2,5\}$. From the figure 1(c), we are in a good position to get better clusters by applying rejoining cells (finding the minimal cover) as it is done in [1].

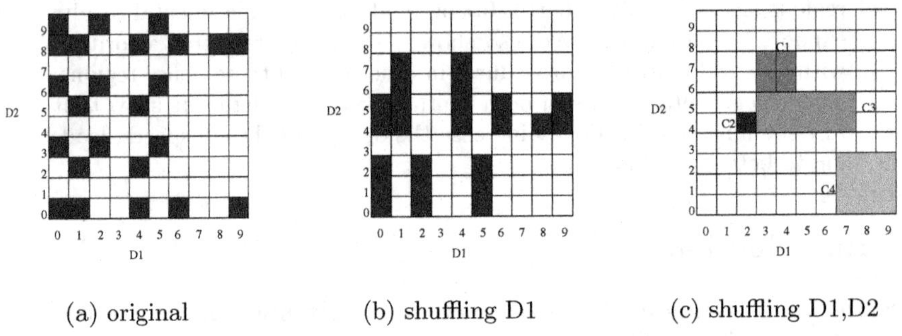

(a) original (b) shuffling D1 (c) shuffling D1,D2

Fig. 1. Illustration of row-shuffling

In this paper, we focus on the design and implementation of a row-shuffling algorithm that helps to increase the density of regions of the cube and in how to integrate it into grid-based cluster methods. We also apply it to increase the efficiency of our approximate querying system[4], which uses statistical models to characterize subspaces in a hyper-dimensional space, using the models to approximately answer queries.

The rest of the paper is organized as follows. We first discuss related work in Section 2. In Section 3, we describe in detail our approach. In Section 4, we present the experimental evaluation of the effectiveness and efficiency of our approach using synthetic datasets and real datasets. Finally in Section 5, concluding remarks and future work are offered.

2 Related Work

Clustering has received a lot of attention in the recent years. Commonly, the clustering methods can be classified into partitioning algorithms, hierarchical algorithms, density based algorithms and grid based algorithms. Partitioning algorithms aim to construct a partition of the database by starting with an initial model and using an iterative control strategy that tries to optimize an objective function. Examples of partitioning algorithms are K-Means [5], and CLARANS [10]. Hierarchical algorithms create a hierarchical decomposition of the database. An example of such methods is BIRCH[13], which uses CF-tree, a hierarchical data structure, to incrementally and dynamically cluster the incoming data points. Density Based Algorithms rely on a density-based notion of clusters. For instance, in DBSCAN [6], for each cluster, the neighborhood of a given radius must contain at least a minimum number of points. In Grid-Based algorithms a cluster is usually a region that has a higher density of points than its surrounding region. Grid-based clustering algorithms [7,12] project the space into a subspace and quantize the projected subspace into a finite number of cells and then perform all the operations on the quantized space. The authors in [1] proposed a bottom-up scheme (similar to the Apriori algorithm for mining association rules) to project the original space to a subspace and find clusters in that subspace. We believe our row shuffling algorithm can be integrated with the above method to deal with some unordered categorical attributes.

3 Our Approach

3.1 Definitions and Problem Statement

Definition 3.1 Data space Density Let $A = \{A_1, A_2, \cdots A_n\}$ be a set of categorical attributes with domains $D_1, D_2, \cdots, D_n$, respectively. Let the dataset T be a set of tuples where each tuple t: $t \in D_1 \times D_2 \times \cdots \times D_n$, the number of tuples in this dataset is denoted as N. Let the data space D be a hyperspace $D_1 \times D_2 \times \cdots \times D_n$, the size of data space is denoted as $\|D\| = \|D_0\| \times \|D_1\| \times \cdots \times \|D_n\|$. The density of data space D is denoted as $\tau = \frac{N}{\|D\|}$.

Definition 3.2 Interval Region We call $S = S_1 \times S_2 \cdots \times S_n$ an interval region if for all $i \in \{1, \cdots, n\}$, $S_i \subseteq D_i$. Let the dataset T_S be the subset of T where each tuple $t : t \in S_1 \times S_2 \cdots S_n$. The number of tuples in S is denoted as N_S. The size of data space of S is denoted as $\|S\| = \|S_0\| \times \|S_1\| \times \cdots \times \|S_n\|$. The density of region S is denoted as $\tau_S = \frac{N_S}{\|S\|}$.

Definition 3.3 Density-based Cluster We call S is a density based cluster C iif it satisfies:
1. $\tau_S \geq c\tau$, where c is a predefined constant.
2. There exists no another cluster S' such that $S \subset S'$.

Problem 3.1 Given dataset D and constant c, find the complete cluster set $CSET = \{C_1, C_2, \cdots, C_k\}$, where
1. C_i, $i \in \{1, 2, \cdots, k\}$, is a density based cluster (Definition 3.3).

2. $C_i \cap C_j = \emptyset$ for all $i, j \in \{1, 2, \cdots, k\}, i \neq j$.
3. There exists no cluster $C' \notin CSET$ such that there exists some tuple $t \in C'$ and $t \notin C_i$ for all $C_i \in CSET$.

Figure 1 (c) shows the $CSET = \{C_1, C_2, C_3, C_4\}$ in a two dimension dataset.

Many clustering methods assume the number of clusters is given k. The clustering problem can be formalized as Problem 3.2. We will talk more about these two problems and give two algorithms, namely $CLUSTER1$ for Problem 3.1 and $CLUSTER2$ for Problem 3.2. We will show the row-shuffling can improve the result of both methods in experimental evaluation section.

Problem 3.2 Given dataset D and a predefined constant k, find the cluster set $CSET = \{C_1, C_2, \cdots, C_k\}$, where C_i, $i \in \{1, 2, \cdots, k\}$,is determined by maximizing the average density and $C_i \cap C_j = \emptyset$ for all $i, j \in \{1, 2, \cdots, k\}, i \neq j$.

Unfortunately, there are no efficient algorithms to find optimal solutions to problems 3.1 and 3.2 (and none are likely to be developed). In this paper, we present a heuristic that aims to find a sub-optimal, but good solution to the problems.

3.2 Row Shuffling Algorithm

In this subsection, we discuss the row-shuffling algorithm and how it can be applied to a projected subspace. The data space D with n dimensions can be projected to the subspace D_p with m dimensions, usually with $m << n$. If we view the whole data space as one n-dimension hyper-rectangle, the projected subspace D_p can be viewed as an m-dimension hyper-rectangle. The values of the cells in this new hyper-rectangle can be assigned in many ways. For instance, we could assign a cell a value equal to the number of non-empty cells in the original space that map to this cell when the projection is done. (We use this method in our experiments.) Alternatively, we could assign a cell a value equal to the aggregation value of cells in the original space that map to this cell when the projection is done. (In fact, there are many mappings that can be used between cell values in the original space and those in the projected subspace.) The reason behind projecting some dimensions out of the original space is that the tuples in a given data space are approximately randomly distributed along those dimensions (e.g., date). Those dimensions do not affect the result of the clustering, so grid-based clustering methods just project out those dimensions. It is obvious that the projected subspace is denser (and smaller) than the original data space and usually the number of cells in the projected subspace $\|D_p\|$ is far less than the number of cells N in the original data space. If we view those cells which has values exceeding some threshold as dense units, we can apply the techniques[1] to merge those dense units into clusters. However, before applying that technique, we can increase the density of the regions by moving around unordered categorical values. To do so, however, we need to decide which "rows" are to be moved closer to each other by formulating some notion of similarity between the rows.

The similarity notion that we use is based on the distribution of the cells in the projected subspace. If we view attribute values of one fixed dimension D_i as rows and the combination of all other dimensions' attribute values as columns, the projected subspace can be viewed as a spreadsheet. It is obvious the count of row is $\|D_i\|$ and the count of column is $\prod_{j \neq i} \|D_j\|$. The similarity between two rows i_1, i_2 can be computed by using the difference between the cell values $\hat{C}_{i_1,j}, \hat{C}_{i_2,j}$ for each column j , where $j = \{1, 2, \cdots, \prod_{j \neq i} \|D_j\}$. The difference between two rows can be measured by the p-norm distance.

Figure 2 shows the row-shuffling algorithm. After we compute the similarity between each pair of rows, we get a $\|D_i\| \times \|D_i\|$ similarity matrix SIM_i for dimension i. For each pair of two rows, we need to compare the values of every column in the spreadsheet. So the cost of computing SIM_i for dimension i is $O(\|D_i\|\|D_p\|)$, where $\|D_i\|$ is the domain size of dimension i, $\|D_p\| = \prod_{j=1}^{m} D_j$ is the size of subspace D_p. The total cost of computing SIM for all dimensions is $O(\sum_{i=1}^{m} \|D_i\|\|D_p\|)$. Usually, the similarity matrix SIM_i could be fitted in memory due to the fact that the domain size of the meaningful categorical attribute D_i is relatively small. If the subspace $\|D_p\|$ can be fitted in memory (remember $\|D_p\| << N$), we only need one scan of disk I/O. Otherwise, we need several scans of disk I/O to read part of rows in memory each time. As the cost of CPU is dominant, the I/O cost is small. In fact, the categorical attributes often have hierarchy. The similarity matrix SIM_i can be defined and computed on some coarser hierarchical levels. In that case, the computation cost is really trivial, however, the experiment shows row shuffling still achieves good effectiveness.

Now we can exploit the SIM to assign the new index to each attribute value. The idea is straight forward. First, we choose the largest number in SIM_i, assume $sim(i_1, i_2)$, so row i_1 and row i_2 should be adjacent to each other. We get the order list $\cdots, i_1, i_2, \cdots$. Then we choose the next largest value in row i_1 and i_2 in SIM_i, assume $sim(i_1, i_3)$. So row i_3 and row i_1 should be adjacent neighbor. We insert the i_3 into the order list, so the order list is $\cdots, i_3, i_1, i_2, \cdots$. We continue to find the next neighbor of row i_3 or row i_2. In each step, we set those cells in SIM_i with the rows already in the order list to zero, so we can always find the new neighbor which is not in the order list. It is obvious the above method may not optimal: finding the optimum is, in general, a very expensive procedure. The next step is just to assign each row's index as the index in the order list. Here we should point out that the mapping result for each dimension does not depend on the processing sequence of dimensions.

3.3 Clustering Algorithms

A dense hyper-rectangle is a region that contains many non-zero cells. As we can see from Figure 1, a cluster can be viewed as a set of adjacent dense hyper-rectangles. For each hyper-rectangle as well as for the cluster, we have the following structure :

- start-point $sp[m]$, end-point $ep[m]$, center-point $cp[m]$. These three m dimension array can determine the exact position and the range of the region.

```
row-shuffling()
BEGIN
        forall dimension i ∈ {1, 2, ···, m} (1)
                compute SIM_i (2)
                assign new index by scanning SIM_i (3)
END
```

Fig. 2. Row-shuffling Algorithm

- *size* which can be computed by the start-point and the end-point.
- *Ntuple*, number of tuples in this region.
- density, τ, which can be computed from the size and the number of tuples in this region.

We denote by the name of *unit* a set of adjacent cells (it can be as simple as just one cell). Figure 3 shows the clustering algorithm $CLUSTER1$ according to Problem 3.1 where predefined constant c decides the cluster density threshold. Figure 4 shows the clustering algorithm $CLUSTER2$ according to Problem 3.2 where a predefined constant k is known to be the number of clusters in data space. Both methods aim to merge dense units into big regions by applying bottom-up strategy. The dense units can be determined by scanning the projected subspace to see whether its density exceeds some threshold. The left units can be seen as sparse units and we do not need keep structure information for these sparse units. Instead we can estimate the number of tuples in the sparse unit during the merge process if some sparse units are included in the merged regions. The average number of tuples in the sparse unit can be easily estimated, subtracting the number of tuples in dense units from the total number of tuples and then dividing by number of sparse units. The number of dense unit is usually far less than the number of cells, so we can keep the dense unit structure list $ULIST$ in memory. The difference between $CLUSTER1$ and $CLUSTER2$ lies in how the merge procedure is applied. (The merge procedure is shown in Figure 5.) $CLUSTER1$ tries to merge the nearest two dense units into one dense unit by calling the process merge. The condition for merging is that the density τ' after the merge satisfies $\tau' > c\tau$, where τ is the average density of the whole data space. On the other hand, $CLUSTER2$ tries to merge dense units until k clusters are found. In line 6 in Figure 5 the number of tuples in the merged regions also includes the estimated tuples of sparse units, which lie in the merged regions. If we want to get the precise number of tuples in each region, we only need one more scan of the dataset. We should also compute and store the p-norm distance between each pair of dense regions in order to merge the nearest ones.

```
CLUSTER1()
BEGIN
        scan dataset to generate the projected subspace D_p (1)
        scan subspace to generate dense unit list ULIST (2)
        compute the distance for every pair of units in ULIST(3)
        do
            find the nearest two units u_i, u_j (4)
            if u = merge(u_i, u_j) is dense unit (5)
              insert u and delete u_i, u_j from ULIST (6)
              recompute the distance for every pair of units with u_i or u_j (7)
            else
              set the distance between u1 and u2 ∞ (8)
              continue
        while{the distance between each pair of unit in ULIST is ∞}(9)
END
```

Fig. 3. Cluster Method 1 $CLUSTER1$

```
CLUSTER2()
BEGIN
        scan dataset to generate the projected subspace D_p (1)
        scan subspace to generate dense unit list ULIST (2)
        compute the distance for every pair of units in ULIST (3)
        do
            find two units u_i, u_j when the density after merge is maximum (4)
            u = merge(u_i, u_j) (5)
            insert u and delete u_i, u_j from ULIST (6)
            recompute the distance for every pair of units with u_i or u_j (7)
        while{elements in ULIST is more than k}(8)
END
```

Fig. 4. Cluster Method 2 $CLUSTER2$

```
merge(u_1, u_2)
BEGIN
        For each dimension i in {1, 2, ···, m} do (1)
            u.sp[i] = min{u_1.sp[i], u_2.sp[i]} (2)
            u.ep[i] = max{u_1.ep[i], u_2.ep[i]} (3)
            u.cp[i] = 0.5 × (u.ep[i] + u.sp[i]) (4)
        compute u.size (5)
        u.Ntuple = u_1.Ntuple + u_2.Ntuple + estimated (6)
        u.τ = u.Ntuple / u.szie (7)
        return u (8)
END
```

Fig. 5. Merge Method

3.4 Discussion

- We do not discuss how to get the projected subspace from the original data space. There are several articles [9,7,1] that focus on this dimension reduction problem.
- The processing time of grid-based algorithms is typically independent of the number of data objects, the space size and the number of dimensions. It is determined only by the size of the projected subspace, which in turn is determined by the quantized size of each projected dimension. So high dimensionality does not play an important role for grid-based cluster algorithm. This is the reason why we combine the row shuffling method with grid-based cluster algorithms and apply them in our Quasi-Cube system[4]. However, we believe row shuffling algorithm can easily be integrated into other partitioning algorithms[5,10,1] and density based algorithms[6].
- It is worth pointing out that density is not always a correct measure for good clusters. It is possible that two clusters with different behaviors may be merged into one by using row shuffling based on the density similarity definition. However, this can be eliminated by adopting a different method to assign values to cells.
- For some hierarchical categorical attributes, we must preserve the hierarchical information after row-shuffling. For example, there may be hierarchy in our example product→type→category on attribute product. Shuffling a soda (beverages) next to a shirt (clothes) is not admissible. A simple approach to avoid this problem is restricting the row-shuffling to the children of each parent (i.e., rows of "clothes" can be shuffled among each other, but not outside of the class "clothes").

4 Empirical Evaluation

In this section, we show the performance of our row-shuffling algorithm by comparing the results of grid-based clustering algorithms when the row shuffling is used and when it is not. We do not plan to address the issue of comparing grid-based clustering algorithms with other clustering algorithms, since this falls out of the scope of this paper. We use several synthetic datasets that explicitly vary some parameters to explore the performance of our approach. We also show the effectiveness of our approach by doing experiments with several real datasets (Due to the space limit, we only show one synthetic dataset and one real dataset here. The detailed information is in [3]).

4.1 Synthetic Data Sets

The synthetic data set DS1 we generated in this section has 4 categorical attributes A, B, C, D with domain size 100. The position of the points distributed randomly along attribute D while there are some clusters along dimension A, B, C. The number of clusters K is 20, the cluster size is fixed (5,5,5,100), the density of cluster τ_c is 0.08, the noise N_x is varied. After generating the dataset, we reassign the attribute value to some random index to disturb the attribute distribution. We aim to show we can restore the original dataset by applying row-shuffling algorithm.

Figure 6 shows the result of using $CLUSTER1$ on DS1 with different numbers of noisy points, with and without row-shuffling. We measure the number of clusters obtained and the average points found in the clusters. Notice that in every experiment we recovered the original clusters.

N 10^3	$Noise N_x$ No. pts. ($\text{x}10^3$)	c	without RS No. of clusters	average size	with RS No. of clusters size 1,000	size 2,000	size 3,000	average size($\text{x}10^3$)
20	0	50	1371	14.6	8	6	0	1.43
25	5	50	1485	13.5	9	4	1	1.43
30	10	50	1535	13.0	16	2	0	1.11
40	20	50	1724	11.6	16	2	0	1.11
120	100	8	1371	14.8	11	3	1	1.33

Fig. 6. DS1: Cluster method 1 with and without row-shuffling (RS) for different noise levels. (The RS "number of clusters" columns show the number of clusters according to their sizes: 1,000, 2,000, and 3,000 respectively. The clusters generated in DS1 were of size 1,000. Some clusters –distributed uniformly– are placed together by the clustering algorithm, since they are close to each other. Hence, clusters of size 2,000 and 3,000 are formed.

Figure 7 shows the result of DS1 with different noise size N_x under the clustering method 2 $CLUSTER2$. The measure includes minimum, maximum, and average cluster density.

		cluster density τ ($\text{x}10^{-2}$) without RS			cluster density τ ($\text{x}10^{-2}$) with RS		
N(10^3)	Noise N_x (10^3)	min	max	average	min	max	average
20	0	0.013	0.060	0.027	5.04	8	7.79
25	5	0.013	0.060	0.027	6.13	8.02	7.87
30	10	0.013	0.060	0.027	5.52	8.03	7.81
40	20	0.013	0.060	0.027	4.67	8.64	7.81
120	100	0.013	0.060	0.027	6.66	8.14	7.94

Fig. 7. DS1: Cluster method 2 with and without RS for different noise levels. The number of clusters used K is equal to 20.

4.2 Real Data Sets

PKDD99 Discovery Challenge Dataset. PKDD99 Discovery Challenge [11] provides a dataset of bank transactions include seveal tables. The transaction table include the following fields: trans-id, account-id, date, type, operation, amount, balance,k-symbol, bank of the partner,account of the partner. Here we aim to find the clusters in transaction table such as some specific accounts (clients) are clustered together with some kinds of operations in some date periods. (Our ultimate aim is to model the clusters and use the models to speedup the EDA analysis[2,4].) From the transaction table, we get a dataset with four categorical attributes: account-id, date, type, operation. Accordingly, the domain size is 4500, 2191,3, 6. There are 651,237 entries in this dataset.

In our experiment, we project the space into a subspace with three dimensions, account-id, type and operation. Figure 8 shows the result of Bank Dataset under clustering method 1 $CLUSTER1$. Figure 9 shows the result of Bank Dataset under clustering method 2 $CLUSTER2$. In both experiments, sizable gains are obtained. When applying $CLUSTER1$, the number of clusters decreases while the number of points inside clusters increases dramatically. (The gains range from 4.65 times the average number of points in a cluster to 34 times.) When applying $CLUSTER2$, the average cluster density is substantially increased. (An average of 3.5 times.)

	cluster without RS		cluster with RS	
c	No. of clusters	avg points in cluster	No. of clusters	average points in cluster
8	1190	191	140	1629
10	755	209	21	7143
15	369	167	23	2686
20	79	197	16	917

Fig. 8. Bank Dataset: Cluster method 1 with and without RS under different c.

	cluster density τ (x10^{-2}) without RS			cluster density τ (x10^{-2}) with RS		
k	min	max	average	min	max	average
10	0.87	1.11	1.00	0.76	5.47	2.81
20	0.80	1.35	1.00	0.73	6.32	3.80
40	0.90	2.14	1.15	0.90	7.40	4.44

Fig. 9. Bank Dataset: Cluster method 2 with RS and without RS for different number of clusters (k).

We also applied row shuffling algorithm to increase the efficiency of our approximate querying system[4]. By increasing the density of the modeled regions, row-shuffling helps to improve the accuracy and performanc of modeling. Figure 10 shows the result of compression ratio using loglinear model with and without row shuffling, where compression ratio is the size of model parameter plus the size of outlier over the size of the cells.

The cell is kept as an outlier if the relative error of the estimated cell is larger than predefined threshold which is shown on X axis. In experiments, sizable gains are obtained. When applying row shuffling, the compression ratio is nearly as half as that without applying rowshuffling. It is important to remark that every cell is bounded by the relative error shown on X axis in Figure 10. When the selectivity of the queries increases(OLAP user cares more about range query), the error in the answer decreases drastically[4].

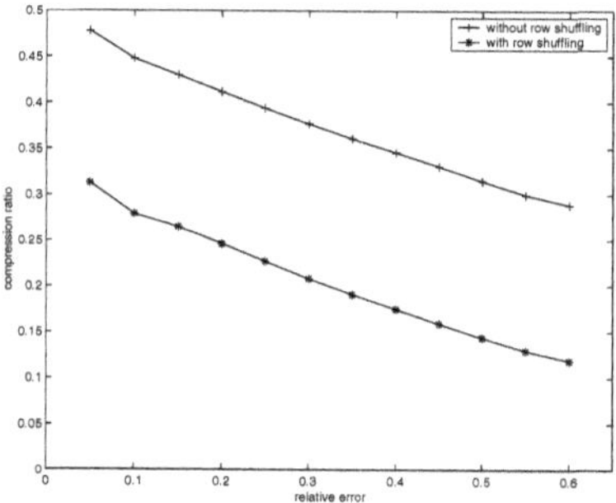

Fig. 10. Compression ratio obtained using the loglinear model over the bank dataset with and without row shuffling. The Y axis shows the compression ratio.The X axis shows the relative error threshold for each cell.

5 Conclusions

In this paper, we have presented a row-shuffling algorithm that has the potential of substantially increasing the density of subspaces in a multidimensional database. The algorithm can be easily integrated with grid-based clustering methods. We evaluated this algorithm using both synthetic and real datasets, showing that the increase in density is substantial.

The algorithm is useful not only as a pre-processing tool for grid-clustering methods, but it can also be applied to increase the efficiency of other techniques as well. For instance, we are currently using it to enhance our our approximate querying system[4], which uses statistical models to characterize subspaces in a hyper-dimensional space, using the models to approximately answer queries.

The idea is to trade space and latency for accuracy in the answers. By increasing the density of the modeled regions, row-shuffling helps to improve the accuracy and performance of modeling. We have shown that in real datasets we achieved much better compression ratio when we combined row shuffling algorithm into approximate modeling techniques. Similar gains can be experienced when using row-shuffling before subjecting the data to approximate data mining techniques, such as the one described in [2], where we aim to perform exploratory data analysis in large datasets in an approximate way in order to scale the technique to large data sets.

References

1. R.Agrawal, J.Gerhrke, D.Gunopulos, and P.Raghavan. Automatic subspace clustering of high dimensional data for data mining. In *Proceedings of the ACM SIGMOD International Conference on Management of Data, Seattle, Washington*, 1998.
2. D. Barbará, X. Wu. Using Approximations to Scale Exploratory Data Analysis in Datacubes. In *Proceedings of the Fifth ACM SIGKDD International Conference on Knowledge Discovery and Data Mining, San Diego, California*, 1999.
3. D. Barbará, X. Wu. Finding Dense Clusters in Hyperspace: An Approach Based on Row Shuffling. Technical Report, George Mason university, ISE Dept, August 2000 .
4. D. Barbará, X. Wu. Using Loglinear Models to Compress Datacubes. In *Proceedings of the first International Conference on Web-Age Information Management,Shanghai,China*, 2000.
5. P. Bradley, U. Fayyad, and C. Reina, Scaling Clustering Algorithms to Large Databases. In *Proceedings of the 1998 ACM-SIGKDD International Conference on Knowledge Discovery and Data Mining*, August 1998.
6. M.Ester, H.Kriegel, J.Sander, and X.Xu A Density-Based Algorithm for Discovering Clusters in Large Spatial Databases with Noise. In*Proceedings of 1996 ACM-SIGKDD International Conference on Knowledge Discovery and Data Mining*, 1996.
7. A. Hinneburg, D.A.Keim Optimal Grid-Clustering: Towards Breaking the Curse of Dimensionality in High-Dimensional Clustering. In *Proceedings of the 25rd VLDB Conference, Edinburgh, Scotland*, 1999.
8. International Business Machines IBM Intelligent Miner User's Guide, 1996
9. Piotr Indyk. Dimensionality Reduction Techniques for Proximity Problems.
10. R.T.Ng, J.Han Efficient and Effective Clustering Methods for Spatial Data Mining. In *Proceedings of the 20th Very Large Data Bases Conference*,1994.
11. PKDD99 Discovery Challenge Download the Data. http://lisp.vse.cz/pkdd99/chall.htm
12. W.Wang, J.Yang, R. Muntz STING: A Statistical Information Grid Approach to Spatial Data Ming. In *Proceedings of the 23rd VLDB Conference, Athens, Greece*, 1997.
13. T.Zhang, R.Ramakrishnan, and M. Livny. Birch: An efficient data clustering method for large databases. In *Proceedings of the ACM SIGMOD International Conference on Management of Data, Montreal, Quebec*, June 1996.

Modelling Classification Performance for Large Data Sets

An Empirical Study

Baohua Gu[1], Feifang Hu[2], and Huan Liu[3]

[1] Department of Computer Science, National University of Singapore
gubh@comp.nus.edu.sg
[2] Department of Statistics & Applied Probability, National University of Singapore
stahuff@nus.edu.sg
[3] Department of Computer Science & Engineering, Arizona State University, USA
hliu@asu.edu

Abstract. For many learning algorithms, their learning accuracy will increase as the size of training data increases, forming the well-known *learning curve*. Usually a learning curve can be fitted by interpolating or extrapolating some points on it with a specified model. The obtained learning curve can then be used to predict the maximum achievable learning accuracy or to estimate the amount of data needed to achieve an expected learning accuracy, both of which will be especially meaningful to data mining on large data sets. Although some models have been proposed to model learning curves, most of them do not test their applicability to large data sets. In this paper, we focus on this issue. We empirically compare six potentially useful models by fitting learning curves of two typical classification algorithms—C4.5 (decision tree) and LOG (logistic discrimination) on eight large UCI benchmark data sets. By using all available data for learning, we fit a *full-length* learning curve; by using a small portion of the data, we fit a *part-length* learning curve. The models are then compared in terms of two performances: (1) how well they fit a *full-length* learning curve, and (2) how well a fitted *part-length* learning curve can predict learning accuracy at the full length. Experimental results show that the power law ($y = a - b * x^{-c}$) is the best among the six models in both the performances for the two algorithms and all the data sets. These results support the applicability of learning curves to data mining.

1 Introduction

1.1 Motivation

When an induction algorithm (e.g., a classification algorithm) is run on a data set, it 'learns' from the data and produces a generalized model (e.g., a decision tree, or a set of classification rules). Generally speaking, the more instances the learner sees during the learning, the higher the model accuracy. Such a relation is depicted by a so-called *learning curve*. On a typical learning curve, the horizontal axis represents *Size*, the number of instances used for training (so

X.S. Wang, G. Yu, and H. Lu (Eds.): WAIM 2001, LNCS 2118, pp. 317–328, 2001.

called training data), while the vertical axis represents *Acc*, the accuracy rate of the model produced on the training data and tested against a set of instances unseen during the training (so called testing data). Theoretical and empirical studies have suggested that learning curves typically have a fast increasing portion early in the curve, following with a relatively slow increasing portion and finally a plateau portion when the learning accuracy no longer increases with more training data [13].

In practice, the learning curve can be modelled by fitting a group of $(Size, Acc)$ points (called *learning points* hereafter in this paper), in order to avoid the redundant and expensive work of learning every size of a data set [9]. The learning curve, if available, can be very useful: (1) to predict what is a reachable learning accuracy for a given amount of data, (2) to estimate how many data should be used to achieve a desired learning accuracy, and (3) when to stop a learning process according the predictable gain in learning accuracy [5]. Such uses can find many practical applications by data mining practitioners who frequently deal with large data sets.

For large data sets, it will be more preferable to fit learning points that only cover a small amount of all available data. Mathematically, such a fitting can be implemented by interpolating the front portion of a learning curve then extrapolating to its later portion until the full length. The result of the fitting depends on how many learning points to fit and which model to use. As we are restricted to use too many learning points that may involve costly computation of learning a large amount of data, the choice of the model is actually more important.

Theoretically, given a set of points, one can fit the curve with as many models as he will, as long as he tries more functions to fit or uses more parameters to tune and can afford the subsequent complexity. Practically however, models with simpler expression and less parameters are more preferable because of easier operations. Another, the exact behavior of a learning curve is founded differing with the used learning algorithm as well as the used data set [1,7]. A natural question is thus that if there exists a common model that can well fit various learning curves with respect to different learning algorithms and various data sets.

Hopefully, for its application to data mining, we need a model that satisfies the following properties: (1) be simple (with less parameters), (2) to be able to well fit a full-length learning curve, (3) to be able to well extrapolate to the full length by interpolating the early part of the learning curve, and (4) be applicable to different learning algorithms and different data sets. When models are similar in the former two properties, the last two properties are more significant to data mining. Then which model is the desired?

1.2 Related Research

The common feature in the shape of learning curves suggests a possibility of fitting with a common model, of which the parameters are tuned to fit the exact shapes. The famous power law seems more often suggested to take this job [4,5,8].

Frey and Fisher [5] use $y = a * x^{-b}$ to model C4.5 decision tree performance, where y is error rate of learning, x is training data size, $a > 0$ and $b > 0$ are parameters to be fitted. After comparing the two-parameter power law with other three two-parameters models, namely linear model, logarithm model and exponential model, they conclude that it is the best among the four models and usable to predict error rate of unseen larger size. Note that modelling learning error is equivalent to modelling learning accuracy, their work does show that the power law is potentially suitable in fitting learning curves. However, all data sets they use are relatively small: most of them only have hundreds of instances and the largest only has about three thousand instances. Moreover, the compared linear model ($y = a * x + b$)and exponential model ($y = a * exp(-b * x)$) are inherently not suitable in fitting learning curves due to their too fast increase with x, and this will become even worse for large data sets.

John and Langley[8] use $y = a - b * x^{-c}$ to fit learning curves for a naive Bayesian classifier, where y is learning accuracy, x is data size, $a > 0, b > 0, c > 0$ are parameters to estimate. They apply it to some large data sets, however, they do not consider other fitting models. Moreover, in each of the above works, only one learning algorithm is considered. Therefore, these researches do not consider the following questions: whether there is another model better than the power law, and whether a model such as the power law can apply to large data sets as well as other learning algorithms. In this work, we address our attention to these unsolved issues.

1.3 Our Contribution

In this study, we empirically compare six models found in the mathematical community and potentially usable for fitting learning curves, investigate which model performs best (in the sense of the above mentioned properties) for eight large UCI benchmark data sets and two typical classification algorithms, namely C4.5 (decision tree approach) and LOG (logistic discrimination approach). The six models, namely two-parameters power law, three-parameters power law, logarithm model, vapor pressure model, Morgan-Mercer-Flodin (MMF) model, and weibull model [16], come from three function families with two to four parameters. All of them have shapes similar to that of a typical learning curve.

Learning points are obtained by running the two classification algorithms on eight UCI data sets. By using all available data of a data set for learning, we fit a *full-length* learning curve; by using a small portion of the data, we fit a *part-length* learning curve. The models are then compared in terms of two performances: (1) how well they fit a *full-length* learning curve (called *fitting performance* hereafter in this paper), and (2) how well a fitted *part-length* learning curve can predict (extrapolate) the learning accuracy at the full length (called *predicting performance* hereafter in this paper). Our experiments show that the three-parameter power law ($y = a - b * x^{-c}$) is overall the best model in both the performances for the two algorithms and all the data sets. This result provides empirical support for applying the power law to fitting learning curves for large data sets, thus paves the way for applying learning curves to data mining.

2 Candidate Models, Algorithms, and Data Sets

The six candidate models used in this study are briefly described in Table 1. All of them are non-linear and respectively belong to three different major function families: *Power Law* family, *Exponential* family and *Sigmoidal* family. Figure 1 roughly illustrates their shapes, compared to the shape of a typical learning curve. From Figure 1, we can see that all the six models have the potential to fit a learning curve probably by tuning their parameters. Note that their parameters vary from two to four. From the view of mathematics, a model with too many parameters is either hard to converge or subject to over-fitting [16]. From the view of practice, such a model is also difficult to use. Therefore, we do not consider models with more than four parameters.

Table 1. The 6 Candidate Fitting Models

Model Name	Notion	Formula	Remarks
2-parameters Power Law	Pow1	$y = a * x^b$	$a > 0, b > 0$, Power Law family
Logarithm	Log	$y = a + b * log(x)$	Exponential family
3-parameters Power Law	Pow2	$y = a - b * x^{-c}$	$a > 0, b > 0, c > 0$, Power Law family
Vapor Pressure	Vap	$y = exp(a + b/x + c * log(x))$	Exponential family
MMF model	MMF	$y = (a * b + c * x^d)/(b + x^d)$	Sigmoidal family
Weibull	Wbl	$y = a - b * exp(-c * x^d)$	$a > 0, b > 0, c > 0$, Sigmoidal family

To facilitate the fitting process, we use the *Levenberg-Marquardt* method [2, 17] to solve nonlinear regression. This method combines the steepest-descent method and a Taylor series based method and has been proven to be a fast reliable technique for nonlinear optimization. We use the following setting in fitting with all models: random-guessed initial values for regression, $1.0e-06$ for the tolerance value of stopping iterations, the maximum iterations 100, and the maximum diverging iterations 100.

We choose C4.5 [15] and LOG [11] as representatives of two main categories of classification algorithms: decision tree method and statistical method [12]. The C4.5 is a popular decision tree induction system, and the **LOG** is a FORTRAN 90 implementation of logistic discriminant analysis. A comprehensive comparison of many classifiers [10] has reported that both algorithms tend to produce high classification accuracy. The eight large UCI benchmark data sets [3] used in this study are summarized in Table 2. Note that the number of instances of these

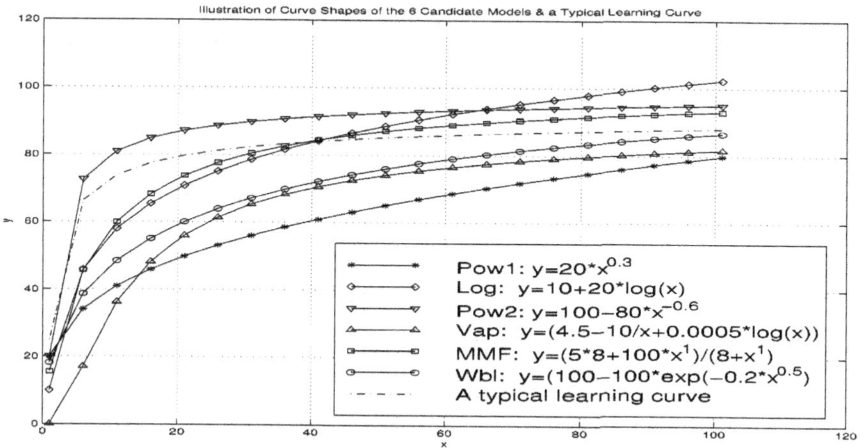

Fig. 1. Illustration of Curve Shapes of the 6 Candidate Models and a Typical Learning Curve

data sets range from three thousands to eighty thousands. Although they are not "very large" from the view of many real world applications of data mining [14], they are fairly "large" from the view of research.

Table 2. Descriptions of 8 UCI data sets

Data Set Name	Notion	Nominal Attribute	Numeric Attribute	Instances # for Training	Instances # for Testing	C4.5 max accuracy	LOG max accuracy
abalone	aba	1	7	3000	1177	45.0	25.6
adult	adu	8	6	36000	12842	85.8	83.1
letter	let	0	16	15000	5000	87.7	78.1
mushroom	mus	22	0	8000	2992	99.6	99.9
pendigits	pen	0	16	8000	2992	96.4	95.3
satellite	sat	0	36	4435	2000	91.5	83.8
thyroid	thy	15	6	3772	3428	99.6	95.9
waveform	wav	0	21	80000	40000	99.0	87.5

3 Fitting Performance

3.1 Criterion of Comparison

We use standard error of the estimates S to measure the performance of non-linear curve fitting and report correlation coefficient r for reference. The standard error of the estimate is defined as $S = \sqrt{(\sum_{i=1}^{n}(y_i - f(x_i))^2)/(n-m)}$, where n is number of points, m is number of parameters in the model, $n-m$ is actually the number of degrees of freedom, (x_i, y_i) is the ith point to be fitted, and $f(x)$ is the fitted model. The correlation coefficient is defined as $r = \sqrt{(S_t - S_r)/S_t}$, where S_t is the deviation of the points from their mean value $\bar{y} = (\sum_{i=1}^{n} y_i)/n$, $S_t = \sum_{i=1}^{n}(y_i - \bar{y})^2$, S_r is the deviation of the points from the fitted curve, $S_r = \sum_{i=1}^{n}(y_i - f(x_i))^2$. For a perfect fit, there will be $S_r = 0$, thus $r = 1$.

3.2 Results of Fitting

For each data set, we fit its C4.5 learning curve and LOG learning curve respectively. To get learning points for fitting a full-length learning curve, we use an uniform sampling size scheme: 1%, 5%, 10%, 20%, 30%, 40%, 50%, 60%, 70%, 80%, 90%, and 100% of the all available data. For each size, a random sample is drawn from the total training data and used to train a classifier, which is then tested against the testing data. This procedure is repeated 10 times to get an average learning accuracy for the size. Finally, twelve learning points are obtained for each data set. Then each of the six candidate models is used to fit these learning points. Due to the space limit, we omit the results of fitting C4.5 and LOG learning curves. Readers can refer to [6] for detailed results. The overall ranking of the six models in terms of S value on the eight data sets are shown in Table 3 and Table 4. From the four tables, we observe that:

Table 3. Ranks of C4.5 Fitting

Models	Sum of S ranks over 8 data sets	Average	Overall Rank
Pow1	$6+6+6+6+6+6+6+5=47$	5.9	6
Log	$5+5+5+5+5+5+5+4=39$	4.9	5
Pow2	$1+3+2+2+2+3+3+3=19$	2.4	3
Vap	$2+4+4+4+4+4+4+6=32$	4.0	4
MMF	$3+1+3+3+1+1+2+1=15$	1.9	1
Wbl	$4+2+1+1+3+2+1+2=16$	2.0	2

Table 4. Ranks of LOG Fitting

Models	Sum of S ranks over 8 data sets	Average	Overall Rank
Pow1	$6+6+6+6+6+6+6+6=48$	6.0	6
Log	$5+5+5+5+5+5+5+5=40$	5.0	5
Pow2	$3+1+4+3+3+4+3+3=24$	3.0	3
Vap	$4+3+3+4+4+5+4+4=31$	3.9	4
MMF	$1+4+2+1+2+1+1+1=13$	1.6	2
Wbl	$2+1+1+1+1+2+2+2=12$	1.5	1

(1) In most cases, the models with more parameters tend to have smaller S values, thus are ranked in front, suggesting their higher performance in fitting. This is not surprising from the view of mathematics.
(2) In most cases, the models with the same number of parameters tend to have close S values, suggesting their similar performance in fitting. This is also not surprising from the view of mathematics.
(3) In most cases, the models with three and four parameters are significantly better than the two models with two parameters, while the S values between three-parameters models and four-parameters models are not significantly different.

Note that using one more parameter does increase the complexity of the fitting process. But, if it did not significantly increase the fitting accuracy, we would rather not use it. The above observations suggest that models with two parameters seems not enough to fit well a full-length learning curve, while using four parameters seems redundant. Therefore, in fitting learning curves, a model with three parameters seems a trade-off between model complexity and model accuracy. In this sense, the three-parameters power law should be the best in fitting the full-length learning curves.

However, this result is less attractive to data mining, because obtaining a full-length learning curve requires the fitted learning points cover the x-axis range from a small size up to the full size of the data set. And to obtain the learning accuracy at the large or full size, we must run the learning algorithm on a large amount of the available data thus involve high computational cost. This is obviously opposite to our motivation of applying learning curve to data mining. Therefore, it is necessary to examine the predicting performance of the models as we describe in the next section.

4 Predicting Performance

A model may become less attractive to learning on large data sets if it is strong in *fitting performance* but weak in *predicting performance*. Given two models with similar fitting performance, the one with higher predicting performance is more desirable to data mining. In this section, we compare the six candidate models with respect to this performance. Instead of fitting a *full-length* learning curve for each data set, we intentionally fit a *part-length* one on a small portion of the whole available data, then we extrapolate it to the full length to see whether it can predict the learning accuracy at that size accurately. The predicted accuracy is compared to the observed full-size learning accuracy given in Table 2. The model that gives the less difference between the predicted and the observed is considered the better.

However, this implies an essential but still open issue: how many instances are adequate to support a good extrapolation. Although we hope to use as fewer instances as possible to obtain enough learning points (the pairs of $(Size, Acc)$), the learning points corresponding to too small amount of instances will exhibit too little information about the shape of the whole learning curve so that no model can properly "guess" the latter trend of the curve. This is obvious in mathematics: given a segment of a curve, one can arbitrarily extend it to any shape. Frey and Fisher [5] mention this issue, however, they only test a 15% portion of a data set. Intuitively, the larger the portion, the more accurate the extrapolation. To find out how the predicting performance will be affected by size of the portions, we intentionally test four portions for each data set, covering 5%, 10%, 15%, and 20% of the total data. For each portion, A part-length learning curve is fitted from 10 learning points that equally span the interval of the portion. Like in the previous section, learning accuracy at each size is averaged from 10 runs on random samples with that size.

The differences (in percentage) between the prediction and the observation on the 100% size (i.e., $diff = y_{predicted} - y_{observed}$) for the two classification algorithms are reported respectively in Table 5 and Table 6, for all data sets and the four portions. In both tables, for each portion of a data set, the names of models that rank the first three in terms of $|diff|$ is reported in the rightmost three columns of that portion, while the bottom six rows report the ranking of the six models averaged on the eight data sets for each portion and the overall ranking for the four portions. From the two tables, we have the following observations:

(1) The predicting performance of a model may differ greatly with data sets. For example, the logarithm model can predict LOG learning accuracy very well in *adult* ($|diff| < 1.5\%$ for all the portions) but very bad in *letter* ($|diff| > 20\%$ for the 5% portion and 10% portion).

(2) The predicting performance of a model may greatly differ with algorithms. This can be seen from their ranking. For example, the Pow2 overall ranks best for both C4.5 and LOG, however, in its C4.5 predicting, for all data sets and all portions, it ranks in the first three, while in its LOG predicting, for some portions of some data sets, it ranks out of the first three. This can also be seen from the $|diff|$. For example, in the C4.5 predictions of Pow2, the $|diff|$ values for all data sets and all portions are less than 3%, except 4.27% for *abalone* and 3.4% for *waveform* on the 5% portion, while in its LOG predictions, the $|diff|$ becomes 16% for *abalone* and 11.72% for *waveform* on the 5% portion.

(3) There is no model that consistently makes the best prediction for all portions on all data sets.

(4) The averaged ranking show that the three-parameters power law tends to have the best predicting performance.

The first two observations are not out of our expectations, because similar observations have been shown by previous studies (but typically for small data sets). And the two observations may also account much for the third observation. In the presence of the three observations, the fourth observation shows that the three-parameters power law is more robust than the others with respect to the two classification algorithms as well as the eight data sets, and also more robust with respect to the amount of data used in fitting the *part-length* learning curves. Although the MMF and Weibull are better than the three-parameter power law in accuracy when fitting *full-length* learning curves, they lose to the latter in the predicting performance. This is probably because given only a segment of a whole learning curve, models with four parameters tend to overfit it, while

Table 5. Predicting Performance Comparison of C4.5

Data	Portion	Pow1	Log	Pow2	Vap	MMF	Wbl	Rank 1,2,3
aba	5%	14.12	9.34	4.27	7.97	2.78	3.35	MMF, Wbl, Pow2
	10%	12.64	9.67	-0.04	-0.03	-1.85	-2.32	Vap, Pow2, MMF
	15%	3.09	2.67	-0.58	-0.17	-1.43	-1.67	Vap, Pow2, MMF
	20%	1.84	1.62	1.05	1.70	-0.59	0.62	MMF, Wbl, Pow2
adu	5%	7.28	6.56	0.39	2.38	-0.69	-1.65	Pow2, MMF, Wbl
	10%	2.04	1.91	1.03	1.72	0.19	0.99	MMF, Wbl, Pow2
	15%	1.59	1.51	1.00	1.83	0.52	1.70	MMF, Pow2, log
	20%	1.64	1.58	0.50	0.93	-0.17	0.26	MMF, Wbl, Pow2
let	5%	24.89	9.31	1.22	14.56	-8.85	-15.81	Pow2, MMF, Log
	10%	13.27	6.05	-0.11	5.58	-2.85	-5.27	Pow2, MMF, Wbl
	15%	9.73	5.02	0.62	5.48	-3.16	-7.44	Pow2, MMF, Vap
	20%	8.32	4.75	1.08	3.85	-2.60	-3.31	Pow2, MMF, Wbl
mus	5%	23.82	18.75	-2.46	-1.06	-2.48	-3.10	Vap, Pow2, MMF
	10%	10.81	9.40	0.07	2.12	-0.07	-0.81	Pow2, MMF, Wbl
	15%	6.76	6.11	-0.42	0.57	-0.48	-0.64	Pow2, MMF, Vap
	20%	4.69	4.34	-0.64	-0.14	-0.65	-0.74	Vap, Pow2, MMF
pen	5%	31.85	21.31	-0.69	6.13	-0.81	-1.53	Pow2, MMF, Wbl
	10%	15.20	11.75	0.80	4.67	0.65	0.36	Wbl, MMF, Pow2
	15%	9.24	7.60	0.57	2.93	-1.47	-2.35	Pow2, MMF, Wbl
	20%	6.04	5.15	-0.06	1.46	-0.97	-1.28	Pow2, Wbl, MMF
sat	5%	23.15	17.76	-2.34	-0.72	-2.49	-3.49	Vap, Pow2, MMF
	10%	7.78	6.68	-3.02	-3.11	-3.52	-3.62	Pow2, Vap, MMF
	15%	3.60	3.14	-1.40	-0.28	-1.62	-1.77	Vap, Pow2, MMF
	20%	1.95	1.71	-0.93	-0.11	-1.21	-1.07	Vap, Pow2, Wbl
thy	5%	12.02	10.52	-1.68	-0.62	-1.77	-2.07	Vap, Pow2, MMF
	10%	5.80	5.35	0.68	2.20	0.22	0.41	MMF, Wbl, Pow2
	15%	3.17	3.00	0.63	1.47	0.03	0.13	MMF, Wbl, Pow2
	20%	2.69	2.57	0.42	1.00	-0.73	-0.14	Wbl, Pow2, MMF
wav	5%	-2.02	-2.39	-3.40	2.14	5.40	7.83	Pow1, Vap, Log
	10%	0.77	0.32	-0.68	2.24	3.20	2.43	Log, Pow2, Pow1
	15%	1.69	1.28	-0.01	2.07	1.97	2.15	Pow2, Log, Pow1
	20%	1.66	1.32	0.38	2.79	2.20	2.87	Pow2, Log, Pow1
Rank	**Portion**	**Pow1**	**Log**	**Pow2**	**Vap**	**MMF**	**Wbl**	**Remarks**
Aver-age	5%	6	5	1	3	3	4	average over 8 data sets for each portion
	10%	6	5	1	4	2	3	
	15%	6	5	1	3	2	5	
	20%	6	5	1	4	2	3	
Overall Rank		6	5	1	3	2	4	over all portions

Table 6. Predicting Performance Comparison of LOG

Data	Portion	Pow1	Log	Pow2	Vap	MMF	Wbl	Rank 1,2,3
aba	5%	-9.40	-14.98	-16.89	-3.80	-21.22	-23.67	Vap, Pow1, Log
	10%	-14.84	-16.85	-11.65	-12.70	-20.10	-21.17	Pow2, Vap, Pow1
	15%	-15.03	-16.59	-14.14	-14.30	-19.94	-21.26	Pow2, Vap, Pow1
	20%	-16.14	-17.05	-14.51	-17.45	-19.20	-19.59	Pow2, Pow1, Log
adu	5%	1.91	1.40	0.35	7.00	8.64	8.31	Pow2, Log, Pow1
	10%	1.29	1.04	-3.34	-2.87	-3.38	-3.51	Log, Pow1, Vap
	15%	-1.54	-1.61	-2.07	-1.32	-2.16	-1.38	Vap, Wbl, Pow1
	20%	0.60	0.45	-0.39	0.19	-1.66	-0.77	Vap, Pow2, Log
let	5%	68.47	20.24	8.17	31.88	10.82	5.50	Wbl, Pow2, MMF
	10%	44.62	20.68	13.97	38.73	-5.21	-11.12	MMF, Wbl, Pow2
	15%	23.63	13.42	4.52	9.53	-3.08	-9.74	MMF, Pow2, Vap
	20%	11.80	7.34	-5.49	-5.40	-7.01	-10.72	Vap, Pow2, MMF
mus	5%	5.04	4.73	0.04	1.39	-0.85	-1.65	Pow2, MMF, Vap
	10%	3.56	3.42	1.02	1.92	0.75	0.78	MMF, Wbl, Pow2
	15%	2.59	2.51	0.72	1.26	0.64	0.59	Wbl, MMF, Pow2
	20%	1.57	1.54	0.90	1.14	0.77	1.12	MMF, Pow2, Wbl
pen	5%	20.01	13.81	1.36	8.07	-1.34	-1.10	Wbl, MMF, Pow2
	10%	5.92	4.42	-5.35	-3.88	-6.48	-7.37	Vap, Log, Pow2
	15%	3.67	2.70	0.65	2.07	-0.11	0.72	MMF, Pow2, Wbl
	20%	4.60	3.71	1.96	3.85	2.23	3.10	Pow2, MMF, Wbl
sat	5%	10.36	3.92	-18.56	-22.93	-19.36	-19.54	Log, Pow1, Pow2
	10%	-0.25	-3.10	-5.29	16.63	48.74	16.57	Pow1, Log, Pow2
	15%	5.90	2.77	0.50	12.50	-0.95	2.39	Pow2, MMF, Wbl
	20%	-1.26	-2.85	-4.21	7.14	-3.11	3.01	Pow1, Log, Wbl
thy	5%	5.43	3.55	0.88	15.30	-4.65	8.43	Pow2, Log, MMF
	10%	7.50	5.89	3.33	11.87	-4.03	7.80	Pow2, MMF, Log
	15%	3.97	3.30	0.86	2.37	-3.63	-0.94	Pow2, Wbl, Vap
	20%	4.15	3.58	-0.82	0.38	-1.74	-3.05	Vap, Pow2, MMF
wav	5%	-8.19	-8.29	-11.72	-12.15	-11.80	-11.88	Pow1, Log, Pow2
	10%	-10.26	-10.28	-11.69	-11.95	-11.76	-11.44	Pow1, Log, Wbl
	15%	-10.97	-10.97	-11.48	-11.35	-11.60	-11.06	Pow1, Log, Wbl
	20%	-11.18	-11.18	-11.51	-11.43	-11.54	-11.20	Pow1, Log, Wbl
Rank	**Portion**	**Pow1**	**Log**	**Pow2**	**Vap**	**MMF**	**Wbl**	**Remarks**
Aver-age	5%	4	2	1	6	3	5	average over 8 data sets for each portion
	10%	3	2	1	5	4	6	
	15%	6	5	1	3	4	2	
	20%	6	3	1	2	4	5	
Overall Rank		6	2	1	4	3	5	over all portions

models with two parameters tend to underfit it, thus both negatively affect their extrapolation. Combined with the results of fitting performance as shown in the previous section, these results show that the three-parameter power law is the best in both performance thus should be the first considered model to fit learning curve for the large data sets in our experiments.

5 Conclusion and Future Research

The benefit of obtaining an accurate learning curve of large data sets lies in that we are able to use it to predict: (1) what is the achievable learning accuracy for a given amount of training data, (2) how many training data is needed to reach a desirable learning accuracy, and (3) when to stop the learning process according the predictable gain in learning accuracy. The benefit of choosing a good model for fitting learning curves lies in that we are able to use it to obtain the desired learning curve without too much learning effort that may cover a large amount of data, thus can save much computation cost.

In this empirical study, aiming at finding a model that fits well learning curves for large data sets, we compare six candidate models that come from three functional families with two to four parameters. We compare their fitting performance (how well they fit a *full-length* learning curves) and predicting performance (how well they extrapolate to the full length by a fitted *part-length* learning curve), for eight large UCI benchmark data sets and two typical classification algorithms. Our experimental results show that the three-parameters power law ($y = a - b * x^{-c}$) is the best among the six models in both the performances. It also exhibits another salient advantage: it is less susceptible to the two classification algorithms and the eight benchmark data sets than the other models. This suggests its possible applicability to other learning algorithms and various data sets. Therefore our results should be useful in facilitating various data mining tasks with large data sets.

Our experiments also reveal that even the best model also has varying predicting performance; sometimes the performance could vary significantly with learning algorithms as well as data sets. Therefore, we should not simply rule out the other models. More detailed study should be conducted with more learning algorithms and more data sets to investigate under which circumstances which models are more appropriate. Another more pressing issue on our immediate agenda is that as the predicting performance depends on the amount of data used in generating learning points for fitting, how we can confidently decide this amount effectively.

References

1. S. Amari, N. Fujita, and S. Shinomoto. Four types of learning curves. *Neural Computation*, 4(4):605–618, 1992.
2. Yonathan Bard. *Nonlinear Parameter Estimation.* Academic Press, 1974.
3. C.L. Blake and C.J. Merz. UCI repository of machine learning databases, 1998. (http://www.ics.uci.edu/~mlearn/MLRepository.html).

4. C. Cortes. *Prediction of Generalization Ability in Learning Machines.* PhD thesis, Department of Computer Science, University of Rochester, New York, 1993.
5. L.J. Frey and D.H. Fisher. Modeling decision tree performance with the power law. In *Proceedings of the Seventh International Workshop on Artificial Intelligence and Statistics.* Morgan Kaufmann, 1999.
6. B.H. Gu, F.F. Hu, and H. Liu. An empirical study of fitting learning curves. Technical report, Department of Computer Science, National University of Singapore, 2001.
7. H. Gu and H. Takahashi. Exponential or polynomial learning curves?—-case-based studies. *Neural Computation*, 12(4):795–809, 2000.
8. G.H. John and P. Langley. Static versus dynamic sampling for data mining. In *Proceedings of the Second International Conference on Knowledge Discovery and Data Mining (KDD'96).* AAAI / MIT Press, 1996.
9. C.M. Kadie. *Seer: Maximum Likelihood Regression for Learning-Speed Curves.* PhD thesis, Department of Computer Science, University of Illinois at Urbana-Champaign, 1995.
10. T. Lim, W. Loh, and Y. Shih. A comparison of prediction accuracy, complexity, and training time of thirty-three old and new classification algorithms. *Machine Learning*, 1999.
11. Tjen-Sien Lim. Users' guide for logdiscr version 2.0, 1999. (http://recursive-partitioning.com/logdiscr/).
12. D. Michie, D.J. Spiegelhalter, and C.C. Taylor. *Machine Learning, Neural and Statistical Classification.* Ellis Horwood Limited, Campus 400, Maylands Avenue, Hemel Hempstead, Hertfordshire, HP2 7EZ, England, 1994.
13. F. Provost, D. Jensen, and T. Oates. Efficient progressive sampling. In *Proceedings of the fifth ACM SIGKDD international conference on Knowledge discovery and data mining(KDD'99)*, pages 23–32. AAAI/MIT Press, 1999.
14. F. Provost and V. Kolluri. A survey of methods for scaling up inductive algorithms. *Machine Learning*, pages 1–42, 1999.
15. J.R. Quinlan. *C4.5: Programs for Machine Learning.* Morgan Kaufmann, San Mateo, CA, 1993. (http://www.cse.unsw.edu.au/ quinlan/).
16. D. A. Ratkowsky. *Handbook of Nonlinear Regression Models.* Marcel Dekker, INC., 1990.
17. G.A.F. Seber and C.J. Wild. *Nonlinear regression.* Wiley & Sons, 1989.

Mapping Referential Integrity Constraints from Relational Databases to XML[1]

Xiaochun Yang and Guoren Wang

Dept. of Computer Science & Engineering, Northeastern University, Shenyang, 110006, P.R.China
yangxc73@263.net wanggr@mail.neu.edu.cn

Abstract. XML is rapidly emerging as the dominant standard for exchanging data on the WWW. Most of application data are stored in relational databases due to its popularity and rich development experiences over it. Therefore, how to provide a proper mapping approach from relational data to XML documents becomes an important topic. Referential integrity constraints are useful for semantic specification that plays the important roles in relation schema definition. So far, there are about a dozen of XML schema languages have been proposed. Although most languages are based on DTD, they have different grammar resulting in the XML world more complicated. In this paper, we investigate referential integrity constraints for XML. An extended DTD with several kinds of constraints-DTD_C is proposed, and a corresponding equivalent mapping approach, ICMAP is presented. Finally, the comparison on the respect of constraint representation capability is performed, which proves that ICMAP is more effective than other known approaches.

1 Introduction

With the booming development of network, the requirement for sharing information becomes one of key problems. However, in the foreseeable future, most business data will continue to be stored in relational database systems because of the widely uses and rich developing experiences associated with relational database systems. On the other hand, XML is rapidly emerging as a standard for exchanging business data on the WWW[1]. Therefore, transformation from relational data to XML data becomes one of the primary research problems in the field of current information exchanging, sharing and integration.

As a standard for exchanging business data on the WWW, XML should provide the ability of expressing data and semantics among heterogeneous data sources on the WWW. How to express integrity constraints in XML is a very important research issue because they play the key roles in specifying semantics[2], maintaining data consistency[3], optimizing queries[4], and integrating information[5]. In the relational

[1] This work is partially supported by the Teaching and Research Award Program for Outstanding Young Teachers in Higher Education Institutions and the Cross Century Excellent Young Teacher Foundation of the Ministry of Education of China, the Natural Science Foundation (69803004) of China.

X.S. Wang, G. Yu, and H. Lu (Eds.): WAIM 2001, LNCS 2118, pp. 329-340, 2001.

model, there are mainly three kinds of integrity constraints including domain constraints, referential integrity constraints, and general constraints. Referential integrity constraints are considered to be a fundamental part of the relational data model and paid more attentions in most commercial systems, and consist of primary key, candidate key and foreign key.

So far, there are mainly six XML schema languages that have been proposed, such as XML DTD[1], XML Schema[6], XDR[7], SOX[8], Schematron[9] and DSD[10], among which XML Schema and Schematron are superior with respect to the expressiveness of constraints. XML Schema is an ongoing effort of W3C to aid DTD in the XML world. Different languages have different grammars that result in the XML world more complicated. Moreover, the philosophies by which each language has been designed are quite different. Therefore, one language should not be regarded as superior to the others[11]. Most languages have a common property that they are based on the existing DTD. The ID/IDREF(s) mechanism of DTD has similarities to both the identity-based notions of references from object-oriented database and keys/foreign keys from relational databases. It helps to refer to an element easily in an XML document. Therefore, this paper focuses on an equivalent mapping method from relational data to XML data based on DTD's unary ID/IDREF(s).

A number of recent proposals aimed at transformation from popular databases to XML documents. The YAT system[12] developed by INRIA is a semistructured data conversion and integration system that adopts XML as a middleware model for wrappers, mediators to communicate data, structures and operations. IBM Almaden Research Center [13] characterized the solution space based on the main differences between XML documents and relations, studied on the mapping problems at data level and provided a significant performance benefit. Pennsylvania University [14,15] studied constraint implication problems, concerning path and type constraints, object identifier, and inverse reference. The AT&T labs developed a general, dynamic and efficient tool, SilkRoute[16], for viewing and querying relational data in XML. However, as we know, the existing researches mostly focused on querying underlying popular databases and exporting the query results into XML data. This kind of approach is suitable for exchanging data between different applications. However, from the point of view to keep constraint semantics, the existing researches have the following problems to be studied further.

1. Mapping Keys. Papers [12,15] only considered constraint mapping for object-oriented databases. Each object identifier was mapped into an XML ID attribute. Unfortunately, it did not describe how to map keys into XML data. While paper [13] mainly considered the issues of data mapping for relational databases, by which, the keys in a table are mapped into XML attributes directly. Paper [15] studied on integrity constraint mapping for object-oriented databases and relational databases. The mapping mechanism is similar to [12-14]. These approaches have the same problems that if keys are mapped into XML ID attributes, they will become invisible data in XML document. In fact, the role of keys not only identifies a tuple, but also has explicit meaning, e.g., attribute SSN(Social Security Number) can be regarded as a key in a table. The above mapping can not represent equivalently the data originating from relational database.
2. Mapping Foreign Keys. Every table arising from a relationship has referential integrity constraints. Each primary key in a table for the relationship is a foreign key. Mapping many-to-many relationships with attributes is still an unresolved problem. Most proposals[12,13] merely provided solutions for transformation of

foreign keys associated with one-to-one and one-to-many relationships. Other methods [14,15] used two inverse one-to-many relationships to represent a many-to-many relationship. All of these approaches did not consider how to map relationships with attributes.

3. Mapping Composite Keys and Composite Foreign Keys. The above approaches have another common problem that they provided mapping approaches only for simple keys and simple foreign keys, not for composite keys and composite foreign keys.

Keeping constraints semantic is useful for optimizing and maintaining distributed semantic constraints[17]. In order to provide an effective mechanism to solve the above problems, this paper presents a Document Type Definition with Constraints(DTD_C) and corresponding XML document with Constraints(XML_C), designs a DTD_C based mapping approach (ICMAP) to map relational data and its referential integrity constraints into XML_C document. DTD_C is an extended DTD that is used to define the referential integrity constraints for XML_C by ignoring the exact syntax definition. XML_C is an XML document conforming to DTD_C definition whose instances still conform to XML grammar. ICMAP only extends DTD, without changing the primary XML document instances. In order to ensure semantic-lossless mapping, keys/foreign keys are mapped into elements as well as ID/IDREF attributes, the mapped elements and attributes are used to represent data and semantics, respectively. As for composite keys/foreign keys, ICMAP only changes the constructing method for attribute values, and reduces the scope and type of an ID/IDREF attribute by specifying key attributes. Moreover, a bi-directional referential mechanism is constructed to support path constraints in semistructured data by defining multi-valued foreign key constraints. According to the four different options of enforcing referential integrity constraints, the hierarchy based and constraint based mapping rules are proposed. Both of these two mapping rules can transform many-to-many relationships with attributes that was not studied by any existing mapping approaches to the best of our knowledge.

The rest of the paper is organized as follows. Section 2 discusses the representation ability of XML and relational databases for referential integrity constraints. Section 3 proposes DTD_C and XML_C. Section 4 presents the ICMAP approach including mapping rules and construction method. Section 5 performs the comparison on the respect of constraint representation capability, which proves that ICMAP is more effective than other known approaches. Finally, Section 6 concludes the whole paper.

2 Referential Integrity Constraints in RDB and XML

Neither relational model nor XML is a semantic model having deficient semantic description capability. Relational database adopts flat table to express the relationship among entities, and uses DDL to define integrity constraints to express semantics among data implicitly. XML adopts a nested structure, and uses DTD's ID/IDREFs to support the referential mechanism.

Here is a simple example of teaching database. *char* and *integer* distinguish the domain constraints of each attribute, *primary key* defines primary keys of each table, *foreign key* defines foreign keys referring to other tables. Attribute *ano* is the primary key of *advisor*, while *ano* field of *student* is a foreign key and refers to *advisor*.

```
Create table advisor (ano char(10) NOT NULL,
   ano char(20) NOT NULL, primary key (ano) );
Create table student (sno char(10) NOT NULL,
   ano char(10), age integer, primary key(sno),
   foreign key(ano) references advisor,
   on delete cascade);
```

Different from relational databases, XML documents are in hierarchical format having arbitrary nested structures with a singleton root element. Each element has a tag associated with it. An element can have attributes and values or nested sub-elements. ID annotation indicates that the associated elements should be uniquely identified by it. IDREF(s) are logic pointer(s) referring to the associated elements with the same ID attribute value. ID and IDREF(s) are both based on unary attribute, and attributes are invisible when browsing XML documents.

3 XML Documents with Constraint Type

We first introduce some notations to facilitate expression. Given an XML document, let E be a set of instances of all elements in the document, τ be an element type in the document, $Attr(\tau)$ be a set of attribute of type τ, *Atom* be a set of all atomic types. We use $Ext(\tau)$ to denote the set of nodes labeled by τ in E, we use $\tau.l$ to indicate the value of the attribute l of τ. Furthermore, we use $p \quad q$ to represent that p implicates q.

Definition 1 DTD with Constraints (DTD$_C$). A DTD$_C$ is an extended DTD with constraints. A DTD$_C$ is denoted by (D, V, Σ), where:

- D is a standard DTD structure, $D = ((T, r, P), K)$,
  - (T, r, P) is a context free grammar represented by EBNF. T is a finite set of element types τ in E; r is the element type of the root, $r \quad T$; P is a function: $T \quad \alpha\bullet\alpha \quad E$, $\alpha ::= \quad | \alpha^* | \alpha^+ | \alpha? | \alpha,\alpha | \tau | Atom$, α is a regular expression covering all nodes ($E \quad$ #PCDATA) in XML, denotes the empty value, „*" stands for the Kleene closure, „+" for at least one α, „?" for zero or one α, and „," stands for the concatenation.
  - K is a partial function identifying the ID and IDREF(s) attributes: $\bigcup_{\tau \quad T} Attr(\tau) \quad$ {ID,IDREF, IDREFs},
- V is a value constraint function $Ext(\tau) \quad Attr(\tau)$, denotes that the values of $Attr(\tau)$ are originated from $Ext(\tau)$,
- Σ is a set of basic XML constraints recording all kinds of constraints that can be mapped into XML document instances.

Definition 2 Primary Key Constraint. Suppose $l \quad Attr(\tau)$, if $\forall x,y \quad Ext(\tau)(x.l = y.l \quad x = y)$, the attribute l is the primary key of type τ. Primary key constraint can be expressed in the formula (1).

$$\tau.l \quad \tau \tag{1}$$

In XML documents, references are based on unary attributes, hence l $Attr(\tau)$. Formula (1) denotes that if $\tau.l$ τ, then for any l' l, we have $\tau.l' / \tau$, i.e., l is the primary key of type τ.

Definition 3 Foreign Key Constraint. Suppose l $Attr(\tau)$, $\tau'.l'$ τ', if $\forall x$ $Ext(\tau)\exists y$ $Ext(\tau')$ $(x.l=y.l')$, the attribute l of type τ is the foreign key referring to type τ'. Foreign key constraint can be defined as Formula (2). Clearly, if there is a foreign key constraint $\tau.l$ $_{f}$ $\tau'.l'$, then $\tau'.l'$ τ' must be true.

$$\tau.l \quad _{f}\,\tau'.l' \tag{2}$$

Definition 4 Multi-valued Foreign Key Constraint. Suppose l $Attr(\tau)$, $\tau'.l'$ τ', if $\forall x$ $Ext(\tau)\exists Y$ $Ext(\tau')(x.l=Y.l')$, then the attribute l of type τ is the multi-valued foreign key referring to type τ'. Multi-valued foreign key constraint can be defined as Formula (3). Clearly, if there is a multi-valued foreign key constraint $\tau.l$ $_{mf}\tau'.l'$, then $\tau'.l'$ τ' must be true.

$$\tau.l \quad _{mf}\,\tau'.l' \tag{3}$$

In relational databases, the implication and finite implication problems for candidate keys are undecidable[14], so we only provide mapping approaches for primary keys and foreign keys.

Definition 5 Document with Constraints (XML$_C$). An XML document: (E, A, V_o, *entry*) can be said as a document with constraints respecting to a DTD$_C$, if and only if there is a mapping $f: E$ A V_o T {*Atom*}, such that:

- E is a set of instances of all elements in XML$_C$,
- A is a set of all attribute values in XML$_C$,
- V_o is the set of type of all atomic values, $\forall$value V_o, f(value)=*Atom*,
- *entry* is the root of the XML$_C$ document, $f(r)$=*entry*,
- XML$_C$ logically implicates the constraint set Σ.

4 ICMAP Mapping Approach

4.1 Basic Table Mapping

Rule 1 Basic Table Mapping. Given a table R(A) in a relational database. $\forall$a1,a2,…,an A, the mapping rule for the basic table is listed as follows.

- The table name and attribute name are mapped into the tags of the associated elements of XML$_C$: $T_{new} = T_{old}$ {R, a_1, a_2,…, a_n},
- All tuples of the table R are mapped into sub-elements of root element of XML$_C$: P_{new}(r) = P_{old}(r) {R*},
- All attribute values of table R are mapped into sub-elements of elements labeled by tag R: P_{new}(R)={ a_1, a_2,…, a_n },
- $\Sigma_{new} = \Sigma_{old}$.

4.2 Primary Key Mapping

In most existing approaches, keys in relational databases are transformed to ID attributes to maintain referential semantics in XML. Actually, in relational databases, keys have concrete application meaning besides identifying tuples in a table. Because an attribute is invisible in XML document, the concrete application meaning will be lost if a key is only mapped into an ID attribute. In addition, a key can be composite in relational databases, while the ID is a unary attribute of XML. Therefore, it is impossible to map a composite key to an ID attribute. In our mapping approach, a primary key is mapped into elements and an associated attribute. The following mapping rule only focuses on how to construct a mapped attribute for a primary key while construction of mapped elements is already discussed in the mapping for basic tables.

Rule 2 Primary Key Mapping. Given a table R(A, B) in a relational database. Let X denote the primary key of R. $\forall a_1,a_2,\ldots,a_n$ X, $\forall b_1,b_2,\ldots,b_m$ Y, the mapping rule for primary key X is given as follows.

- Let l be ID attribute of element R to express primary key in relational table R: *Attr*(R)={l}, *K*(R.l) = ID,
- The value of ID attribute l is constructed by the value of primary key in table R: $V(R.l)= {}_{i=1}^{n} a_i$,
- Add primary key constraint into the constraint set: $\Sigma_{new}= \Sigma_{old}$ {R.l R}.

Generally, in a table, the size of key values is small, thus we can duplicate the key values to construct ID attributes in an XML_C document. In Fig. 1a, = is a symbol to express that the value of attribute l comes from the composite values of the associated elements. Thus the mapped data can be displayed lossless by mapping keys into elements besides ID attributes, i.e., if the primary key of a table is a composite attribute, it is enough to construct an one-to-one mapped attribute value corresponding with the unary ID (e.g., let ${}_{i=1}^{n} a_i$ be the mapped value of $\{a_1,a_2,\ldots,a_n\}$).

It should be noted that the primary keys of two different relational tables may have same values. It results in that $\tau.l$ τ, $\tau'.l'$ τ', $\forall x$ $Ext(\tau)\exists y$ $Ext(\tau')$ $(x.l=y.l')$ in the same mapped XML_C, i.e., the ID attributes of two different element types τ and τ' may have the same values. In XML specification, the scope and type of the ID/IDREF(s) are limited in the whole document. While in XML_C, we use constraints $\tau.l$ τ and $\tau'.l'$ τ' to limit the scope of the ID in the same element type by changing slightly the constraints on the attributes involved.

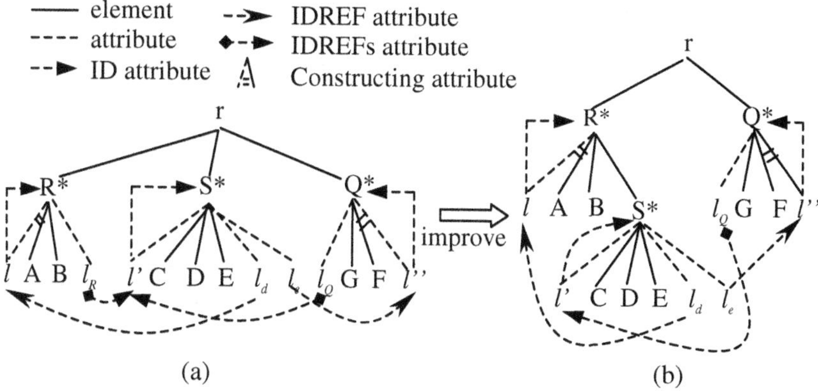

Fig. 1. Mapping Primary Key/Foreign Key into DTD_C. (a) Constraint based mapping, (b) Hierarchy based optimized mapping

4.3 Foreign Key Mapping

In relational databases, a table having foreign keys referring to other tables can be an entity as well as a relationship between entities. For convenience, we will use three tables R(A, B), S(C, D, E) and Q(F, G) to represent multiple tables R_i, S_j and Q_k(1 i n,1 j m,1 k p) respectively.

Rule 3 Foreign Key Mapping. Given tables R(A, B), S(C, D, E) and Q(F, G) in a relational database, and suppose attributes A and F are primary keys of tables R and Q respectively, attributes D and E are foreign keys referring to tables R and Q respectively. A, B, …, and G can represent an attribute or a set of attributes: $A=\{a_1,a_2,\ldots,a_n\}$, $D=\{d_1,d_2,\ldots,d_l\}$, $E=\{e_1,e_2,\ldots,e_n\}$, $F=\{f_1,f_2,\ldots,f_l\}$, then the mapping rule for foreign key is given as follows.

- Let l_d, l_e be IDREF attributes of element S to express foreign keys referring to element R, Q in table S respectively: *Attr*(S)= *Attr*(S) $\{l_d, l_e\}$, $K(S.l_d)$ = IDREF, $K(S.l_e)$ = IDREF,
- Let l_R, l_Q be IDREFs attributes of element R, Q respectively to express inverse reference to element S: *Attr*(R)=*Attr*(R) $\{l_R\}$, *Attr*(Q)= *Attr*(Q) $\{l_Q\}$, $K(R.l_R)$ = IDREFs, $K(Q.l_Q)$ = IDREFs,
- The value of IDREF attributes l_d, l_e are constructed by the value of foreign keys D, E respectively in table S: $V(S.l_d)= \; {}_{i=1}^{l} d_i$, $V(S.l_e)= \; {}_{i=1}^{n} e_i$,
- Add foreign key constraints into the constraint set: $\Sigma_{new}=\Sigma_{old}$ $\{R.l_R \;{}_{mf} S.l', S.l_d \;{}_f R.l', S.l_e \;{}_f Q.l'', Q.l_Q \;{}_{mf} S.l'\}$,
- Constructs IDREFs attribute values from K and Σ_{new} of the mapped DTD_C, the algorithm is given as follows.

```
Algorithm CustIDREFS(dtdc: DTDC definition,
    mainElemExt: elements corresponding to main table,
    subElemExt: elements corresponding to sub table)
Begin
   count := 0;
   repeat   //search the subElemExt in relational table
      num := 0;
      repeat         // iterate mainElemExt
         tmpElem := mainElemExt[num];
         if (tmpElem.id=subElemExt[count].idref)
            InsertAttrValue(tmpElem.idrefs,
                                subElemExt[count].id);
         endif
         num := num +1;
      until iterate mainElemExtent over
      count := count +1;
   until search over
end
```

The mapped result of tables R, S and Q to DTD_C is shown in Fig. 1a. By constructing attributes l_R and l_Q, the bi-directional referential mechanism is implemented. Bi-directional referential mechanism can support the path constraints in semistructured data, e.g., if we start from root *r*, any element that is reached from *r* by following a R's edge followed by an l_R edge can also be reached from *r* by following a S's edge[2,15]. (The research of path constraints is out of the scope of this paper, so we will not discuss it in details).

Rules 1~3 give general mapping rules based on constraints. Intuitively, the hierarchy is more suitable for XML specification as well as the relationships in real world. Thus we tend to adopt hierarchy to represent the relationships between tables. By this way, some constraints can be replaced by hierarchy, so that the size of constraint set Σ can be reduced, and the corresponding cost of constraints evaluation and maintenance can be cut down.

Rule 4 Mapping Rule Optimization. Given element types R and S in an XML_C document, and assume that S is the sub-element of the root, elements A, B are sub-elements of R, elements C, D, E are sub-elements of S, attributes *l*, *l'* are ID attributes of R, S respectively, attribute l_R is IDREFs attribute of R referring to S, and attributes l_d is IDREF attribute referring to R. The optimization mapping rule for elements R and S is given as follows.

- $T_{new} = T_{old}$,
- Let S be sub-element of R, remove the attribute l_R and the edge between the *r* and S: P_{new}(r)=P_{old}(r)-{S*}, P_{new}(R)=P_{old}(R) {S*}, $Attr_{new}$(R)=$Attr_{old}$(R) −{l_R},
- Reduce constraint set Σ: Σ_{new}=Σ_{old} −{R.l_R $_{mf}$ S.*l'*}.

The procedure of optimized mapping is shown in Fig. 1b. In the hierarchical format of XML implies that element S can not be the sub-element of element R and element Q simultaneity. When S is associated with R and Q simultaneity, we only change one pair of constraints, e.g., constraints between R and S into hierarchy, and keep the other pair of constraints. In fact, the hierarchy like R and S can solve most of the instances in the real world, e.g., the relationships among university, department, faculty, student can be substituted for hierarchy.

4.4 Options for Enforcing Referential Integrity Constraints

Review the example in Section 2. As we know, the insertions of student tuples that violate referential integrity will be rejected. SQL-92 and the later SQL specifications provide several alternative ways to handle the deletions of *advisor* tuples that violate referential integrity by choosing the four options including *no action*, *cascade*, *set default*, and *set null* on *delete* and *update* operations.

The options are specified as part of the foreign key declaration. The default option is *no action*, which means that the action (*delete* or *update*) violating constraints is to be rejected. Let's analyse these options on the two mapping rules (Rule 3 and Rule 4) for foreign keys. Look at the mapping structures shown in Fig. 1.

1. CASCADE

- Using Rule 3: If a deletion of R elements violates referential integrity, ICMAP first searches the elements matching type S, then deletes the R elements and associated S elements. If an update of R elements violates referential integrity, R elements and the matched elements of type S are changed simultaneity.
- Using Rule 4: If a deletion of R elements violates referential integrity, the subtree begin from these R elements are deleted. If an update of R elements violates referential integrity, ICMAP only updates the sub-elements' inverse IDREF attributes of these R elements subtrees.

2. NO ACTION

- Using Rule 3: If a deletion/update of R elements' IDREFs is not *null*, it is means that the operation violates referential integrity, the deletion/update will be rejected.
- Using Rule 4: If delete/update an element with sub-elements, the deletion/update will be rejected.

3. SET DEFAULT

- Using Rule 3: Suppose there is an element *e'* of type R is regarded as the defalt element. If a deletion of R element *e* violates referential integrity, ICMAP first searches the matched S elements, changes these matched elements' IDREF to refer to *e'*, adds IDREFs in *e'* to refer to these matched elements, then deletes *e*. The update operation is similar to the deletion operation.
- Using Rule 4: Suppose there is an element *e'* of type R is regarded as the defalt element. If a deletion of R element *e* violates referential integrity, ICMAP first moves the elements rooted by *e* as the sub-element of *e'*, changes the content of inverse IDREF to refer to *e'*, then deletes *e*. The update operation is similar to the deletion operation.

4. SET NULL

- Using Rule 3: If a deletion of R element *e* violates referential integrity, ICMAP first searches the matched S elements, changes IDREF attribute of these matched elements to *null*, deletes *e*. Update operation is similar to the deletion operation.
- Using Rule 4: The hierarchy is not suitable for this option because we can not construct a format with null parent element.

We can summarize the above comparsion as follows. The hierarchy based mapping rule is suitable for saft type maintenance for referential integrity constraint, such as the option is *no action* or *cascade*, while the constraints based mapping rule is suitable for unsafe type maintainment, such as the option is *set default* or *set null*.

5 Comparison of Semantic Representation Capability

There are three primary existing mapping approaches having the ability to describe semantics indirectly. Paper [13] adopted a simple hierarchy to map foreign keys from tables, paper [14] proposed an extended DTD approach, and paper [15] presented an object reference based approach. For example, there are three relationships in the teaching database. Each *advisor* advises many *students*. Each *student* can select many *courses*, and each *course* can be enrolled by many *students*. The sketch maps of these three approaches and ICMAP are shown in Fig. 2 by using the description of ICMAP. For convenience, we called them as MAP, E_MAP and OO_MAP respectively.

MAP builds a hierarchy between *advisor* and *student* according to their actual

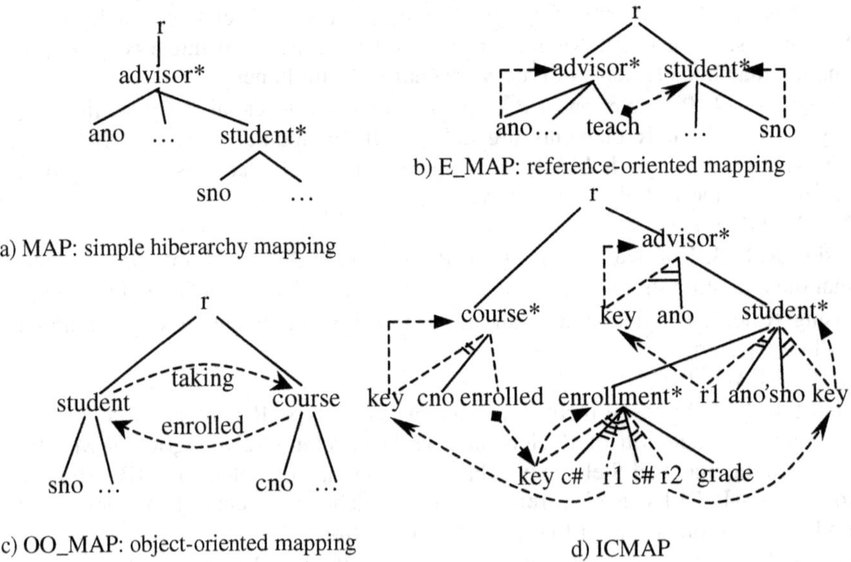

Fig. 2. Comparison of different mapping approaches

meanings. This approach can describe the one-to-one and one-to-many relationships between tables, but it is difficult to maintain the data consistency without capability to define referential integrity constraints. E_MAP extends DTD specification, each table is mapped into an element type, all table instances are mapped into the extension of the mapped element type. Each element can be a referential attribute referring to other elements. The fatal disadvantage of this approach is that it neglects the difference between attribute and element in XML specification. In fact, only attribute can be ID/IDREF(s) in XML specification. OO_MAP is based on object model. Similar to E_MAP, each class is mapped into an element type, the extent of the class is mapped into the set of instances of the mapped element type. This approach can describe bi-directional referential semantics and many-to-many relationships without attributes, for example, in Fig. 2c, the *taking* and *enrolled* are IDREFs attributes referring to *course* and *student* respectively. However, when the many-to-many relationship has attributes, e.g. if *enrolled* has attribute *grade*, it can not describe this semantic, i.e., attribute *grade* can be neither the attribute of element *student* nor the attribute of element *course*. Fortunately, the ICMAP approach overcomes all these shortcomings. The detail comparative information is listed in Table 1.

Table 1. Comparison Table for Different Mapping Approaches

Contents of Comparison		MAP	E_MAP	OO_MAP	ICMAP
Distinguish attributes &elements		N	N	N	Y
Degree of semantic representation		None	Lower	Secondary	Higher
Domain constraint		N	N	N	N
Generic constraint		N	N	N	N
Primary Key		N	Y[2]	Y[3]	Y
Composite Primary Key		N	N	N	Y
Candidate Key		N	N	N	N
Foreign Key		N	Y	Y	Y
one-to-one relationship	Without attribute	Y(implicit)	Y	Y	Y
	With attribute	Y (implicit)	Y	Y	Y
one-to-many relationship	Without attribute	Y (implicit)	Y	Y	Y
	With attribute	Y (implicit)	Y	Y	Y
many-to-many relationship	Without attribute	N	N	Y	Y
	With attribute	N	N	N	Y

6 Conclusion

This paper proposed an extended XML DTD, DTD_C, to solve the referential integrity constraints mapping problems from relational databases to XML document data. More specifically, the characteristics of ICMAP are listed as follows: (1) In XML, referential integrity constraints from relation schema were preserved, concerning primary key constraints and foreign key constraints. (2) The concept of multi-valued foreign key supporting bi-directional referential mechanism between element types was presented. (3) The mapping problem on many-to-many relationship with attributes was solved. (4) Two optional mapping rules enforcing referential integrity constraints were provided. (5) The semantics-lossless mapping for keys was ensured. (6) Mapping for composite keys and composite foreign keys were supported.

The study of mapping referential integrity constraints provides stable foundation for mapping integrity constraints from relational model to XML specification. The integrity constraints consist of domain constraints, general constraints besides referential integrity constraints. General constraints provide rich definitions for semantic constraints. User can use *check* and *assertion* to define constraints intra-table or inter-table. General constraints can be mapped by incorporating active node

---

[2] missing some data on display

[3] mapping object identifiers rather than keys for OO model

in XML_C in our ICMAP approach. Due to the length limited, we did not discuss it in detail here. The detail description should be referred to [18]. On the practical side, especially for extracting constraints and the associated data automatically, we believe that the ICMAP approach proposed here is promising.

References

1. Bray, T., Paoli, J., Sperberg-McQueen, C.M(eds.).: Extensible Markup Language (XML) 1.0. W3C. (1998) http://www.w3.org/TR/REC-xml
2. Abiteboul, S., Vianu, V.: Rugular Path Queryies with Constraints. Proc. of 16th ACM PODS. ACM Press, Tucson, Arizona(1997)51-61
3. Labrinidis, A., Roussopoulos, N.: WebView Materialization. Proceedings ACM SIGMOD Int. Conference on Management of Data. ACM Press, Dallas, Texas(2000)14-19
4. Papakonstantinou, Y., Vassalos, V.: Query Rewriting for Semistructured Data. Proceedings ACM SIGMOD Int. Conference on Management of Data. ACM Press, Philadephia(1999)455–466
5. Cluet, S., Delobel, C., Siméon, J., Smaga, K.: Your Mediators Need Data Conversion!. SIGMOD Record Vol.27(2). Association for Computing Machinery, Inc., New York (1998)177-188
6. Thompson, H.S., Beech, D., Maloney, M., Mendelsohn. N (eds.).: XML Schema Part 1: Structures. W3C. (2000) http://www.w3.org/TR/xmlschema-1
7. Microsoft.: XML Schema Developer's Guide. Internet Document. (2000) http://msdn.microsoft.com/xml/XMLGuide/schema-overview.asp
8. Davidson, A., Fuchs, M., Hedin, M., et al.: Schema for Object-Oriented XML 2.0. W3C. (1999) http://www.w3.org/TR/NOTE-SOX
9. Jelliffe, R.: Scematron. Internet Document. (2000) http://www.ascc.net/xml/resource/schematron/
10. Klarlund, N., Moller, A., Schwatzbach, M.I.: DSD: A Schema Language for XML. Proc. of 3rd ACM Workshop on Formal Methods in Software Practice(2000)
11. Lee, D., Chu. W.: Comparative analysis of Six XML Schema Languages. SIGMOD Record, Vol.29(3). Association for Computing Machinery, Inc., New York (2000)76-87
12. Christophides, V., Cluet, S., Siméon, J.: On Wrapping Query Languages and Efficient XML Integration. In: Chen, W., Naughton, J., Bernstein, P. (eds.): SIGMOD Record, Vol.29(2). Association for Computing Machinery, Inc., New York (2000)141-152
13. Carey, M., Lindsay, B., Pirahesh, H., Reinwald, B.: Efficiently Publishing Relational Data as XML Documents. Proc. of 26th VLDB. Morgan Kaufmann, Cairo, Egypt(2000)65-76
14. Fan, W., Siméon, J.: Integrity Constraints for XML. Proc. of 19th ACM PODS. ACM Press, Dallas, Texas (2000)23-34
15. Buneman, P., Fan, W., Weinstein, S.: Path Constraints on Semistructured and Structured Data. Proc. of 17th ACM PODS. ACM Press, Seattle, Washington(1998)129-138
16. Fernández, M., Tan, W.C., Suciu D.: SilkRoute: Trading between Relations and XML. Proc. of 9th Int. Conf. on World Wide Web.(2000)
17. Yang, X., Wang, G., Yu, G., Wang, D.: Study on Information Cooperation in Virtual Enterprise Information Systems. Proc. of 3rd CODAS. IEEE Computer Society Press. Beijing, China(2001)
18. Yang, X., Wang, G., Yu, G.: Mapping General Constraints from Relational Database to XML. Technique Report of Northeastern University, TR-CS-2001-02(2001)

Session 5A
Data Integration & Filtering

Regular Research Paper (30 minutes)
Attribute Value Extraction and Standardization in Data Integration

Regular Research Paper (30 minutes)
Indexing Attributes and Reordering Profiles for XML Document Filtering and Information Delivery

Short Research Paper (15 minutes)
An Approach for Data Filtering Based on Rough Set Theory

Attribute Value Extraction and Standardization in Data Integration[1]

Hongjun Lu[1] and Zengping Tian[2]

[1] Hong Kong University of Science & Technology, Hong Kong, China
luhj@cs.ust.hk

[2] Fudan University, Shanghai 200433, China
zptian@fudan.edu.cn

Abstract. Most database systems and data analysis tools work with relational or well-structured data. When data is collected from various sources for warehousing or analysis, extracting and formatting the input data into required form is never a trivial task, as it seems. We present in this paper a pattern-matching based approach for extracting and standardizing attribute values from input data entries in the form of character strings. The core component of the approach is a powerful pattern language, which provides a simple way for specifying the semantic features, length limitations, external references, element extraction and restructure of attributes. Attribute values can then be extracted from input strings by pattern matching. Constraints on attributes can be enforced so that the attribute values are standardized even the input data is from different sources and in different formats. The pattern language and matching algorithms are presented. A prototype system based on the proposed approach is also described.

1 Introduction

There are a number of exciting developments in the area of data management recently. The Internet and the World Wide Web (the Web) brings millions data sources available on-line. OLAP and data warehousing technology supports on-line decision-making using large volumes of data. Data mining technology makes it possible to discover knowledge from huge amount of available data. However, the success of all the above requires one common task, integrating data from disperse sources, which is never a trivial task as it seems.

In this paper, we study one of the problems related to data integration: extracting attributes from input data and standardizing them according to a predefined format. This problem can be illustrated using the following example. In the process of integrating customer records, the sample input data entries are as follows:

---

[1] This work is partially supported by a grant from the Research Grant Council of the Hong Kong Special Administrative Region, China (HKUST6092/99E) a grant from the National 973 project of China (No. G1998030414).

X.S. Wang, G. Yu, and H. Lu (Eds.): WAIM 2001, LNCS 2118, pp. 343-354, 2001.

John Smith 900 East Hamilton Avenue, Suite 100, Campbell, CA 95008, USA. Tel: (408)879-7215, Fax: (408)879-7205, jsmith@decisionism.com, Rogers Communications Inc.

David London 7601 Lewinsville Road, McLean, Texas 75201, USA, Tel: 847-9500, Fax: 556-0089 dlondon@dbesoftware.com, DBsoftware Inc.

With these input data records, the objective is to have a single relational table with attributes *Fname, Lname, Phone, Fax, Email, Street, City*, and *Zip-Code*. Furthermore, each attribute has its own specific format. For example, the phone number and fax number should be in the form of 999-999-9999 where first three digits represent the area code and the seven-digit number is separated by a hyphen. The *Zip-Code* should be the abbreviation of a state name followed by five digits. Therefore, given the above two data entries, the following relational records are expected.

Fname	Lname	Tel.	Fax	Email	Street	City	Zip Code
John	*Smith*	*408-879-7215*	*408-879-7205*	*jsmith@decisionism.com*	*900 East Hamilton Avenue*	*Campbell*	*CA 95008*
David	*London*	*214-847-9500*	*214-556-0089*	*dlondon@dbesoftware.com*	*7601 Lewinsville Road*	*McLean*	*TX 75201*

Comparing the input data entries and the final records, we can see that, in order to obtain the final two records, we need (1) to extract attributes from the input text, (2) to format each attribute into the specified format, and (3) to rearrange them according to the given schema. We refer this process as *attribute value extraction and standardization.* The need of an elegant solution to this problem is obvious. While most applications, such as data warehousing and data mining, expect a uniform structure of input, real world data, such as data available from the Web, is often not well-structured. Furthermore, even the original data is well structured, e.g., from relational database systems, structural difference always exists when data is from various sources.

One classical technique for extracting sub-string from texts is pattern matching. Usually, the pattern is defined by regular expression. Hopecroft and Ullman gave a standard account of the relation between regular language and finite automata, and presented algorithms for the conversion of a regular expression to a non-deterministic finite automaton [1]. Aho et al. presented a number of algorithms that use regular expression to search text [2]. Aho gave a good survey on algorithms of matching keywords, looking up dictionaries, and searching regular expressions [3]. Recently, Clarke and Cormack developed a shortest-match substring search algorithm to search text from SGML documents [4]. More recently, Atzeni and Mecca proposed a computational completeness language, *Editor*, which employs an *Aho-Corasick* algorithm [5] like method to conduct text searching, and uses Cut & Paste to restructure document [6].

Although the problem of string matching has been well studied, most of the work was conducted in the environment of text processing. In order to apply the technique to the problem of attribute value extraction and standardization, the classical technique must be re-developed and enhanced. In this paper, we propose a pattern-matching based approach to attribute value extraction and standardization. The unique features of the approach include a simple but powerful pattern language and efficient pattern-matching algorithms for processing large number of data records. The proposed language can specify both the structure of an attribute and constraints on it, such as its length, the alphabet and range of its values. We also developed related algorithms that extract attributes conforming to the defined patterns from text strings. A module for extracting and standardizing attribute values based on the proposed approach has been developed for a data integration system.

The remainder of the paper is organized as follows. Section 2 discusses the characteristics to be described for an attribute followed by the definitions of our pattern languages. The sketch of the algorithm for matching pattern instances in free text data is described in Section 3. Section 4 briefly describes the attribute extraction and standardization module in our data integration system based on the proposed language and matching algorithms. Finally, Section 5 concludes the paper.

2 A Pattern Language for Attribute Value Extraction and Standardization

In this section, we present an informal introduction to a pattern language for specifying the required features of an attribute first and then a formal definition of the syntax and semantics of our pattern language is given.

2.1 Using a Pattern to Describe an Attribute

One of the major difficulties in developing a language for describing an attribute is that it is highly data and application dependant. For the purpose of attribute extraction, we need a language that can describe both the output and the input patterns. Furthermore, the simplicity of the language is another important consideration for ease of use by various users.

As mentioned earlier, the *regular expression* is probably the most popular and powerful tool to describe string patterns. However, there are some deficiencies to directly use regular expressions to specify the attributes. First, as used in database schema definition, most attributes have length requirement. Although regular expression with *Kleene closure* operator * and *positive closure* operator $^+$ can also define both fixed length string instance and patterns with infinite length, fixed length string can only be described by repeating patterns.

Second, attributes in a data record need often to satisfy certain constraints. Such constrains could be syntactic. For example, telephone numbers should be in the form as 408-879-7215, 703-847-9500, and a person's name should be in the form of *J. D. London*. In addition to such structural, or syntactic constraints, some constraints are related to the semantics of the attribute. For example, although zip code is a 5-digit number, not every 5-digit number is a valid zip code.

Third, for the purpose of attribute value extraction and standardization, we need certain mechanism to extract sub-patterns and re-order them in the output. For example, in searching for a pattern to match the telephone numbers, sometimes only the local number, not the country code and the area code, is in need. We refer this as *element extraction* from a pattern.

Based on the above observations, we propose a pattern language that extends the concept of regular expressions to define patterns for extracting attribute values. In this language, the length of a pattern is defined explicitly. The constraints on the pattern are expressed using predicates. To define data element extraction and restructuring, pattern expression is introduced. All these features are integrated into the language in a uniform and consistent fashion. In this section, we use certain examples to illustrate those features and the formal definition of the language will be given in the next subsection.

A 5-digit zip code can be specified as *X*[5; *isDigital*] where *X* is a *pattern variable*, 5 is the length restriction of pattern instances, and *isDigital* is a predicate that specifies a constraint on the value of the pattern variable. A system should support both built-in and user-defined predicates. The following are some examples of such predicates and their semantics:

isUpperCase(s): string *s* is in upper case;
isDigital(s): *s* is a digital string, that is, all characters are in the set {0, 1, …, 9};
isMixedCD(s): all characters in *s* are in the set {a, b, …,z, A, B, …,Z, 0, 1, …, 9};

By the definition, the above pattern matches all 5-digital numbers. Most people write US zip code using the abbreviations of states followed by a 5-didgit number, which can be expressed as follows:

Y[2; *isAlphabetic, isUpperCase*] *X*[5; *isDigital*]

This is a concatenation of three patterns. The first one is *Y*[2; *isAlphabeticr, isUpperCase*], the second one a space, and the third one is *X*[5; *isDigital*]. An instance of the pattern is a string that matches each part of the pattern. In the pattern, *isAlphabetic* and *isUpperCase* are two predicates. They form a conjunctive predicate, and require that the 2-character string should be in upper case.

Although this pattern can match zip codes like *CA 95008*, it will fail to match the zip code *Virginia 22102*. To incorporate these two cases into one pattern, we can modify the previous one into

Y[2; *isAlphabetic, isUpperCase*|4-15; *isInStateNameDic, isAlphabetic*] *X*[5; *isDigital*]

In this definition, pattern variable *Y* can match either an upper case 2-character string or a string of length 4 to 15. Here, *isInStateNameDic* is a predicate that employs the external dictionary to check if a string is a state name. A simple method to validate such constraints is table look-up. We can build various dictionaries to serve the purpose. The following are few examples and their semantics.

isInStateNameDic (s): *s* is in the dictionary containing names of the US states;
isInCountryNameDic (s): *s* is in the dictionary of name countries.

This pattern can match exactly the two types of zip codes like *CA 95008* and *Virginia 22102*. To simplify the expression, the common predicates are put at end in the […] part and are delimited by '||'. For example, the expression above can be simplified as following:

Y[2; *isUpperCase*|3-15; *isInStateNameDic*||*isCharacter*] *X*[5; *isDigital*].

To set a consistent syntax and sound semantics for the language, we will present the formal definition of the language in next subsection.

To facilitate element extraction, we introduce pattern expressions as follows.

X <= *Y*[2; *isCharacter, isUpperCase*|3-15; *isInStateNameDic,*] *X*[5; *isDigital*]

In a pattern expression, '<=' means to extract out the value of certain pattern variables, *X* in this example, as the output. The above pattern expression can be used to match zip codes from a text and extract 5-digit codes from them.

To improve the expressive power of the pattern language to define pattern instances with arbitrary length, we introduce *Kleene closure* * and *positive closure* $^+$ in the pattern (expression) definition. With such extension, regular expressions are describable in the language.

2.2 The Pattern Language

We will first describe the syntax of the pattern language, and then discuss the semantics.

2.2.1 Syntax

A pattern language can be defined as < , Γ,*V*>, where:

= {a, b, …, z, A, B, …Z, 0, 1, …,9, -, …,<, >}, This is a finite set of symbols. Here it denotes the set of all printable characters. *is the *Kleene closure* over .

$\Gamma = \{p_1, p_2, \ldots, p_n\}$, it is a finite set of predicates.

$V = \{X, Y, Z, \ldots\}$, it is a finite set of variables.

Predicates are defined over strings in *, which assert some properties over the pattern instances. For example, *isUpperCase*(s) is true if all characters in string s are in upper case; otherwise, it is false.

The syntactic elements include pattern and pattern expression. They are defined as following:

Definition 2.1 *Patterns* are defined as followings:

(1) If *s* *, *s*, $(s)^*$, and $(s)^+$ are *constant patterns*. Here we distinguish ( ) from ( ). The former is a meta mechanism used to enclose the effective scope of * and $^+$, and pattern definition is closed in them while the later are two symbols in the alphabet.

(2) If *X* is a variable over *, $X[n_{11}, \ldots, n_{1h(1)}\ ; p_{11}, \ldots, p_{1m(1)} | \ldots | n_{k1}, \ldots, n_{kh(k)}\ ; p_{k1}, \ldots, p_{km(k)}]$, $X^*[n_{11}, \ldots, n_{1h(1)}\ ; p_{11}, \ldots, p_{1m(1)} | \ldots | n_{k1}, \ldots, n_{kh(k)}\ ; p_{k1}, \ldots, p_{km(k)}]$, and $X^+[n_{11}, \ldots, n_{1h(1)}\ ; p_{11}, \ldots, p_{1m(1)} | \ldots | n_{k1}, \ldots, n_{kh(k)}\ ; p_{k1}, \ldots, p_{km(k)}]$ are *variable patterns*, where X V, p_{kl} Γ, and n_{ij} *N*. *X* is called *pattern variable* and [...] is the *pattern condition*. The pattern condition can have more than one sub-conditions separated by '|'. In each sub-condition, the natural numbers limit the length of the pattern and the predicates define the constraints on the pattern instances. All sub-conditions are in disjunction relationship, that is, a string satisfying any sub-condition is an instance of the pattern.

(3) If *P* and *Q* are patterns, *PQ*, $(PQ)^*$, and $(PQ)^+$ are *complex patterns*.

Both constant patterns and variable patterns are *basic patterns*. Constant patterns are simple patterns, such as *abcd* and *efgh*. A variable pattern defines a set of strings that satisfy the predicates and the length limitations given in it.

Definition 2.2 *Pattern expression* is defined as *T* <= *R* where *R* is a pattern, and *T* is a string consisting of constant strings from * and pattern variables from *R*.

T and R are named the *head* and *body* of the pattern expression, respectively. When the pattern contains the closure operators, the element can be extracted by pattern expressions are defined as follows.

1) If R is in the form of $X^{+}[\ldots]$ or $X^{*}[\ldots]$, X is allowed to appear in T.
2) If R is in the form of $(uX[\ldots]v)^{+}$ or $(uX[\ldots]v)^{*}$, X is allowed to appear in T.
3) If R is in the form of $(PQ)^{+}$ or $(PQ)^{*}$, some pattern variables of P' and Q' are allowed to appear in T, where P' and Q' are patterns P and Q without the condition parts of variable patterns, respectively.

2.2.2 Semantics

In previous subsection we gave some explanations of the semantics of the pattern language intuitively. In this section, the formal semantics of the language is defined. Here we adopt a kind of semantics using active domain. That is, defining the semantics of a pattern against a document over which the pattern will be searched.

For a pattern language < , Γ, V>, a document d and d *, supposing $SUBSTR(d)$ is a set that contains all the substrings of d, and then we define a searching operator $\mathbf{S}$, which assigns semantics to patterns over document d as following.

Definition 2.3 *Semantics for patterns* are defined as followings:

For constant patterns s, $(s)^{*}$, and $(s)^{+}$, if s $SUBSTR(d)$, then

$\mathbf{S}\,[\,s(d)\,] = \{\,s\,\}$

$\mathbf{S}[\,(s)^{+}(d)\,] = \{t\,|t \quad (\{s\}^{+} \quad SUBSTR(d))$ and $|t|$ should be the maximum possible length $\}$

$\mathbf{S}[\,(s)^{*}(d)\,] = \mathbf{S}\,[\,(s)^{+}(d)\,] \quad \{\varepsilon\}$

where $|t|$ denotes the length of string t. The intuitive meaning of this definition is that, while searching a constant string over a document, if the string is a substring of the document, it is returned as the searching result.

For a pattern $X[n_{11}, \ldots, n_{1h(1)}\,;\, p_{11},\ldots, p_{1m(1)}\,|\ldots|\, n_{k1}, \ldots, n_{kh(k)}\,;\, p_{k1},\ldots, p_{km(k)}]$, if X is a pattern variable over $SUBSTR(d)$, then

$\mathbf{S}\,[X[n_{11}, \ldots, n_{1h(1)}\,;\, p_{11},\ldots, p_{1m(1)}\,|\ldots|\, n_{k1}, \ldots, n_{kh(k)}\,;\, p_{k1},\ldots, p_{km(k)}](d)\,]$

$= \mathbf{S}\,[X[n_{11}, \ldots, n_{1h(1)}\,;\, p_{11},\ldots, p_{1m(1)}](d)] \;\ldots\; \mathbf{S}[X[\,n_{k1}, \ldots, n_{kh(k)}\,;\, p_{k1},\ldots, p_{km(k)}](d)\,]$

where

$\mathbf{S}[X[n_{i1}, \ldots, n_{ih(i)}\,;\, p_{i1},\ldots, p_{im(i)}](d)]$

$= \{s\,|\,s \quad SUBSTR(d)$, $|s|$ should be the maximum possible length,

and $p_{i1}(s) \;\ldots\; p_{ih(i)}(s) \quad (|s|= n_{i1} \;\ldots\; |s|= n_{im(i)})$ holds$\}$, 1 i k.

In the definition, pattern instances are circumscribed from both semantic and syntax aspects. Sets of predicates pose semantic constraints to the pattern instances. Syntactically, the length of pattern instances is confined in the set $\{n_{ij}\}$. For a pattern instance, its length should be some n_{ij} given in the set. Moreover, we adopt *maximum length semantic*. That is, if a string and some of its sub-strings are instances of the searched pattern at the same time, the string with the maximum length is always chosen as the semantic of the searched pattern, not considering those sub-strings with short lengths. Formally, if s $\mathbf{S}[X[\ldots](d)]$ and $|s|= n_{ij}$, then there is no string $t = wsv$, t $SUBSTR(d)$, and $|\,t\,|= n_{ik}$, such that n_{ik} $\{\,n_{i1}, \ldots, n_{im(i)}\,\}$, $n_{ik} > n_{ij}$, and $p_{i1}(t) \;\ldots\; p_{ih(i)}(t)$ holds.

For patterns $X^*[\ldots]$, and $X^+[\ldots]$, if X is a pattern variable over *SUBSTR*(d), then
S $[X^+[\ldots](d)] = \{ s_1 s_2 \ldots s_k \mid s_1 s_2 \ldots s_k$ *SUBSTR*(d) and $\mid s_1 s_2 \ldots s_k \mid$ should be the maximum possible length, and s_i **S**$[X[\ldots](d)]$, 1 i k }
S $[X^*[\ldots](d)] =$ **S** $[X^+[\ldots](d)]$ $\{\varepsilon\}$
For complex pattern PQ, $(PQ)^*$ and $(PQ)^+$, if P and Q are sub-patterns, then
S $[PQ(d)] = \{ pq \mid pq$ *SUBSTR*(d), p **S** $[P(d)]$, and q **S** $[Q(d)]\}$
S $[(PQ)^+(d)] = \{ p_1 q_1 p_2 q_2 \ldots p_k q_k \mid p_1 q_1 p_2 q_2 \ldots p_k q_k$ *SUBSTR*(d), $\mid p_1 q_1 p_2 q_2 \ldots p_k q_k \mid$ should be the maximum possible length, p_i **S** $[P(d)]$, and q_i **S** $[Q(d)]$, 1 i k }
S $[PQ^*(d)] =$ **S** $[PQ^+(d)]$ $\{\varepsilon\}$
The complex pattern defines that the concatenations of patterns are still legal patterns, which allows patterns to combine with each other arbitrarily.

Definition 2.4 For a pattern expression T <= R, while searching it against document d and d *, it is denoted as T <= $R(d)$, and its semantic is defined as following.

For a pattern expression X <= $uX[\ldots]v$, if u, v *SUBSTR*(d) and X is a pattern variable, then

S $[X$ <= $uX[\ldots]v(d)] = \{ s \mid usv$ **S** $[uX[\ldots]v(d)]\}$

The intuitive meaning of the simple pattern expression is to extract out some element from a pattern. The extracted element can be used as a string. In the definition, pattern variable X is extracted out from the pattern in the body.

For a pattern expression uP'vQ'w <= PQ(d), if u, v, w *, P' and Q' are variable strings and they only contain variables from P and Q, respectively, then

S[uP'vQ'w <=PQ(d)] = {$upvqw$ |pq *SUBSTR*(d), p **S**[P'<=PQ(d)], and q **S**[Q'<= PQ(d)] }

Element extraction provides some flexibility in manipulating data. This kind of pattern expression allows not only extracting, but also restructuring data, which is very useful. In the definition, *P'* and *Q'* are extracted from pattern PQ(d) to form a set of strings with the form uP'vQ'w. Such kind of capability is useful in information extraction and restructure.

Pattern expressions involving the closure operators are defined as follows:

For pattern expressions sXt <= $X^+[\ldots]$(d), where s, t *,
S$[sXt$ <= $X^+[\ldots](d)] = \{ ss_1t, ss_2t, \ldots, ss_kt \mid s_1 s_2 \ldots s_k$ *SUBSTR*(d), $\mid s_1 s_2 \ldots s_k \mid$ should be the maximum possible length, and s_i **S**$[X[\ldots](d)]$, 1 i k }
For pattern expressions sXt <= $X^*[\ldots]$(d), where s, t *,
S$[sXt$ <= $X^*[\ldots](d)] =$ **S**$[sXt$ <= $X^+[\ldots](d)]$ $\{st\}$
For pattern expressions sXt <= $(uX[\ldots]v)^+(d)$, where s, t *,
S$[sXt$ <= $(uX[\ldots]v)^+(d)] = \{ ss_1t, ss_2t, \ldots, ss_kt \mid us_1vus_2v \ldots s_kv$ *SUBSTR*(d), $|us_1vus_2v \ldots s_kv|$should be the maximum possible length, and s_i **S**$[X[\ldots](d)]$,1 i k }
For pattern expressions sXt <= $(uX[\ldots]v)^*(d)$, where s, t *,
S$[sXt$ <= $(uX[\ldots]v)^*(d)] =$ **S**$[sXt$ <= $(uX[\ldots]v)^+(d)]$ $\{st\}$

So far, we have presented the syntax and semantics of the pattern language. We claim that the pattern language is more powerful than regular expressions in the following theorem.

Theorem 2.1 Given a regular set R on *, we can find a pattern P in a pattern language < , Γ, V> so that the set of all instances of P is R.

The proof of the theorem is straightforward. The pattern language is open in the senses that predicates can be introduced to enrich it. If only Γ contains for each letter in a character predicate that can differentiate it from other letters, each regular expression on * can be defined by a constant pattern. Thus, the conclusion of the theorem is justified. It seems that the pattern language is strictly more powerful than regular expressions for pattern expressions can extract strings according to the context information. Furthermore, the extensible predicate set makes the language more powerful.

3 Extracting/Formatting Attribute Values Using Patterns

In this section we discuss issues related to extract from a document the patterns defined in the language. Limited by space, we omitted the detailed data structures and algorithm descriptions, which can be found in [7]. The system consists of three major components: *Pattern Preprocessor*, *Matcher*, and *Predicate Library*. The Pattern Preprocessor accepts a user-defined pattern, transforms it into a *label pattern*, and finally, outputs a *transition graph*, an intermediate data structure, to the Matcher as its input. The Matcher gets transition graph as one of its input, and then, simulates an extended deterministic finite automaton (DFA) on an input document. During the process of simulation, the Matcher may call some external functions in the predicate library to determine whether a string satisfies defined constraints. The predicate library consists of both system- and user-defined functions that check whether a string satisfies a predicate. Facilities are also available so that the Matcher can find the corresponding function for a predicate appeared in a pattern definition.

3.1 Pre-processing of Patterns

The major work of the Pattern Preprocessor is to transform the user-defined pattern into some intermediate data structure that can be further processed by the Matcher. Since the pattern definitions in our language are in fact quite similar to regular expressions [1], and the recognition of regular expressions is a well-studied problem, we would like to use the results of previous work as much as possible.
Comparing pattern X[2-20;*isInCustomerDic*]Y^{+}[1;*isMixedCD*]Z[3-20;*isInStreetDic*]U^{+}[1; *isMixedCD*] with regular expression $l_1 l_2^{+} l_3 l_4^{+}$, both of them have the same structure, except the differences in the basic components. Therefore, a reasonable approach is to first convert a pattern definition into a sort of restricted regular expression, *label pattern*, and then, employ the techniques developed for recognizing regular expressions to process it.

3.1.1 Label Pattern

The label pattern is actually a simplification of the pattern. In a label pattern, all basic patterns, both constant patterns and variable patterns, are replaced by labels, which are some symbols from the finite set $\boldsymbol{L} = \{l_1, l_2, l_3, l_4, l_5, \ldots\}$. Given a pattern P, a *label mapping* m_p is defined, which maps each constant pattern and variable pattern in P into a label in $\boldsymbol{L}$. Likewise, a *pattern mapping* M_p maps the pattern P into a label pattern. Formally, it can be defined as following:

$$m_p: \{ c_1, c_2, c_3, \ldots, v_1, v_2, v_3, \ldots\} \rightarrow \{l_1, l_2, l_3, l_4, l_5, \ldots\}$$
$$M_p: P \rightarrow E$$

where c_i and v_j are constant and variable patterns in P; E is a label pattern that replaces constant pattern c_i and variable pattern v_j in P with $m_p(c_i)$ and $m_p(v_j)$, respectively. The suffixes of both mappings will be omitted if it is clear in the context.

Theorem 3.1. Given a pattern P, a label mapping m_p, and a pattern mapping M_p, the label pattern $M_p(P)$ is a regular expression that does not contain '|' operators.

To process a pattern expression, the pattern mapping M should be extended. For a pattern expression R <= P, a given label mapping m on basic patterns of both R and P, and a pattern mapping M, the pattern expression is converted into a *label expression*, a 2-tuple, in which the head and the body of the pattern expression are converted, respectively. That is,

$$M(R <= P) = <M(R), M(P)>$$

In the expression above, since P is a pattern, $M(P)$ should be a label pattern. To get M(R), the label mapping m should also be extended since R only contains variables, no variable patterns. That is,

$$m(v[\ldots]) = m(v) = l_i, \text{ where } v \quad \boldsymbol{V}.$$

3.1.2 Label Pattern Processing

As we mentioned above, each user defined pattern or pattern expression can be converted into a label pattern or label expression. For label expression, we only concern the label pattern converted from the body of pattern expression. Currently, the focus of our work is concentrated on the processing of label pattern. A label pattern is actually a restricted regular expression. We therefore use the techniques used in recognizing regular expressions to assist our work.

As the first step to process a label pattern, a *Deterministic Finite Automaton* (DFA) is constructed for the label pattern. Formally, a DFA is a 5-tuples $<\mathbf{Q}, \mathbf{M}, \delta, q_0, \mathbf{F}>$ [1]. For our cases, we define the items as followings:

$\boldsymbol{Q} = \{q_0, q_1, q_2, \ldots\}$;

$\boldsymbol{M} = \boldsymbol{L}$; that is, the input alphabet is the set of labels we use in the label patterns.

δ is implemented by a *Trans* function. That is, if $\delta(q_i, l) = q_j$, then $Trans(q_i, l) = q_j$.

q_0 is the initial state.

$\boldsymbol{F}$ is a set of accepting states, that is, $\boldsymbol{F} \quad \boldsymbol{Q}$.

Given a label pattern, its corresponding DFA can be constructed using available algorithms [1, 3]. Among the five items in a DFA, the three ones δ, q_0, $\boldsymbol{F}$ are different for different label patterns and should be kept for each DFA. The data structures for keeping them can be found in [7].

The label expressions are different from regular expressions in that labels are not input symbols, thus the DFA cannot be used in recognizing the instances of the user defined pattern. The DFA, however, do give us a great help in recognizing the pattern instances since it provides a framework for the recognizing. The most important operation in the processing is that, given a state q_i, all the labels defined on it are checked to find the label (its corresponding pattern) that can be satisfied by the current input string. And then the transition function $Trans(q_i, l) = q_j$ is employed to send the DFA from current state to the next one. To support this operation, we have to derive a function *Follow* from the transition function *Trans* as following.

Follow: $\mathbf{Q} \rightarrow 2^{L}$

Follow(q_i) = {l | *Trans*(q_i, l) **Q**}

From the definition of the *Follow* function, it is obviously that this function attaches each state of the DFA a set of labels, which can send the DFA from the given state to a legal DFA state.

3.2 Pattern Matcher

The Matcher scans through the input document and searches for the instances of the user defined pattern or pattern expression. It works in two phases: *simulation* and *collection.* During the simulation phase, it simulates the behaviors of the DFA of the label pattern. The DFA, however, does not transmit from one state to another by looking only one input character as the usual DFA. It looks forward for a finite number of characters to see which pattern can be satisfied, thus gets the corresponding label of the pattern, and decides the following state of the DFA. That an accepting state is reached means an instance of the pattern has been found successfully. The Matcher then enters the collection phase. At this time, a pattern or pattern expression instance is assembled according to the definition.

The above description gives a rough idea of how the Matcher working on label expressions, that is, pattern expressions. Label patterns and hence patterns, are special cases of label expressions. With a small modification, i.e., making the instance of the body pattern as a matching result, and concatenating all the values of the labels together, the Matcher can work on both label expressions and label patterns.

3.3 Cost Based Sub-pattern Matching Sequence

The basic algorithm for searching pattern instances in free text described above simulates a DFA of the pattern and tries to find pattern instance of each sub-pattern in the pattern definition from left to right. Given pattern *X[3;IsDigital]W[3-8;IsAscii]Y[4-5;IsDigital]" Street",* the algorithm first tries to find instance of *X[3;IsDigital],* then those of *W[3-8;IsAscii],* and *Y[4-5;IsDigital].* At last, it tries to match the constant string *Street.* However, it is obvious that fixed length instances like " *Street*" and *X[3;IsDigital]* are much easier to find than those variable length ones. The larger the range of the variable length pattern, the more costly to search.

Based on this observation, an optimization can be applied to the basic DFA-based pattern matching algorithm, where the *cost* is defined as the maximum length variation of the instances of a sub-pattern. . The rationale is that more possible strings that can match a sub-pattern with large length variations, more costly searching for the matches in the input string. Based on this definition, the cost of a constant sub-pattern is zero; those of '+' or '*' sub-patterns are infinite. With the defined cost, instead of searching for matches based on the lexical order of sub-patterns in a pattern definition, those sub-patterns with less cost will be searched first.

4 A Prototype System

The pattern language and matching algorithms described in the previous sections are implemented as a module, *Standardizer*, in a data integration system being developed at Hong Kong University of Science & Technology. The system consists of a number of tools for cleansing data for integration, warehousing and mining. The *Standardizer* is one of such tools. Figure 5.1 is the screen dump of the system when the module is to be invoked. The data shown on screen is hotel information obtained from the Web. Four attributes, *rid, hotel_name, telephone* and *fax* are shown. It can be seen that the real world data is really dirty. For example, the telephone numbers are in quite different format for different records, such as "806-353-3541", "303 371-0700" and "719-589-2567, Toll Free Reservations 1-". For such an attribute, the function of the module is to extract the useful information and to standard them into the same format.

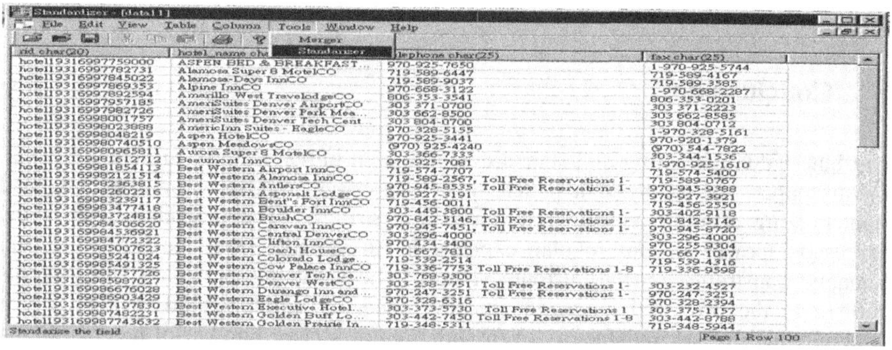

Fig. 5.1. Initial Screen Dump for the Standardizer

After the Standardizer is invoked, a user can specify the left-hand side and right-hand side of a pattern expression for an attribute. In the example, user chose the attribute telephone for value extraction and standardization. A pattern *X*[3; isDigital]"-"*Y*[3; isDigital]"-"*Z*[4; isDigital] was specified and the attribute should be standardized into "Tel: "*X*"-"*YZ* if the defined pattern was matched. This can be represented as

"Tel: "*X*"-"*YZ* <= *X*[3; isDigital]"-"*Y*[3; isDigital]"-"*Z*[4; isDigital]

What shown in the data window in Figure 5.2 is the result after applying the above given pattern expression. Those records highlighted failed to match the pattern and remained unchanged. The system allows user to modify the patterns so that those unmatched records can be covered by the pattern and standardized to the specified format. The system also provides other related functions, such as saving the patterns for later use, management of the dictionaries, etc.

In addition to the expressive power of the language, the efficiency of our implementation of the matching algorithms is also a concern. We conducted certain experiments to investigate the performance of the system. The results indicated that the performance is satisfactory.

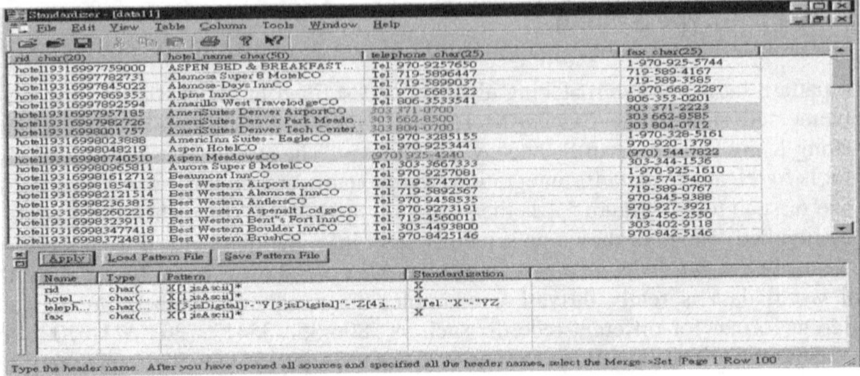

Fig. 5.2. The Standardizer at Work

5 Conclusions

Attribute value extracting and standardization is an important task in data cleansing. In this paper, we proposed a pattern matching based approach for extracting and standardizing attribute values from input text strings. The language extends the expressive power of the regular expressions to support both the structural and semantic constraints on the attribute values. The matching algorithms for patterns defined in the proposed language are developed and implemented in a prototype system, which works satisfactory even with data of a large number of records. Some preliminary experiments were conducted.

The future work includes further polishing the language. More comprehensive study is planned.

References

1. Hopcroft, J.E., Ullman, J.D.: *Introduction to Automata Theory, Languages, and Computation*. Addison-Wesley Publishing Company, 1979.
2. Aho, A.V., Hopcroft, J.E., Ullman, J.D.: *The Design and Analysis of Computer Algorithms*. Addison-Wesley, Reading, Massachusetts, 1974.
3. Aho, A.V.: Algorithms for Finding Patterns in Strings. In: Leeuwen, J.V. (ed): *Handbook of Theoretical Computer Science*. Elsevier Science Publishers, (1990) 256-300.
4. Clarke, C.L.A., Cormack, G.V.: On the Use of regular Expressions for Searching Text. *Technical Report* CS-95-07, Department of Computer Science, University of Waterloo.
5. Aho, A.V., Corasick, M.J.: Efficient String Matching-An Aid to Bibliographic Search. *Communications of the ACM*, 18(6), (1975) 333-340.
6. Atzeni,P., Mecca, G.: Cut and Paste. In: Ozsoyoglu, Z. M. (ed): *Proceedings of the Sixteenth ACM SIGACT-SIGMOD-SIGART Symposium on Principles of Database Systems*, May 12-14, 1997, Tucson, Arizona. ACM Press, (1997) 144-153.
7. Lu, H., Tian, Z., Ng, Y.Y.: Attribute Value Extraction and Standardization by Pattern Matching, *submitted for publication*, May 2000.

Indexing Attributes and Reordering Profiles for XML Document Filtering and Information Delivery

Wang Lian, David W. Cheung, and S.M. Yiu

Department of Computer Science and Information Systems,
The University of Hong Kong, Pokfulam, Hong Kong.
{wlian, dcheung, smyiu}@csis.hku.hk

Abstract. With the ever increasing volume of information generation, selective dissemination of information becomes more and more important since it only brings users the necessary information. Traditional selective dissemination methods usually depend on keyword matching and focus on effectiveness rather than efficiency and scalability. **XFilter** [1], which adopts XML and XPath, changes the focus to efficiency and scalability. However, the filtering system built in XFilter is mainly based on XML elements without considering the use of attributes. In this paper, we describe two mechanisms, one for reordering user profiles and the other for indexing XML attributes, which can be seamlessly combined with the filtering algorithm of XFilter to give significant improvement on XML document dissemination over the original filtering algorithm of XFilter. Experiments were carried out to verify our claim.

Keywords: XML, XPath, Elements, Attributes, Selective Dissemination of Information

1 Introduction

Due to the increasing volume of data available in electronic forms and the popularity of Internet, the need to continuously deliver a large volume of timely and relevant information to a large group of interested users based on user profiles has accelerated the development of SDI (Selective Dissemination of Information) [1] applications.

In Information Retrieval community, matching between user profiles and documents has been extensively investigated [4] [5] [6]. Typical IR-style user profiles are intended for unstructured text-based systems and keywords are used to represent these user profiles. Most of these approaches focus on effectiveness rather than efficiency and scalability which, however, are some critical requirements of an Internet-based SDI system. The key insight to build high-performance, scalable SDI systems is that in such systems, the roles of profiles and data are reversed [7]. In database society, data are indexed, while in SDI systems, profiles are indexed instead. Therefore the sophisticated techniques in database such as

X.S. Wang, G. Yu, and H. Lu (Eds.): WAIM 2001, LNCS 2118, pp. 355–366, 2001.

triggers [8] [9] may not be suitable for achieving high scalability for SDI systems. The need for a more efficient SDI system using a different approach is obvious.

XML [10], being the new standard for data representation and exchange on the Web, embeds structural information in documents using elements (tags). This kind of structural information can help us define more accurate user profiles, thus may be used to increase the efficiency of a SDI system. In [1], an XML-based SDI system: XFilter is built. In this system, XPath language [2] is used to represent user profiles. The inputs are XML documents. Basically, when an XML document comes in, the *relevant* user profiles are checked and the document will be delivered to the users whose profiles *match* the input document.

In XFilter, each XPath expression representing a user profile is converted to a modified Finite State Machine (FSM). Together with a sophisticated indexing structure, the matching of user profiles and XML documents can be done efficiently. However, the indexing structure built in XFilter is mainly on XML elements without considering the use of attributes. In this paper, we extend the work in XFilter, by (1) indexing also the attributes; and (2) reordering the input sequence of user profiles, to further reduce the number of profile comparisons. The experimental results show that significant improvement is gained using these two enhancements.

The remaining of the paper is organized as follows. We will give an overview on the filtering mechanism of XFilter and the motivations to extend this mechanism in Section 2. How to index the attributes and reorder the user profiles will be presented in Section 3. Experimental results are shown in Section 4 and we will give the conclusion in Section 5. Note that we assume the readers have knowledge about XML and XPath, please refer to [2] [10] for relevant information.

2 Background and Motivations

In this section, we give an overview on the filtering mechanism used in XFilter and discuss the motivations for enhancing this filtering mechanism. For details of XFilter, please refer to [1].

2.1 The Filtering Mechanism in XFilter

In XFilter, each user profile is represented by an XPath expression. Each XPath expression is decomposed into a set of *path nodes* with each path node corresponds to an XML element in the expression. No path node is generated for the wildcard ("*") symbol. For example, the XPath expression //a/*/b/c will have three path nodes corresponding to the elements a, b, and c respectively. XFilter then groups and indexes user profiles according to path nodes in an inverted index [3] which is organized as a hash table based on the element names that appear in the XPath expressions.

In order to handle the matching process efficiently, each XPath expression is converted to a Finite State Machine (FSM) in which a state corresponds to a path node. When an XML document comes in, the FSMs of *relevant* XPath expressions are executed while the document is being parsed. A user profile is considered to match an XML document when the final state of its FSM is reached. To simulate the FSM, two lists of path nodes, the *Candidate List* and *Wait List*, are attached to each unique element name in the inverted index. The path node corresponding to the current state of FSM of each expression is placed on the Candidate List under the corresponding element name. All other path nodes representing future states are stored in the Wait Lists under the corresponding element names. A state transition is simulated by promoting a path node from the Wait List to the Candidate List. In other words, when parsing an XML document, if an element x appears, all FSMs with path nodes appearing in the Candidate List under x will be executed. Figure 1 shows an example of the inverted index on five simple XPath expressions.

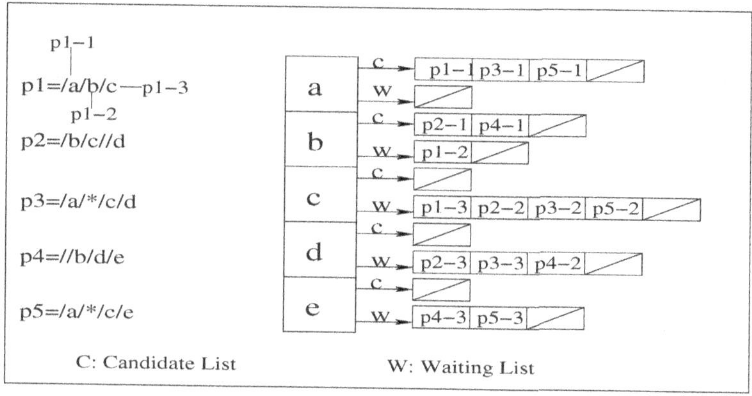

Fig. 1. Naive Inverted List Structure

To initialize the Candidate and Wait Lists, one trivial approach is to put the start state of each FSM (ie., the first path node of each XPath expression) in the corresponding Candidate List and all other states in the corresponding Wait Lists. As indicated in [1], this approach is usually not efficient as the first few path nodes tend to be the same among a lot of XPath expressions. As a result, some Candidate Lists will be long which may affect the performance of the matching process. The authors then propose a *List Balancing* method to reduce the length difference of Candidate Lists of different elements. The idea is quite simple. When adding a new profile in the index, the path node corresponding to the shortest Candidate List is made to be the "start" state of the FSM and inserted in the Candidate List. The path nodes before this one are kept as a "prefix" attached to the start state, while all other nodes are inserted in the corresponding Wait Lists. When this FSM is started, the prefix will be checked against the document with the help of a stack to make sure that all the preceding states match with the document.

Figure 2(i) and (ii) show the resulting inverted list structures built by the straightforward and the List Balancing methods respectively based on the input user profiles sequence 1. According to the experimental results in [1], List Balancing gives a better result than the straightforward method and it shows that the initial distribution of the path nodes to the Candidate and Wait Lists will greatly affect the performance of a SDI system.

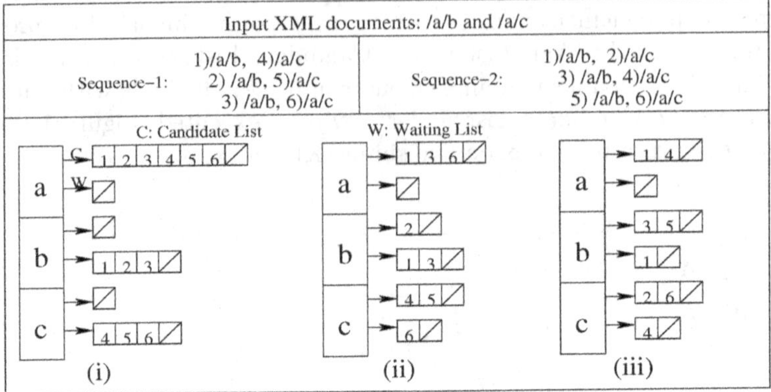

Fig. 2. Different Inverted List Structures

2.2 Motivations

In this subsection, we discuss some motivations to extend the fitering mechanism used in XFilter. First of all, we show that List Balancing is not the best way to distribute the path nodes in the Candidate and Wait Lists. Consider the example in Figure 2.

Suppose the input XML documents are $/a/b$ and $/a/c$. For the inverted list structure in (i), we have to perform 9 comparisons of path nodes and 6 movements from Wait List to Candidate List for each document. For the inverted list structure in (ii) which is the result of applying the List Balancing method, we have to perform 7 comparisons and 3 movements for document $/a/b$ and 8 comparisons and 3 movements for document $/a/c$. The factor that affects the performance is the length difference of the Candidate Lists among different elements. General speaking, the smaller the difference, the better is the performance.

According to this observation, we notice that in (ii), the difference of Candidate lists of element a and b is 2, if we can reduce this difference, the performance may still be improved. In fact, this is possible by reordering the six profiles as follows: $/a/b$, $/a/c$, $/a/b$, $/a/c$, $/a/b/$, $/a/c$ (ie, sequence 2 in Figure 2). Figure 2(iii) shows the structure using this sequence and List Balancing method. All the Candidate Lists are of the same length. For both documents $/a/b$ and $/a/c$, we only need 7 comparisons and 2 movements for each. In the next section, we will present an algorithm which will reorder the user profiles based on this observation.

The second observation is that in XFilter, the index is built on elements only. However, in NITF [10] DTD, which is used in all the experiments in testing XFilter performance, there are 158 elements and 588 attributes. On average one element has four attributes. Therefore if we can utilize the information from attributes, we may have chance to do better. Consider the following simple example. Given an XML document $/a/b/c$ and a user profile $/a/b/c[...]$, obviously they do not match as the profile has attribute requirement on c while the document does not have the attribute at all. In fact, [1] also reports that making use of attributes can greatly reduce the number of profiles to be checked.

However, to index the attribute values may generate a huge index and may mean a lot of work which cannot compensate the benefit gained. In the next section, we will describe an approach to index only the presence of attributes without checking the actual values.

3 Reordering Profiles and Indexing Attributes

3.1 Reordering Profiles

Definition 1. *Two XPath expressions xp_1 and xp_2 are said to have the same formulation if after removing all "*", "[", "]", contents between "[" and "]" and changing all "//" to "/" from both expressions, the two resulting expressions are the same.*

For example, $//a/b[...]/*/c$ and $/a//b/c$ have the same formulation. The rationale behind the reordering algorithm is to evenly distribute profiles of same formulation on the input sequence. The reordering algorithm is shown below.

```
/* Input : IN, a sequence of original profiles */
/* Output: OUT, a new sequence of profiles */
Step 1: Grouping all the profiles in IN of the same formulation in
one cluster
Step 2: Give tag number to each cluster from 1,2,...,n-1,n
Step 3: for (int i=1,i<=n;i++)
          if group i is not empty, then
             pick out a profile from it, insert it into OUT;
             remove this profile from group i
```

Although we cannot guarantee that this kind of reordering of profiles is optimal, the experimental results show that it is much better than pure List Balancing.

3.2 Indexing Profiles on Attributes Appearance

For ease of illustration purpose, we assume that the given set of XPaths do not contain "//" and recursion if they have the same formulation. The algorithm for building the index on attributes appearance is shown below.

```
/* Input : XP, a set of XPathes */
/* Output : INDEX, an index array */
for(i = 1; i <= XP.size; i++)
    for(j = 1; j <= XP[i].size; j++){
        if(XP[i][j]! = "*")
            if(XP[i][j] has attribute requirement)
                item.attributeappear = 1
            else
                item.attributeappear = 0
            item.profileid = XP.id
            INDEX[j].add(item)
```

Fig. 3. Algorithm for Indexing Attribute Appearance

Here, each index item is a record of two fields:profile id and attribute appearance. Note that if *any* of the attributes of the corresponding element appear, the index will be set to 1, otherwise it is 0. Figure 4 shows an example of an index on attributes appearance.

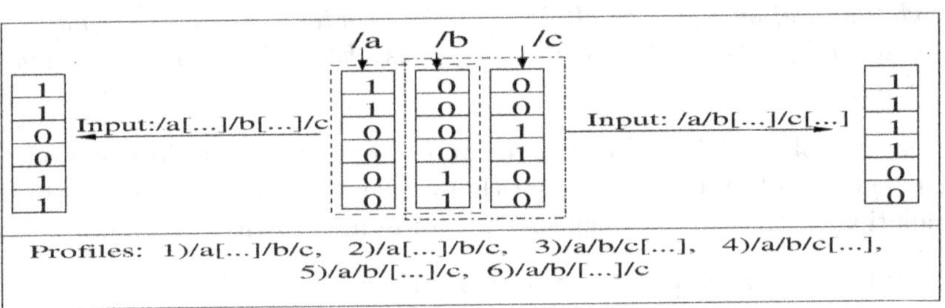

Fig. 4. Bit indexing of attributes

In this example, we have six profiles: $/a[...]/b/c$, $/a[...]/b/c$, $/a/b/c[...]$, $/a/b/c[...]$, $/a/b[...]/c$, $/a/b[...]/c$. The three columns in center is the index array we build on them, each element a, b, c has an index. And each index has six entries for six profiles, the 1 or 0 value in each record indicates attribute appearance (we omit profile id for simplicity, the order of records in index is the same as the order of profilese). Profiles 1 and 2 have attribute requirement on element a, so the first and second entries of element a's index are set to 1. Suppose now the input XML document is $/a[...]/b[...]/c$, because both elements a and b have attributes, so we only need to check the profiles listed in indices of element a and b without consider the profiles in index of element c. Therefore, only profile 1,2,5,6 will be sent for further checking. Just as the left most column indicates. Similarily for the case when the input document is $/a/b[...]/c[...]$.

Readers may find that the index we build on attribute appearance for an element does not consider the number of attributes appeared in the expression. The index will perform worse if the distribution of attributes on elements is highly skewed, that is, few elements have many attributes. According to Theorem 1, we can avoid this by redistributing attributes from the element with lots of attributes to elements with few attributes. This can be done by maintaining an additional DTD with attributes more evenly distributed, and modifying user profiles accordingly. The modification can be done transparent to users. The details will be discussed in the full paper.

Theorem 1. *Given two elements, A and B, where A has* $n+1 (n > 1)$ *attributes,* a_1, a_2,...,a_{n+1} *and B has no attributes. If the distribution of attributes on both profiles and documents are evenly distributed on all elements, then moving one attribute from A to B will reduce the average number of profiles for further checking over all documents.*

Proof (sketch): We only consider A, B and their attributes, and keep other elements and attributes in XML document and profiles unchanged. Because we assume that the document's attribute requirement is evenly distributed on all elements, so the input XML document's attribute requirements of all possible attribute combinations on A and B are equal.

Let us first count the number of possible combinations of attribute requirements on A and B before moving one attribute from A to B. The possible number of XML documents has only one attribute requirement on A is C^1_{n+1}, the possible number of XML documents has only two attribute requirements on A is C^2_{n+1}, and the possible number of XML documents has n+1 attribute requirements on A is C^{n+1}_{n+1}. Summing up all of them, we have the following number of possible XML documents.

$$2^{n+1} - 1 \tag{1}$$

In all the above possible cases, the number of profiles in element A's index are the same. So, the total number of profiles that will be checked is $(2^{n+1} - 1) * |A(a_1, a_2, ...a_{n+1})|$ (where $|A(a_1, a_2, ...a_{n+1})|$ denotes the number of profiles with "attributeappear=1").

Now we move a_{n+1} from A to B and recompute the number of XML documents on all possible combinations of attributes on A and B. We have the following number of combinations.

$$(2^n - 1)|A(a_1, a_2, ...a_n)| + |B(a_{n+1}| + (2^n - 1)|A(a_1, a_2, ..., a_n)B(a_{n+1})| \tag{2}$$

Because

$$|A(a_1, a_2, ...a_{n+1})| = |A(a_1, a_2, ..., a_n)B(a_{n+1})| \tag{3}$$

By reducing Expression 1 and 2 by Expression 3 we have

$$(2^n)|A(a_1, a_2, ...a_{n+1})| \tag{4}$$

and

$$(2^n - 1)|A(a_1, a_2, ..., a_n)| + |B(a_{n+1})| \tag{5}$$

Obviously, Expression 4>5, so, moving one attribute from A to B will reduce the number of profiles for further checking in FSM.
end of Proof

Indexing attributes has some limitations which need more investigation. One of the limitations is that it cannot be used on profiles beginning with "//" operator. Therefore, if there are a large number of profiles which begin with "//", then the benefit may not be significant. However, we may be able to rewrite some of these profiles to replace "//" with some segments having only "/". After rewriting a profile, we can again index attributes on it. For those profiles with "//" in the middle, we cannot build index for all elements of these profiles. However we can still build index on the elements from the beginning of the profile up to the appearance of "//" to increase the benefit as much as possible. Another limitation is that it does not allow recursion in profiles. But we believe that recursion seldomly appear in *user's profiles.* And the portion of profiles before the appearance of recursion can still be indexed.

4 Performance Analysis

In this section we evaluate the performance of the filtering algorithm in XFilter and our enhancements. We examine three algorithms: (1) List Balancing with prefiltering (LBP) (Prefiltering is to eliminate profiles that contain an element which is not present in document); (2) LBP with reordering profiles (O+LBP); (3) O+LBP with indexing attributes (A+O+LBP). LBP, which is used in XFilter, acts as a control.

4.1 Experiment Settings

The experiments were carried out on a Dell Optiplex Celeron-500 PC with 128MB memory running simplified chinese windows98. All structures are built and kept in memory in all experiments.

In order to make the experiments comparable, we also used the NITF DTD which were used as the benchmark in XFilter experiments. We used the same XML documents generation tools as in XFilter: IBM's XML Generator Tool [11], which can automatically create random XML documents based on a given DTD according to some user provided constraints. We also implemented a simple profile generator for generating random profiles. For each experiment, we first generated a set of profiles and then built all the structures. After that, we fed randomly generated XML documents in. For each experimental setting, we generated and filtered XML documents until the 90% confidence intervals for the measured filter times are within plus or minus 3% of the mean. Two groups of experiments were performed. One that does not allow attributes for testing O+LBP and the other that allows attributes for testing A+O+LBP.

Table 1 list four important parameters for our experiments. P denotes the number of profiles, which is used to measure the scalability of the system in terms of the number of users. D denotes the maximum depth of the XML document

Table 1. Input parameters of data generation

Parameter	Meaning	Range
P	Number of profiles	20,000 to 100,000
D	Maximum depth of the XML document and profile	4 to 10
W	Probability of a wildcard ('*') appear in a profile	0 to 80%
A	Generate attribute or not	1/0

and profiles. For a given experiment, D is the same for both XML documents and profiles. W denotes the probability of wildcard that appears in profiles. A denotes whether attribute is generated for profiles. When A is set to 1 then each profile has one attribute. And the position of attribute is evenly distributed over all profiles.

4.2 Analysis of Experimental Results on LBP versus O+LBP

Experiment 1: Varying P (D=5, W=0, A=0)

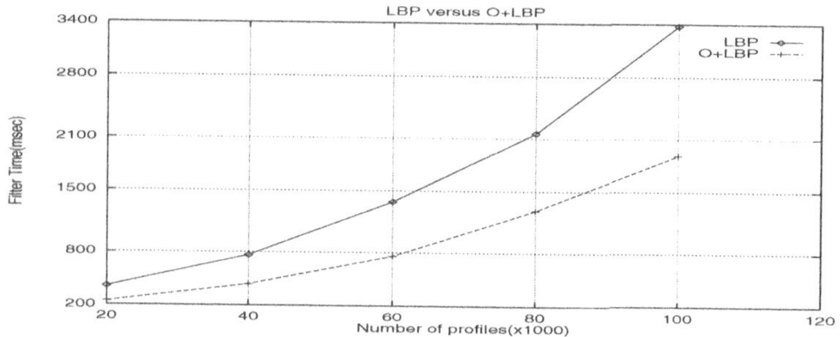

Fig. 5. Varying P, (D=5, W=0, A=0)

Experiment 2: Varying D (P=50,000, W=0, A=0)

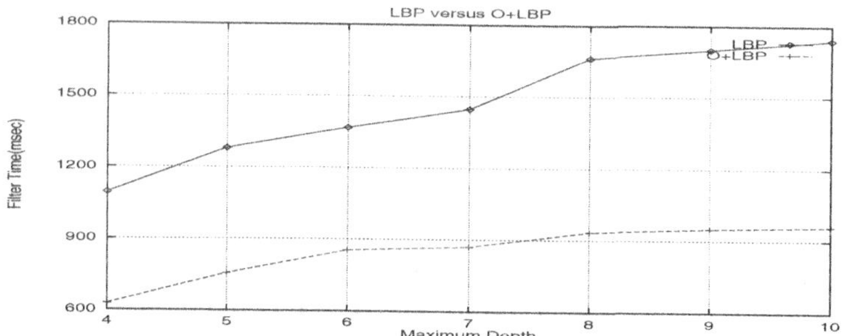

Fig. 6. Varying D, (P=50,000, W=0, A=0)

Experiment 3: Varying W (P=50,000, D=5, A=0)

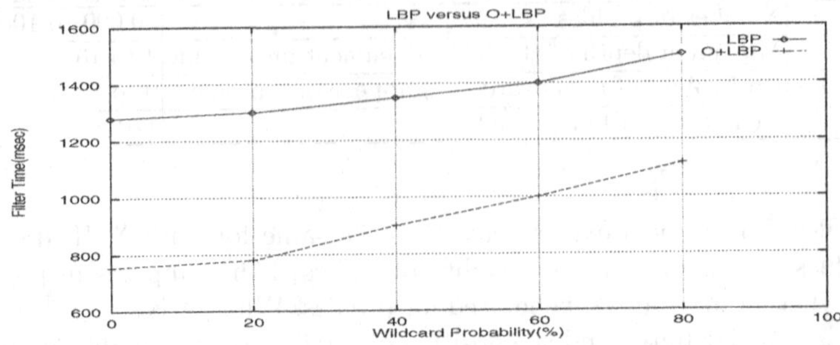

Fig. 7. Varying W, (P=50,000, D=5, A=0)

The results are shown in Figures 5, 6, and 7 respectively. In Figure 5, we can see that with reordering of profiles, the average filter time used by O+LBP is only around 60% of that of LBP. In Figure 6, although the filter time in both LBP and O+LBP increase as D increases, O+LBP increases slower than LBP. In Figure 7, O+LBP performs better than LBP, but as the number of wildcards increases, the effect of reordering profiles reduces as the reordering does not take into account of wildcards.

4.3 Analysis of Experimental Results on LBP, O+LBP versus A+O+LBP

Experiment 4: Varying P (D=5, W=0, A=1)

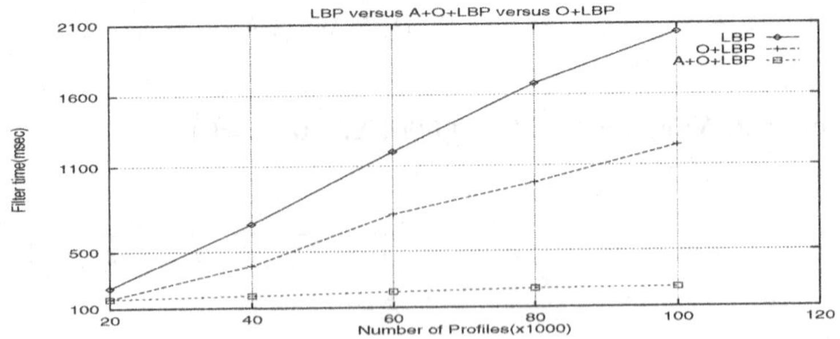

Fig. 8. Varying P, (D=5, W=0, A=1)

Experiment 5: Varying D (P=50,000, W=0, A=1)
Experiment 6: Varying W (P=50,000, D=5, A=1)

The results are shown in Figures 8, 9, and 10 respectively. In all three experiments, it is quite clear that A+O+LBP is the winner. However, from Figure

10, we can see that the performance of A+O+LBP drops as the number of wildcards increases. This is obvious because reordering profiles does not take into account of wildcards and wildcards also reduce the probability that a profile can be identified to be irrelevant in attribute appearance index.

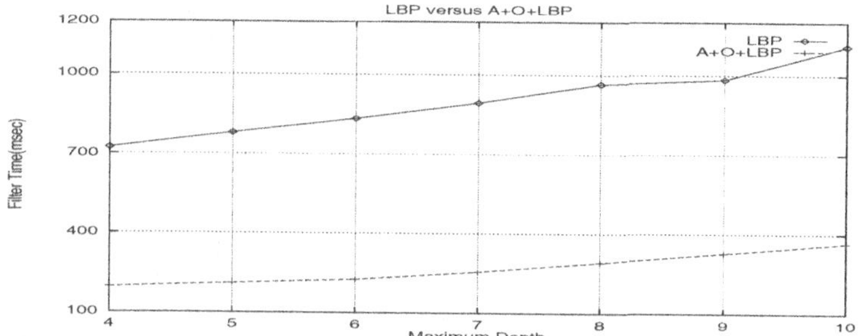

Fig. 9. Varying D, (P=50,000, W=0, A=1)

Summary of Experiments: The experiments show that the combination of reordering profiles and indexing attributes can give us good speed up compared with the original XFilter. In fact, reordering profile does not require more memory and indexing attributes only increases the memory requirement by a small amount. Therefore, the performance of these two mechanisms is verified.

5 Conclusion and Future Work

In this paper, we have designed two mechanisms: **reordering of profiles** and **indexing attributes**, which can greatly improve XFilter's efficiency. Future work include the design of an optimal distribution of profiles in the Candidate and Wait Lists and the extension of our work to allow user modify profiles online.

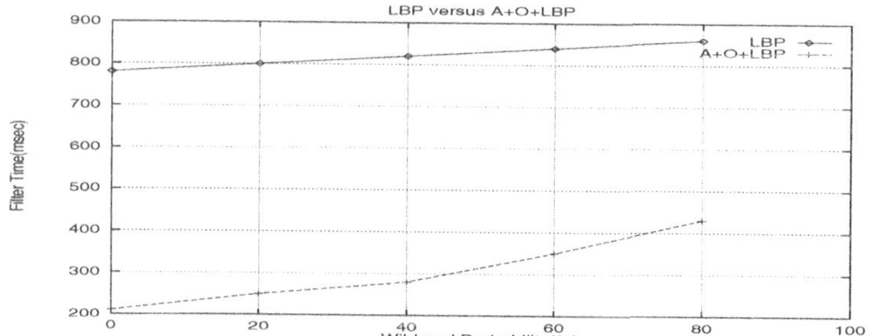

Fig. 10. Varying W, (P=50,000, D=5, A=1)

References

1. Mehmet Altinel, Michael J. Franklin, Efficient Filtering of XML Documents for Selective Dissemination of Information, In *Proc. of the 26th Conf. VLDB*, Cairo, Egypt, August 2000.
2. J.Clark, S. DeRose, XML Path Language (XPath) Version 1.0, In *W3C Recommendation*, http://www.w3.org/TR/xpath, November,1999
3. G. Salton, Automatic Text Processing, Addison Wesley, 1989
4. D. Aksoy, M. Altinel, R. Bose, U. Cetintemel, M. Franklin, J. Wang, S. Zdonik, Research in Data Broadcast and Dissemination, In *Proc. of the 1st Intl. Conf. on Advanced Multimedia Content Processing*, Osaka, Japan, November, 1998
5. M. Franklin, S. Zdonik, Data in your Face: Push Technology in Perspective, In *Proc. of ACM SIGMOD Conf.*, Seattle, WA, June, 1998
6. P. W. Foltz, S. T. Dumais, Personalized Information Delivery: An Analysis of Information Filtering Methods, CACM, 35(12):51-60, December 1992
7. T. W. Yan, H. Garcia-Molina, Index Structures for Selective Dissemination of Information Under Boolean Model, In *Proc. of ACM TODS*, 19(2):332-364, 1994
8. M. Stonebraker, A. Jhingran, J. Goh, S. Potamianos, On Rules, Procedures, Caching and Views in Data Base Systems, In *Proc. of ACM SIGMOD Conf.*, pp.281-290, 1990
9. J. Widom, S. J. Finklestein, Set-Oriented Production Rules in RElational Database Systems In *Proc. of ACM SIGMOD Conf.*, pp.177-186,1995
10. R. Cover, The SGML/XML Web Page, http://www.oasis-open.org/cover/sgml-xml.html December, 1999
11. A. L. Diaz, D. Lovell, XML Generator, http://www.alphaworks.ibm.com/tech/xmlgenerator, September, 1999

An Approach for Data Filtering Based on Rough Set Theory

Xuri Yin, Zhihua Zhou, Ning Li, and Shifu Chen

National Laboratory for Novel Software Technology, Nanjing University
Nanjing, 210093, P.R.China

adam@ai.nju.edu.cn, {zhouzh, ln, chensf}@nju.edu.cn

Abstract. Rough set theory is an important tool to deal with uncertain or vague knowledge. In this paper, the Rough set theory is deeply investigated, and an approach for data filtering based on rough set theory is proposed. The important feature of this approach is that the internal dependency structure of the system is kept intact, and that no additional parameters are needed. Theoretical analysis and experimental results show this approach can effectively reduce granularity of attribute measurement and improve the statistical signification of rules.

1 Introduction

As the amount of information in the world is steadily increasing, there is a growing demand for tools of analyzing the data and finding patterns in terms of implicit dependencies in data. Although simple statistical techniques for data analysis have been used for many years, advanced techniques for intelligent data analysis are not yet mature. As a result, there is a growing gap between data generation and data understanding. Therefore, it is very important to find a fast, effective and intelligent method for data analysis.

Rough set theory [1] which has been developed by Z. Pawlak and his co–workers since the early 1980s, and has recently received more and more attention as a means of knowledge discovery and data mining. This approach was designed as a tool to deal with uncertain or vague knowledge in AI applications, and has shown to provide a theoretical basis for the solution of many problems within knowledge discovery. The original view behind the rough set model was the observation that the information about a decision is usually vague because of uncertainty and imprecision coming from many sources and vagueness may be caused by granularity of representation of the information [2]. Knowledge representation in rough set model is done via information system, which is a tabular form of an OBJECT →ATTRIBUTE VALUE relationship. When granularity of representation of the information in information system is too high, and the number of objects in each equivalence class is very small, the classification rules generated from this information system will possibly has low correct prediction for unseen objects. Thus, it is very necessary to filter data in database in order to remove unnecessary granularity while keeping essential information.

X.S. Wang, G. Yu, and H. Lu (Eds.): WAIM 2001, LNCS 2118, pp. 367–374, 2001.

In [3,4,5,6], some more sophisticated methods for data filtering were proposed, but these methods require additional model assumptions such as the representability of the collected sample, prior probabilities, fuzzy functions, or degrees of belief. In [7], Düntsch developed a simple data filtering procedure that is compatible with the rough set approach and may improve significance of rules while keeping the dependency information [8]. The main tool is 'binary information systems', in which every attribute has exactly two values. Because we can obtain a binary system from an information system by replacing a non–binary attribute q with a set of attributes, the number of attributes in binary system is the sum of $|V_q|$ for all attribute q in original information system. Thus, this method generally results in an increased complexity. In this paper, the Rough set theory is deeply investigated, and a rough set based algorithm for data filtering in Information system is proposed. Theoretical analysis and experimental results show this algorithm can effectively reduce granulation of attribute measurement and obtain a higher strength of prediction in terms of the statistical significance of rules.

In section 2, we give an introduction to Rough sets theory. Then, in the following section, we present a rough sets theory based algorithm for data filtering and theoretical analysis of the algorithm. In section 4 we give the results of experiments by using our method to filter data in information system. In the last section we summarized work done in this paper.

2 Rough Set Theory

In this section, we illustrate the main concept of rough set theory,which are necessary for our further formulation.

Knowledge representation in rough set theory is done via information system.

Definition 1. (Information System) An information system

$$I = \langle U, \Omega, V_q, f_q \rangle_{q\in\Omega}$$

consists of

1. A finite set U of objects, $U = \{x_1, x_2, ..., x_n\}$,
2. A finite set Ω of attributes, $\Omega = \{q_1, q_2, ..., q_m\}$,
3. For each $q \in \Omega$
   (a) A set V_q of attribute values,
   (b) An information function $f_q: U \to V_q$,

A *Decision system* is an $I = \langle U, \Omega, V_q, f_q \rangle_{q\in\Omega}$ for which the attributes in Ω are further classified into disjoint sets of *condition attributes* C and *decision attributes* D.($\Omega = C \cup D, C \cap D = \varnothing$).

An *equivalence relation* is a reflexive, symmetric, and transitive binary relation on U. With each subset Q of Ω we associate an equivalence relation θ_Q on U by setting

$$x\ \theta_Q\ y \Leftrightarrow (\text{all } q \in Q)\ f_q(x) = f_q(y)$$

The partition associated with θ_Q is denoted by U/IND(Q). We denote by the symbol $[x]_Q$ the equivalence class in U/IND(Q) which contains x

$$[x]_Q = \{y : x\ \theta_Q\ y\}$$

Given Q, P $\subseteq\Omega$, each class X of θ_Q intersects one or more classes Y_i, $i \le k_X$,of_θ_P. This leads to Q, P –*rules* of the form

Deterministic rules: $x\in X \rightarrow x\in Y_0$

Indeterministic rules: $x\in X\rightarrow (x\in Y_0)\vee(x\in Y_1)\vee \ldots\vee(x\in Y_{kx})$, where $k_X > 0$, and $X\cap Y_i\neq\emptyset$, for $i \le k_X$

Class $X\in U/IND(Q)$ is called *P–deterministic* if it is contained in a class of P. We use Q→P for the conjunction over all Q, P– rules, and call *Q→P deterministic* if all Q, P – rules are deterministic. In this case, we write Q⇒P.

Definition 2. (Approximation Quality)The *approximation quality* [8] $\gamma(Q\rightarrow P)$ of a rule Q→P is defined as

$$\gamma(Q \quad P) = \frac{|\{X \quad U/IND(Q): X \quad is \quad P - Deter\min istic\}|}{|U|} \qquad \textbf{(1)}$$

Note that Q⇒P if and only if $\gamma(Q\rightarrow P) = 1$.

Let σ be a permutation of U, and $P\subseteq\Omega$, We define a new information function $f_r^{\sigma(p)}$ by

$$f_r^{\sigma(P)} = \begin{matrix} f_r(\sigma(x)) & if\ r \quad P, \\ f_r(x) & otherwise, \end{matrix} \qquad \textbf{(2)}$$

The resulting information system I_σ permute the values within the P–rows according to σ, while leaving the Q–columns constant. We let $\gamma(Q\rightarrow\sigma(P))$ be the approximation quality of the prediction of $\sigma(P)$ by Q in I_σ.

We denote by the symbol $p(\gamma(Q \quad P)\,|\,H_0)$ the extremeness of the observed approximation quality, where H_0 means the null hypothesis "Objects are randomly assigned to rules".

Definition 3. (Statistical Significance) The *statistical significance* [8] of a rule Q→P is defined as

$$p(\gamma(Q \quad P)\,|\,H_0) = \frac{|\{\gamma(Q \quad \sigma(P)) \quad \gamma(Q \quad P):\sigma \quad \Sigma\}|}{|U|!} \qquad \textbf{(3)}$$

This is the number of all permutations σ of U for which the approximation quality $\gamma(Q\rightarrow\sigma(P))$ is at least as large as the original one, normalized by the number of all permutations. If $p(\gamma(Q \quad P)\,|\,H_0)$ is low, traditionally below 5%, then the rule Q→P is deemed *significant*, otherwise, we call the rule *casual*.

Given $P\subseteq\Omega$, of particular interest in rough set theory are those attribute sets Q which are minimal with respect to the property that Q⇒P. A set Q with this property is called a *rule reduct* of P. If $P=\Omega$, we call Q simply a *reduct*. Intersection of all reducts of Ω is called as *core* of the information system I, denoted by core(I).

In rough set theory, the core elements are essential for the knowledge representation, and an empty core indicates a high substitution rate among the attributes. This may be due to high granularity in an information system.

3 Data Filtering Algorithm

3.1 Data Filtering Algorithm

When mining classification rules in a decision system I, we usually use approximation quality $\gamma(Q \to P)$ of a rule $Q \to P$ as a measure of the quality of Q with respect to P. If $\gamma(Q \to P)=1$, then the prediction is perfect. However, a perfect or high approximation quality is not a guarantee for validity of rule. If, for example, the rough set method discovers a rule $Q \to P$ that is based on only a few observations, the approximation quality of the rule may be due to chance. Although the approximation quality of the rules is high,even 1.0, the rule will still be rather useless for a different data sample. Thus, the validity of inference rules for prediction must be validated by statistical techniques.

If information granulation in an information system is high, the values of the statistical signification of rules are usually large. So, it is necessary to reduce the values of the statistical signification of rules in order to improve their strength of prediction. A possible method that could reduce the values of statistical signification is introducing data filtering to the information system.

In this section, we present a Rough sets theory based algorithm for data filtering. The basic idea is to merge the equivalence classes of θ_Q. In this way, the information granulation can be effectively reduced and the statistical signification of rules can be improved while the dependency information is reserved.

The following is a Rough sets theory based algorithm for data filtering.

Input: $I = \langle U, \Omega, V_q, f_q \rangle_{q\in\Omega}$, where $\Omega = C \cup D$, $C \cap D = \varnothing$, C and D is condition attributes and decision attributes respectively

Output: $I^R = \langle U, \Omega, V_q^R, f_q^R \rangle_{q\in\Omega}$, where $\Omega = C \cup D$ and $C \cap D = \varnothing$, C and D are condition attributes and decision attributes respectively

Step 1: For each attribute $q \in \Omega$ in I,

Calculate the sets of the equivalence classes of $\theta_{\{q\}}$, U/IND({q}) ;

Step 2: For each attribute $q \in C$ in I ,

1. Sorts the value of attribute q. Those values sorted are denoted as $q_0, q_1, \ldots q_{k-1}$;
2. Let $q_0=0$, $q_1=1$, … , $q_{k-1}=k-1$;
3. j=0;
4. $v=q_{j+1}$, $q_{j+1}=q_j$. If $[q_j]_q$ and $[q_{j+1}]_q$ are D-deterministic, and there is $Y_{i0} \in U/IND(D)$ that holds $[q_j]_q \subseteq Y_{i0}$ and $[q_{j+1}]_q \subseteq Y_{i0}$,

   then $q_{j+2}=q_{j+2}-1, \ldots , q_{k-1}=q_{k-1}-1$;

   else $q_{j+1}=v$;
5. j=j+1.If j=k then input $q_0, q_1, \ldots q_{k-1}$; else goto 4 ;

Step 3: End

3.2 Theoretical Analysis

In order to illuminate the validity of the algorithm proposed in section 3.1, we give a theoretically analysis in this section. First, we show that this algorithm can keep the approximation quality of a rule , then show that this algorithm does not decrease the statistical signification of a rule.

Theorem 1 If rule Q→D is generated from the information system I , and rule Q*→D the information system I^R, then

$$\gamma(Q\to D)=\gamma(Q^*\to D)$$

PROOF : For every attribute $q\in Q$, let q_i and q_j are its different value , and their corresponding objects are u_i and u_j, $[u_i]_q$ and $[u_j]_q$ are D–deterministic.

We denote by the symbol q* the corresponding attribute of q in the information system I^R .By the algorithm proposed in section 3.1, the object sets that are merged from $[u_i]_q$ and $[u_j]_q$ holds $[u_{ij}]_q\in U/IND(\{q^*\})$, and is D–deterministic.

By the definition of approximation quality , we have

$$\gamma(\{q\}\to D)=\gamma(\{q^*\}\to D)$$

Thereby

$$\gamma(Q\to D)=\gamma(Q^*\to D)$$

Theorem 2 If rule Q→D is generated from the information system I , and rule Q*→D the information system I^R, then

$$p(\gamma(Q \quad P)\,|\,H_0)=p(\gamma(Q^* \quad D)\,|\,H_0)$$

PROOF : Let $\sigma\in\Sigma$. First, we prove

$$\gamma(Q\to\sigma(D))\geq\gamma(Q^*\to\sigma(D))$$

Let $Q\subseteq\Omega$, there are two equivalence classes $[u_i]_Q$ and $[u_j]_Q$ that hold the condition of the algorithm. Note that they are merged to an equivalence class,denoted by $[u_i]_{Q^*}$, of Q* in the information system I^R after data-filtering。 When $[u_i]_Q$ and $[u_j]_Q$ have the same decision attribute value, the equivalence class $[u_i]_{Q^*}$ is D–deterministic. But if $[u_i]_Q$ and $[u_j]_Q$ have the different decision attribute value, then $[u_i]_{Q^*}$ is not D–deterministic.

Thus $$\gamma(Q\to\sigma(D))\geq\gamma(Q^*\to\sigma(D))$$

The following is the proof of the Theorem 2.

Because of $\gamma(Q^*\to\sigma(D))\geq\gamma(Q^*\to D)$, by the Theorem 1, we have

$$\gamma(Q\to D)=\gamma(Q^*\to D)$$

Thus $$\gamma(Q\to\sigma(D))\geq\gamma(Q^*\to\sigma(D))\geq\gamma(Q^*\to D)=\gamma(Q\to D)$$

$$\gamma(Q\to\sigma(D))\geq\gamma(Q\to D)$$

Consequently

$$|\{\gamma(Q\to\sigma(D))\geq\gamma(Q\to D):\sigma\in\Sigma\}|\geq|\{\gamma(Q^*\to\sigma(D))\geq\gamma(Q^*\to D):\sigma\in\Sigma\}|$$

By the definition of statistical signification , the conclusion follows.

Thus, it can be seen that the before-mentioned theoretical analysis shows that our algorithm for data filtering not only can keep the dependency information in the information system, but also can effectively improve the statistical signification of rules.

4 Experiments

In the first experiment, we use the example presented in reference [7] to test the algorithm proposed in this paper. The information system is displayed in Table 1.

Table 2 is the information system obtained from the information system in table 1 by using before-mentioned algorithm for data filtering.

Table 1. An information system

U	M	P	H
x_1	1	3	0
x_2	3	2	0
x_3	2	1	0
x_4	3	3	0
x_5	2	4	1
x_6	4	1	1
x_7	1	5	1
x_8	5	4	1

Table 2. Filtered information system

U	M	P	H
x_1	0	1	0
x_2	2	1	0
x_3	1	0	0
x_4	2	1	0
x_5	1	2	1
x_6	3	0	1
x_7	0	2	1
x_8	3	2	1

After data filtering, we use the GROBIAN software [9] to calculate the value of γ and α. Table 3 shows the value of γ and α before and after data-filtering (1000 times simulations) . It is easily seen that the value of γ keeps constant and the value of α has been reduced.

Table 3. The values of γ and α of the example before and after data-filtering

Parameter	Before data-filtering			After data-filtering		
	M	P	M , P	M	P	M , P
γ	0.5	0.75	1	0.5	0.75	1
α	0.773	0.417	1	0.766	0.050	0.427

In the second experiment, we use our algorithm to test the Iris data. Iris data contains 150 samples, 5 attributes (4 for condition attribute and 1 decision attribute) and 3 classes.

Fig.1 shows the number of classes of Iris data before and after data filtering, from which we can observe a dramatic fall in the number of classes of attributes.

The some values of γ and α of Iris data before and after data-filtering is given in Table 4 (1000 times simulations) .

The results of the above experiments also show that the algorithm presented in this paper can effectively improve the statistical signification of rules while keeping the dependency information

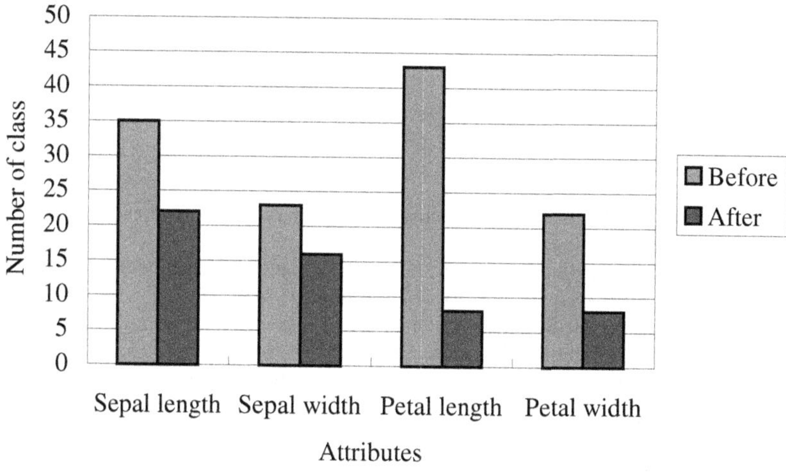

Fig. 1. The number of classes of Iris data before and after data-filtering

Table 4. The values of γ and α of Iris data before and after data-filtering

Attributes	Before filtering		After filtering	
	γ	α	γ	α
SL,SW,PL,PW	1	0.036	1	0.001
SL,SW.PL	1	0.002	1	0.001
SW,PL,PW	1	0.002	1	0.001
SL,SW	084	0.001	0.84	0.001
SL,PL	0.99	0.001	0.99	0.001
SW	0.13	0.001	0.13	0.001
SL	0.21	0.001	0.21	0.001

5 Conclusions

Rough set approach is an important tool to deal with uncertain or vague knowledge in AI applications. In this paper, the Rough set theory is deeply investigated, and a Rough set theory based algorithm for data filtering in Information system is proposed. The important feature of this approach is that the internal dependency structure of the system is kept intact, and that no additional parameters are needed. Theoretical analysis and experimental results show this algorithm can effectively reduce granularity of attribute measurement and obtain a higher strength of prediction in terms of the statistical significance of rules.

Acknowledgements. The National Science Foundation of P. R. China and the Science Foundation of Jiangsu Province, P. R. China, supported this research.

Refereces

[1] Z.Pawlak. Rough Sets. International Journal of Information and Computer Science, 11(5): 341-356, 1982.

[2] Z.Pawlak and R.Slowinski, Rough set approach to multi-attribute decision analysis, ICS Research Report 36,Warsaw University of Technology, 1993.

[3] Skowron, A. Nguyen, H. S. Quantization of real value attributes: Rough set and Boolean reasoning approach. Bulletin of International Rough Set Society, 1, 5–16,1996.

[4] Nguyen, H. S., Nguyen, S. H. Skowron, A. Searching for features defined by hyperplanes. In Z. Ras & M. Michalewicz (Eds.), ISMIS-96, Ninth International Symposium on Methodologies for Intelligent Systems, vol. 1079, 366–375, Berlin. Springer–Verlag, 1996.

[5] Skowron, A. Polkowski, L. Analytic morphology: Mathematical morphology of decision tables. Fundamenta Informaticae, 27, 255–271,1996.

[6] Düntsch.I Gediga.G. Relation restricted prediction analysis, http://www.infj.ulst.ac.uk/~cccz23/papers/ordrel.html.

[7] Düntsch.I and Gediga.G Simple data filtering in rough set systems. International Journal of Approximate Reasoning, 18, 93–106,1998.

[8] Düntsch.I and Gediga.G. Statistical evaluation of rough set dependency analysis. International Journal of Human-Computer Studies, 46, 589-604,1997.

[9] Düntsch.I and Gediga.G. The rough set engine GROBIAN. http://www.infj.ulst.ac.uk/~cccz23/papers/grobian.html.

Session 5B
Workflow & Adaptive Systems

Regular Research Paper (30 minutes)
Web-based Workflow Evolution in ADOME-WFMS

Short Research Paper (15 minutes)
Meta-Data Objects as the Basis for System Evolution

Short Research Paper (15 minutes)
Adaptive Web Meta-Search Enhanced by Constraint-based Query Constructing and Mapping

Short Research Paper (15 minutes)
A Mixed Data Dissemination Strategy for Mobile Computing Systems

Web-Based Workflow Evolution in ADOME-WFMS

Dickson K.W. Chiu[1], Qing Li[2], and Kamalakar Karlapalem[3]

[1]Dickson Computer Systems, 7A Victory Avenue, 4th floor, Homantin, Kowloon, Hong Kong
kwchiu@ieee.org

[2]Department of Computer Science, City University of Hong Kong, Tat Chee Avenue, Kowloon, Hong Kong
csqli@cityu.edu.hk

[3] Indian Institute of Information Technology, Gachibowli, Hyderabad, INDIA
kamal@iiit.net

Abstract. Workflow is automation of a business process. A Workflow Management System (WFMS) is a system that assists in defining, managing and executing workflows. Most of the current WFMSs are built on traditional relational database systems and/or are using an object-oriented database system for storing the definition and run-time data about the workflows. However, to support flexible definition and adaptive features, such as on-line workflow evolution and exception handling, a WFMS requires advanced modeling functionality. In this paper, we describe our approach towards flexible workflow definition and workflow evolution, with a meta-modeling approach supported by an integrated advanced object environment (ADOME). Web-based mechanisms are also devised as part of the ADOME-WFMS system supporting workflow evolution.

1 Introduction

Workflow management system technology, though recent, has been regarded as one of the main types of advanced information systems. It is perceived that workflow technology not only requires the support for complex data model functionality, but also flexibility for dynamically modifying the workflow specifications, especially in cases of exception handling. Because of unanticipated possibilities, special cases, changes in requirement and operation environment, exceptions may occur frequently during the execution of a business process. An exception is an event (i.e., something that happens), which deviates from normal behavior or may prevent forward progress of a workflow. Upon unexpected exceptions, a comprehensive WFMS should support *cooperative exception handling*, i.e., provide assistance for the users to reallocate resources (data / object update) or to amend the workflow, such as adding alternatives (*workflow evolution*). Further, frequent occurrences of similar exceptions have to be incorporated into workflow specifications as *expected exceptions*. Such workflow evolution can help avoid unnecessary exceptions by eliminating error-prone activities,

X.S. Wang, G. Yu, and H. Lu (Eds.): WAIM 2001, LNCS 2118, pp. 377-389, 2001.

adding alternatives, or by enhancing the operation environment. This can lead to a WFMS that supports workflow adaptation through exceptions. Thus, in contrast with traditional software systems, workflows usually evolve more frequently.

To support for flexible workflow definition, enactment and evolution, the support for powerful data model functionality is necessary. Using extended object oriented meta-modeling is a promising approach, as illustrated in this paper. With this approach, we can have a simple but expressive core data dictionary (meta-schema). From this meta-schema, users can define all other classes for the WFMS, including activity schemas, exceptions and handlers. Further, from these schemas WFMS objects (in particular, activity instances) can be instantiated. This contributes a substantial improvement to WFMS modeling based on relational models because the entity modeling and implementation is tied together in a straightforward manner. Extensive reuse can also be facilitated as discussed in [10].

In this paper, we present our approach towards flexible workflow definition and online workflow evolution in an advanced object environment, with reference to ADOME-WFMS [8,10]. Different from our other papers such as [8] which presented a classification of exceptions and handlers, [9] which detailed ADOME-WFMS exception driven workflow recovery, and [10] which focused on our error handling mechanisms, the objectives and contributions of this paper are as follows: (i) We present a coherent practical solution from workflow modeling, definition to evolution. Moreover, the meta-modeling approach to activity modeling, which facilitates flexible workflow definition and evolution, is novel. (ii) We demonstrate the use of ADOME-WFMS in supporting flexible workflow definition and workflow evolution through effective web interface facilities. Such a web-based workflow evolution approach is trendy and promising. (iii) While many other works concentrate on theoretic aspects of workflow evolution, we demonstrate the mechanisms for workflow evolution and various workflow evolution policies with detailed but simple algorithms, based on our expressive activity meta-model. (iv) Even though there have been numerous works in workflow evolution and workflow exception, our proposal of an augmented solution for exception handling based on workflow evolution is novel. Furthermore, because our underlying ADOME environment is essentially an active OODBMS, many techniques presented in this paper should be applicable to WFMSs based on similar environments.

The rest of our paper is organized as follows. Section 2 presents a meta-modeling approach to activity modeling, which facilitates reuse, flexible workflow enactment and evolution. Section 3 explains the mechanisms of workflow evolution in ADOME-WFMS and how various workflow evolution policies are supported. Section 4 presents the web-based mechanism of ADOME-WFMS supporting workflow evolution. Section 5 compares related work. Finally, we conclude the paper with our plans for further research in Section 6.

2 Flexible Activity META-modeling

The activity model of ADOME-WFMS is in accordance with the WfMC standard [24]. Typically, an activity is recursively decomposed into *sub-activities* and eventually down to the unit level called *tasks* (as illustrated by the example in Fig. 1). Sibling sub-activities / tasks belonging to the same parent activity form a directed graph that defines the execution dependencies among them. These dependencies, including sequence, parallel, conditional and synchronization, are expressed graphically as follows: An arc pointing from activity A1 to A2 denotes A2 is to be executed immediately after A1 (i.e. A2 is a successor of A1). Outgoing arcs from activity A to more than one successor denote parallel execution branches of all the successors after A is completed (called *split*). Transition predicates may be associated with these splits. Only those arcs where transition predicate evaluates to true are executed. If the transition predicates of a split are in mutual exclusion, the split is called an OR-split (representing decision), otherwise it is called an AND-split (representing parallel execution). Incoming arcs towards an activity A from more than one predecessor are called *join*. AND-join synchronization activates A when all predecessors of A finish. OR-join activates A when any predecessor finishes (i.e., no synchronization is involved).

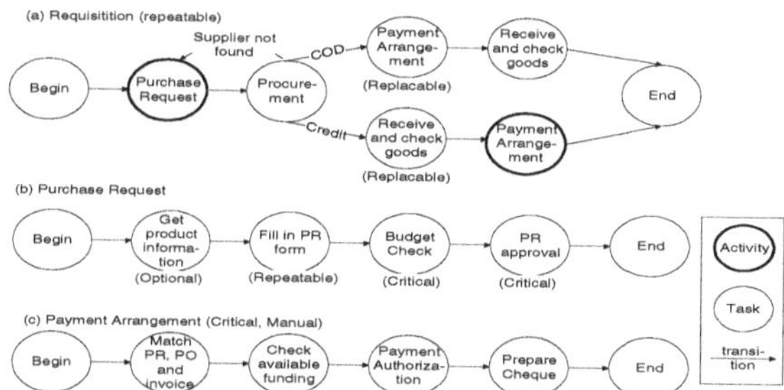

Fig. 1. Example Workflow of Requisition Procedures

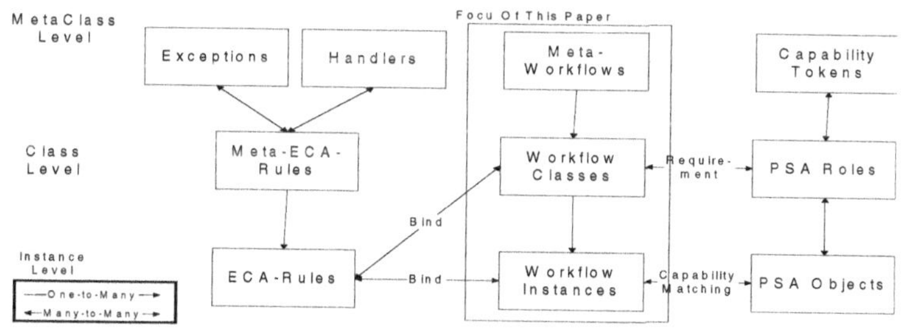

Fig. 2. Three-Level Meta-Modeling for ADOME-WFMS

Many of the earlier WFMSs [12] are built on top of traditional database technologies (e.g., relational databases). They fall short in facilitating / offering flexibility of modeling, ease of implementation, and/or in handling dynamic run-time requirements. Advanced features — objects, rules, roles, active capability and the flexibility — of object-oriented database systems are needed to facilitate the development of a versatile WFMS [7], especially with meta-modeling approach. In ADOME-WFMS, we advocate a three-level meta-modeling approach wherein workflows, capabilities, exceptions, and handlers are defined at a meta-level as depicted in Fig. 2.

Workflow templates are defined at the meta-level so that actual workflows can be instantiated for specific applications. For example, a generic requisition workflow template can be declared at the meta-level, so that specific requisition workflows have customized rules and sub-activities can be instantiated. Capability tokens are defined at the meta-level so that they can be combined to form PSA-roles, which capture requirements of task classes (cf. [8]). Exceptions (which are events) and handlers (which correspond to conditions and actions) are defined at the meta-level. Exceptions are associated to handlers in the form of meta-Event-Condition-Action-rules (meta-ECA-rules). Specific ECA-rules can then be bound to workflow for versatile exception handling (cf. [10]).

```
class WFMS_class
class_attributes:
  Class_Description: string;
  Class_Date_Created: date;
Attributes:
  Instance_Date_Created: date;
  Name: string;
  Instance_Description: string;
end

   class Task isa Activity
   attribute_initilization:
      Activity_Graph = NIL;
    attributes:
     Task_Need: set of Token;
     Allow_Partial_Match: bool;

          ...
   methods
     Match_Cost,
         Partial_Match,
     Match_Cost_Ext...
   end

class Arc isa WFMS_class
   Source, Destination:
      Activities;
   Transisition_Condition:
      Boolean;
end;
```

```
class Graph_Node isa WFMS_class
attributes:
  Subactivity: Activity;
  Predecessor_Join: (AND_join, OR_join, NIL);
  Successor_Split: (AND_split, OR_split, NIL);
end;

class Activity isa WFMS_class
 /* all activities are sub-classes of this
  meta-activity class because each different
  activity class can have multiple instance */
class_attributes:
  Input_Parameters, Output_Parameters,
  IO_Parameters: set of Parameter;
events:
  execute, finish, abort ...
exceptions:
  no_PSA, PSA_reject, cannot_proceed ...
rules:
  Manditory_handlers: set of rules;
  Handlers: set of rules;
attributes:
  Activity_Graph:
   (Activity_Node set of Graph_Node;
    Transisition set of Arc;)
  Reexecution_Pattern:
      (optional, repeatable, replacable…);
  /* parameters for execution of instance */
  Priority: integer;
  PSA_chosen: set of PSA;
methods
  Decomposition, PSA_for_Activity, Execution, ....
end
```

Fig. 3. Meta-level Specification of Activities and Tasks

To illustrate further, the meta-level design for activity schemas is shown in Fig. 3 with the following features. All activity schemas are treated as sub-classes of the meta-class `Activity`. `WFMS_class` serves as the root class of all class definitions in the WFMS for easy maintenance of the classes and objects. The meta-activity schema contains all features for defining activity schemas, such as input/output parameters, and the activity graph, which describes the sub-activities and their incoming/outgoing transitions, join/split types, mandatory/regular handlers. Class-attributes (which is a feature supported in many advanced object-oriented systems [17]) are used for storing either attributes of the class object (such as class description) or attributes of the same value among all objects of the class (such as the input / output specifications). All sub-class objects inherit the definition attributes of the super-class object but each of the classes can have their own value of class attributes. WFMS related events for activities (such as `execute`, `finish`, `abort`), standard workflow exceptions (such as `no_PSA`, `PSA_reject`, `cannot_proceed`) are declared with the meta-class so that these features are applicable to all activities schemas.

When an activity instance is started, it has its own copy of the activity graph and re-execution pattern. This allows both instance and schema level workflow evolution. On the other hand, rule objects can be declared outside of the scope of activities first, and then bound to individual activity schemas (or specific instances) to facilitate reuse. This full object-oriented approach enables full inheritance of various activity properties (such as rules and re-execution mode) down the composition hierarchy and applies to each of the activity / task instances. From this meta-level schema, users can define all other classes for the WFMS, including activity schemas, PSAs, roles, exceptions and handlers. Further, from these schemas WFMS objects (in particular, activity instances) can be instantiated. This contributes a substantial improvement to WFMS modeling based on relational models (such as [18]) because the entity modeling and implementation is tied together in a straightforward manner. Extensive reuse is also facilitated as discussed in [10].

3 Flexible Workflow Evolution

ADOME-WFMS has the required facilities for supporting various types of workflow evolution (cf. [8]). In particular, besides conventional exception handling resolutions, the *Human Intervention Manager* sub-module also accepts update of workflow on-line. In contrast, there are currently few WFMSs having such facilities for supporting the whole spectrum of exception-handling resolutions, especially those relating to workflow evolution. In ADOME-WFMS, the user can choose any of the suggested resolutions to be persistent, or enter schema evolution operations, update of workflow and/or enter new ECA rules (but subject to the enforcement strategies as described in the next section). As workflow evolution requires the modification of workflow definitions or adding ECA rules to the system during work in progress, an advanced schema evolution capability is required at run-time. Due to ADOME's support of dynamic schema evolution [19], ADOME-WFMS readily provides exception resolutions based on schema evolution. It should be noted that the resolutions based on schema evolution are general-purpose ones, which can help reduce the occurrence of additional exceptions.

3.1 Workflow Evolution Primitives

In [2], a complete, minimal, and consistent set of workflow evolution primitives is proposed. Workflow evolution primitives can be used for static and dynamic workflow evolution, including for migration of individual workflow instances. They are divided into two parts: (i) *declaration primitives* modify the declaration of workflow variables (including their default values), (ii) *flow primitives* modify the flow structure of the workflow schema. In this section, we show how this set of primitives are adapted and supported in the ADOME-WFMS framework.

```
PROCEDURE AppendNode (n, a: Activity, G: Activity_Graph)
   IF (a=END) OR (n IN G.Subactivity) THEN RETURN ERROR;
   G.Arc = G.Arc U (a, n, true)
   G.Graph_node = G.Graph_node U (n, NIL, a.Successor_Split)
   FOREACH j in G.Arc where j.Source=a
       j = (n,  j.Destination, j.Transition_Condition)
   END
END

PROCEDURE SplitNode (n, a: Activity, b: Boolean, G: Activity_Graph)
   IF (n=a) OR (n IN a.Successor) OR
      (a.Successor_Split=AND_Split)OR (n.Predecessor_Join=AND_join)
   THEN RETURN ERROR
   G.arc = G.arc U (a, n, b)
   a.Successor_Split = OR_split;  n.Predessor_Join = OR_join
END

PROCEDURE JoinNode (a: Activity, w: set of Activity; G: Activity_Graph)
   FOREACH j in w do
      IF (j.Succesor_Split=OR_split) or (a IN j.Successor)
      THEN RETURN ERROR
   END
   IF (a IN w) OR (a.Predecessor_Join =OR_join)
   THEN RETURN ERROR
   FOREACH j in w do
      G.arc = G.arc U (j, a, true); j.Successor_Split = AND_split
   END
   a.Predessor_Join = AND_join
END

PROCEDURE ModifyCondtion(s, t: Activity, b: Boolean; G: Activity_Graph)
    IF (s, t, *) not IN G.arc THEN RETURN ERROR
    UPDATE j.Transition_Condition = b
         WHERE j IN G.arc AND j.source=s AND j.destination=t
END

PROCEDURE InsertBefore (n, a: Activity, G: Activity_Graph)
   IF (a=BEGIN) OR (n IN G.Subactivity) THEN RETURN ERROR;
   G.arc = G.arc U (n, a, true)
   G.graph_node = G.Graph_Node U (n, a.Predecessor_Join)
   FOREACH j in G.Arc where j.Destination=a
     j = (j.Source, n,  j.Transition_Condition)
   END
END

PROCEDURE DeleteNode (n: Activity, G: Activity_Graph)
   replace n in G.graph_node by a null node.
END
```

Fig. 4. Algorithms for ADOME-WFMS Workflow Evolution Primitives

Declarative primitives modify the declaration of workflow variables and their default values. This is well supported in ADOME-WFMS, since the underlying ADOME layer, actually has the same corresponding primitives for schema evolution. Declarative primitives include:

1. *Addvar (a: Activity, v: Variable_Name, t: Type, d: DefaultValue)* adds an attribute *v* of type *t* with initial value to the schema declaration of an activity / task *a* if the attribute does not exist in the activity schema. We add the following feature for convenience: if the attribute *v* exists, the default value is changed to *d* while the

type parameter must be unchanged. In both cases, the value *d* must conform to type *t*.

2. RemoveVar (*a: Activity, v: Variable_Name*) removes the attribute *v* from the schema declaration of an activity / task *a*. However, we do not allow attributes of the activity schema that capture important activity semantic information (*workflow system variables*) to be deleted. These attributes, such as `Activity_Graph`, `PSA_chosen`, `priority`, `task_need`, etc., are listed in the meta-activity schema declaration (cf. Fig. 3),

In particular, changing default values of *workflow system variables* have important semantics, such as change of task capability requirement, default rule binding (cf. Fig. 3). Thus, the *Addvar* primitive should support change of default value, because we do allow deleting this protected variable and later adding it back with a new default value to implement this effect.

Flow primitives modify the flow structure of the activity schema. With reference to the meta-activity schema declaration, all these primitives, in essence, update the default value of the initial value of the workflow system variable `Activity_Graph`. On the other hand, if we want to apply flow primitives to evolve an activity instance, we update the `Activity_Graph` attribute of the instance instead. Flow primitives include:

1. AppendNode (*n, a: Activity*) inserts a new sub-activity named *n* in the activity graph, as a successor of sub-activity named *a*; former successors of a will become successors of *n* in the new schema. Activity *a* can be *START* node, but not the *END* node. If we want to add another sub-activity instance that already exists, we can create a new activity class *n2* that is a sub-class of *n*, and add *n2* instead. For example, the second occurrence of the "Payment_Arrangement" sub-activity in the activity graph is defined as another sub-activity called "Payment_Arrangment2", which is a sub-class of the former one.
2. SplitNode (*n, a: Activity; b: Boolean*) adds an existing task *n* among the successors of *a*, (i.e., adds *a* transition from *a* to *n* in the activity graph), with transition condition *b*. Now, *a* becomes an OR-split node and *n* becomes an OR-join node. Activity *n* should be different from *a* and *n* should not already be a successor of *a*. Moreover, *a* should not be an AND-split, while *n* should not be an AND-join node. (If *a* is an AND-split node, append a dummy node *a2* to *a* first. If *n* is an AND-join node, insert a dummy *n2* node before *n* first.)
3. JoinNode (*a: Activity; w: set of Activity*) makes all activities in *w* become predecessors of *a* in AND-join mode. Activity *a* should not be in *w* and or in the set of *w*'s successors. Moreover, *a* should not be an OR-join node, while all activities in *w* should not be an OR-split node. (If *a* is an OR-join node, insert a dummy node *s2* before *s* first. If any task *j* in *w* is an OR-split node, append a dummy node for each *j* first.)
4. ModifyCondition(*s,t: Activity; b: Boolean*) change the transition condition of the arc from *s* to *t* to *b*. The arc must exist for such a modification.

Based on the above primitives, other common operators can be derived, according to [2]. Fig. 4 illustrates how these primitives are implemented in ADOME-WFMS.

Another operator InsertBefore (*n, a: Activity*) is included to illustrate how other operators can be directly implemented in ADOME-WFMS. This operator inserts a new sub-activity named *n* in the activity graph, as a predecessor of sub-activity named *a*; former predecessors of *a* will become successors of *n* in the new schema. Similarly, DeleteNode (*n : Activity*) can also be implemented by replacing the target node with a null node.

From a user's perspective, these primitives may be too low-level. Some typical workflow evolution methods for ADOME-WFMS at a higher-level (as explained [8]) are illustrated in Table 1. These are specified with the above-mentioned workflow primitives so that users can easily choose their desired workflow evolution. Furthermore, these workflow evolution actions are typical solutions for avoiding some currently anticipated exceptions.

Table 1. Sample Specification for Workflow Evolutions in ADOME-WFMS

Other Workflow Evolution Actions	*Expression in ADOME-WFMS Workflow Evolution Primitives*
Add sub-activity which recruits more PSAs before *a* with capability requirement *cap*, budget *b* and deadline *t*	`InsertBefore(a, RecuitPSA(cap, b, t))`
Force PSA assignment to task *a* with an expression *e*	`Addvar(a, PSA_Chosen, PSA, e)`
Change capability requirement for task *a* to *tok*	`Addvar(a, Task_Need, set of Token, tok)`
Delete branch arc from activity s to t	`Modify_Condition(s, t, false)`

Add preparation work step *p*, which will be executed upon condition *c*, before transition from sub-activity *a* to *b*	`InsertBefore(b, p);`
	`SplitNode(a, b, not c);`
	`ModifyCondition(a, p, c)`

Add procedural handler *p* to activity *a* upon exception condition *c* (*p* resumes execution to *a*'s successor)	`InsertAfter(a, p);`
	`SplitNode(a, a.Succesor, not c);`
	`ModifyCondition(a, p, c)`

Add constraint *c* in the form of an ECA rule to activity *a*	`Addvar(a, Manditory_Handler, set of rules, a.Manitory_Handler.Init U c)`
Add ECA rule handler to activity *a*	`Addvar(a, Handler, set of rules, a.Handler.Init U c)`

3.2 Workflow Evolution Policies

Workflow evolution policies refer to how workflow instances adopt newly evolved workflow schema, while they are executing. Because ADOME-WFMS uses activity decomposition, upon workflow evolution (i.e., modification of a certain sub-activity class definition), the side effects of affecting other activities containing this sub-activity are very much confined. At the time of the workflow evolution, only those activities having the same sub-activity currently executing are affected. Other activities having the same sub-activity but not currently executing are unaffected since the sub-activity is encapsulated, and behaves as a black box to activities at a higher level. In order to allow further control over the semantics and implications of workflow evolution, users can choose the following workflow evolution policies: (1) *Temporary change*: only change the current instance (e.g., as a trial). (2) *Delayed change*: change the current and future instances, the other sub-activity instances currently executing continue using the old definition (e.g., the user judges that the extra costs in affecting other ongoing jobs is not worthwhile since the exception case may or may not happen). (3) *Abrupt change*: abort the current and other executing instances of the sub-activity; re-execute with the new definition or alternate paths as determined by the exception handling mechanism for the parent activity (e.g., because of a critical problem observed in activity definition). (4) *Immediate change*: all the instances suddenly use the new definition. The user should judge whether this has inconsistency impact. Valid examples include: adding new alternative branches, adding exception handlers, etc. (5) *Progressive change*: allow different instance to take different decisions on whether to hand over to the new schema.

Progressive change needs the most attention. In [20], a mechanism called hand-over policy is used, in which hand-over rules (in the form of ECA rules) are used to specify how individual affected workflow instances adopt the new schema for execution. The main issue considered is the position of a running instance, i.e., the current task of that instance being executed (specified with the "ON" clause). The condition part can be any user-defined condition, including those referring to past execution history. Because ADOME-WFMS Recovery Manager (cf. [9]) keeps track of the sequence of executing tasks and sub-activities for backtracking, not only the current position but also any pattern specification on the execution history can be specified.

The action part can be as follows: (1) The "rollback to *t*" primitive specifies to semantically undo some work back to the execution position *t* so that the running instance can comply with the new workflow schema. The ADOME-WFMS Recovery Manger supports this primitive as described in [9]. (2) The "change over to *t*" primitive specifies migration to the new schema and resumes by jumping to task/sub-activity *t*, which can be specify as the same position of the old schema. Under our ADOME-WFMS activity and execution model, the corresponding action is to update the value of the activity graph to the new one, and then to trigger *t*'s start event. (3) The "go ahead" primitive specifies continuing with the old schema, i.e. nothing should be done to that instance. Furthermore, [20] showed how these hand-over primitives could be used to specify various workflow evolution policies. Since ADOME-WFMS can support these primitives, ADOME-WFMS can support various workflow evolution policies described in this section.

4 Web-Based Interface for Workflow Evolution

We have also designed a web-based interface for workflow evolution. Upon pressing the *Workflow Evolution* button, the user can access a workflow evolution menu page as shown Fig. 5, where a set of possible high-level workflow evolution options (cf. Table 2) are presented. However, a full-fledged graphical interface for workflow evolution (accessible with the *Workflow Editor* button) is under construction and is beyond the scope of this paper. In addition, the user may press the *Other Workflow Evolution* button to access Advanced Workflow Evolution menu page for entering workflow evolution primitives (as described in Section 3.1). Multiple primitive steps can be entered and edited, so that the workflow definition can be changed to a desired new one in one shot, and evolution policy can be defined accordingly.

As for workflow evolution policies (cf. Section 3.2), simple ones (viz. temporary change, immediate change, delayed change, and abrupt change) are accessible with buttons as shown in Fig. 5. If progressive change is required, the user can press the *Go and Set Evolution Policy* button to access the detailed Workflow Evolution Policy menu page. Here, evolution policy rules can be entered in the form of event-condition-action rules. To simplify frequently used operation, the condition part can be entered in the form of "Before / At / After" a task/activity (accessible with a pull-down menu) of the original workflow, while the action part can be entered in the form of "Rollback / Change Over / Go Ahead" to a task/activity of the new workflow.

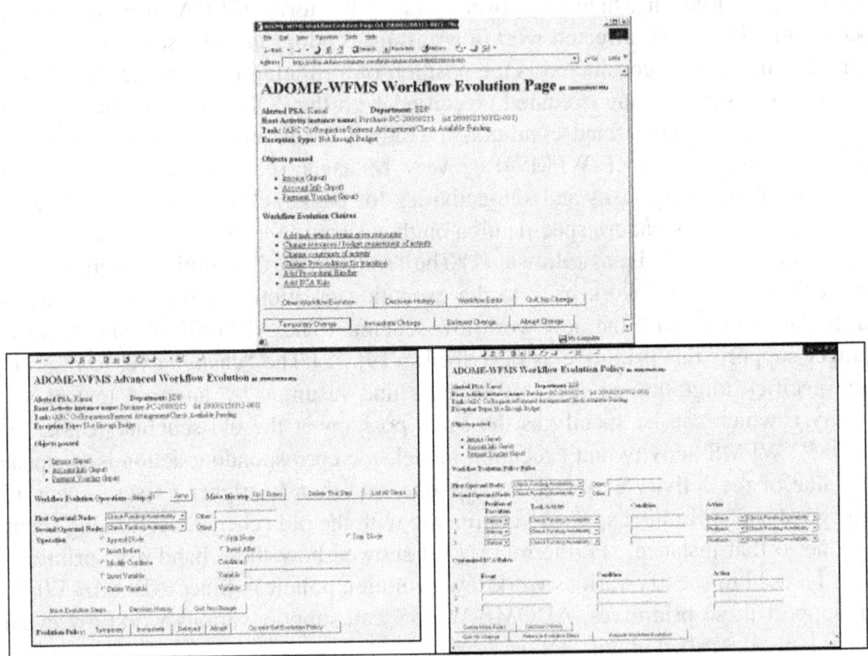

Fig. 5. ADOME-WFMS Workflow Evolution Web Pages

5 Related Work

Dartflow [4] is one of the first web-based WFMS, using transportable agents, CGI and Java technologies. Eflow [3] is one of the closest commercial systems with features like E-ADOME in handling e-Services. However, Eflow does not address matching of agents directly with tasks. Instead, it uses the concept of generic service node and service selection rules. Currently, several commercial WFMSs such as TIB/InConcert [21] and Staffware 2000 [23], provide web user interface too. In addition, I-Flow [14] has a Java workflow engine. However, not all the above-mentioned WFMSs support for web-based cooperative exception handling, workflow evolution or active paging of clients with Internet message facilities like ICQ.

One of the earliest work in workflow evolution is [13], where correctness criteria for instance migration are defined based on the definition of the set of all valid node sequences, i.e., a change is valid if the execution sequence can be obtained with the new workflow definition. As discussed in Section 3, We apply the techniques of [2] and [20] in designing ADOME-WFMS workflow evolution primitives and operations. PROSYT [11], ADEPTflex [22] and [1] are works on adapting workflow at instance level, but not for schema or workflow evolution.

In summary, few systems have advocated (let alone supported) an extensive meta-modeling approach (based on agents, match-making, exception handling, etc.). Most related work addresses exceptions caused by inappropriate workflow evolution rather than how workflow evolution can contribute to exception handling and avoidance. They do not provide a web interface for workflow evolution.

6 Conclusions

This paper has presented, in details, a coherent practical solution from workflow modeling to evolution, based on a meta-modeling approach in ADOME-WFMS. We have demonstrated the simplicity and expressiveness of this approach, where the entity modeling and implementation is tied together in a straightforward manner. In particular, we have shown the mechanisms for workflow evolution and various workflow evolution policies with detailed but simple algorithms, based on our activity meta-model. The resultant system (i.e. ADOME-WFMS) can therefore gracefully support flexible exception handling with a novel augmented solution based on workflow evolution. We have also illustrated the use of ADOME-WFMS, through effective web interface facilities being built upon the ADOME prototype system, in supporting flexible workflow enactment and workflow evolution. Furthermore, because our ADOME environment is essentially an active OODBMS, many techniques presented in this paper should be applicable to WFMSs based on similar environments. We consider further research issues on interfacing and interoperability important for extending the applicability of an advanced WFMS engine, which includes: expanding the possible interfaces and coordinating different types of agents, graphical workflow evolution tools, and inter-operating with other WFMS. On the other hand, we are interested in the application of ADOME-WFMS in various advanced real-life e-commerce environments [6], such as procurement, finance, stock trading and insurance. As mentioned, a web-based user interface environment supporting the whole range of activities is being devised for ADOME-WFMS; we believe such an interface environment is particularly suitable for the advanced e-commerce applications which we plan to target at.

References

1. Borgida A., Murata, T.: A Unified Framework for Tolerating Exceptions in Workflow/Process Models - A Persistent Object Approach, International Joint Conference on Work Activities Coordination and Collaboration (WACC '99), San Francisco (1999)
2. Casati, F.: Models, Semantics, and Formal Methods for the Design of Workflows and their Exceptions. PhD thesis, Dipartimento di Elettronica e Informazione, Politecnico di Milano, Milano, Italy (1998)
3. Casati, F., et al.: Adaptive and Dynamic Service Composition in eFlow. HP Laboratories Technical Report HPL-2000-39 (2000)
4. Cai, T., Gloor, P., Nog, S.: DartFlow: A Workflow Management System on the Web using Transportable Agents, Technical Report PCS-TR96-283, Dartmouth College, Hanover, N.H., 1996
5. Chan, L.C., Li, Q.: An Extensible Approach to Reactive Processing in an Advanced Object Modeling Environment. In Proceedings of 8th Intl. Conf. on Database and Expert Systems Applications (DEXA '97). LNCS(1308), Toulouse, France (1997) 38-47
6. Chiu, D.K.W., Karlapalem, K., Li, Q.: E-ADOME: A Framework For Enacting E-services. VLDB Workshop on Technologies for E-Services, Cairo, Eygpt (2000)
7. Chiu, D.K.W., Li, Q.: A Three-Dimensional Perspective on Integrated Management of Rules and Objects. International Journal of Information Technology, **3**(2) (1997) 98-118
8. Chiu, D.K.W., Li, Q., Karlapalem, K.: A Meta Modeling Approach for Workflow Management Systems Supporting Exception Handling, Special Issue on Method Engineering and Metamodeling, Information Systems, Elsevier Science, 24(2) (1999)159-184
9. Chiu, D.K.W., Li, Q., Karlapalem, K.: Facilitating Exception Handling with Recovery Techniques in ADOME Workflow Management System, Journal of Applied Systems Studies, Cambridge International Science Publishing, Cambridge, England, **1**(3) (2000)
10. Chiu, D.K.W., Li, Q., Karlapalem, K.: Web Interface-driven Cooperative Exception Handling in ADOME Workflow Management System, Information Systems, Elsevier Science, 26(2) (2001)
11. Cugola, G.: Inconsistencies and Deviations in Process Support Systems, PhD Thesis, Politecnico di Milano (1998)
12. Dogac, A., Ozsu, T., Sheth, A. (eds): Proceedings of the NATO Advanced Study Institute (ASI) Workshop on Workflow Management Systems and Interoperability, Istambul,Turkey (1997)
13. Ellis, S., et al: Dynamic Change within Workflow Systems, Proceedings of the Conference on Organizational Computing Systems (1995).
14. Enix Consulting Limited. An Independent Evaluation of i-Flow Version 3.5, 2000 (available at http://www.i-flow.com).
15. GHG Corp: Clips Architecture Manual, Version 5.1 (1992) available at http://www.ghg.net/clips/CLIPS.html
16. Hagen, C., Alonso, G.: Flexible Exception Handling in the OPERA Process Support System, 18th International Conference on Distributed Computing Systems (ICDCS 98), Amsterdam, The Netherlands (1998)
17. Ibex Corporation: Itasca Reference Manual, 1994.
18. Karlapalem, K., Yeung, H. P., Hung, P. C. K.: CapBaseED-AMS - A Framework for Capability-Based and Event-Driven Activity Management System. In Proceeding of COOPIS '95 (1995) 205-219

19. Li, Q., Lochovsky, F. H.: ADOME: an Advanced Object Modeling Environment. IEEE Transactions on Knowledge and Data Engineering, **10**(2) (1998) 255-276
20. Liu, C., Orlowska, M., Li. H.: Automating handover in dynamic workflow environments. In Proceedings of the 10th International Conference on Advanced Information Systems Engineering CAiSE'98, Pisa, Italy (1998)159-172
21. McCarthy, D., Sarin, S.: Workflow and Transactions in InConcert. IEEE Data Engineering,16(2) (1993) 53-56
22. M. Reichert and P. Dadam. ADEPTflex - supporting dynamic changes of workflows without losing control. *Journal of Intelligent Information Systems*, 10(2):93-129, Mar. 1998
23. Staffware Corporation: Staffware Global - Staffware's Opportunity to Dominate Intranet based Workflow Automation (2000) http://www.staffware.com
24. Workflow Management Coalition: The Workflow Reference Model. (WFMC-TC-1003, 19-Jan-95, 1.1) (1995)

Meta-data Objects as the Basis for System Evolution

Florida Estrella[1], Zsolt Kovacs[2], Jean-Marie Le Goff[2], Richard McClatchey[1], and Norbert Toth[1]

[1]Centre for Complex Cooperative Systems, UWE, Frenchay, Bristol BS16 1QY UK
Richard.McClatchey@cern.ch
[2]EP Division, CERN, Geneva, Switzerland
Jean-Marie.Le.Goff@cern.ch

Abstract. One of the main factors driving object-oriented software development in the Web-age is the need for systems to evolve as user requirements change. A crucial factor in the creation of adaptable systems dealing with changing requirements is the suitability of the underlying technology in allowing the evolution of the system. A reflective system utilizes an open architecture where implicit system aspects are reified to become explicit first-class (meta-data) objects. These implicit system aspects are often fundamental structures which are inaccessible and immutable, and their reification as meta-data objects can serve as the basis for changes and extensions to the system, making it self-describing. To address the evolvability issue, this paper proposes a reflective architecture based on two orthogonal abstractions - model abstraction and information abstraction. In this architecture the modeling abstractions allow for the separation of the description meta-data from the system aspects they represent so that they can be managed and versioned independently, asynchronously and explicitly. A practical example of this philosophy, the CRISTAL project, is used to demonstrate the use of meta-data objects to handle system evolution.

1 Reflection

The capability of a system to reflect upon itself and be able to inspect and change its own state and behavior is called reflection. A reflective system utilizes an open architecture where implicit system aspects are reified to become explicit first-class meta-objects [1]. These implicit aspects are often fundamental structures which are inaccessible and immutable. Meta-objects are the self-representations of the system describing how its internal elements can be accessed and manipulated. These self-representations are causally connected to the internal structures they represent, i.e. changes to these self-representations immediately affect the underlying system.

The use of reflection in computing creates a mutable and extensible system [2]. In a mutable system, the behavior of existing constructs can be modified. On the other hand, an extensible system allows new features to be added. The ability to dynamically augment, extend and re-define system specifications can result in a considerable improvement in flexibility. This leads to dynamically modifiable systems which can adapt and cope with evolving requirements.

X.S. Wang, G. Yu, and H. Lu (Eds.): WAIM 2001, LNCS 2118, pp. 390-399, 2001.

A reflective open architecture likewise increases a system's potential for reuse [3]. The customization mechanisms inherent in this architecture permit the system to be modified and reused for different needs. Making the components of the system self-representing or self-describing allows dynamic system re-configuration. It is therefore essential for such a self-describing system to have the capability to store descriptions about its dynamic structure, and make these descriptions available to the rest of the infrastructure as a consequence of how the system is connected.

The separation of system descriptions from the system aspects they represent is essential in the specification of evolvable OO system. To address the evolvability issue, this paper proposes a reflective architecture based on two orthogonal abstractions - model abstraction and information abstraction. In this architecture the modeling abstractions allow for the separation of description meta-data from the system aspects they represent so that they can be managed and versioned independently, asynchronously and explicitly.

Meta-Object Protocol (MOP), a concrete manifestation of the open implementation technique, opens up language abstractions and its implementations to the programmers [1][4]. Consequently, programmers are capable of adjusting the language semantics and implementation better to suit their needs. Such flexibility in altering language semantics, and possibly improving performance through alternative implementation strategies, results in considerable benefit and program clarity for programmers in being able to customize the language semantics, and encourages programmers to participate in the language design process. MOP-based open languages are also called reflective programming languages. In general, a reflective system is a system which incorporates structures representing aspects of itself [5]. Such capability can only be attained if the language provides mechanisms which explicitly represent implicit aspects of the language itself, i.e. its descriptions and behavior.

Some descriptions which play major roles in defining a language behavior are class, attribute, association, inheritance, operation invocation, instance representation and the schema. To be able to dynamically modify these descriptions, they need to be turned into objects, thus creating class objects, attribute objects, association objects, etc. These objects are called meta-objects, as compared to application objects which are called base objects. Meta-objects control and manage the operations of base objects. The interface to these meta-objects is the MOP. In other words, the MOP is a set of operations used with meta-objects to define and configure system behavior.

The promotion of implicit system descriptions to become explicit objects is called reification. The advantage of reifying system descriptions as meta-objects is that operations can be carried on them, like composing and editing, storing and retrieving, organizing and reading. Since these meta-objects represent system descriptions, their manipulation can result in change in system behavior. For reifying language descriptions like class, attribute and association, which themselves act as classes, what is needed is a mechanism for defining the class of a class. In OO programming, the class of a class object is a meta-class. Meta-objects, therefore, are implemented as meta-classes. The concept of meta-classes is a key design technique in improving the reusability and extensibility of these languages. VODAK [6], Prometheus [7], ADAM [8] and OM [9] are some of the next generation database management systems which have adopted the meta-class approach for tailoring the data model to adapt to evolving specifications. A meta-class may, typically, define properties about object creation, encapsulation, inheritance rules, message passing and the like.

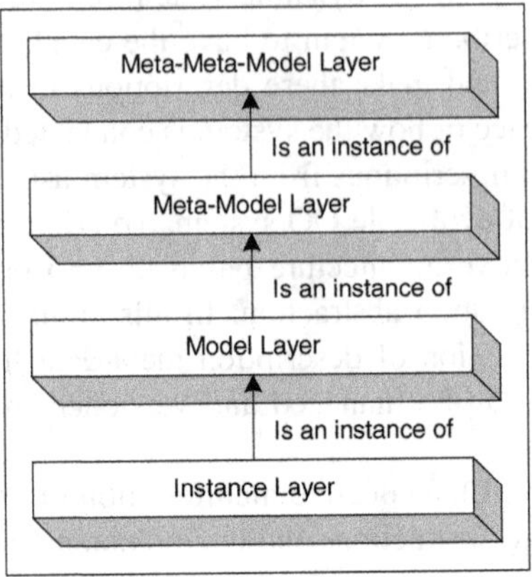

Fig. 1. Four Layer Modeling Architecture

2 Modeling Architectures

In modeling complex information systems, it has been shown that at least four modeling layers are required (see Figure 1) [10]. Each layer provides a service to the layer above it and serves as a client to the layer below it. The meta-meta-model layer defines the language for specifying meta-models. Typically more compact than the meta-model it describes, a meta-meta-model defines a model at a higher level of abstraction than a meta-model. Elements of the meta-meta-model layer are called meta-meta-objects. Examples of meta-meta-objects include MetaClass, MetaAttribute and MetaAssociation. These meta-meta-objects are also meta-classes whose instances are constructs corresponding to meta-model constructs.

The meta-model layer defines the language for specifying models. A meta-model is an instance of a meta-meta-model. It is also more elaborate than the meta-meta-model that describes it. Elements of the meta-model layer are called meta-objects, examples of which include Class, Attribute and Association. The model layer defines the language for specifying information domains. In this case, a model is an instance of a meta-model. Elements like Student, Teacher and Course classes are domain-specific examples of elements of the model layer. The bottom layer contains user objects and user data. The instance layer describes a specific information domain. Domain examples of user objects include the instances of Student, Teacher and Course classes. The Object Management Group (OMG) [11] standards group has a similar architecture based on model abstraction, with the Meta-Object Facility (MOF) model and the Unified Modeling Language (UML) [12] model defining the language for the meta-meta-model and meta-model layers, respectively.

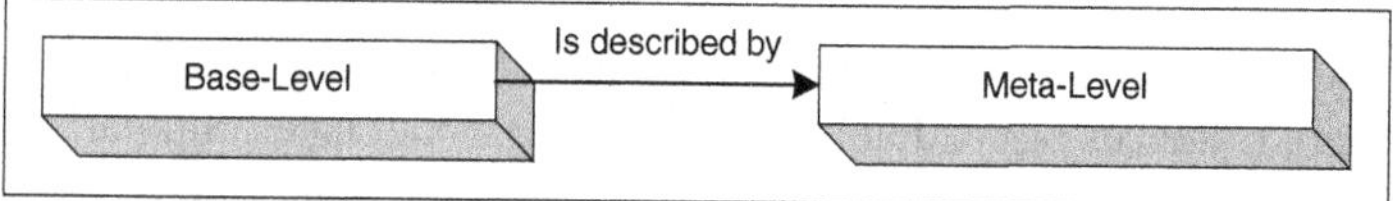

Fig. 2. Meta-Level Architecture

Orthogonal to the model abstraction inherent in multi-layered meta-modeling approach is the information abstraction which separates descriptive information from the data they are describing. These system descriptions are called meta-data, as they are information defining other data. A reflective open architecture typifies this abstraction. A reflective open architecture is divided into two levels - the meta-level where the descriptive information reside and the base-level which stores the application data described by the meta-level elements. The meta-level contains the meta-data objects (also referred to as meta-objects in this paper) which hold the meta-data. These meta-objects manage the base-level objects. A two-layer architecture is shown in Figure 2.

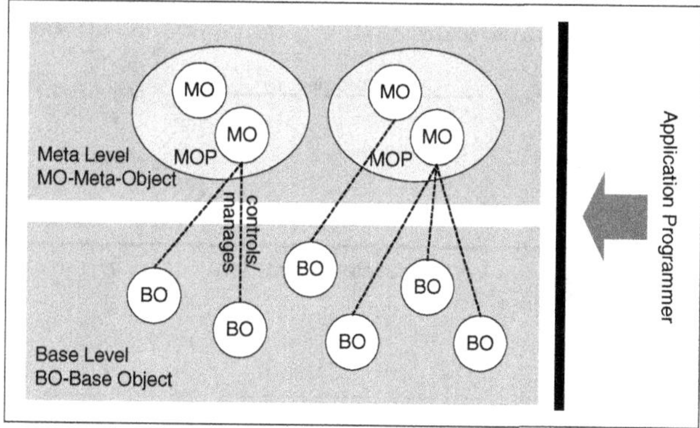

Fig. 3. Separation of Meta-Objects from Base Objects

The separation of meta-objects from base objects (see Figure 3) is essential in establishing the difference between what an object does (in the base-level) from how it does it (in the meta-level). A meta-level architecture gives access to meta-objects and ensures that changes on the meta-objects lead to changes on the intended system aspects represented by the meta-objects, i.e. the two levels are causally connected. For example, changes on the class Meta-object in the meta-level, via the class MOP, should result in the appropriate changes to all application objects in the base-level.

3 A Description-Driven Architecture

This paper proposes an architecture which combines the multi-layered meta-modeling approach with the meta-level architecture [13]. The description-driven architecture is illustrated in Figure 4. The layered architecture on the left hand side is typical of the layered systems and the multi-layered architecture specification of the OMG discussed earlier.

The relationship between the layers is Is an instance of. The instance layer contains data which are instances of the domain model in the model layer. Similarly, the model layer is an instance of the meta-model layer. On the right hand side of the diagram is another instance of model abstraction. It shows the increasing abstraction of information from meta-data to model meta-data, where the relationship between the two is Is an instance of as well. These two architectures provide layering and hierarchy based on abstraction of data and information models.

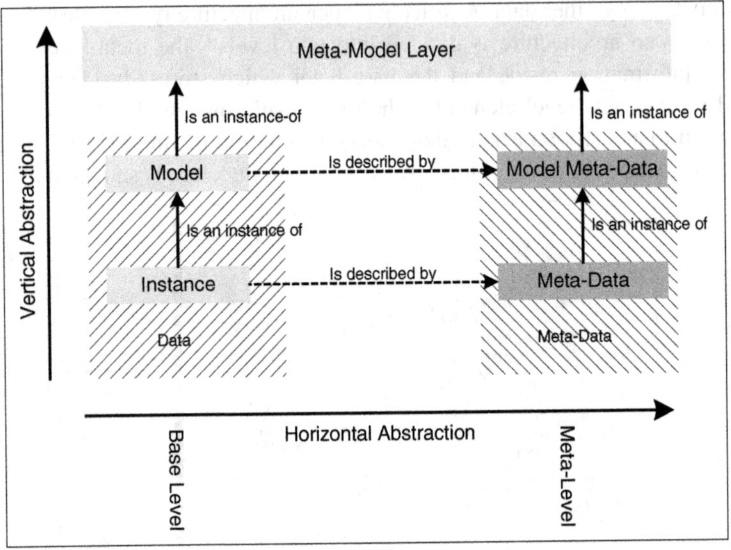

Fig. 4. Description-Driven Architecture

The horizontal view provides an alternative abstraction where the relationship of meta-data and the data they describe are made explicit. This view is representative of the information abstraction and the meta-level architecture discussed earlier. The meta-level architecture is a mechanism for relating data to information describing data, where the link between the two is Is described by. As a consequence, the dynamic creation and specification of object types is promoted. The separation of system type descriptions from their instantiations allows the asynchronous specification and evolution of system objects from system types, consequently, descriptions and their instances are managed independently and explicitly. The dynamic configuration (and re-configuration) of data and meta-data is useful for systems whose data requirements are unknown at development time.

4 A Practical Example

This research has been carried out at the European Centre for Nuclear Research (CERN) [14] based in Geneva, Switzerland. CERN is a scientific research laboratory studying the fundamental laws of matter, exploring what matter is made of, and what forces hold it together. Scientists at CERN build and operate complex accelerators and detectors. Accelerators are huge machines to speed up particles very close to the speed of light, and then to let them collide with other particles. Detectors, on the other hand, are large instruments to observe what happens during these collisions.

The Compact Muon Solenoid (CMS) is a general purpose experiment that will be constructed from an order of a million parts and will be produced and assembled in the next decade by specialized centres distributed worldwide (see Figure 5). As such, the construction process is very data-intensive, highly distributed and ultimately requires a computer-based system to manage the production and assembly of detector components.

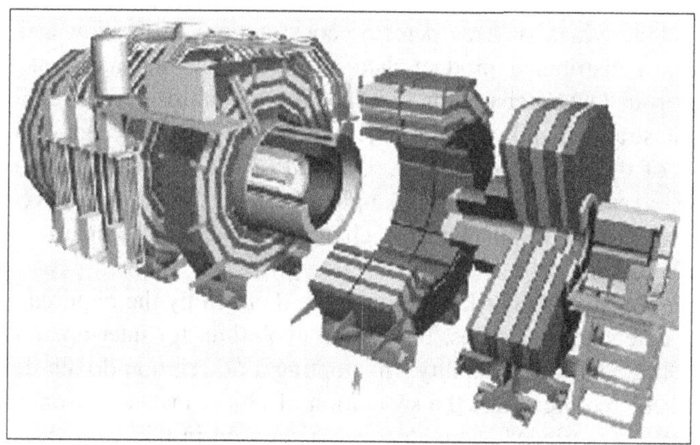

Fig. 5. The CMS Detector

In constructing detectors like CMS, scientists require data management systems that are able of cope with complexity, with system evolution over time (primarily as a consequence of changing user requirements) and with system scalability, distribution and inter-operation. No commercial products provide the workflow and product data management capabilities required by CMS [15]. The design constraints imposed by CMS which are not currently satisfied by any commercial offering include:

- The workflow and product-related descriptions tend to evolve rapidly over time. The software must cater for the development of a high physics detector over an extended period of time (1999-2005) and whose design will naturally advance as time elapses. Hence the need to support long-running and potentially nested workflow activities, with natural consequences on transaction handling.
- The construction of CMS is one-of-a-kind. The evolution of workflows and product data must be allowed to take place as production continues. Consequently, versions of workflow and product descriptions coexist in the production process for the dura-

tion of the CMS construction. This is in contrast to industrial production lines where the process is seldom one-of-a-kind.

- The CMS construction is highly distributed. Production of (versions) of CMS products will take place in disparate areas all over the world. Each of these production centres must cater for multiple versions of evolving workflow and product descriptions in an autonomous manner but centrally coordinated from CERN.
- The data store must be reliably secure and available for a variety of purposes. Many users require different access to the CMS data, e.g. construction engineers interpret data using an assembly-oriented view, physicists view the detector data in terms of a set of electronically-decoded channels and mechanical engineers view the detector data in terms of constituent three-dimensional volumes aligned in space.

A research project, entitled CRISTAL (Cooperating Repositories and an Information System for Tracking Assembly Lifecycles) [16][17] has therefore been initiated, using OO computing technologies where possible, to facilitate the management of the engineering data collected at each stage of production of CMS. CRISTAL captures all the physical characteristics of detector components, which are, later, required by the physicists for activities such as detector construction, calibration and maintenance. CRISTAL is a distributed product data and workflow management system which makes use of an OO database for its repository, a multi-layered architecture for its component abstraction and dynamic object modeling for the design of the objects and components of the system. CRISTAL is based on a DDS using meta-objects. These techniques are critical to handle the complexity of such a data-intensive system and to provide the flexibility to adapt to the changing production scenarios typical of any research production system.

The design of the CRISTAL prototype was dictated by the requirements for adaptability over extended timescales, for system evolution, for inter-operability, for complexity handling and for reusability. In adopting a description-driven design approach to address these requirements, the separation of object instances from object descriptions instances was needed. This abstraction resulted in the delivery of a three layer description-driven architecture. The model abstraction (of instance layer, model layer, meta-model layer) has been adopted from the OMG specification, and the need to provide descriptive information, i.e. meta-data, has been identified to address the issues of adaptability, complexity handling and evolvability.

Figure 6 illustrates CRISTAL architecture. The CRISTAL model layer is comprised of class specifications for CRISTAL type descriptions (e.g. *PartDescription*) and class specifications for CRISTAL classes (e.g. *Part*). The instance layer is comprised of object instances of these classes (e.g. *PartType#*1 for *PartDescription* and *Part#1212* for *Part*). The model and instance layer abstraction is based on model abstraction and *Is an instance of* relationship. The abstraction based on meta-data abstraction and *Is described by* relationship leads to two levels - the meta-level and the base-level. The meta-level is comprised of meta-objects and the meta-level model which defines them (e.g. *PartDescription* is the meta-level model of *PartType#1* meta-object). The base-level is comprised of base objects and the base-level model which defines them (e.g. *Part* is the base-level model of the *Part#1212* object).

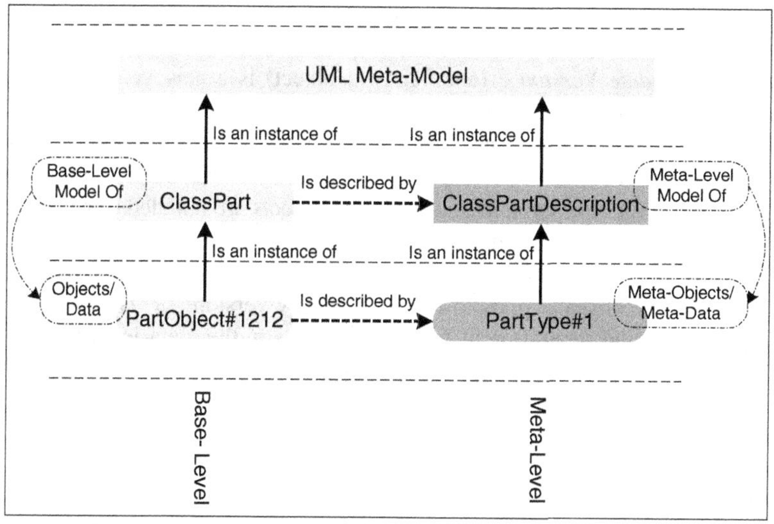

Fig. 6. The CRISTAL Architecture

In the CMS experiment, production models change over time. Detector parts of different model versions must be handled over time and coexist with other parts of different model versions. Separating details of model types from the details of single parts allows the model type versions to be specified and managed independently, asynchronously and explicity from single parts. Moreover, in capturing descriptions separate from their instantiations, system evolution can be catered for while production is underway and therefore provide continuity in the production process and for design changes to be reflected quickly into production. As the CMS construction is one-of-a-kind, the evolution of descriptions must be catered for.

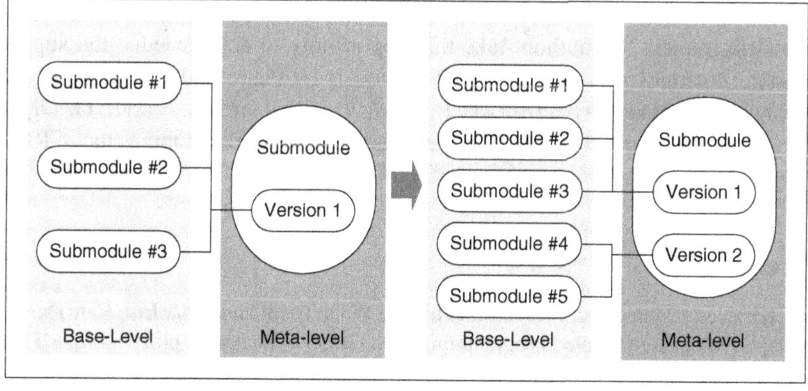

Fig. 7. Evolving CMS Descriptions

The evolving CMS descriptions is illustrated in Figure 7. *Submodule Version 1* is a type object describing physical detector parts *Submodule#1*, *Submodule#2* and *Submodule#3*. *Submodule Version 2* (another type object) is a new version of the same type specification, and coexists with *Submodule Version 1* and its instances. In this example, *Submodule Version 1* and *Submodule Version 2* are instances of *ClassPartDescription* (in the meta-level). As new instances can be dynamically added into the system, consequently new versions and new type objects are handled transparently and automatically. In the base-level, *Submodule#1* is an instance of *ClassPart*. The *Is described by* relationship between the meta-level and the base-level elements allows for instantiations of physical parts to be described by versions of type objects in the meta-level. Hence, the separation of type descriptions in the meta-level from the data objects they describe caters for evolving system specifications.

5 Conclusions

The ubiquity of change in current information systems have contributed to the renewed interest in improving underlying system design and architecture. Reflection, meta-architectures and layered systems are the main concepts this paper has explored in providing a description-driven architecture which can cope with the growing needs of many computing environments. The description-driven architecture has two orthogonal abstractions combining multi-layered meta-modeling with open architectural approach allowing for the separation of description meta-data from the system aspects they represent. The description-driven philosophy facilitated the design and implementation of the CRISTAL project which required mechanisms for handling and managing evolving system requirements. In conclusion, it is interesting to note that the OMG has recently announced the so-called Model Driven Architecture as the basis of future systems integration [18]. Such a philosophy is directly equivalent to that expounded in this and earlier papers on the CRISTAL description-driven architecture.

Acknowledgments. The authors take this opportunity to acknowledge the support of their home institutes. The support of P. Lecoq, J-L. Faure and M. Pimia is greatly appreciated. N. Baker, A. Bazan, T. Le Flour, S. Lieunard, L. Varga, G. Organtini and G. Chevenier are thanked for their assistance in developing the CRISTAL prototype.

References

1. G. Kiczales, "Metaobject Protocols: Why We Want Them and What Else Can They Do?", Chapter in Object-Oriented Programming: The CLOS Perspective, pp 101-118, MIT Press, 1993.
2. B. Foote, "Objects, Reflection and Open Languages", *Workshop on Object-Oriented Reflectionn and Meta-Level Architectures, European Conference for Object-Oriented Programming (ECOOP)*, Uthrect, Netherlands, 1992.

3. B. Foote and J. Yoder, "Metadata and Active Object Models", *Fifth Conference on Pattern Languages of Programs (PLOP 98)*, Illinois, USA, August 1998.
4. G. Kiczales, J. des Rivieres and D. Bobrow, "The Art of Metaobject Protocol", MIT Press, 1991.
5. D. Riehle and K. Matzel, "Using Reflection to Support System Evolution", *Proceedings of the Annual Conference on Object-Oriented Programming Languages, Systems and Applications (OOPSLA)*, 1998.
6. W. Klas, et. al., "Database Integration using the Open Object-Oriented Database System VODAK", In O. Bukhres and A. Elmagarmid (Eds.), Object Oriented Multidatabase Systems: A Solution for Advanced Applications, Chapter14, Prentice Hall, 1995.
7. C. Raguenaud, J. Kennedy and P. Barclay, "The Prometheus Database Model", Prometheus technical report 2, Napier University, School of Computing, 1999.
8. N. Paton, "ADAM: An Object-Oriented Database System Implemented in Prolog", *In M.H.Williams (Ed.), Proceedings of the 7th British National Conference On Databases (BNCOD)*, Cambridge University Press, 1989.
9. The Object Model (OM) and the Object Model System (OMS), URL http:// www.globis.ethz.ch/research/oms/.
10. M. Staudt, A. Vaduva and T. Vetterli, "Metadata Management and Data Warehousing", Technical Report 21, Swiss Life, Information Systems Research, July 1999.
11. The Object Management Group (OMG), URL http://www.omg.org.
12. The Unified Modeling Language (UML) Specification, URL http://www.omg.org/technology/uml/.
13. F. Estrella, "Objects, Patterns and Descriptions in Data Management", PhD Thesis, University of the West of England, Bristol, England, December 2000.
14. The European Centre for Nuclear Research (CERN), URL http://cern.web.cern.ch/CERN.
15. Z. Kovacs, "The Integration of Product Data with Workflow Management Systems", PhD Thesis, University of West of England, Bristol, England, April 1999.
16. R. McClatchey, et. al., "The Integration of Product Data and Workflow Management Systems in a Large Scale Engineering Database Application", *Proceedings of the 2nd IEEE International Database Engineering and Applications Symposium*, Cardiff, United Kingdom, July 1998.
17. F. Estrella, et. al., "Using a Meta-Model as the Basis for Enterprise-Wide Data Navigation", *Proceedings of the Third IEEE Metadata Conference*, Maryland, USA, April 1999.
18. OMG Publications., "Model Driven Architectures - The Architecture of Choice for a Changing World". See http://www.omg.org/mda/index.htm

Adaptive Web Meta-search Enhanced by Constraint-Based Query Constructing and Mapping

Lieming Huang, Ulrich Thiel, Matthias Hemmje, and Erich J. Neuhold

GMD-IPSI, Dolivostr. 15,
D-64293, Darmstadt, Germany
{lhuang, thiel, hemmje, Neuhold}@darmstadt.gmd.de

Abstract. This paper introduces an adaptive method that can be used to construct the query user interfaces for the information integration systems (IIS) on the Web, and a constraint-based method for mapping queries from such IISs into the specific formats of heterogeneous Internet sources. The fuse of this research was ignited by witnessing that WWW information searching becomes harder and harder due to the tremendous development of the Internet and the explosive growth of digital information on the World Wide Web. Incorporating adaptive and constraints-coordinated mechanisms into an information integration system can overcome the diversity of heterogeneous sources and utilize the functionality of the individual sources to the fullest extent.

1 Introduction

On the World Wide Web (WWW or Web for short) there are innumerable information sources containing useful information that cannot be indexed by general-purpose search engines and hence invisible to most common users. It will facilitate users easy and accurate access to specific information (e.g., scientific publications) through an

Fig. 1. NCSTRL

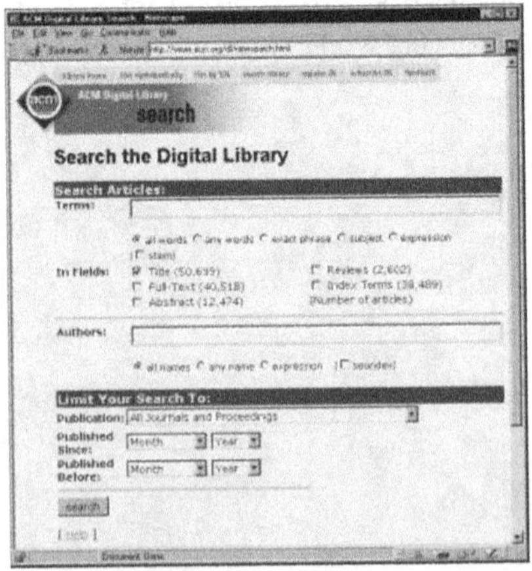

Fig. 2. ACM-Digital Library

X.S. Wang, G. Yu, and H. Lu (Eds.): WAIM 2001, LNCS 2118, pp. 400-407, 2001.

integrated information retrieval system (IIRS) that integrates all kinds of information sources and (general/specific-purpose) search engines.

Considering the great discrepancies among heterogeneous, distributed information sources, it is not an easy thing to integrate them. From Figures 1-2, we can see the differences in the user interfaces (and query capabilities) of these three sources. Current IIRSs employ simple uniform user interfaces that can be supported by all sources in order to mask the diversity. However, this method will inevitably discard the rich functionality provided by specific information sources, and it is difficult for users to input complicated queries and retrieve (or pinpoint) more specific information.

In order to make full use of the query capabilities of sources and improve the precision of retrieved information, some systems adopt static mixed user interfaces that integrate almost all controls from various sources. Nevertheless, three obstacles need to be overcome by such a mixed user interface: (1) it will increase the users' cognitive load and make the system hard to use for novice users; (2) the constraints between the user interfaces of heterogeneous sources may cause a user query to be inconsistent with an underlying source and make the query mapping difficult; (3) considering the instability of information sources on the Internet, it is hard to maintain mixed interfaces. In addition, the static user interface lacks flexibility and the interactive nature of information retrieval.

This paper tries to attack this dilemma by combining the mechanism of adaptive query input interface construction with the constraints-based query translation method. Our meta-search engine prototype dynamically generates the query input interface that will benefit both the expression of users' information needs and the utilization of the information sources' query capabilities. The constraints-based query mapping method will make the query translation more accurate, thus utilizing the query capability of target source as much as possible. The rest of this paper is organized as follows. Section 2 discusses related work. Section 3 discusses the mechanisms of adaptive UI construction and the constraints-based query mapping. Finally, section 4 concludes this paper.

2 Related Work

The idea of querying and collating results from multiple databases is not new. Internet meta-search engines, online catalogues, multi-databases and other kinds of information integration systems have attracted a lot of attention since the advent of the network. There are many meta-search engines (such as Meta-crawler, AskJeeves, Savvysearch, ProFusion, etc. they merge the results from some well-known search engines) and information integration systems (such as Lexis-Nexis, DIALOG, etc. they integrate the results of multiple heterogeneous databases).

The issue of providing a common user interface for distributed networked services can trace back to 70s and 80s (e.g., [6]). However, this problem remains unresolved. Most current meta-search engines only use a simplest user interface. Some systems provide more sophisticated user interfaces for distributed search (e.g., [1, 3]). However, these systems do not consider the coordination of various constraints among the controls of information sources' user interfaces. Considering the great diversity in schematic, semantic, interface and domain aspects, building an efficient user interface for integration purposes is quite difficult. This paper proposes a method for dynamically generating user interface, which can achieve the following advantages: (1) It will benefit the progressively self-refining construction of users' information needs; (2) Conflicts among heterogeneous sources can be coordinated efficiently; (3) User queries will match the queries supported by target sources as much as possible. Many papers (e.g., [2, 5, 7]) describe the query capabilities of sources and deal with the query translation problems. Paper [2] applies user-defined mapping rules to subsume queries for translation between different sources and describes some problems involved in predicate rewriting. Our paper proposes a more generic model for translating arbitrary queries supported by various sources. Our two-phase method for coping with query subsuming (relaxing and decomposing) and post-processing (tightening with common filters and composing with special filters) can well coordinate the functional discrepancies among heterogeneous information sources. Papers [5] and [7] do not consider some special constraints, such as the limitations of term modifiers, logical operators and the order of terms. This paper sufficiently describes all kinds of constraints between the query models (as embodied in the user interfaces) of various sources, and therefore can utilize the functionality of each source to the fullest extent.

There are a lot of efforts towards laying down all kinds of standards or protocols for distributed information retrieval, such as Z39.50[Z95], STARTS[GCGMP97], etc. However, for a number of reasons (such as a large amount of legacy information; producers are unwilling to comply with strict rules; great differences from one domain to another, etc.), these standards are not being applied extensively.

3 Adaptive User Interface Construction with Constraints-Based Query Mapping

From Figures 1-2, we know that there are many discrepancies among the user interfaces of heterogeneous sources and it makes integration difficult. However, all the controls available in user interfaces can be divided by function into three groups (in this paper, we use scientific publication-oriented search engines as examples):

(1) **Classification Selection Controls (CSC)**, a classification selection control is a component on the user interface to a search engine, by selecting one or more items of which, users can limit their information needs to certain domains, subjects, categories, etc. For example, **CSC** = {Category CSC, Journal CSC, Search Engine CSC, Language CSC, etc.};

(2) **Result Display Controls (RDC)**, A result display control can be used by users to control the formats, sizes or sorting methods of the query results. For example, **RDC** = {Sorting Criteria RDC, Grouping Size RDC, Description RDC}. **Sorting Criteria RDC** = {<Relevance ranking>, <Author>, <Date>, etc.}; **Grouping Size RDC** = {<10>, <20>, etc.}; **Description RDC** = {<full>, <brief>, <URL >, etc.};
(3) **Query Input Controls (QIC)**, All terms, term modifiers and logical operators of a search engine constitute a query input controls group, through which users can express their information needs (queries). **<Terms (T)>**: A term is the content keyed into an input box on the user interface. **<Term Modifiers (M)>**: A term modifier is used to limit the scope, the quality or the form of a term. For example, Field Modifiers: {<Title>, <Full-Text>, <Keywords>, <Abstract>, <Author>, etc.}; Term Qualifiers: {<Exactly Like>, <Multiple Words>, <Using Stem Expansion>, etc.}. **<Logical Operators (L)>**: A logical operator is used to logically combine two terms to perform a search, the results of which are then evaluated for relevance. For example, {<AND>, <OR>, etc.}

Various constraints exist among the controls in the user interfaces of search engines. Here we only list some cases: (1) Invalid modifiers for a term. For example, a term with wildcard (e.g., comput*) cannot use the <Exactly Like> qualifier. (2) Incompatible modifiers. For example, <Date> field cannot be combined with <Sound Like> qualifier. (3) Incompatible CSCs. For example, the <Computer Sciences> category with the selection of the <Zoological Journal of the Linnean Society> journal will retrieve nothing. Now we give the definition of control constraint rules. Suppose there are *n* **controls** on the user interface and each control has several **items** (e.g., a <field modifier> control has such items: <Title>, <Abstract>, etc.). Due to the constraints among the controls of one search engine or among the controls of several different search engines, if users select *p* **items** from these n **controls**, there are other *q* **items** from these n **controls** that must be disabled (users cannot select these q items unless they change their previous manipulations) or must be enabled (these q items are selected automatically). Disabling some items of a control does not mean that the other items of this control will be enabled; it means that users can select one or more of these remaining items of the control or select nothing. Enabling an item means that this value has been selected and will be sent to the target search engine. For example, in the rule "(Field_modifier_1).**ENABLE**(<Abstract>) (Term_qualifier_1). **DISABLE** (<Sound Like>, <Spelled Like>, <Before>, <After>)", if users select the <Abstract> item in a field modifier, according to the rule, some items (e.g. <Sound like>, <Spelled like>, etc) in the corresponding term qualifier are disabled. Control constraint rules can be employed to dynamically generate the query user interface of a meta-search engine.

The user interface of a meta-search engine changes in accordance with both the user manipulations and the control constraint rules. When users gradually express their information needs by manipulating controls (especially the classification selection controls) and inputting keywords, the number of search engines that can satisfy the information needs of users may decrease. Suppose that only some of the underlying search engines may be relevant, then when dynamically constructing the user interface, the system need not consider the irrelevant controls and items that cannot be supported by these search engines. Synthesizing an integrated interface will coordinate the conflicts arising from heterogeneous sources with differing query syntax. There are many differences between the user interfaces and query models of search engines for different domains. For example, it is difficult for a meta-search engine to provide a uniform interface that can be efficiently used by users searching for information on scientific publications (they share fields such as 'Author', 'Article title', 'Abstract', etc.), vehicles (fields such as 'Makers', 'Models', 'Cylinders', etc.) and weather forecasting (fields such as 'Temperature', 'Relative humidity', 'Wind', etc.). Each time users execute a query, their information needs are on a certain domain or subject. In addition, search engines for similar domains have many similarities in their user interfaces. Therefore, taking these characteristics into account, the user interface dynamically generated by such an adaptive meta-search engine can facilitate the expression of both the query capabilities of information sources, and the information needs of users. Fig. 3 displays four screen shots of the user interfaces in which a query has been input progressively. Fig. 3(a) shows the initial interface and in Fig. 3(d), the query construction completes.

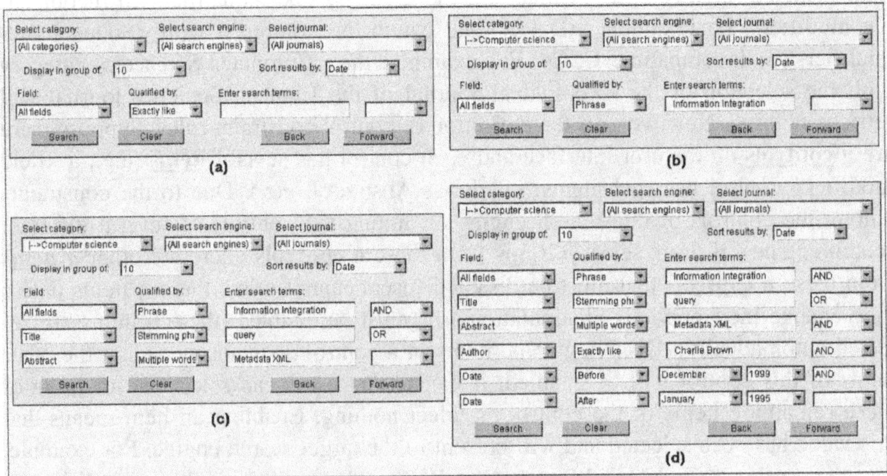

Fig. 3. Dynamically-generated user interfaces for meta-search engines

Up to now, we have discussed the method of dynamically constructing the user interface for a meta-search engine. However, discrepancies inevitably exist between the user interface of a meta-search engine and that of an underlying search engine. Therefore, the meta-search engine needs to transform the user query into the format supported by the target source. Sometimes, query subsuming and results post-processing are employed to compensate for the functional discrepancies between a meta-search engine and sources. When the system translates the original query Q^o into the target query Q^t, one of the following three cases will occur.

Fig. 4 illustrates these three cases. In the following, we will discuss them separately and at the same time introduce how the common filters (these kinds of filters occur frequently and most of them can be applied to refine the results, so we call them "Common") and the special filters (these kinds of filters occur not often and most of them cannot be applied to refine the results, so we call them "special") are generated and how they later will be used to post-process the raw results. The "merger" module will (1) sort and group all results according to certain criteria; (2) revisit search engines (some search engines need to be accessed more than one time to get complete information); (3) dynamically reorganize the displayed results when the results come from some slow-responding search engines; and so on.

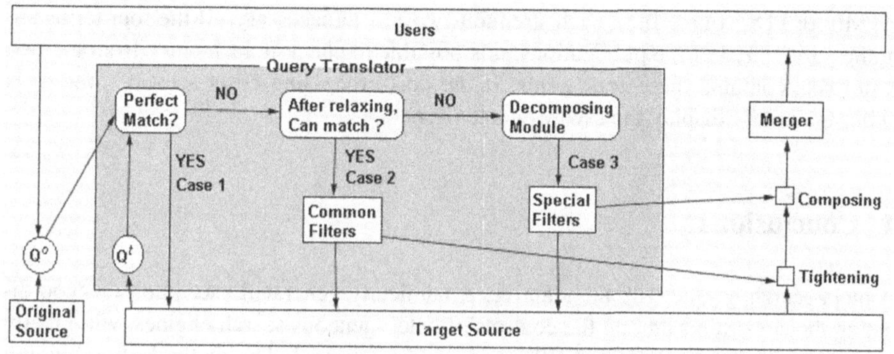

Fig. 4. Three cases of query translation

<u>**Case 1:**</u> In this case, each term in Q^o can be put into a certain term in Q^t, and the field modifier and the term qualifier of this term can also be supported by the corresponding term in Q^t. Furthermore, each logical operator in Q^o can also be supported in Q^t, and the logical value of the new query is equivalent to the original query if the order of terms is changed.. We call this case as "Perfect Match" because the results need not be post-processed.

<u>**Case 2:**</u> Some field modifiers, term qualifiers or logical operators in Q^o cannot be supported by Q^t, but after relaxing them (i.e. broadening the scope of the limitation and therefore enabling that more results may be retrieved), for example, <u><NEAR> <AND></u>, <u><Phrase> <Multiple Words></u>, <u><Title> <Abstract> <Full Text></u>, etc., the newly-generated Q^o can be supported by Q^t. In this case, the system dispatches the relaxed query, and when the results come, the results are post-processed according to the previous relaxing information. For the relaxed field modifiers, term qualifiers and logical operators, the system uses some filters to record such information and later use them to refine the results in order to compensate for the relaxing of constraints. We call such filters "common filters" and call the result refining process as "Tightening" (See Fig. 4).

<u>**Case 3:**</u> In this case, Q^o cannot be supported by Q^t even after relaxing some modifiers or logical operators. The system will break Q^o into several sub-queries, then translate

and dispatch each sub-query separately. We use special filters to record such decomposition information (See Fig. 4). When the corresponding results come, these "special filters" are employed to compose the results. However, in most cases, either because we cannot obtain relevant information from target sources or because result post-processing will cost unreasonable CPU-time, result composing is impossible. For example, suppose that a four-term query is (A *AND* B *AND* C *AND* D) and the target query only supports two terms. Now we decompose the original expression into two sub-expressions (A *AND* B) and (C *AND* D). If the four terms are limited to the "Abstract" field or the "Full-Text" field of the publications, we cannot intersect the two result sets from (A *AND* B) and (C *AND* D) because we cannot check whether a term is in such fields. Even if we can get such information (e.g. by analyzing the PS, HTML, or PDF source file), such strenuous work is unnecessary. If the four terms are in the "title" field of the publications, it is possible to check if each entry from the two result sets contains these four terms. If the post-processing costs a lot of time, it is better to directly display the raw results to users.

4 Conclusions

A meta-search engine with an adaptive, dynamically generated user interface, coordinating the constraints among the controls of heterogeneous search engines, will greatly improve the effectiveness of WWW information retrieval. The method of combining adaptive user interface construction and constraints-based query translation proposed in this paper can be applied to all kinds of distributed information retrieval systems (such as digital libraries, meta-search engines, agent-based information providers, etc.) that integrate online repositories or search engines (search tools) with quite different user interfaces and query models. With the help of source wrapping tools, they can also be used to integrate queryable information sources delivering semi-structured data, such as product catalogues, weather reports, software directories, and so on.

References

1. Baldonado, M., Winograd, T.: SenseMaker: An Information-Exploration Interface Supporting the Contextual Evolution of a User's Interests, Proc. of CHI '97. Atlanta, GA, USA, Apr. 1997, pp 11-18.
2. Chang, C., Garcia-Molina, H., Paepcke, A.: Predicate Rewriting for Translating Boolean Queries in a Heterogeneous Information System. ACM Transactions on Information Systems, 17(1), Jan. 1999, pp 1-39.
3. Cousins, S., Paepcke, A., Winograd, T., Bier, E., Pier, K.: The Digital Library Integrated Task Environment (DLITE), Proc. of ACM Digital Libraries. Philadelphia, PA, USA, July 1997, pp 142-151.
4. Gravano, L., Chang, K., Garcia-Molina, H., Paepcke, A.: STARTS: Stanford Proposal for Internet meta-searching. Proc. of the ACM SIGMOD. Tucson, AZ, USA, May 1997, pp. 207-218.

5. Levy, A., Rajaraman, A., Ordille, J.: Querying Heterogeneneous Information Sources Using Source Descriptions. Proc. of the 22nd VLDB Conf. Bombay, India, Sep. 1996, pp 251-262.
6. Negus, E.: Development of the Euronet-Diane Common Command Language, in Proceedings of Online Information Meetings, pp 95-98. 1979.
7. Vassalos, V., Papakonstantinou, Y.: Describing and Using Query Capabilities of Heterogeneous Sources. Proc. of the 23rd VLDB Conf. Athens, Greece, Aug. 1997, pp 256-265.
8. Z39.50 Maintenance Agency. Information Retrieval (Z39.50): Application Service Definition and Protocol Specification. ftp://ftp.loc.gov/pub/z3950/official/. 1995.

A Mixed Data Dissemination Strategy for Mobile Computing Systems

Guohong Cao[1], Yiqiong Wu[1], and Bo Li[2]

[1] Department of Computer Science and Engineering,
The Pennsylvania State University
{gcao,ywu}@cse.psu.edu

[2] Department of Computer Science and Engineering,
Xi'an Jiaotong University, Xi'an, China
boblee@summit.com.cn

Abstract. Broadcasting is a very effective technique to disseminate information to a massive number of clients when the data size is small. However, if the data size is large, the broadcast cycle may be long, and hence the access delay becomes a problem. Caching frequently accessed data at the client side can reduce the access latency and improve the bandwidth utilization. However, caching techniques may not perform well when the data are frequently updated. In this paper, we propose to apply different techniques (broadcasting and caching) to deal with different components of the data based on their update frequency. Compared to previous schemes, the proposed solution not only reduces the query latency, but also improves the throughput and the bandwidth utilization.

1 Introduction

With the explosion of Internet techniques and the popularity of mobile terminals (MTs) such as laptops, personal digital assistants, people with battery powered MTs wish to access various kinds of web services over wireless networks at any time any place. However, existing wireless Internet services are limited by the constraints of mobile environments such as narrow bandwidth, asymmetric communication channels, unstable connectivity, and limitations of battery technologies. Thus, mechanisms to efficiently transmit information from the server to the massive number of clients (running on MTs) have received considerable attention [1,4,6].

There are two fundamental models [4] of providing clients with information: *data broadcasting* and *on-demand*. In the broadcasting model, data is periodically broadcasted on a communication channel. Accessing broadcasted data does not require uplink transmission and is "listen only". Since the cost of broadcasting does not depend on the number of users, this method has good scalability and can be used to address the low bandwidth issue in mobile computing systems. In the on-demand model, clients request data on the uplink channel and the server responds by sending the data to the clients.

X.S. Wang, G. Yu, and H. Lu (Eds.): WAIM 2001, LNCS 2118, pp. 408–416, 2001.

Although broadcasting has good scalability and low bandwidth requirements, it has some drawbacks. For example, since a web page may contain a large volume of data (especially in the multimedia era), the data broadcast cycle may be long. Hence, the clients have to wait for a long time before getting the required data. Caching frequently accessed data on the client side is an effective technique to improve performance in a mobile environment. It can reduce the number of uplink message for a particular data item, and the number of downloads of the same data item. However, the disconnection and mobility of the clients make cache consistency a challenging problem. Effective cache invalidation strategies are required to ensure the consistency between the cached data at the clients and original data stored in the server.

Barbara and Imielinski [1] provide a solution which is suitable for mobile environments. In this approach, the server periodically broadcasts an invalidation report (IR) in which the changed data items are indicated. Rather than querying a server directly regarding the validation of cached copies, clients can listen to these invalidation reports over wireless channels. Cao [2] proposed an UIR-based approach to address the long query latency problem of the IR-based approach. In this approach, a small fraction of the essential information (called updated invalidation report (UIR)) related to cache invalidation is replicated several times within an IR interval, and hence the client can answer a query without waiting until the next IR. However, if there is a cache miss, the client still needs to wait for the data to be delivered. In this paper, we propose a scheme to further improve the cache hit ratio. Instead of passively waiting, clients intelligently prefetch the data that are most likely used in the future. Although caching data at the client site can improve performance and conserve battery energy, caching may not be the best solution if the broadcasted data are frequently updated, in which case, a combination of different techniques may be required. We propose to apply different techniques (broadcasting and caching) to deal with different components of the data based on their update frequency. Detailed experiments are provided to evaluate the proposed methodology. Compared to previous schemes, the proposed solution not only reduces the query latency, but also improves the throughput and the bandwidth utilization.

The rest of the paper is organized as follows. Section 2 presents the necessary background. In Section 3, we propose techniques to improve the cache hit ratio, and deal with frequently updated data. Section 4 evaluates the performance of the proposed scheme. Section 5 concludes the paper.

2 Preliminaries

To ensure cache consistency, the server broadcasts invalidation reports (IRs) every L seconds. The IR consists of the current timestamp T_i and a list of tuples (d_x, t_x) such that $t_x > (T_i - w * L)$, where d_x is the data item id, t_x is the most recent update timestamp of d_x, and w is the invalidation broadcast window size. In other words, IR contains the update history of the past w broadcast intervals. Every client, if active, listens to the IRs and invalidates its cache accordingly. To answer a query, the client listens to the next IR and uses it to decide whether its cache is valid or not. If there is a valid cached copy of the requested data item, the client returns the item immediately. Otherwise, it sends a query request to the server through the uplink.

In order to reduce the query latency, Cao [2] proposed to replicate the IRs m times; that is, the IR is repeated every $(\frac{1}{m})^{th}$ of the IR interval. As a result, a client only needs to wait at most $(\frac{1}{m})^{th}$ of the IR interval before answering a query. Hence, latency can be reduced to $(\frac{1}{m})^{th}$ of the latency in the previous schemes (when query processing time is not considered).

Since the IR contains a large amount of update history information, replicating the complete IR m times may consume a large amount of broadcast bandwidth. In order to save the broadcast bandwidth, after one IR, $m-1$ *updated invalidation reports* (UIRs) are inserted within an IR interval. Each UIR only contains the data items that have been updated after the last IR was broadcasted. In this way, the size of the UIR becomes much smaller compared to that of the IR. As long as the client downloads the most recent IR, it can use the UIR to verify its own cache. The idea of the proposed technique can be further explained by Figure 1. In Figure 1, $T_{i,k}$ represents the time of the kth UIR after the ith IR. When a client receives a query between $T_{i-1,1}$ and $T_{i-1,2}$, it can answer the query at $T_{i-1,2}$ instead of T_i. Thus, to answer a query, the client only needs to wait for the next UIR or IR, whichever arrives earlier. However, if there is a cache miss, the client still needs to fetch data from the server, which increases the query latency. Also, if the data are frequently updated, the latency will be significantly increased. Next, we propose a scheme to improve the cache hit ratio and dealing with the frequently updated data.

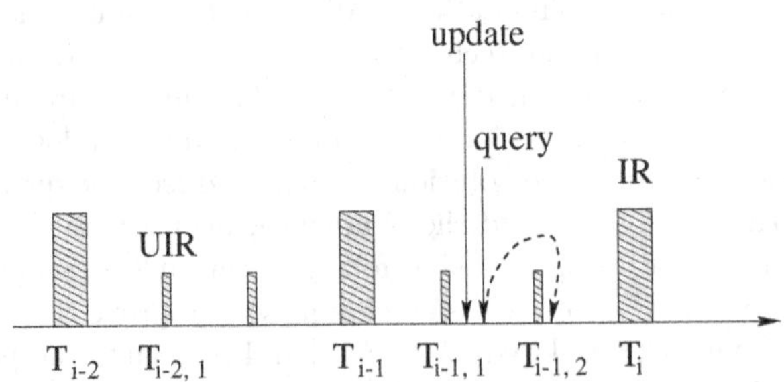

Fig. 1. Reducing the query latency by replicating UIRs

3 A Mixed Data Dissemination Strategy

3.1 Improving the Cache Hit Ratio

To improve the cache hit ratio, clients prefetch data that may be used in the near future. For example, if a client observes that the server is broadcasting a data item which is an invalid entry of its local cache, it is better to download the data; otherwise, the client may have to send another request to the server, and the server will have to broadcast the data item again in the near future. To save power, clients may only wake up during the IR broadcasting time, and then how to prefetch data becomes an issue. As a solution, after broadcasting the IR, the server first broadcasts the *id* list of the data items whose real data will be broadcasted next, and then broadcasts the data items whose *ids* are in the *id* list. Each client should always listen to the IR if it is not disconnected. At the end of the IR, the client downloads the *id* list and finds out when the interested data will come, and wakes up at that time to download the data. With this approach, power can be saved since clients stay in the doze mode most of the time; bandwidth can be saved since the server may only need to broadcast the updated data once.

3.2 Dealing with Frequently Updated Data

The IR-based approach is very useful in applications where data items do not change frequently, and then clients can cache these data items and use them to serve queries locally. However, if the data are frequently updated, caching may not be helpful. In this case, broadcasting the data on the air may be a good solution. Following this idea, many indexing techniques [4,6] have been proposed to address the tradeoff between query latency and power consumption. In most of the indexing techniques, the index and the real data are both broadcasted. Since some data items may contain a large amount of data (especially in the multimedia era), the clients may have to wait for a long time before getting the required data. In short, the indexing (broadcasting) techniques are good for small data size while the IR-based approach is good for large data size with less update frequency. However, in real life, most applications may not work well with either approach. For example, although the stock price of a company is updated frequently, the company related news such as the company profile, financial news, new product release, and broker coverage, may only be updated several times in a day. Since the stock price is updated too often, the IR-based approach is not suitable. Similarly, broadcasting techniques should not be used to maintain company related news due to large data sizes that need to be updated. We propose to apply multiple techniques to deal with the problem. The central idea is to differentiate the frequently updated data part from others. In other words, a data item can be divided into two *data components*: the hot component and the cold component. The hot component is the data part which is frequently updated, while the cold component is the data part which is not frequently updated. Indexing techniques are used to access those data components that are frequently updated, whereas IR-based techniques are used to access those data components which are not frequently updated. Considering the above example, broadcasting techniques are used to access the stock prices, whereas IR-based techniques are used to access the company news.

To implement the idea, we modify the UIR-based approach so that it can be used to deal with frequent updates. The idea is to broadcast the frequently updated data components multiple times during an IR interval. This can be done by broadcasting them after each UIR or IR. Since most of the frequently updated data components have small data size, broadcasting them should not add too much overhead. If the client access pattern is known, the hot data components should be broadcasted more often than the cold data components to reduce the average query latency. If multiple channels are available, the server can use one channel to deliver the frequently updated data components using broadcasting techniques, and use another channel to deliver the cold components using the UIR-based techniques. The process of dividing a data item into two components should be mutually agreed by the clients and the server. When a client needs to serve a query, it has to know where to locate the components of the data item. It may have to access one component from the local cache and download the other one from the broadcast channel.

4 Performance Evaluation

In order to evaluate the efficiency of various cache management algorithms, we develop a model which is similar to that employed in [2,3,5]. It consists of a single server that serves multiple clients. The database can only be updated by the server whereas the queries are made on the client side. From the server point of view, the database is divided into two subsets: the *hot* data subset and the *cold* data subset. The hot data subset includes data items from 1 to 100 (out of 2000 items) and the cold data subset includes the remaining data items of the database. From the client point of view, the database is divided into three subsets: the *hot* data subset, the *medium* data subset, and the *cold* data subset. The hot data subset includes 20 randomly (based on the client *id*) chosen items from the first 100 items. The medium data subset includes the remaining 80 items in the first 100 items. The cold data subset includes the remaining data items of the database. Table 1 lists the parameters used in our model.

4.1 The Query Latency

The left graph of Figure 2 shows the query delay as a function of the data size for the broadcast approach under different update arrival time. As can be seen, the query delay is proportional to the data size. When the data size is small, the delay is small. When the data size increases to 2000 bytes, the delay is too high to be tolerable. Thus, the broadcast approach is not suitable for applications which have very large data sizes and have strict delay requirements. As can be seen, the query delay of the broadcast approach is not affected by the mean update arrival time.

The right graph of Figure 2 shows the query delay as a function of the mean update arrival time for the UIR approach under different data item sizes (S = 2000 bytes, S = 200 bytes, and S = 20 bytes). When the mean update arrival time decreases, the data is updated more frequently, and more clients have cache misses. As a result, the query delay increases. As the mean update arrival

Table 1. The Simulation Parameters

Database items D	2000 items
Hot data items D_h	20 items
Medium data items D_m	80 items
Cold data items D_c	(2000-100)=1900 items
Number of clients n	200
Cache size c	20 to 200 items
Broadcast interval L	20 seconds
The UIR replicate times m	5
Broadcast window size w	10 intervals
Mean hot component update arrival time T_h	0.001s to 10000s
Mean cold component update arrival time T_c	0.1s to 10000s
Mean info. query generate time T_q	10s to 300s
Hot data update prob. p_u	0.33
Hot data access prob. q_h	0.75
Medium data access prob. q_m	0.10
Cold data access prob. q_c	0.15
Hot component data size S_h	16 bits
Cold component data size S_c	10 bytes to 2048 bytes
The timestamp size S_{tmp}	32 bits
The id size S_{id}	16 bits
Broadcast bandwidth R	20000 bits/s

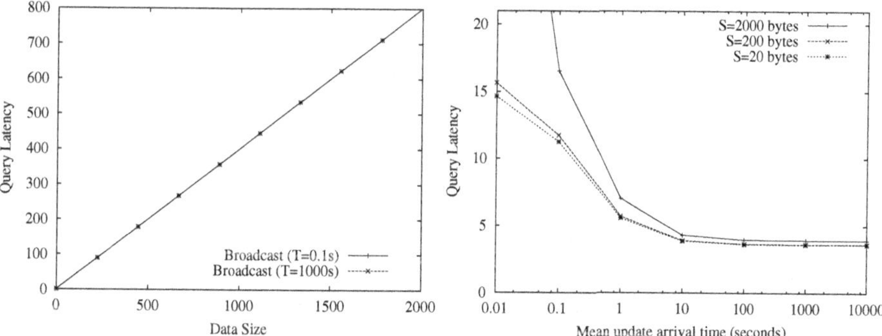

Fig. 2. A comparison of the query latency. The left figure shows the query latency as a function of data size for the broadcast approach. The right figure shows the query latency as a function of the mean update arrival time for the UIR approach ($T_q = 100s, c = 200, n = 100$).

time becomes very small, many clients have cache misses and their requests form a queue at the server. Since it takes a longer time to send a large data item than a small data item, clients may need to wait for a longer time if the data size is large. For example, the query delay of $S = 2000$ is much higher than that of $S = 20$ as the mean update arrival time drops below $1s$.

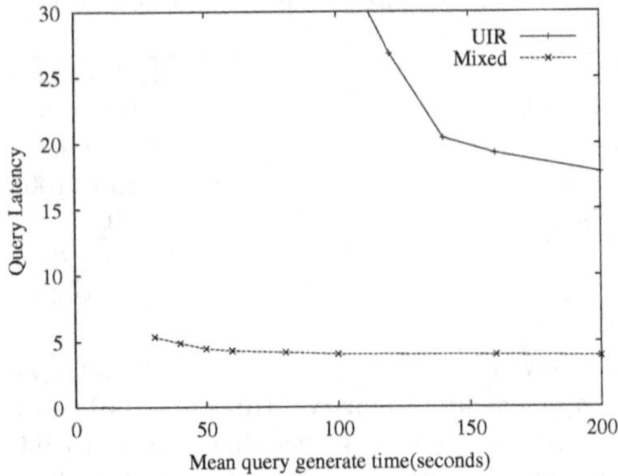

Fig. 3. A comparison of the query delay ($T_c = 100s, T_h = 0.01s, c = 200, n = 100$)

Each client generates queries according to the mean query generate time. The generated queries are served one by one. If the queried data is at local cache, the client can serve the query locally; otherwise, the client has to request the data from the server. If the client cannot process the generated query due to waiting for the server reply, it queues the generated queries. Since the broadcast bandwidth is fixed, the server can only transmit a limited amount of data during one IR interval, and then it can only serve a maximum number (α) of queries during one IR interval. If the server receives more than α queries during one IR interval, some queries are delayed to the next IR interval. If the server receives more than α queries during each IR interval, many queries may not be served, and the query delay may be out of bound. Due to the difference of the data size in different approach, the value of α varies. For example, with $T_h = 0.01s$, the query delay of $S = 200$ is still around $15s$, but the the query delay of $S = 2000$ becomes infinitely high. Note that when $T_h = 0.01s$, broadcasting the IR and UIR occupies a large amount of bandwidth since many data items are updated and their *ids* must be added to the IR and UIR.

Figure 3 compares the query delay of the UIR approach and the mixed approach. As can be seen, the mixed approach outperforms the UIR approach in terms of query delay. In the mixed approach, most of the queries can be served after an UIR is broadcasted, and then the query delay is very low. The query delay of the UIR approach becomes infinitely high when T_q drops below $100s$. This is due to the fact that the cache hit ratio of the UIR approach is much smaller than the mixed approach. Since the UIR approach does not differentiate between the hot component and the cold component, the mean update arrival time equals the hot component update arrival time $T_h = 0.01s$, and then its cache hit ratio is near 0. In the mixed approach, the mean update arrival time is $T_c = 100s$, and then their cache hit ratio is pretty high.

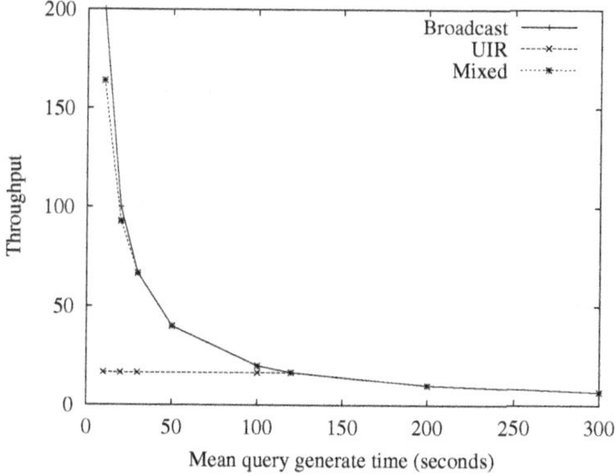

Fig. 4. The number of queries served per IR interval ($T_c = 100s, T_m = 0.01, c = 200, n = 100$)

4.2 The Throughput

As explained in the last subsection, with limited broadcast bandwidth, the server can only serve a maximum number (α) of client requests during one IR interval. However, the throughput (the number of queries served per IR interval) may be larger than α since some of the queries can be served by accessing the local cache. Since the mixed approach has much higher cache hit ratio than the UIR approach, the throughput of the mixed approach is much higher than the UIR approach. As shown in Figure 4, the broadcast approach has the highest throughput, while the UIR approach has the lowest throughput. The mixed approach has the same throughput as the broadcast approach when $T_q > 40s$. When the mean query generate time drops below 40s, the throughput of the mixed approach becomes lower than the broadcast approach.

5 Conclusions

We proposed a mixed approach to deal with the limitations of the broadcasting techniques and cache techniques. In our approach, based on the data update frequency, each data item is divided into two components: the hot component and the cold component. The UIR-based approach is used to deal with the cold component and broadcasting techniques are used to deal with the hot component. In this way, the proposed mixed data dissemination approach can be extended to many different application environments. Simulation results showed that the proposed solution can not only reduce the query latency, but also improve the throughput and the bandwidth utilization.

References

1. D. Barbara and T. Imielinski: Sleepers and Workaholics: Caching Strategies for Mobile Environments. ACM SIGMOD. (1994) 1–12
2. Cao, G.: A Scalable Low-Latency Cache Invalidation Strategy for Mobile Environments. ACM Int'l Conf. on Mobile Computing and Networking (MobiCom). (2000) 200–209
3. Hu, Q. and Lee, D.: Cache Algorithms based on Adaptive Invalidation Reports for Mobile Environments. Cluster Computing. (1998) 39–48
4. Imielinski, T., Viswanathan, S., Badrinath, B.: Data on Air: Organization and Access. IEEE Transactions on Knowledge and Data Engineering, vol. 9, no. 3, (1997) 353–372
5. Jing, J., Elmagarmid, A., Helal, A., Alonso, R.: Bit-Sequences: An Adaptive Cache Invalidation Method in Mobile Client/Server Environments. Mobile Networks and Applications. (1997) 115–127
6. W. Lee, Q. Hu, and D. Lee: Lee, W., Hu, Q., Lee, D.: A Study on Channel Allocation for Data Dissemination in Mobile Computing Environments. ACM/Baltzer Mobile Networks and Applications. (1999) 117–129

Author Index

Lecture Notes in Computer Science

For information about Vols. 1–2015
please contact your bookseller or Springer-Verlag

Vol. 2016: S. Murugesan, Y. Deshpande (Eds.), WebEngineering. IX, 357 pages. 2001.

Vol. 2018: M. Pollefeys, L. Van Gool, A. Zisserman, A. Fitzgibbon (Eds.), 3D Structure from Images – SMILE 2000. Proceedings, 2000. X, 243 pages. 2001.

Vol. 2019: P. Stone, T. Balch, G. Kraetzschmar (Eds.), RoboCup 2000: Robot Soccer World Cup IV. XVII, 658 pages. 2001. (Subseries LNAI).

Vol. 2020: D. Naccache (Ed.), Topics in Cryptology – CT-RSA 2001. Proceedings, 2001. XII, 473 pages. 2001

Vol. 2021: J. N. Oliveira, P. Zave (Eds.), FME 2001: Formal Methods for Increasing Software Productivity. Proceedings, 2001. XIII, 629 pages. 2001.

Vol. 2022: A. Romanovsky, C. Dony, J. Lindskov Knudsen, A. Tripathi (Eds.), Advances in Exception Handling Techniques. XII, 289 pages. 2001

Vol. 2024: H. Kuchen, K. Ueda (Eds.), Functional and Logic Programming. Proceedings, 2001. X, 391 pages. 2001.

Vol. 2025: M. Kaufmann, D. Wagner (Eds.), Drawing Graphs. XIV, 312 pages. 2001.

Vol. 2026: F. Müller (Ed.), High-Level Parallel Programming Models and Supportive Environments. Proceedings, 2001. IX, 137 pages. 2001.

Vol. 2027: R. Wilhelm (Ed.), Compiler Construction. Proceedings, 2001. XI, 371 pages. 2001.

Vol. 2028: D. Sands (Ed.), Programming Languages and Systems. Proceedings, 2001. XIII, 433 pages. 2001.

Vol. 2029: H. Hussmann (Ed.), Fundamental Approaches to Software Engineering. Proceedings, 2001. XIII, 349 pages. 2001.

Vol. 2030: F. Honsell, M. Miculan (Eds.), Foundations of Software Science and Computation Structures. Proceedings, 2001. XII, 413 pages. 2001.

Vol. 2031: T. Margaria, W. Yi (Eds.), Tools and Algorithms for the Construction and Analysis of Systems. Proceedings, 2001. XIV, 588 pages. 2001.

Vol. 2032: R. Klette, T. Huang, G. Gimel'farb (Eds.), Multi-Image Analysis. Proceedings, 2000. VIII, 289 pages. 2001.

Vol. 2033: J. Liu, Y. Ye (Eds.), E-Commerce Agents. VI, 347 pages. 2001. (Subseries LNAI).

Vol. 2034: M.D. Di Benedetto, A. Sangiovanni-Vincentelli (Eds.), Hybrid Systems: Computation and Control. Proceedings, 2001. XIV, 516 pages. 2001.

Vol. 2035: D. Cheung, G.J. Williams, Q. Li (Eds.), Advances in Knowledge Discovery and Data Mining – PAKDD 2001. Proceedings, 2001. XVIII, 596 pages. 2001. (Subseries LNAI).

Vol. 2037: E.J.W. Boers et al. (Eds.), Applications of Evolutionary Computing. Proceedings, 2001. XIII, 516 pages. 2001.

Vol. 2038: J. Miller, M. Tomassini, P.L. Lanzi, C. Ryan, A.G.B. Tettamanzi, W.B. Langdon (Eds.), Genetic Programming. Proceedings, 2001. XI, 384 pages. 2001.

Vol. 2039: M. Schumacher, Objective Coordination in Multi-Agent System Engineering. XIV, 149 pages. 2001. (Subseries LNAI).

Vol. 2040: W. Kou, Y. Yesha, C.J. Tan (Eds.), Electronic Commerce Technologies. Proceedings, 2001. X, 187 pages. 2001.

Vol. 2041: I. Attali, T. Jensen (Eds.), Java on Smart Cards: Programming and Security. Proceedings, 2000. X, 163 pages. 2001.

Vol. 2042: K.-K. Lau (Ed.), Logic Based Program Synthesis and Transformation. Proceedings, 2000. VIII, 183 pages. 2001.

Vol. 2043: D. Craeynest, A. Strohmeier (Eds.), Reliable Software Technologies – Ada-Europe 2001. Proceedings, 2001. XV, 405 pages. 2001.

Vol. 2044: S. Abramsky (Ed.), Typed Lambda Calculi and Applications. Proceedings, 2001. XI, 431 pages. 2001.

Vol. 2045: B. Pfitzmann (Ed.), Advances in Cryptology – EUROCRYPT 2001. Proceedings, 2001. XII, 545 pages. 2001.

Vol. 2047: R. Dumke, C. Rautenstrauch, A. Schmietendorf, A. Scholz (Eds.), Performance Engineering. XIV, 349 pages. 2001.

Vol. 2048: J. Pauli, Learning Based Robot Vision. IX, 288 pages. 2001.

Vol. 2051: A. Middeldorp (Ed.), Rewriting Techniques and Applications. Proceedings, 2001. XII, 363 pages. 2001.

Vol. 2052: V.I. Gorodetski, V.A. Skormin, L.J. Popyack (Eds.), Information Assurance in Computer Networks. Proceedings, 2001. XIII, 313 pages. 2001.

Vol. 2053: O. Danvy, A. Filinski (Eds.), Programs as Data Objects. Proceedings, 2001. VIII, 279 pages. 2001.

Vol. 2054: A. Condon, G. Rozenberg (Eds.), DNA Computing. Proceedings, 2000. X, 271 pages. 2001.

Vol. 2055: M. Margenstern, Y. Rogozhin (Eds.), Machines, Computations, and Universality. Proceedings, 2001. VIII, 321 pages. 2001.

Vol. 2056: E. Stroulia, S. Matwin (Eds.), Advances in Artificial Intelligence. Proceedings, 2001. XII, 366 pages. 2001. (Subseries LNAI).

Vol. 2057: M. Dwyer (Ed.), Model Checking Software. Proceedings, 2001. X, 313 pages. 2001.

Vol. 2059: C. Arcelli, L.P. Cordella, G. Sanniti di Baja (Eds.), Visual Form 2001. Proceedings, 2001. XIV, 799 pages. 2001.

Vol. 2060: T. Böhme, H. Unger (Eds.), Innovative Internet Computing Systems. Proceedings, 2001. VIII, 183 pages. 2001.

Vol. 2062: A. Nareyek, Constraint-Based Agents. XIV, 178 pages. 2001. (Subseries LNAI).

Vol. 2064: J. Blanck, V. Brattka, P. Hertling (Eds.), Computability and Complexity in Analysis. Proceedings, 2000. VIII, 395 pages. 2001.

Vol. 2065: H. Balster, B. de Brock, S. Conrad (Eds.), Database Schema Evolution and Meta-Modeling. Proceedings, 2000. X, 245 pages. 2001.

Vol. 2066: O. Gascuel, M.-F. Sagot (Eds.), Computational Biology. Proceedings, 2000. X, 165 pages. 2001.

Vol. 2068: K.R. Dittrich, A. Geppert, M.C. Norrie (Eds.), Advanced Information Systems Engineering. Proceedings, 2001. XII, 484 pages. 2001.

Vol. 2070: L. Monostori, J. Váncza, M. Ali (Eds.), Engineering of Intelligent Systems. Proceedings, 2001. XVIII, 951 pages. 2001. (Subseries LNAI).

Vol. 2071: R. Harper (Ed.), Types in Compilation. Proceedings, 2000. IX, 207 pages. 2001.

Vol. 2072: J. Lindskov Knudsen (Ed.), ECOOP 2001 – Object-Oriented Programming. Proceedings, 2001. XIII, 429 pages. 2001.

Vol. 2073: V.N. Alexandrov, J.J. Dongarra, B.A. Juliano, R.S. Renner, C.J.K. Tan (Eds.), Computational Science – ICCS 2001. Part I. Proceedings, 2001. XXVIII, 1306 pages. 2001.

Vol. 2074: V.N. Alexandrov, J.J. Dongarra, B.A. Juliano, R.S. Renner, C.J.K. Tan (Eds.), Computational Science – ICCS 2001. Part II. Proceedings, 2001. XXVIII, 1076 pages. 2001.

Vol. 2075: J.-M. Colom, M. Koutny (Eds.), Applications and Theory of Petri Nets 2001. Proceedings, 2001. XII, 403 pages. 2001.

Vol. 2076: F. Orejas, P.G. Spirakis, J. van Leeuwen (Eds.), Automata, Languages and Programming. Proceedings, 2001. XIV, 1083 pages. 2001.

Vol. 2077: V. Ambriola (Ed.), Software Process Technology. Proceedings, 2001. VIII, 247 pages. 2001.

Vol. 2078: R. Reed, J. Reed (Eds.), SDL 2001: Meeting UML. Proceedings, 2001. XI, 439 pages. 2001.

Vol. 2081: K. Aardal, B. Gerards (Eds.), Integer Programming and Combinatorial Optimization. Proceedings, 2001. XI, 423 pages. 2001.

Vol. 2082: M.F. Insana, R.M. Leahy (Eds.), Information Processing in Medical Imaging. Proceedings, 2001. XVI, 537 pages. 2001.

Vol. 2083: R. Goré, A. Leitsch, T. Nipkow (Eds.), Automated Reasoning. Proceedings, 2001. XV, 708 pages. 2001. (Subseries LNAI).

Vol. 2084: J. Mira, A. Prieto (Eds.), Connectionist Models of Neurons, Learning Processes, and Artificial Intelligence. Proceedings, 2001. Part I. XXVII, 836 pages. 2001.

Vol. 2085: J. Mira, A. Prieto (Eds.), Bio-Inspired Applications of Connectionism. Proceedings, 2001. Part II. XXVII, 848 pages. 2001.

Vol. 2086: M. Luck, V. Mařík, O. Štěpánková, R. Trappl (Eds.), Multi-Agent Systems and Applications. Proceedings, 2001. X, 437 pages. 2001. (Subseries LNAI).

Vol. 2089: A. Amir, G.M. Landau (Eds.), Combinatorial Pattern Matching. Proceedings, 2001. VIII, 273 pages. 2001.

Vol. 2091: J. Bigun, F. Smeraldi (Eds.), Audio- and Video-Based Biometric Person Authentication. Proceedings, 2001. XIII, 374 pages. 2001.

Vol. 2092: L. Wolf, D. Hutchison, R. Steinmetz (Eds.), Quality of Service – IWQoS 2001. Proceedings, 2001. XII, 435 pages. 2001.

Vol. 2093: P. Lorenz (Ed.), Networking – ICN 2001. Proceedings, 2001. Part I. XXV, 843 pages. 2001.

Vol. 2094: P. Lorenz (Ed.), Networking – ICN 2001. Proceedings, 2001. Part II. XXV, 899 pages. 2001.

Vol. 2095: B. Schiele, G. Sagerer (Eds.), Computer Vision Systems. Proceedings, 2001. X, 313 pages. 2001.

Vol. 2096: J. Kittler, F. Roli (Eds.), Multiple Classifier Systems. Proceedings, 2001. XII, 456 pages. 2001.

Vol. 2097: B. Read (Ed.), Advances in Databases. Proceedings, 2001. X, 219 pages. 2001.

Vol. 2098: J. Akiyama, M. Kano, M. Urabe (Eds.), Discrete and Computational Geometry. Proceedings, 2000. XI, 381 pages. 2001.

Vol. 2099: P. de Groote, G. Morrill, C. Retoré (Eds.), Logical Aspects of Computational Linguistics. Proceedings, 2001. VIII, 311 pages. 2001. (Subseries LNAI).

Vol. 2101: S. Quaglini, P. Barahona, S. Andreassen (Eds.), Artificial Intelligence in Medicine. Proceedings, 2001. XIV, 469 pages. 2001. (Subseries LNAI).

Vol. 2105: W. Kim, T.-W. Ling, Y-J. Lee, S.-S. Park (Eds.), The Human Society and the Internet. Proceedings, 2001. XVI, 470 pages. 2001.

Vol. 2106: M. Kerckhove (Ed.), Scale-Space and Morphology in Computer Vision. Proceedings, 2001. XI, 435 pages. 2001.

Vol. 2109: M. Bauer, P.J. Gymtrasiewicz, J. Vassileva (Eds.), User Modelind 2001. Proceedings, 2001. XIII, 318 pages. 2001. (Subseries LNAI).

Vol. 2110: B. Hertzberger, A. Hoekstra, R. Williams (Eds.), High-Performance Computing and Networking. Proceedings, 2001. XVII, 733 pages. 2001.

Vol. 2118: X.S. Wang, G. Yu, H. Lu (Eds.), Advances in Web-Age Information Management. Proceedings, 2001. XV, 418 pages. 2001.

Vol. 2119: V. Varadharajan, Y. Mu (Eds.), Information Security and Privacy. Proceedings, 2001. XI, 522 pages. 2001.

Vol. 2121: C.S. Jensen, M. Schneider, B. Seeger, V.J. Tsotras (Eds.), Advances in Spatial and Temporal Databases. Proceedings, 2001. XI, 543 pages. 2001.

Vol. 2126: P. Cousot (Ed.), Static Analysis. Proceedings, 2001. XI, 439 pages. 2001.